T0224292

The Azure Data Lakehouse Toolkit

Building and Scaling Data Lakehouses on Azure with Delta Lake, Apache Spark, Databricks, Synapse Analytics, and Snowflake

Ron L'Esteve

Apress®

The Azure Data Lakehouse Toolkit: Building and Scaling Data Lakehouses on Azure with Delta Lake, Apache Spark, Databricks, Synapse Analytics, and Snowflake

Ron L'Esteve
Chicago, IL, USA

ISBN-13 (pbk): 978-1-4842-8232-8 ISBN-13 (electronic): 978-1-4842-8233-5
https://doi.org/10.1007/978-1-4842-8233-5

Managing Director, Apress Media LLC: Welmoed Spahr
Acquisitions Editor: Jonathan Gennick
Development Editor: Laura Berendson
Coordinating Editor: Jill Balzano

Cover designed by eStudioCalamar

Cover image designed by Freepik (www.freepik.com)

Distributed to the book trade worldwide by Springer Science+Business Media New York, 1 New York Plaza, Suite 4600, New York, NY 10004-1562, USA. Phone 1-800-SPRINGER, fax (201) 348-4505, e-mail orders-ny@springer-sbm.com, or visit www.springeronline.com. Apress Media, LLC is a California LLC and the sole member (owner) is Springer Science + Business Media Finance Inc (SSBM Finance Inc). SSBM Finance Inc is a **Delaware** corporation.

For information on translations, please e-mail booktranslations@springernature.com; for reprint, paperback, or audio rights, please e-mail bookpermissions@springernature.com.

Apress titles may be purchased in bulk for academic, corporate, or promotional use. eBook versions and licenses are also available for most titles. For more information, reference our Print and eBook Bulk Sales web page at http://www.apress.com/bulk-sales.

Any source code or other supplementary material referenced by the author in this book is available to readers on GitHub via the book's product page, located at www.apress.com/. For more detailed information, please visit http://www.apress.com/source-code.

Printed on acid-free paper

For Cayden and Christina

Table of Contents

About the Author

Ron L'Esteve is a professional author, trusted technology leader, and digital innovation strategist residing in Chicago, IL, USA. He is well known for his impactful books and award-winning article publications about Azure Data and AI architecture and engineering. He possesses deep technical skills and experience in designing, implementing, and delivering modern Azure Data and AI projects for numerous clients around the world.

Having several Azure Data, AI, and Lakehouse certifications under his belt, Ron has been a trusted and go-to technical advisor for some of the largest and most impactful Azure implementation projects on the planet. He has been responsible for scaling key data architectures, defining the roadmap and strategy for the future of data and business intelligence needs, and challenging customers to grow by thoroughly understanding the fluid business opportunities and enabling change by translating them into high-quality and sustainable technical solutions that solve the most complex challenges and promote digital innovation and transformation.

Ron is a gifted presenter and trainer, known for his innate ability to clearly articulate and explain complex topics to audiences of all skill levels. He applies a practical and business-oriented approach by taking transformational ideas from concept to scale. He is a true enabler of positive and impactful change by championing a growth mindset.

About the Technical Reviewer

Diego Poggioli is an analytics architect with over ten years of experience managing big data and machine learning projects.

At Avanade, he is currently helping clients to identify, document, and translate business strategy and requirements into solutions and services that help clients to achieve their business outcomes using analytics.

With a passion for software development, cloud, and serverless innovations, he has worked on various product development initiatives spanning IaaS, PaaS, and SaaS.

He is also interested in the emerging topics of artificial intelligence, machine learning, and large-scale data processing and analytics.

He holds several Microsoft Azure and AWS certifications.

His hobbies are handcraft with driftwood, playing with his two kids, and learning new technologies. He currently lives in Bologna, Italy.

Acknowledgments

The journey to completing this book has inspired me to learn more, dream more, and do more. I am thankful to my family, friends, and supporters who have fueled me with the determination and inspiration to write this book.

Introduction

With the rise of data volume, velocity, and variety in the modern data and analytics platform on Azure, there is an ever-growing demand for innovative low-cost storage and on-demand compute options that are centered around their decoupled capabilities. This book will enhance your understanding around some of the practical methods of designing and implementing the Data Lakehouse paradigm on Azure by demonstrating the capabilities of Apache Spark and Delta Lake to build cutting-edge modern Lakehouse solutions on Databricks, Synapse Analytics, and Snowflake. You will gain an understanding of these various technologies and how they fit into the modern data and analytics Lakehouse paradigm by supporting the needs of ingestion, processing, storing, serving, reporting, and consumption. You'll also gain a better understanding of how machine learning, data governance, and continuous integration and deployment play a role in the Lakehouse.

The Data Lakehouse paradigm on Azure, which leverages Apache Spark and Delta Lake heavily, has become a popular choice for big data engineering, ELT (extraction, loading, and transformation), AI/ML, real-time data processing, reporting, and querying use cases. In some scenarios of the Lakehouse paradigm, Spark coupled with MPP is great for big data reporting and BI Analytics platforms that require heavy querying and performance capabilities since MPP is based on the traditional RDBMS and brings with it the best features of SQL Server, such as automated query tuning, data shuffling, ease of analytics platform management, even data distribution based on a primary key, and much more. As the Lakehouse matures, specifically with Delta Lake, it begins to demonstrate its capabilities of supporting many critical features, such as ACID (atomicity, consistency, isolation, and durability)-compliant transactions for batch and streaming jobs, data quality enforcement, and highly optimized performance tuning.

In the upcoming chapters of this book, we will unravel the many complexities of understanding the technologies used within the Lakehouse paradigm along with their capabilities through hands-on, scenario-based exercises. You will learn how to implement advanced performance optimization tools and patterns for Spark performance improvement in the Lakehouse by using partitioning, indexing, and other tuning options. You will also learn about the capabilities of Delta Lake which include schema evolution, change feed, Live Tables, sharing, and clones. Finally, you will gain more knowledge about some of the advanced capabilities within the Lakehouse, such as building and installing custom Python libraries, implementing security and controls, and working with event-driven autoloading data on the Lakehouse platform. The chapters presented within this book are intended to equip you with the right skills and knowledge to design and implement a modern Lakehouse by serving as your Data Lakehouse Toolkit.

PART I

Getting Started

CHAPTER 1

The Data Lakehouse Paradigm

In this chapter, you will learn about the Lakehouse architectural best practices, patterns, and Apache Spark capabilities in the Lakehouse. You will also learn about the many Azure-centric technologies that support Spark for ELT, advanced analytics, storage, compute, and reporting to form the modern Data Lakehouse architecture.

Background

Prior to the introduction of massively parallel processing (MPP) architectures in the early 1990s, the analytics database market was dominated by symmetrical multiprocessing (SMP) architecture since around the 1970s. SMP had drawbacks around sizing, scalability, workload management, resilience, and availability, and the MPP architecture addressed many of these SMP drawbacks related to performance, scalability, high availability, and read/write throughput. MPP had drawbacks related to cost, a critical need for data distribution; downtime for adding new nodes and redistributing data; limited ability to scale up compute resources on-demand for real-time processing needs; and potential for overcapacity given the limitations to isolate storage from compute.

A Resilient Distributed Dataset (RDD) in Spark is similar to a distributed table in MPP in that many of the RDD operations have an equivalent MPP operation. RDD does, however, offer better options for real-time processing needs, ability to scale up nodes for batch processing, while also scaling storage (Data Lake) independently and cost-effectively from compute. Also, it is recommended over MPP for highly unstructured data processing (text, images, video, and more). Additionally, it offers the capability for large-scale advanced analytics (AI, ML, text/sentiment analysis, and more). Seeing the many benefits that Spark and the modern Data Lakehouse platform have to offer, customers are interested in understanding and getting started with the Data Lakehouse paradigm.

R. L'Esteve, *The Azure Data Lakehouse Toolkit*, https://doi.org/10.1007/978-1-4842-8233-5_1

Given the multitude of cloud offerings which include Amazon Web Services (AWS), Google Cloud Platform (GCP), and Microsoft Azure, there are clearly multiple cloud-based offerings for building out a Lakehouse. Many large organizations leverage multi-cloud platforms and product offerings as part of their technology stack. This book will focus on the Azure Data Lakehouse paradigm since it integrates well with a variety of other cloud platforms and service providers.

The Data Lakehouse paradigm on Azure leverages Apache Spark and Delta Lake heavily. Apache Spark is an open source unified analytics engine for large-scale data processing which provides an interface for programming clusters which includes data parallelism and fault tolerance. Similarly, Delta Lake is also open source and provides a reliable Data Lake Storage layer which runs on top of an existing Data Lake. It provides ACID-compliant transactions, scalable metadata handling, unified streaming, and batch data processing and is fully compatible with Apache Spark–based APIs. Both Spark and Delta Lake have become popular choices for big data engineering, ELT, AI/ML, real-time data processing, reporting, and querying use cases. In some scenarios of the Lakehouse paradigm, Spark coupled with MPP is great for big data reporting and BI Analytics platforms that require heavy querying and performance capabilities since MPP is based on the traditional RDBMS and brings with it the best features of SQL Server, such as automated query tuning, data shuffling, ease of analytics platform management, even data distribution based on a primary key, and much more. This may be a more common scenario as the Lakehouse paradigm is in its infancy. As the Lakehouse matures, specifically with Delta Lake, it can support critical features such as ACID transactions for batch and streaming jobs, data quality enforcement, and highly optimized performance tuning.

While Spark has traditionally been designed for large data processing, the advancement of Spark is a hot industry topic that would help with aligning the Lakehouse paradigm with the best features of traditional RDBMS to address Lakehouse performance issues.

Architecture

As numerous modern Data Lakehouse technologies become generally available on the Azure data platform with demonstrated capabilities of outperforming traditional on-premises and cloud databases and warehouses, it is important to begin understanding this Lakehouse architecture, the typical components utilized in the Lakehouse paradigm, and how they all come together and contribute to realizing the modern Data Lakehouse architecture. Azure's modern resource-based consumption model for PaaS and SaaS services empowers developers, engineers, and end users to use the platforms, tools, and technologies that best serve their needs. That being said, there are many Azure resources that serve various purposes in the Lakehouse architecture. The capabilities of these tools will be covered in greater detail in subsequent sections. From a high level, they serve the purpose of ingesting, storing, processing, serving, and consuming data.

From a compute perspective, Apache Spark is the gold standard for all things Lakehouse. It is a multi-language engine for executing data engineering, data science, and machine learning on single-node machines or clusters and is prevalent in Data Factory's Mapping Data Flows (DF), Databricks, and Synapse Analytics and typically powers compute of the Lakehouse. As we grow and evolve the Lakehouse paradigm, Photon (`https://databricks.com/product/photon`), a new execution engine on the Databricks Lakehouse platform, provides even better performance than Apache Spark and is fully compatible with Apache Spark APIs. When there is an opportunity to utilize Photon for large data processing initiatives in supported platforms such as Databricks, it would certainly be a sound option.

With storage being cheap within the Data Lake comes the idea of the Lakehouse; however, there is a lack of ACID-compliant features within Data Lakes that persist files as parquet format. Delta Lake is an open source storage layer that guarantees data atomicity, consistency, isolation, and durability in the lake. In short, Delta Lake is ACID compliant. In addition to providing ACID transactions, scalable metadata handling, and more, Delta Lake runs on an existing Data Lake and is compatible with Apache Spark APIs. There are a few methods of getting started with Delta Lake. Databricks offers notebooks along with compatible Apache Spark APIs to create and manage Delta Lakes. Alternatively, Azure Data Factory's (ADF) Mapping Data Flows, which uses scaled out Apache Spark clusters, can be used to perform ACID-compliant CRUD operations through GUI-designed ETL pipelines.

From a data serving and consumption perspective, there are a variety of tools on the Azure platform including Synapse Analytics Serverless and Dedicated Pools for storage and ad hoc querying, along with Power BI (PBI) for robust reporting dashboards and visualizations. Outside of the Azure platform, Snowflake also serves as a strong contender to the Synapse Dedicated Pool (SQL DW) as a dedicated data warehouse. All of these various tools and technologies serve a purpose in the Lakehouse architecture which make it a necessity to include them for the particular use case that they best serve rather than choosing between one and the other. The Lakehouse architecture, shown in Figure 1-1, also supports deep advanced analytics and AI use cases with cognitive services, Azure ML, Databricks ML, and Power BI AI/ML capabilities. Finally, it is critical to build in DevOps best practices within any data platform, and the Lakehouse supports multi-environment automated continuous integration and delivery (CI/CD) best practices using Azure DevOps. All these modern Lakehouse components can be automated with CI/CD, scheduled and monitored for health and performance with Azure Monitor and App Insights, secured with Key Vault, and governed with Purview.

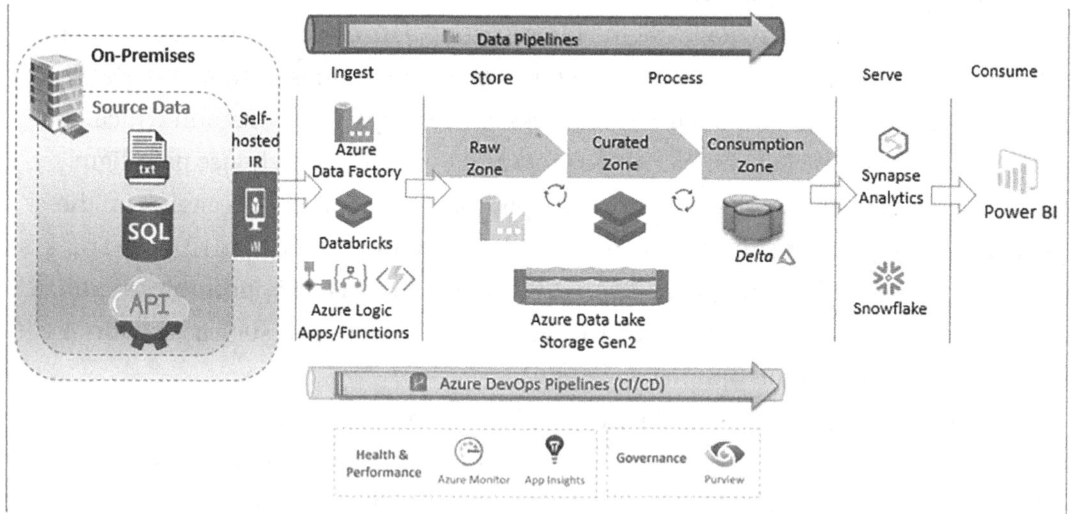

***Figure 1-1.** Lakehouse architectural paradigm*

Ingestion and Processing

This initial portion of any data architecture is the ingestion process. Data sources range from on-premises to a variety of cloud sources. There are a few Azure resources that are typically used for the data ingestion process. This includes Data Factory, Databricks, and custom functions and connectors. This section will further explore some of these components and their capabilities.

Data Factory

Azure Data Factory is a cloud-based ELT platform used for data integration and transformation within its graphical user interface, much like Microsoft's traditional SQL Server Integration Services (SSIS) on-premises toolset. Data Factory supports tight integration with on-premises data sources using the self-hosted Integration Runtime (IR). The IR is the compute infrastructure used by Data Factory and Synapse Pipelines to provide data integration capabilities across different network environments including on-premises. This capability has positioned this service as a tool of choice for integrating a combination of on-premises and cloud sources using reusable and metadata-driven ELT patterns. For cloud sources, the Azure IR is recommended, and the SSIS IR is used for running the SSIS engine which allows you to natively execute SSIS packages. An Integration Runtime is the compute resource infrastructure used by Azure Data Factory to provide data integration capabilities, such as data flows and data movement, which has access to resources in either public, private, or hybrid network scenarios.

Within ADF, Integration Runtimes (IR) are the compute resource infrastructure used to provide data integration capabilities, such as data flows and data movement. ADF has the following three IR types:

- **Azure Integration Runtime**: All patching, scaling, and maintenance of the underlying infrastructure are managed by Microsoft, and the IR can only access data stores and services in public networks.
- **Self-hosted Integration Runtimes**: The infrastructure and hardware are managed by you, and you will need to address all the patching, scaling, and maintenance. The IR can access resources in both public and private networks.
- **Azure-SSIS Integration Runtimes**: VMs running the SSIS engine allow you to natively execute SSIS packages. All the patching, scaling, and maintenance are managed by Microsoft. The IR can access resources in both public and private networks.

Data Factory also supports complex transformations with its Mapping Data Flow service which can be used to build transformations, Slowly Changing Dimensions (SCD), and more. Mapping Data Flow utilizes Databricks Apache Spark clusters under the hood and has a number of mechanisms for optimizing and partitioning data.

Mapping Data Flows are visually designed data transformations in Azure Data Factory. Data flows allow data engineers to develop data transformation logic without writing code. The resulting data flows are executed as activities within Azure Data Factory pipelines that use scaled out Apache Spark clusters. We will explore some of the capabilities of Mapping Data Flows in Chapters 11 through 15 for data warehouse ETL using Slowly Changing Dimensions (SCD) Type I, big Data Lake aggregations, incremental upserts, and Delta Lake. There are many other use cases around the capabilities of Mapping Data Flows that will not be covered in this book (e.g., dynamically splitting big files into multiple small files, manage small file problems, Parse transformations, and more), and I would encourage you to research many of these other capabilities of Mapping Data Flows.

Additionally, data can be transformed through Stored Procedure activities in the regular Copy Data activity of ADF.

There are three different cluster types available in Mapping Data Flows: general purpose, memory optimized, and compute optimized. The following is a description of each:

- **General purpose**: Use the default general-purpose cluster when you intend to balance performance and cost. This cluster will be ideal for most data flow workloads.
- **Memory optimized**: Use the more costly per-core memory optimized clusters if your data flow has many joins and lookups since they can store more data in memory and will minimize any out-of-memory errors you may get. If you experience any out-of-memory errors when executing data flows, switch to a memory-optimized Azure IR configuration.
- **Compute optimized**: Use the cheaper per-core-priced compute-optimized clusters for non-memory-intensive data transformations such as filtering data or adding derived columns

ADF also has a number of built-in and custom activities which integrate with other Azure services ranging from Databricks, Functions, Login Apps, Synapse, and more. Data Factory also has connectors for other cloud sources including Oracle Cloud, Snowflake, and more. Figure 1-2 shows a list of the various activities that are supported by ADF. When expanded, each activity contains a long list of customizable activities for ELT. While Data Factory is typically designed for batch ELT, its robust event-driven scheduling triggers can also support event-driven real-time processes, although Databricks Structured Streaming is typically recommended for all things streaming. Data Factory also has robust scheduling and monitoring capabilities with verbose error logging and alerting to support traceability and restart capabilities of pipelines. Pipelines that are built in ADF can be dynamic and parameterized, which contribute to the reusability of pipelines that are driven by robust audit, balance, and control (ABC) ingestion frameworks. Data Factory also securely integrates with Key Vault for secret and credential management. Synapse Pipelines within Synapse Analytics workspace has a very similar UI as Databricks as it continues to evolve into the Azure standard unified analytics platform for the Lakehouse. Many of the same ADF pipelines can be built with Synapse Pipelines with a few exceptions. For features and capabilities that are available in the more Data Factory V2 toolbox, choose Data Factory V2 as the ELT tool.

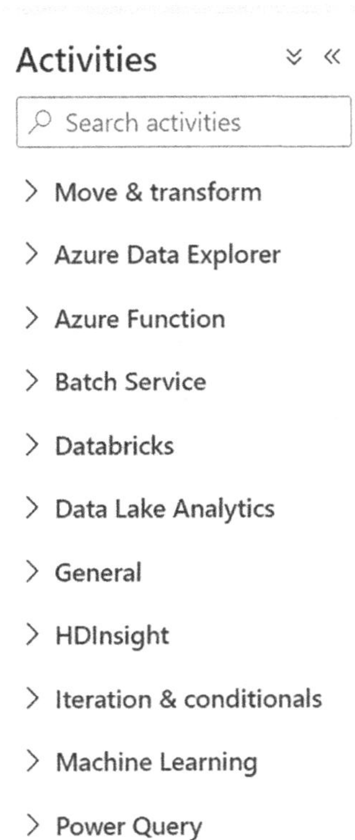

Figure 1-2. *ADF activities*

Data Factory supports over 90 sources and sinks as part of its ingestion and load process. In the subsequent chapters, you will learn how to create pipelines, datasets, linked services, and activities in ADF. The following list shows and defines the various components of a standard ADF pipeline:

- **Pipelines** are logical grouping of activities that together perform a task.
- **Activities** define actions to perform on your data (e.g., copy data activity, ForEach loop activity, etc.)

- **Datasets** are named views of data that simply points or references the data you want to use in your activities within the pipeline.
- **Linked Services** are much like connection strings, which define the connection information needed for Data Factory to connect to external resources.

Currently, there are a few limitations with ADF. Some of these limitations include

1. Inability to add a For Each activity or Switch activity to an If activity.
2. Inability to nest ForEach loop, If, and Switch activities.
3. Lookup activity has a maximum of 5,000 rows and a maximum size of 4 MB.
4. Inability to add CRON functions for modular scheduling.

Some of these limitations are either on the ADF product team's roadmap for future enhancement, or there are custom solutions and workarounds. For example, the lack of modular scheduling within a single pipeline can be offset by leveraging tools such as Azure Functions, Logic Apps, Apache Airflow, and more. Ensure that you have a modular design with many pipelines to work around other limitations such as the 40 activities per pipeline limit. Additional limitations include 100 queued runs per pipeline and 1,000 concurrent pipeline activity runs per subscription per Azure Integration Runtime region.

Databricks

Databricks can also be used for data ingestion and is typically well suited for cloud and streaming sources. While Databricks can certainly be connected to an on-premises network using an architecture similar to Figure 1-3, it is an unnecessarily complex path to access on-premises data sources given the robust capabilities of ADF's self-hosted IR. When connecting to on-premises sources, try to use ADF as much as possible. On the other hand, from a streaming perspective, Databricks leverages Apache Spark to ingest and transform real-time big data sources with ease. It can store the data in a variety of file formats including parquet, Avro, delta, and more. These storage formats will be covered in more detail within the storage section. When combined with ADF for ingestion, Databricks can be a powerful customizable component in the Lakehouse data ingestion framework.

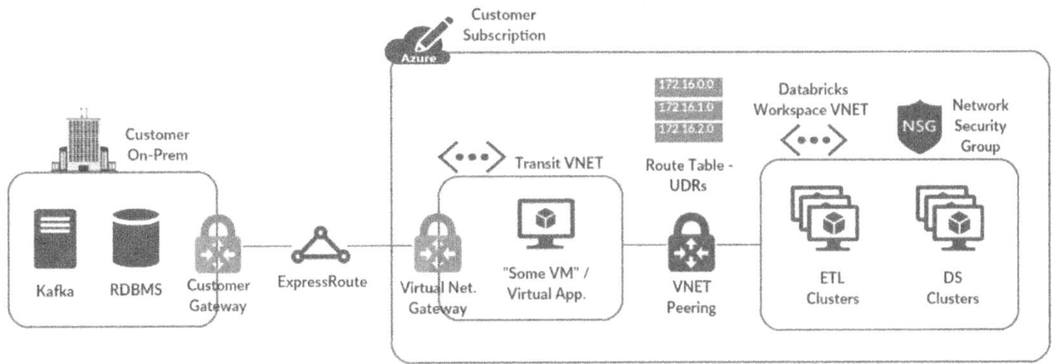

Figure 1-3. *Databricks connect to on-premises architecture*

Apache Spark's structured streaming is a stream processing framework built on the Spark SQL engine. Once a computation and the source and destination are specified, the structured streaming engine will run the query incrementally and continuously as new data is available. Structured streaming treats a stream of data as a table and continuously appends data. Databricks does an excellent job of implementing structured streaming solutions using events fed into an Azure IoT Hub and processed by Apache Spark through a Databricks notebook and into a Delta Lake to persist the data. Structured streaming provides the robust capability of applying advanced schema evolution, data aggregations, and transformation on datasets in real time. The concept of event-driven ELT paradigms is a best practice within the Lakehouse. Databricks' "Auto Loader" is designed for event-driven structured streaming ELT and advanced schema evolution patterns.

Functions and Logic Apps

With Serverless Functions, developers can create custom event-driven serverless code that can solve complex data integration and orchestration challenges. Functions can be called from both Databricks notebooks and Data Factory pipelines via APIs or through regular out-of-the box ADF activities that can be integrated with other activities and pipelines through the ADF canvas. With Logic Apps, creating and running automated workflows that integrate your apps, data, services, and systems has never been easier. With this platform, you can quickly develop highly scalable integration solutions.

Synapse Analytics Serverless Pools

Synapse Analytics plays a strong role in the Lakehouse architecture due to its ever-growing and flexible feature set which includes dedicated MPP SQL big data warehouses, Serverless SQL, and Apache Spark Pools. In addition, Synapse Analytics also has its very own workspace environment for writing and executing custom code along with creating, scheduling, and monitoring pipelines. With Serverless Apache Spark Pools, you can leverage Apache Spark for compute resources that are similar to Databricks Spark clusters. There is no need to set up any underlying infrastructure to maintain clusters. With its pay per use model, serverless pool charges are calculated per terabyte for data that is processed by each query that is run. This model separates storage from compute costs to promote a cost-efficient Lakehouse architecture that provides fine-grained insights into storage and compute costs. Note also that external tables can also be created with Data Lake delta format files. The default Spark node size is memory optimized, and it has a few options: small (~4 vCores/32 GB), medium (~8 vCores/64 GB), large (~16 vCores/128 GB), XLarge (~32 vCores/256 GB), XXLarge (~64 vCores/432 GB), and XXXLarge (~80 vCores/2504 GB). Auto-scaling can be enabled and is determined by the number of nodes defined in the scale settings. Synapse Analytics also supports Spark Structured Streaming capabilities.

The following code sample demonstrates how developers can write SQL scripts with Serverless SQL Pools to query the Azure Data Lake Storage gen2 account by using standard SQL commands along with the OPENROWSET function. The format can include parquet, delta, and others. Queries can contain complex joins with orders and groupings. Also, wild cards such as "*.parquet" are permitted in the ADLS gen2 folder path. Once a SQL endpoint is created, it can be connected to BI services such as Power BI and more. The user will be able to easily retrieve the tables through the UI while the underlying data is actually in parquet file format.

```
SELECT
        YEAR(pickup_datetime) AS year,
        passenger_count,
        COUNT(*) AS cnt
FROM
    OPENROWSET(
        BULK 'https://adls2.blob.core.windows.net/delta-lake/data/*.
        parquet',
```

```
        FORMAT='DELTA'
    ) nyc
WHERE
    nyc.year = 2021
    AND nyc.month IN (1, 2, 3)
    AND pickup_datetime BETWEEN CAST('1/1/2021' AS datetime) AND
    CAST('12/31/2021' AS datetime)
GROUP BY
    passenger_count,
    YEAR(pickup_datetime)
ORDER BY
    YEAR(pickup_datetime),
    passenger_count;
```

Stream Analytics

Azure Stream Analytics is an event-processing engine which allows examining high volumes of data streaming from devices, sensors, websites, social media feeds, applications, etc. It is easy to use and based on simple SQL query language. Additionally, it is a fully managed (PaaS) offering on Azure that can run large-scale analytics jobs that are optimized for cost since users only pay for streaming units that are consumed.

Azure Stream Analytics also offers built-in machine learning functions that can be wrapped in SQL statements to detect anomalies. This anomaly detection capability coupled with Power BI's real-time streaming service makes it a powerful real-time anomaly detection service. While there are a few use cases that can benefit from Stream Analytics, the Lakehouse architecture has been adopting Databricks Structured Streaming as the stream processing technology of choice since it can leverage Spark for compute of big delta and parquet format datasets and has other valuable features including advanced schema evolution, support for ML use cases, and more. As we wrap up this section on Stream Analytics, the following script demonstrates just how easy it is to write a Stream Analytics SQL query using the anomaly detection function. Stream Analytics is a decent choice for a stream processing technology that is needed to process real-time data from an IoT Hub which can then also be read in real time by a Power BI dashboard.

```
WITH AnomalyDetectionStep AS
(
    SELECT
        EVENTENQUEUEDUTCTIME AS time,
        CAST(temperature AS float) AS temp,
        AnomalyDetection_SpikeAndDip(CAST(temperature AS float), 95, 120,
        'spikesanddips')
            OVER(LIMIT DURATION(second, 120)) AS SpikeAndDipScores
    FROM IoTHub
)
SELECT
    time,
    temp,
    CAST(GetRecordPropertyValue(SpikeAndDipScores, 'Score') AS float) AS
    SpikeAndDipScore,
    CAST(GetRecordPropertyValue(SpikeAndDipScores, 'IsAnomaly') AS
    bigint) AS
    IsSpikeAndDipAnomaly
INTO IoTPowerBIOutput
FROM AnomalyDetectionStep
```

In time-streaming scenarios, performing operations on the data contained in temporal windows is a common pattern. Stream Analytics has native support for windowing functions, enabling developers to author complex stream processing jobs with minimal effort. The following windowing functions are available within Stream Analytics:

- **Tumbling window** allows you to segment data into distinct time segments (count of tweets per time zone every ten seconds).
- **Session window** allows group streaming events that arrive at similar time and filter our no data (count of tweets that occur within five minutes of each other).
- **Hopping window** looks backward to determine when an event occurs (every five seconds, count of tweets in the last ten seconds).

- **Sliding window** produces output when an event occurs (count of tweets for a single topic over the last ten seconds).
- **Snapshot window** groups events that have the same timestamp. You can apply a snapshot window by adding System.Timestamp() to the GROUP BY clause.

Messaging Hubs

Azure's IoT Hub and Event Hub are cloud service offerings which can ingest and support large volumes of low-latency and high-reliability, real-time device data into the Lakehouse. Azure IoT Hub connects IoT devices to Azure resources and supports bidirectional communication capabilities between devices. IoT Hub uses Event Hubs for its telemetry flow path. Event Hub is designed for high-throughput data streaming of billions of requests per day. Both IoT and Event Hub fit well within both Stream Analytics and Databricks Structured Streaming architectures to support the event-driven real-time ingestion of device data for further processing and storage in the Lakehouse, as shown in Figure 1-4.

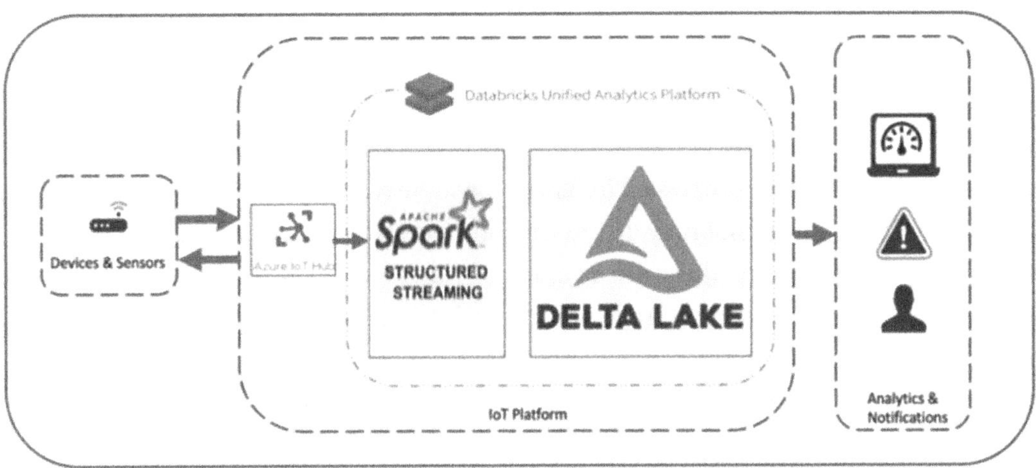

***Figure 1-4.** Delta Lake Structured Streaming architecture*

Table 1-1 lists the differences in capabilities between Event Hubs and IoT Hubs.

Table 1-1. *Event Hubs vs. IoT Hubs*

IoT capability	IoT Hub standard tier	IoT Hub basic tier	Event Hubs
Device-to-cloud messaging	Yes	Yes	Yes
Protocols: HTTPS, AMQP, AMQP over webSockets	Yes	Yes	Yes
Protocols: MQTT, MQTT over webSockets	Yes	Yes	
Per-device identity	Yes	Yes	
File upload from devices	Yes	Yes	
Device provisioning service	Yes	Yes	
Cloud-to-device messaging	Yes		
Device twin and device management	Yes		
Device streams (preview)	Yes		
IoT edge	Yes		

Storing and Serving

Once data is ingested and processed in Azure, it will be ready for storage and serving to a variety of consumers that may be internal and external to an organization. Within the Lakehouse architecture, there are a variety of platforms available for storing and serving data. ADLS gen2 is the storage platform of choice for the Lakehouse due to its cheap storage costs and compatibility with Delta Lake, which provides ACID-compliant transactions along with strong features for optimizing, indexing, and performance tuning in the Lakehouse. In this section, you will learn more about Delta Lake and a variety of other big data storage systems including Synapse Analytics Dedicated Pools, Snowflake, SQL databases, and NoSQL databases and how they fit into the Lakehouse.

Delta Lake

Delta Lake is an open source storage layer within the Lakehouse which guarantees data atomicity, consistency, isolation, and durability (ACID compliance) in the lake. Delta Lake runs on an existing Data Lake and is compatible with Apache Spark APIs. Numerous Azure resources are Delta compatible including Synapse Analytics, Databricks, Snowflake, Data Factory, and others. Databricks and Synapse Analytics workspaces support queries that can be run on delta format files within the lake through a variety of languages within notebooks. Additionally, Delta supports Apache Spark APIs to create and manage Delta Lakes. Azure Data Factory's Mapping Data Flows can perform ACID-compliant Delta Lake CRUD operations through GUI-designed ETL pipelines. Many of the ACID-compliant features of Delta Lake are included in the following list:

- **Atomicity**: *Write either All Data or Nothing.* Apache Spark save modes do not utilize any locking and are not atomic. With this, a failed job may leave an incomplete file and may corrupt data. Additionally, a failing job may remove the old file and corrupt the new file. While this seems concerning, Spark does have in-built data frame writer APIs that are not atomic but behaves so for append operations. This however does come with performance overhead for use with cloud storage.
- **Consistency**: *Data is always in a valid state.* If the Spark API writer deletes an old file and creates a new one and the operation is not transactional, then there will always be a period of time when the file does not exist between the deletion of the old file and creation of the new. In that scenario, if the overwrite operation fails, this will result in data loss of the old file. Additionally, the new file may not be created. This is a typical spark overwrite operation issue related to consistency.
- **Isolation**: *Multiple transactions occur independently without interference.* This means that when writing to a dataset, other concurrent reads or writes on the same dataset should not be impacted by the write operation. Typical transactional databases offer multiple isolation levels. While Spark has task and job-level commits, since it lacks atomicity, it does not have isolation types.

- **Durability**: *Committed data is never lost.* When Spark does not correctly implement a commit, then it overwrites all the great durability features offered by cloud storage options and either corrupts or loses the data. This violates data durability.

When designing a Data Lake, it is important to design the appropriate zones and folder structures, as shown in Figure 1-5. Typically, the Lakehouse can contain multiple zones including raw, staging, and curated. In its most simplistic form, there exists a raw and curated zone, as shown in Figure 1-5. The raw zone is basically the landing zone where all disparate data sources including structured, semi-structured, and unstructured data can land. The data in this zone is typically stored as parquet format but can also support JSON, CSV, XML, images, and much more. Parquet files, in columnar format, can be further compressed with what is called snappy compression which offers a 97.5% compression ratio. As data moves toward curation and consumption, there can be various other zones in between ranging from data science zone to staging zone and more. Databricks typically label their zones as Bronze, Silver, and Gold. Once the data is ready for final curation, it would move to a curated zone which would typically be in delta format and also serves as a consumption layer within the Lakehouse. It is typically in this zone where the Lakehouse would store and serve their dimensional Lakehouse models to consumers. A Data Lake can have multiple containers to segregate access, and each Data Lake Storage account has up to five petabytes of storage capacity. There are a variety of security-level access controls ranging from role-based access control (RBAC) to shared access signature (SAS) that need to be considered when designing a Data Lake. For more information on designing a Data Lake, check out my MSSQLTips article here: `www.mssqltips.com/sqlservertip/6807/design-azure-data-lake-store-gen2/`. Once curated data is available in the Delta Lake, it can be accessed via a variety of BI tools including Synapse Analytics workspace for further analysis and insights, all within the Lakehouse.

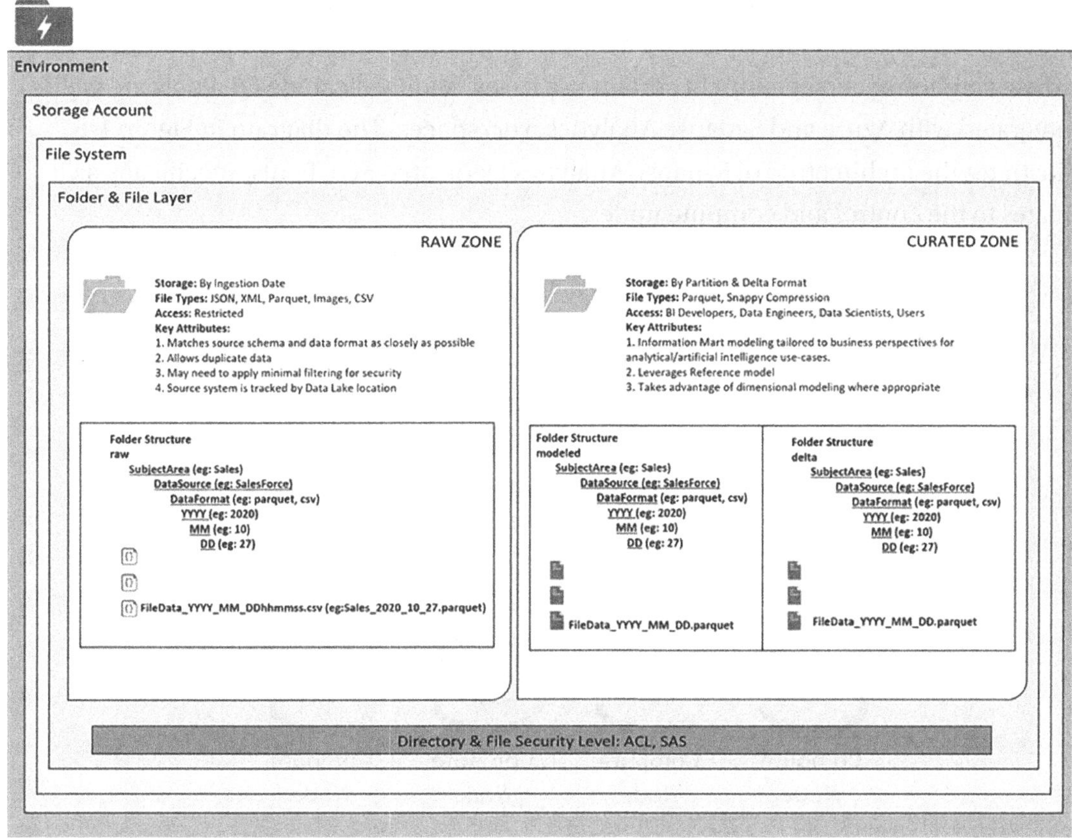

Figure 1-5. *Data Lake zones and hierarchies*

Synapse Analytics Dedicated SQL Pools

Dedicated SQL Pools, formerly called Azure SQL data warehouse, is a big data warehouse system that leverages a scale-out architecture to distribute the compute resources for data processing across multiple nodes. A control node optimizes queries for parallel processing and passes the operations to the compute nodes for parallel processing. Dedicated SQL Pools decouple storage from compute which supports sizing of compute independently of storage, much like Snowflake's architecture. It also supports pausing and resuming of the compute resources as needed. It stores data in a relational table with columnar storage. Data Warehousing Units (DWU) are used to measure the size of a Dedicated SQL Pool. Dedicated SQL Pools represent a traditional big data warehouse and oftentimes fit into the Lakehouse architecture in the form of a serving layer which can easily connect to a variety of BI tools including

Power BI and non-Azure tools such as Tableau and more. Dedicated SQL Pools are similar to Snowflake data warehouse and oftentimes are compared with Snowflake as a data warehouse choice. Both fit certain use cases, and Dedicated SQL Pools are well integrated with Azure and Synapse Analytics workspaces. The diagram in Figure 1-6 illustrates the architecture of Synapse Analytics Dedicated SQL Pools, specifically as it relates to the control and compute nodes.

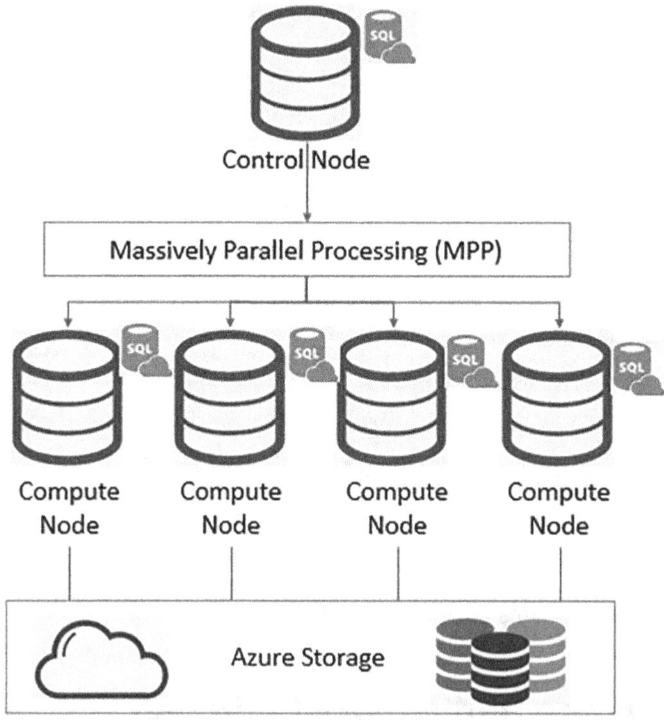

Figure 1-6. *Synapse Dedicated SQL Pool appliance architecture*

The two types of main data distributions that are used in Dedicated SQL Pools are hash and round-robin distributed tables. Round robin is the default distribution type for a table in a Dedicated SQL Pool, and the data for a round-robin distributed table is distributed evenly across all the distributions. As data gets loaded, each row is simply sent to the next distribution to balance the data across distributions. Usually, common dimension tables or staging tables or tables that don't distribute data evenly are good candidates for round-robin distributed tables. A hash distributed table's data gets distributed across multiple distributions and eventually gets processed by multiple compute nodes in parallel across all the compute nodes. Fact tables or large tables are good candidates for hash distributed tables. You select one of the columns from the table to use as the distribution key column when creating a hash distributed table, and then Dedicated SQL Pools automatically distribute the rows across all 60 distributions based on distribution key column value. Replicated tables eliminate the need to transfer data across compute nodes by replicating a full copy of the data of the specified table to each compute node. The best candidates for replicated tables are tables with sizes less than 2 GB compressed and small dimension tables. For more details on getting a better understanding of this section from a deeper technical perspective, check out my MSSQLTips article on this topic that can be found here: `www.mssqltips.com/sqlservertip/4889/design-and-manage-azure-sql-data-warehouse/`

Relational Database

Interestingly, relational databases still play a role in modern Data Lakehouse architectures because of their reliability and vast battle-hardened feature set from decades of iterations and product releases. Since the Lakehouse is still in its infancy and many fully native Lakehouse technologies are still evolving and growing, organizations prefer to have a hybrid architectural model where data can be served in both the Lakehouse and a traditional relational database. This approach solves for learning curve issues for getting ramped up with the Lakehouse's capability along with the connectivity limitations for existing BI tools to seamlessly connect to parquet and/or delta format data in the Lakehouse. There are various options for relational databases on the Azure platform including SQL options, MariaDB, PostgresSQL, and MySQL, so the database of choice will always be dependent on a variety of factors driven by the particular need and use case. This section will focus on Azure SQL database, specifically its purchasing models, service tiers, and deployment models.

Azure SQL database is a cloud-computing database service (database as a service), which is offered by Microsoft Azure Platform which helps to host and use a relational SQL database in the cloud without requiring any hardware or software installation. We will be using the standard Azure SQL database in many of the chapters in this book as a source, sink, and metadata-driven control database.

Purchasing Models (SQL DTU vs. vCore Database)

There are a vast number of SQL database options in Azure including DTU vs. vCore. DTU and vCores are two different purchasing models for Azure SQL which include variations in computation, memory, storage, and IO. Azure pricing calculator can help with aligning cost and capability with the appropriate SQL database solution.

A DTU unit is a combination of CPU, memory, and read and write operations and can be increased when more power is needed. It is a great solution if you have a preconfigured resource configuration where the consumption of resources is balanced across CPU, memory, and IO. You can increase the number of DTUs reserved once you reach a limit on the allocated resources and experience throttling, which translates into slower performance or timeouts.

The disadvantage of DTUs is that you don't have the flexibility to scale only a specific resource type, like the memory or the CPU. Because of this, you can end up paying additional resources without needing or using them.

The vCore model allows you to scale each resource (CPU, memory, IO) independently. You could scale the storage space up and down the database based on how many GB of storage is needed, and you can also scale the number of cores (vCores). The disadvantage is that you can't control the size of memory independently. Also, it is important to note that vCore serverless compute resources are twice the price of provisioned compute resources, so a constant high load would cost more in serverless than it would in provisioned. vCores can use the SQL Server licenses that you have from your on-premises environment.

Service Tiers

There are three available service tiers for Azure SQL database:

- **General-purpose/standard** service tier is designed for common workloads. It offers budget-oriented balanced compute and storage options.
- **Business-critical/business-premium** service tier is designed for online transaction processing (OLTP) applications with high transaction rate and lowest-latency I/O. It offers the highest resilience to failures by using several isolated replicas.
- **Hyperscale** service tier is designed for big data OLTP databases and the ability to scale storage and compute gracefully.

Deployment Models

There are two available deployment models for Azure SQL database:

- **Single database** represents a fully managed, isolated database. You might use this option if you have modern cloud applications and microservices that need a single reliable data source. A single database is similar to a contained database in the SQL Server database engine.
- **Elastic pool** is a collection of single databases with a shared set of resources, such as CPU or memory, and single databases can be moved into and out of an elastic pool.

Non-relational Databases

NoSQL databases also play a role in the Lakehouse paradigm due to their flexibility in handling unstructured data, millisecond response time, and high availability. Cosmos DB is one such fully managed NoSQL database service, which offers automatic and instant scalability, data replication, fast multi-region reads/writes, and open source APIs for MongoDB and Cassandra. With Cosmos DB's Azure Synapse Link, users can get near real-time insights on data stored in a transactional system. Azure Synapse Link for Azure Cosmos DB is a cloud-native hybrid transactional and analytical processing (HTAP) capability that allows users to run near real-time analytics over operational data in Azure Cosmos DB. Data engineers, business analysts, and data scientists now have the ability to use Spark or SQL Pools to get near real-time insights into their data without impacting the performance of their transactional workloads in Cosmos DB.

There are numerous advantages to Azure Synapse Link for Azure Cosmos DB including reduced complexity since a near real-time analytical store either reduces or eliminates the need for complex E-T-L or change feed job processes. Additionally, there will be little to no impact on operational workloads since the analytical workloads are rendered independently of the transactional workloads and do not consume the provisioned operational throughput. Additionally, it is optimized for large-scale analytics workloads by leveraging the power of Serverless Spark and SQL Pools which makes it cost effective due to the highly elastic Azure Synapse Analytics compute engines. With a column-oriented analytical store for workloads on operational data including aggregations and more, along with decoupled performance for analytical workloads,

Azure Synapse Link for Azure Cosmos DB enables and empowers self-service, near real-time insights on transactional data. Figure 1-7 illustrates the role Azure Synapse Link plays between a transactional Cosmos DB and the analytical Synapse Analytics workspace.

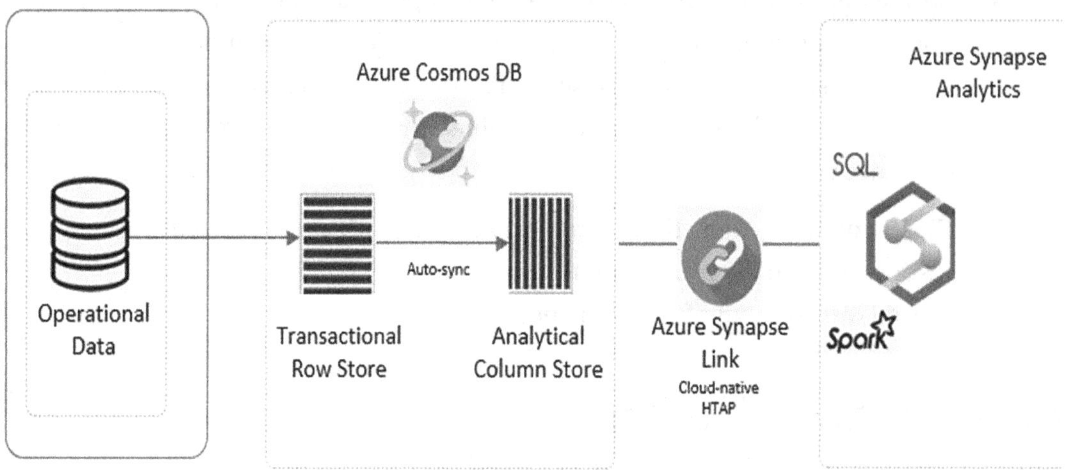

***Figure 1-7.** Azure Synapse Link connected to Cosmos DB and Synapse Analytics*

When deciding when to choose between a SQL and NoSQL database for your data solution, ensure that you take the following comparison factors into consideration, as shown in Table 1-2.

***Table 1-2.** SQL vs. NoSQL*

	SQL	NOSQL
Definition	SQL databases are primarily called RDBMS or relational databases	NoSQL databases are primarily called as non-relational or distributed database
Design for	Traditional RDBMS uses SQL syntax and queries to analyze and get the data for further insights. They are used for OLAP systems	NoSQL database systems consist of various kinds of database technologies. These databases were developed in response to the demands presented for the development of the modern application
Query language	Structured query language (SQL)	No declarative query language

(continued)

Table 1-2. *(continued)*

	SQL	NOSQL
Type	SQL databases are table-based databases	NoSQL databases can be document based, key-value pairs, graph databases
Schema	SQL databases have a predefined schema	NoSQL databases use dynamic schema for unstructured data
Ability to scale	SQL databases are vertically scalable	NoSQL databases are horizontally scalable
Examples	Oracle, Postgres, and MS-SQL	MongoDB, Redis, Neo4j, Cassandra, Hbase
Best suited for	An ideal choice for the complex query-intensive environment	It is not a good fit for complex queries
Hierarchical data storage	SQL databases are not suitable for hierarchical data storage	More suitable for the hierarchical data store as it supports key-value pair methods
Variations	One type with minor variations	Many different types which include key-value stores, document databases, and graph databases
Development year	It was developed in the 1970s to deal with issues with flat file storage	Developed in the late 2000s to overcome issues and limitations of SQL databases
Consistency	It should be configured for strong consistency	It depends on DBMS as some offers strong consistency like MongoDB, whereas others offer only eventual consistency, like Cassandra
Best used for	RDBMS database is the right option for solving ACID problems	NoSQL is best used for solving data availability problems
Importance	It should be used when data validity is super important	Use when it's more important to have fast data than correct data
Best option	When you need to support dynamic queries	Use when you need to scale based on changing requirements
ACID vs. BASE model	ACID (atomicity, consistency, isolation, and durability) is a standard for RDBMS	BASE (basically available, soft state, eventually consistent) is a model of many NoSQL systems

The following APIs are available in Cosmos DB:

- **SQL**: Provides capabilities for data users who are comfortable with SQL queries. Even though the data is stored in JSON format, it can easily be queried by using SQL-like queries.
- **MongoDB**: Existing instances of MongoDB can be migrated to Azure Cosmos DB without major effort.
- **Gremlin**: Can be used for storing and performing operations on graph data and supports native capabilities for graph modeling and traversing.
- **Casandra**: Dedicated data store for applications created for Apache Cassandra where users have the ability to interact with data via CQL (Cassandra Query Language)
- **Table**: Can be used by applications prepared natively for close working with Azure Storage tables.

Snowflake

Snowflake is a modern cloud data warehouse platform which integrates well with the Azure platform and does not require dedicated resources for setup, maintenance, and support. Snowflake's architecture, shown in Figure 1-8, runs on cloud infrastructure and uses a central data repository for persisted data that is accessible from all compute nodes in the platform which is beneficial for data management, known as shared disk architecture. Snowflake also processes queries using MPP compute clusters where each node in the cluster stores a portion of the entire dataset locally, also known as shared nothing architecture, which is beneficial for performance management. Multiple compute clusters are grouped together to form virtual warehouses. Multiple virtual warehouses can be created to access the same storage layer without needing multiple copies of the data in each warehouse. These virtual warehouses can be scaled up or down with minimal downtime or impact to storage. Snowflake also provides a variety of services including infrastructure, security and metadata management, optimizers, and robust authentication and access control methods. These services manage the storage and compute layers and ensure security and high availability of the platform. Snowflake's architecture also includes and supports zero-copy cloning, time travel, and data sharing. With zero-copy cloning, the CLONE command allows users to create copies of their schemas, databases, and tables without copying the underlying data while having access to close to real-time production data in various environments. With time travel, historical data that has been changed or deleted can be retrieved within a defined time period. With data sharing, Snowflake producers and consumers can easily share and consume data from a variety of unique avenues without having to physically copy or move the data. Snowflake costs are based on usage; therefore, users only pay for storage and compute resources that are used.

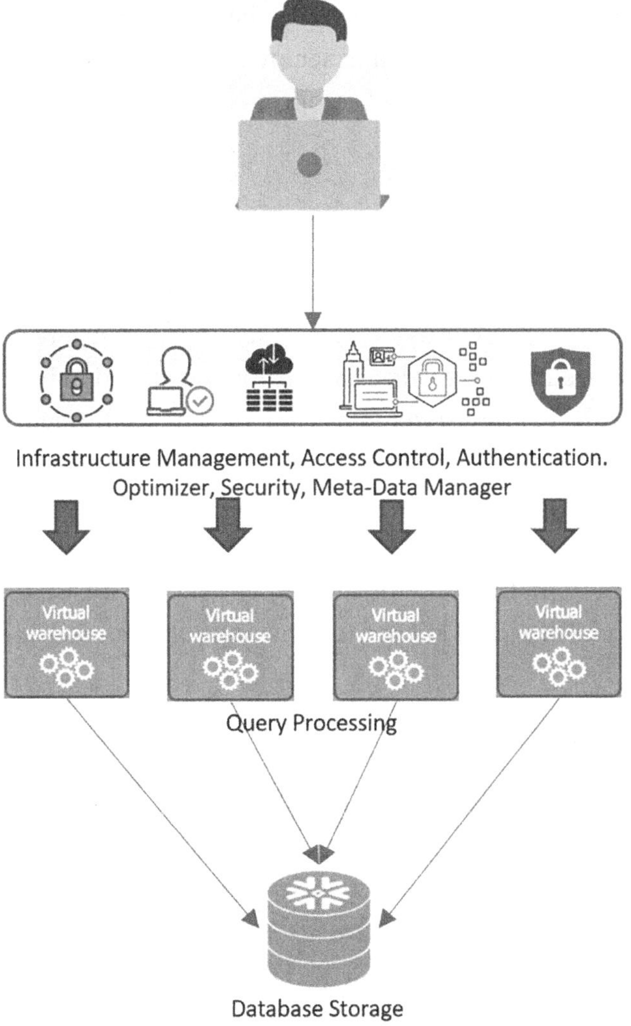

Figure 1-8. *Snowflake architecture*

Snowflake provides a number of capabilities including the ability to scale storage and compute independently, data sharing through a Data Marketplace, seamless integration with custom-built applications, batch and streaming ELT capabilities, complex data manipulation functions and features, support for a variety of file formats, and more. Snowflake provides a variety of connectivity options including command-line clients such as Snow SQL, ODBC/JDBC drivers, Python/Spark connectors, and a list of third-party connectors. These capabilities make Snowflake a strong complementary choice during the design and implementation of your Lakehouse because it offers unique capabilities which include reasonably priced big data storage and compute resources, multiple secure data sharing offerings, and secure and protected integration with Azure services, along with data encryption and compression capabilities.

Consumption

Storing and serving data is a pivotal step in the end-to-end life cycle from sourcing data to consuming it. It is within the storage and serving layer where the cleansed, transformed, and curated data is made available for consumption by the end users. Consumption can come in many different variations such as through Azure-native BI tools including Power BI, Analysis Services, Power Platform, etc. Data within the Lakehouse can also be consumed by a variety of non-Azure BI tools such as Tableau, Informatica, and more. A good Lakehouse serving layer offers flexibility for consuming the data from a variety of BI tools. In this section, our efforts will focus on understanding the capabilities of some of these Lakehouse consumption options within Azure.

Analysis Services

Azure Analysis Services (AAS) is a fully managed platform as a service (PaaS) that provides enterprise-grade data models in the cloud. With Analysis Services, users can create secured KPIs, data models, metrics, and more from multiple data sources with a tabular semantic data model. Analysis Services integrates well with a variety of Azure services and can connect to Synapse Analytics Dedicated Pools. Figure 1-9 shows a sample AAS workspace which can be accessed through Visual Studio (VS).

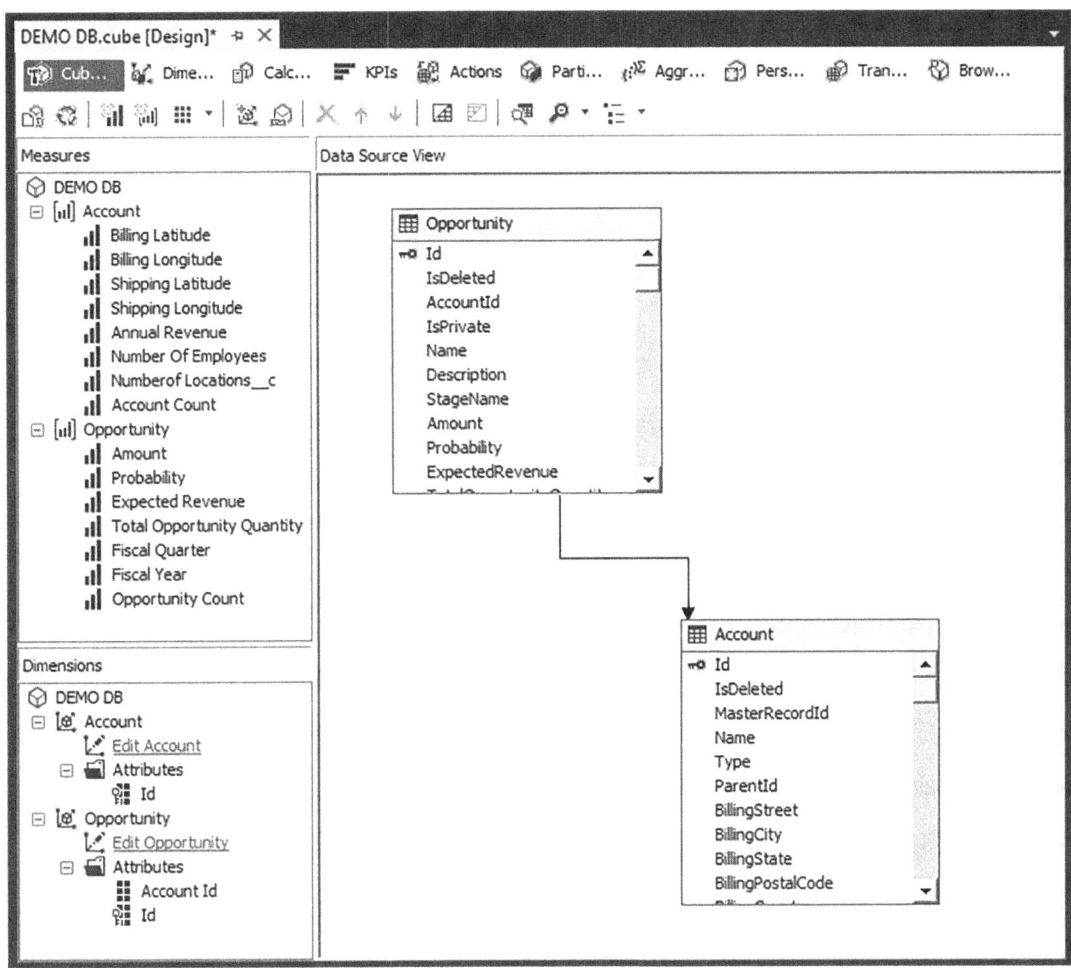

***Figure 1-9.** Azure Analysis Services*

When comparing Analysis Services with Power BI Premium (PBI), Analysis Services (AAS) may offer better scale-out capabilities, metadata translations, object-level security, and perspective feature set; however, in the modern Lakehouse, organizations and users are strongly considering and choosing Power BI Premium over AAS due to its vast features including paginated reports, data flows, AI workloads, pay per user models, and much more. Table 1-3 lists many of these comparisons between PBI and AAS.

Table 1-3. *Power BI Premium vs. Azure Analysis Services*

	Power BI Premium	Azure Analysis Services
Unlimited Power BI content viewing	Yes	No
Paginated reports	Yes	No
Data flows	Yes	No
AI workload	Yes	No
Multi-model memory management	Yes	No
Pre-aggregated tables	Yes	No
Composite models	Yes	No
Automated incremental refresh	Yes	No
Large datasets	Yes	Yes
Third-party application support	Yes	Yes
Bring your own key (BYOK)	Yes	No
Scale out	Not yet	Yes
Metadata translations	Not yet	Yes
Object-level security	Not yet	Yes
Perspectives	Not yet	Yes

Power BI

Power BI (PBI) is an Azure-native reporting technology which provides interactive visualizations and business intelligence capabilities which empower users to create their own visually appealing, accurate, and highly performant reports and dashboards. While Power BI dashboards can be custom built, there are a variety of dashboards that can be either purchased or are publicly available on open source platforms. For example, the following GitHub Repository: `https://github.com/Azure/ccodashboard` provides a variety of dashboards which can leverage Azure REST APIs to gain insights into critical monitoring, operations, and infrastructure components within your Azure Data Lakehouse platform. Figure 1-10 shows the sample home page of Power BI where developers can get started with building their reports and dashboards.

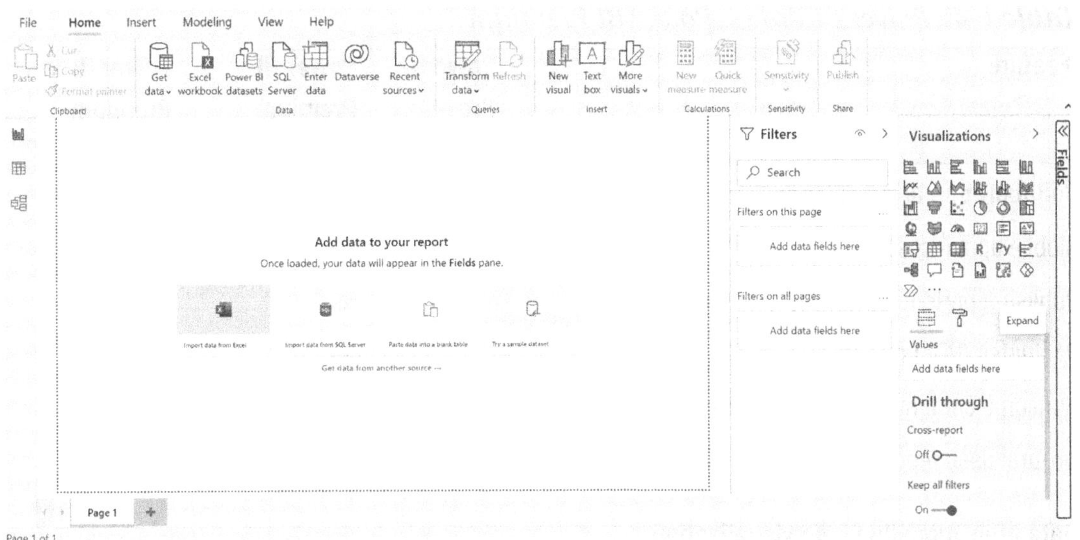

Figure 1-10. *Power BI UI*

With Power BI, users can directly query the Lakehouse parquet files using the OPENROWSET function within a SQL query after specifying a SQL serverless endpoint in the connection credentials. Within the Synapse Analytics workspace, you can create a PBI linked service and use that within the various services of the Synapse Analytics unified analytics platform. Power BI also supports connectivity to a variety of other Lakehouse tools including Databricks, Snowflake, REST APIs, and many more. From a cost optimization perspective, parquet will perform optimally due to its columnar storage format benefits; therefore, the view on parquet files in Synapse Serverless SQL Pools will result in low-cost compute resources. For a high number of queries across extremely large datasets, Dedicated SQL Pools may be the better storage choice to prevent from high costs incurring per query. Materialized views with external tables on Dedicated SQL Pools may help with these high query volumes against the large datasets. When selecting a PBI service option, there are a few options to choose from which include Premium vs. Pro. Each option comes with its own capabilities and price points. Table 1-4 shows a side-by-side comparison between Power BI Pro and Premium to help with choosing the right feature for your reporting needs.

Table 1-4. *Power BI Pro vs. Power BI Premium*

Feature	Power BI Pro	Power BI Premium Per user	Power BI Premium Per capacity
Collaboration and analytics			
Mobile app access	Yes	Yes	Yes
Publish reports to share and collaborate	Yes	Yes	
Paginated (RDL) reports		Yes	Yes
Consume content without a per user license			Yes
On-premises reporting with Power BI Report Server			Yes
Data prep, modeling, and visualization			
Model size limit	1 GB	100 GB	400 GB
Refresh rate	8/day	48/day	48/day
Connect to 100+ data sources	Yes	Yes	Yes
Create reports and visualizations with Power BI Desktop4	Yes	Yes	Yes
Embed APIs and controls	Yes	Yes	Yes
AI visuals	Yes	Yes	Yes
Advanced AI (text analytics, image detection, automated machine learning)		Yes	Yes
XMLA endpoint read/write connectivity		Yes	Yes
Data flows (direct query, linked and computed entities, enhanced compute engine)		Yes	Yes
Analyze data stored in Azure Data Lake Storage		Yes	Yes
Governance and administration			
Data security and encryption	Yes	Yes	Yes
Metrics for content creation, consumption, and publishing	Yes	Yes	Yes

(*continued*)

Table 1-4. (*continued*)

Feature	Power BI Pro	Power BI Premium Per user	Power BI Premium Per capacity
Application life cycle management		Yes	Yes
Multi-geo deployment management			Yes
Bring your own key (BYOK)			Yes
Auto-scale add-on availability (preview)			Yes
Maximum storage	10 GB/user	100 TB	100 TB
Continuous integration and deployment			
Deployment pipelines (including paginated reports management)		Yes	Yes

Power Apps

Power Apps is a suite of apps, services, connectors, and data platform that provides a rapid application development environment to build custom apps for your business needs. There are two styles of these apps: canvas apps and model-driven apps. Canvas apps provide you with a blank canvas onto which you can drag and drop components in any formation to design a user interface. Model-driven apps are based on underlying data stored in Common Data Service (CDS), which is a secure, cloud-based storage space that organizations can use to store business application data. Canvas apps are ideal for building task-based or role-based applications. Model-driven apps, on the other hand, are better for creating end-to-end solutions. Within the Lakehouse, Power Apps fits within the consumption layer since users are able to build custom apps to interact with data in the storage and serving layer using GUI-based BI tools to interact with the data through read and write back operations.

Advanced Analytics

As data makes its way into the storage, serving, and consumption layers of the Lakehouse, a subset of your data consumers, including from business stakeholders, data scientists, and others, may be interested in the data from the perspective of performing advanced analytics on the Lakehouse datasets. These various stakeholders and data consumers would be interested in understanding the capabilities that the Lakehouse provides as it relates to cognitive services and machine learning. With the benefit of having data stored in the Lakehouse which supports a variety of file formats such as images, parquet, JSON, AVRO, xml, REST APIs, and more, Azure cognitive and machine learning services can seamlessly connect to these various Lakehouse datasets through their Azure-native tools and technologies.

Cognitive Services

Cognitive services brings AI to developers through APIs and offers a variety of services to provide the ability for AI to see, hear, speak, search, understand, and accelerate decision making into apps. Developers of all skill levels and those that do not have an expertise in machine learning can easily add AI capabilities to their apps. The current available Azure cognitive services include the following. Each of these services has the capability of connecting to Lakehouse datasets store and served in Azure Storage (ADLS gen2 and BLOB).

- **Anomaly Detector**: Identifies potential problems early on
- **Content Moderator**: Detects potentially offensive or unwanted content
- **Metrics Advisor**: Monitors metrics and diagnoses issues
- **Personaliser**: Creates rich, personalized experiences for every user
- **Immersive Reader**: Helps comprehend text using audio and visual cues
- **Language Understanding**: Builds natural language understanding in apps
- **QnA Maker**: Creates a conversational question and answer layer over data
- **Text Analytics**: Detects sentiment, key phrases, and named entities
- **Translator**: Detects and translates more than 90 supported languages
- **Speech to Text**: Transcribes audio speech into readable text

- **Text to Speech**: Converts text to lifelike speech for natural interfaces.
- **Speech Translation**: Integrates real-time speech translation into apps.
- **Speaker Recognition**: Identifies and verifies speaking based on audio
- **Computer Vision**: Analyzes content in images and video.
- **Custom Vision**: Customizes image recognition to fit your business needs
- **Face**: Detects and identifies people and emotions in images
- **Form Recognizer**: Extracts text, key-value pairs, and tables from documents
- **Video Indexer**: Analyzes visual and audio of video and index content
- **Search**: Provides developers with APIs and tools for building a rich search experience over private, heterogeneous content in web, mobile, and enterprise applications

Machine Learning

Azure Machine Learning is a service that delivers a complete data science platform. It supports both code-first and low-code experiences. Azure Machine Learning studio is a web portal in Azure Machine Learning that contains low-code and no-code options for project authoring and asset management and can connect to a variety of Lakehouse services including ADLS gen2, Azure SQL database, and more. Azure Machine Learning also integrates well with other Databricks, Data Factory, and Kubernetes services for model deployment. The three main machine learning techniques include the following:

- **Supervised learning**: Algorithms make predictions based on a set of labeled examples that you provide. This technique is useful when you know what the outcome should look like.
- **Unsupervised learning**: Algorithms label the datasets for you by organizing the data or describing its structure. This technique is useful when you don't know what the outcome should look like.

- **Reinforcement learning**: Algorithms learn from outcomes and decide which action to take next. After each action, the algorithm receives feedback that helps it determine whether the choice it made was correct, neutral, or incorrect. It's a good technique to use for automated systems that have to make a lot of small decisions without human guidance.

Continuous Integration, Deployment, and Governance

Once you've fully built out your ingestion, processing, serving, storage, and consumption layers of your Lakehouse platform, there are various options for continuously integrating and deploying automated code to multiple environments along with applying robust data governance policies and practices on data. This section will cover CI/CD and data governance (Purview) within the Azure Data Lakehouse platform.

DevOps

A CI/CD pipeline is used to automate the process of continuous integration and continuous deployment. The pipeline facilitates the software delivery process via stages like build, test, merge, and deploy. Azure DevOps Server is a Microsoft product that provides version control, reporting, requirements management, project management, automated builds, testing, and release management capabilities. It covers the entire application life cycle and enables DevOps capabilities such as CI/CD within the Lakehouse. This section will cover the various CI/CD pipelines and processes including SQL database, Data Factory, and MLOps deployments that can be built within the Lakehouse.

There are a few methods of deploying Azure Data Factory environments with Azure DevOps CI/CD. Source-control repository options can range from GitHub to DevOps Git, and implementation architectures can range from utilizing adf_publish branches to using working and master branches instead. Azure DevOps build and release pipelines can be used for CI/CD, and custom PowerShell scripts can be used for deploying the CI/CD Data Factory resources automatically within upper environments. Figure 1-11 illustrates the CI/CD process for ADF.

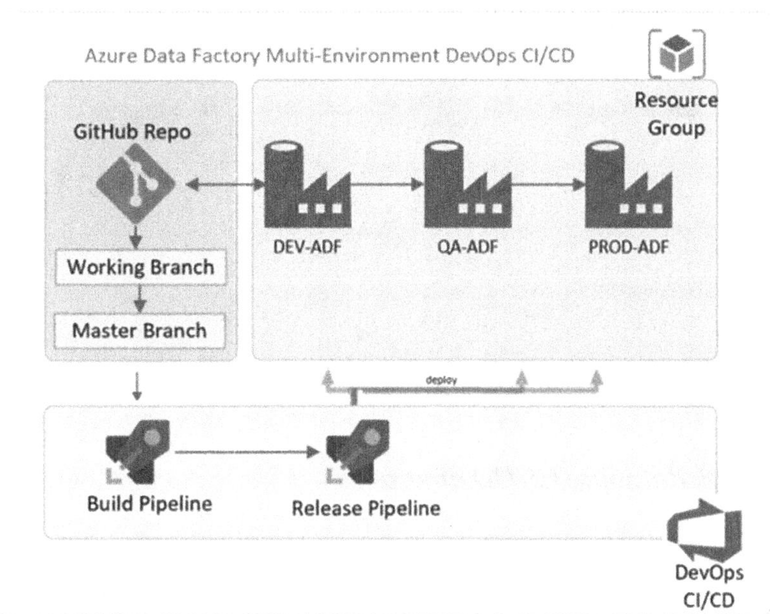

Figure 1-11. *ADF CI/CD diagram*

CI/CD within Azure SQL databases and Synapse Dedicated SQL Pools is also possible with Azure DevOps. The best way to work with change control to prepare for CI and CD for databases is to perform all development using Visual Studio. There are a few source-control options within Visual Studio. GitHub is one of these source-control options and offers a number of benefits including advanced security options. Integrating multiple applications such as Visual Studio, GitHub, Azure DevOps, and Azure SQL databases for a seamless CI/CD process is a growing need for many enterprises that are on a journey to modernize their data and infrastructure platform. The architectural flow diagram shown in Figure 1-12 illustrates how to deploy local SQL DDL and DML scripts from Visual Studio to an Azure SQL database through a GitHub repository which is then picked up with an Azure DevOps build (CI) and release (CD) pipeline that tests and deploys the changes to the upper environments.

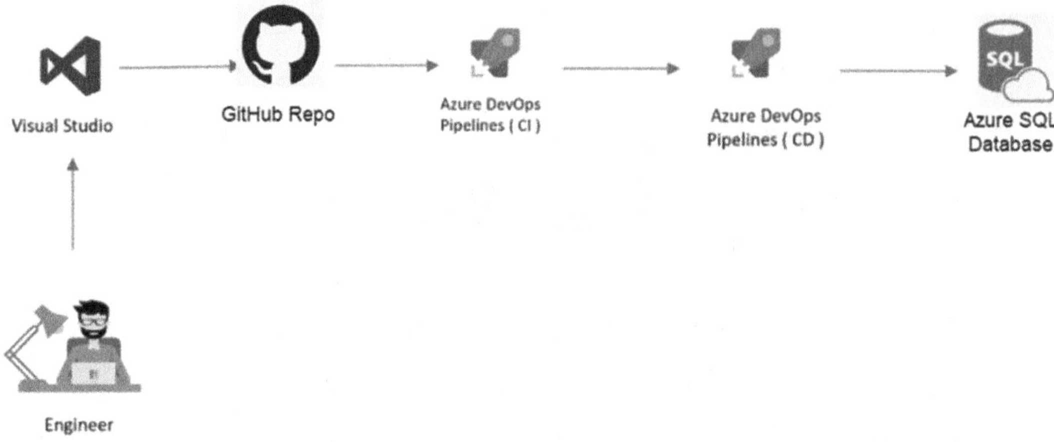

Figure 1-12. *SQL database CI/CD diagram*

The DevOps CI/CD paradigm is prevalent across a variety of Azure PaaS services. DevOps for machine learning, also known as MLOps, enables data science, IT, and business teams to increase the pace of model development and deployment through automated continuous integration and deployment best practices. Well-designed MLOps paradigms support monitoring, validation, and governance of machine learning models. Large globally distributed organizations are seeking methods of success for deploying MLOps Frameworks across their organizations for multiple data science teams. They are seeking to clearly understand Azure MLOps Frameworks and patterns of success as they champion MLOps across their organizations. Figure 1-13, containing a generic Azure MLOps Framework architecture diagram, illustrates just how Azure Machine Learning, coupled with Azure DevOps, makes the concept of the Azure MLOps Framework a reality.

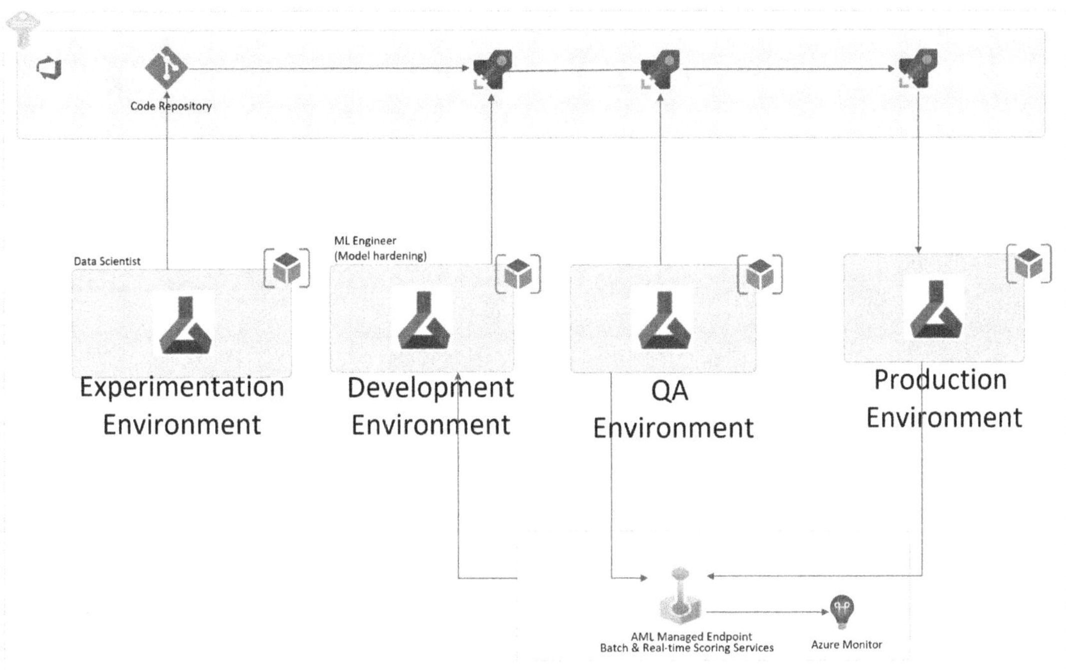

Figure 1-13. *MLOps CI/CD diagram*

Purview

Purview is an Azure-native cloud-based SaaS data governance technology which brings with it an easy-to-use UI and catalog for easily discovering and understanding data sources by the users who register and manage the data assets. Users can maintain a copy of the indexed metadata as well as a reference to the source location. Figure 1-14 shows the home page of the Purview UI.

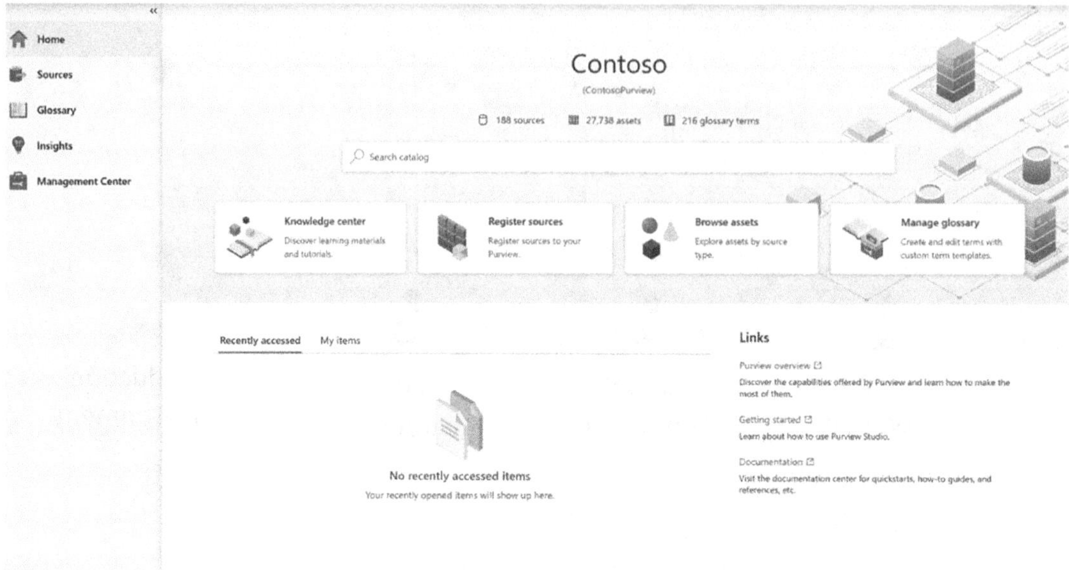

Figure 1-14. *Purview home page UI*

Additionally, this metadata can be further enriched in Purview through tags, descriptions, and more. Figure 1-15 shows a sample of how lineage can be tracked within Purview for an Azure Data Factory copy activity. Lineage can also be registered with the Purview REST API and can be integrated with Azure Functions for a more customized and code-driven experience that can be used with other Azure Data Lakehouse services such as Databricks. Lineage from Power BI can also be captured within Purview for scanning and retrieving lineage of PBI assets. Please see the following GitHub Repository: `https://github.com/franmer2/AzurePurviewFullPBILineage_US` to learn more about the technical details for integrating Purview with Power BI.

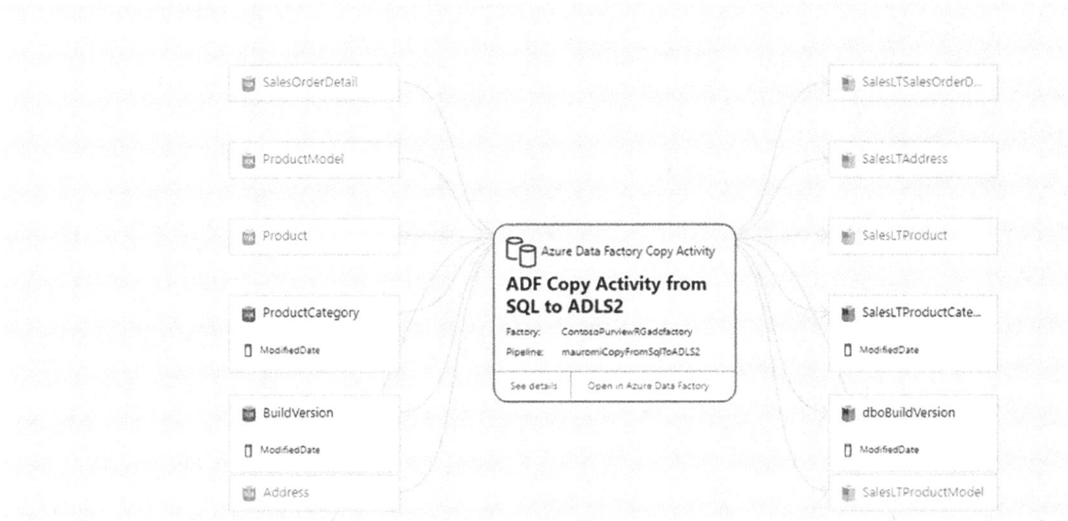

Figure 1-15. *Purview Lineage for ADF copy activity*

Summary

The Modern Azure Data Lakehouse is quickly becoming a pivotal architectural paradigm in the cloud services and data warehousing domain. It offers a seamless native integration with ingestion, processing, storing, serving, and consumption layer technologies in Azure. Its advantages of low-cost, high-performance, and exceptionally secure cloud ELT, storage, compute, optimization, and querying capabilities are catching the eye of many organizations as they search for a futuristic solution that encompasses all of these benefits. Organizations are seeking to move away from low-performing, high-cost, infrastructure-bound architectures and technologies and into the Lakehouse where they will be able to reap the benefits of automated testing, continuous integrations and deployment, and advanced analytics capabilities.

PART II

Data Platforms

CHAPTER 2

Snowflake

Snowflake, a modern cloud data warehouse platform, provides a number of capabilities including the ability to scale storage and compute independently, data sharing through a Data Marketplace, seamless integration with custom-built applications, batch and streaming ELT capabilities, complex data manipulation functions and features, and more. These capabilities make Snowflake a strong complementary choice during the design and implementation of the Lakehouse paradigm since it offers unique capabilities which include reasonably priced big data storage and compute resources, multiple secure data sharing offerings, and secure interaction with numerous Azure services through APIs and out-of-the-box Snowflake connectors. Customers are often unaware of the various capabilities of Snowflake along with how they could get started with exploring Snowflake.

There are many benefits to Snowflake including its elastic ability to scale up its virtual warehouse to improve performance and speed and scale down afterward. There are also a variety of SQL-based functions and support options to combine both structured and semi-structured data for analysis and ELT. Snowflake's multi-cluster architecture is built for highly concurrent workloads and easy accessibility for multiple stakeholders. Snowflake's architecture enables data sharing among Snowflake users and external customers with ease. Snowflake also offers high availability and security on Azure. It is SOC 2 Type II certified and supports additional levels of security for HIPAA customers and encryption across all network communications. In this chapter, you will learn about the various capabilities of Snowflake which include its security, governance, and replication/failover feature sets. In addition, you will learn more about Snowflake's capabilities around data sharing, data applications, and its data import, export, and transformation integrations with Azure resources. The topics you will learn will help with applying it toward practical Lakehouse decisions, implementations, and ELT integrations with Azure.

R. L'Esteve, *The Azure Data Lakehouse Toolkit*, https://doi.org/10.1007/978-1-4842-8233-5_2

Architecture

Snowflake's architecture, shown again in Figure 2-1, runs on cloud infrastructure and includes a new SQL query engine. Snowflake uses a central data repository for persisted data that is accessible from all compute nodes in the platform which is beneficial for data management, known as shared disk architecture. Snowflake also processes queries using MPP compute clusters where each node in the cluster stores a portion of the entire dataset locally, also known as shared nothing architecture, which is beneficial for performance management. Multiple compute clusters are grouped together to form virtual warehouses. Multiple virtual warehouses can be created to access the same storage layer without needing multiple copies of the data in each warehouse. These virtual warehouses can be scaled up or down with minimal downtime or impact to storage. Snowflake also provides a variety of services including infrastructure, security and metadata management, optimizers, and robust authentication and access control methods. These services manage the storage and compute layers and ensure security and high availability of the platform.

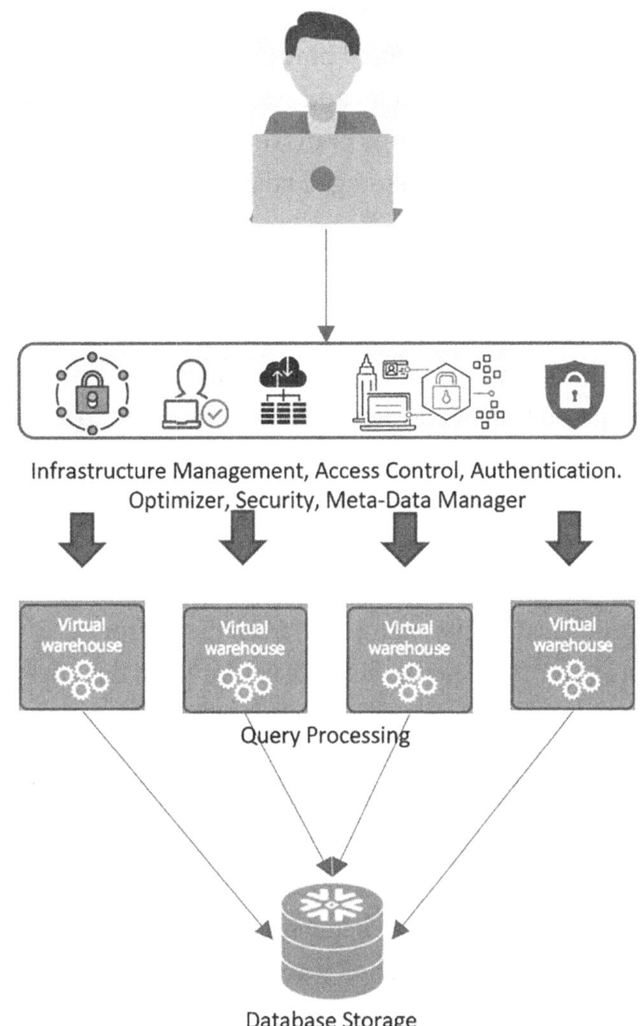

Figure 2-1. *Snowflake architecture diagram*

When data is loaded into Snowflake, it is optimized, compressed as AES-256 encryption, and stored in cloud storage. Queries are processed using virtual warehouses, which are basically MPP compute clusters with multiple nodes. From a connectivity perspective, Snowflake provides a variety of connection options including its robust UI, command-line clients such as Snow SQL, ODBC/JDBC drivers, Python/Spark connectors, and list of third-party connectors. Snowflake's architecture also includes and supports zero-copy cloning, time travel, and data sharing. With zero-copy cloning, the CLONE command allows users to create copies of their schemas, databases, and tables without copying thc underlying data while having access to close to real-time production data in various environments. With time travel, historical data that has been changed or deleted can be retrieved within a defined time period. With data sharing, Snowflake producers and consumers can easily share and consume data from a variety of unique avenues without having to physically copy or move the data. Snowflake costs are based on usage; therefore, users only pay for storage and compute resources that are used.

Cost

Before we dive into cost, it is important to note that Snowflake offers a 30-day free trial with up to $400 of usage, so from a cost perspective, this may help with building out a use case to test certain storage and compute features. Snowflake's pricing model is based on storage and compute resource usage within the Snowflake platform. These final costs can exponentially increase when your Lakehouse architecture includes Snowflake as the consumption layer coupled with Azure Data Lake Storage Gen2 as the storage layer and Power BI as the reporting layer. That being said, from the perspective of the Snowflake data warehouse, storage is priced per terabyte of compressed data per month, and compute is based on processing units (credits) that are billed on usage per second. In the United States, storage costs begin at $23/terabyte and $0.00056/second for each credit used. Since virtual warehouses come in many sizes, Snowflake supports the following compute credit usage per hour. The costs for storage and compute are also determined by the edition (standard, enterprise, business critical), the region, and whether the account is on-demand (no long-term licensing requirements) or capacity (up-front commitment). The warehouses can be configured to auto-suspend when no queries are being run and it is in idle state, which contributes to further cost savings. This is quite a paradigm shift from traditional on-premises systems, along with a variety of other cloud data warehouses. Figure 2-2 shows the sizes and credit usage per hour for Snowflake.

Snowflake Warehouse Sizes and Credit Usage per Hour								
Size	X-Small	Small	Medium	Large	X-Large	2X-Large	3X-Large	4X-Large
Credit Usage per Hour	1	2	4	8	16	32	64	128

***Figure 2-2.** Snowflake warehouse sizes and credit usage per hour*

The annual pricing of Snowflake typically depends on the number of users, pipelines, and data. Figure 2-3 shows the estimated annual Snowflake cost based on these various factors. As with any cloud-based service, it is important to prevent misuse of any Snowflake features which may run up the bill, such as long and inefficient running compute jobs, the warehouse running 24/7, failing to enable auto-suspend and query timeout features, replicating very large datasets, and more.

Users	Pipelines	Data	Cost
Less than 20	Less than 20	Less than 5 TB	Between $30K and $80K
Between 30 and 50	Between 30 and 50	Less than 50TB	Between $100K and $200K
Greater than 100+	Between 100s to 1000s	Greater than 100+ TB	Between $300K and $500K

Figure 2-3. *Estimated annual Snowflake cost*

Security

Snowflake has a suite of strong security for both data and account users. From its vast compliance support features to its data and object security capabilities, Snowflake standard and advanced security features its various editions and offerings. Snowflake also offers private connectivity to a variety of external services and cloud providers including Azure via Azure Private Link for its business-critical or higher editions. Snowflake uses System for Cross-domain Identity Management (*SCIM*) to manage user identities and groups and supports Microsoft Azure Active Directory as a SCIM identity provider. From a user and authentication point of view, Snowflake supports MFA, OAuth, and SSO authentication types in addition to key-pair authentication as an alternative to basic authentication and key-pair rotation to support multiple active keys. Additionally, Snowflake offers tight access control and data encryption capabilities. In this section, we will take a closer look at Snowflake's integration with Azure-native tools, specifically Key Vault and Private Link.

Azure Key Vault

With Snowflake's business-critical edition, data encryption with customer-managed keys for Azure can be enabled with an Azure Key Vault that Snowflake has access to use. After customers create an RSA 4K key in their Azure tenant, they can grant a Snowflake service principal access to use the key for a variety of activities. Within Azure Data Factory, Snowflake database credentials can also be stored in Key Vault and configured in the Snowflake connector's linked service in ADF.

Azure Private Link

Azure Private Link enables private connectivity and access to Snowflake through a private IP address with traffic being routed from the customer virtual network (VNet) to the Snowflake VNet using Microsoft rather than the public Internet.

Azure Private Link on Snowflake can be enabled either through a virtual machine or through peering, which can then connect to the Azure Private Link endpoint in your virtual network, which then connects to the Private Link Service and routes to Snowflake.

Applications

Snowflake integrates well with data applications that use Snowflake as the analytical engine. The Snowflake SQL API allows users to access and update data, along with executing queries and DDL and DML statements in Snowflake DB. Snowflake also offers a number of connectors (Kafka, Python, Spark) and drivers (JDBC, .NET, Node.js, ODBC, PHP) to support and enable building custom data, reporting, and analysis applications. These custom-tailored solutions extend even further with user-defined functions (UDFs) to perform custom operations with either SQL, JavaScript, or Java. Snowflake also supports creating UDF in Azure Functions to simplify the integration with other external APIs. Branching and looping programming methods are supported in Snowflake Stored Procedures since it is combined with JavaScript.

Replication and Failover

Replication can be enabled for existing databases and will set the database as primary. Only databases are supported for replication. The secondary replica database would typically reside in a separate region and can be used in read-only mode. All DML and DDL operations will be run against the primary database, with the ability for data to be refreshed on a defined period from snapshots of the primary database. During replication, Snowflake encrypts the database files in transit from source to target. Limitations around replication include (1) restrictions on refreshes when external tables exist on the primary database and (2) prevention of replication for databases created from shares. Once replication is enabled for a primary database with at least one secondary replica database along with an active refresh schedule, failover can be enabled at that point.

Data Integration with Azure

While Snowflake is external to the Azure platform, it does integrate quite well with Azure from a security, identity, and data integration perspective. Between connectors, drivers, and plug-ins, both Snowflake and Azure support cross-platform integrations quite seamlessly. In this section, I will discuss some of these integration capabilities between Azure and Snowflake. Figure 2-4 illustrates an architectural pattern for integrating Snowflake with ADLS gen2, Data Factory, Databricks, and Power BI. This is a common pattern which uses Data Factory for data ingestion of source data; Databricks notebooks for transformations; Snowflake for the audit, balance, and control (ABC) frameworks and data warehouse; and finally Power BI for the reporting layer.

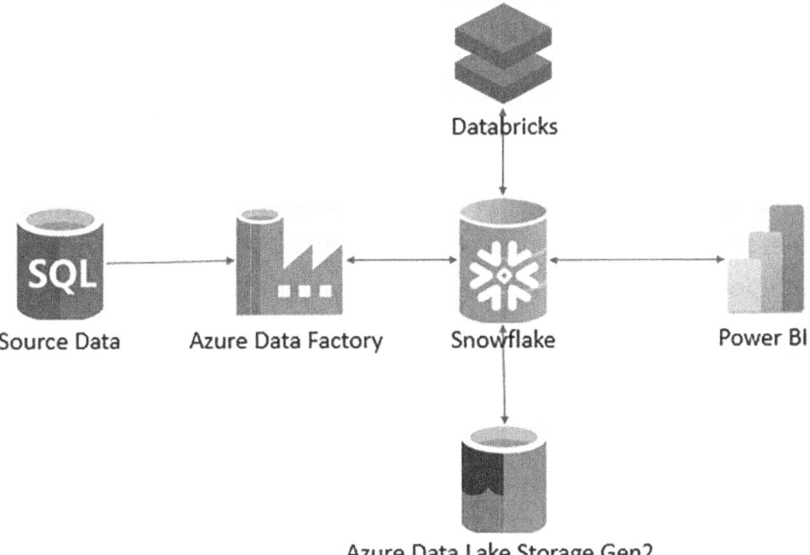

***Figure 2-4.** Snowflake with ADLS gen2, Data Factory, Databricks, and Power BI*

Data Lake Storage Gen2

Oftentimes, customers intend to store their data in a cloud-based storage service such as Amazon S3 or Azure Data Lake Storage Gen2. Snowflake provides ways for connecting to these services. For Azure Data Lake Storage Gen2, Snowflake supports both SAS Key and service principal identity access, with the general recommendation being to use the latter service principal identity access since it avoids having to use a key. The following Snow SQL script demonstrates an example of how to begin creating an ADLS gen2 storage integration with Snowflake. You can copy and paste this script within your Snowflake Query execution UI. The comments separate out the various stages that are executed by the full script. It begins by creating the storage integration and a stage to the ADLS gen2 account and container with parquet file format using SAS token credentials and then copies data into a Snowflake table from the ADLS gen2 stage using pattern matching. Finally, data is copied from the Snowflake table into ADLS gen2.

```
-- create a storage integration

create storage integration azure_int
  type = external_stage
  storage_provider = azure
  enabled = true
  azure_tenant_id = 'TENANAT-ID'
  storage_allowed_locations = ('azure://myaccount.blob.core.windows.
  net/mycontainer1/mypath1/', 'azure://myaccount.blob.core.windows.net/
  mycontainer2/mypath2/')
  storage_blocked_locations = ('azure://myaccount.blob.core.windows.net/
  mycontainer1/mypath1/sensitivedata/', 'azure://myaccount.blob.core.
  windows.net/mycontainer2/mypath2/sensitivedata/');

-- create a stage with SAS token and parquet file format

create or replace stage ADLS2
  url='azure:// myaccount.blob.core.windows.net/ mycontainer1'
  credentials=(azure_sas_token='SASTOKEN')
  file_format = PARQUET_FILE_FORMAT;

-- copy into Snowflake Table from ADLS2 Stage

copy into SnowflakeTable1
  from @ADL2
  pattern='.*sales.*.parquet';

-- copy into ADLS2 stage and new folder called d1 from Snowflake Table

copy into @ADLS/d1 from SnowflakeTable1;
```

```
-- copy into specified ADLS gen2 account, container, and folder from
Snowflake Table

copy into azure://myaccount.blob.core.windows.net/data/Table1/ from
SnowflakeTable1 storage_integration = myint;
```

Real-Time Data Loading with ADLS gen2

Snowflake's Snowpipe is a serverless data loader which enables loading of real-time data from ADLS gen2 as soon as it is available in a stage. Snowpipe's architectural diagram shown in Figure 2-5 depicts the flow of data from Azure sources to a target Snowflake data warehouse through Snowpipe and Azure Event Hubs.

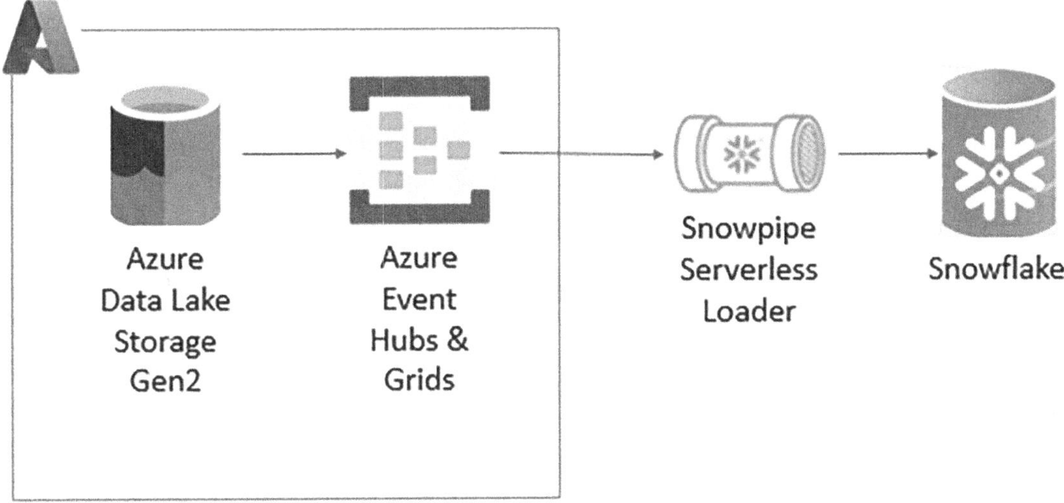

Figure 2-5. *Architecture showing ADLS gen2 to Snowflake using Snowpipe*

When a Snowpipe is created, it leverages the COPY INTO statement to load data. The following Snow SQL script shows how to create a notification integration using an Azure Event Grid subscription. It then moves on to describe how to create a Snowpipe with a number of parameters including the auto-ingest parameter which determines whether to automatically load data files from the specified external stage when event notifications are received from a configured message service. The last part of the Snowpipe script specifies the COPY INTO commands along with file formats.

```
-- create a notification integration

CREATE NOTIFICATION INTEGRATION notification_int
  ENABLED = true
  TYPE = QUEUE
  NOTIFICATION_PROVIDER = AZURE_STORAGE_QUEUE
  AZURE_STORAGE_QUEUE_PRIMARY_URI = '<queue_URL>'
  AZURE_TENANT_ID = '<directory_ID>';

-- create a Snowpipe

create pipe azure_pipe
  auto_ingest = true
  integration = 'notification_int'
  as
  copy into db_snowpipe.public.table
  from @db_snowpipe.public.stage
  file_format = (type = 'JSON');
```

Data Factory

Snowflake continues to integrate well with other Azure services including Data Factory V2. With its built-in Snowflake connector, developers can instantly connect to Snowflake using account credentials along with database and warehouse names. ADF supports Snowflake as both a source and sink and can be used with ADF's Mapping Data Flow activities to enhance the level of transformations with the pipeline, as shown in Figure 2-6.

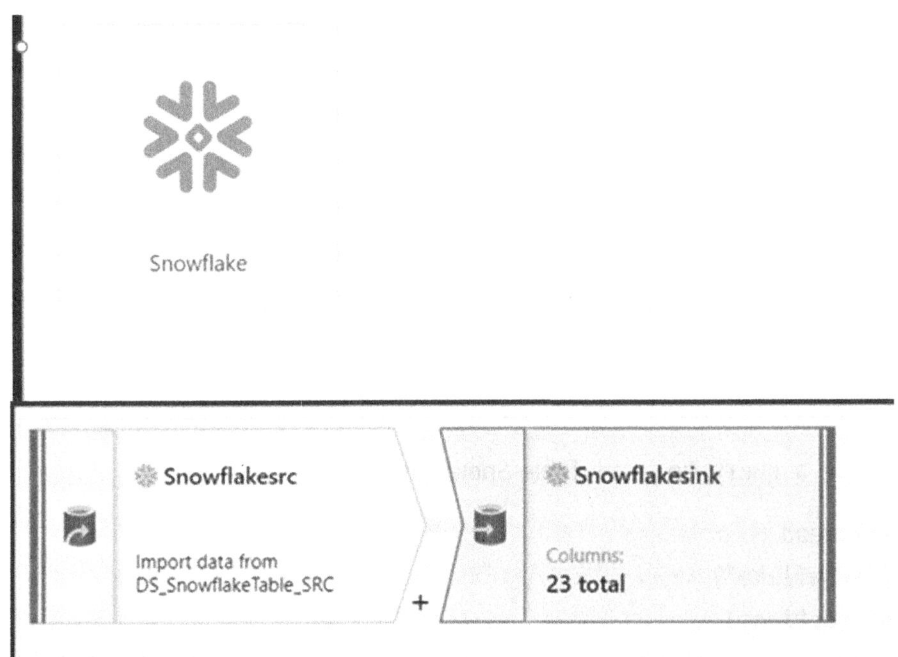

Figure 2-6. *Snowflake activities in ADF*

Databricks

Databricks offers connectors and scripts for reading and writing to Snowflake in both Scala and Python languages. These notebooks can then also be integrated with Data Factory activities, processes, and for scheduling. The following script shows an example of how to read and write data to Snowflake. The script begins by setting the ADLS gen2 context and keys. It goes on to show how to set the various Snowflake options. Finally, it shows how to write a SQL query to read from Snowflake and to write five rows into Snowflake. Note that the select query can be more complex to accommodate complex joins as well.

```
-- connecting to ADLS2 account

spark.conf.set(
  "fs.azure.account.key.rl001adls2.dfs.core.windows.net",
  "ENTER-KEY"
)
```

```
-- setting Snowflake options

# snowflake connection options
options = {
  "sfUrl": "snow.east-us-2.azure.snowflakecomputing.com",
  "sfUser": "accountadmin",
  "sfPassword": "Admin123!",
  "sfDatabase": "snowflake_sample_data",
  "sfSchema": "tpcds_sf10tcl",
  "sfWarehouse": "COMPUTE_WH"
}
-- executing a query to read from Snowflake table

df = spark.read
.format("snowflake")
.options(**options)
.option("query",  "select * from snowflake_sample_data.tpcds_sf10tcl.
item").load()
 df.show()

-- writing to Snowflake

spark.range(5).write
.format("snowflake")
.options(**options2)
.option("dbtable", "TEST_DEMO")
.save()
```

Data Transformation

Since there are numerous methods of transforming data before, during, or after it lands in Snowflake, this section will discuss some of these various transformation options and their capabilities. DBT (Data Build Tool) is an open source tool which manages Snowflake's ELT workloads by enabling engineers to transform data in Snowflake but simply writing SQL select statements, which DBT then converts to tables and views. DBT provides DataOps functionality and supports ETL and data transformation using the standard SQL language. These models can be versioned and unit tested within Snowflake.

Snowflake also supports transforming while loading it into a table using the COPY INTO command in order to avoid using numerous staging or temp tables. Some features supported by the COPY INTO command include casts using SQL select statements, column reordering, adding sequence columns, including auto-increment identity columns, and more. Snowflake also supports loading of semi-structured data into separate columns. An example of transforming data while loading it using the COPY INTO command can be seen in this script shown in the following which basically replaces the ~ character from the columns before loading it from ADLS gen2 into Snowflake:

```
-- Transforming data while loading it into Snowflake from ADLS gen2

COPY INTO AUTHOR (AUTHOR_CODE, DESCRIPTION)
FROM
(SELECT REPLACE($1,'~',''),REPLACE($2, '~','')
FROM @MY_ADLS2_ACCOUNT/raw/AUTHOR.txt)
FILE_FORMAT = AUTHOR_FILE_FORMAT;
```

Snowflake also supports the FLATTEN command, which produces a lateral view of an OBJECT or ARRAY within a VARIANT column. The VARIANT data type imposes a 16 MB size limit on individual rows, and Snowflake recommends using this data type when you are not sure what operations you intend to perform on your semi-structured data which may include OBJECTs or ARRAYs. An Array is used to represent dense or sparse arrays of arbitrary size, where index is a nonnegative integer, and an Object is used to represent collections of key-value pairs, where the key is a non-empty string. The following script shows an example of flattening JSON and XML data. It begins by showing you how to create a table with VARIANT data type, along with scripts for creating both JSON and XML file formats. It then provides sample XML, JSON, and nested JSON data along with the corresponding SQL statements containing the FLATTEN commands. These SQL statements can also be used in the COPY INTO command to transform and FLATTEN data while loading it into a Snowflake table from your ADLS gen2 account.

```
-- Creating a new Snowflake table with VARIANT column

CREATE TABLE "DEMO_DB"."PUBLIC"."FLATTEN_RAW_JSON_TABLE" ("FLATTEN_RAW_COL"
VARIANT)
COMMENT = 'Store JSON Data';
```

```
-- Creating a JSON file format

CREATE FILE FORMAT "DEMO_DB"."PUBLIC".JSON
TYPE = 'JSON'
COMPRESSION = 'AUTO'
ENABLE_OCTAL = FALSE
ALLOW_DUPLICATE = FALSE
STRIP_OUTER_ARRAY = TRUE
STRIP_NULL_VALUES = FALSE
IGNORE_UTF8_ERRORS = FALSE;

-- Creating an XML file format

CREATE FILE FORMAT "DEMO_DB"."PUBLIC".XML
TYPE = 'XML'
COMPRESSION = 'AUTO'
PRESERVE_SPACE = FALSE
STRIP_OUTER_ELEMENT = TRUE
DISABLE_SNOWFLAKE_DATA = FALSE
DISABLE_AUTO_CONVERT = FALSE
IGNORE_UTF8_ERRORS = FALSE;

-- Sample XML data

<?xml version='1.0' encoding='UTF-8'?>
<dataset>
 <AUTHOR AUTHOR_UID = 1>
    <FIRST_NAME>Ron</FIRST_NAME>
    <MIDDLE_NAME/>
    <LAST_NAME>LEsteve</LAST_NAME>
 </AUTHOR>
 <AUTHOR AUTHOR_UID = 2>
    <FIRST_NAME>Sam</FIRST_NAME>
    <MIDDLE_NAME>Smith</MIDDLE_NAME>
    <LAST_NAME>Broadwhick</LAST_NAME>
 </AUTHOR>
 <AUTHOR AUTHOR_UID = 3>
    <FIRST_NAME>Kathy</FIRST_NAME>
```

```
    <MIDDLE_NAME>L</MIDDLE_NAME>
    <LAST_NAME>Salisbery</LAST_NAME>
 </AUTHOR>
 <AUTHOR AUTHOR_UID = 4>
    <FIRST_NAME>Levi</FIRST_NAME>
    <MIDDLE_NAME/>
    <LAST_NAME>Bastille</LAST_NAME>
 </AUTHOR>
 <AUTHOR AUTHOR_UID = 5>
      <FIRST_NAME>John</FIRST_NAME>
    <MIDDLE_NAME/>
    <LAST_NAME>Doe</LAST_NAME>
 </AUTHOR>
 <AUTHOR AUTHOR_UID = 6>
    <FIRST_NAME>Kelly</FIRST_NAME>
    <MIDDLE_NAME/>
    <LAST_NAME>Jacobs</LAST_NAME>
 </AUTHOR>
</dataset>

-- Query to FLATTEN the XML data

SELECT
FLATTEN_RAW_COL:"@AUTHOR_UID" as AUTHOR_ID
,XMLGET(FLATTEN_RAW_COL, 'FIRST_NAME'):"$"::STRING as FIRST_NAME
,XMLGET(FLATTEN_RAW_COL, 'MIDDLE_NAME'):"$"::STRING as MIDDLE_NAME
,XMLGET(FLATTEN_RAW_COL, 'LAST_NAME'):"$"::STRING as LAST_NAME
FROM FLATTEN_RAW_XML_TABLE;

-- Sample JSON data

{
        "id": 55388352846278,
        "inventory_quantity": 19,
        "sku": "sku6"
      },
      {
```

```
    "id": 98388391387998,
    "inventory_quantity": 37,
    "sku": "sku4"
  },
  {
    "id": 93394420142283,
    "inventory_quantity": 16,
    "sku": "sku2"
  },
  {
    "id": 95794426007123,
    "inventory_quantity": 28,
    "sku": "sku7"
  },
  {
    "id": 89794429022894,
    "inventory_quantity": 32,
    "sku": "sku9"
  },
  {
    "id": 45694431414982,
    "inventory_quantity": 28,
    "sku": "sku6"
  },
  {
    "id": 23594455597765,
    "inventory_quantity": 76,
    "sku": "sku8"
  },
  {
    "id": 45694459856987,
    "inventory_quantity": 10,
    "sku": "sku1"
  }
```

```
-- Query to FLATTEN the JSON data

SELECT FLATTEN_RAW_COL:id::varchar AS ID,
       FLATTEN_RAW_COL:sku::varchar AS SKU,
       FLATTEN_RAW_COL:inventory_quantity AS INVENTORY_QUANTITY
FROM FLATTEN_RAW_JSON_TABLE,
LATERAL FLATTEN(input => FLATTEN_RAW_JSON_TABLE.FLATTEN_RAW_COL);

-- Sample nested JSON data

[{
  "book_title":"The Definitive Guide to Azure Data Engineering",
  "year_published":2021,
  "authors": [
       {
       "first_name":"Ron",
       "middle_name":null,
       "last_name":"LEsteve"
       },
       {
       "first_name":"Sam",
       "middle_name":"Smith",
       "last_name":"Broadwhick"
       }
       ]
 }
{
  "book_title":"Baby Talks",
  "year_published":2021,
  "authors":
       [{
       "first_name":"Kathy",
       "middle_name":"L",
       "last_name":"Salisbery"
       }
       ]
 }
```

```
{
  "book_title":"BBQ Recipes",
  "year_published":2021,
  "authors":
       [{
       "first_name":"Levi",
       "middle_name":null,
       "last_name":"Bastille"
       }
       ]
 }
{
  "book_title":"Game Of Tech",
  "year_published":2020,
  "authors":
       [{
       "first_name":"John",
       "middle_name":null,
       "last_name":"Doe"
       }
       ]
 }
{
  "book_title":"Corgi Dreams",
  "year_published":2021,
  "authors":
       [{
       "first_name":"Kelly",
       "middle_name":null,
       "last_name":"Jacobs"
       }
       ]
 }
```

```
-- Query to FLATTEN the nested JSON data

SELECT
    value:first_name::VARCHAR AS FIRST_NAME,
    value:middle_name::VARCHAR AS MIDDLE_NAME,
    value:last_name::VARCHAR AS LAST_NAME,
    FLATTEN_RAW:book_title::VARCHAR AS BOOK_TITLE,
    FLATTEN_RAW:year_published::VARCHAR AS YEAR_PUBLISHED
FROM FLATTEN_RAW_NESTEDJSON_TABLE
,LATERAL FLATTEN(input => FLATTEN_RAW:authors);
```

Governance

The governance of data assets is a critical need, and many organizations are turning to dedicated data governance technologies including Purview, Azure's native data governance service offering. Purview offers an out-of-the-box integration with Snowflake for the purpose of extracting metadata from all Snowflake assets. It also supports tracking lineage of relationships. In addition to Purview, Snowflake also offers a variety of options for governing data assets on their platform for enterprise editions or higher which we will discuss in this section. These features include the following.

Column-Level Security

Within Snowflake, it is possible to apply masking policies to columns within a table or view with the Dynamic Data Masking and External Tokenization. Data Masking selectively masks plain-text data in table and view columns at query time. The data administration of definition of the policies is managed by security or privacy officers and not the object owner. External Tokenization tokenizes data by replacing sensitive data with an undecipherable token before loading it into Snowflake and de-tokenizes the data at query runtime and uses external functions. Dynamic Data Masking supports data sharing, but tokenization does not.

Here is a sample script which details on how to create masking policies. Within the External Tokenization script, creditcard_decrypt is the external function needed for unprotecting the tokenized data. When creating masking policies, regex, timestamps, UDF, and custom decryption scripts are supported.

```
-- create a custom masking policy admin role

create role masking_policy_admin;

-- grant privileges to masking_policy_admin role.

grant create masking policy on schema <schema_name> to role masking_
policy_admin;

grant apply masking policy on account to role masking_policy_admin;

-- Dynamic Data Masking
create masking policy mask_creditcard as (val string) returns string ->
  case
    when current_role() in ('FINANCE') then val
    else '******'
  end;

-- External Tokenization

  create masking policy detokenize_creditcard as (val string) returns
string ->
  case
    when current_role() in ('FINANCE') then decrypt_creditcard(val)
    else val -- sees tokenized data
  end;

-- Apply Masking Policy to Column in Table
create or replace table tbl_customer_data (creditcard string masking policy
mask_creditcard);

-- Apply Masking Policy to Column in View
create or replace view vw_customer_data (creditcard string masking policy
mask_creditcard) as select * from tbl_customer_data;
```

Row-Level Security

With row-level security, policies can be applied to determine which rows to include in a query's results. These policies can be based on roles and/or mapping tables and can also include conditions and functions to transform the data at runtime when certain conditions are met.

Here is a sample row access policy to allow regional managers the ability to view only their region's sales based on a mapping table called region_manager_mapping. If the manager's current role is in the mapping table, they will only be able to see data for their respective region. Additionally, the leadership_role is a custom role that would supersede the manager's role in terms of privilege; therefore, this role would not be bound to a particular region and would have full access to all data for their subordinate regional managers.

```
-- Create manager and leadership roles and grant access to sales table
create role manager_role;
create role leadership_role;
grant select on table sales to role manager_role;
grant select on table sales to role leadership_role;

-- Create row access policy

create or replace row access policy security.sales_policy as (sales_region
varchar) returns boolean ->
  'leadership_role' = current_role()
      or exists (
            select 1 from region_manager_mapping
              where manager = current_role()
                and region = region
          )
;

-- Applying newly create row access policy to existing sales table

alter table sales add row access policy security.sales_policy on (region);
```

Access History

Snowflake provides an ACCESS_HISTORY view containing a record for each query which lists the base table columns that were directly accessed in order to provide insights on frequently accessed tables and columns by the user to support audit of data access for regulatory and governance initiatives. In addition to regulatory compliance auditing, this view can help with discovering unused data for the purpose of archival or deletion.

Here are some sample queries that can be run using the access_history view:

```
-- Query to obtain user access history

select user_name
       , query_id
       , query_start_time
       , direct_objects_accessed
       , base_objects_accessed
from access_history

-- Query to determine who accessed a sensitive table(object_id) in the
last 30 days
select distinct user_name
from access_history
     , lateral flatten(base_objects_accessed) f1
where f1.value:"objectId"::int=<fill_in_object_id>
and f1.value:"objectDomain"::string='Table'
and query_start_time >= dateadd('day', -30, current_timestamp())
;
```

Object Tagging

Tags enable tracking of sensitive data for compliance, discovery, protection, and resource usage. A tag is a schema-level object that can be associated with another Snowflake object. Tags are stored as key-value pairs (e.g., cost_center = 'data'). The following script shows how to create custom tags:

```
-- create a custom tag_admin role

use role useradmin;
create role tag_admin;
```

```
use role accountadmin;
grant create tag on schema <schema_name> to role tag_admin;
grant apply tag on account to role tag_admin;

-- create a new tag

use role tag_admin;
use schema my_db.my_schema;
create tag cost_center;

-- create a tag on a new warehouse

use role tag_admin;
create warehouse mywarehouse with tag cost_center =      'data     ';

-- create a tag on an existing table's column

alter table <table_name> modify column <column_name> set tag <tag_key>
=      '<tag_value>      ' [ , <tag_key> = '<tag_value>' ,      ... ];
alter table <table_name> modify column <column_name> unset <tag_key>
[ , <tag_key> , ... ];

-- view all available tags

select * from snowflake.account_usage.tags
order by tag_name;
```

Sharing

Snowflake offers secure data sharing products that include Direct Share, Data Marketplace, and Data Exchange via secure data sharing. With secure data sharing, read-only database objects ranging from tables, secure views, external tables, secure materialized views, and secure UDFs can be shared by a data provider's account and consumed by a data consumer's account using underlying metadata. This means that no actual data is transferred between accounts, and therefore, the data consumer will not incur storage costs but rather only compute costs to run queries on the shared data. Additionally, data providers will have access to the data consumer's consumption metadata details. Data providers can provide data consumers that do not have Snowflake accounts what is known as reader accounts. These read-only accounts are owned by the data provider and allow the data consumer to access the data without needing a Snowflake account. The limitation with this approach to data consumers is that they cannot perform DML operations since the accounts are read only. Table 2-1 outlines the capabilities of each data sharing option offered by Snowflake.

Table 2-1. *Snowflake's Data Sharing vs. Data Marketplace vs. Data Exchange*

	Data Sharing	Data Marketplace	Data Exchange
Secure data sharing protocol	Yes	Yes	Yes
Account-to-account sharing	Yes	Yes	Yes
Zero-copy sharing	Yes	Yes	Yes
Share tables	Yes	Yes	Yes
Share external tables	Yes	Yes	Yes
Share secure views	Yes	Yes	Yes
Share secure materialized views	Yes	Yes	Yes
Share secure UDFs	Yes	Yes	Yes
Read-only consumer database	Yes	Yes	Yes
Share multiple databases	Yes	Yes	Yes
Create and manage reader accounts	Yes	Yes	Yes
Cross-region and cloud platform sharing	Yes	Yes	Yes
Private data shared 1:1 between two parties	Yes	No	No
Invitation-only private data shared from 1 provider to multiple consumers	No	Yes	No
Public data shared and administered by Snowflake Data Marketplace	No	No	Yes
Standard or personalized data sharing	No	Yes	Yes
Gives non-Snowflake users access to data	Yes	Yes	No

(*continued*)

Table 2-1. (*continued*)

	Data Sharing	Data Marketplace	Data Exchange
Allows consumers to search for and discover data	No	Yes	Yes
Control who can publish data and see your listings	No	Yes	No
Easily obtain usage metrics	No	Yes	Yes
Seamless UI for connecting data consumers with providers	No	Yes	Yes
Access third-party data from several different vendors	No	Yes	Yes
Seamless avenue for market data Monetization	No	Yes	Yes

Direct Share

Direct Share supports account-to-account data sharing using Snowflake's secure data sharing with the benefit of not having to copy the data from account to account. Here is a sample script which demonstrates just how easy it is to create a share, grant usage to database objects, and then allow specified accounts access to the share. Shares can be even more complex to allow sharing of multiple databases across regions and cloud providers. The last script in this section shows how to create a Dynamic Secure View that can then be shared via account-to-account or reader account access. This method enforces row-level security by only allowing consumers access to data that they are permitted to view based on their current account. A well-defined mapping table and appropriate key across tables will be needed for this approach to be set up. Once successfully set up, it allows for seamless data sharing across vendors and clients.

```
-- create a Share on a database and schema

create share share_data;

grant usage on database db_data to share share_data;
grant usage on schema db_data.dim to share share_data;
grant select on table db_data.dim.customers to share share_data;

-- show grants to the Share

show grants to share share_data;
```

```
-- add accounts to the Share
alter share share_data add accounts=Account1, Account2;

-- create a Dynamic Secure View
CREATE or replace SECURE VIEW SHARED_VIEW AS
SELECT
        NAME,
       SALES,
       PRODUCT,
       ID
FROM FACT_SALES fs
JOIN DIM_CUSTOMER dc
ON fs.ID = dc.ID
AND UPPER(SNOWFLAKE_ACCNT) = CURRENT_ACCOUNT();
```

Data Marketplace

The Snowflake Data Marketplace is a location for accessing a variety of datasets, and it uses secure data sharing to connect data providers with consumers. As a data consumer, you can access and query third-party datasets in your Snowflake account and join it with your own data or other third-party datasets. As a data provider, you can publish real-time live datasets securely to the Marketplace to make it available for others to consume, without having to build and maintain APIs and ELT pipelines for customers. Data in the Marketplace can be standard data listings where the data can be available without needing to request permission. Alternatively, it can be personalized data listings that would need approvals for request submissions and may even have a fee for consumption.

Data Exchange

The Snowflake Data Exchange is a private data hub for securely sharing data across a group of members that are invited to discover and consume the data. This differs from the Marketplace in that this Exchange is a private and customized secure avenue to share and consume data with fine-grained permissions for who can produce and consume the data. The Data Exchange can be integrated with Azure's Private Link as well.

Continuous Integration and Deployment

The principles and architectural patterns of continuous integration and deployment (CI/CD) are prevalent in numerous technologies and domains. The benefits of CI/CD can be realized in a number of platforms to promote code from a development environment to upper environments in order to automatically test and streamline the deployment of production-ready code from one environment to another which has traditionally been known as DevOps. Within Snowflake's data ecosystem, this is called DataOps. Users can create multiple virtual warehouses ranging from DEV to QA to PROD, which can be sized independently and are completely isolated from each other. Developers can also create Feature Branch Databases in a matter of seconds to work on their own use cases and development efforts. With zero-copy cloning, production databases can be cloned quickly without having to duplicate actual data. Snowflake also supports auto-scaling of databases to test and validate a variety of tests. In this section, we will go over two methods (Jenkins and Azure DevOps) for integrating and building CI/CD pipelines with Snowflake.

Jenkins

Jenkins is a Java-based open source automation tool which supports CI/CD in a variety of applications including Snowflake. Sqitch is a database change management application used for automating and deploying changes to Snowflake's various environments. Figure 2-7 illustrates the architecture for building CI/CD pipelines to promote code from a GitHub source repo to the Jenkins CI/CD server to the Sqitch Docker Container, where the Sqitch docker image for Snowflake is the execution environment. This process then deploys the changes to various environments. A similar process can also be integrated with Azure DevOps, AWS, or other cloud providers.

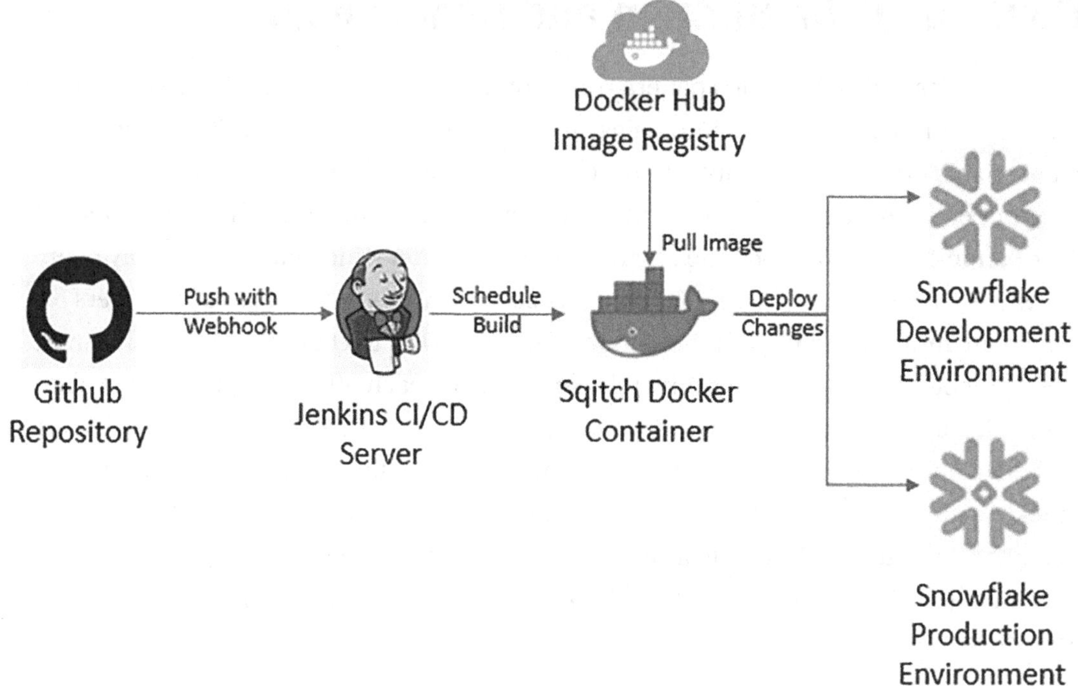

***Figure 2-7.** Snowflake integration with Jenkins for CI/CD*

Azure DevOps

Similar to Jenkins, Azure DevOps (ADO) also supports the CI/CD build and deployment of database changes from one Snowflake environment to another using GIT repositories within Azure DevOps for source control, along with Azure CI and CD pipelines, shown in Figure 2-8. Schemachange, also called snowchange, is a Python-based tool which can manage all Snowflake database changes and objects and can be integrated and deployed through Azure DevOps YAML pipelines. It is important to note that there are a variety of other database change management tools, much like Liquidbase, that could also be used as an alternative to schemachange. Similarly, GitHub could be used as an alternative to Git. There are always multiple architectural customizations that could be applied to custom tailor your Snowflake CI/CD solution in Azure and/or with other cloud providers.

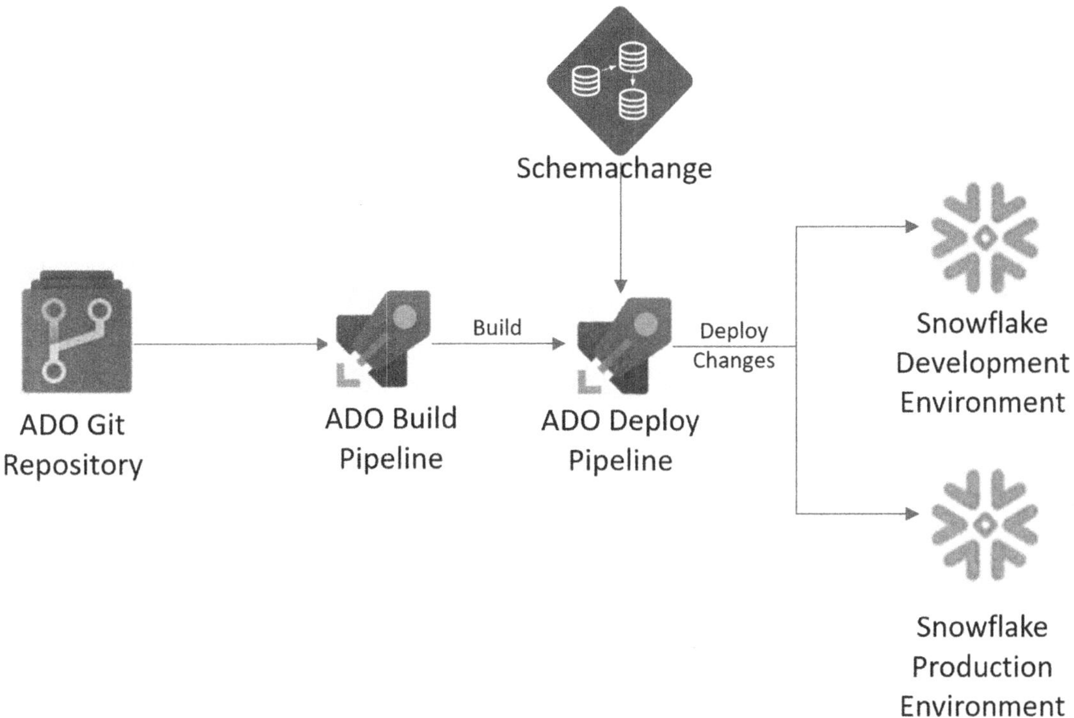

Figure 2-8. *Snowflake integration with Azure DevOps (ADO) for CI/CD*

Reporting

The capability of building robust and visually appealing reports, metrics, and dashboards is a critical need within the modern data and analytics platform and Lakehouse paradigm. There are a variety of reporting tools available on the market that can connect to data warehouses and platforms such as Synapse and Snowflake. From the perspective of Azure, Microsoft's Power BI Reporting platform has a variety of connectors including a Snowflake connector along with multiple connectivity modes and authentication methods for Snowflake, which we will explore in this section.

Power BI

In Figure 2-9, notice the variety of databases that can be connected to Power BI (PBI). This can be set up through Power BI's Get Data UI shown in the figure. Snowflake is one such connection option available that we will explore in this section. Simply select Snowflake and click Connect.

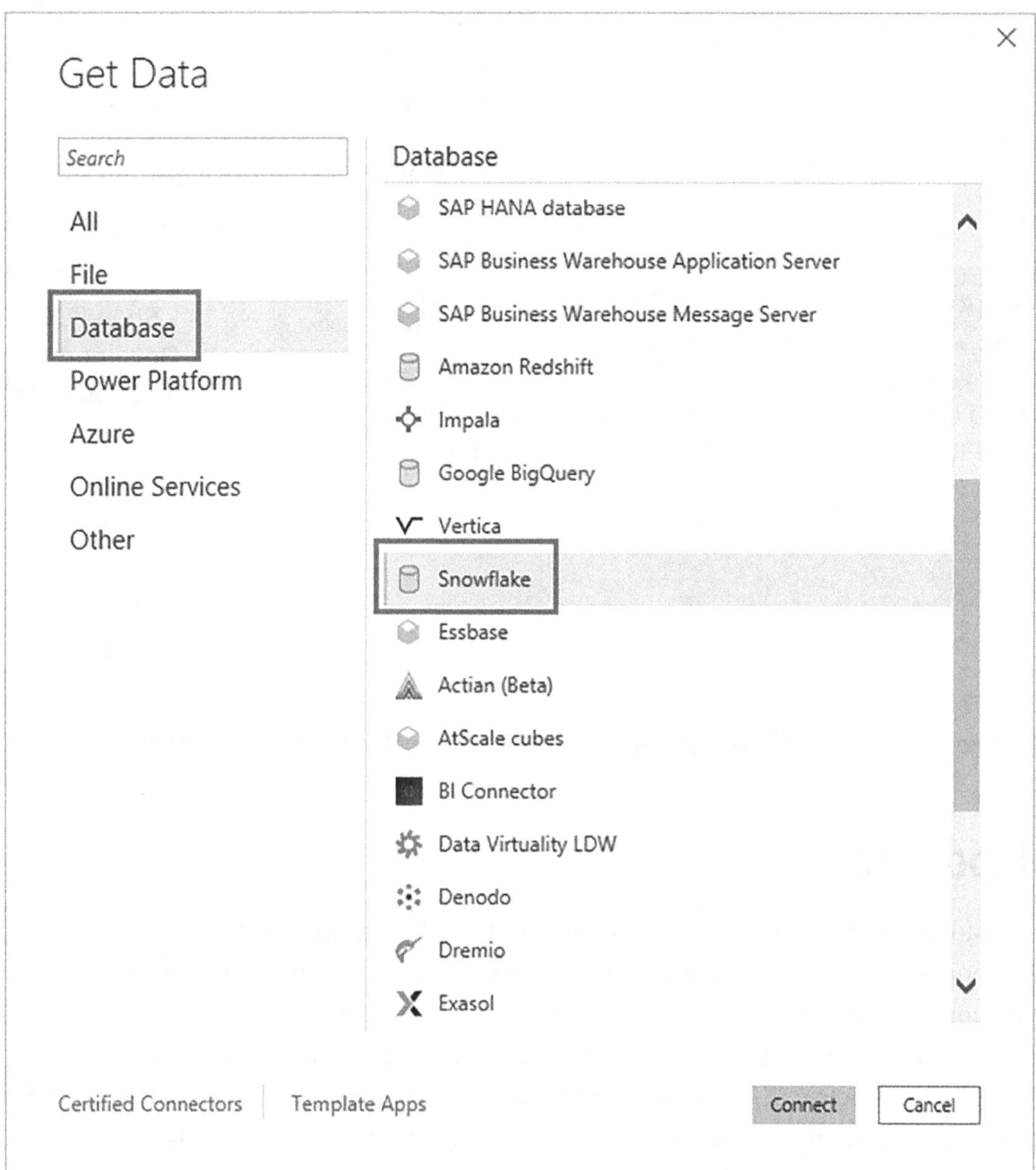

Figure 2-9. *Snowflake connector within Power BI*

An advanced UI will appear, shown in Figure 2-10, which requires you to enter the Snowflake server and warehouse name. In addition, advanced optional values such as role names, timeout settings, and relationship columns allow you to specify the granularity of the connection, as needed. Also, notice that both Import and Direct

Query data connectivity modes are supported through this PBI Snowflake connector. With Direct Query, your dashboard will directly query the data sources at runtime with faster refreshes at 15-minute increments, and no data will be imported into Power BI, thus reducing the overall file's footprint. This may translate to slower performance since you may have to compete with other users for bandwidth and since compression of the Vertipaq performance engine is not taken advantage of with this Direct Query method. With Direct Query, there may also be some limitations around transformations, specifically DAX functions.

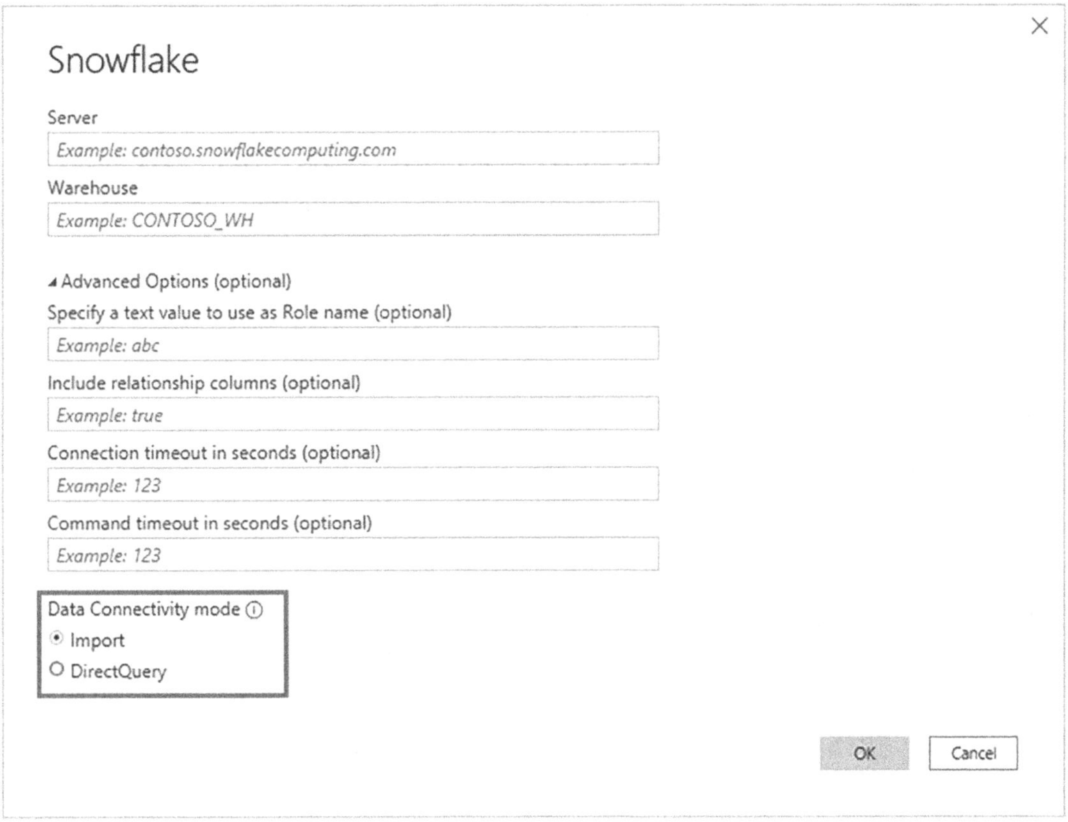

Figure 2-10. *PBI Snowflake connector configuration details*

On the other hand, the Import method will cache the data that is being connected to and will create a point in time snapshot of the data and will leverage the Vertipaq storage engine to access the cached source rather than the actual source data, which can lead to improved performance.

Additionally, with this method, you'll be able to use M and DAX functions with no limitations to modeling data and combine various data sources. Disadvantages of this method include a limited number of refreshes per day, at up to 48 for Premium SKUs. Also, import caches are limited to 10 GB per dataset for Premium SKUS. One other thing to keep in mind is the lack of ease in transitioning back to Direct Query mode once you have opted for Import mode. Power BI has also introduced a newer mode called Composite (dual) mode which can mix Import and Direct Query modes. This new setting allows the Power BI service to determine the most efficient mode to use on a query-by-query basis.

After the Snowflake server and warehouse details along with the data connectivity modes have been configured, this Snowflake PBI connector offers two methods of connecting to your Snowflake data warehouse. These include (1) basic authentication through a username and password, as shown in Figure 2-11, and (2) Microsoft Account authentication which we will discuss shortly. For the basic authentication, simply enter your username and password and click "Connect."

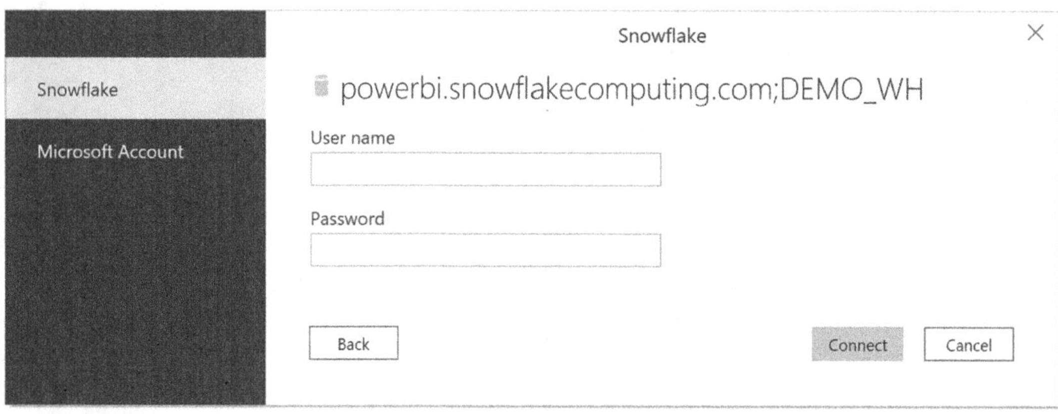

***Figure 2-11.** PBI Snowflake connector basic authentication*

For Microsoft Authentication shown in Figure 2-12, Power BI can connect to Snowflake using identity provider credentials and OAuth for a seamless single-sign-on (SSO) experience which also prevents the need for on-premises PBI gateways since PBI will use a Snowflake driver instead. When PBI connects to Snowflake, it obtains a Snowflake token as part of the connection string which is validated and mapped to the Snowflake user and then creates a session for PBI to access data.

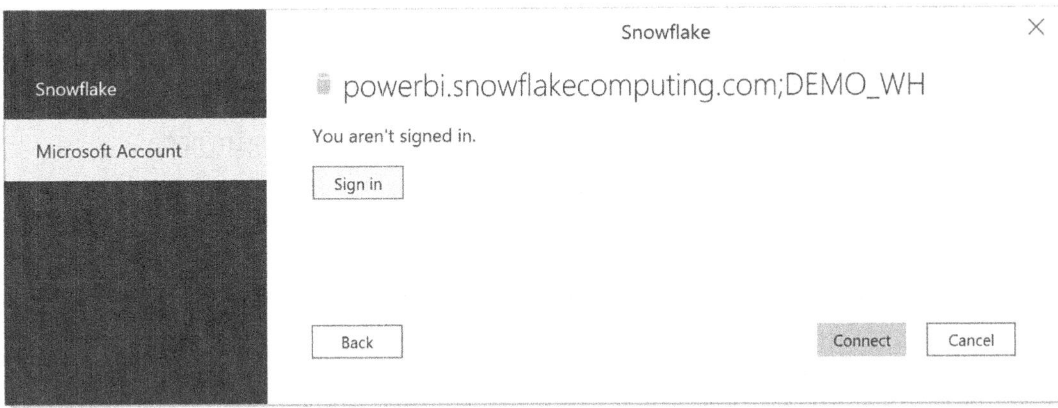

Figure 2-12. *PBI Snowflake connector Microsoft Authentication*

By default, the ACCOUNTADMIN or SECURITYADMIN Snowflake roles are not allowed to instantiate a Snowflake session from PBI. Also, if Network Policies are being used, ensure to include the Microsoft Azure IP ranges for the Azure region where the Snowflake account is hosted. Note that Azure Private Link does not support this process and a Power BI Gateway will need to be used if Azure Private Link is being used.

Here is the script that will need to be run in Snowflake to create the Security Integration. Note that only the ACCOUNTADMIN or a role with global CREATE INTEGRATION permissions will be allowed to run this script.

The <AZURE_AD_ISSUER> value for the external_oauth_issuer parameter includes the TENANT_ID (e.g., `https://sts.windows.net/TENANT_ID/`) and can be found in the About section in your Power BI tenant. Once this script executes successfully, be sure to test connectivity from Power BI to Snowflake using SSO to ensure that you can authenticate and connect successfully.

```
-- create Power Bi Security Integration

create security integration powerbi
    type = external_oauth
    enabled = true
    external_oauth_type = azure
    external_oauth_issuer = '<AZURE_AD_ISSUER>'
    external_oauth_jws_keys_url = 'https://login.windows.net/common/
    discovery/keys'
```

```
external_oauth_audience_list = ('https://analysis.windows.net/powerbi/
connector/Snowflake')
external_oauth_token_user_mapping_claim = 'upn'
external_oauth_snowflake_user_mapping_attribute = 'login_name'
external_oauth_any_role_mode = 'ENABLE';
```

Delta Lake, Machine Learning, and Constraints

Both Databricks and Synapse Analytics provide Delta Lake support which enable support for workloads that are run on open source Apache Spark compute through well-integrated APIs. The support for delta format is less well known with Snowflake. Organizations that are considering Snowflake as part of their Lakehouse are also interested to know about the machine learning capabilities of Snowflake. In the following sections, you will learn more about this support for delta format which Snowflake offers in addition to its machine learning capabilities and support for constraints.

Delta Lake

While Snowflake does support integration with delta format, it is both an experimental and proprietary process. Snowflake supports the reading of Delta Tables by using a manifest file which contains a list of data files to read for querying the Delta Table. This integration can be achieved by first generating a manifest file using Databricks. As an example, the following code can be used to generate this manifest file with a SQL query within the Databricks workspace:

```
GENERATE snowflake_delta_manifest FOR TABLE DeltaDimCustomer
```

After this, Snowflake can be configured to read this manifest file through either an external table or view. You'll need to begin by first creating a stage using code similar to the following from Snowflake. A Snowflake Stage is used to reference inside and outside of Snowflake. For external Stages, Snowflake supports ADLS gen2, AWS S3, and GCP buckets.

```
create or replace stage delta_stage_table url='<path-to-delta-table>'
```

Once this Stage is created, you can create an external table using the code as follows:

```
CREATE OR REPLACE EXTERNAL TABLE delta_DimCustomer(
    filename VARCHAR AS split_part(VALUE:c1, '/', -1)
  )
  WITH LOCATION = @delta_stage_table/snowflake_delta_manifest/
  FILE_FORMAT = (TYPE = CSV)
  PATTERN = '.*[/]manifest'
  AUTO_REFRESH = true;
```

When the Delta Table is updated, the manifest file must be regenerated through either explicit or automatic updates. Be sure to understand the limitations around data consistency and schema evolution. When the manifest file is updated, it overwrites the existing manifest file. If the table is partitioned, the partitioned manifest files will be updated automatically; however, since all manifests of the partitions cannot be updated concurrently, this may lead to versioning issues or other errors. Since Snowflake uses a schema defined in its table definition, it does not support Delta Lake's schema evolution capability since it will not query the updated schema until after the table definition is updated to the new schema. For more information on Snowflake to Delta Lake integration, please see the following Snowflake article: `https://docs.databricks.com/delta/snowflake-integration.html`

Machine Learning

Databricks and Synapse Analytics workspaces support machine learning through various libraries, runtimes, APIs, and other out-of-the-box functionality. When considering a Lakehouse, customers are interested in understanding if Snowflake also provides support for machine learning workloads and model development. Snowflake supports executing Python, Spark, and Java code; therefore, models can be trained and executed in Snowflake for development purposes by using custom code. Once developed, these models will need a separate environment to run. The samples shown in the following GitHub Repository demonstrates that models can be pushed inside Snowflake UDFs to run the model as part of SQL: `https://github.com/avadhoot-agasti/snowflake-demos/blob/master/ml_classifier_lending_club.ipynb`. While this is not as robust as having access to open source libraries, packages, runtimes, APIs, and compute on Spark, it does demonstrate that Snowflake can support ML model development initiatives through custom scripts and processes.

Constraints

Snowflake provides support for constraints including UNIQUE, PRIMARY KEY, FOREIGN KEY, and NOT NULL. A table can have multiple unique and foreign keys but only one primary key. NOT NULL constraints are always enforced, while other constraints can be defined as not always explicitly enforced. When a table is copied using a CREATE TABLE..LIKE or CREATE TABLE ..CLONE command, all constraints are also copied over. Constraints can be defined on single or multi-columns. Oftentimes, customers look closely at the capabilities of constraints when choosing an enterprise data warehouse platform, so having an understanding of Snowflake's capabilities around constraints will be useful.

Summary

In this chapter, you learned more about the capabilities of Snowflake and how it has the potential to complement the modern Data Lakehouse paradigm. Snowflake has oftentimes been compared to Synapse Analytics Dedicated SQL Pools (SQLDW) as organizations evaluate a persistent data warehouse consumption layer for their Data Lakehouse platform. At its core, the Synapse Analytics offerings are well integrated with other Azure-native technologies and support native DELTA and Spark-based analytics on top of your Data Lake in addition to its persistent data warehouse, Dedicated SQL Pools. It is also great at handling ML, AI, and steaming workloads. Snowflake, on the other hand, is designed for conventional BI workloads while also offering robust support for streaming. Additionally, Snowflake supports ML and DELTA format, with certain limitations and less robustness than Synapse. Snowflake offers unlimited scale, superior partner integrations and marketplace offerings, and great value out of the box, while Synapse may have a slightly elevated learning curve due to its advanced offerings.

Snowflake offers a cost-efficient, highly secure architecture with fully managed infrastructure to support a variety of data warehouse use cases including batch and real-time ELT pipelines. It also offers tight integration with Azure resources including Private Endpoints, Functions, Data Lake Storage Gen2, DevOps, Power BI, and more. With the ability to build highly customized data applications along with continuous integration and deployment solutions across a variety of platforms, Snowflake is becoming a complementary solution option that fits a number of use cases within the Data Lakehouse. Customers are seeing the vast benefits and value from its data sharing platforms that allow them to directly consume datasets from a variety of vendors to avoid having to build and maintain interim ELT pipelines which need to land the data into intermediate staging tables, which also adds to storage and compute costs. Overall, Snowflake brings with it a vast variety of features and capabilities that have been challenging architects and organizations to take a closer look at Snowflake to determine and understand its place in the modern Data Lakehouse paradigm. Table 2-2 lists out some of the comparisons between Snowflake and Synapse Analytics Dedicated SQL Pools which may help you and your organization as you meticulously compare and contrast the two data warehousing solutions. For more details on getting started with Snowflake, check out the robust "Getting Started" documentation from Snowflake that can be found here: `https://docs.snowflake.com/en/user-guide-getting-started.html`

Table 2-2. *Snowflake vs. Synapse Analytics Dedicated SQL Pools*

	Snowflake	**Synapse Analytics Dedicated SQL Pools**
Ability to segregate compute and storage pricing	Yes	Yes
Scale/pause/resume compute	Yes	Yes
ANSI-SQL compliant	Yes	Yes
Structured and semi-structured source data support	Yes	Yes
Data virtualization support: (ability to query CSV/parquet/JSON, etc.)	Yes	Yes
Delta Lake support (Snowflake requires additional manifest file)	Yes	Yes
Azure Data Lake Storage Gen2 source and sink support	Yes	Yes
Azure Data Factory source and sink support	Yes	Yes
Azure Databricks source and sink support	Yes	Yes
Power BI Reporting layer support	Yes	Yes

(*continued*)

Table 2-2. *(continued)*

	Snowflake	Synapse Analytics Dedicated SQL Pools
Enterprise business-critical security and protection in a single pricing tier	No	Yes
Compute is dedicated per customer and billed per usage unit (DWU)	No	Yes
Supports high security and dedicated compute at a higher price point	Yes	No
Support for manual indexing	No	Yes
Massively parallel processing (MPP) backend	No	Yes
Automatically indexes data	Yes	Yes
Data sharing (Synapse supports Azure data sharing while Snowflake has Direct Share, Data Exchange, and Data Marketplace)	Yes	Yes
Cross-database queries	Yes	No
Multiple databases	Yes	No
Trigger-based file loads	Yes	Yes
Per hour pricing structure support	No	Yes
Per credit pricing structure support	Yes	No

CHAPTER 3

Databricks

Databricks is a technology platform that is available on Azure along with other multi-cloud environments. It is intended to serve as a unified data and analytics platform that supports data warehousing in the lake, advanced analytics use cases, real-time streaming analytics, and much more. With its various workspaces including machine learning, data science, SQL analytics, and data engineering, Databricks is truly a unified platform which offers services to support all stakeholders within the data and advanced analytics domain. With its robust support for Delta Lakes and advanced performance optimization capabilities, it supports cutting-edge Lakehouse capabilities. It is an industry-leading platform that has been outperforming query speed and cost benchmarks when compared with Snowflake and other similar platforms. This record performance is a result of the compute engines which include both Apache Spark and Photon, which is an MPP engine that is built from scratch in C++ and does heavy parallel query processing.

Navigating through the many service offerings within the Databricks platform can be challenging. In this chapter, you will learn about some of the fundamental offerings and advanced capabilities of Databricks. We will begin by exploring the various components of workspaces, compute, and storage. As data engineers, citizen data integrators, and various other Databricks enthusiasts begin to understand the various benefits of Spark as a valuable and scalable compute resource to work with data at scale, they would need to know how to work with this data that is stored in their Azure Data Lake Storage Gen2 (ADLS gen2) containers. Azure Databricks offers the capability of mounting a Data Lake Storage account to easily read and write data in your lake. While there are many methods of connecting to your Data Lake for the purposes of reading and writing data, in the storage section of this chapter, you will learn how to securely mount and access your ADLS gen2 account from Databricks. Finally, toward the end of this chapter, you will learn more about Delta Lake, real-time and advanced analytics, security, governance, and continuous integration and deployment for Databricks.

R. L'Esteve, *The Azure Data Lakehouse Toolkit*, https://doi.org/10.1007/978-1-4842-8233-5_3

Workspaces

Within Databricks, there are a few different workspaces which are designed for different personas including data science, data engineering, machine learning, SQL, and business analysts. Workspaces are environments for accessing your Databricks services which include notebooks, libraries, dashboards, experiments, and more. In this section, we will explore these various workspaces along with the features that they offer.

Data Science and Engineering

The data science and engineering workspace, shown in Figure 3-1, is the most common workspace used by data engineering and data science professionals. Within this workspace, you will be able to create notebooks for writing code in either Python, Scala, SQL, or R languages. Notebooks can be shared, secured with visibility and access control policies, organized in hierarchical folder structures, and attached to a variety of high-powered compute clusters. These compute clusters can be attached at either the workspace or notebook level. It is within these notebooks where you will also be able to render your code execution results in either tabular, chart, or graph format.

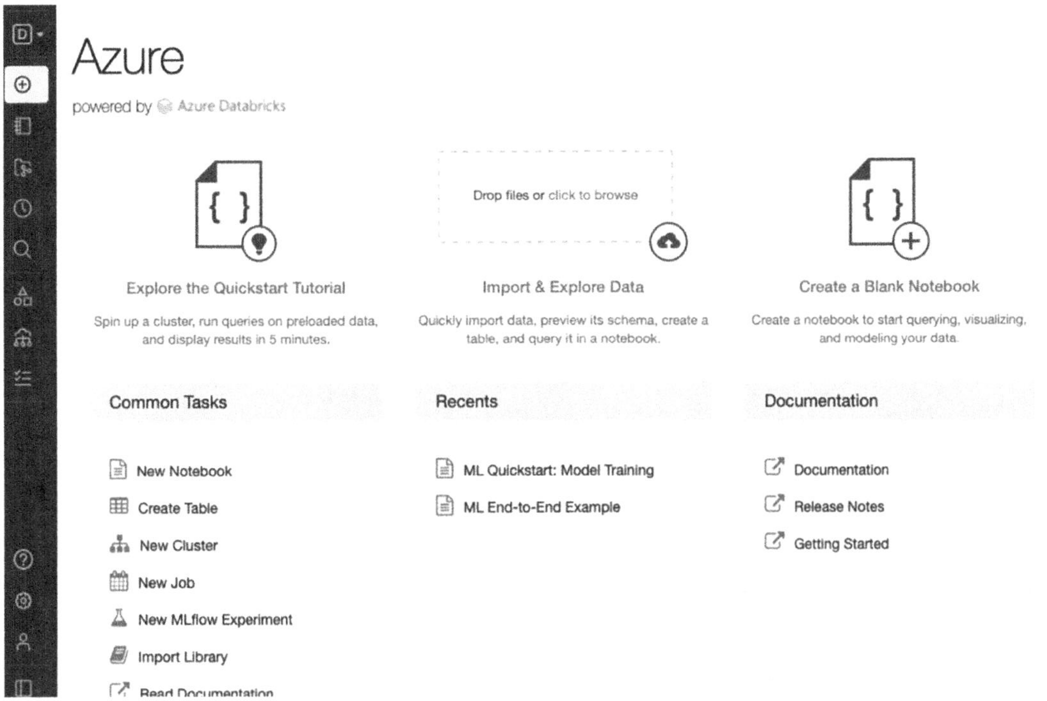

***Figure 3-1.** Data science and engineering workspace*

Once you have completed your code development in your notebook, you will also have the option of adding it to repos, shown in Figure 3-2, which provides integration with remote Git repository providers. With repos, you will be able to clone remote repos, manage branches, push and pull changes, and visually compare differences on commit.

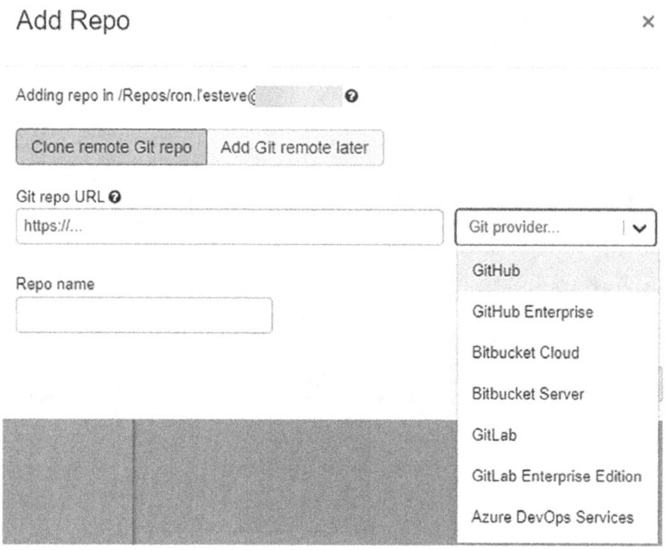

***Figure 3-2.** Databricks repos UI*

The Databricks workspace also offers Library UI, shown in Figure 3-3, which provides you with the option of having either third-party (e.g., PyPI, Maven, CRAN) or custom code (e.g., .whl, .egg, JAR) available for notebooks and jobs within the workspace that run on clusters. These libraries can be written in Python, Java, Scala, and R languages.

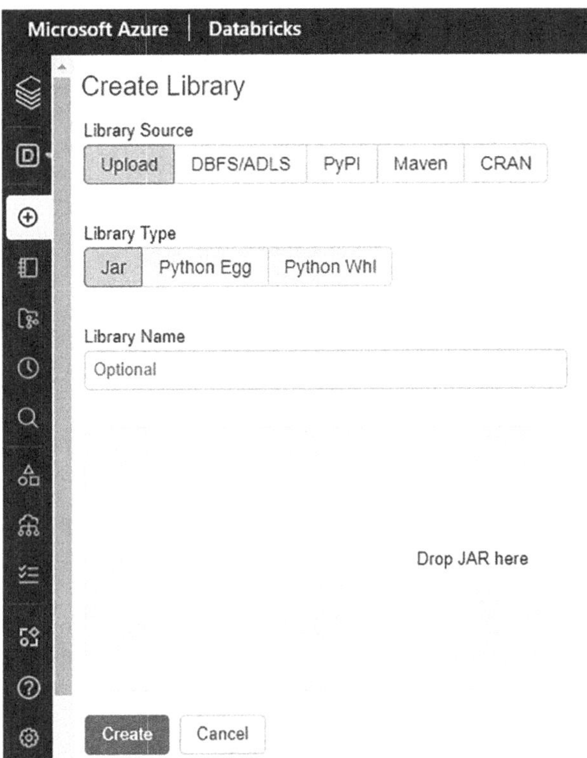

Figure 3-3. *Databricks library UI*

In a scenario where you would be interested in running your notebook code which may contain ELT and other data engineering scripts on a recurring basis, you could create and schedule a job from your notebook. The Job Scheduler UI, shown in Figure 3-4, is where you would need to specify whether this is a manual or scheduled job along with the date and time intervals. The compute must be specified, and you could also add status email alerts and parameters as needed.

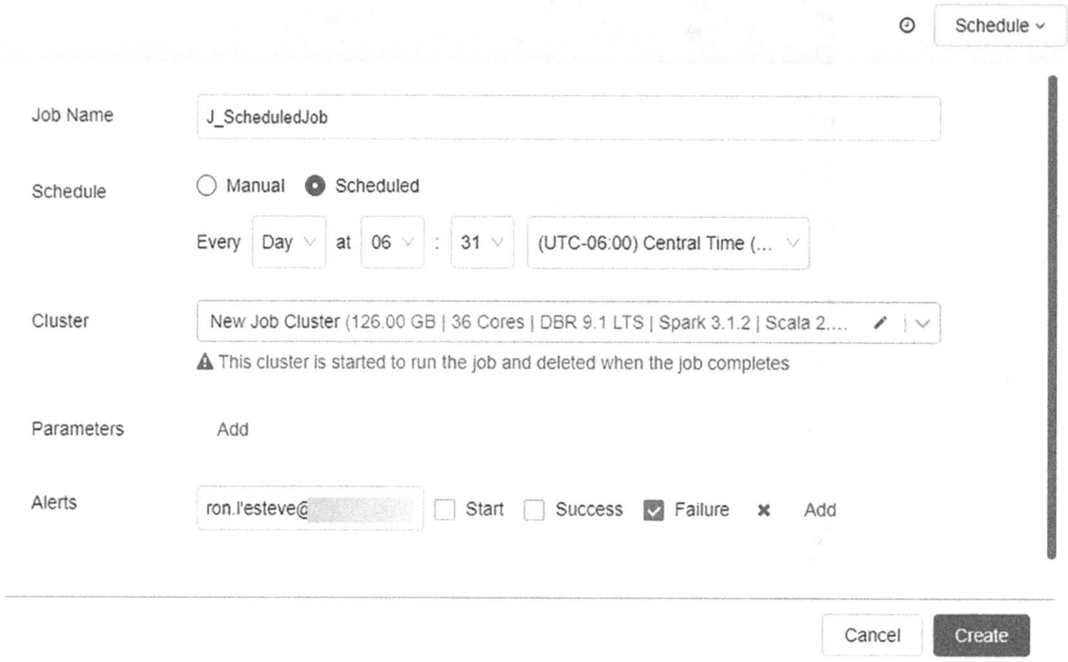

Figure 3-4. *Databricks Job Scheduler UI*

Data within the workspace can be accessed via the Databricks File System (DBFS) which is mounted to the workspace. Hive tables can also be created programmatically in the notebook or with the out-of-the-box Create New Table UI, shown in Figure 3-5, which allows you to create tables and import data.

Figure 3-5. *Create New Table UI*

Your workspace also comes equipped with Partner Connect, shown in Figure 3-6, which allows you to easily integrate your Databricks SQL endpoints and Databricks clusters with a variety of other data ingestion, transformation, visualization, and advanced analytics tools.

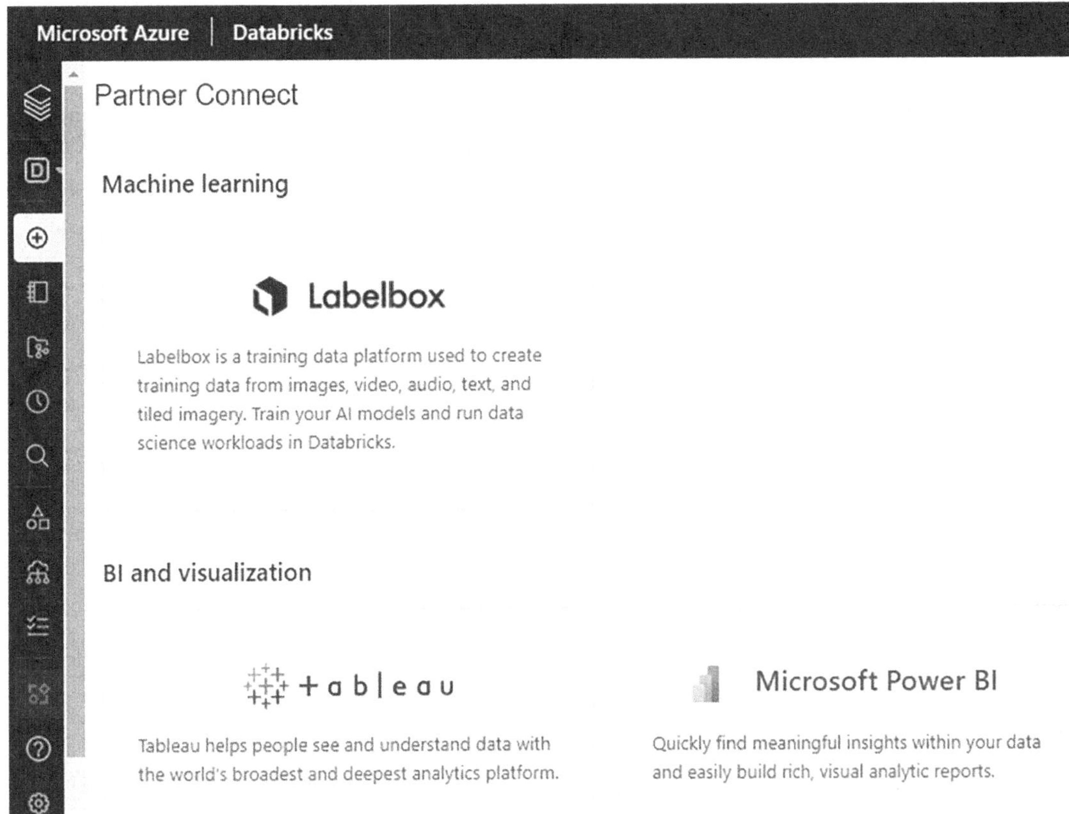

Figure 3-6. *Partner Connect UI*

The data science and engineering workspace also supports the capability of creating MLflow Experiments, shown in Figure 3-7, which let you organize and control access to MLflow runs for an experiment. There are robust features available within MLflow Experiments for visualizing, searching for, comparing runs, downloading run artifacts, and serving models.

With MLflow Model Serving, you can host machine learning models from the Model Registry as REST endpoints that are updated automatically based on the availability of model versions and stages and can be queried with these APIs with standard authentication. When enabled, Databricks automatically creates, deploys, and syncs versions of the model on the cluster, restarts the cluster if an error occurs, and terminates the cluster when model serving is disabled.

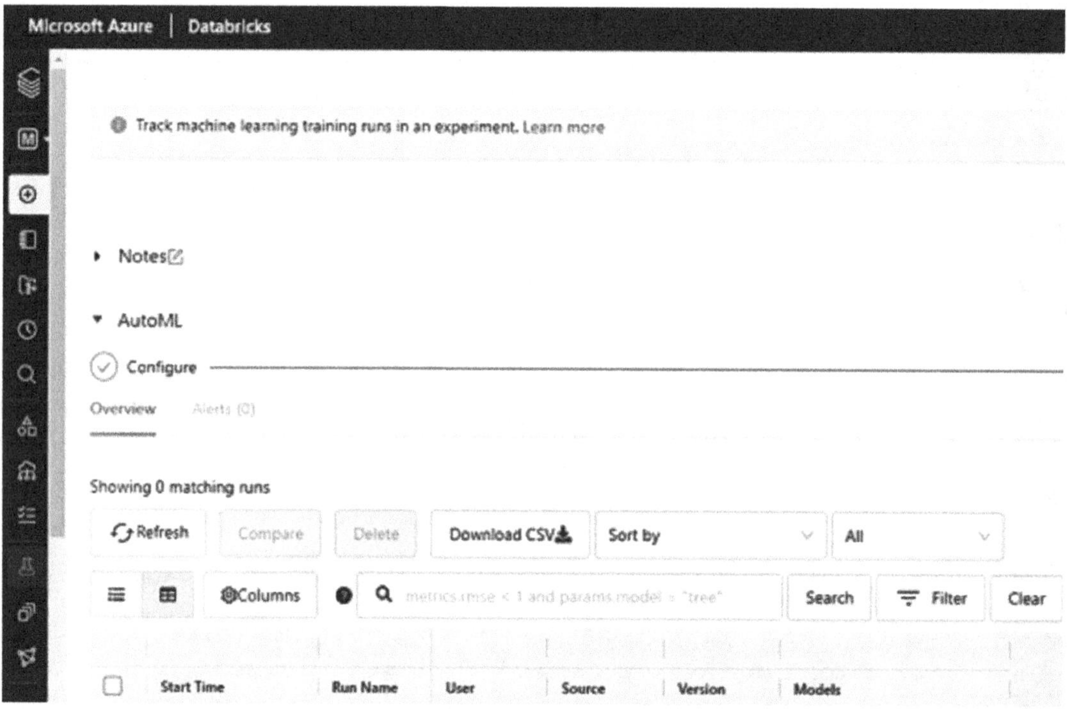

***Figure 3-7.** Experiments tab for creating manual or auto-ML experiments*

Finally, within the workspace, you will also have access to a variety of user, group, and workspace administrator settings within the Admin Console, shown in Figure 3-8. You will be able to control fine-grained permissions around admin privileges, workspace access, SQL access, and cluster creation at a user level. Groups can also be created with members that have certain entitlements. Finally, Workspace Settings within the Admin Console allow you to define access control, storage, job, cluster, and advanced-level settings.

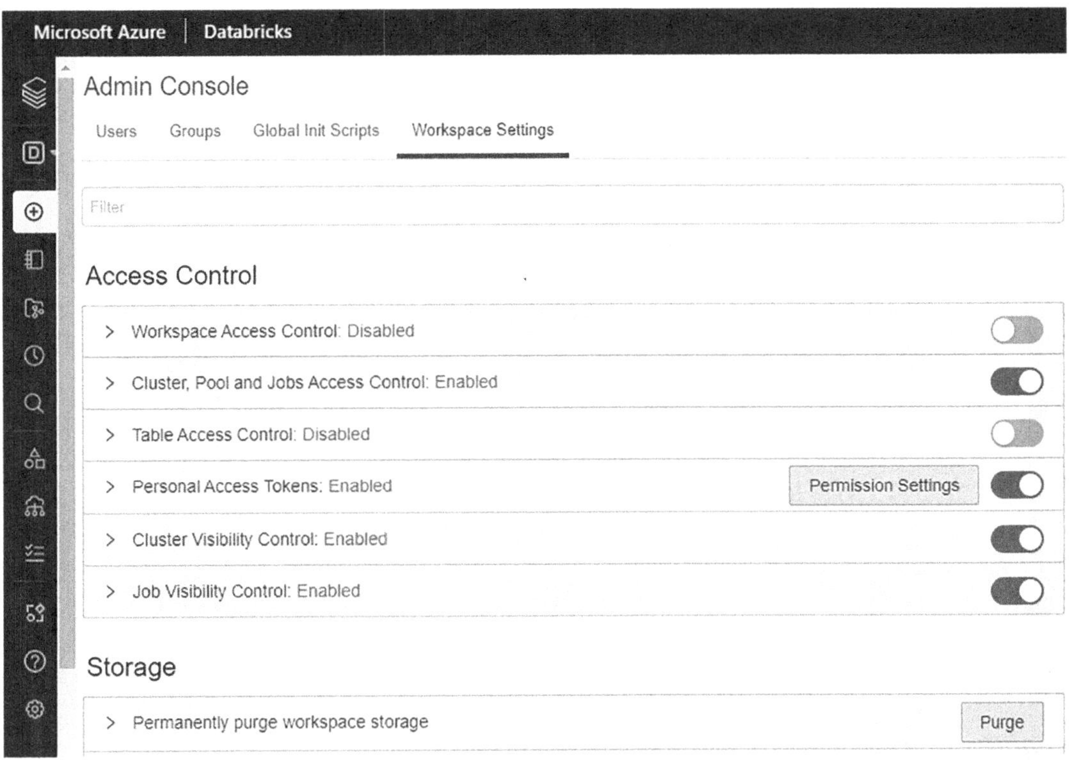

Figure 3-8. *Admin Console UI*

Machine Learning

The machine learning workspace, shown in Figure 3-9, is like the data science and engineering workspace in that it offers many of the same components. In addition, this machine learning workspace offers added components for Experiments, Feature Stores, and ML Models. This workspace supports an end-to-end machine learning environment including robust components for managing feature development, model training, model serving, and experiment tracking. Models can be trained manually or through AutoML. They can be tracked with MLflow tracking and support the creation of feature tables for model training and inferencing. Models can then be stored, shared, and served in the Model Registry. For more details on how to create an MLflow Experiment, install the MLflow Library, enable notebook logging, register, promote, and serve a model, please see my MSSQLTips article on this topic: `www.mssqltips.com/sqlservertip/6806/mlflow-azure-databricks/`

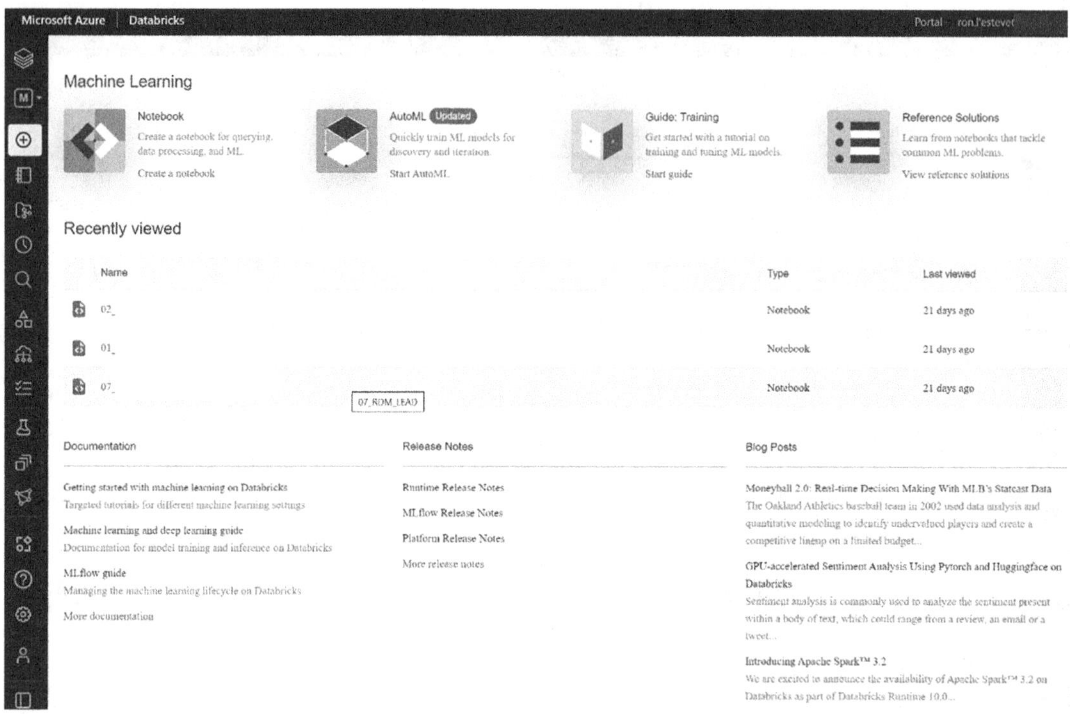

Figure 3-9. *Databricks machine learning workspace*

Figure 3-10 shows the Feature Store UI within the machine learning workspace, which is a centralized repository of discovery and sharing of features which can be used for model training and inference.

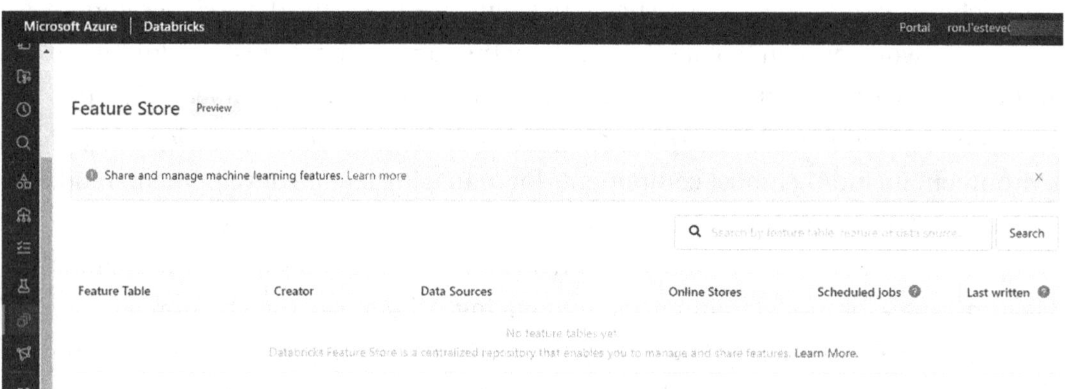

Figure 3-10. *Feature Store UI*

The Registered Models UI, shown in Figure 3-11, provides a Model Registry for managing the life cycle of MLflow Models. It provides model versioning, stage promotion details, and model lineage and supports email notifications.

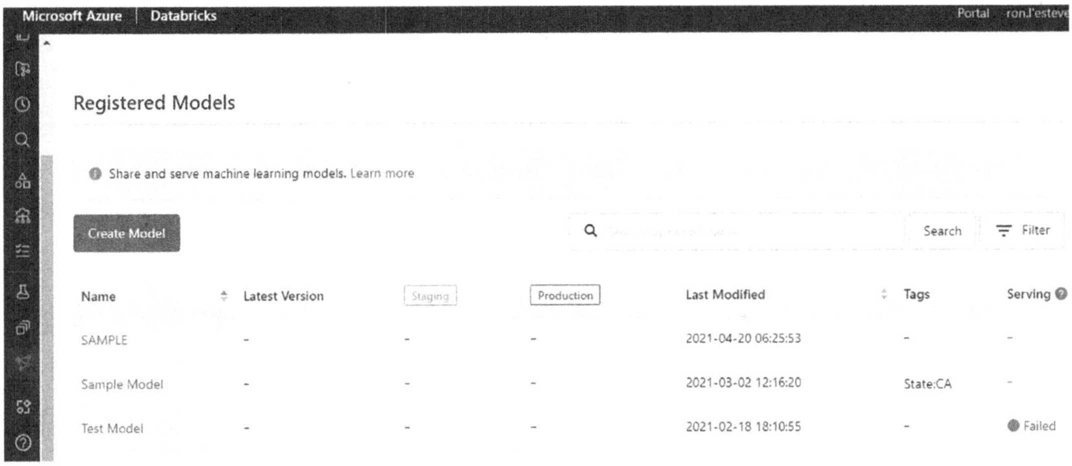

Figure 3-11. Model Registry UI

SQL

As customers and organizations continue adopting the Lakehouse paradigm, it is critical for them to have similar capabilities of their traditional data and BI systems when applying business intelligence and SQL-based analysis on their Lakehouse data. With pioneering Lakehouse architectures, there has been a need to persist aggregated and dimensional data within SQL server–based systems in addition to the lake. This parallel effort to persist data in both the lake and a SQL database has been adopted to address the challenges associated with easily querying, visualizing, and analyzing dimensional data with traditional SQL and BI tools such as SSMS and Power BI. Since there are inefficiencies and cost implications with persisting data in multiple systems, leading cloud providers now provide a variety of tools to support the seamless integration of BI and SQL analysis on Lakehouse data with experiences much like the traditional BI and data tools on the market. Microsoft's Synapse Analytics offers this capability through its SQL endpoints which provides users the ability to query, analyze, and perform BI on their Lakehouse data using traditional tools including SSMS and Power BI. Databricks introduced SQL Analytics to address some of these Lakehouse paradigm challenges. Customers are interested in learning more about Databricks' SQL Analytics.

The Databricks SQL workspace, shown in Figure 3-12, provides a native SQL interface and query editor, integrates well with existing BI tools, supports the querying of data in Delta Lake using SQL queries, and offers the ability to create and share visualizations. With SQL Analytics, administrators can granularly access and gain insights into how data is being accessed within the Lakehouse through usage and phases of the query's execution process. With its tightly coupled integration with Delta Lake, SQL Analytics offers reliable governance of data for audit and compliance needs. Users will have the ability to easily create visualizations in the form of dashboards and will not have to worry about creating and managing complex Apache Spark–based compute clusters with SQL serverless endpoints.

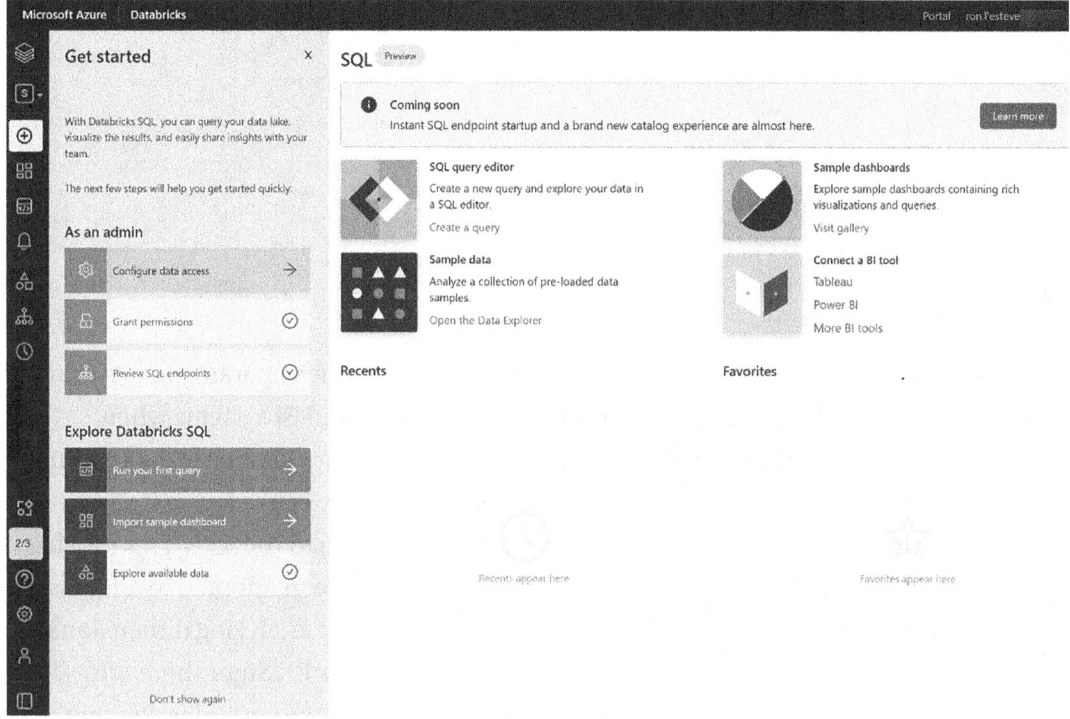

***Figure 3-12.** Databricks SQL Analytics workspace*

Figure 3-13 shows the SQL queries UI along with how easy it is to query your Lakehouse data either in the Databricks DBFS or ADLS gen2 account by writing simple SQL statements. Notice also that with this SSMS-like UI experience, you can easily see your schemas and tables to the left, can write your SQL query easily with live auto complete, and view the query results and stats in a single UI.

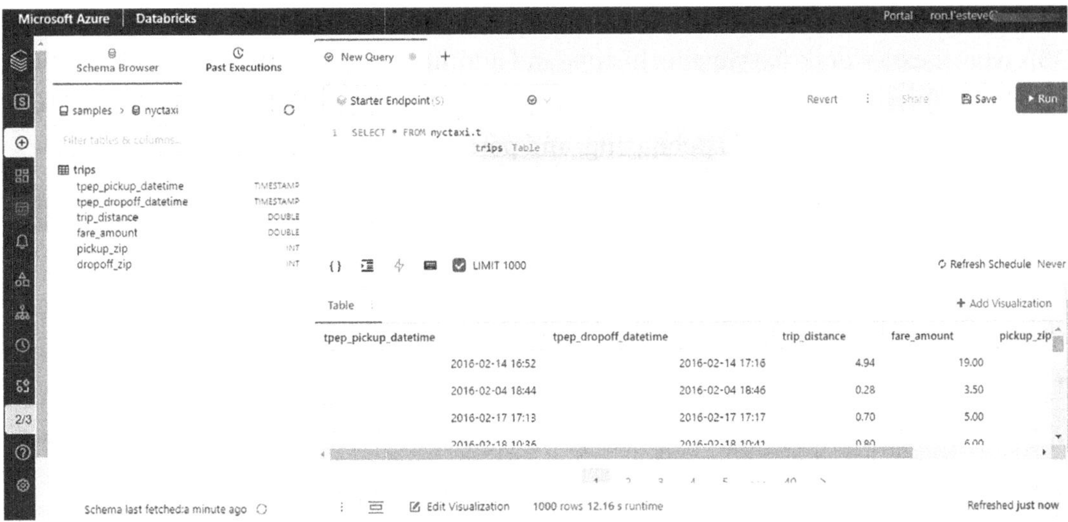

Figure 3-13. *Display of SQL query UI*

Additionally, by writing SQL code like the following script, you could also create tables using parquet files stored within your ADLS gen2 account. Remember to ensure that your lake is appropriately mounted to the right ADLS gen2 path. In the following code, the root mount path begins with "/data":

```
CREATE TABLE nyc_taxi.yellowcab
USING parquet
LOCATION '/data/nyc_taxi/parquet/yellowcab.parquet
```

Figure 3-14 shows the SQL Dashboard UI. Custom Dashboards can be easily created, pinned, and visualized within the UI. Additionally, there are various sample dashboards that are available in the gallery.

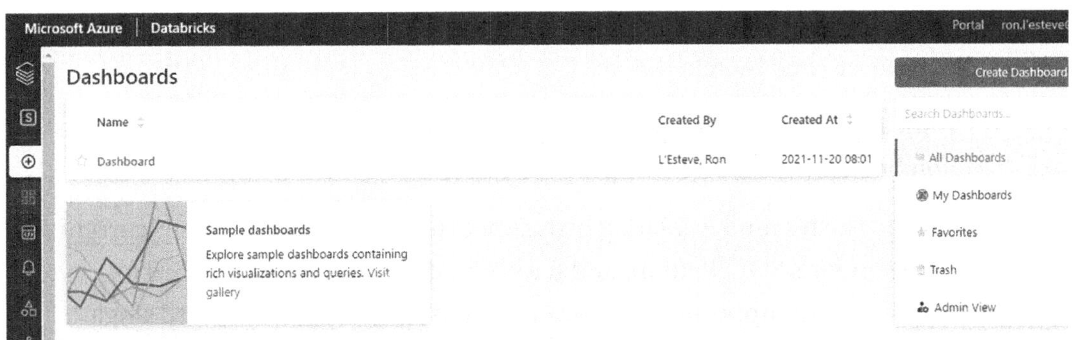

Figure 3-14. *Display of Dashboards UI*

Figure 3-15 shows the Query History UI which is an easy-to-use UI that offers a SQL DBA type of experience for viewing history and additional pertinent statistics of how SQL queries performed using SQL endpoints. From a SQL DBA standpoint, this can be used for monitoring, management, debugging, and performance optimization.

Query	SQL Endpoint	Started At	Duration	User
Listing tables 'catalog : %, schemaPattern : %, tableTypes : n...	Starter Endpoint	2021-11-20 06:53	4.16 s	ron.l'esteve
Listing tables 'catalog : %, schemaPattern : %, tableTypes : n...	Starter Endpoint	2021-11-20 06:53	17.81 s	ron.l'esteve
Listing catalogs	Starter Endpoint	2021-11-20 06:52	2 ms	ron.l'esteve
Listing catalogs	Starter Endpoint	2021-11-20 06:52	181 ms	ron.l'esteve
show tables in `default` -- user_id: {}	Starter Endpoint	2021-11-18 18:22	271 ms	ron.l'esteve
show grant on DATABASE `default` -- user_id: {}	Starter Endpoint	2021-11-18 18:22	324 ms	ron.l'esteve
show databases -- user_id: {}	Starter Endpoint	2021-11-18 18:22	320 ms	ron.l'esteve
describe database extended `default` -- user_id: {}	Starter Endpoint	2021-11-18 18:22	461 ms	ron.l'esteve

Figure 3-15. *Display of sample Query History*

Compute

Notebooks and jobs within Databricks are run on a set of compute resources called clusters. All-purpose clusters are created using the UI, CLI, or REST API and can be manually started, shared, and terminated. The second type of cluster is called a job cluster which is created, started, and terminated by a job. The following workloads utilize these all-purpose and job clusters:

- **Data engineering** workloads are automated and will run on job clusters created by schedulers.
- **Data analytics** workloads are interactive and will run Databricks notebook commands on all-purpose clusters.

The available cluster modes include high concurrency (optimized for concurrent workloads and supports SQL, Python, and R workloads), standard (optimized for single-user clusters and supports SQL, Python, R, and Scala workloads), and single node (contains no workers and is ideal for single-user clusters that need to compute low data volumes). As for runtime versions, they include the core components that run on Databricks plus some preinstalled standard libraries. There are a few available options which include the following:

- **Databricks Runtime** includes Apache Spark and other components that enhance big data analytics and workloads.
- **Databricks Runtime for machine learning** includes machine learning and data science libraries such as TensorFlow, Keras, PyTorch, and XGBoost.
- **Databricks Runtime for genomics** includes components for working with genomic and biomedical data.
- **Databricks light** includes Apache Spark and can be used to run JAR, Python, or spark-submit jobs but is not recommended for interactive notebook job workloads.

Databricks Connect is a client library for Databricks Runtime which allows you to connect your favorite IDE, notebook server, and other custom applications to Databricks clusters for running large Spark jobs without needing IDE plug-ins. It allows you to develop and debug code in your IDE to write jobs using Spark APIs without losing your work during cluster shutdown, since the cluster is decoupled from the application. For more details on setting up Databricks Connect, read the following documentation: `https://docs.databricks.com/dev-tools/databricks-connect.html`

Many of the runtimes include Apache Spark, which is a multi-language engine for executing data engineering, data science, and machine learning on single-node machines or clusters. There have been recent advancements toward a newer engine called Photon which is a vectorized engine developed in C++ and is intended to improve Spark and SQL query performance. Databricks offer auto-pilot options for auto-scaling between a minimum and maximum number of nodes, along with the capability of terminating the cluster after a period of inactivity to prevent incurring unnecessary costs. Cluster nodes have a single driver node which runs the main function and executes parallel operations on the worker nodes which read and write data. The min and max worker specification setting allows you to set the auto-scaling range. There are quite a few options for worker and driver types, and Databricks recommends Delta Cache Accelerated worker types which creates local copies of files for faster reads and supports delta, parquet, DBFS, HDFS, blob, and ADLS gen2 format files. To save costs by accessing unused capacity at deep discounts, you can toggle on "Spot instances" in the "New Cluster" UI. Finally, with ADLS gen2 credential pass-through enabled, the user's Active Directory credentials will be passed to Spark to give them access to data in ADLS gen2. Figure 3-16 shows the details required to create a cluster from the Databricks UI.

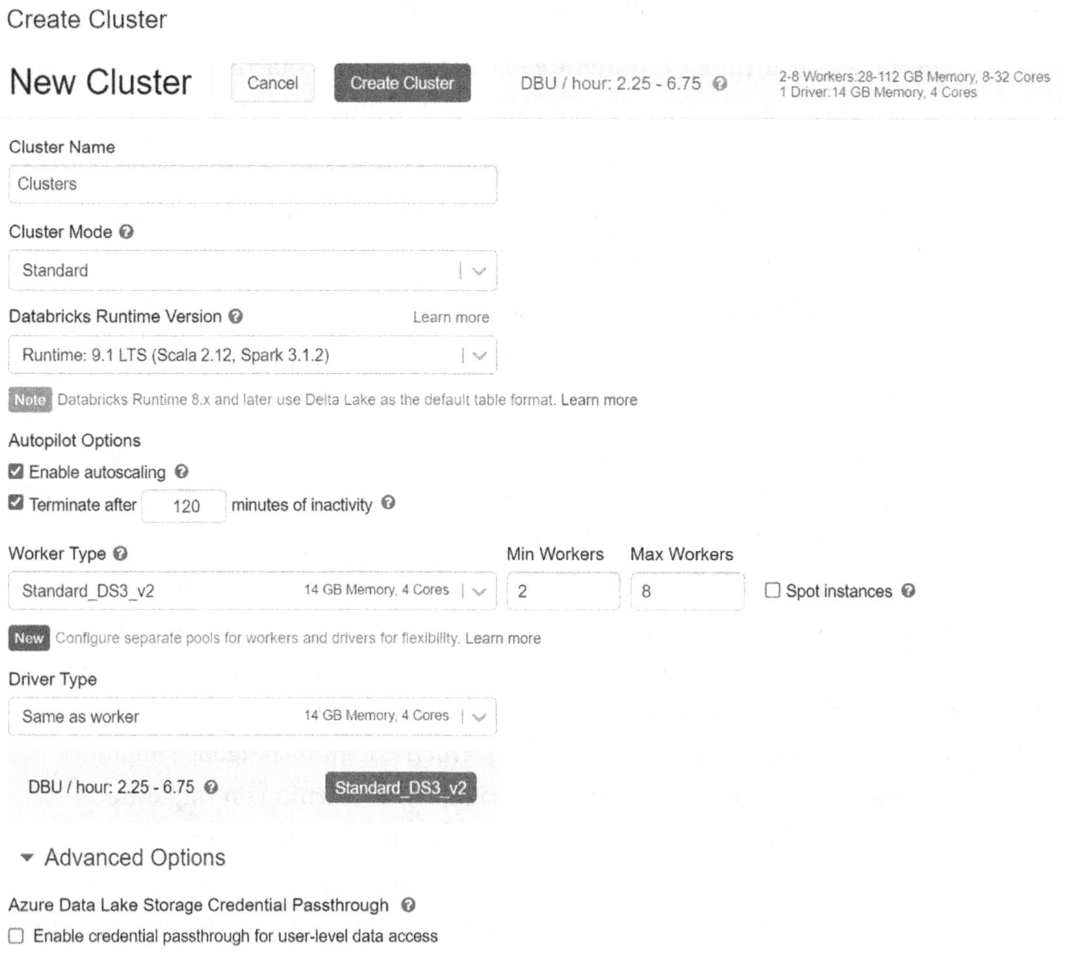

Create Cluster

New Cluster
Cancel
Create Cluster
DBU / hour: 2.25 - 6.75
2-8 Workers:28-112 GB Memory, 8-32 Cores
1 Driver:14 GB Memory, 4 Cores

Cluster Name
Clusters

Cluster Mode
Standard

Databricks Runtime Version
Learn more
Runtime: 9.1 LTS (Scala 2.12, Spark 3.1.2)
Note Databricks Runtime 8.x and later use Delta Lake as the default table format. Learn more

Autopilot Options
Enable autoscaling
Terminate after 120 minutes of inactivity

Worker Type
Min Workers
Max Workers
Standard_DS3_v2 14 GB Memory, 4 Cores
2
8
Spot instances
New Configure separate pools for workers and drivers for flexibility. Learn more

Driver Type
Same as worker 14 GB Memory, 4 Cores

DBU / hour: 2.25 - 6.75
Standard_DS3_v2

Advanced Options

Azure Data Lake Storage Credential Passthrough
Enable credential passthrough for user-level data access

***Figure 3-16.** Display of configuration options for creating new clusters*

In addition to clusters, pools within Databricks are a set of idle instances that can reduce cluster startup and auto-scaling times by attaching clusters and allocating worker and driver nodes from the pool. Figure 3-17 shows the configurations required within the "Create Pool" UI.

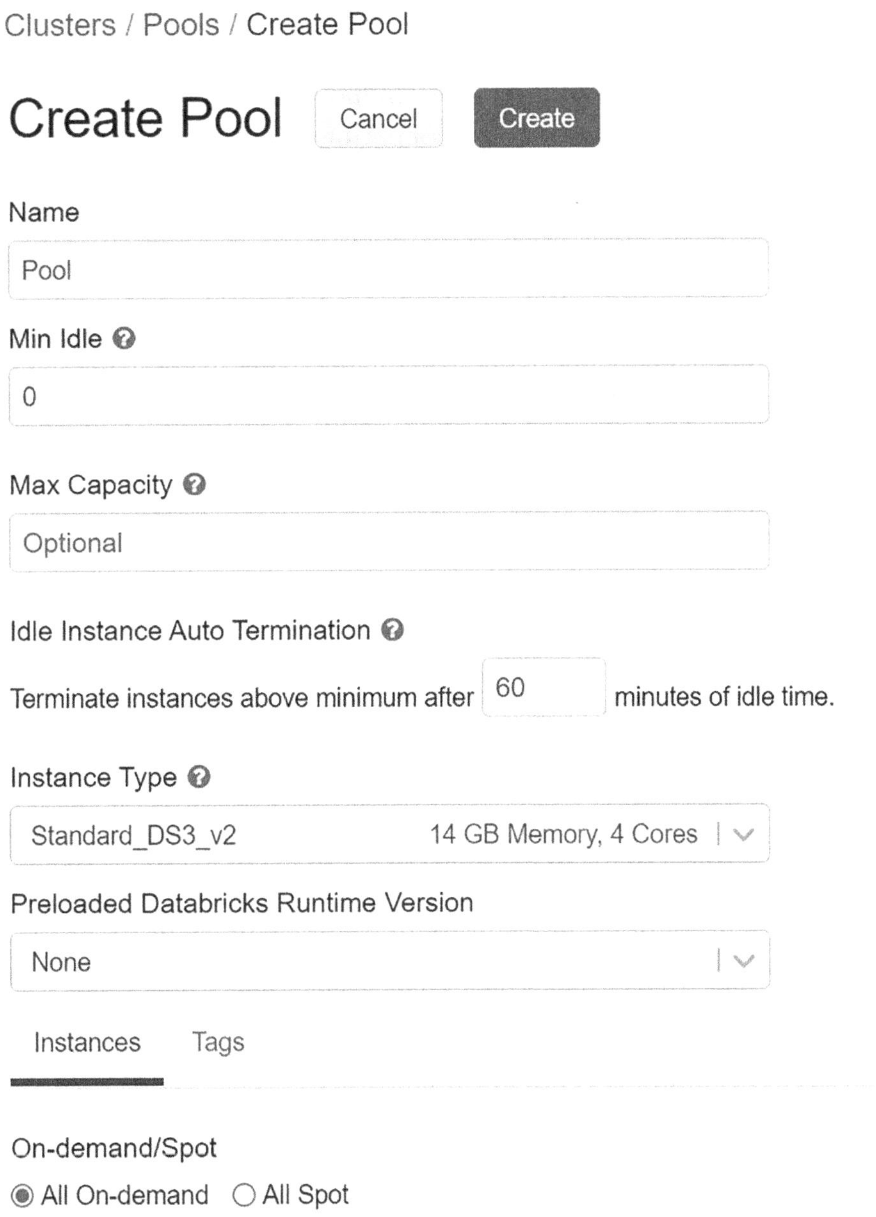

Clusters / Pools / Create Pool

Create Pool Cancel Create

Name

Pool

Min Idle

0

Max Capacity

Optional

Idle Instance Auto Termination

Terminate instances above minimum after 60 minutes of idle time.

Instance Type

Standard_DS3_v2 14 GB Memory, 4 Cores

Preloaded Databricks Runtime Version

None

Instances Tags

On-demand/Spot

All On-demand All Spot

***Figure 3-17.** Display of Create Pool configuration settings*

Databricks also offers serverless compute capabilities for its SQL workspace. Serverless SQL operates on a pool of servers which is fully managed by Databricks and runs on Kubernetes containers and can be quickly assigned to users and scaled up during heavy load times. Another benefit of Serverless SQL is that users will not need to wait for clusters to start up or scale out since compute will be instantly available. With Serverless SQL, users can easily connect to the endpoints with BI tools such as Power BI using built-in JDBC/ODBC driver–based connectors. Figure 3-18 shows the UI for creating and configuring Serverless SQL endpoints.

Figure 3-18. *SQL Endpoints configuration properties*

Storage

Databricks File System (DBFS) is available on Databricks clusters and is a distributed file system mounted to a Databricks workspace. DBFS is an abstraction over scalable object storage which allows users to mount and interact with files stored in ADLS gen2 in delta, parquet, json, and a variety of other structured and unstructured data formats. Developers can store files in a FileStore which is a folder in DBFS where you can save files and have them accessible to your web browser. There are a variety of Databricks datasets that come mounted with DBFS and can be accessed through the following Python code: `display(dbutils.fs.ls('/databricks-datasets'))`. DBFS, Spark, and local file APIs can be used to read and write to DBFS file paths. Databricks also supports Apache Hive, which is a data warehouse system for Apache Hadoop that provides SQL querying capabilities for data in HDFS. Hive supports structure on unstructured data. A variety of Apache Spark tables are supported including managed and external tables. DBFS can be accessed through the UI or mount points, which you will learn more about in the following section.

Mount Data Lake Storage Gen2 Account

While there are a few methods of connecting to ADLS gen2 from Databricks, this section will cover an end-to-end process of securely mounting your ADLS gen2 account in Databricks. Toward the end of this section, you will learn how to read data from your mounted ADLS gen2 account within a Databricks notebook.

Getting Started

To proceed with this exercise, you will need to create the following Azure resources in your subscription:

1. **Azure Data Lake Storage Gen2 account:** Please create an Azure Data Lake Storage Gen2 account, shown in Figure 3-19. While creating your Azure Data Lake Storage Gen2 account through the Azure Portal, ensure that you enable hierarchical namespace in the Advanced configuration tab so that your storage account will be optimized for big data analytics workloads and enabled for file-level access control lists (ACLs).

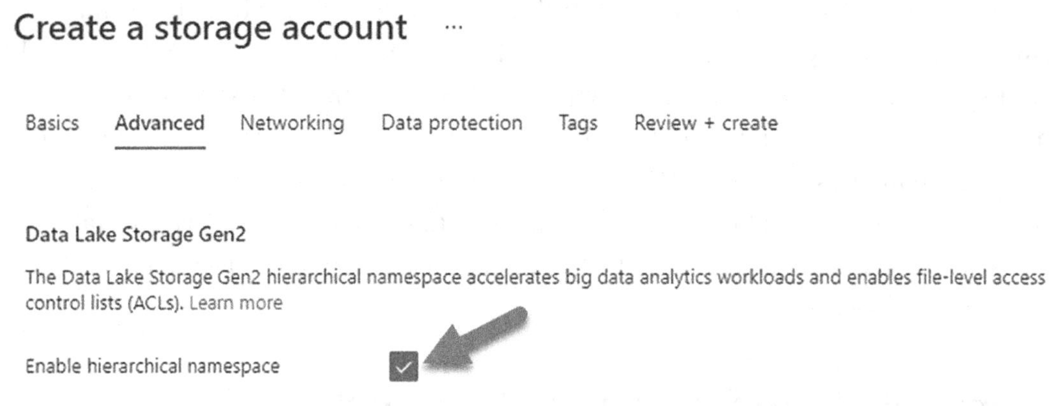

Figure 3-19. *Enable hierarchical namespace for ADLS gen2*

Also remember to create a container in your ADLS gen2 account once your storage account is successfully deployed. For the purposes of this exercise, you will also need a folder (e.g., raw) along with some sample files that you can test reading from your Databricks notebook once you have successfully mounted the ADLS gen2 account in Databricks.

2. **Azure Databricks workspace (Premium Pricing Tier):** Please create an Azure Databricks workspace, shown in Figure 3-20. While creating your Databricks workspace through the Azure portal, ensure that you select the Premium Pricing Tier which will include Role-based access controls. This Premium Pricing Tier will ensure that you will be able to create an Azure Key Vault–backed Secret Scope in Azure Databricks. Additionally, this tier selection will prevent you from encountering any errors while creating this secret scope in Databricks.

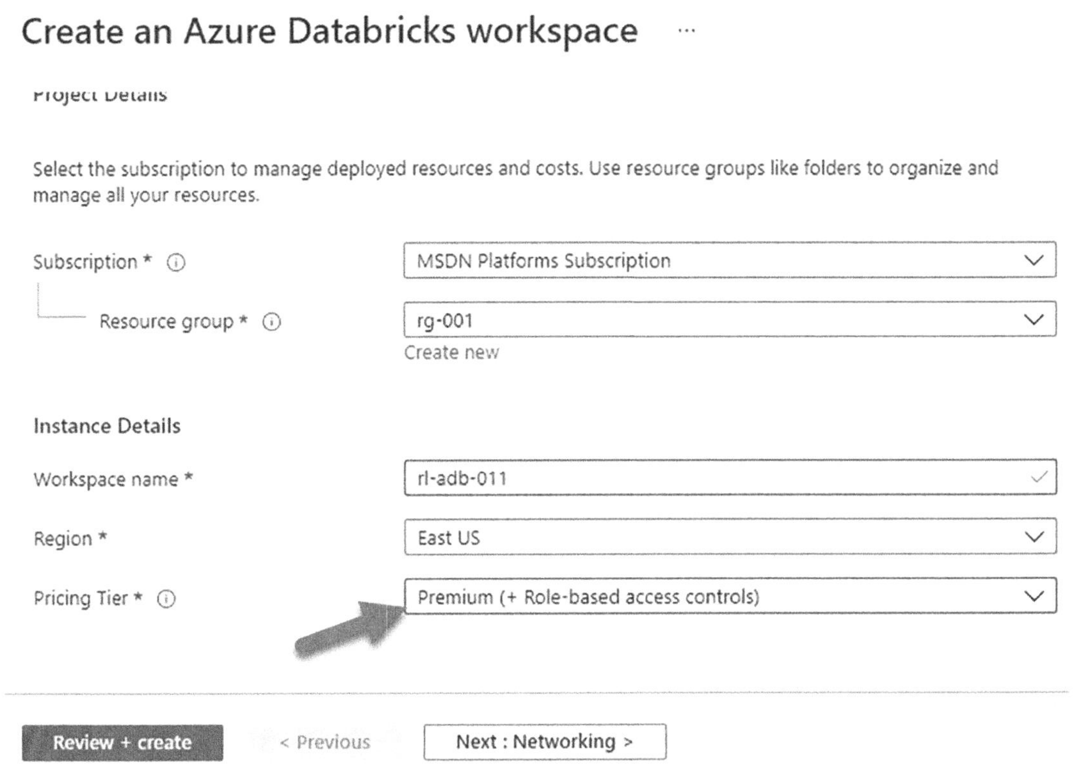

***Figure 3-20.** Create Databricks Premium account*

3. **Azure Active Directory App registration:** Please register an application by navigating to Azure Active Directory, clicking +New registration, as shown in Figure 3-21.

Register an application ···

* Name

The user-facing display name for this application (this can be changed later).

ADLS

Supported account types

Who can use this application or access this API?

- (•) Accounts in this organizational directory only (Default Directory only - Single tenant)
- ( ) Accounts in any organizational directory (Any Azure AD directory - Multitenant)
- ( ) Accounts in any organizational directory (Any Azure AD directory - Multitenant) and personal Microsoft accounts (e.g. Skype, Xbox)
- ( ) Personal Microsoft accounts only

Help me choose...

By proceeding, you agree to the Microsoft Platform Policies

Register

***Figure 3-21.** Register an app for ADLS gen2 access*

Once your App is registered, navigate to the Overview tab of your newly registered app, and copy the Application (client) ID and Directory (tenant) ID, shown in Figure 3-22, and save them in a notepad for now. These values will need to be entered and stored as Key Vault secrets in the next step of the process.

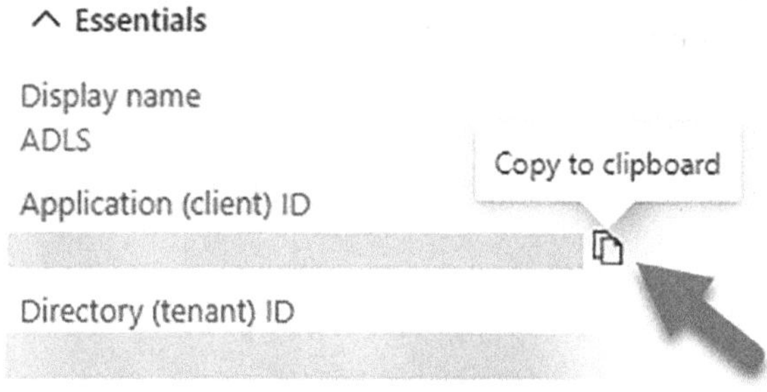

***Figure 3-22.** Copy the Tenant and Client IDs*

To complete the App registration process, you will need one last value, which is the Client Secret. Figure 3-23 shows you how to obtain this value. Navigate to the Certificates & secrets tab within your registered app, create a new client secret, copy the value, and save it in your notepad as Client Secret. You will need to add this to the Key Vault secrets in the next step.

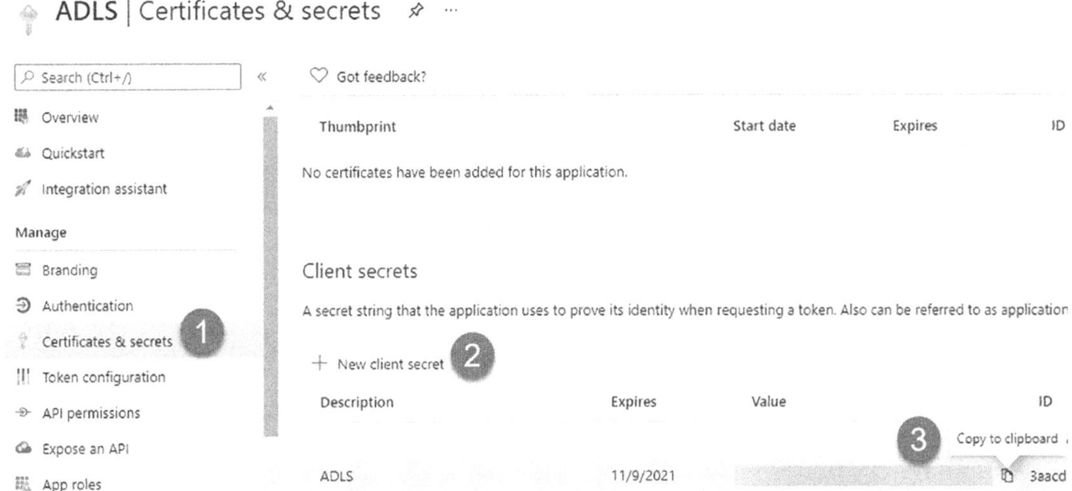

Figure 3-23. *Add new client secret*

Now that your app is registered, you will need to navigate to the Access Control settings of the ADLS gen2 storage account and give the app role access-level Storage Blob Data Contributor rights to the Storage account, as shown in Figure 3-24.

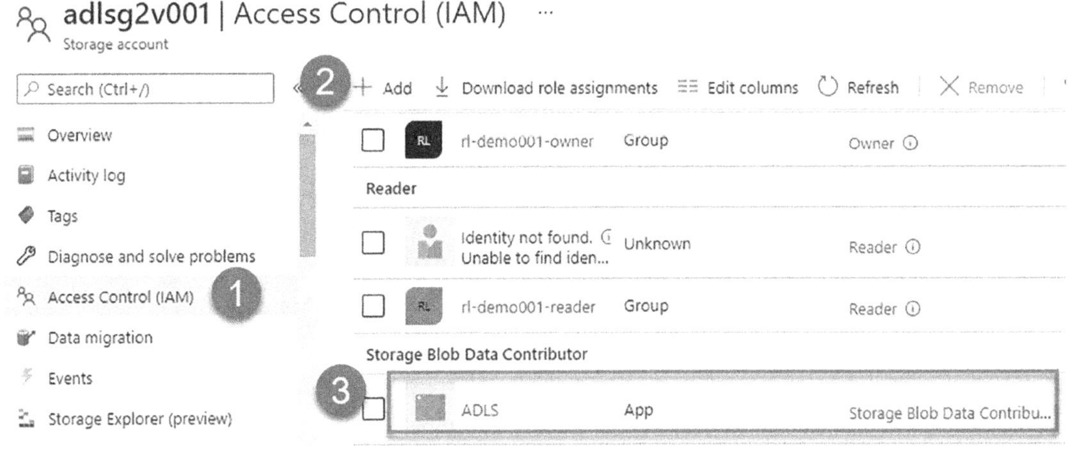

Figure 3-24. *Give the app access to ADLS gen2 account*

4. **Azure Key Vault:** Please create a Key Vault in your Azure subscription, and add the ClientID, TenantID, and ClientSecret as Secrets. Once created, ensure that these secrets have a status of enabled, as shown in Figure 3-25.

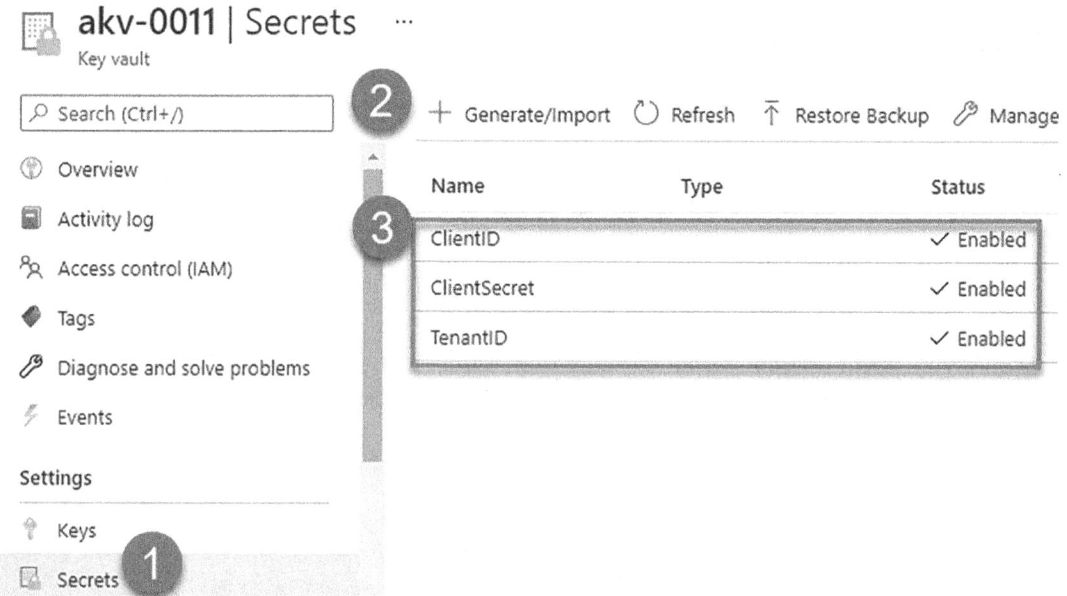

Figure 3-25. *Add the app secrets in Key Vault*

Create a Secret Scope

In Azure Databricks, you will need to create an Azure Key Vault–backed secret scope to manage the secrets, as seen in Figure 3-26. A secret scope is a collection of secrets identified by a name. Prior to creating this secret scope in Databricks, you will need to copy your Key Vault URI and Resource ID from the Properties tab of your Key Vault in the Azure portal.

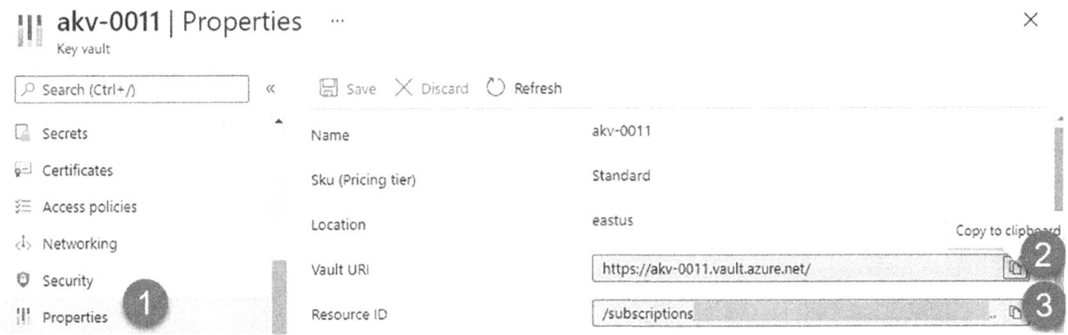

Figure 3-26. *Copy the Key Vault properties*

To create this secret scope in Databricks, navigate to `https://<DATABRICKS-INSTANCE>#secrets/createScope` and replace `<DATABRICKS-INSTANCE>` with your own Databricks URL instance. This URL will take you to the UI where you can create your secret scope. Paste the Key Vault URI and Resource ID which you copied in the previous step into the respective DNS Name and Resource ID section, as shown in Figure 3-27.

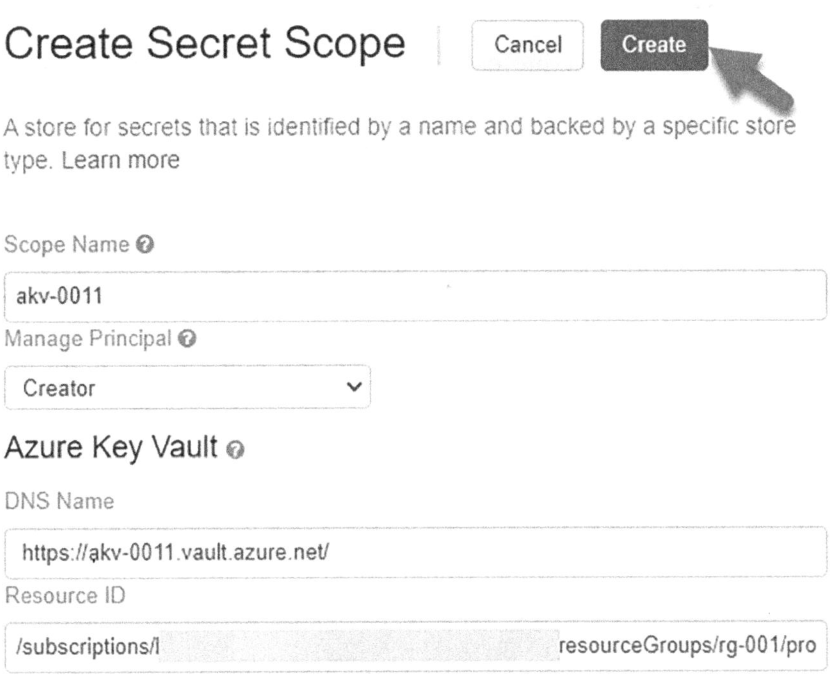

Figure 3-27. *Create a secret scope in Databricks*

Finally, by clicking Create, notice in Figure 3-28 that the secret scope will be successfully added. This confirms that you have successfully created a secret scope in Databricks and you are now ready to proceed with mounting your ADLS gen2 account from your Databricks notebook.

The secret scope named akv-0011 has been added.

Manage secrets in this scope in Azure KeyVault with manage principal = creator

Figure 3-28. *Confirmation window showing the secret scope is added*

Mount Data Lake Storage Gen2

All the steps that you have created in this exercise until now are leading to mounting your ADLS gen2 account within your Databricks notebook. Before you prepare to execute the mounting code, ensure that you have an appropriate cluster up and running in a Python notebook, as shown in Figure 3-29.

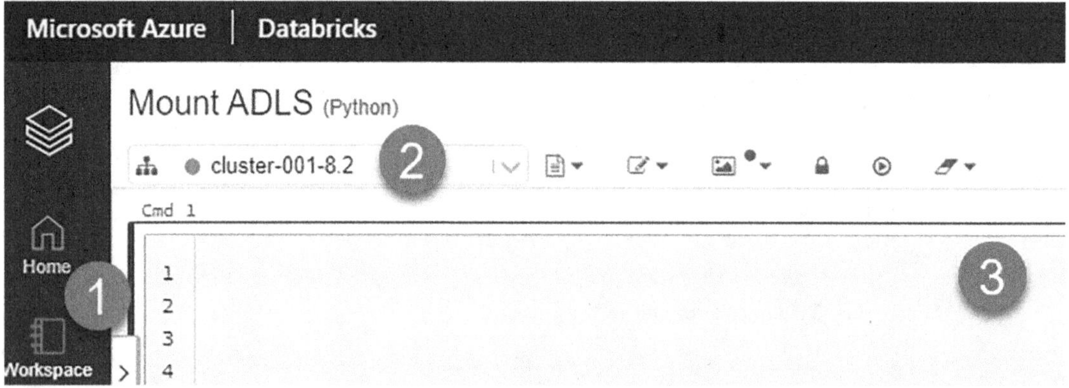

Figure 3-29. *Prepare the Databricks cluster and workspace*

Paste the following code into your Python Databricks notebook, and replace the adlsAccountName, adlsContainerName, adlsFolderName, and mount point with your own ADLS gen2 values. Also ensure that the ClientId, ClientSecret, and TenantId match the secret names that you provided in your Key Vault in Azure portal.

```
# Python code to mount and access Azure Data Lake Storage Gen2 Account from
Azure Databricks with Service Principal and OAuth

# Define the variables used for creating connection strings
adlsAccountName = "adlsg2v001"
adlsContainerName = "data"
adlsFolderName = "raw"
mountPoint = "/mnt/raw"

# Application (Client) ID
applicationId = dbutils.secrets.get(scope="akv-0011",key="ClientId")

# Application (Client) Secret Key
authenticationKey = dbutils.secrets.get(scope="akv-0011",key="Clie
ntSecret")

# Directory (Tenant) ID
tenandId = dbutils.secrets.get(scope="akv-0011",key="TenantId")

endpoint = "https://login.microsoftonline.com/" + tenandId + "/
oauth2/token"
source = "abfss://" + adlsContainerName + "@" + adlsAccountName + ".dfs.
core.windows.net/" + adlsFolderName

# Connecting using Service Principal secrets and OAuth
configs = {"fs.azure.account.auth.type": "OAuth",
           "fs.azure.account.oauth.provider.type": "org.apache.hadoop.
           fs.azurebfs.oauth2.ClientCredsTokenProvider",
           "fs.azure.account.oauth2.client.id": applicationId,
           "fs.azure.account.oauth2.client.secret": authenticationKey,
           "fs.azure.account.oauth2.client.endpoint": endpoint}
```

```
# Mount ADLS Storage to DBFS only if the directory is not already mounted
if not any(mount.mountPoint == mountPoint for mount in dbutils.
fs.mounts()):
  dbutils.fs.mount(
    source = source,
    mount_point = mountPoint,
    extra_configs = configs)
```

Finally, run the code in the notebook, and notice the successful completion of the Spark job in Figure 3-30. Congratulations, your ADLS gen2 storage account has successfully been mounted, and you are now ready to work with the data.

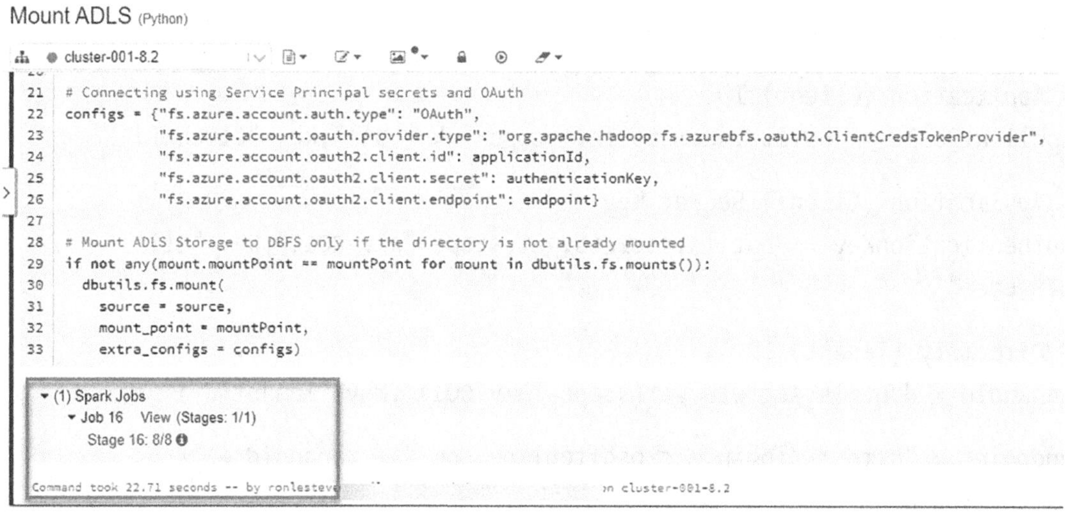

Mount ADLS (Python)

cluster-001-8.2

```
# Connecting using Service Principal secrets and OAuth
configs = {"fs.azure.account.auth.type": "OAuth",
           "fs.azure.account.oauth.provider.type": "org.apache.hadoop.fs.azurebfs.oauth2.ClientCredsTokenProvider",
           "fs.azure.account.oauth2.client.id": applicationId,
           "fs.azure.account.oauth2.client.secret": authenticationKey,
           "fs.azure.account.oauth2.client.endpoint": endpoint}

# Mount ADLS Storage to DBFS only if the directory is not already mounted
if not any(mount.mountPoint == mountPoint for mount in dbutils.fs.mounts()):
  dbutils.fs.mount(
    source = source,
    mount_point = mountPoint,
    extra_configs = configs)
```

▾ (1) Spark Jobs
▾ Job 16 View (Stages: 1/1)
Stage 16: 8/8

Command took 22.71 seconds -- by ronlesteve ... on cluster-001-8.2

Figure 3-30. Code that has been run in the notebook to mount ADLS gen2

Run the following command to list the mounts that have been created on this account:

```
display(dbutils.fs.mounts())
```

Notice in Figure 3-31 that the mount you created in this exercise is in the list, along with other mount points that have previously been created.

Cmd 6

```
display(dbutils.fs.mounts())
```

▸ (3) Spark Jobs

	mountPoint	source
1	/databricks-datasets	databricks-datasets
2	/databricks/mlflow-tracking	databricks/mlflow-tracking
3	/databricks-results	databricks-results
4	/mnt/raw	abfss://data@adlsg2v001.dfs.core.windows.net/raw
5	/databricks/mlflow-registry	databricks/mlflow-registry
6	/	DatabricksRoot

***Figure 3-31.** Code to list the mounts on the account*

Run the following command to unmount the mounted directory:

```
# Unmount only if directory is mounted
if any(mount.mountPoint == mountPoint for mount in dbutils.fs.mounts()):
  dbutils.fs.unmount(mountPoint)
```

Notice in Figure 3-32 that mount /mnt/raw has successfully been unmounted by this command.

Cmd 7

```
# Unmount only if directory is mounted
if any(mount.mountPoint == mountPoint for mount in dbutils.fs.mounts()):
  dbutils.fs.unmount(mountPoint)
```

▸ (1) Spark Jobs

/mnt/raw has been unmounted.

Command took 20.70 seconds -- by ronlesteve(on cluster-001-8.2

***Figure 3-32.** Code to unmount the ADLS mount*

Read Data Lake Storage Gen2 from Databricks

In the previous section, you learned how to securely mount an ADLS gen2 storage account from within your Databricks notebook. In this section, you will learn about some commands that you can execute to get more information about your mounts and read data, and finally, you will also learn how to unmount your account if needed.

Run the following command to list the content on your mounted store:

```
dbutils.fs.ls('mnt/raw')
```

Notice in Figure 3-33 that this dbutils.fs.ls command lists the file info which includes the path, name, and size.

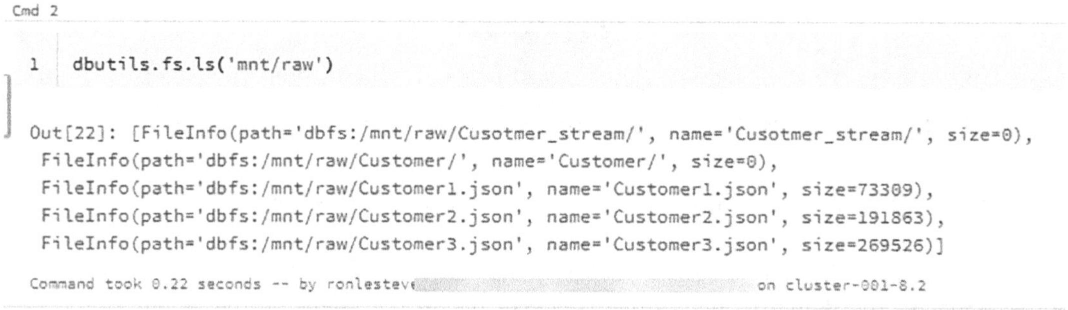

```
Cmd 2

dbutils.fs.ls('mnt/raw')

Out[22]: [FileInfo(path='dbfs:/mnt/raw/Cusotmer_stream/', name='Cusotmer_stream/', size=0),
 FileInfo(path='dbfs:/mnt/raw/Customer/', name='Customer/', size=0),
 FileInfo(path='dbfs:/mnt/raw/Customer1.json', name='Customer1.json', size=73309),
 FileInfo(path='dbfs:/mnt/raw/Customer2.json', name='Customer2.json', size=191863),
 FileInfo(path='dbfs:/mnt/raw/Customer3.json', name='Customer3.json', size=269526)]

Command took 0.22 seconds -- by ronlesteve on cluster-001-8.2
```

Figure 3-33. *Code to view the mount list*

Alternatively, use the %fs magic command to view the same list in tabular format:

```
#dbutils.fs.ls('mnt/raw')
%fs
ls "mnt/raw"
```

By running this, you will notice an error, shown in Figure 3-34. I deliberately added the commented out `#dbutils.fs.ls` code to show that if you happen to have comments in the same code block as the `%fs` command, you will receive an error.

```
Cmd 3

#dbutils.fs.ls('mnt/raw')
%fs
ls "mnt/raw"

SyntaxError: invalid syntax
Command took 0.08 seconds -- by ronlesteve on cluster-001-8.2
```

***Figure 3-34.** Code to view the mount list with error*

To get around this error, remove any comments in the code block which contains the `%fs` command:

```
%fs
ls "mnt/raw"
```

Notice that the same results as the dbutils command are displayed in Figure 3-35, this time in a well-organized tabular format.

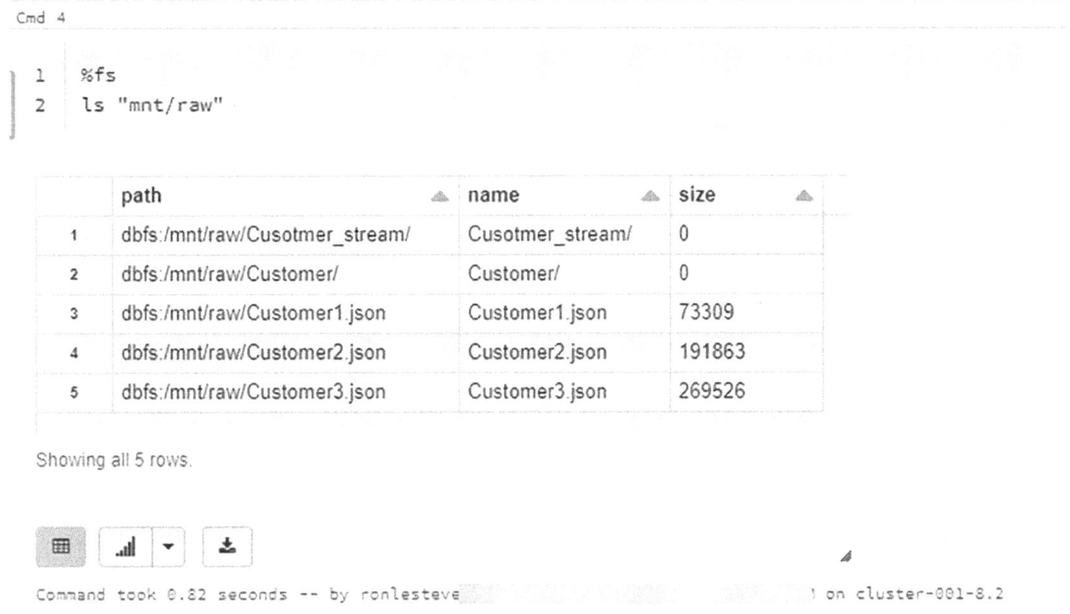
Cmd 4
%fs
ls "mnt/raw"
Showing all 5 rows.
Command took 0.82 seconds -- by ronlesteve
on cluster-001-8.2

	path	name	size
1	dbfs:/mnt/raw/Cusotmer_stream/	Cusotmer_stream/	0
2	dbfs:/mnt/raw/Customer/	Customer/	0
3	dbfs:/mnt/raw/Customer1.json	Customer1.json	73309
4	dbfs:/mnt/raw/Customer2.json	Customer2.json	191863
5	dbfs:/mnt/raw/Customer3.json	Customer3.json	269526

***Figure 3-35.** Code to view the mount list without error*

Read the data from the mount point by simply creating a data frame to read the file by using the spark.read command:

```
df = spark.read.json("/mnt/raw/Customer1.json")
display(df)
```

For this scenario, we are reading a json file stored in the ADLS gen2 mount point. Notice in Figure 3-36 that the data from the file can be read directly from the mount point.

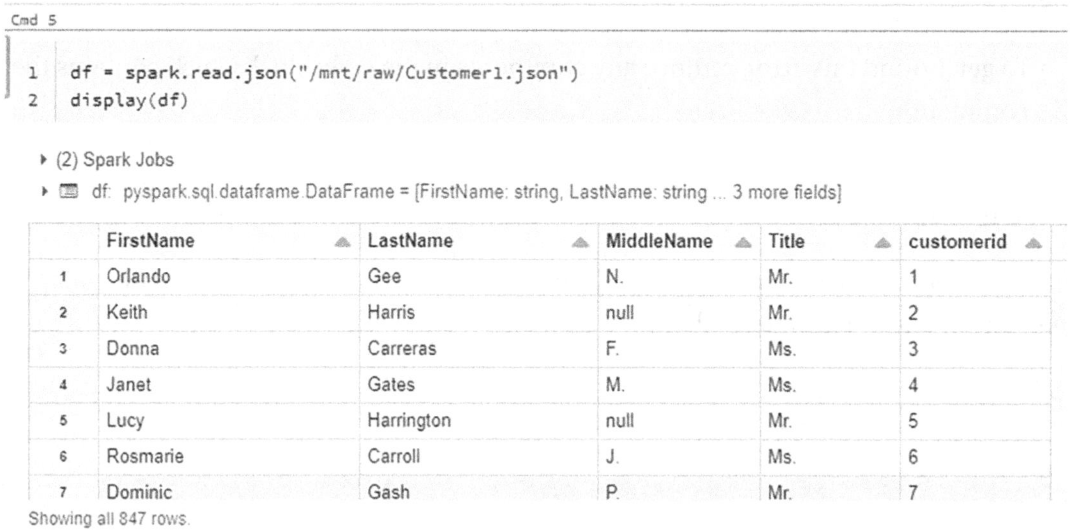

Cmd 5

```
df = spark.read.json("/mnt/raw/Customer1.json")
display(df)
```

▸ (2) Spark Jobs

▸ df: pyspark.sql.dataframe.DataFrame = [FirstName: string, LastName: string ... 3 more fields]

	FirstName	LastName	MiddleName	Title	customerid
1	Orlando	Gee	N.	Mr.	1
2	Keith	Harris	null	Mr.	2
3	Donna	Carreras	F.	Ms.	3
4	Janet	Gates	M.	Ms.	4
5	Lucy	Harrington	null	Mr.	5
6	Rosmarie	Carroll	J.	Ms.	6
7	Dominic	Gash	P.	Mr.	7

Showing all 847 rows.

Figure 3-36. *Code to read file from ADLS gen2*

Delta Lake

Delta Lake is an open source storage layer which runs on an ADLS gen2 account, is compatible with Apache Spark APIs, and provides ACID-compliant transactions, capabilities for streaming and batch data processing, and handling of metadata. With Databricks, you also gain access to the Delta Engine, which is an Apache Spark–compatible query engine which is optimized for performant interactive queries, data operations within the lake, and ELT workloads. You will learn more about performance optimization techniques using Delta Engine within the chapters in Section 5. Specifically, you will learn about dynamic partition pruning for Querying Star Schemas, Z-Ordering, Data Skipping, Adaptive Query Execution (AQE), Bloom Filter Indexes, and Hyperspace.

It is within your Delta Lake where you will be able to perform both batch and real-time advanced analytics on your data. Some of these Delta features will be covered within the chapters of Section 4. Specifically, you will learn more about some of these features which include schema evolution, change feed, clones, Live Tables, and sharing.

Reporting

Databricks can be accessed through Power BI by using the built-in Power BI connector. This connector supports both Azure Active Directory (AAD) and Single Sign On (SSO). Additionally, the ODBC driver is optimized for highly performant queries. Figure 3-37 shows Power BI's Databricks source configuration UI which requires the Databricks Server Hostname and HTTP Path of the cluster. Optionally, a database can be specified. Notice that both Import and DirectQuery modes are supported. Finally, Fast Evaluation enables faster processing of large DirectQuery- and Import-based datasets.

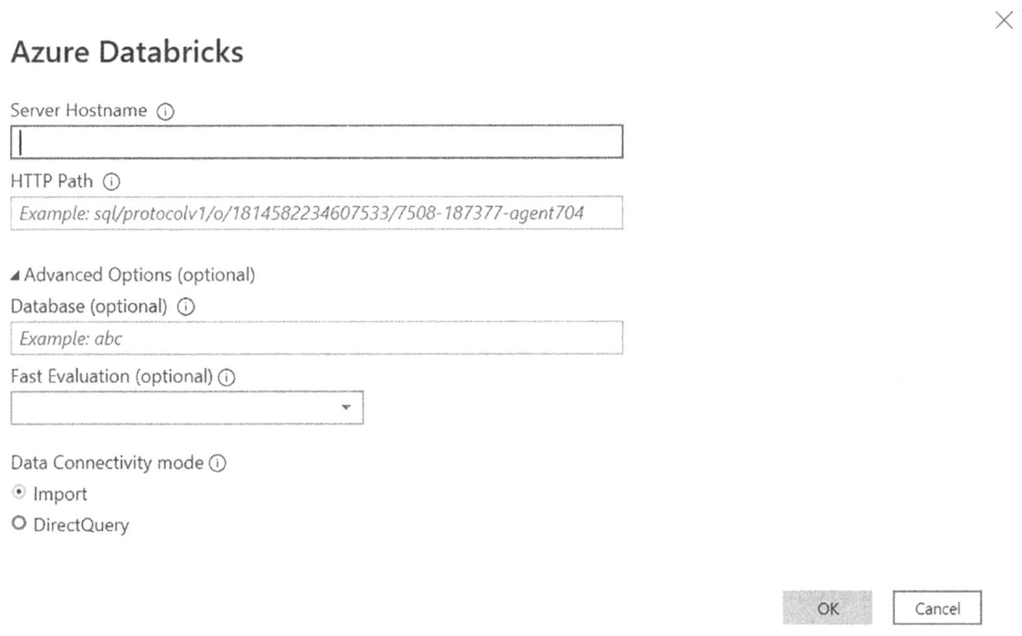

Figure 3-37. *Databricks source connector within Power BI Desktop*

The Databricks Partner Connect tab within the workspace simplifies the process of connecting Databricks SQL endpoints to Power BI. With the Databricks Partner Connect UI, you can seamlessly create new or link to existing endpoints or clusters. Figure 3-38 shows how Databricks cluster and SQL endpoints can connect to Power BI. Once the compute is selected, the connection credentials are then passed to a Power BI Desktop File (.pbids) which will be downloaded onto your local drive.

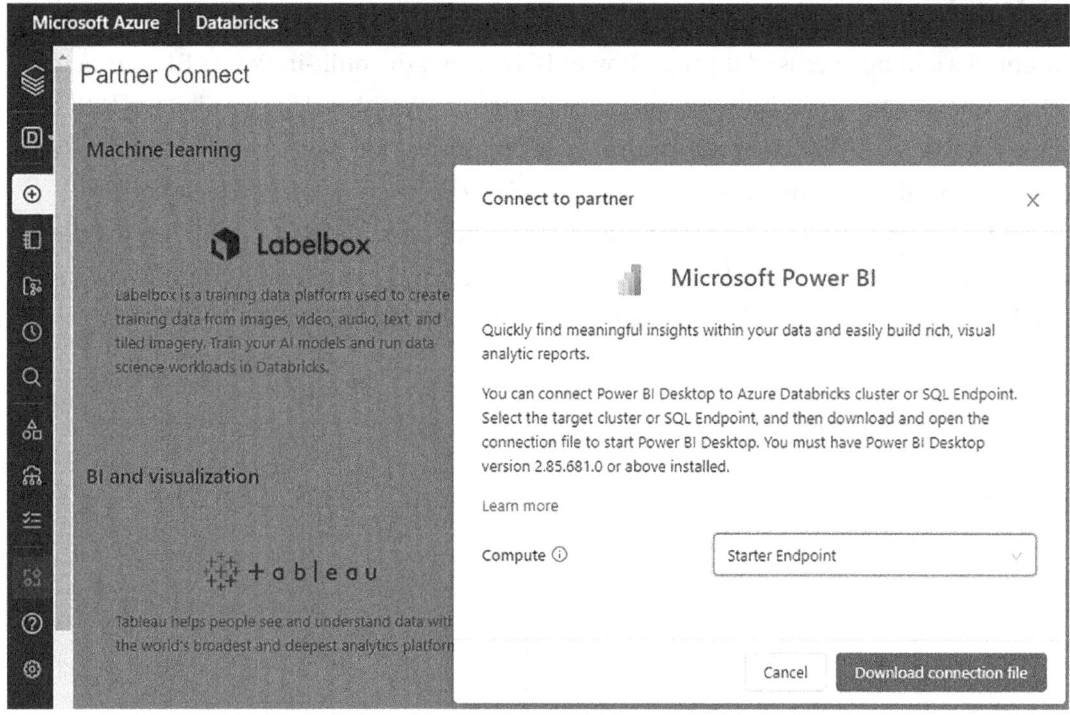

***Figure 3-38.** Databricks Partner connection setup for Power BI*

After opening the file, you will need to provide your connection credentials either through Active Directory, Databricks Personal Access Token (PAT), or Databricks Username and Password. Once fully authenticated from Power BI, you will be able to access the source data directly from Power BI based on the connection credentials included in the file, as shown in Figure 3-39. Partner Connect offers this seamless connectivity between Databricks and a variety of other BI and reporting tools in addition to Power BI.

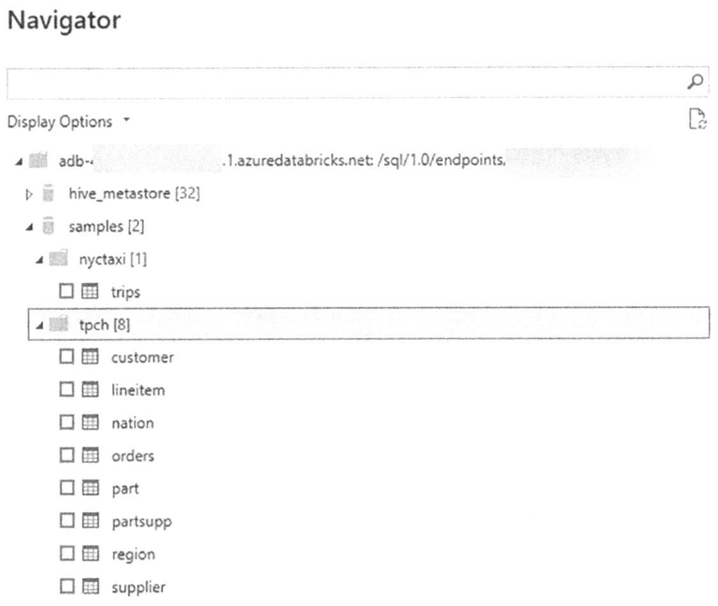

Figure 3-39. *Display of source data available from SQL endpoint connection file*

Real-Time Analytics

Databricks provides an Apache Spark Structured Streaming service built on the Spark SQL engine which will run queries incrementally and continuously append incoming data as it becomes available directly from your IoT devices, sensors, social networks, and online transactions. It integrates well with both IoT and Event Hubs and supports a variety of data output modes including append (only add new records to the output sink), update (update changed records in place), and complete (rewrite the full output) modes. Figure 3-40 shows the architectural pattern that structured streaming typically supports within Databricks.

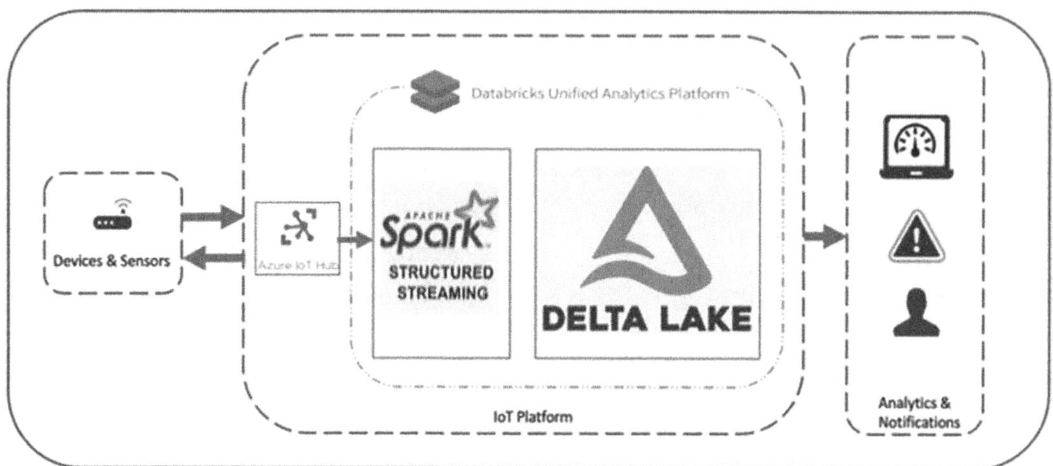

Figure 3-40. *Structured Streaming Delta Lake architecture*

Real-time Change Data Capture (CDC) has been a key requirement for numerous ELT and data warehousing processes. The same is true for the Lakehouse paradigm, and Databricks simplifies this process with its Change Data Feed service which enables you to only read a Delta Table's change feed rather than the entire table to capture and manage changes. It requires you to manually enable a Delta Table's Change Data Feed properties. This configuration can be set at either the table for individual tables or cluster level for all tables associated with the cluster, and the process will capture and store related metadata. There are a variety of connectors for other transactional systems such as Azure Cosmos DB for integrating the change feed process of data into the Lakehouse which can be processed by Databricks.

Databricks also provides an Auto Loader service which is designed for event-driven structured streaming ELT patterns and is constantly evolving and improving with each new runtime release. Auto Loader's cloudFile source supports advanced schema evolution. With schema inference capabilities, there is no longer the need to identify and define a schema. Databricks also offers a service called Delta Live Tables (DLT) which provides the tools for building and managing reliable real-time pipelines within your Delta Lake. These pipelines can be built on data from cloudFiles sources which are integrated with Auto Loader, Event Hubs, and IoT Hubs to support a process for performing real-time ELT on your data. Delta Live Tables can be created using the syntax shown in the following code and can be chained to other scripts in the form of dependencies to develop ELT scripts for multiple stages (raw, staging, curated).

These pipelines which capture lineage and dependencies can be visually tracked, tested, restarted, and maintained both manually and automatically.

```
CREATE live TABLE nyc_taxi
COMMENT "Raw Table for nyc_taxi"
AS
SELECT * FROM cloud_files("/data/nyc_taxi", "parquet")
```

When writing Delta Live Table notebook code, temporary views can also be used for staging and lookup purposes. Live Tables created in previous stages can be used in subsequent stages, with added data quality and integrity checks in the higher staging and curated zones. Table properties, comments, and integrity checks can easily be added through SQL syntax to the Delta Live Tables. After code has been written to create various Delta Live Tables for defining the ELT logic through multiple stages, a new pipeline can be created to orchestrate the process of populating the data in the tables. Figure 3-41 shows the UI to create a new pipeline. The notebook where you created your Delta Live Table code will need to be specified. Pipelines can be triggered on a schedule or run continuously to incrementally update the tables as new data arrives.

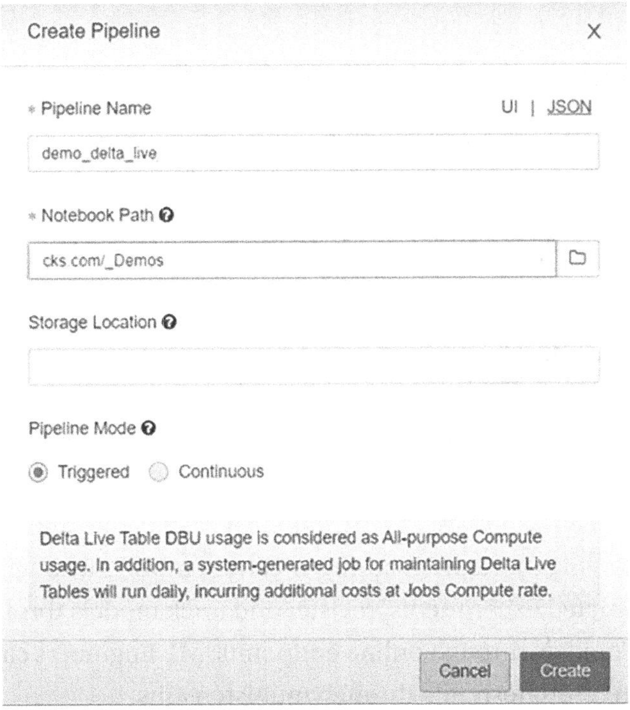

***Figure 3-41.** Display of the UI to create pipelines in Databricks*

Once the job is set up and run, Figure 3-42 shows the full graph that is produced as a result of Databricks' interpretation of the notebook code since it understands the pipeline's graph as it relates to semantics, transformations, and infrastructure needs. Clusters will be started and optimized for the Delta Live Table pipelines. The graph shows connections between tables, as well as real-time testing and log updates. These jobs can be scheduled using the scheduler.

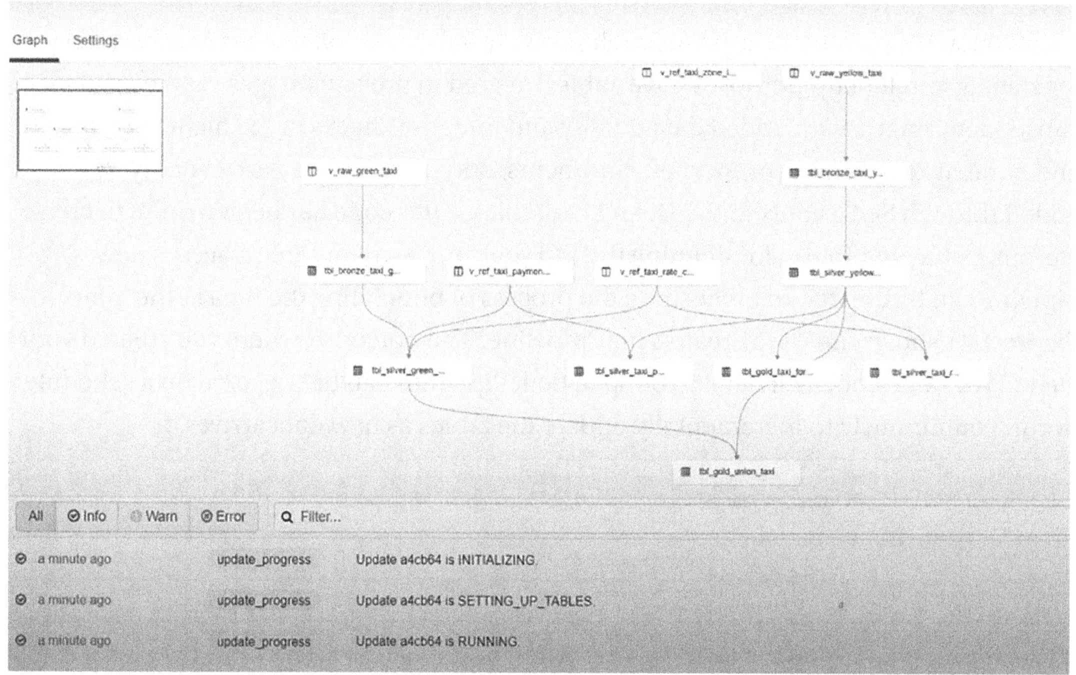

***Figure 3-42.** Display of Delta Live Table graph*

Advanced Analytics

From an advanced analytics capability standpoint, Databricks supports the full cycle of machine learning model development and serving. With its machine learning workspace, data scientists and ML engineers can create and manage feature development and serving through a feature store, train models through a variety of custom and automated experiments, register and track models through a Model Registry, and serve models through online endpoints. ML Engineers can also create ML Pipelines which can be orchestrated through multistep jobs.

Within the workspace, you will have access to a variety of libraries, packages, languages, and visualizations to support a robust experience for building custom-advanced analytics solutions. Databricks Runtime ML clusters include many machine learning libraries, such as TensorFlow, PyTorch, Keras, and XGBoost. Packages such as Maven, CRAN, PyPI, and JAR can be imported into notebooks and integrated directly with your code. A variety of visualizations can also be built in the notebook cells to support additional advanced analytics use cases.

Databricks offers a few other features for advanced analytics which include AutoML, MLflow, and R notebooks. With Auto ML, you will be able to automatically generate machine learning models based on source data and gain deep insights into the results from its included Python notebook with source code for each run, along with summary statistics on the data. MLflow is an open source platform for managing the end-to-end machine learning life cycle by tracking experiments to compare and record parameters and results, packaging ML code to share with other data scientists or transfer to production, managing and deploying ML Models using a variety of available libraries, and registering models for easy model management and serve models to host them as REST endpoints. Finally, with R notebooks in Databricks, you will be able to write SparkR for advanced statistics and visualization use cases with seamless access to a variety of R packages.

Security and Governance

Security and data governance in Databricks includes the policies for securely managing data within your Lakehouse. Databricks offers robust capabilities around governing data at the row and column levels and extends to covering cluster, pool, workspace, and job access controls. Databricks also offers other access and visibility features including workspace, cluster, and job visibility controls. Cluster policies enable administrators to control access to compute resources.

Databricks Unity Catalog solves many organizational challenges around sharing and governing of data in the Lakehouse by providing an interface to govern all Lakehouse data assets with a security model that is based on ANSI SQL GRANT command, along with federated access and easy integration with existing catalogs. It offers fine-grained permissions on tables, views, rows, and columns from files persisted in the Lakehouse. For example, in the code shown as follows, the SQL GRANT statement will delegate permissions on a table to a group. Permissions can be fine-grained to certain columns as well.

```
GRANT SELECT ON tbl_nyctaxidata TO datadevs
GRANT SELECT (mileage, city, state, zip) ON nyctaxidata TO dataanalysts
```

The Unity Catalog also supports SQL view–based access control which allows you to create complex aggregated views for certain users or groups:

```
CREATE VIEW sum_nyctaxi_mileage AS
  SELECT date, country, city, state SUM(*) AS Total_Miles FROM tbl_nyctaxidata
  GROUP BY date, country, city, state

GRANT SELECT ON sum_nyctaxi_mileage TO dataanalysts
```

With the Unity Catalog's attribute-based controls, you can tag columns as PII and manage access to all columns tagged as PII in a single rule:

```
ALTER TABLE tbl_nyctaxidata ADD ATTRIBUTE pii ON credit_card_number
ALTER TABLE tbl_nyctaxicustomers ADD ATTRIBUTE pii ON email

GRANT SELECT ON TABLE tbl_nyctaxidata
  HAVING ATTRIBUTE NOT IN (pii)
  TO datamanagers
```

Note that attribute-based controls can also be applied to MLflow models using the following sample SQL command:

```
GRANT EXECUTE ON MODELS HAVING ATTRIBUTE (midwest_churn)
  TO midwest_regionalmanagers
```

Unity Catalog streamlines access to a variety of Lakehouse assets including Data Lake files, SQL databases, Delta Shares, and ML Models. It also offers centralized audit logs for best practice compliance management standards. Unity Catalog minimizes the challenges around enforcing reliable data governance with its fine-grained permissions; governing various data assets such as SQL databases, ML Models, and metastores; and keeping these data assets in sync with up-to-date security models.

Databricks offers numerous security features including tightly coupled integration with the Azure platform with access through Azure Active Directory (AAD) credential pass-through. Databricks also supports SSO authentication for other identity and authentication methods for technologies such as Snowflake. Audit logging can be enabled to gain access to robust audit logs on actions and operations on the workspace. Keys and secrets can be integrated with Azure Key Vault. Databricks also supports creating secret scopes which are stored in an encrypted database owned and managed by Databricks.

Databricks supports several compliance standards including GDPR, HIPAA, HITRUST, and more. With its support for virtual networks (vNets), your infrastructure will have full control of network security rules, and with Private Link, no data will be transmitted through public IP addresses.

When working with SQL in Databricks, the security model follows a similar pattern as you would find with traditional SQL databases which allows for setting of fine-grained access permissions using standard SQL statements such as `GRANT` and `REVOKE`. With access control lists (ACLs), administrators can configure and manage permissions to access Databricks SQL alerts, dashboards, data, queries, and SQL endpoints. Figure 3-43 shows a list of how the available visibility and access controls are presented within the Databricks Admin Console. The following list outlines some of these visibility and access controls:

- **Workspace Visibility Control:** Prevents users from seeing objects in the workspace that they do not have access to.
- **Cluster Visibility Control:** Prevents users from seeing clusters they do not have access to.
- **Job Visibility Control:** Prevents users from seeing jobs they do not have access to.
- **Cluster, Pool, and Jobs Access Control:** Applies controls related to who can create, attach, manage, and restart clusters, who can attach and manage pools, and who can view and manage jobs.
- **Workspace Access Control:** Applies controls related to who can view, edit, and run notebooks in a workspace.
- **Table Access Control:** Applies controls related to who can select and create databases, views, and functions from Python and SQL. When enabled, users can set permissions for data objects on that cluster.
- **Alert Access Control:** Applies controls related to who can create, run, and manage alerts in Databricks SQL.
- **Dashboard Access Control:** Applies controls related to who can create, run, and manage dashboards in Databricks SQL.

- **Data Access Control:** Applies data object-related controls using SQL commands such as GRANT, DENY, REVOKE, etc., to manage access to data objects.
- **Query Access Control:** Applies controls related to who can run, edit, and manage queries in Databricks SQL.
- **SQL Endpoint Access Control:** Applies controls related to who can use and manage SQL endpoints in Databricks SQL. A SQL endpoint is a computation resource that lets you run SQL commands on data objects within the Databricks environment.

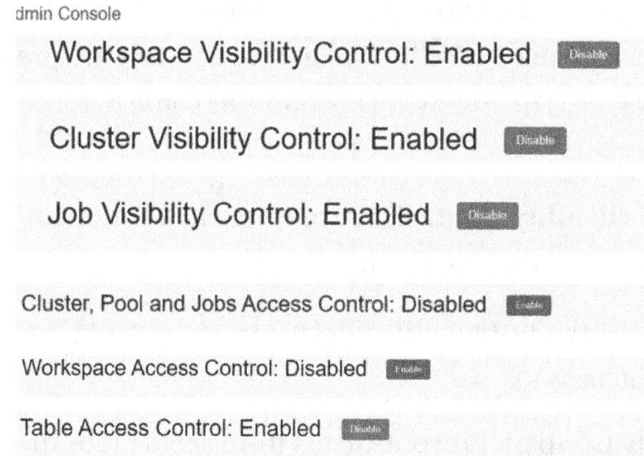

Figure 3-43. *Databricks Admin Console access and visibility controls*

Azure Purview is a data governance service that helps manage and govern a variety of data sources including Azure Databricks and Spark Tables. Using Purview's Apache Atlas API, developers can programmatically register data lineage, glossary terms, and much more into Purview directly from a Databricks notebook. Figure 3-44 illustrates how lineage from a Databricks transformation notebook could potentially be captured in Purview because of the Apache Atlas API running code to capture and register lineage programmatically. More details can be found about this topic at the following GitHub Code Repository, which is created, owned, and maintained by Intellishore: https://github.com/intellishore/data-lineage-databricks-to-purview

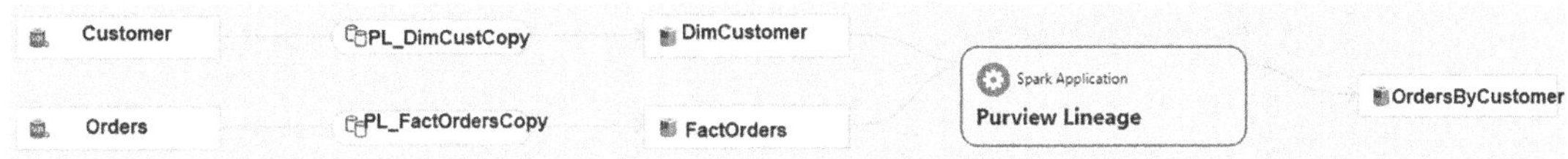

***Figure 3-44.** Purview Lineage tracking for Spark applications*

Continuous Integration and Deployment

Continuous integration and deployment standards are prevalent across a variety of Azure data services which use Azure DevOps (ADO) for this CI and CD process. Similarly, Databricks supports CI/CD within Azure DevOps by relying on repos that store code that needs to be promoted to higher Databricks environments. Once these repositories are connected and synchronized to Azure DevOps, the CI and CD pipelines can be built using YAML code or the classic editor. The build pipeline will use the integrated source repo to build and publish the artifact based on automated continuous integration, and the release pipeline will continuously deploy the changes to the specified higher environments. The Databricks release pipeline tasks shown in Figure 3-45 requires the installation of the Databricks Script Deployment Task by Data Thirst from the Visual Studio Marketplace. The marketplace link can be found here: `https://marketplace.visualstudio.com/items?itemName=DataThirstLtd.databricksDeployScriptsTasks`. These tasks support the deployment of Databricks files such as .py, .csv, .jar, .whl, etc., to DBFS. In addition, there are tasks available for the deployment of Databricks notebooks, secrets, and clusters to higher environments. As with any ADO CI/CD process, once the pipelines are built, there is also the capability of adding manual approval gates, code quality tests, and more within the pipelines to ensure that the best quality code is being promoted to higher environments.

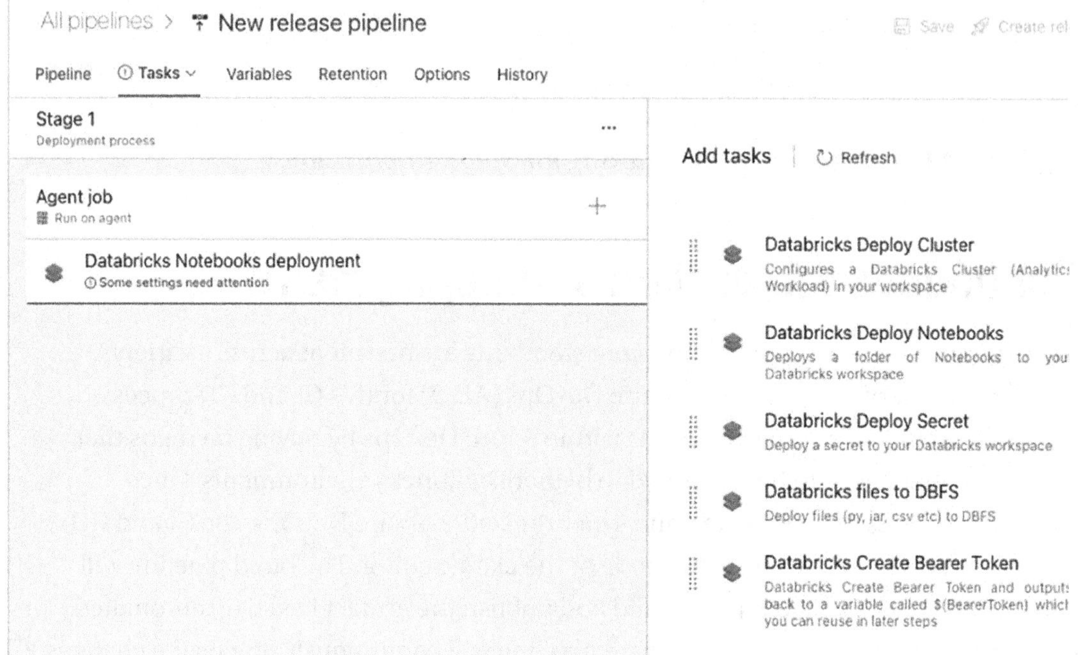

***Figure 3-45.** Databricks CI/CD tasks available in Azure DevOps*

Integration with Synapse Analytics

There are a few options for reading and writing data to Synapse Analytics Dedicated SQL Pools from Databricks as part of ELT processes by using a JDBC connector coupled with the power of the COPY INTO command. This can be achieved by providing a username and password or OAuth 2.0 with a service principal for authentication. The following Python script demonstrates just how easy it is to read, write, and transform data in Synapse Analytics Dedicated SQL Pools directly from a Databricks notebook.

```
# Read data from Synapse SQL table.
df = spark.read \
  .format("com.databricks.spark.sqldw") \
  .option("url", "jdbc:sqlserver://<connection-string>") \
  .option("tempDir", " https://adlsg2v001.dfs.core.windows.net/data/raw") \
  .option("forwardSparkAzureStorageCredentials", "true") \
  .option("dbTable", "<table-name>") \
  .load()
```

```
# Read Azure Synapse query and load into Databricks Dataframe.
df = spark.read \
  .format("com.databricks.spark.sqldw") \
  .option("url", "jdbc:sqlserver://<connection-string>") \
  .option("tempDir", "https://adlsg2v001.dfs.core.windows.net/data/raw") \
  .option("forwardSparkAzureStorageCredentials", "true") \
  .option("query", "select * from table group by n") \
  .load()

# Apply data transformations and write back to a Synapse SQL Table.

df.write \
  .format("com.databricks.spark.sqldw") \
  .option("url", "jdbc:sqlserver://<connection-string>") \
  .option("forwardSparkAzureStorageCredentials", "true") \
  .option("dbTable", "<table-name>") \
  .option("tempDir", " https://adlsg2v001.dfs.core.windows.net/data/
  raw ") \
  .save()
```

In this section, you will learn more about the advanced features related to data encryption, data and query profiling, constraints, and merging using Delta Live Tables.

Dynamic Data Encryption

Encrypting and decrypting data is a critical need for many organizations as part of their data protection regulations. With the new Databricks Runtime 10.3, there are two new functions, aes_encrypt() and aes_decrypt(), that serve this very purpose. They can be combined with row-level security features to only display the decrypted data to those who have access. The function works by simply writing a SQL statement similar to the following code by specifying what to encrypt as well as a 32-bit encryption key: `SELECT aes_encrypt('MY SECRET', 'mykey')`. To decrypt your data, simply run the aes_decrypt () function with code that is similar to the following, which wraps your encrypted value and key within the decrypt function and casts it as a string: `SELECT CAST(aes_decrypt(unbase64('encryptedvalue'), 'mykey') as string)`

For scenarios where you are seeking added row-level security-based decryption, you could start by creating the following tables shown in Figure 3-46. The first table, tbl_encrypt, contains the encryption key used in the encryption function and group name which matches the name of the corresponding security groups that have been in the Databricks Admin UI. The next table, tbl_data, contains the data that needs to be protected along with the same group name that can be mapped to tbl_encrypt.

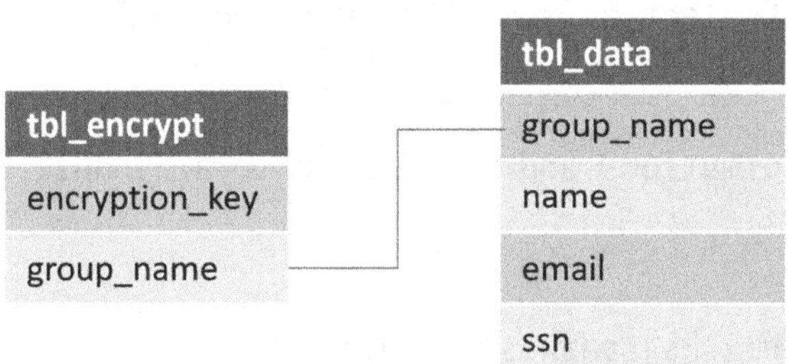

***Figure 3-46.** Dynamic Data Encryption data model*

The is_Member function can be used as a filter in a SQL statement to only retrieve rows for which the current user has access to. The following SQL code creates a view on tbl_encrypt to only show groups that a user has access to:

```
CREATE VIEW vw_decrypt_data
AS
SELECT * FROM tbl_encrypt where is_Member(group_name)
```

Finally, you could write another SQL query similar to the following to decrypt your data dynamically based on the group that you have row-level access to. Additionally, if an encryption key is ever deleted from tbl_encrypt, then the following query will return "nulls" for the rows that you may still have access to, but since the encryption is no longer part of the lookup table, you will not be able to decrypt the data and will only see "nulls" in place of the actual data. This pattern prevents the need from having to store duplicate versions of data by dynamically decrypting row-level data based on group-based membership.

```
SELECT
       cast(aes_decrypt(a.name, DA.encryption_key) as string) Name,
       cast(aes_decrypt(a.email, DA.encryption_key) as string) Email,
       cast(aes_decrypt(a.ssn, DA.encryption_key) as string) SSN,
FROM
        tbl_data a
        LEFT JOIN vw_decrypt_data b ON a.group_name = b.group_name
```

Data Profile

Within Databricks notebooks, data distributions and computing summary statistics can be visualized on an exploratory basis directly by running the display(df) command to display the data frame within a notebook as part of the data profiling feature within the notebooks. This can be seen in Figure 3-47, where a data profile will be generated in the data frame across the entire dataset to include summary statistics for columns along with histograms of the columns' value distributions.

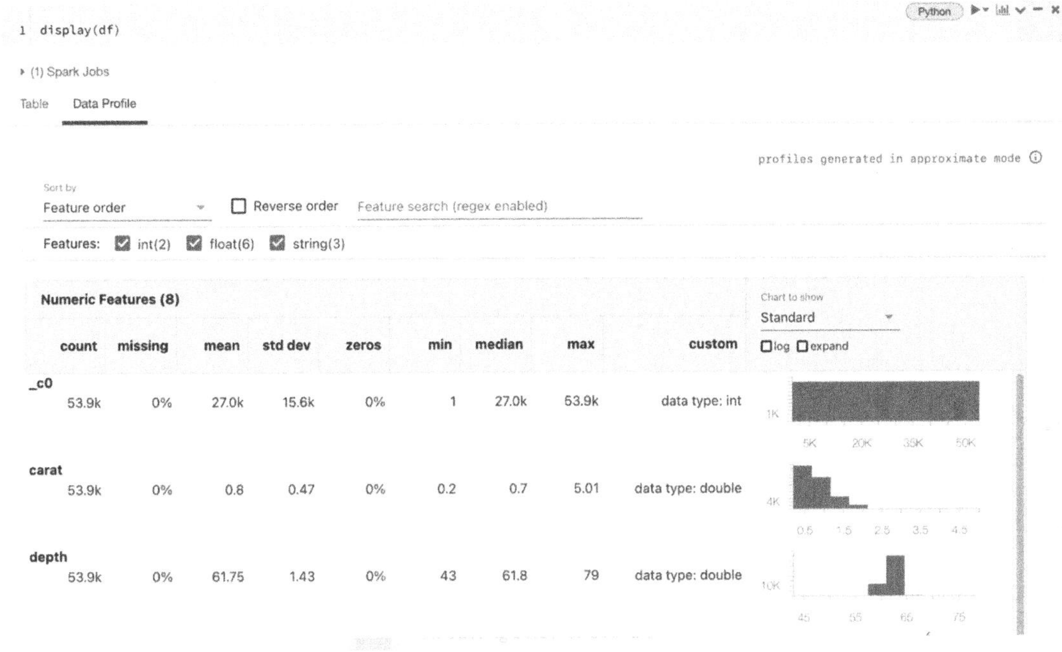

***Figure 3-47.** Sample Data Profile results in Databricks notebook*

Query Profile

The Databricks data engineering and data science workspaces provide a Databricks UI including visual views of query plans and more. The SQL Analytics workspace provides the ability to view details on Query History. In addition, it provides a nice feature to profile your SQL queries in detail to identify query performance bottlenecks and performance optimization opportunities. These details include multiple graphs, memory consumption, rows processed, and more which can also be downloaded and shared with others for further analysis.

For example, within the Databricks data engineering workspace, I run a sample SQL query using a small starter endpoint on the sample tpch data that is included with the workspace, as shown in Figure 3-48.

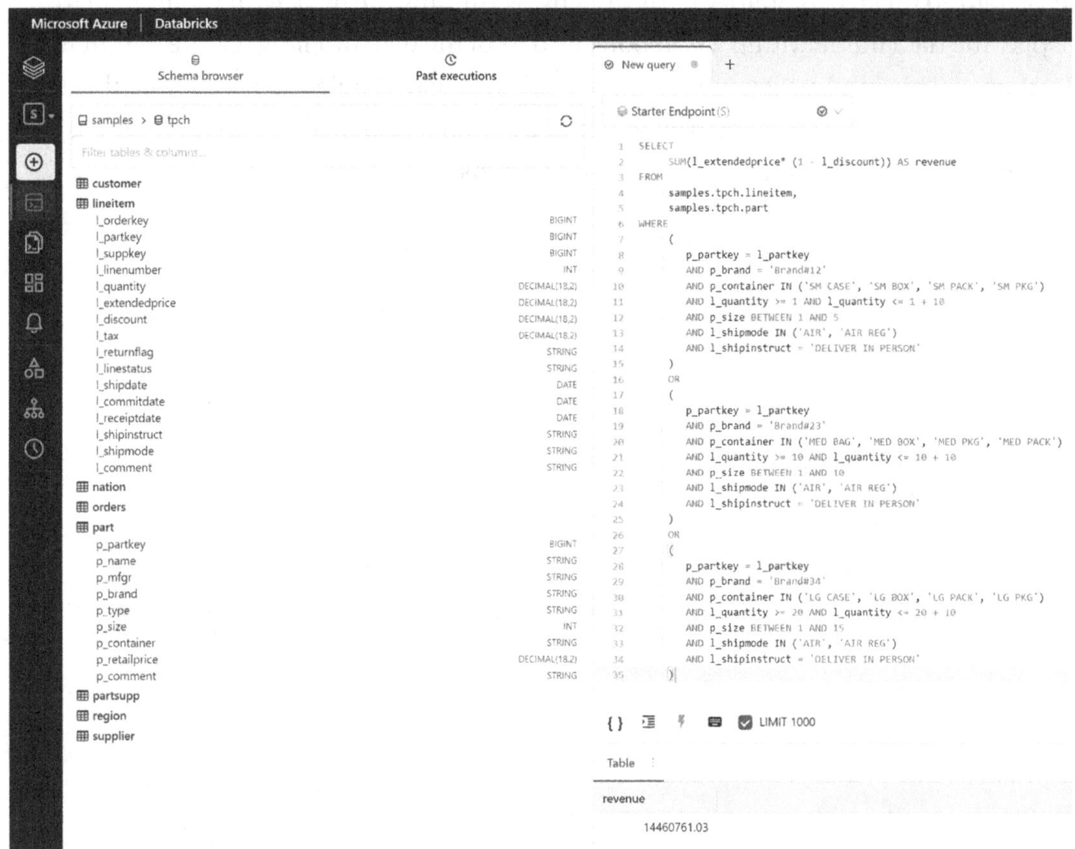

Figure 3-48. *Sample Databricks SQL Analytics workspace query run*

Here is the sample SQL query which I ran in the Databricks SQL Analytics workspace:

```
SELECT
    SUM(l_extendedprice* (1 - l_discount)) AS revenue
FROM
    samples.tpch.lineitem,
    samples.tpch.part
```

```
WHERE
    (
            p_partkey = l_partkey
            AND p_brand = 'Brand#12'
            AND p_container IN ('SM CASE', 'SM BOX', 'SM PACK', 'SM PKG')
            AND l_quantity >= 1 AND l_quantity <= 1 + 10
            AND p_size BETWEEN 1 AND 5
            AND l_shipmode IN ('AIR', 'AIR REG')
            AND l_shipinstruct = 'DELIVER IN PERSON'
    )
    OR
    (
            p_partkey = l_partkey
            AND p_brand = 'Brand#23'
            AND p_container IN ('MED BAG', 'MED BOX', 'MED PKG',
            'MED PACK')
            AND l_quantity >= 10 AND l_quantity <= 10 + 10
            AND p_size BETWEEN 1 AND 10
            AND l_shipmode IN ('AIR', 'AIR REG')
            AND l_shipinstruct = 'DELIVER IN PERSON'
    )
    OR
    (
            p_partkey = l_partkey
            AND p_brand = 'Brand#34'
            AND p_container IN ('LG CASE', 'LG BOX', 'LG PACK', 'LG PKG')
            AND l_quantity >= 20 AND l_quantity <= 20 + 10
            AND p_size BETWEEN 1 AND 15
            AND l_shipmode IN ('AIR', 'AIR REG')
            AND l_shipinstruct = 'DELIVER IN PERSON'
    )
```

As a next step, when you navigate to the “Query History” tab and click “View Query Profile,” you will be able to see the detailed query profile, as shown in Figure 3-49. You will have the option to toggle either graph or tree view. Also, you can view these details by time spent, rows, or peak memory. Toward the right, you can see the duration, IO, files, partitions, spilling, and task details. Finally, you can easily share or download this query plan with a click of a button.

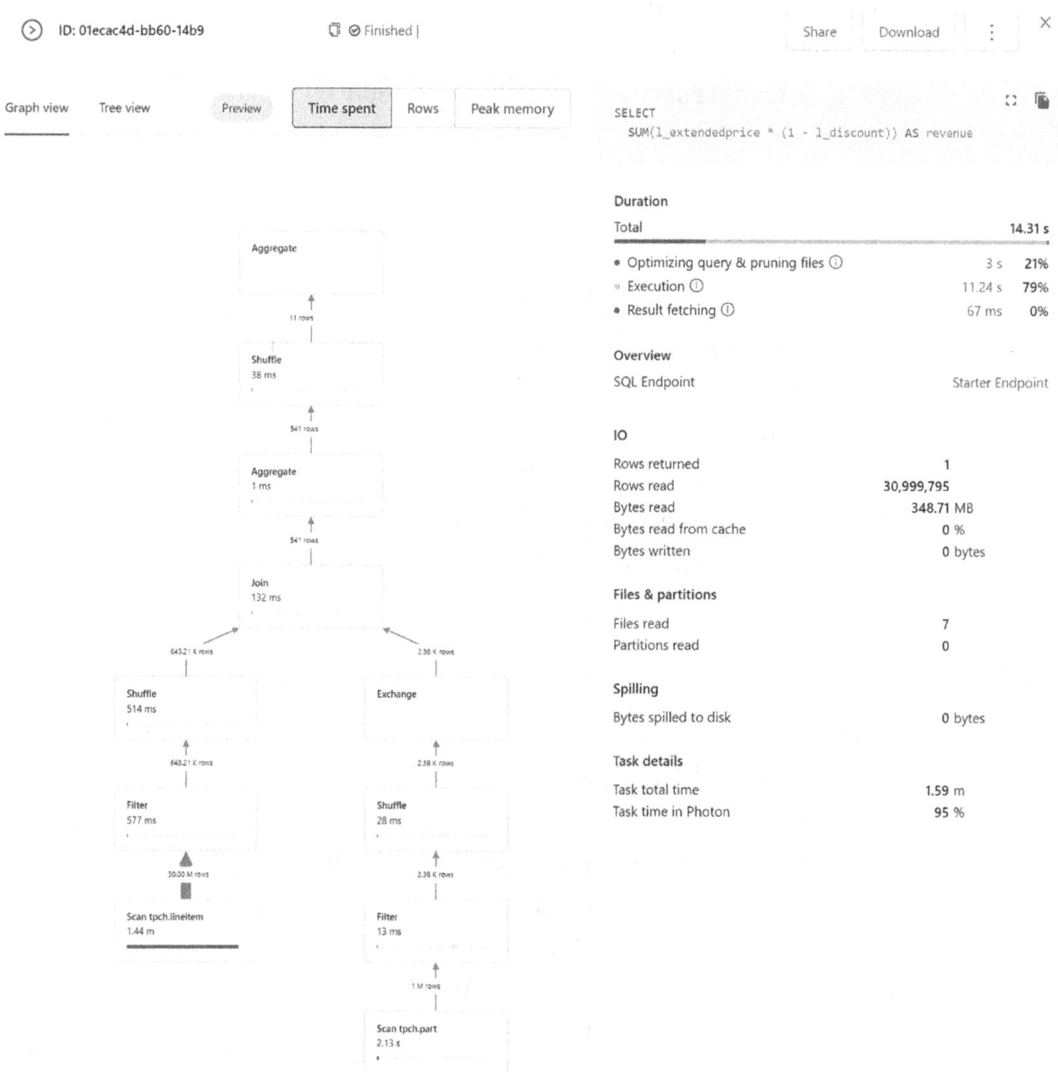

Figure 3-49. SQL Analytics workspace SQL query profile in graph view

Constraints

Delta Tables in Databricks support SQL constraint management clauses including NOT NULL and CHECK to ensure quality and integrity of data is automatically verified. Upon violation of constraints, the InvariantViolationException will be thrown when new data cannot be added.

For the NOT NULL constraint, you can add this within the create table statement's schema definition, as shown in the following code:

```
CREATE TABLE Customers (
    id INT NOT NULL,
    FirstName STRING,
    MiddleInitial STRING NOT NULL,
    LastName STRING,
    RegisterDate DATETIME
  ) USING DELTA;
```

You can also drop a NOT NULL constraint or add a new NOT NULL constraint by using an ALTER TABLE command, as shown in the following code:

```
ALTER TABLE Customers CHANGE COLUMN MiddleInitial DROP NOT NULL;
ALTER TABLE Customers CHANGE COLUMN FirstName SET NOT NULL;
```

The CHECK constraint can be added using an ALTER TABLE ADD CONTRAINT and ALTER TABLE DROP CONTRAINT commands. This will ensure that all rows meet the desired constraint conditions prior to adding it to the table, as shown in the following code:

```
ALTER TABLE Customers ADD CONSTRAINT ValidDate CHECK (RegisterDate >
'1900-01-01');
```

Identity

Historically, within Databricks, the `monotonically_increasing_id()` function has been used to generate the Identity column. It works by giving a partition ID to each partition of data within your data frame, and each row can be uniquely valued. As a first step to achieve this method, let's assume you are using a Customer table with CustomerID,

CustomerFirstName, and CustomerLastName. You will need to begin by obtaining the max value of the CustomerID column by running the following PySpark code:

```
 maxCustomerID = spark.sql("select max(CustomerID) Customer ID from
Customer").first()[0]
```

The next block of code will use the maxCustomerID created in the previous code, and it will apply a unique ID to each record:

```
 Id = (
             Id.withColumn("CustomerID, maxCustomerID= monotonically_
             increasing_id())
)
```

While this method is fast, the issue with this method is that your new identity column will have big gaps in the surrogate key values since each surrogate key will be a random number rather than following a sequential pattern. Yet another method uses the `row_number().over()` partition function which leads to slow performance. This pattern will give you the sequentially increasing numbers for the identity columns which were limitation in the previous function, but with huge cost and performance implications due to the sort that will need to happen. The PySpark code to achieve this would be as follows:

```
window = Window.orderBy("CustomerFirstName")
Id = (
            Id.withColumn("CustomerID", maxCustomeID=row_number().
            over(window))
)
```

Databricks now offers the ability to specify the Identity column while creating a table. It currently works with bigint data types. The following `CREATE TABLE` SQL code shows how this works in practice. The `ALWAYS` option prevents users from inserting their own identity columns. `ALWAYS` can be replaced with `BY DEFAULT` which will allow users to specify the Identity values. `START WITH 0 INCREMENT BY 1` can be altered and customized as needed.

```
CREATE TABLE Customer
(
```

```
CustomerID bigint GENERATED ALWAYS AS IDENTITY (START WITH 0
INCREMENT BY 1),
CustomerFirstName string,
CustomerLastName string
)
```

Delta Live Tables Merge

Delta Live Tables (DLT), which are an abstraction on top of Spark which enables you to write simplified code such as SQL MERGE statement, support Change Data Capture (CDC) to enable upsert capabilities on DLT pipelines with delta format data. With this capability, data can be merged into the Silver zone of the medallion architecture in the lake using a DLT pipeline. Previously, these incremental data updates were achieved through appends from the source into the Bronze, Silver, and Gold layers. With this capability, once data is appended from the source to the Bronze layer, the Delta merges can occur from the Bronze to Silver and Silver to Gold layers of the Delta Lake with changes, lineage, validations, and expectations applied.

Let's look at a sample use case to better understand how this feature works. Delta Live Tables (CDC) will need to be enabled within the pipeline settings of each pipeline by simply adding to the following configuration settings:

```
{
  "configuration": {
    "pipelines.applyChangesPreviewEnabled": "true"
  }
}
```

Once enabled, you will be able to run the `APPLY CHANGES INTO` SQL command or use the `apply_changes()` Python function. Notice that the following code does not accept the MERGE command and that there is no reference to the MERGE command at the surface. Since this feature provides an abstraction layer which converts your code for you and handles the MERGE functionality behind the scenes, it simplifies the inputs that are required. Notice from the following code that `KEYS` are accepted to simplify the JOIN command by joining on the specified keys for you. Also, changes will only be applied WHERE a condition is met. There is also an option to make no updates if nothing has changed with `IGNORE NULL UPDATES`. Like applying changes into a target table, you can APPLY AS DELETE WHEN a condition has been met rather than upserting the data. SEQUENCE BY will define the logical order of the CDC events to handle data which arrives out of order.

```
APPLY CHANGES INTO LIVE.tgt_DimEmployees
FROM src_Employees
KEYS (keys)
[WHERE condition]
[IGNORE NULL UPDATES]
[APPLY AS DELETE WHEN condition]
SEQUENCE BY orderByColumn
[COLUMNS {columnList | * EXCEPT (exceptColumnList)}]
```

DLT's CDC features can be integrated with streaming cloudFile sources, where we would begin by defining the cloudFile configuration details within a data frame, as shown in the following Python code which can be run in a Python Databricks notebook. This was also covered in greater detail in Chapter 17.

```
cloudfile = {
"cloudFiles.subscriptionID": subscriptionId,
"cloudFiles.connectionString": queueconnectionString,
"cloudFiles.format": "json",
"cloudFiles.tenantId": tenantId,
"cloudFiles.clientId": clientId,
"cloudFiles.clientSecret": clientSecret,
"cloudFiles.resourceGroup": resourceGroup,
"cloudFiles.useNotifications": "true",
"cloudFiles.schemaLocation": "/mnt/raw/Customer_stream/_checkpoint/",
"cloudFiles.schemaEvolutionMode": "rescue",
"rescueDataColumn":"_rescued_data"
}
```

Once the cloudFile configuration details are defined within a data frame, create a dlt view for the Bronze zone, as shown in the following code. This code will read the streaming cloudFile source data and incrementally maintain the most recent updates to the source data within the Bronze DLT view.

```
@dlt.view(name=f"bronze_SalesLT_DimCustomer")
```

```
def incremental_bronze();
   df = (spark
      .readStream
      .format"cloudFiles")
      .options(**cloudfile)
      .load("/mnt/raw/Customer_stream/_checkpoint/")

return df
```

After the Bronze view is created, you'll also need to create the target Silver table with the following Python code:

```
dlt.create_target_table("silver_SalesLT_DimCustomer")
```

The next block of Python code will apply the DLT changes from the DimCustomer Bronze source view to the DimCustomer Silver target table with CustomerID as the commonly identified join key on both tables and with UpdateDate as the sequence_by identifier:

```
dlt.apply_changes(
      target = "silver_SalesLT_DimCustomer",
      source = "bronze_SalesLT_DimCustomer",
      keys = ["CustomerID"],
      sequence_by = col("UpdateDate")
)
```

The code defined within this notebook can then be added to a new Databricks pipeline, which will then create a graph as shown in Figure 3-50.

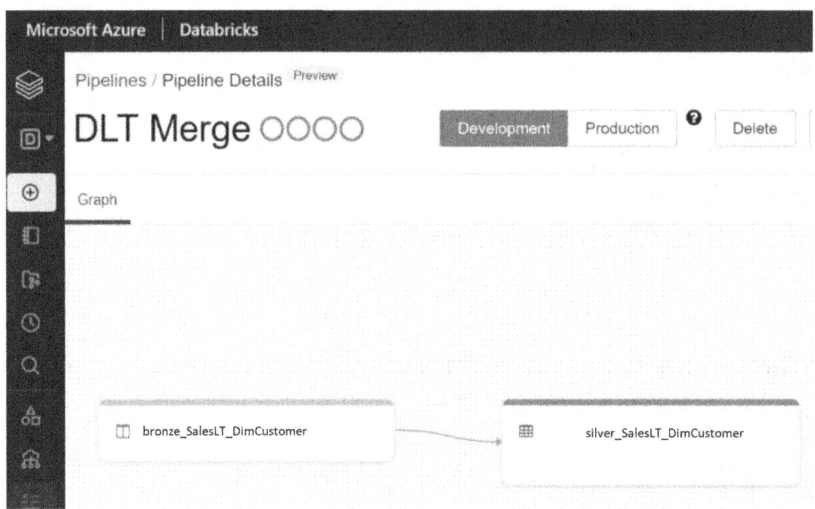

Figure 3-50. *DLT Merge Bronze to Silver pipeline details*

The silver_SalesLT_DimCustomer schema will contain additional derived system columns for _Timestamp, _DeleteVersion, and UpsertVersion. Additionally, Delta logs will be created which will indicate that a MERGE operation has been applied with details regarding a predicate, which will indicate that an ANSI SQL MERGE statement has been created behind the scenes from the inputs of the `apply_changes` function. The logs will also reference and utilize these newly created system columns. Finally, the logs will also capture additional operational metrics such as rows read, copied, deleted, and much more.

Summary

In this chapter, you learned more about the capabilities of the Databricks unified analytics platform including workspaces, compute, and storage. Within the storage section, you learned how to mount an Azure Data Lake Storage Gen2 account to an Azure Databricks notebook by creating and configuring the Azure resources needed for the process, how to write and execute the script needed to create the mount, how to read files, and how to list mounts that have been created, and how to unmount previously mounted directories. Toward the end of the chapter, you gained a deeper understanding of Delta Lake features, real-time analytics, advanced analytics, security, governance, and

CI/CD capabilities for Databricks. For more information on Databricks best practices, please read the contents of the following GitHub Repository: `https://github.com/Azure/AzureDatabricksBestPractices/blob/master/toc.md`. With a strong focus on technological innovations in the field of data and AI, Databricks is growing a Lakehouse Fund for early-stage innovators and open source platform projects in the Lakehouse ecosystems through Databricks Ventures. All these existing and upcoming capabilities in the Databricks ecosystem are equipping developers and organizations with the right tools for building out their Data Lakehouse platform.

CHAPTER 4

Synapse Analytics

Synapse Analytics is a data and analytics platform as a service that unifies data integration, data warehousing, big data analytics, reporting, CI/CD, and much more within the Modern Azure Data platform. It supports a variety of tools such as workspaces for developing code for BI, ML, and ELT within the Lakehouse. It also offers serverless and dedicated compute capabilities for querying data of all volumes, velocities, and varieties at scale. Synapse Analytics does a good job of isolating storage in ADLS gen2 from a variety of compute options including Serverless and Dedicated Spark and SQL Pools. With Serverless Spark and SQL Pools, Synapse Analytics is able to easily scale compute independent of storage, which offers more control over storage and compute costs within your Lakehouse. With Dedicated SQL Pools, Synapse Analytics is able to maintain the former MPP-style SQL data warehouse within its ecosystem. Synapse Analytics integrates well with other Azure Data platform services for data governance, storage, secured credential and identity management, reporting, real-time analytics, advanced analytics, and CI/CD.

Cloud-based unified data and analytics platforms offer a robust set of features to promote development through a workspace, which supports notebook and pipeline development, scheduling, monitoring, reporting, collaboration through repos, and more. Within notebooks, you could write custom code in either Python, Scala, SparkSQL, or .Net for Spark C# to query your Delta Lakehouse files. This notebook code can be integrated with repos. You can also develop ELT pipelines with a GUI which is very similar to Azure Data Factory (ADF). Also similar to ADF, you can schedule and monitor your Synapse Pipelines. Creating Lake databases within Synapse Analytics has never been easier with database templates, which include schemas, columns, relationship, and connectors to support the reusability of industry standardized business models. Database designers are also available when designing your Lake database. Power BI Reporting is also well integrated with Synapse Analytics in that you could develop Power BI datasets from the workspace and you can also connect to Synapse Analytics Dedicated SQL Pools or the workspace as an out-of-the-box source for Power BI.

R. L'Esteve, *The Azure Data Lakehouse Toolkit*, https://doi.org/10.1007/978-1-4842-8233-5_4

Synapse Analytics supports a number of real-time analytics and advanced analytics scenarios. With Synapse Link, a direct connect link can be established between Synapse Analytics and a variety of transactional source systems such as Cosmos DB, Dataverse, and on-premises SQL Server 2022. Azure Data Explorer has also been integrated into Synapse Analytics to support the querying and analytics of log and telemetry data. Structured Streaming and Change Data Capture use cases are also supported within Synapse Analytics. From an advanced analytics perspective, Synapse ML supports the development of production grade ML Models.

From its tight integration with Azure Active Directory, Managed Identity, Private Endpoint capabilities, and more, Synapse Analytics offers extremely robust security features. From a data governance standpoint, Synapse Analytics can be integrated with Azure Purview to discover assets, report lineage, and more. Synapse Analytics also integrates well with Azure DevOps for implementing continuous integration and deployment pipelines. In this chapter, you will learn more about all of these great capabilities of Azure Synapse Analytics to help with your understanding of how it may fit within your Azure Data Lakehouse.

Workspaces

Synapse Analytics workspace is an Azure-native unified data and analytics platform that supports data integration, data warehousing, advanced analytics, and real-time analytics on data of any volume, velocity, and variety. With Synapse Analytics workspaces, you can build ELT pipelines, analyze, and query big data in your data lakes through the secure and well-governed features within the platform. In the following section, you will learn more about some of the feature offerings of Synapse Analytics workspaces which include robust storage offerings, extensive development notebooks which include scripts and templates, and integration capabilities through pipelines similar to Data Factory along with reusable templates. Finally, you will learn more about the monitoring and management capabilities within Synapse Analytics workspaces including compute, repos, and more. Figure 4-1 shows the home page of Synapse Analytics workspace.

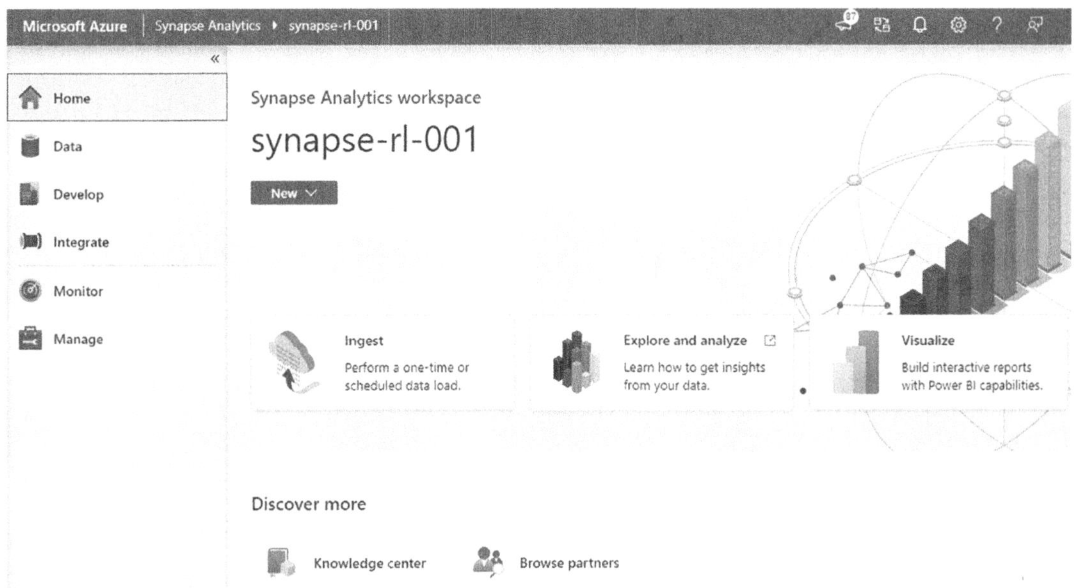

***Figure 4-1.** Synapse Analytics workspace home page*

The Knowledge center, shown in Figure 4-2, offers open datasets and sample code via a gallery containing reusable templates for notebooks, scripts, datasets, pipelines, and databases. If you are new to the workspace, you will have the option to tour the Synapse Studio as well.

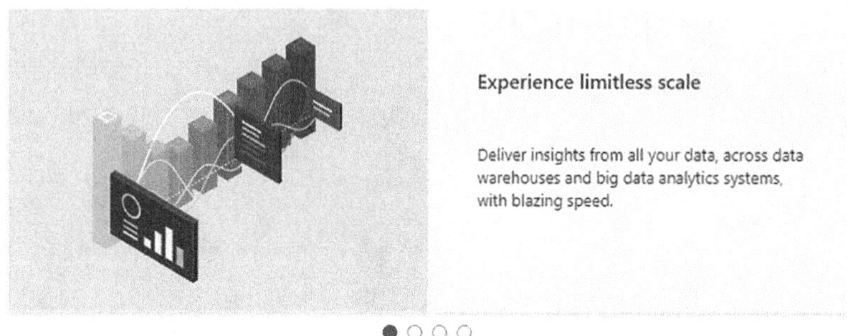

Knowledge center
Get started with Azure Open Datasets and sample code. Return to the knowledge center periodically as we provide updated content.
Experience limitless scale
Deliver insights from all your data, across data warehouses and big data analytics systems, with blazing speed.
Use samples immediately
Click once and we'll create everything you need, from scripts and notebooks to pools and data.
Browse gallery
Select from sample code and Azure Open Datasets to quickly get started in your workspace.
Tour Synapse Studio
Familiarize yourself with key features of Synapse Studio. Start by taking a tour of the homepage.

Figure 4-2. *Synapse Analytics workspace Knowledge center*

Storage

Synapse Analytics offers a variety of data storage options from within its workspace, as shown in Figure 4-3. These options include SQL databases, Lake databases, and Data Explorer databases. You will also have the ability to connect to external data, integration datasets, and a selection of openly available datasets from the gallery.

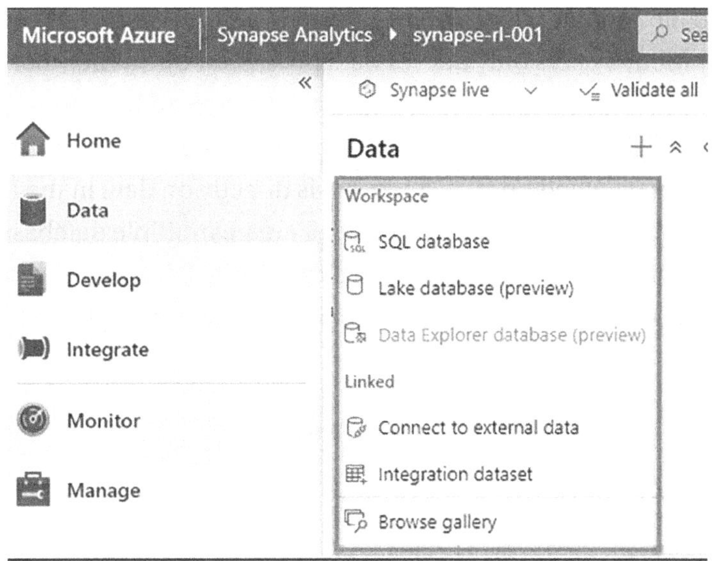

Figure 4-3. *Synapse Analytics workspace data hub*

SQL Database (SQL Pools)

When creating a pool of SQL resources within the Synapse Analytics workspace, you will have the option to select from either Serverless or Dedicated SQL Pools, shown in Figure 4-4. The Dedicated SQL Pool option is a provisioned MPP style SQL data warehouse measured in Data Warehousing Units (DWU). An MPP engine runs on a control node to orchestrate the execution of queries in parallel, while the compute nodes execute queries by distributing the work equally among them from 1 to 60 based on the Data Warehouse Units (DWU). With Dedicated SQL Pools, you will have the benefit of sharding patterns such as round-robin, replicated, and hash distributions. Dedicated SQL Pools also bring the benefit of indexes such as clustered column store indexes. You'll also have access to partitioning options within Dedicated SQL Pools. From a use case perspective, the Dedicated SQL Pools can be used for specific workloads where performance requirements are well understood and require an optimized compute strategy to meet the SLAs that customers have agreed to with their business users since customers will have the ability to invest in reserved instances for the compute that is allocated to the Dedicated SQL and optimize their predictable workloads. With a Serverless SQL Pool, Microsoft provisions and manages the compute, and it is created when a Synapse workspace is created. Since storage and compute are segregated at a higher degree than Dedicate SQL Pools, users can store a variety of different structured and unstructured file formats which can be queried by standard SQL. Additionally, with its pay-per-query model, users only pay for data processed by queries that are run. This model may work well for use cases centered around building a Lakehouse platform where the data will reside in ADLS gen2 and be queried by advanced analysts, data scientists, and others on an ad hoc per query basis directly on data in the Lakehouse. Additionally, with Serverless SQL Pools, users can create multiple databases and easily split out costs per database. However, with Dedicated SQL Pools, users can only create a SQL data warehouse per Dedicated SQL Pool which makes it harder to track costs across users.

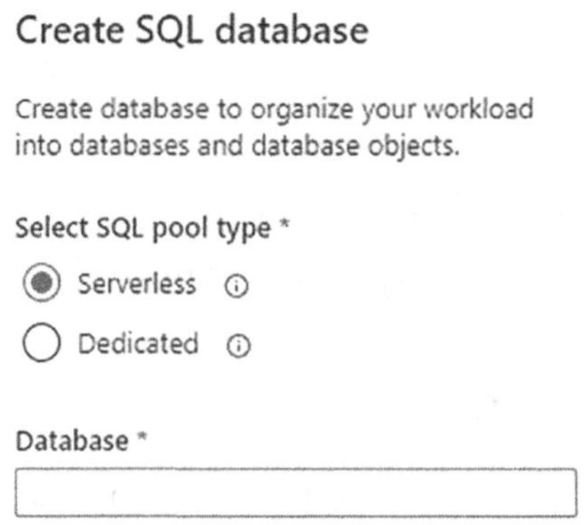

Figure 4-4. *Synapse Analytics SQL database options*

Lake Database

With Lake databases, you will be able to create, organize, and manage external tables in Synapse Analytics workspace from data stored in your ADLS gen2 account. In addition, you will have access to a collection of database templates and a UI-driven database designer, shown in Figure 4-5, which also allows you to create a data model and refine relationships, metadata, and much more. When you query data in your Lake database, it would be using Apache Spark Pool so you would only pay per query executed. The available database templates are specific to industry schemas and data models and can easily be customized.

Figure 4-5. *Synapse Analytics database designer view*

With Lake databases, you will also be able to run cross-database queries across ADLS gen2 accounts in different regions that have been persisted as an external table within the Lake database. Since Lake databases leverage Apache Spark heavily, you will have access to its open source indexing subsystem called Hyperspace. Similar to a SQL Server non-clustered index, Hyperspace will allow you to create an index across a specified data frame, create a separate optimized and reorganized data store for the columns that are being indexed, and include additional columns in the optimized and reorganized data store, much like a non-clustered SQL Server index. A practical example of Hyperspace for Synapse Analytics will be covered in Chapter 16 of this book.

Integration Dataset

Since your Synapse Analytics workspace is truly a unified data platform, you will have the ability to create ELT Synapse Pipelines and data flows, much like how you would create them in Data Factory (ADF). Like ADF, you'll need to create linked services and datasets containing connection strings and references to your source data. An integration dataset within Synapse Analytics workspace follows this same concept. When configuring a new integration dataset, as shown in Figure 4-6, you will have access to a variety of Azure and non-Azure services that you'll be able to create datasets for.

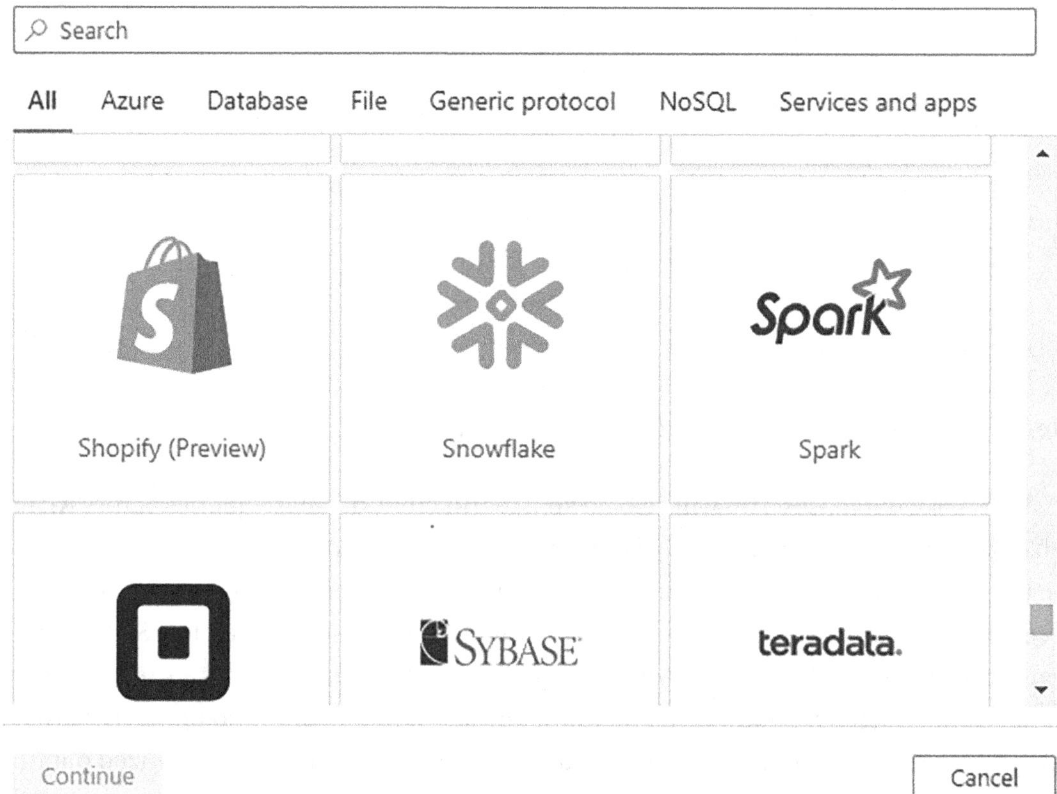

Figure 4-6. *Integration dataset sources*

External Datasets

By default, when you create a Synapse Analytics workspace, you will need to link an ADLS gen2 account. You will be able to run queries against data in this and other accounts that you add by creating additional external tables to these sources which can include Cosmos DB (MongoDB and SQL API), ADLS gen2, Blob, and Data Explorer. Once your connection is verified and you have created the external table, you can run an OPENROWSET command within your SQL query, similar to the script shown in Figure 4-7. For more details on learning how to mount your ADLS gen2 account to

Synapse workspace, please see Microsoft's article on the topic here: `https://docs.microsoft.com/en-us/azure/synapse-analytics/spark/synapse-file-mount-api`

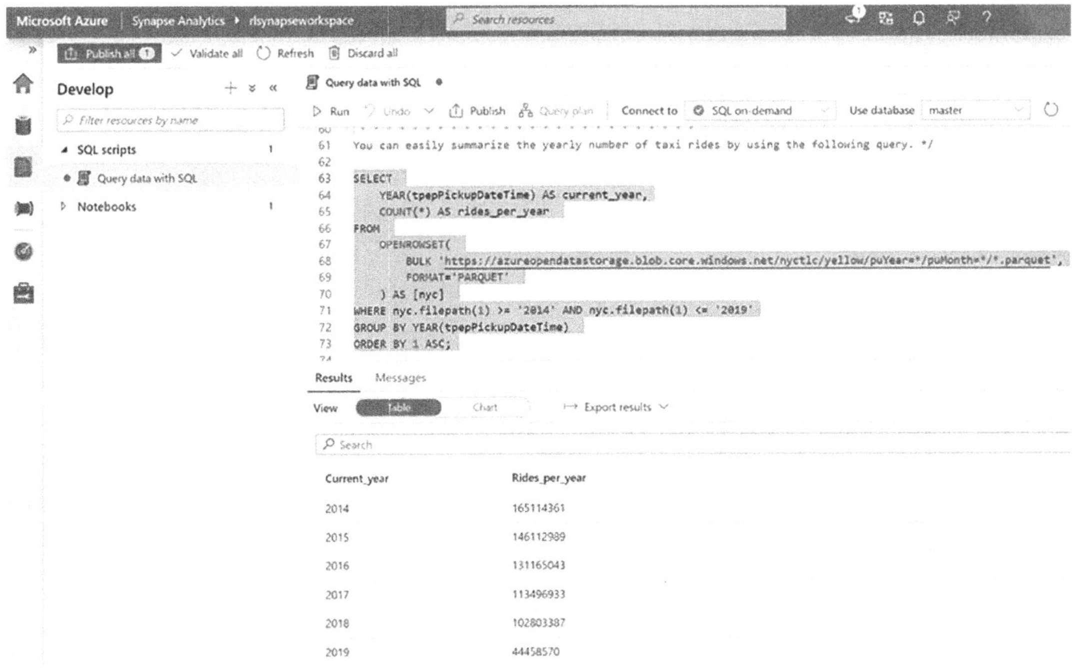

***Figure 4-7.** OPENROWSET command within your SQL query*

Development

There are a few ways to get started with development in Synapse Analytics workspaces, as shown in Figure 4-8. You can write SQL scripts, which run on Serverless SQL Pools to query either your Lake or SQL database. Since Data Explorer is also integrated with Synapse Analytics workspaces, you can query logs and telemetry data from the workspace by writing Kusto Query Language (KQL) scripts. You can also create a notebook to write scripts in either PySpark (Python), Spark (Scala), .NET Spark (C#), or Spark SQL. If your scripts are developed and published, they can be run on Apache Spark Pools. With data flows, you are able to create Apache Spark–based custom GUI-driven transformations, similar to Mapping Data Flows in ADF. Apache Spark job definitions allow you to upload definition and reference files along with customize submission details related to Spark Pools, executors, and more. Finally, within the gallery, you will have access to notebooks containing reusable scripts that can be customized for a variety of use cases across multiple languages.

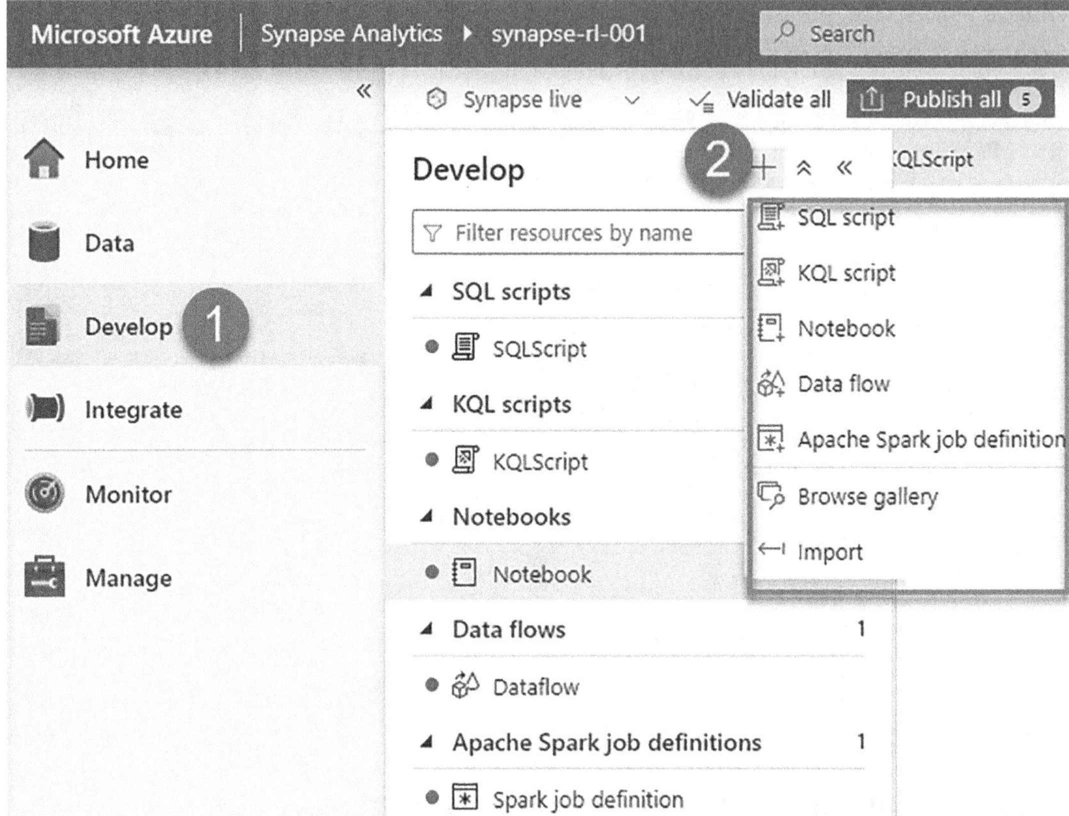

Figure 4-8. Development Hub in Synapse Analytics workspaces

Integration

Integrating data within Synapse Analytics workspaces has never been easier with its Data Factory like UI experience. With Synapse Pipelines, shown in Figure 4-9, you can create custom ELT workloads to move, transform, and integrate a variety of data platform services and functions such as ADLS gen2, Databricks, Snowflake, Functions, SQL database, Lake database, and Dedicated SQL Pools using Spark jobs, stored procedures, data flows, and more.

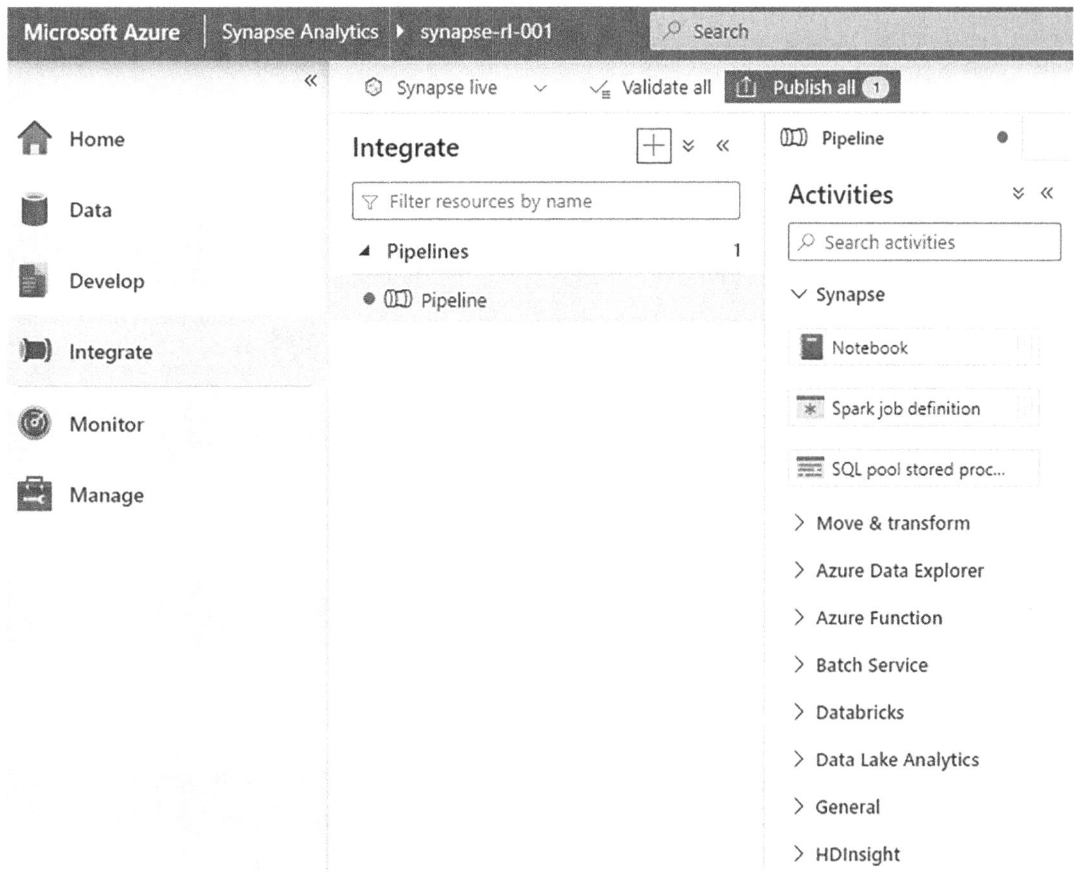

***Figure 4-9.** Synapse Pipeline activities*

The Copy Data Tool, shown in Figure 4-10, provides a GUI-driven experience for building reusable pipelines based on templates to copy data from over 90+ sources to various sinks, which also include Synapse Dedicated SQL Pools and more. By entering the configurations required in the UI, the Copy Data Tool will generate artifacts including pipelines, datasets, and linked services and will create a task cadence and schedule for you. Similarly, the metadata-driven copy task will provide you with parameterized pipelines and a control table. The pipelines will come preconfigured to connect to this control table and read metadata. You will be able to access and update this control table without the need to re-deploy your pipelines. Other Integration Services offered by Synapse Analytics workspaces include gallery pipeline templates which include numerous reusable use case ELT pipelines, along with the capability of importing pipeline templates and resources from support files.

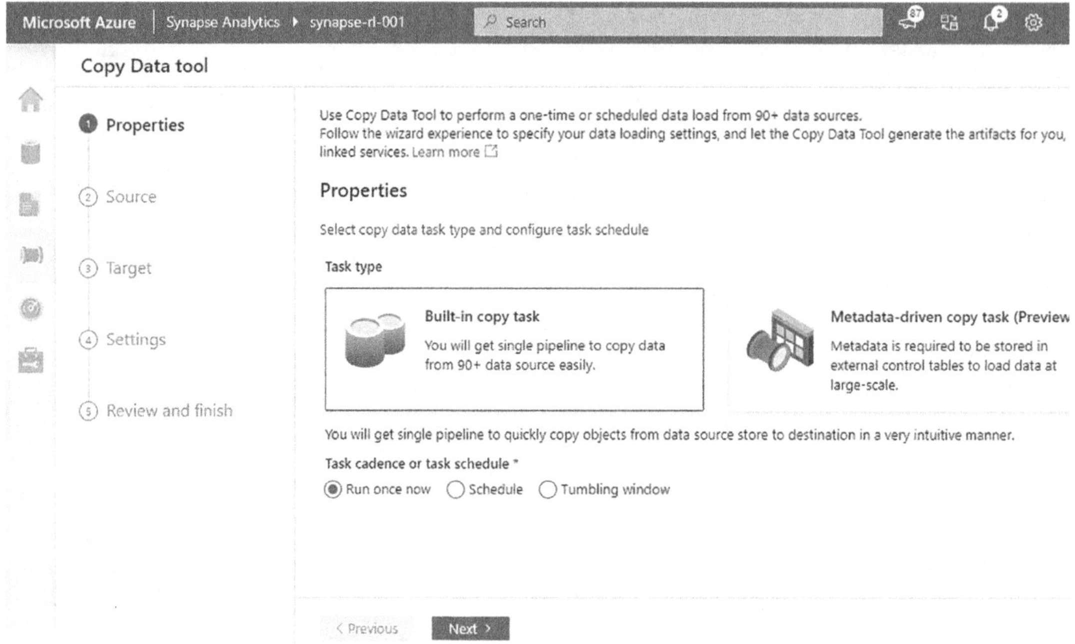

Figure 4-10. *Copy Data Tool UI*

Synapse Pipelines are slowly but surely progressing in its feature offerings to closely align with the available capabilities of Data Factory (ADF). Currently, SSIS integrations and cross-region IR sharing are only a capability of ADF. On the other hand, the robust monitoring of Spark jobs for data flows is a capability of Synapse Pipelines with its Spark Pools and is not a feature of ADF. Based on the trends of these and other features, Synapse Pipelines are growing its feature set to closely align with the current offerings of ADF and other more mature ELT tools such as SSIS. For example, ADF is continuing to expand its feature offerings with its several sources and activities including ADLS gen2 and Cosmos DB's options for "Change Feed/Change Data Capture" (persists changed records to your destination) and "Start from beginning" (initial load of full snapshot followed by changes in subsequent runs). As Synapse Pipelines soon become the standard ELT tool on the Modern Azure Data Lakehouse platform, it will continue to add and enhance many more features to support its Spark Pools, serverless capabilities, Lake database, and much more.

Table 4-1 shows a comparison between Data Factory V2 and Synapse Analytics pipelines. For fully cloud advanced analytics and ELT use cases which include Serverless SQL Pools, Synapse Analytics would be a better choice since it supports Spark notebook activities, job definitions, and SQL Pool stored procedures. On the other hand, for use cases requiring Data Wrangling (Power Query), SSIS IR setup and package execution, IR sharing, and cross-region IR requirements, Azure Data Factory V2 would be a better choice.

Table 4-1. *Data Factory V2 vs. Synapse Analytics Pipelines*

	Data Factory V2	**Synapse Analytics Pipelines**
Codeless data integration capabilities	Yes	Yes
Scripting capabilities	Yes	Yes
Linked services	Yes	Yes
Datasets	Yes	Yes
Activities	Yes	Yes
Triggers	Yes	Yes
Activities	Yes	Yes
Spark notebook activity	No	Yes
Spark job definition activity	No	Yes
SQL Pool stored procedure activity	No	Yes
SSIS package execution activity	Yes	No
Support for Power Query activity (Data Wrangling)	Yes	No
Template gallery and Knowledge center	Yes	Yes
GIT integration	Yes	Yes
Monitoring of Spark jobs for data flow	No	Yes
SSIS Integration Runtime (IR)	Yes	No
Support for cross-region IR (data flows)	Yes	No
IR sharing	Yes	No
Azure Purview integration	Yes	Yes

Monitoring

The Synapse Analytics workspace Monitor Hub, shown in Figure 4-11, provides a GUI-based experience for monitoring workloads related to SQL, Apache Spark, and Data Explorer Pools. You will be able to track status of these analytics pools including if they are online, size, CPU, and memory utilization. You will also be able to track activities related to SQL and KQL requests, Spark applications, and data flow debug sessions. Some of the metrics that you can track for these activities include request content, submission times, duration, data processed, submitter, and status. Finally, like ADF, you will be able to monitor pipeline and trigger runs and Integration Runtimes.

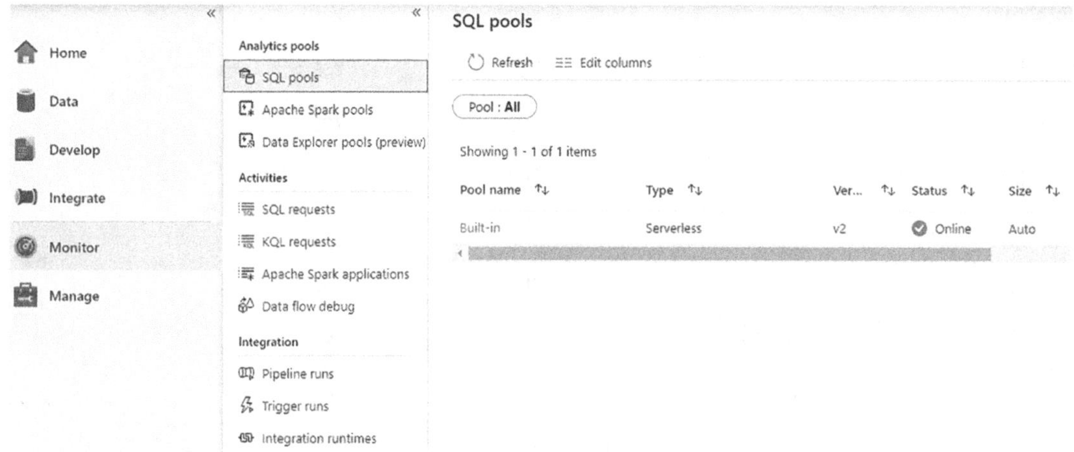

Figure 4-11. Synapse Analytics Monitor Hub

Management

It is within the Manage Hub of Synapse Analytics workspace, shown in Figure 4-12, where you will be able to create and configure SQL, Spark, and Data Explorer Pools which will be available immediately for your workspace. External connections such as linked services and connectivity to your Azure Purview account can also be created in this hub. From an integration standpoint, you will be able to create a variety of triggers such as tumbling windows, storage, and custom events with custom recurrences along with Integration Runtimes which could include either Azure or self-hosted IRs. From the perspective of security management, access controls can be managed from this hub to grant others access to the workspace or workspace items using role-based access controls (RBAC). Credentials can be created through managed identities and service principals based on Azure Active Directory (AAD) authentications.

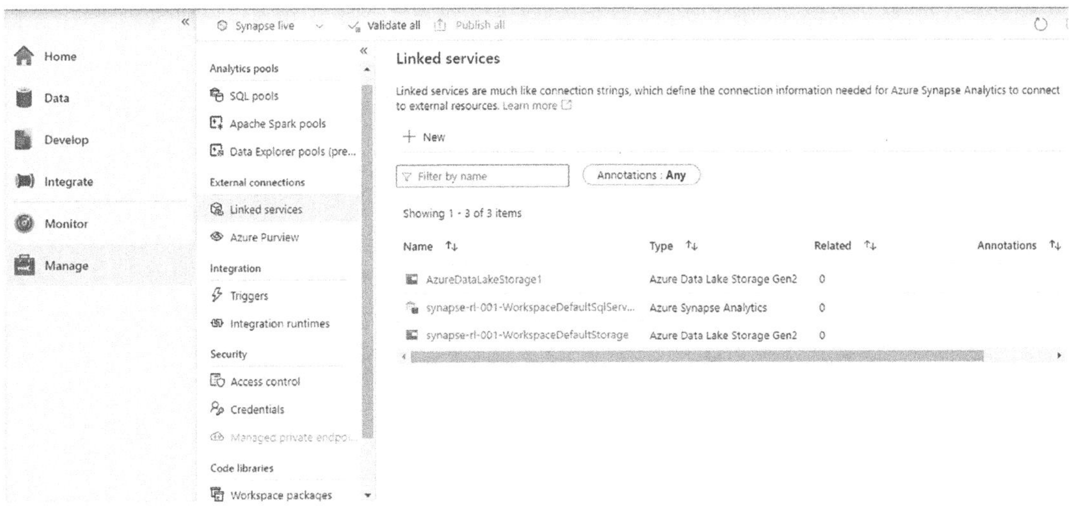

Figure 4-12. *Synapse Analytics Management Hub*

For source controls and configurations, by default, your Synapse Analytics workspace will be connected to Synapse Live, which is like the Data Factory's publish branch which basically offers the capability of collaborating and committing code without the need for a repo. Since there are numerous benefits of checking your code into a source repository, the Synapse Analytics workspace also offers the capability of connecting your entire workspace to the source-control repository, shown in Figure 4-13, which includes Azure DevOps (ADO) as an option. This enables collaborative development and the ability to build CI/CD pipelines to incrementally test and deploy development changes to the higher environments. Once you are connected to your development repo, you will be able to commit and publish changes incrementally.

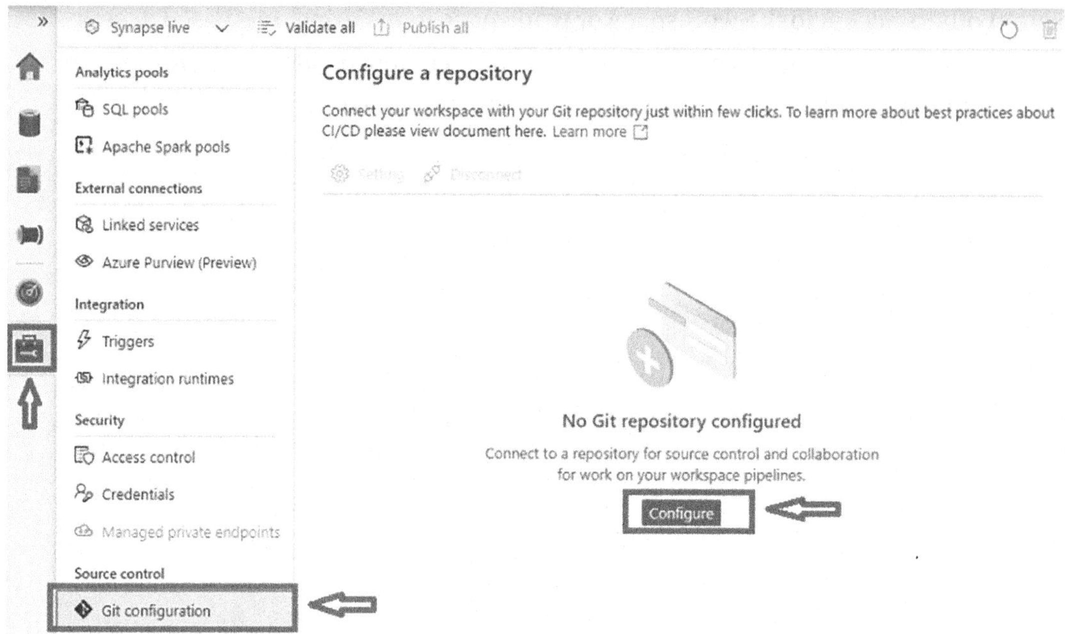

Figure 4-13. *Synapse Analytics source control*

Reporting

Your Synapse Analytics workspaces and all databases can connect to Power BI through its out-of-the-box connectors. The connectors, shown in Figure 4-14, support previewing of data before import, identification of related tables and import of relationships, data transformation using Power Query, and more. Synapse Analytics can also connect to Azure Analysis Services. This is valuable for organizations that used Analysis Services as an intermediary between the data and Power BI Reporting layers. With Power BI's Azure Active Directory Single Sign-On (AAD SSO) integration, security and identity management is seamless, so only users who have access to data will be able to directly query and retrieve it from Power BI.

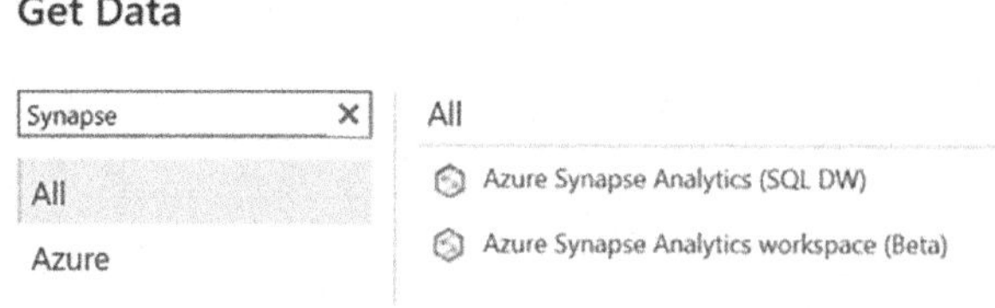

Figure 4-14. *Power BI connectors for Synapse Analytics*

With Lake databases that leverage ADLS gen2 files in either delta or parquet format, connecting directly to Power BI further promotes the Lakehouse paradigm. It is possible to query parquet files directly from SQL endpoints within Power BI. Simply retrieve the endpoints from the Overview tab within your Synapse Analytics workspace blade in the Azure Portal. The endpoints would be like the following and can be specified within a SQL Server database data source connection in Power BI for either Import or Direct Query connectivity modes. When working with the preferred parquet file format, creating pre-aggregated views in Serverless SQL Pools will lead to better performance and lower costs. For analytics workloads that require many queries across large datasets, it may be beneficial to use Dedicated SQL Pools as the storage layer since you would pay a fixed cost which may result in being lower than paying per query for this scenario.

```
Dedicated SQL endpoint
synapse-rl-001.sql.azuresynapse.net

Serverless SQL endpoint
synapse-rl-001-ondemand.sql.azuresynapse.net

Development endpoint
https://synapse-rl-001.dev.azuresynapse.net
```

In your Synapse Analytics workspace, you have the capability of connecting to a Power BI workspace for report development through a linked service, shown in Figure 4-15. This is available in the Manage Hub of the workspace. Once connected, you will have access to all of your datasets and reports within the linked Power BI workspace, and you will be able to develop reports in the Development Hub of the Synapse Analytics workspace using a similar Power BI experience as you would have access to from within Power BI desktop.

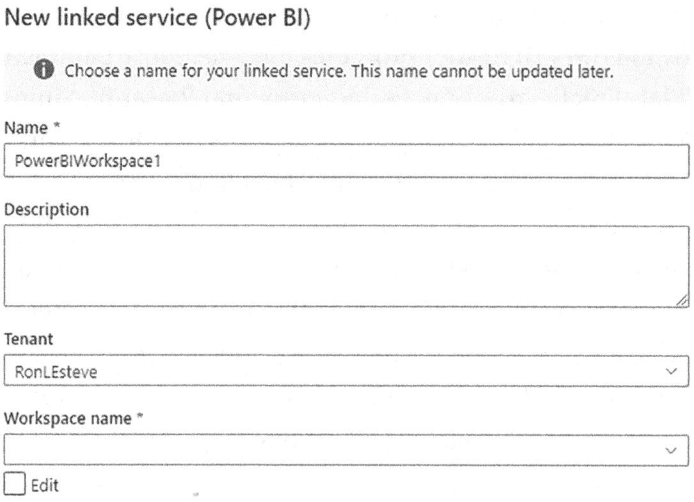

***Figure 4-15.** New linked service for Power BI in Synapse Analytics*

Continuous Integration and Deployment

Once your workspace is linked with an Azure DevOps repo, you will be able to commit and publish the relevant artifact changes. Azure's continuous integration and deployment pipelines would then orchestrate the testing and promotion of the incremental changes from DEV to UAT to PROD. Within your build pipeline, you will need to first add a Copy Files task to copy your Synapse publish templates from your GIT repo to the artifact staging repo. You will also need a Publish Artifact: drop task to publish the artifact to Azure pipelines.

Once the build pipeline is completed, the release pipeline will need to be created. The VS Marketplace offers a variety of tasks that can be integrated with your ADO pipelines, and the Synapse workspace deployment task, shown in Figure 4-16, can be configured to deploy the workspace to higher environments. Note that this deployment task will deploy the Synapse Analytics workspace and assets within it; however, since Synapse Analytics also includes Dedicate SQL Pools, there will need to be a different CI/CD process for this.

Figure 4-16. *Synapse workspace deployment task in VS Marketplace*

Dedicated SQL Pool is the Synapse Analytics flagship MPP data warehouse; therefore, its continuous integration and deployment process will be like the process of incrementally deploying a SQL database dacpac file from development to production. The pattern, shown in Figure 4-17, is common across SQL databases where a developer would be using their local development software such as Visual Studio to develop their data warehouse code. This local environment would be synced with ADO's GIT repo that commits dacpac file changes, and this dacpac file would then be integrated with Azure CI and CD pipelines to deploy the dev data warehouse to the upper environments by using dacpac deployment tasks in the CD release pipeline.

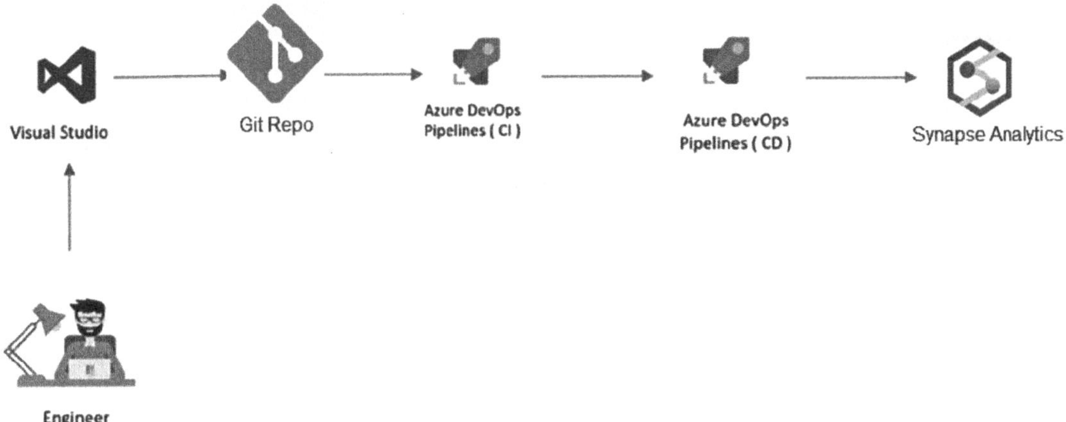

Figure 4-17. *CI/CD flow for Synapse Analytics database deployment*

Real-Time Analytics

With the increase of volume and velocity of data flowing into the Lakehouse, there is a growing demand for real-time analytics for quicker insights. Synapse offers many capabilities around Structured Streaming, Live Links to source systems, Change Data Capture (CDC) capabilities with Tumbling window triggers in Synapse Pipelines, and more. In this section, you will learn more about Structured Streaming and Live Synapse Links within Synapse Analytics workspaces.

Structured Streaming

With Synapse Analytics Structured Streaming capabilities, integrating with IoT and Event Hubs is seamless with its libraries for Spark that can be called within a notebook by using `spark.readStream`, and the transformed data can be written out as delta format within your Lakehouse. With the integration of Structured Streaming within Synapse notebooks, it is possible to perform analytics on real-time data. You can then create a Lakehouse external table to directly query the data in either Synapse Analytics workspaces or within Power BI.

Synapse Link

With Synapse Link, operational data stores including Azure Cosmos DB, Dataverse, On-premises SQL Server 2022, and Data Explorer can be directly connected to Synapse Analytics to support real-time analytics use cases. Figure 4-18 shows what the Synapse Link architecture would look like for one of these technologies, Cosmos DB. Azure Synapse Link for Azure Cosmos DB is a cloud-native hybrid transactional and analytical processing (HTAP) capability that allows users to run near real-time analytics over operational data in Azure Cosmos DB. Data engineers, business analysts, and data scientists now have the ability to use Spark or SQL Pools to get near real-time insights into their data without impacting the performance of their transactional workloads in Cosmos DB.

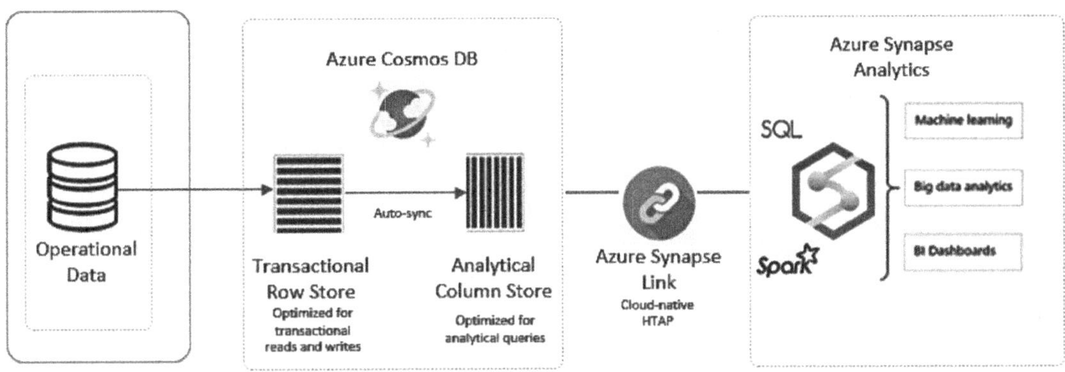

Figure 4-18. *Synapse Link for Cosmos DB architecture*

There are numerous advantages to Azure Synapse Link for Azure Cosmos DB including reduced complexity since a near real-time analytical store either reduces or eliminates the need for complex ETL or change feed job processes. Additionally, there will be little to no impact on operational workloads since the analytical workloads are rendered independently of the transactional workloads and do not consume the provisioned operational throughput. Additionally, it is optimized for large-scale analytics workloads by leveraging the power of Spark and SQL On-demand Pools which makes it cost effective due to the highly elastic Azure Synapse Analytics compute engines. With a column-oriented analytical store for workloads on operational data including aggregations and more, along with decoupled performance for analytical workloads, Azure Synapse Link for Azure Cosmos DB enables and empowers self-service, near real-time insights on transactional data.

Like Cosmos DB, Synapse Link is also available for Dataverse, SQL Server 2022, and Data Explorer. Synapse Link for Dataverse supports integrating data from Power Apps and Dynamics 365 into Synapse Analytics workspaces. With Synapse Link for SQL Server 2022, you will be able to run near real-time analytical queries against your on-premises SQL Server data with minimal impact to your operational system. Finally, from a real-time analytics perspective, Synapse Analytics enables data exploration of your logs and telemetry data with its Data Explorer offering. You will be able to unlock insights and trends on your log and time-series data by running queries in real time.

Advanced Analytics

Unified data and analytics platforms such as Synapse Analytics workspaces bring with it a vast feature set around advanced analytics, specifically for machine learning and cognitive services. Synapse ML simplifies the end-to-end machine learning model development and deployment process through its open source library. It unifies ML Frameworks into a scalable API that is accessible by Python, R, Scala, and Java scripting languages.

A variety of machine learning and cognitive services use cases can be achieved by using Synapse ML. Synapse ML notebooks are like Databricks data science notebooks since users can leverage a variety of programming languages, data science packages, and Spark compute, all within the web user interface. Azure ML, on the other hand, has more robust code-free GUI-based features for model development, training, and registering. Synapse ML provides more of a code- and notebook-based interface for machine learning, cognitive services, and advanced analytics. With its pre-built APIs for cognitive services, Synapse ML provides ready-to-use libraries on Apache Spark such as Form Recognizer, Anomaly Detection, Vision, Translator, Text Analytics, and more. Synapse ML also offers support for Open Neural Network Exchange (ONNX) frameworks and runtimes for ML use cases such as deep learning and more. With access to ONNX tools and model hubs, you will have easy access to over 120 pre-trained models.

In addition to SynapseML, Synapse Analytics workspaces offer many other features that support ML and cognitive services use cases. With the cognitive services wizards, you will be able to select from pre-trained models for Anomaly Detection, Sentiment Analysis, and more, to make predictions on your dataset. Simply right-click your dataset and select Machine Learning ä Predict with a model, as shown in Figure 4-19. Notice that you will also have the option to Train a new model using classification, regression, and time-series forecasting. Once configured, the wizard will generate PySpark code within a new notebook that is connected to your dataset. When compared to Databricks, Synapse ML supports open source MLflow, whereas Databricks supports managed and hosted versions of MLflow with integrated enterprise security integrated with Databricks-specific capabilities. Finally, with Synapse Analytics workspaces, you will be able to integrate and execute Azure Machine Learning pipelines and code within Synapse Pipelines and notebooks. The Summary section of this chapter will contain a table that compares and contrasts the capabilities of Synapse Analytics and Databricks workspaces.

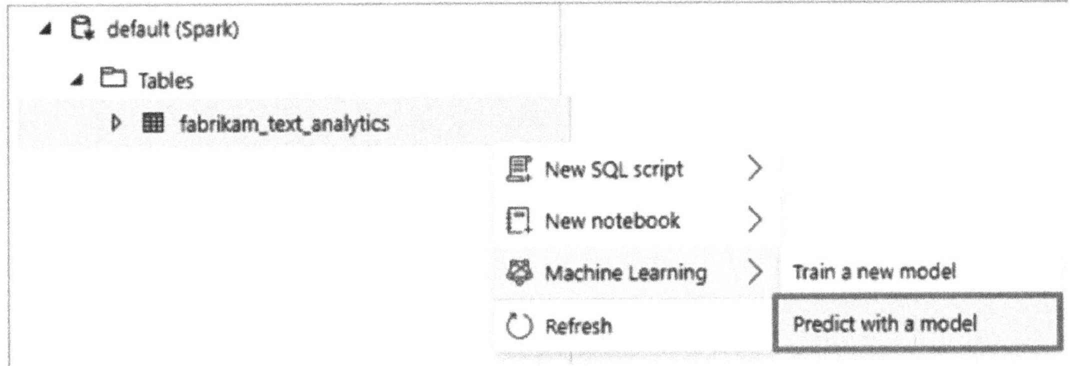

Figure 4-19. *Cognitive services wizard for ML Models*

Security

With Synapse Analytics being an Azure-native platform as a service (PaaS) solution offering, it brings with it the Azure security baseline controls for private network access with Private Endpoints, network attack protection with Firewalls, implementing network security rules, and securing domain name services. With Private Endpoints, a private IP address is used from within a virtual network (vNet) to connect to Synapse Analytics workspace endpoints. Workspaces can configure outbound data traffic to resources in any Azure AD tenant over Private Endpoints. Figure 4-20 shows how to create a private link–enabled Synapse workspace from the Azure Portal.

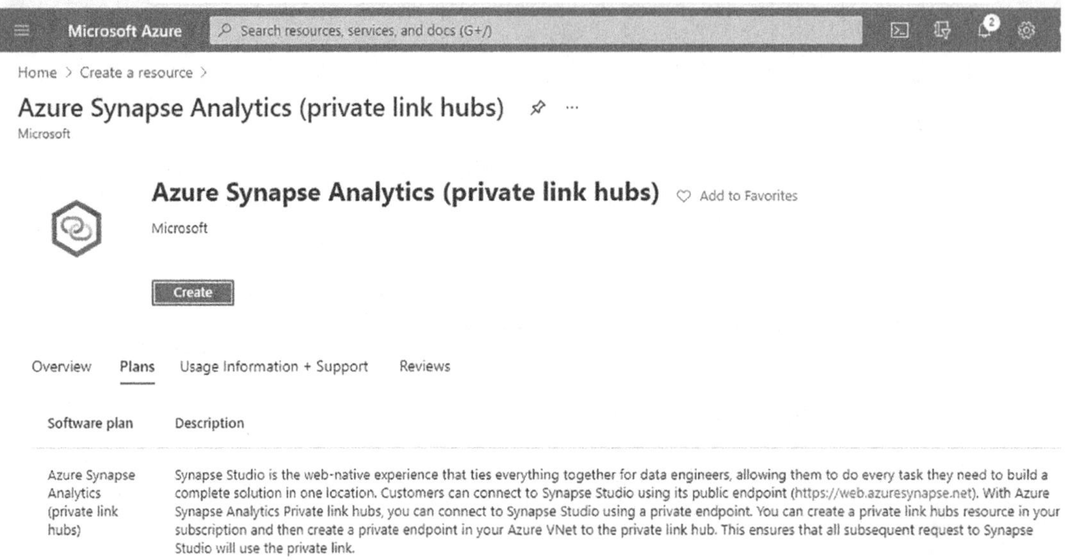

Figure 4-20. *Synapse Analytics Private Link Hubs in Azure Portal*

From an identity management standpoint, Synapse Analytics offers the capability of integrating Azure Active Directory (AAD) within its platform for centralized identity and authentication management by securing and automating application identities with Managed Identity and offering an AAD Single-Sign-On (SSO) experience for application access. With managed identities, Azure resources can authenticate to Synapse Analytics without storing credentials in code and can have multiple users assigned managed identities. Figure 4-21 shows how access control to the Synapse workspace can be granted and managed from the "Manage" tab in Synapse Analytics. Access control mechanisms can include Security Groups, Azure Roles, Synapse Roles, SQL Permissions, and GIT Permissions. For more details on how to granularly set up access control in your Synapse workspace, please refer to the following Microsoft article: `https://docs.microsoft.com/en-us/azure/synapse-analytics/security/how-to-set-up-access-control`

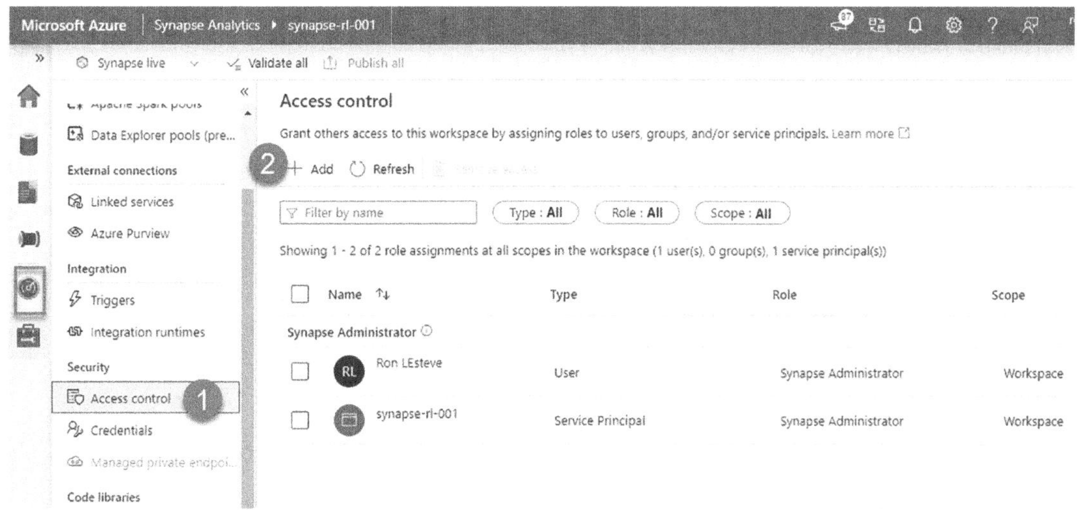

Figure 4-21. *Access controls in Synapse Analytics workspace*

With its role-based access controls (RBAC), it brings with it the principle of privileged access. From a data protection perspective, Synapse Analytics supports the protection of sensitive data through Dynamic Data Masking policies, Transparent Data Encryption (TDE) to protect data at rest and in transit, and robust monitoring capabilities. With TDE, SQL Pools in a workspace can be encrypted with a second layer of encryption with service managed keys and can be enabled at the individual SQL Pool level. Other security features that Synapse Analytics offers include regular automated backups and recoveries, endpoint security, posture and vulnerability management, logging and threat detection, and asset management. Azure SQL Auditing can monitor SQL Pool events and log them to an ADLS gen2 account. Finally, Synapse Analytics is well integrated with Microsoft Defender, which offers vulnerability assessments for SQL resources, advanced security, threat protection alerts, regulatory compliance tracking, and more. Figure 4-22 shows how to access and enable Microsoft Defender within the security section of the Synapse Analytics workspace blade within the Azure Portal. Also, notice the various other security features within the security section which can be enabled and further configured.

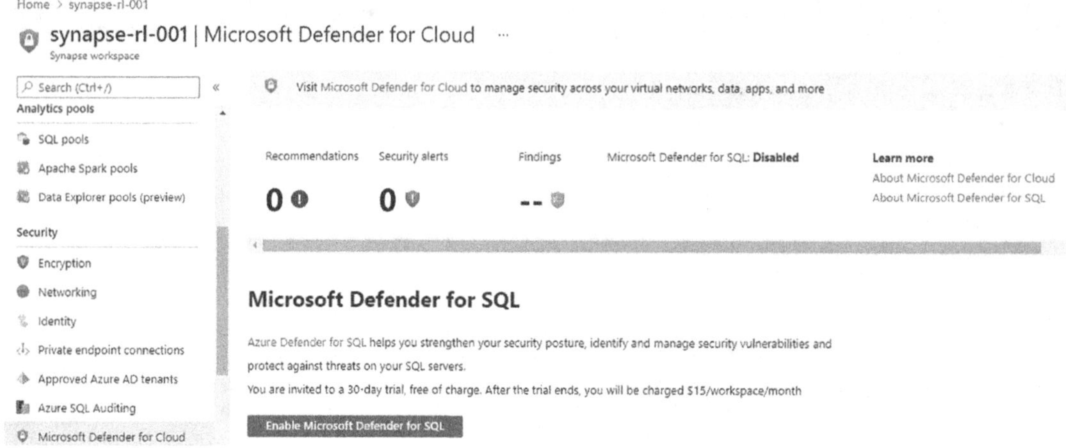

Figure 4-22. *Microsoft Defender for Synapse SQL in Azure Portal*

Governance

Purview is an Azure-native data governance offering from Microsoft. With Purview, data can be discovered, tracked, cataloged, and governed to help businesses map and view their data. Purview can be integrated with Synapse Analytics to discover, classify, map, and evaluate data in workspaces and Dedicated and Serverless SQL Pools. To configure Synapse within Purview, you would simply need to select Azure Synapse Analytics within the "Register sources" UI shown in Figure 4-23, and from there, you will be able to specify details related to your Azure subscription, Synapse Analytics workspace, and more to register and scan your workspace to identify assets and classify data across dedicated or serverless resources.

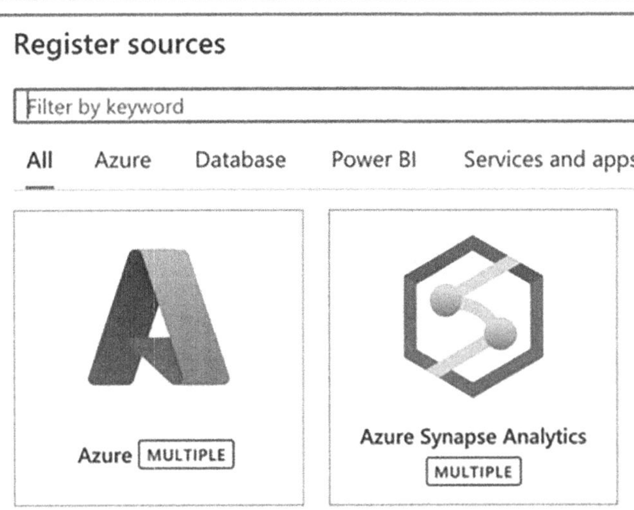

***Figure 4-23.** Synapse Analytics source in Azure Purview*

There are a variety of other benefits and features of integrating Purview with Synapse Analytics. Purview's Apache Atlas Spark Connector is also available to track and register Spark SQL and DataFrame lineage and metadata changes to Purview, when needed. Also, from a security standpoint, Private Endpoints can be used with Purview to secure access from a virtual network (VNet) over a Private Link. With its tightly coupled integration with Azure Active Directory, identity and credential management is seamless with a variety of options including Managed Identity and Service Principle. Additionally, once your Synapse Analytics workspace is registered with Purview, you will have the capability of tracking Synapse Pipeline lineage, shown in Figure 4-24, within Purview.

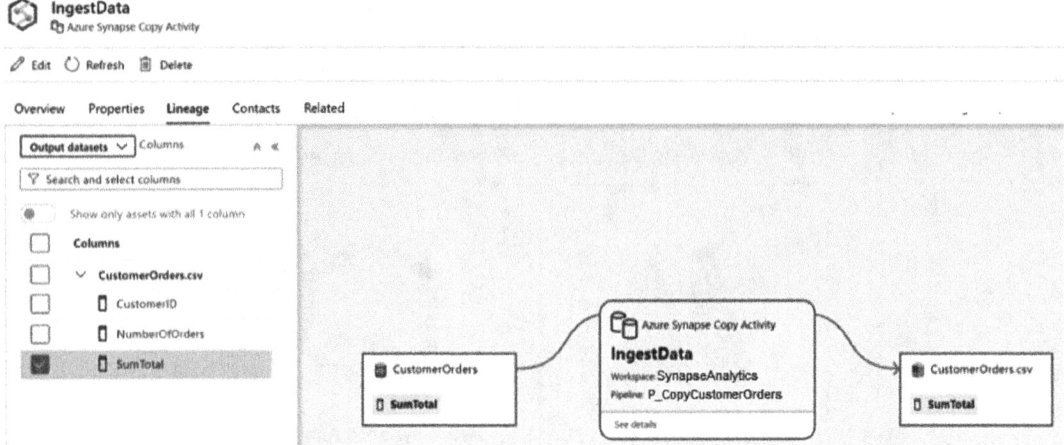

Figure 4-24. *Synapse Pipeline lineage in Azure Purview*

Thus far, we have discussed and explored how we can connect Synapse Analytics to Purview for the purpose of registering, scanning, discovering, and tracking Synapse assets all within the Purview experience. Synapse Analytics and Purview also support the option of discovering Synapse assets that have been registered with Purview directly from the Synapse Analytics workspace. Figure 4-25 shows how to connect your Purview account to the Synapse Analytics workspace from the “Manage” tab.

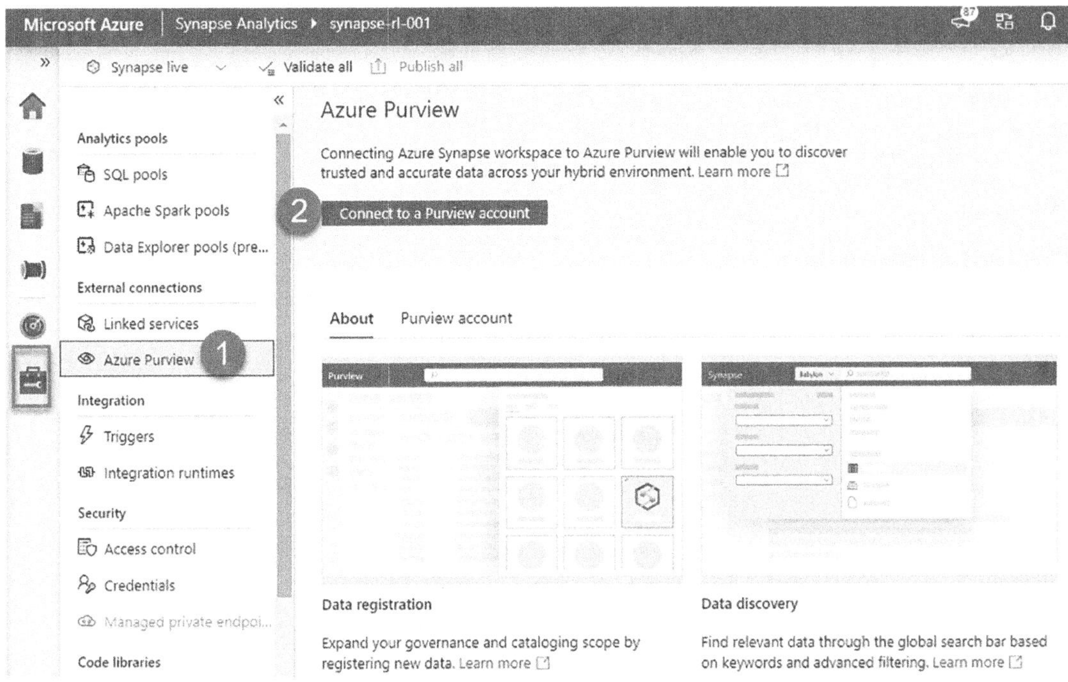

***Figure 4-25.** Connect Azure Purview to Synapse Analytics workspace*

After your Synapse Analytics account has been registered with Purview, you can also connect to your Purview account from the Synapse Analytics workspace. Once connected, you will be able to search for and discover assets directly from the Synapse Analytics workspace search bar, as shown in Figure 4-26. For Synapse Pipelines, Purview registered lineage can also be tracked from the monitoring UI.

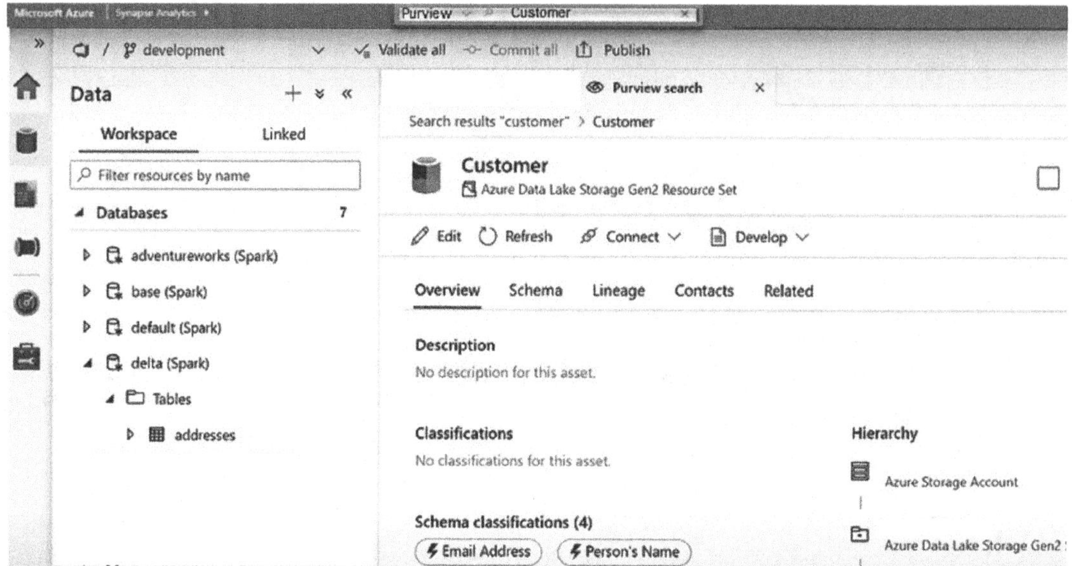

Figure 4-26. *Explore Purview linked assets from Synapse Analytics workspace*

Additional Features

While it is possible to query parquet files from the Synapse Analytics workspace, in the following sections, you will learn more about its support for Delta Lake. Additionally, you will learn about advanced machine learning features, SQL Server Integration Services Integration Runtime support, the availability of constraints within the out-of-the-box data warehouses and databases, out-of-the-box Azure SQL DB incremental support, data sharing capabilities, and the new Map Data Tool.

Delta Tables

Working with Spark Pools within the Synapse Analytics workspace is like Spark compute clusters within Databricks. Like Databricks, when creating a Delta Table in a Spark database, simply run SQL syntax like the code shown as follows which includes defining the code language using the %%sql magic command, running the create table statement that includes defining the data's schema, and finally specifying the use of delta format along with the ADLS gen2 location folder. Complex merge statements with custom logic can be written to load data into the tables, and the table can be queried using common SQL syntax. If you are running this code, please ensure that your ADLS gen2 account is linked.

```
%%sql
-- Create Delta Lake table, define schema and location
CREATE TABLE Delta_Customer (
  Customer STRING NOT NULL,
  Customer_ID INT NOT NULL,
  BeginDate DATE NOT NULL,
  EndDate DATE NOT NULL,
  CurrentRecord INT NOT NULL
)
USING DELTA
-- specify data lake folder location
LOCATION '/Delta/Customer/'
```

Like the Databricks Delta log, Synapse will also maintain a _delta_log. It also supports the DESCRIBE command to retrieve history of the table operations performed on the Delta Tables. Similarly, the VACCUM command can also be run to remove old data files. The concept of time travel is also a capability to read previous versions of data by running code like the following:

```
# Load a previous version of the Delta_Customer table into a dataframe
df = spark.read.format("delta").option("versionAsOf", 3).load("/Delta/
Customer/")
df.show()
```

Serverless SQL Pools can also query Delta Lake. The advantage of using Serverless SQL Pools includes quicker retrieval of data since there is no wait time for Spark nodes to spin up. Synapse supports querying of Delta Lake using Serverless SQL Pools in multiple languages by running the OPENROWSET function, as shown in the following code. Your URI is a link to the ADLS gen2 account containing your data, so it will be important to ensure that your _delta_log table is contained within the root folder that is specified. Also ensure to specify the delta format. The query can be as simple as the one shown in the following code, or quite complex to include multiple joins, filters, orderings, and groupings. For more information about querying Delta Lake from Azure Synapse Analytics workspace, please see the following Microsoft article: `https://docs.microsoft.com/en-us/azure/synapse-analytics/sql/query-delta-lake-format`. Be sure to stay informed about the limitations of this capability.

```
SELECT *
FROM OPENROWSET(
    BULK 'https://adlsaccount.blob.core.windows.net/data/Delta/Customer/',
--Specify Delta Lake folder
    FORMAT = 'delta') as rows --Specify delta format
ORDER BY Customer
```

Machine Learning

Both Databricks and Synapse Analytics workspaces provide robust machine learning capabilities. With SynapseML, data scientists working in the Synapse Analytics workspace have access to open source libraries to enable the creation of scalable ML Pipelines through its multilingual APIs which will run on your Apache Spark Clusters. It can also be used locally and with Databricks. With Synapse ML, you will have access to a variety of cognitive services such as multivariate anomaly detection, deep learning models, responsible AI, light GBM, OpenCV, and more. More information about getting started with Synapse ML, including code samples, can be found in the following site: `https://microsoft.github.io/SynapseML/`

SQL Server Integration Services Integration Runtime (SSIS IR)

Azure-SSIS Integration Runtime (IR) is one of the two IRs within Synapse Analytics workspace with which developers can lift and shift their on-premises SSIS workloads into Synapse Analytics. They can run packages that have been deployed in SSIS and hosted by Azure SQL database or Managed Instance. In addition, they can run SSIS packages that have been deployed in Azure Files. Once configured, the SSIS IR can be selected from the drop-down within the Execute SSIS package activity, as shown in Figure 4-27. Packages can be chosen from either SSISDB, File Systems (Package or Project), Embedded packages, or Package stores. Other required configuration parameters include Folder, Project, and Package location. Other optional configurations can be included in the Settings tab. Notice that there are a variety of other tabs that can also be included as part of this SSIS IR activity.

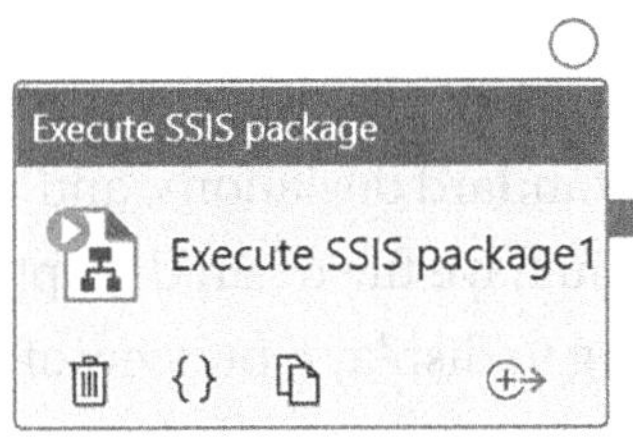

***Figure 4-27.** Execute Azure-SSIS IR activity in Synapse Analytics workspace*

Map Data Tool

The Map Data tool is a GUI-driven, code-free ETL tool to enable users to create their own mappings and data flows from source systems to Synapse Lake database tables. This tool supports quick time to insights since developers can easily build their ELT pipelines without the need to write custom code or scripts. The user will first choose their primary source table, along with the mapping method, source column, and target column, as shown in Figure 4-28. Mapping methods can include common mappings such as surrogate keys composed of multiple columns, lookups, unpivots, and direct mappings. Aggregate mappings are also supported such as averages, standard deviations, and sums. Finally, derived columns are also supported. Once you have the desired mappings established, you can switch on the "Data flow debug" setting to display a preview of the target dataset. If all looks well from a target dataset standpoint, when you click "Create pipeline," a new Execute Pipeline activity will be created for you that contains a Mapping Data Flow activity with the pre-built mappings, aggregations, and derived columns that were selected in the Map Data Tool. This is a neat capability which further demonstrates the code-free features of Synapse Analytics workspaces.

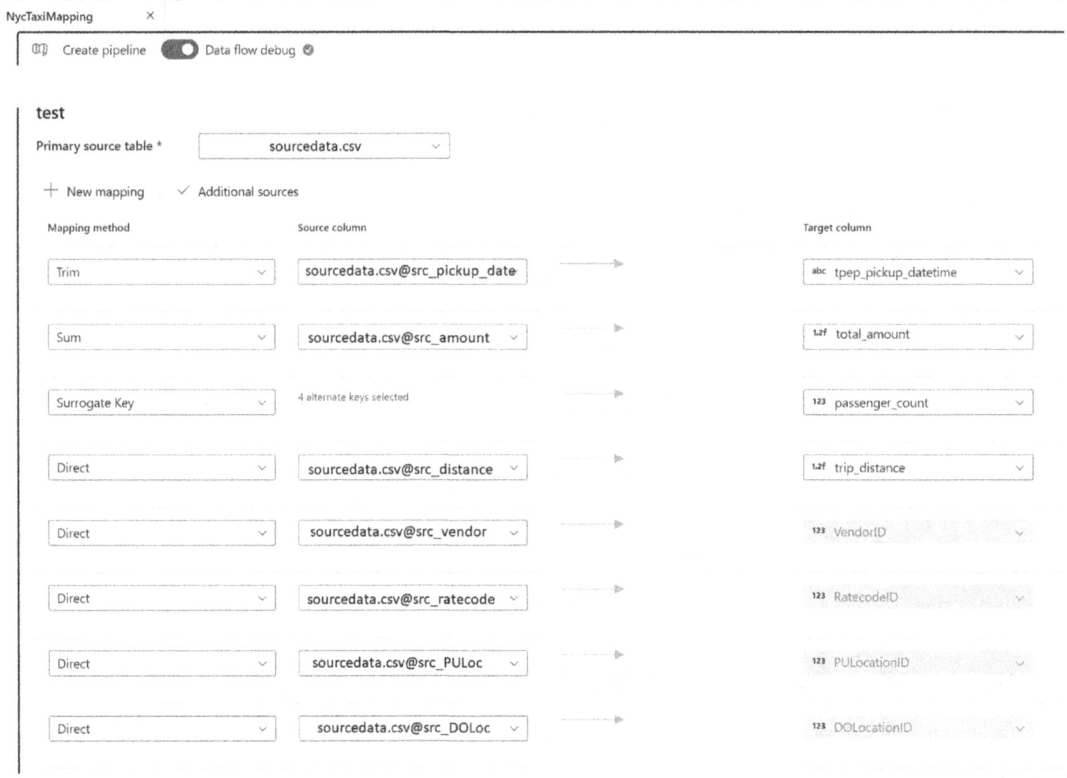

Figure 4-28. *Map Data Tool GUI*

Data Sharing

Sharing data within Synapse Analytics is also supported by a native Azure capability called Azure Data Share. Much like Databricks Delta Sharing and Snowflake Data Sharing, Azure Data Share within Synapse Analytics also provides sharing capabilities for both providers and consumers. With Azure Data Share, data providers can share data from a list of supported data stores with consumers and partners. Currently, ADLS gen2 and Synapse Dedicated SQL Pools are supported data stores. Azure Data Share supports various sharing methods ranging from full or incremental snapshots. It provides robust management and monitoring capabilities to track the shared assets. Consumers can access data that is shared with them through invitations and can integrate Azure Data Share with REST APIs. So if you need to share data with consumers and are not on the Databricks on Snowflake platform, rest assured that you can use Azure Data Share for this use case.

SQL Incremental

Synapse Analytics Pipeline supports a new out-of-the-box feature called "Enable incremental extract" for Azure SQL database sources, as shown in Figure 4-29. When enabled, the source will only read incremental data since a previous run or full data for a first run. Previously, this could be achieved by building custom incremental and Change Data Capture (CDC) pipelines from source to target. By specifying the incremental date column along with other incremental based options in the 'Source options' tab, Data Engineers can easily build incremental ELT patterns without having to write any customer code or design custom pipelines. While this feature is currently only available for Azure SQL database, it is a promising feature that significantly accelerates time to market through this out-of-the-box feature which would have previously taken a significant amount of time to custom develop the full and incremental pipeline.

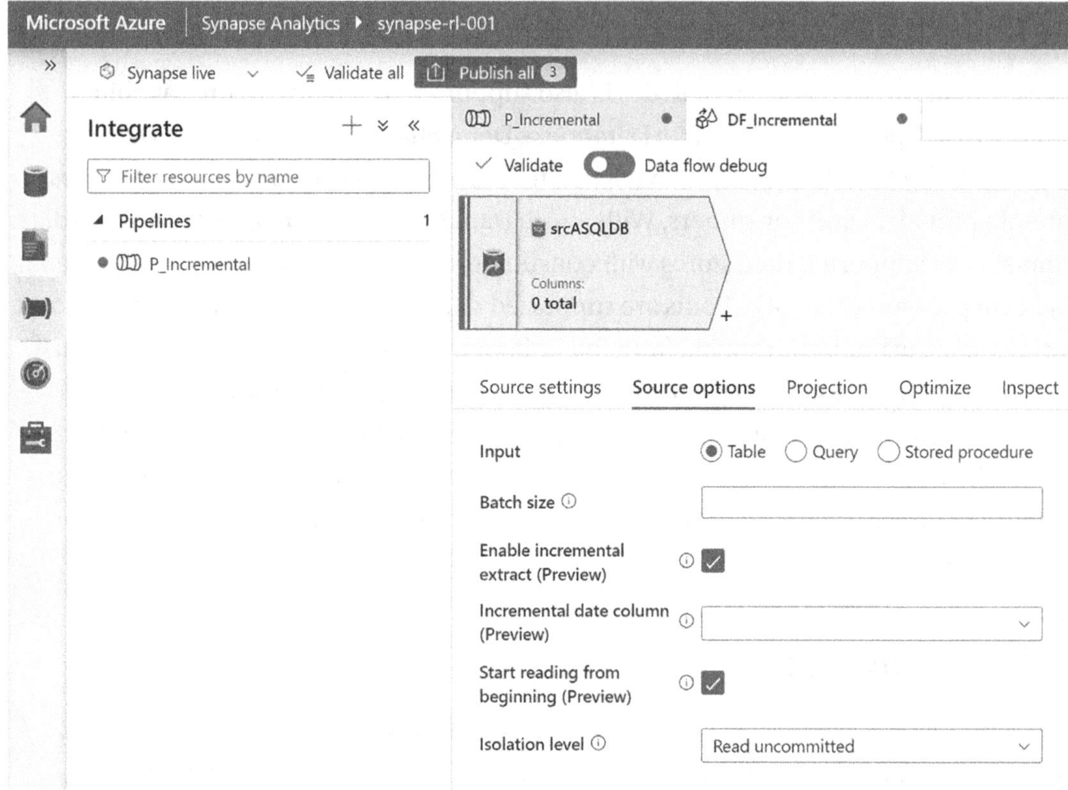

Figure 4-29. *Synapse Mapping Data Flows incremental extract option*

Constraints

While thinking through the concept of the Lakehouse, customers often ask if they will be able to apply constraints to their data in the Lakehouse, much like they would in their traditional SQL-based systems. The concept of keys, relationships, and partitions are all capabilities of Lake databases in Synapse Analytics. Primary, Foreign, and Composite keys are all supported within Lake Databases and their relationships can visually be depicted in the Lake database designer which clearly displays the relationships between multiple tables, as shown in Figure 4-30. As for Synapse Analytics Dedicated SQL Pools (SQLDW), constraints are not well suited for this environment since primary keys and unique keys are allowed but not enforced. Also, there is no foreign key concept. Lastly, primary keys work when not enforced and non-clustered. This means that duplicate entries will be allowed to ensure that your ELT process enforced data quality and cleansing logic. To create a table with constraints, the syntax would need to be similar to the code as follows: `CREATE TABLE Customer(Id int PRIMARY KEY NONCLUSTERED NOT ENFORCED, value int)`

***Figure 4-30.** Lake Database designer relationships*

Summary

Azure Synapse Analytics is a highly secure, well-governed, and powerful tool within the Lakehouse since it is an Azure-native unified data and analytics platform that supports a variety of features across the spectrum of data ingestion and integration, reporting, real-time analytics, advanced analytics, and continuous integration and deployment. By decoupling storage from compute, Synapse Analytics can support a variety of real-time and advanced analytics querying and ELT use cases by keeping costs low and performance high. Synapse also supports an easy approach to designing and implementing industry standard databases with its designer and template capabilities. New features are constantly being added to support the platform's goal of being a one-stop shop for unified data and analytics. One such addition is Synapse Flowlets within Synapse Pipelines, which is a new feature of Mapping Data Flows that enables data engineers to design portions of new data flow logic, or to extract portions of an existing data flow, and save them as separate "Flowlet" artifacts inside their workspace. Data engineers can reuse existing logic and data flows as templates.

Synapse Analytics also offers an MPP style data warehouse, along with a variety of connectors for Purview, Power BI, and Repos. With Synapse Link, you will be able to create live connections to your transactional systems, and with Synapse Pipelines, you can create, schedule, and monitor ELT workloads with ease. Synapse Analytics is truly a unified data and analytics platform that can bring tremendous value to your Data Lakehouse.

Table 4-2 summarizes the comparison of capabilities between Synapse Analytics and Databricks workspaces for machine learning, data lake discovery, real-time integrations, transformations, analysis, reporting, and data warehousing.

Table 4-2. Databricks Workspace vs. Synapse Analytics Workspace

	Databricks Workspace	Synapse Analytics Workspace
Machine Learning		
Choose between standard- and high-concurrency cluster mode	Yes	No
Industry-leading Spark (Databricks Runtime) built on a highly optimized version of Apache Spark offering 50x performance	Yes	No
Open source Apache Spark	No	Yes
Robust developer IDE	Yes	No
ML flow support	Yes	Yes
Data Lake Discovery		
Mount a Data Lake to query	Yes	No
Directly query primary Data Lake without mounting	Yes	No
Delta Lake support	Yes	Yes
Real-Time Integrations and Transformations		
Automated versioning with CI/CD	Yes	Yes
Real-time co-authoring	Yes	Yes
Spark Structured Streaming support	Yes	Yes
SQL Analyses and Data Warehousing		
T-SQL support	Yes	Yes
Dedicated SQL Analytics workspace	Yes	No
Spark SQL support	Yes	Yes
Traditional MPP data warehousing capabilities	No	Yes
Delta Lakehouse capabilities	Yes	Yes
Relational data modeling in workspace	No	Yes

(continued)

Table 4-2. *(continued)*

	Databricks Workspace	Synapse Analytics Workspace
Traditional columnar indexing	No	Yes
Reporting and Self-Service BI		
Use Power BI from the Studio	No	Yes
Easily Integrates with Synapse Dedicated SQL Pools from workspace	No	Yes
Easily Connect to Power BI	Yes	Yes

While considering between Databricks and Synapse Analytics workspace platforms, it would be wise to compare the pros and cons of each platform based on benchmark tests, specific use case, and a variety of other factors to accurately determine whether Databricks, Synapse workspaces, or both might fit within your modern Data Lakehouse platform. Databricks brings the advantage of being an enterprise-ready solution that is capable of handling numerous data varieties, volumes, and velocities, while offering a developer-friendly approach of working with DELTA Tables from its SQL Analytics and data engineering workspaces. With its tremendous DELTA support, ACID transactions and caching are supported. Databricks is also constantly iterating through its product offerings to enhance and speed up its performance. This can be seen with the introduction of its Photon engine as an alternative C++ based compute processing engine. From an advanced analytics perspective, Databricks provides robust support for cognitive services and machine learning through its offerings around ML runtimes, libraries, MLflow, Feature Stores, and more. While these are great feature offerings, there is always room for improvement, and Databricks can improve its endpoint (cluster) startup and shutdown process to be more in-line with a true serverless offering. Also, the process of deciding on the pros and cons of cluster size can be cumbersome when there are so many options with limited guidance on when to choose which option.

Synapse Analytics workspace presents a modern approach managing data engineering and advanced analytics workloads with the advantage of not requiring cluster startups. Synapse provides great support for parquet and supports a variety of data disciplines within its unified platform including Power Bi Reporting, ELT pipelines, machine learning, and much more. Its serverless offering can be accessed directly from commonly used IDEs including Power BI and SQL Server Management Studio (SSMS) through various types of enterprise authentications. While these are all great features of Synapse Analytics workspaces, its support for DELTA and data caching can be improved. When compared to Databricks, there is also more overhead related to access setup of credentials, data formats, and data structure specifications. While Databricks is a more mature Lakehouse platform technology with robust integration and support for DELTA format, it lacks a persistent data warehouse layer technology, which Synapse provides with its Dedicated SQL Pools offering. On the other hand, while Synapse Analytics has room for growth and maturity in the Data Lakehouse platform space, it is quickly growing and evolving its feature offerings to be on par with those of Databricks. As you evaluate if these technologies are a fit for your organization, also consider understanding how these resources can be deployed securely from an infrastructure perspective to enable private connectivity to ensure that organizational security requirements are met.

PART III

Apache Spark ELT

CHAPTER 5

Pipelines and Jobs

There are a few different methods for developing, scheduling, and monitoring Lakehouse ELT pipelines using Apache Spark in Azure. Apache Spark ELT pipelines and jobs can be created and scheduled in Databricks, Data Factory, and Synapse Analytics workspaces. Apache Spark is widely used for processing big data ELT workloads in Azure, and since there are numerous tools and technologies for processing these workloads, understanding the various methods for leveraging Apache Spark for ELT in Azure can be overwhelming.

In this chapter, you will learn about the various methods and applications that can be used to create and support your Data Lakehouse ELT design, development, scheduling, and monitoring of pipelines in Azure. With a focus on Apache Spark for the development of these pipelines, you'll get a deeper understanding of these various options which include Data Factory's Mapping Data Flows and Spark activity, Databricks, and Synapse Analytics workspace jobs and pipelines.

Databricks

Databricks jobs support the orchestration and scheduling of one or more dependent tasks that contain ELT code from a Databricks notebook, Delta Live Table pipelines, or applications written in Scala, SQL, Java, or Python. The environments, parameters, libraries, and clusters can be defined and customized in the jobs. One of the key benefits is the variety of development languages and processes that can be used within the jobs, along with the ability to control the execution order of tasks by specifying dependencies. Tasks within a job can be executed sequentially based on dependencies or in parallel. Figure 5-1 illustrates how you could potentially create a job with a series of sequentially dependent or parallel tasks.

R. L'Esteve, *The Azure Data Lakehouse Toolkit*, https://doi.org/10.1007/978-1-4842-8233-5_5

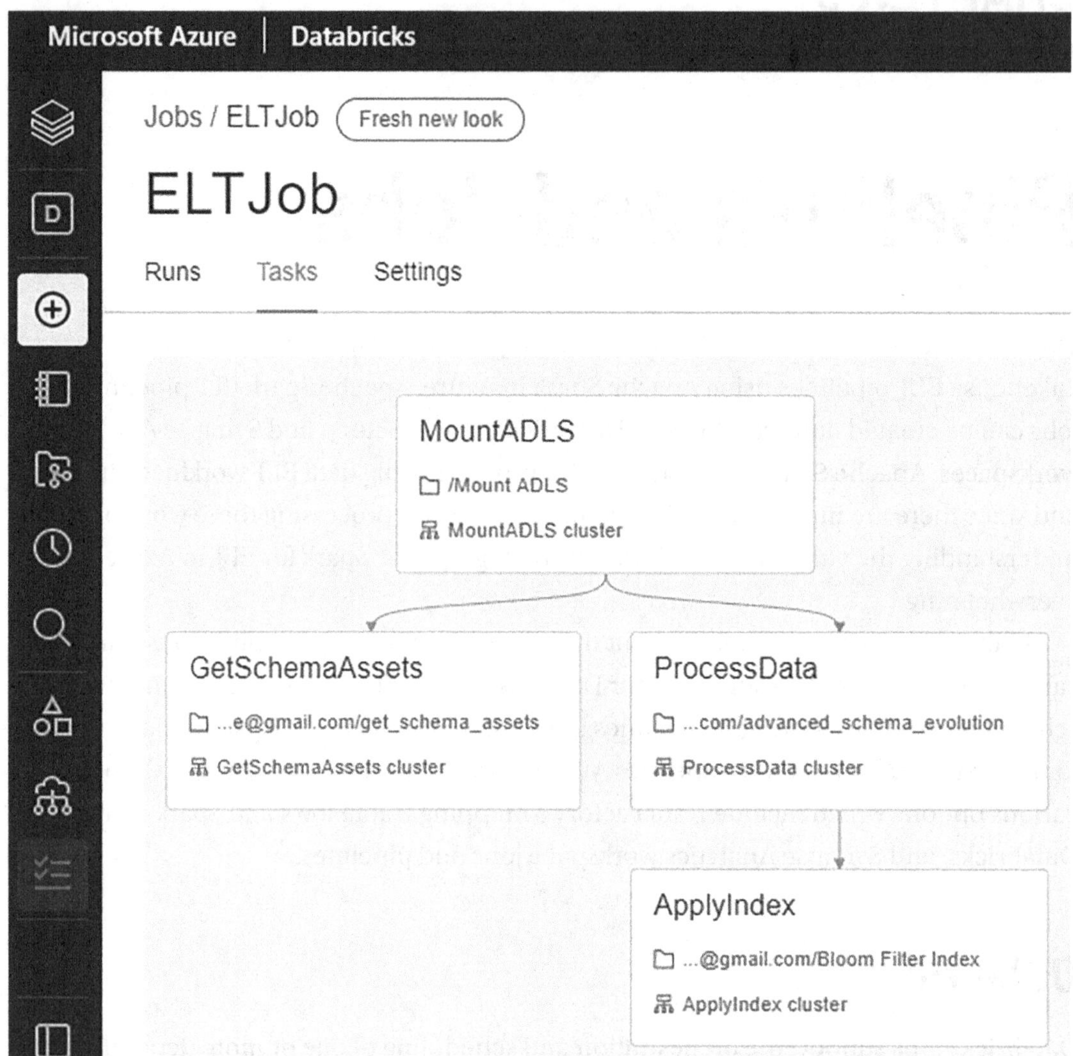

***Figure 5-1.** Tasks tab within Databricks ELT job*

From Figure 5-2, notice that you could easily call your Python, Scala, or SQL Databricks notebook in the task, specify your cluster type, add parameters through UI or JSON, and specify whether the task depends on another task to orchestrate the job.

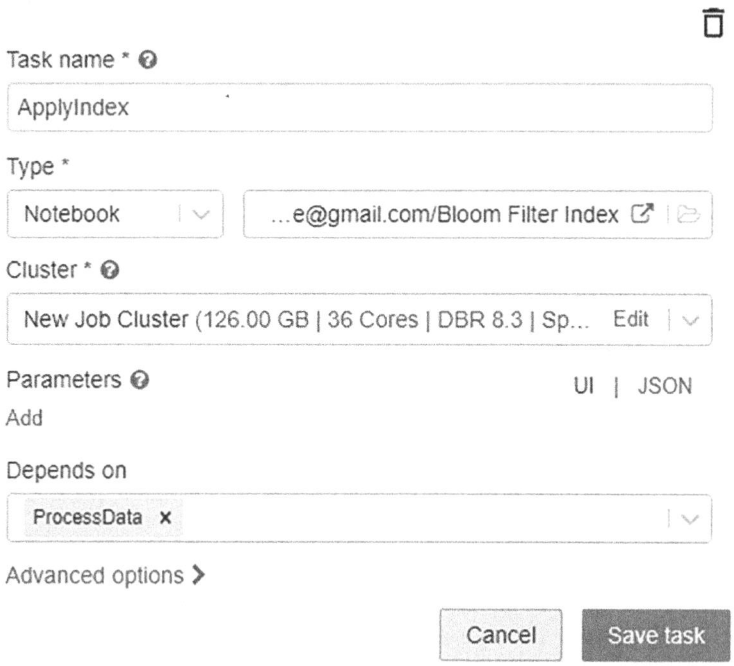

Figure 5-2. *Task details and configuration UI in Databricks ELT job*

Databricks job clusters are highly customizable. Runtime versions are constantly being upgraded to offer better capabilities and support. That said, it is important to ensure that your notebook code is up to date and compatible with newer runtime versions. Within a Databricks cluster, there is an option to enable auto-scaling of the cluster between a min and max number of predefined nodes based on load, as shown in Figure 5-3. Also, auto-termination stops the cluster after a set number of minutes to prevent costs from incurring. It is important to note also that these Databricks clusters can also be used within Data Factory to support more customized cluster configurations. For example, in a Data Factory, you may have a minimum cluster that is running four workers but only need two workers. In such a scenario, you could leverage the Databricks cluster configured for two workers and use that in your Data Factory pipelines.

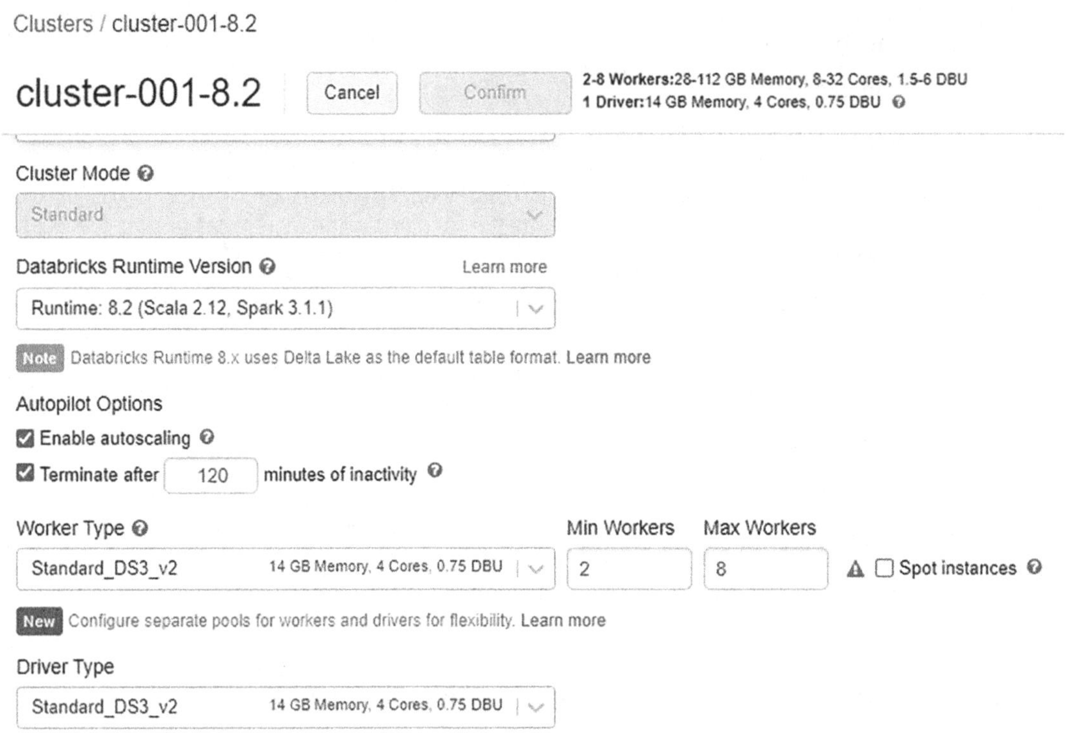

Clusters / cluster-001-8.2

cluster-001-8.2 Cancel Confirm

2-8 Workers:28-112 GB Memory, 8-32 Cores, 1.5-6 DBU
1 Driver:14 GB Memory, 4 Cores, 0.75 DBU

Cluster Mode

Standard

Databricks Runtime Version Learn more

Runtime: 8.2 (Scala 2.12, Spark 3.1.1)

Note Databricks Runtime 8.x uses Delta Lake as the default table format. Learn more

Autopilot Options

Enable autoscaling

Terminate after 120 minutes of inactivity

Worker Type Min Workers Max Workers

Standard_DS3_v2 14 GB Memory, 4 Cores, 0.75 DBU 2 8 Spot instances

New Configure separate pools for workers and drivers for flexibility. Learn more

Driver Type

Standard_DS3_v2 14 GB Memory, 4 Cores, 0.75 DBU

***Figure 5-3.** Databricks cluster configuration UI*

Additional advanced options for the Databricks job allow you to specify custom retry policies along with intervals between policies, shown in Figure 5-4. Within advanced options, you could also add email notifications for the start, success, and/or failure of the task. There are also options for adding dependent libraries to the task and editing timeout values for the task. Each task within the job could be customized with these advanced options.

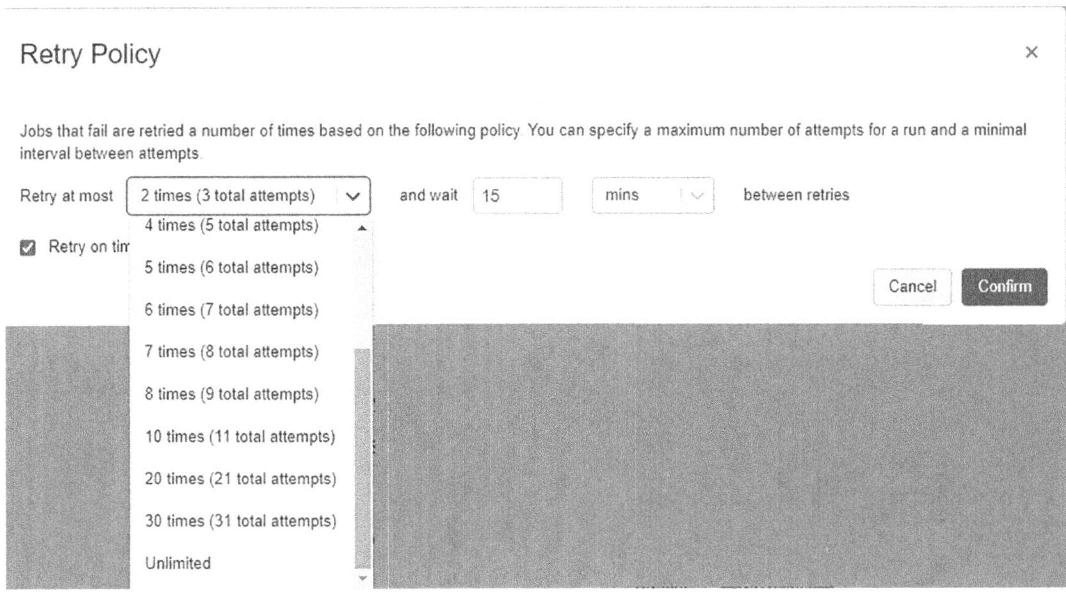

Figure 5-4. *Job retry policy options*

Finally, once your job is developed by combining and orchestrating a collection of tasks, Figure 5-5 shows how you can flexibly schedule the job with the optional Cron Syntax feature to further customize the scheduling experience.

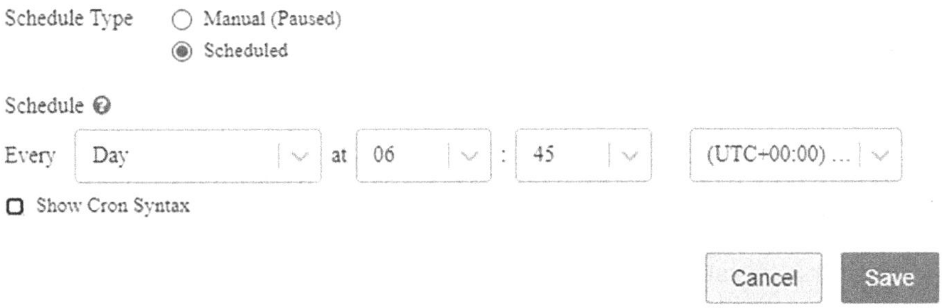

Schedule Type ○ Manual (Paused) ◉ Scheduled

Schedule

Every Day at 06 : 45 (UTC+00:00) ...

☐ Show Cron Syntax

Cancel Save

Figure 5-5. *Detailed scheduling UI for Databricks jobs*

In the Settings tab of the job, shown in Figure 5-6, you could specify the maximum concurrent runs of the job. This is useful if you want to allow successive runs to overlap with each other or if you want to trigger multiple runs that differ by their input parameters. You could also add alerts at the job level in addition to the task level. Lastly, you could add permissions here for who can view, manage, run, and own the job.

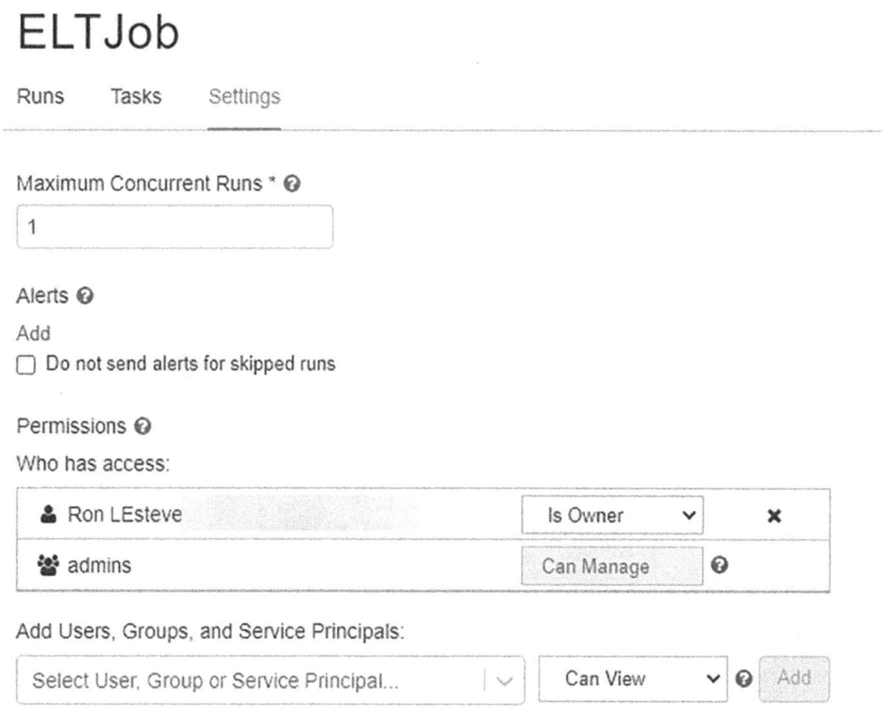

Figure 5-6. *Settings and permissions UI for jobs*

Once the job is scheduled and run, you'll be able to view details around its activity within the Runs tab of the job page. It is on this page where you would be able to visually monitor both active and completed historical runs within the past 60 days. This experience is somewhat similar to Data Factory's visually monitoring UI capability. The added benefit of using Databricks jobs is that you could also combine Delta Live Table pipelines within the tasks of these jobs. Figure 5-7 shows how runs can be monitored in the UI. For a better integration experience with other Azure applications and processes and as an alternative to Databricks jobs, Databricks notebooks can be executed from Data Factory's Databricks job activity; integrated with other Azure applications such as Mapping Data Flows, functions, etc.; and scheduled/monitored in Data Factory. It is possible to set parameters in the ADF job activity that can then be passed to the Databricks notebook to enable the possibility of running different jobs with different parameters.

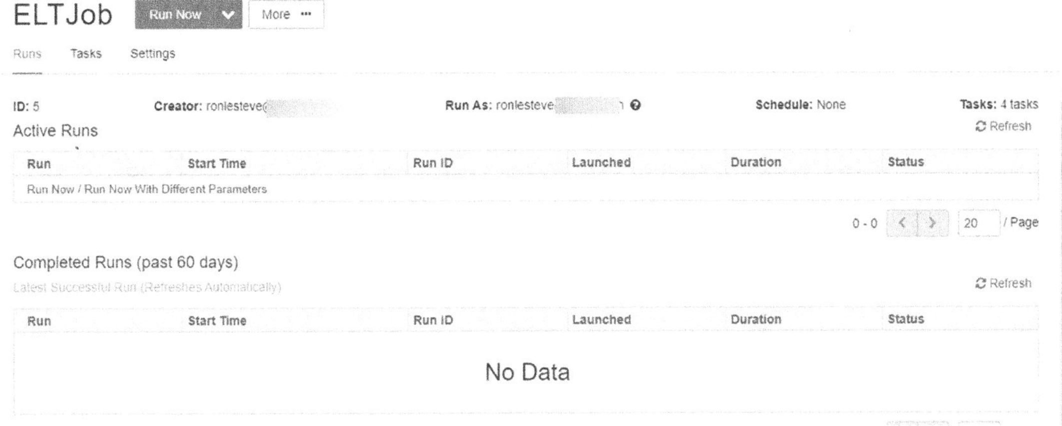

Figure 5-7. *Databricks jobs monitoring UI*

Data Factory

Azure Data Factory offers a robust toolset for developing, scheduling, alerting, and visually monitoring pipeline activity and runs within its UI. Within the Data Factory, Apache Spark can be leveraged for big data ELT workload processing with both Mapping Data Flows and the Spark activity. In this section, you will learn how to optimally create and run Apache Spark jobs in Data Factory.

Mapping Data Flows

Mapping Data Flows are visually designed data transformations within Data Factory that support the design and development of complex transformation logic with minimal code. These data flows can be executed on scaled out Apache Spark clusters that are spun up at runtime and then operationalized using Data Factory scheduling, control, flow, and monitoring capabilities.

Within Mapping Data Flows, data engineers have access to a variety of data transformation activities, as shown in Figure 5-8. These include joins, splits, lookups, complex schema, and row modifiers, along with complex formatters such as flatten and parse transformations. For more details related to transformations using ADF's Mapping Data Flows, please refer to my detailed article on MSSQLTips for data warehouse ETL here: `www.mssqltips.com/sqlservertip/6074/azure-data-factory-mapping-data-flow-for-datawarehouse-etl/`. Refer to the following detailed step-by-step article for big Data Lake aggregations and transformations here: www.mssqltips.com/sqlservertip/6169/azure-data-factory-mapping-data-flows-for-big-data-lake-aggregations-and-transformations/. For detailed options related to incrementally upserting data using ADF's Mapping Data Flows, explore my article that can be found here: www.mssqltips.com/sqlservertip/6729/azure-data-factory-mapping-data-flow-incremental-upsert/

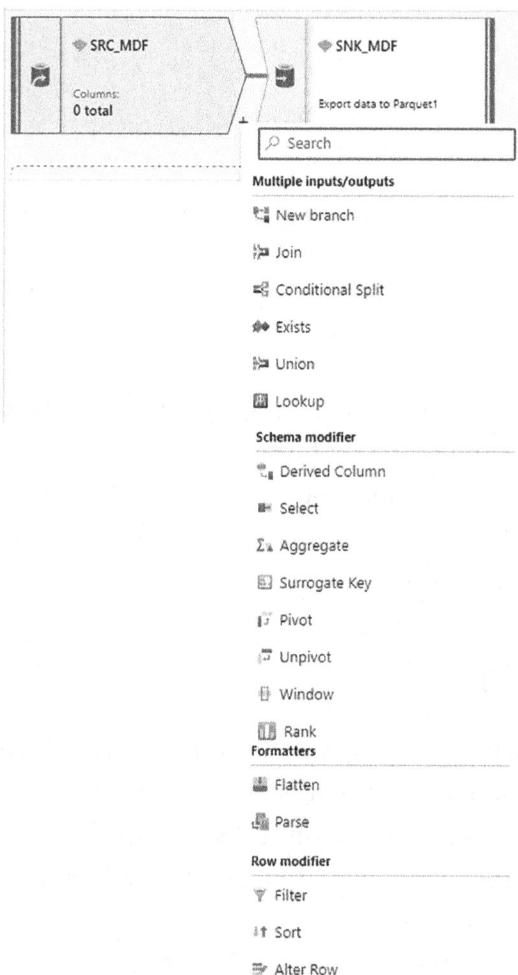

Figure 5-8. *ADF Mapping DF transformations*

Figure 5-9 shows how Mapping Data Flow supports optimizations including defining and configuring the partitioning scheme of the Spark cluster. It supports the repartitioning of data after the transformation has completed and allows you to control the distribution of your data across compute nodes. This is a powerful configuration that must be used with care to ensure that you are optimally partitioning your data.

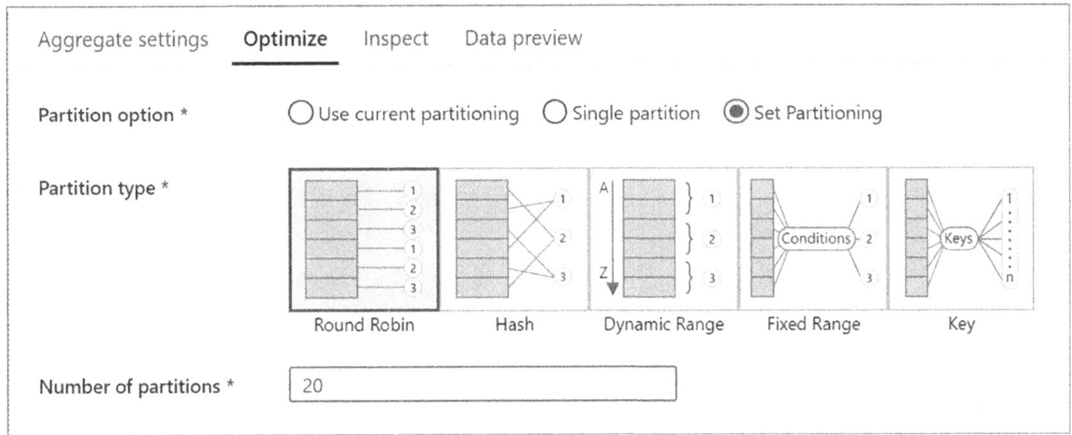

***Figure 5-9.** ADF Optimize tab including partition options, types, and volume*

Once you have completed developing your Mapping Data Flow transformation logic, Figure 5-10 shows the data flow activity that you can add within Data Factory and integrate it with other pipeline processing steps. Additionally, you could also define the compute type, core count, logging levels, and more as you prepare this data flow activity to be scheduled and monitored.

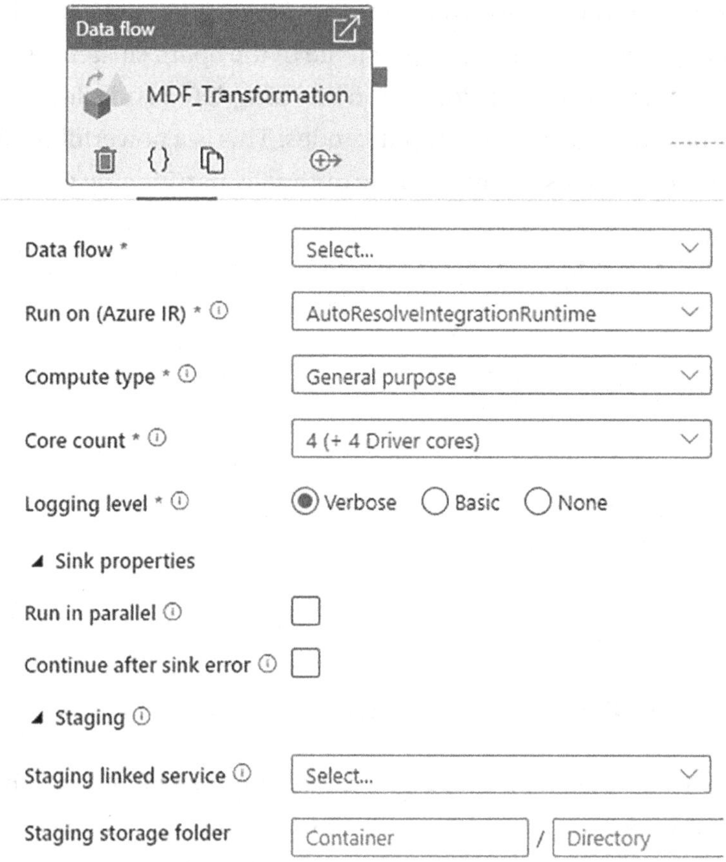

***Figure 5-10.** Graphical user interface, text, and application, for Mapping Data Flows*

The following list captures the various Mapping Data Flow activity configuration requirements:

- **Compute type**: The three available Spark cluster options in Mapping Data Flows are general purpose, memory optimized, and compute optimized. General-purpose clusters are the default, ideal for most workloads, and balance performance and cost. Memory-optimized clusters are ideal for data flows with many joins and lookups since they can store more data in memory to minimize out-of-memory errors and come at a higher price point per core. Finally, compute-optimized clusters are ideal for simple, non-memory-intensive data transformations such as filtering and adding derived columns. They are not recommended for ELT or production workloads and come at a cheaper price per core.

- **Logging level**: For pipeline executions that do not require fully logged activities, Basic or None could be selected. Alternatively, "Verbose" requests ADF to fully log activity at each individual partition level during your data transformation.
- **Time to live**: Data flows spin up new Spark clusters based on the Azure IR configurations. Since these clusters take a few minutes to start up, the time-to-live (TTL) feature specifies how long to keep the cluster running after executing a job. This is a valuable setting when your pipeline contains multiple sequential data flows. The "Quick reuse" feature also minimizes startup time by keeping the compute environment alive for the period specified in the TTL. For parallel data flow executions, ADF does not recommend enabling TTL for the activity's IR since only one job can run on a single cluster at a time and when two data flows start, the second will spin up its own cluster.
- **Core count**: Data flows distribute processing over nodes in a Spark cluster to complete operations in parallel. More cores translate into more nodes which increase processing power and decrease processing time. While the default cluster size is four driver and worker nodes, the cluster is capable of scaling up to the core counts specified in Figure 5-11.

Worker cores	Driver cores	Total cores
4	4	8
8	8	16
16	16	32
32	16	48
64	16	80
128	16	144
256	16	272

Figure 5-11. *Workers, drivers, and total cores available in Mapping Data Flows*

HDInsight Spark Activity

The Spark activity within Data Factory pipelines, shown in Figure 5-12, supports the execution of a Spark program on your own or on-demand HDInsight clusters. The advantage of this Spark activity is that it supports the execution of highly customized Python scripts or JAR files that are stored in your Data Lake Storage Gen2 account. This Spark activity differs from data flows in that it mainly supports the purpose of custom transformation scripts. While data flows can also be integrated with custom transformations, its main goal is to provide a codeless transformation experience. With an on-demand HDInsight Spark activity configured through a linked service, Data Factory will automatically create a Spark cluster to process the data and will then delete the cluster after the processing is completed. Similar to most other Data Factory pipeline activities, the Spark activity supports custom-defined timeouts and retry intervals. Additionally, it can be chained to other Data Factory pipeline activities and can accept variables and parameters. HDInsight clusters come with their own pricing tiers that need to be thoroughly evaluated and compared to other available clusters across Mapping Data Flows, Databricks, and Synapse Spark Pools.

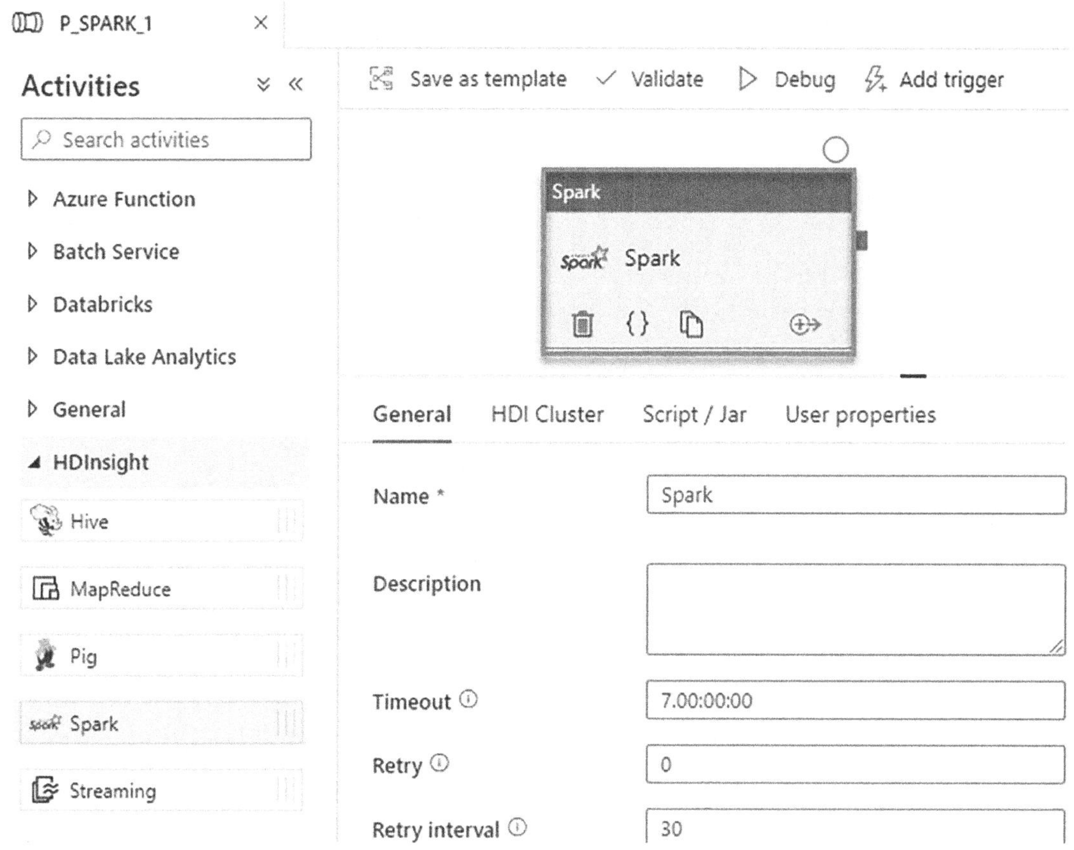

Figure 5-12. *Spark HDInsight activity within ADF*

Azure HDInsight is a managed Apache Hadoop service that lets you run Apache Spark, Apache Hive, Apache Kafka, Apache HBase, and more in the cloud. One of the advantages of this Spark activity is that you can either bring your own HDInsight cluster or use an on-demand HDInsight cluster. When selecting the "On-demand HDInsight" option, you must configure the properties listed in Figure 5-13.

The "Time to live" specifies how long the on-demand HDInsight cluster stays alive after completion of an activity run if there are no other active jobs in the cluster, and the minimal allowed value is five minutes. The "Cluster size" defines the number of worker nodes in the cluster. The HDInsight cluster is created with two head nodes along with the number of worker nodes you specify for this property. The nodes are of size Standard_D3 that has 4 cores, so a 4-worker node cluster takes 24 cores (4*4 = 16 cores for worker nodes, plus 2*4 = 8 cores for head nodes).

New Linked Service (Azure HDInsight)
Name *
AzureHDInsightLinkedService
Description
Type *
Bring your own HDInsight
On-demand HDInsight
Connect via integration runtime *
AutoResolveIntegrationRuntime
Azure Storage Linked Service *
AzureBlobStorage1
Edit Connection
Cluster type *
spark
Spark version
Cluster size *
4
Time to live *
00:05:00
Service principal id *
Service principal key
Azure Key Vault
Service principal key *
Tenant *
Version
3.6
Cluster name prefix
Annotations
New

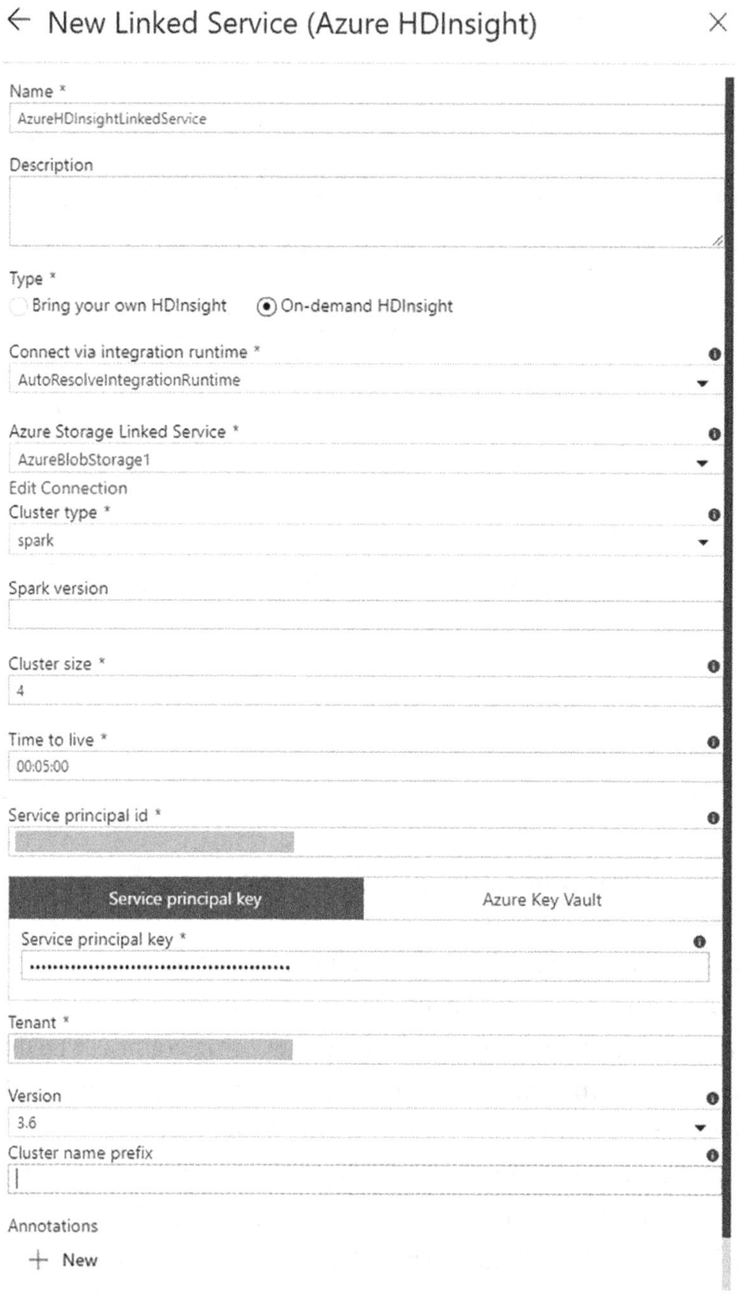

Figure 5-13. *HDInsight linked service settings*

These scripts will be executed on the predefined cluster and are application agnostic in that you will not need an instance of either a Databricks or Synapse Analytics workspace notebook to persist and containerize your code. The code can simply be stored as a .py file in your ADLS gen2 account and be executed on the cluster defined in this Spark activity.

Here is a generic sample Python script file that takes an input sentence, splits the words out on individual lines, and outputs the results to a defined storage account. The following script wordcount.py can be called from the Spark activity:

```
import sys
from operator import add

from pyspark.sql import SparkSession

def main():
    spark = SparkSession\
        .builder\
        .appName("PythonWordCount")\
        .getOrCreate()

    lines = spark.read.text("wasbs://adftutorial@<storageaccountname>.blob.
    core.windows.net/spark/inputfiles/minecraftstory.txt").rdd.map(lambda
    r: r[0])
    counts = lines.flatMap(lambda x: x.split(' ')) \
        .map(lambda x: (x, 1)) \
        .reduceByKey(add)
    counts.saveAsTextFile("wasbs://adftutorial@<storageaccountname>.blob.
    core.windows.net/spark/outputfiles/wordcount")

    spark.stop()

if __name__ == "__main__":
    main()
```

Scheduling and Monitoring

Azure Data Factory pipelines can be triggered manually and through a few scheduling methods. A scheduled trigger, shown in Figure 5-14, invokes a pipeline based on a defined start and end date. It can be customized for recurrences as low as every one minute and as high as monthly schedules. A Tumbling window trigger operates on a periodic interval.

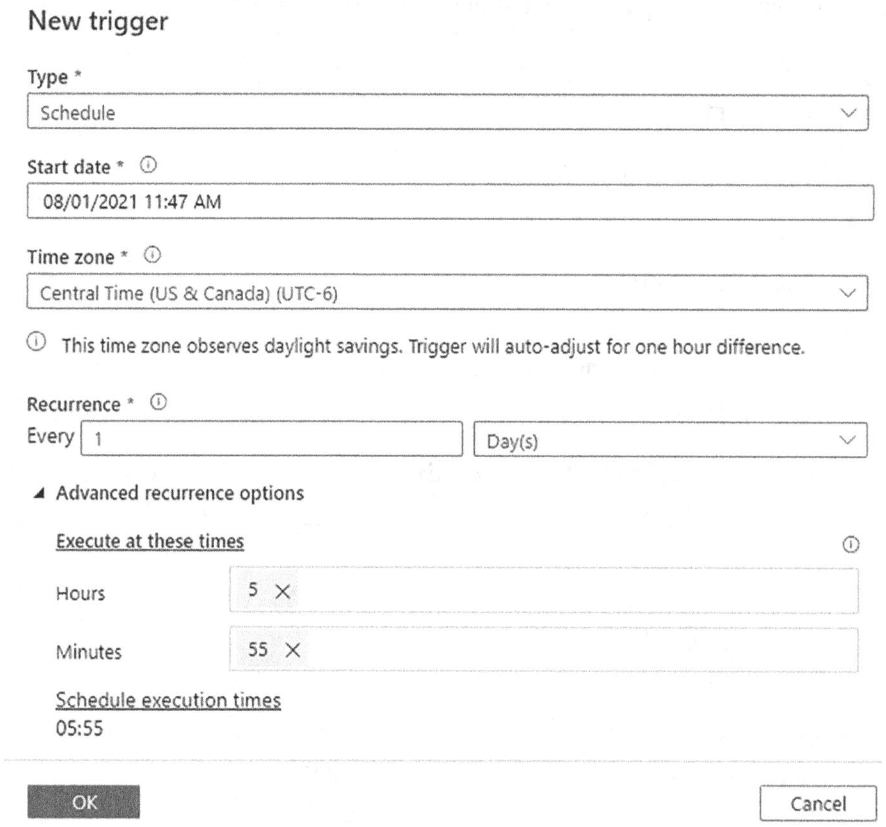

Figure 5-14. *ADF trigger for scheduling pipelines*

An event-based trigger, shown in Figure 5-15, responds to either storage events or custom events. The ADLS gen2 storage account will need to be selected along with the container name. Additional parameters around blob end and begin paths can be configured. The event can be triggered when a blob is created, deleted, or both. There is also an option to ignore empty blobs with zero bytes.

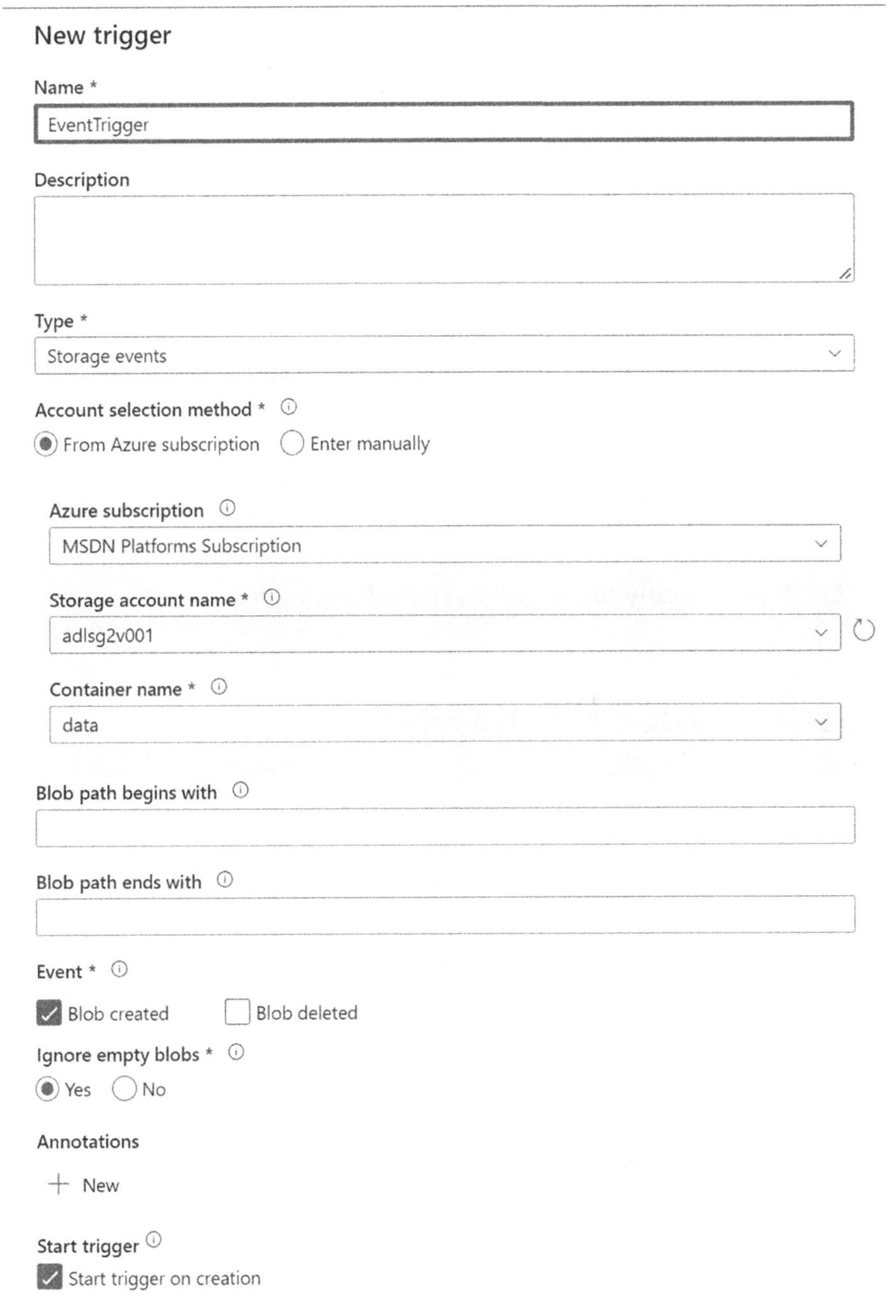

New trigger

Name *

EventTrigger

Description

Type *

Storage events

Account selection method *

From Azure subscription   Enter manually

Azure subscription

MSDN Platforms Subscription

Storage account name *

adlsg2v001

Container name *

data

Blob path begins with

Blob path ends with

Event *

Blob created   Blob deleted

Ignore empty blobs *

Yes   No

Annotations

+ New

Start trigger

Start trigger on creation

Figure 5-15. *ADF event trigger*

Data Factory offers a robust monitoring and alerting framework, shown in Figure 5-16, that allows a variety of customizations for visually monitoring pipeline and detailed activity runs within each pipeline. Within this monitoring UI, you can also manually rerun failed pipelines or cancel running pipelines. There are also options for monitoring consumption and alerting users on a variety of alert condition metrics.

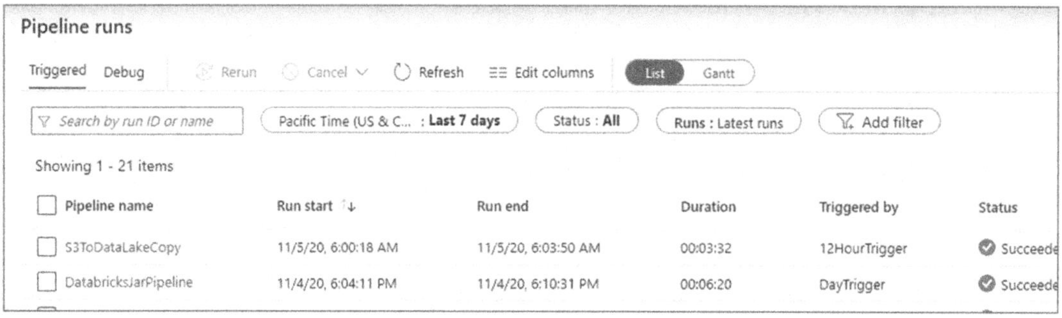

Figure 5-16. *UI for visually monitoring ADF pipeline jobs*

Synapse Analytics Workspace

Azure Synapse Analytics workspace is based on the existing Data Factory UI experience; therefore, many of the scheduling and monitoring capabilities of Data Factory will also be redundant and applicable to workloads that are run within Synapse Analytics workspace.

Within Synapse Analytics workspaces, users have access to Serverless SQL Pools, Dedicated SQL Pools, and Apache Spark Pools. Serverless SQL Pools support the need for ad hoc querying and to further explore data to derive real-time insights. They are created when the Synapse workspace is provisioned, and it is essentially used to query data as a service. In addition, Dedicated SQL Pools can be used when performance requirements are well defined, and there is a need to persist, deliver, and maintain data in a traditional distributed data processing engine. Apache Spark Pools in Synapse Analytics workspaces can be used for analytics using in-memory big data processing engines.

The default Spark node size is memory optimized, and it has a few options: small (~4 vCores/32 GB), medium (~8 vCores/64 GB), large (~16 vCores/128 GB), XLarge (~32 vCores/256 GB), XXLarge (~64 vCores/432 GB), and XXXLarge (~80 vCores/2504 GB).

Auto-scaling can be enabled and is determined by the number of nodes defined in the scale settings. Figure 5-17 shows an example of the UI used to create an Apache Spark Pool along with all of the available configuration options.

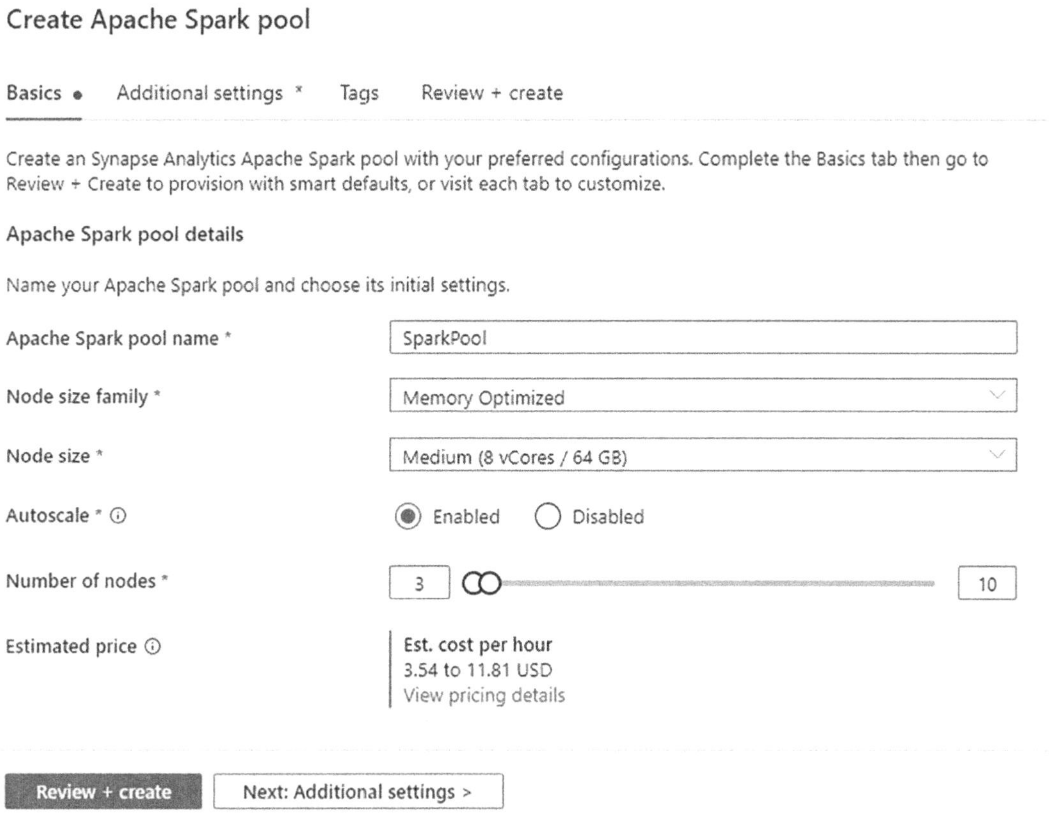

Figure 5-17. *Steps to create and configure Synapse Spark Pool*

In the next step, you'll need to provide additional configuration settings related to pausing the cluster if it has been idle for a certain time, depicted in Figure 5-18. The default setting is 15 minutes. Additionally, there is an option to select the version of Spark to be used and options to upload environment configuration files.

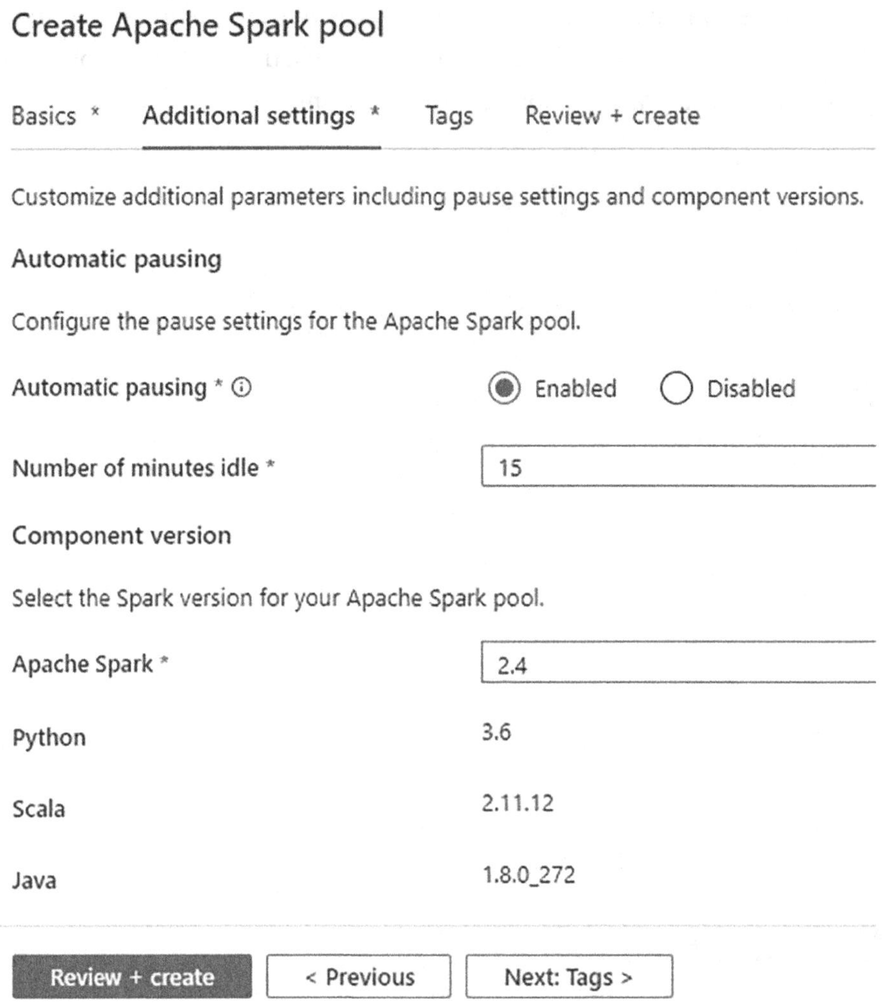

Figure 5-18. *Additional settings for configuring Spark Pool*

After the Spark Pool is created, you'll be able to develop your ELT code within a new notebook in the Synapse Analytics workspace, attach it to the Spark Pool, and then add the notebook to either a new or existing pipeline. This sample notebook is shown in Figure 5-19.

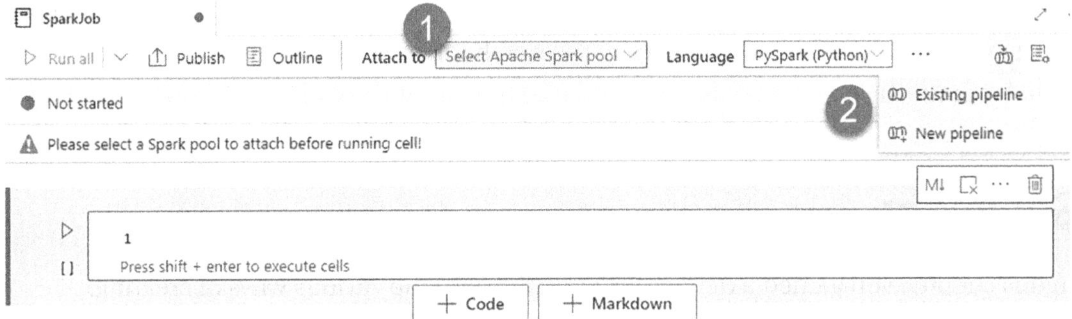

Figure 5-19. *Steps to add notebook to pipeline*

After adding the notebook to a new pipeline, notice the notebook activity within Synapse Pipelines shown in Figure 5-20, which is quite similar to Data Factory pipelines. The notebook is now available to be scheduled and monitored much like how the Data Factory pipelines are triggered and visually monitored. There are other Synapse activities that could be combined with this notebook.

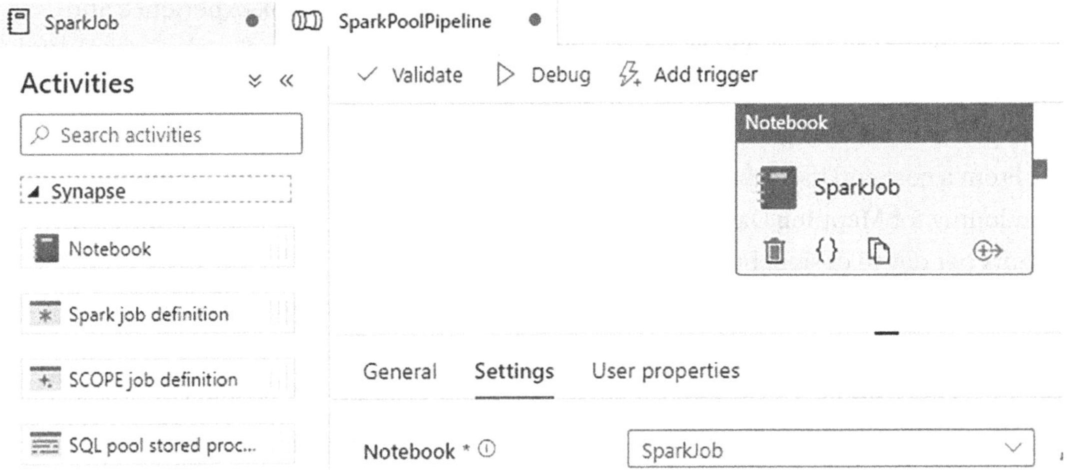

Figure 5-20. *Spark notebook activity within Synapse Pipelines*

As for monitoring the Apache Spark Pools, Synapse Pipeline offers the capability to monitor the Spark Pools visually within the monitor UI. For Spark Pools, users have the ability to monitor the pool size, active users, allocated vCores and memory (GB), and when the pool was created. For Apache Spark applications, users will be able to monitor the status, timestamp, and various other metrics of the notebook that is run on the Spark Pool. The visual monitoring experience is very similar to the monitoring of Data Factory pipelines.

Summary

In this chapter, you gained a deeper understanding of the various ways of creating, scheduling, and monitoring Apache Spark ELT jobs in Azure by using Data Factory's Mapping Data Flows and Spark activity pipelines, Databricks jobs, and Synapse Analytics workspace pipelines. Mapping Data Flow offers a low-code data engineering experience, while the Spark activity offers a more customizable experience within Data Factory's native toolset. The Spark activity may be useful in scenarios where you'll need to bring your own HDInsight cluster. In other scenarios, it may be beneficial to consider Databricks for your ELT and scheduling them within either Databricks or the Data Factory pipeline experience. Synapse Analytics workspaces bring Spark Pools as a service that can be used for custom development in a notebook experience and then scheduled/monitored with Synapse Pipelines. As you continue your journey with implementing the Lakehouse architecture with big data ELT workloads, you'll be better equipped with choosing the right tool for creating and scheduling your ELT jobs.

From a cost and use case perspective, there are a few scenarios that are worth mentioning for Mapping Data Flows. For example, a data engineer that is putting in 8 hours per day to design, build, and test data flows daily can enable the debug mode for data flows, which includes a default TTL of 60 minutes for debug sessions. The daily pricing might be approximately $12 (8 [hours] x 8 [compute-optimized cores] x $0.19 = $12). Similarly, if another team member needs to profile the data or design ELT workloads for 1 hour in debug mode, they might only incur $2 for the 1 hour (1 [hour] x 8 [general-purpose cores] x $0.28 = $2). For production-ready schedule-based and triggered data flows that include light workloads of less than 5 input and output datasets, along with light transformations, and hourly scheduled triggers running on 16 cores of general compute with a time to live (TTL) of 10 minutes, the total pricing would be approximately less than $2. While Synapse Analytics Pipelines also follow a similar cost structure as ADF's Mapping Data Flows, you can always check out the latest pricing updates on Microsoft's Synapse Analytics Pricing page that can be found here:

`https://azure.microsoft.com/en-us/pricing/details/synapse-analytics/`. Finally, Databricks' job resource compute is priced anywhere from $0.15 to $0.30 per DBU hour, respectively, for its standard and premium tiers. You can always check out the latest pricing updates on Microsoft's Databricks Pricing page that can be found here: `https://azure.microsoft.com/en-us/pricing/details/databricks/`. Always thoroughly vet your solution based on use case scenarios to ensure that your final costs are estimated accurately and that you have tight controls around your compute via alerts and metric tracking throughout your development, scheduling, and monitoring process.

CHAPTER 6

Notebook Code

The various data and analytics platforms on Azure support a number of unique methods of designing processes and implementing pipelines for extraction, loading, and transformation (ELT) of your data. With Azure Data Factory and Synapse Pipelines, GUI-driven tasks and activities simplify the design, implementation, and time to market for your ELT pipelines and jobs. Additionally, ADF's Mapping Data Flows and Synapse Pipelines leverage Apache Spark's compute engine under the hood.

Apache Spark's unified analytics engine is a market game changer since it is capable of large-scale data processing and brings the architectural benefits of Resilient Distributed Datasets (RDD), which supports fault tolerance for distributing data over clusters of machines. While there are numerous GUI-based activities for data ingestion and transformation within Data Factory and Synapse Analytics, oftentimes, data engineers that are building these ELT pipelines need more flexibility in their approach to building these ELT pipelines by having the capability to write custom code in multiple languages with access to open source and custom libraries. For example, a data engineer can write custom code to implement a Type 2 Slowly Changing Dimension in either SQL, Python, or Scala for both batch and streaming data. This is just one of many use cases for writing custom notebook code.

With Databricks and Synapse Analytics workspaces, Azure's two flagship unified data and analytics platforms, it is possible to write custom code for your ELT jobs in multiple languages within the same notebook. Apache Spark's APIs provide interfaces for languages including Python, R, Scala, and SQL. Also, these platforms provide the capability of accessing custom and open source libraries at either the cluster or notebook scope to provide data engineers with the right tools for developing their custom code to tailor their ELT scripts and processes to the unique business use cases and scenarios. While it is possible to write custom code in multiple languages with both Databricks and Synapse Analytics, in this chapter, you will gain a deeper understanding of how to write efficient custom code in PySpark, Scala, and SQL for ELT workloads using Databricks notebooks.

R. L'Esteve, *The Azure Data Lakehouse Toolkit*, https://doi.org/10.1007/978-1-4842-8233-5_6

There are a few ways of writing custom code for extracting and loading data from a source to a destination in Azure. With Spark's API support for various languages, ScalaSpark, SparkSQL, and PySpark can all be used within the same notebook when needed. Additionally, the Delta Engine supports these languages as well. In this chapter, you will learn about a few use cases for extracting and loading Excel, XML, JSON, and Zip URL source data with custom PySpark code. Toward the end of this chapter, you will learn about how you could also use Scala, SQL, and user-defined functions (UDFs) within your Databricks ELT notebooks. As a prerequisite to this chapter, it would be important to understand how to manage notebooks which can be found in the following Databricks Link: `https://docs.databricks.com/notebooks/notebooks-manage.html`. You can import notebooks by using the following run command: `%run /Shared/MyNotebook`. For more information related to the %run command along with other notebook workflows, please see the following Microsoft article: `https://docs.microsoft.com/en-us/azure/databricks/notebooks/notebook-workflows`

PySpark

PySpark is an interface for Apache Spark in Python, which allows writing Spark applications using Python APIs and provides PySpark shells for interactively analyzing data in a distributed environment. PySpark supports features including Spark SQL, DataFrame, Streaming, MLlib, and Spark Core. In Azure, PySpark is most commonly used in the Databricks platform, which makes it great for performing exploratory analysis on data of differing volumes, varieties, and velocities. It allows users to build machine learning pipelines and create ELT for the Data Lakehouse. Popular libraries such as Pandas along with custom libraries can be leveraged by PySpark analyses and pipelines. Users often struggle to get started with writing functional PySpark code and regularly search for patterns of success when getting started with PySpark for Lakehouse ELT jobs.

PySpark is widely used by data engineers, data scientists, and data analysts to process big data workloads. PySpark is great because it supports in-memory computations, distributed processing, fault tolerance, immutability, caching, lazy evaluation, built-in optimizations, and support for ANSI SQL. By running initial commands such as `from pyspark.sql.functions import *` and `from pyspark.sql.types import *`, you can easily write PySpark using the ANSI SQL language. This makes applications run on PySpark significantly faster than traditional systems. It seamlessly supports both streaming and machine learning pipelines which make it a popular choice for data engineer and data scientists that are interested in working with their big data residing in the Lakehouse. Databricks on Azure has been widely adopted as a gold standard tool for working with Apache Spark due to its robust support for PySpark. In this section, you will learn the fundamentals of writing functional PySpark code in Databricks for creating databases and tables, reading and writing a variety of file types, creating user-defined functions (UDFs), and working with data frames and the Spark Catalog, along with other useful Lakehouse pipeline-related PySpark code to ingest and transform your data. The following section will demonstrate how to extract and load Excel, XML, JSON, and Zip URL source file types.

Excel

With Databricks notebooks, you can develop custom code for reading and writing from Excel (.xlsx) data sources that are stored in your ADLS gen2 account. Firstly, you'll need to ensure that your ADLS gen2 account is mounted to your Databricks workspace so that your data will be accessible from your notebook. Before you begin development, ensure that your cluster has the following Maven library `com.crealytics:spark-excel_2.12:0.13.5` installed on it. Simply head over to the Libraries tab on your cluster, as shown in Figure 6-1, and search for `spark-excel` in the Maven Central library source. When you find the abovementioned library, install it on your cluster. For this exercise, I have used the following cluster version `9.1 LTS (includes Apache Spark 3.1.2, Scala 2.12)`.

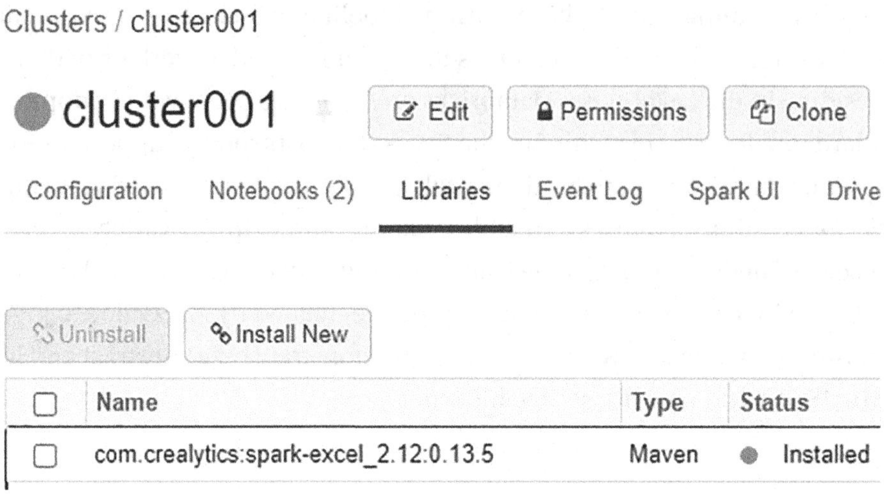

Figure 6-1. Spark Excel Maven installed on cluster

Next, create a new Python notebook and ensure that the cluster that you previously created is attached to it. The PySpark code shown in Figure 6-2 will call the Maven Spark Excel library and will load an Orders Excel file into a data frame. You can find the sample CSV and Excel files that are used in this section within my GitHub Repo here: `https://github.com/ronlesteve/the-azure-data-lakehouse-toolkit/tree/main/ExcelFiles`. Notice the various options that you have at your disposal which include the capability for specifying headers, sheet names, and more. You can also specify the cell range using the dataAddress option.

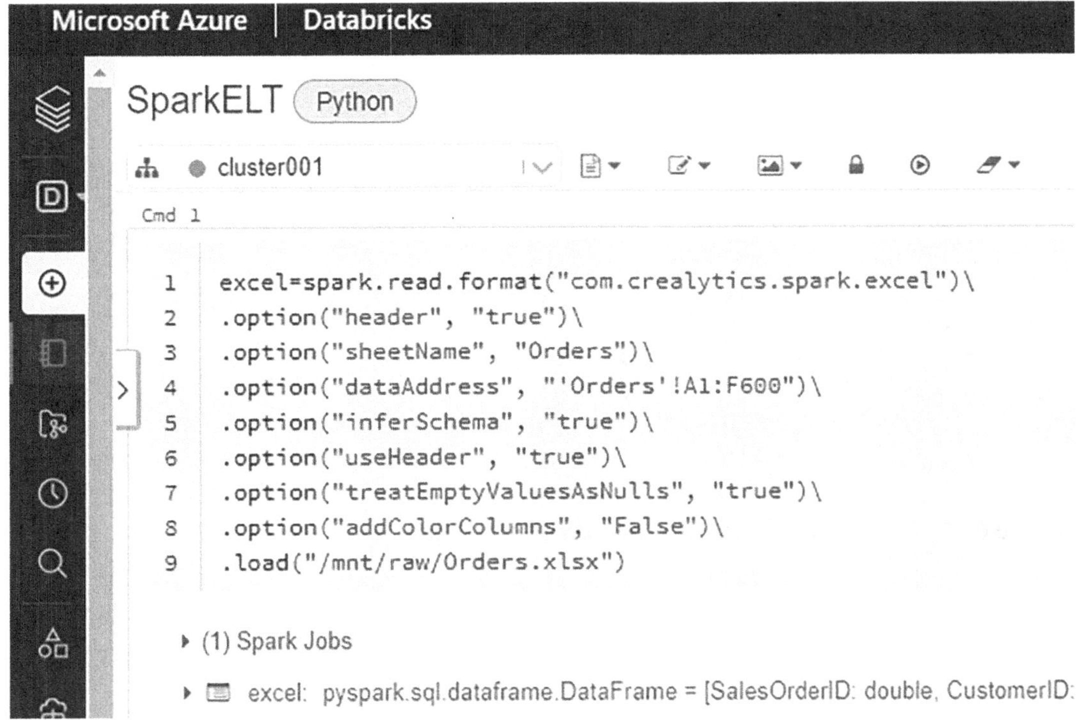

***Figure 6-2.** Read Excel file using Spark Excel format with options*

Here is the PySpark code that you will need to run to recreate the results shown in Figure 6-2:

```
excel=spark.read.format("com.crealytics.spark.excel")\
.option("header", "true")\
.option("sheetName", "Orders")\
.option("dataAddress", "'Orders'!A1:F600")\
.option("inferSchema", "true")\
.option("useHeader", "true")\
.option("treatEmptyValuesAsNulls", "true")\
.option("addColorColumns", "False")\
.load("/mnt/raw/Orders.xlsx")
```

After running the code successfully, run the `display(excel)` command to view the results of the Excel file being loaded to the data frame. Notice from Figure 6-3 that the data is organized into a tabular format which makes this easy to consume for further analysis.

```
display(excel)
```

▸ (3) Spark Jobs

	SalesOrderID	CustomerID	OrderQty	ProductID	UnitPrice	LineTotal
1	71774	2	1	836	356.898	356.898
2	71774	3	1	822	356.898	356.898
3	71776	4	1	907	63.9	63.9
4	71780	5	4	905	218.454	873.816
5	71780	6	2	983	461.694	923.388
6	71780	7	6	988	112.998	406.7928
7	71780	10	2	748	818.7	1637.4

Showing all 542 rows.

***Figure 6-3.** Display of Excel data in tabular format*

The following PySpark code shows how to read the CSV file and load it to a data frame. With this method, there is no need to refer to the Spark Excel Maven library in the code.

```
csv=spark.read.format("csv")\
.option("header", "true")\
.option("inferSchema", "true")\
.load("/mnt/raw/dimdates.csv")
```

Figure 6-4 shows how the `display(csv)` command will then retrieve the results in a similar tabular format as the previous example.

```
display(csv)
```

▸ (1) Spark Jobs

	DateNum	Date	YearMonthNum	Calendar_Quarter	MonthNum	MonthName	MonthShortName
1	19910101	1/1/1991	199101	Qtr 1	1	January	Jan
2	19910102	1/2/1991	199101	Qtr 1	1	January	Jan
3	19910103	1/3/1991	199101	Qtr 1	1	January	Jan
4	19910104	1/4/1991	199101	Qtr 1	1	January	Jan
5	19910105	1/5/1991	199101	Qtr 1	1	January	Jan
6	19910106	1/6/1991	199101	Qtr 1	1	January	Jan
7	19910107	1/7/1991	199101	Qtr 1	1	January	Jan

Truncated results, showing first 1000 rows.

***Figure 6-4.** Display of CSV data in tabular format*

To take the use case a step further, notice from the following sample PySpark code that you have the option to select the content from a CSV file and write it to an Excel file with the help of the Spark Excel Maven library.

```
csv.select("*").write.format('com.crealytics.spark.excel')\
.option("header","true")\
.option("inferSchema","true")\
.save('/mnt/raw/dimdate.xlsx',mode="overwrite")
```

Sure enough, after the code successfully completes running, notice from Figure 6-5 that a new dimdate.xlsx file has been created in your ADLS gen2 account.

dimdate.xlsx	Hot (inferred)
dimdates.csv	Hot (inferred)
Orders.xlsx	Hot (inferred)

Figure 6-5. *Excel file has been created in ADLS gen2*

To further display the contents of this new file, you could run the following PySpark code to read the Excel file into a data frame. Notice how this code to read an Excel file differs from the code to read a CSV file, since you will need to specify the Maven library in this code.

```
csv_to_xls=spark.read.format("com.crealytics.spark.excel")\
.option("header", "true")\
.option("inferSchema", "true")\
.load("/mnt/raw/dimdate.xlsx")
```

When you run the display(csv_to_xls) command, notice from Figure 6-6 that the Excel file now contains the same data as the CSV file.

```
display(csv_to_xls)
```

▸ (1) Spark Jobs

	DateNum	Date	YearMonthNum	Calendar_Quarter	MonthNum	MonthName
1	19910101	1/1/1991	199101	Qtr 1	1	January
2	19910102	1/2/1991	199101	Qtr 1	1	January
3	19910103	1/3/1991	199101	Qtr 1	1	January
4	19910104	1/4/1991	199101	Qtr 1	1	January
5	19910105	1/5/1991	199101	Qtr 1	1	January
6	19910106	1/6/1991	199101	Qtr 1	1	January
7	19910107	1/7/1991	199101	Qtr 1	1	January

Figure 6-6. *Display of the contents of new file*

The XlsxWriter is a Python module for writing text, numbers, formulas, and hyperlinks to multiple worksheets in an Excel (.xlsx) file. It supports highly customizable formatting and more. To install the XlsxWriter, run the pip install xlsxwriter within a cell of your Python notebook, and notice the messages that will be displayed, as shown in Figure 6-7, to confirm that it has been successfully installed.

```
pip install xlsxwriter
```

```
Python interpreter will be restarted.
Collecting xlsxwriter
  Downloading XlsxWriter-3.0.2-py3-none-any.whl (149 kB)
Installing collected packages: xlsxwriter
Successfully installed xlsxwriter-3.0.2
WARNING: You are using pip version 21.0.1; however, version 21.3.1 is available.
You should consider upgrading via the '/local_disk0/.ephemeral_nfs/envs/pythonEnv-
upgrade pip' command.
Python interpreter will be restarted.
```

Figure 6-7. *Code to install xlswriter*

Once installed, you will be able to import the xlsxwriter by using PySpark code similar to the following. You can then write custom PySpark code to extract, transform, and load data within your Excel file.

```
import xlsxwriter
from shutil import copyfile
```

```
workbook = xlsxwriter.Workbook("/mnt/raw/Orders.xlsx")
worksheet = workbook.add_worksheet()
worksheet.write(0, 0, "Key")
worksheet.write(0, 1, "Value")
workbook.close()

copyfile('/mnt/raw/Orders.xlsx', '/mnt/raw/dimdate.xlsx')
```

XML

When working with XML files in Databricks, you will need to install the `com.databricks - spark-xml_2.12` Maven library onto the cluster, as shown in Figure 6-8. Search for spark.xml in the Maven Central Search section. Once installed, any notebooks attached to the cluster will have access to this installed library.

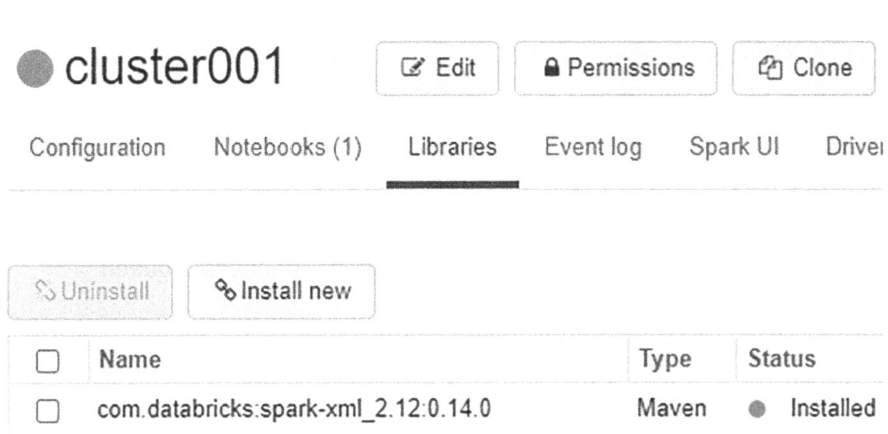

***Figure 6-8.** Display of installed Spark XML Maven library*

After you install the XML library, you'll need to ensure that your xml data file is uploaded to your ADLS gen2 account which is mounted to your Databricks workspace. The following code shows a few sample records of the XML file books.xml that is used in this example. This is a Microsoft sample file that can be found here: `https://docs.microsoft.com/en-us/previous-versions/windows/desktop/ms762271(v=vs.85)`.

In addition, you can find another sample xml file related to Purchase Orders here: https://docs.microsoft.com/en-us/dotnet/standard/linq/sample-xml-file-multiple-purchase-orders

```
<?xml version="1.0"?>
<catalog>
   <book id="bk101">
      <Author>LEsteve, Ron</author>
      <title>The Definitive Guide to Azure Data Engineering</title>
      <genre>Computer</genre>
      <price>44.95</price>
      <publish_date>2020-08-01</publish_date>
      <description>Modern ELT, DevOps, and Analytics on the Azure Cloud
      Platform.</description>
   </book>
   <book id="bk102">
      <Author>Ralls, Kim</author>
      <title>Midnight Rain</title>
      <genre>Fantasy</genre>
      <price>5.95</price>
      <publish_date>2000-12-16</publish_date>
      <description>A former architect battles corporate zombies,
      an evil sorceress, and her own childhood to become queen
      of the world.</description>
   </book>
   <book id="bk103">
      <Author>Corets, Eva</author>
      <title>Maeve Ascendant</title>
      <genre>Fantasy</genre>
      <price>5.95</price>
      <publish_date>2000-11-17</publish_date>
      <description>After the collapse of a nanotechnology
      society in England, the young survivors lay the
      foundation for a new society.</description>
   </book>
</catalog>
```

After your xml file is loaded to your ADLS gen2 account, run the following PySpark script shown in Figure 6-9 to read the xml file into a data frame and display the results. Notice that the format is not tabular, as expected, because we have not yet integrated the Spark xml package into the code.

```
df=spark.read.text("/mnt/raw/books.xml")
display(df)
```

▸ (1) Spark Jobs

▸ df: pyspark.sql.dataframe.DataFrame = [value: string]

	value
1	<?xml version="1.0"?>
2	<catalog>
3	<book id="bk101">
4	<author>LEsteve, Ron</author>
5	<title>The Definitive Guide to Azure Data Engineering</title>
6	<genre>Computer</genre>
7	<price>44.95</price>

***Figure 6-9.** Code to read XML data as text*

Here is the PySpark code that you will need to run to recreate the results shown in Figure 6-9:

```
df=spark.read.text("/mnt/raw/books.xml")
display(df)
```

Next, run the following PySpark code that loads your xml file into a data frame using the previously installed Spark xml maven package and displays the results in tabular format, as shown in Figure 6-10.

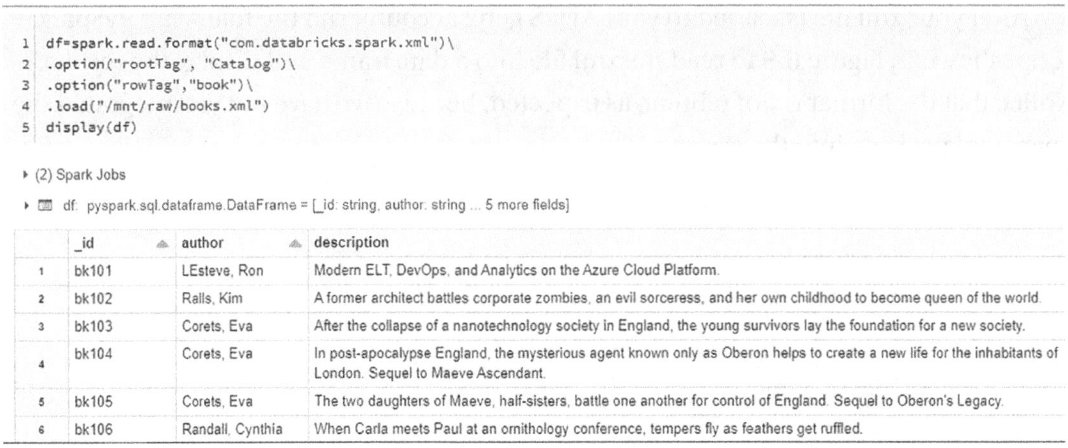

```
df=spark.read.format("com.databricks.spark.xml")\
.option("rootTag", "Catalog")\
.option("rowTag","book")\
.load("/mnt/raw/books.xml")
display(df)
```

▸ (2) Spark Jobs

▸ df: pyspark.sql.dataframe.DataFrame = [_id: string, author: string ... 5 more fields]

	_id	author	description
1	bk101	LEsteve, Ron	Modern ELT, DevOps, and Analytics on the Azure Cloud Platform.
2	bk102	Ralls, Kim	A former architect battles corporate zombies, an evil sorceress, and her own childhood to become queen of the world.
3	bk103	Corets, Eva	After the collapse of a nanotechnology society in England, the young survivors lay the foundation for a new society.
4	bk104	Corets, Eva	In post-apocalypse England, the mysterious agent known only as Oberon helps to create a new life for the inhabitants of London. Sequel to Maeve Ascendant.
5	bk105	Corets, Eva	The two daughters of Maeve, half-sisters, battle one another for control of England. Sequel to Oberon's Legacy.
6	bk106	Randall, Cynthia	When Carla meets Paul at an ornithology conference, tempers fly as feathers get ruffled.

Figure 6-10. *Code to load xml file into a data frame using Spark XML package*

Here is the PySpark code that you will need to run to recreate the results shown in Figure 6-10. rowTag is the row tag to treat as a row, and rootTag is the root tag to treat as the root.

```
df=spark.read.format("com.databricks.spark.xml")\
.option("rootTag", "Catalog")\
.option("rowTag","book")\
.load("/mnt/raw/books.xml")
display(df)
```

With this next block of PySpark code, you will be able to use the Spark xml package to write the results of the data frame back to an xml file called booksnew.xml:

```
df.select("*").write.format('com.databricks.spark.xml')\
.option("rootTag", "Catalog")\
.option("rowTag","book")\
.save('/mnt/raw/booksnew.xml',mode="overwrite")
```

Finally, you could also create a SQL table using the following syntax which specifies the xml format, xml file path, and rowTag. With this table created, you'll be able to write SQL scripts to query your xml data in tabular format.

```
%sql
CREATE TABLE books
USING xml
```

```
OPTIONS (path "/mnt/raw/books.xml", rowTag "book");
SELECT * FROM books;
```

JSON

There are numerous scenarios where you may need to read and write JSON data stored within your ADLS gen2 account from Databricks notebook. The following code json=spark.read.json('/mnt/raw/Customer1.json') defines a data frame based on reading a json file from your mounted ADLS gen2 account. When the display(json) command is run within a cell of your notebook, notice from Figure 6-11 that the results are displayed in tabular format.

```
display(json)
```

▸ (1) Spark Jobs

	FirstName	LastName	MiddleName	Title	customerid
1	Orlando	Gee	N.	Mr.	1
2	Keith	Harris	null	Mr.	2
3	Donna	Carreras	F.	Ms.	3
4	Janet	Gates	M.	Ms.	4
5	Lucy	Harrington	null	Mr.	5
6	Rosmarie	Carroll	J.	Ms.	6
7	Dominic	Gash	P.	Mr.	7

Showing all 847 rows.

***Figure 6-11.** JSON data displayed in tabular format*

For reference, here are the first three rows of the Customer1 file to show the structure of the json format:

```
{"customerid":1,"Title":"Mr.","FirstName":"Orlando","MiddleName":"N.","Last
Name":"Gee"}
{"customerid":2,"Title":"Mr.","FirstName":"Keith","LastName":"Harris"}
{"customerid":3,"Title":"Ms.","FirstName":"Donna","MiddleName":"F.",
"LastName":"Carreras"}
```

This next block of code is SQL syntax which can also be run within your Python notebook by specifying the %sql command in the beginning of the script. With the following scripts, you will be able to create a temporary SQL view of the json format data. You could then write SQL statements to query the view just as you would a regular SQL table to retrieve the results in tabular format.

```
%sql
CREATE TEMPORARY VIEW json_table
USING json
OPTIONS (path "/mnt/raw/Customer1.json")
```

```
%sql
SELECT * FROM json_table
WHERE customerid>5
```

In the next scenario, you can read multiline json data using simple PySpark commands. First, you'll need to create a json file containing multiline data, as shown in the following code. This code will create a multiline.json file within your mounted ADLS gen2 account.

```
dbutils.fs.put("/mnt/raw/multiline.json", """
[
    {"string":"string1","int":1,"array":[0,1,2],"key/value": {"key":
    "value1"}},
    {"string":"string2","int":2,"array":[3,4,5],"key/value": {"key":
    "value2"}},
    {"string":"string2","int":2,"array":[6,7,8],"key/value": {"key":
    "value2"}}
]""",True)
```

After the file is created, you can read the file by running the following script: `multiline_json=spark.read.option('multiline',"true").json("/mnt/raw/multiline.json")`. After that, the `display(multiline_json)` command will retrieve the multiline json data with the capability of expanding the data within each row, as shown in Figure 6-12.

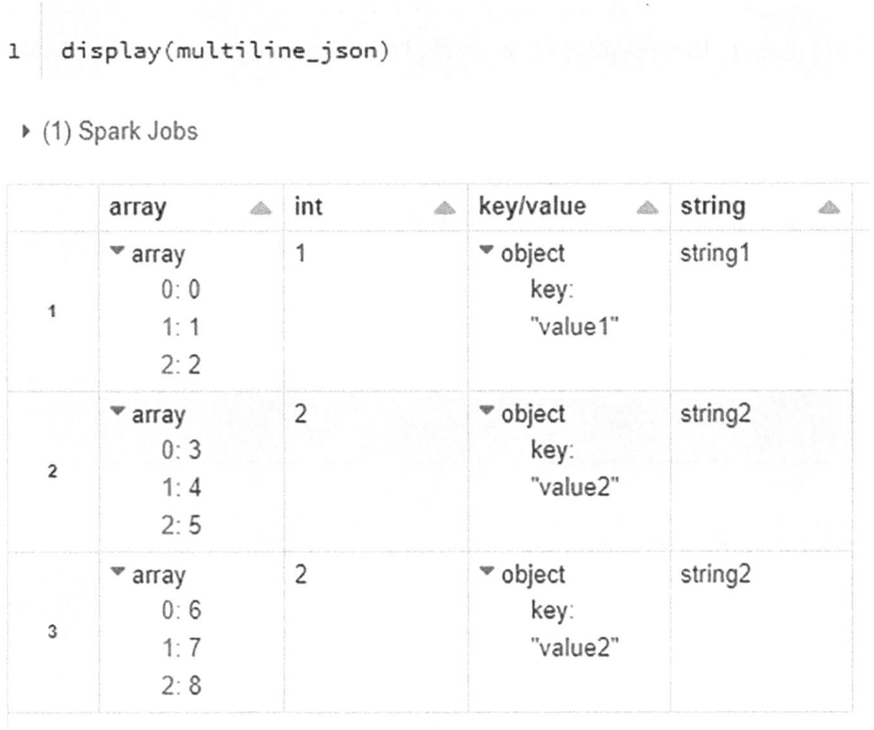

```
display(multiline_json)
```

▸ (1) Spark Jobs

	array	int	key/value	string
1	▾ array 0: 0 1: 1 2: 2	1	▾ object key: "value1"	string1
2	▾ array 0: 3 1: 4 2: 5	2	▾ object key: "value2"	string2
3	▾ array 0: 6 1: 7 2: 8	2	▾ object key: "value2"	string2

Figure 6-12. *Display of multiline JSON in notebook*

Let's go over one last JSON-based scenario which would allow you to create a Resilient Distributed Dataset (RDD), which is a collection of elements that are partitioned across nodes of a cluster that can be operated on in parallel. In the following code shown, you would store the JSON object per string in a data frame, create an RDD using the sc.parallelize command, and finally you'll be able to read the data:

```
# RDD[String] storing a JSON object per string
data = ['{"booktitle":"The Azure Data Lakehouse Toolkit","author":{"firstna
me":"Ron","lastname":"LEsteve"}}']
rdd = sc.parallelize(data)
df = spark.read.json(rdd)
df.printSchema()
```

Since the data has been displayed in a multiline format, shown in Section 1 of Figure 6-13, you can run the following command: `display(df.select("booktitle","author.firstname","author.lastname"))` to select the fields that you want to display in tabular format, shown in Section 2 of Figure 6-13.

Alternatively, you can run this command to display the print format results shown in Section 3 of Figure 6-13: `df.select("booktitle","author.firstname","author.lastname").show()`

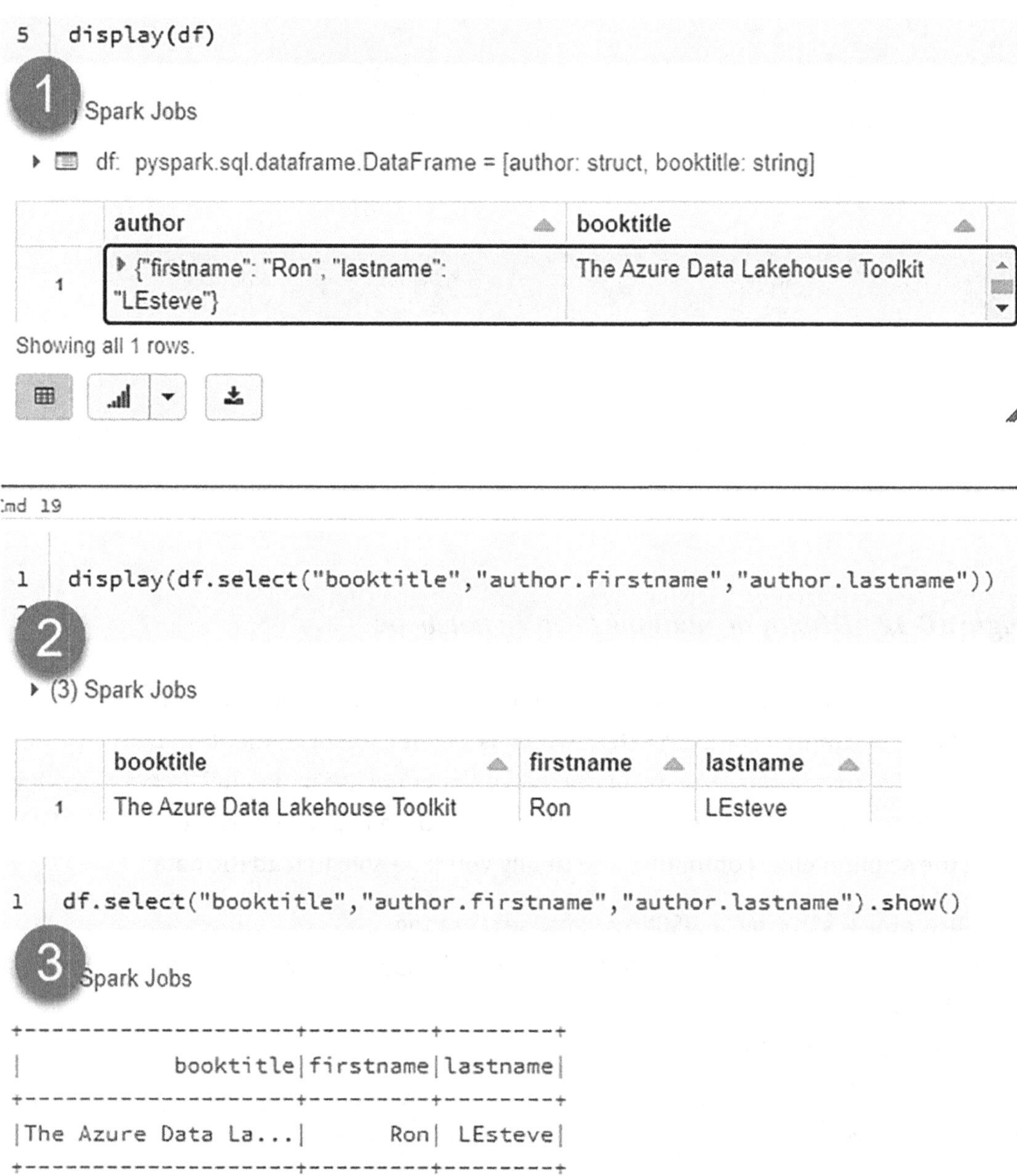

Figure 6-13. *Multi-view display of JSON data and fields*

ZIP

Reading ZIP files from a URL and downloading them both locally within your Databricks notebook and into your ADLS gen2 mounted container is a capability by importing the urllib package into your notebook code. Simply run the following code and specify the URL link to your zip data. Also, note that you will not need to run the pip install command. The second part of the code will use the %sh magic command to unzip the zip file. When you use %sh to operate on files, the results are stored in the directory/ databricks/driver. Before you load the file using the Spark API, you can move the file to DBFS using Databricks utilities. The last block of code in this section of the script will list the files stored in the databricks/driver directory.

```
#Code to import the urllib package and read the contents of the specified
URL zip file.
import urllib
urllib.request.urlretrieve("https://resources.lendingclub.com/LoanStats3a.
csv.zip", "/tmp/LoanStats3a.csv.zip")

#Code the unzip the url zip file
%sh
unzip /tmp/LoanStats3a.csv.zip
tail -n +2 LoanStats3a.csv > temp.csv
rm LoanStats3a.csv

#Code to list the files in the folder
%fs ls file:/databricks/driver/
```

Notice from Figure 6-14 that the temp.csv file exists in `/databricks/driver/`.

```
%fs ls file:/databricks/driver/
```

	path	name	size
1	file:/databricks/driver/preload_class.lst	preload_class.lst	813069
2	file:/databricks/driver/conf/	conf/	4096
3	file:/databricks/driver/ganglia/	ganglia/	4096
4	file:/databricks/driver/eventlogs/	eventlogs/	4096
5	file:/databricks/driver/temp.csv	temp.csv	42408110
6	file:/databricks/driver/logs/	logs/	4096

***Figure 6-14.** Display of Databricks driver where CSV file was downloaded*

Finally, you can run the following script to move the file from the databricks/driver folder to your mounted ADLS gen2 account. The second section of the code will load the unzipped CSV file into a data frame and display it. The final code in this section shows an option for running the %sh magic command to unzip a .zip file, when needed.

```
#Code to move the file from databricks/driver folder to your mounted
ADLSgen2 account.
dbutils.fs.mv("file:/databricks/driver/temp.csv", "/mnt/raw/
LoanStats3a.csv")

#Code to load the unzipped csv file in your ADLSgen2 account into a
dataframe.
df = spark.read.format("csv").option("inferSchema", "true").
option("header","true").load("/mnt/raw/LoanStats3a.csv")
display(df)

#Option for unzipping a zip file in your ADLSgen2 account
%sh
unzip mnt/raw/emp.zip
```

Figure 6-15 depicts the display of the tabular results of the unzipped data which has been loaded into a data frame.

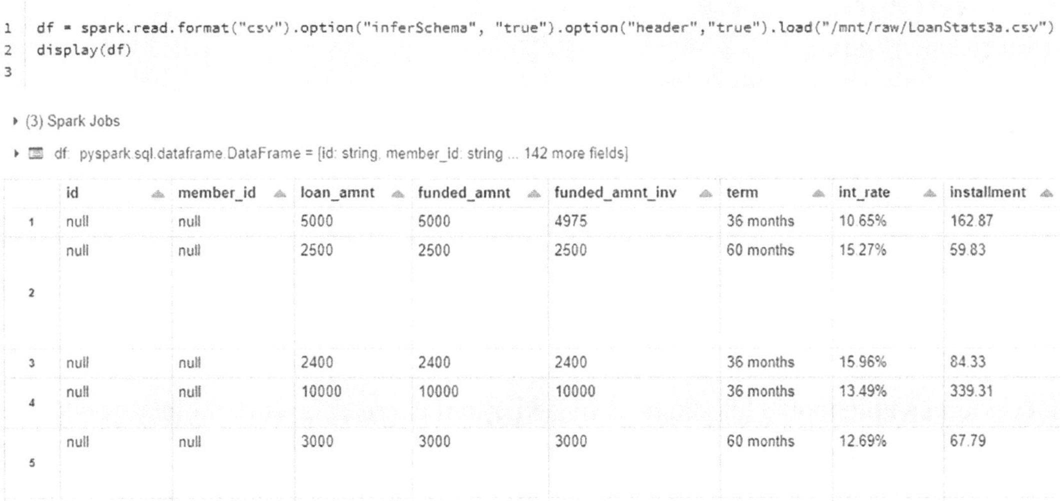

```
df = spark.read.format("csv").option("inferSchema", "true").option("header","true").load("/mnt/raw/LoanStats3a.csv")
display(df)
```

▸ (3) Spark Jobs

▸ df: pyspark.sql.dataframe.DataFrame = [id: string, member_id: string ... 142 more fields]

	id	member_id	loan_amnt	funded_amnt	funded_amnt_inv	term	int_rate	installment
1	null	null	5000	5000	4975	36 months	10.65%	162.87
2	null	null	2500	2500	2500	60 months	15.27%	59.83
3	null	null	2400	2400	2400	36 months	15.96%	84.33
4	null	null	10000	10000	10000	36 months	13.49%	339.31
5	null	null	3000	3000	3000	60 months	12.69%	67.79

Figure 6-15. *Code to read CSV file downloaded from a URL and unzipped*

Scala

Oftentimes, developers may choose to write their code in Scala since it is also object oriented like Python and is ten times faster than Python due to its static type language. Some developers may find it easier and more user-friendly to use than Python. Also, Scala handles concurrency and parallelism very well, while Python doesn't support true multi-threading. All that being said, developers can switch between Scala, Python, SQL, and R languages within their notebooks by simply specifying the language by using the %scala magic command. Multiple languages can be combined in the same notebook by using this process. As an example, the following code will achieve the same goals as the PySpark script in the XML section, with a few obvious syntactical differences. This shows how both PySpark and Scala can achieve the same outcomes.

```
// Infer schema

import com.databricks.spark.xml._ // Add the DataFrame.read.xml() method

val df = spark.read
  .option("rowTag", "book")
  .xml("dbfs:/books.xml")
```

```
val selectedData = df.select("author", "_id")
selectedData.write
  .option("rootTag", "books")
  .option("rowTag", "book")
  .xml("dbfs:/newbooks.xml")
```

SQL

Through a few scenarios in this chapter, we have explored just how easy it is to write SQL code within a notebook. This can be achieved by either creating a new notebook with the default language set to SQL or by specifying the magic %sql command within cells of the notebook. Within the notebooks, Databricks uses ANSI standard SQL dialect by default which makes it much easier to migrate your on-premises SQL workloads to the Lakehouse. Furthermore, with SQL, you can query JSON as well as create user-defined functions (UDFs). The following code shows how to query nested json format data using SQL:

```
SELECT
  book:bookid.author,
  book:bookid.title,
  book:bookid.genre,
FROM book;
```

SQL UDFs are easy to create as either temporary or permanent functions that can be reused across queries, and they allow developers to extend and customize SQL code in Databricks. They simplify the process of creating queries through better readability and modularity. As an example, they can be used to simplify the creation of complex scripts for PII data masking and much more. The following code shows an example of how a function could be created to return the max number of books sold for a specified book ID:

```
/* function to return max amount of books sold
** for the specified book_id
*/

CREATE FUNCTION udf_max_copies_sold_for_title (@book_id CHAR(6))
RETURNS INT
```

```
AS
BEGIN
DECLARE @qty INT
-- initialize the variable at 0:
SELECT @qty = 0

SELECT
    @qty = MAX(qty)
FROM sales
WHERE
book_id = @book_id

/* If there are no books sold for book_id specified
** then return 0:
*/
RETURN ISNULL(@qty, 0)

END
```

As we wrap up this section, it is important to mention that similar to SQL UDFs, Python (https://docs.microsoft.com/en-us/azure/databricks/spark/latest/spark-sql/udf-python), Scala (https://docs.microsoft.com/en-us/azure/databricks/spark/latest/spark-sql/udf-scala), and Pandas (https://docs.microsoft.com/en-us/azure/databricks/spark/latest/spark-sql/udf-python-pandas), UDFs can also be registered and invoked within your Databricks notebook when needed. The sample links provided in this section include sample code for creating, calling, and using Python, Scala, and Pandas UDFs in data frames. These code samples demonstrate the vast multilingual capabilities of Databricks.

Optimizing Performance

In Section 5 and in Chapters 12 through 16 of this book, you will learn more about performance optimization techniques for your Lakehouse platform. When running big data workloads on predefined Apache Spark clusters, you can investigate the cluster configuration by looking at the Ganglia Dashboard, as shown in Figure 6-16. This dashboard will help with the analysis of whether the cluster configurations are right sized based on memory, CPU, and server load distribution on the cluster. The Ganglia Dashboard can be accessed from the Metrics tab within your Databricks Cluster.

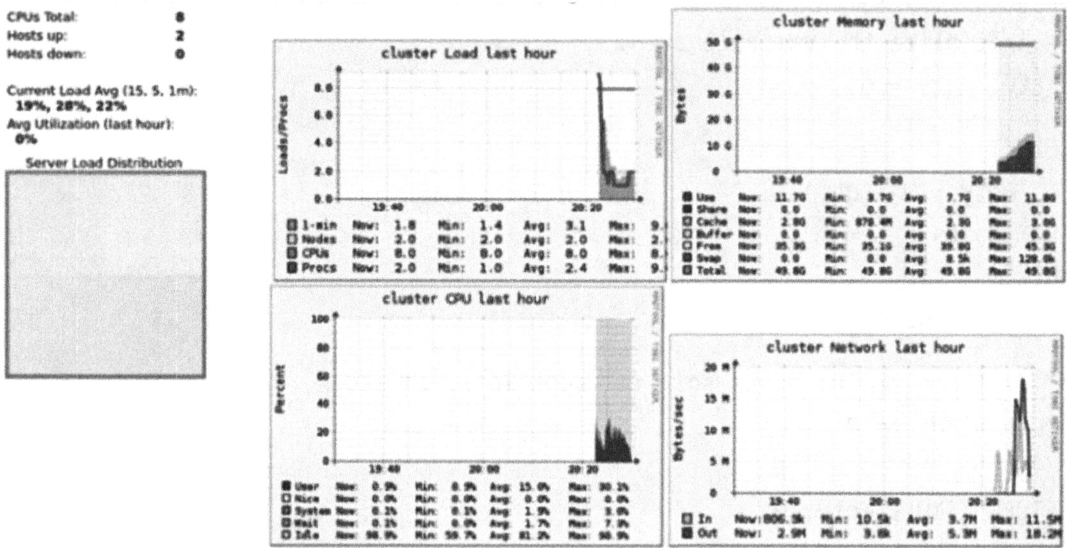

Figure 6-16. *Ganglia Dashboard showing memory, CPU, and load on cluster*

When writing notebook code, Apache Spark optimization tips and techniques will be key for highly performant workloads. Always ensure that you have an optimal partitioning design that avoids small files resulting in too many small partitions, which leads to significant overhead than required for processing the small tasks. Also, avoid extremely large partitions by repartitioning before a large shuffle operation as well as after the transformations occur. If your Spark Executors are idle for a long period of time, consider using the dynamic allocation commands `spark.dynamicAllocation.enabled = True \ spark.dynamicAllocation.minExecutors=n \ spark.dynamicAllocation.maxExecutors=n` to release Executors back into the cluster pool if they meet the specified idle time. For performance associated with sums and counts, know when to use the following functions instead of the standard groupByKey():

1. **groupByKey**: This key may cause "out of disk problems" as data is sent over the network and collected on the reduced workers. The Syntax for a standard groupByKey may look like this:

```
sparkContext.textFile("hdfs://")
                    .flatMap(line => line.split(" ") )
                    .map(word => (word,1))
```

```
                    .groupByKey()
                    .map((x,y) => (x,sum(y)))
```

2. **reduceByKey**: Use when you need to group by a key on a partitioned or distributed dataset to aggregate values for each key. Data are combined at each partition, with only one output for one key at each partition to send over the network. The following code shows an example of reduceByKey:

```
sparkContext.textFile("hdfs://")
                    .flatMap(line => line.split(" "))
                    .map(word => (word,1))
                    .reduceByKey((x,y)=> (x+y))
```

3. **combineByKey**: Use when you need to group by a key on a partitioned or distributed dataset to aggregate values for each key with different inputs and outputs for the "reduce" functions. The following code shows an example of combineByKey:

```
val result = rdd.combineByKey(
                        (v) => (v,1),
                        ( (acc:(Int,Int),v) => acc._1 +v , acc._2 +1 ) ,
                        ( acc1:(Int,Int),acc2:(Int,Int) =>
                        (acc1._1+acc2._1) , (acc1._2+acc2._2))
                        ).map( { case (k,v) => (k,v._1/v._2.toDouble) })
        result.collect.foreach(println)
```

4. **foldByKey**: Use when you need to aggregate values based on keys to perform an operation which yields a zero value. The following code shows an example of foldByKey:

```
val Scores = Array(("Ron", 90.0), ("Cayden", 100.0), ("Christina", 93.0),
("Ron", 95.0), ("Cayden", 70.0), ("Dee", 98.0))
val scoreData = sc.parallelize(Scores).cache()

scoreData.foldByKey(0)(_+_).collect
```

Summary

Writing custom code within your Lakehouse's unified data and analytics platform is a capability with both Databricks and Synapse Analytics. In this chapter, you learned more about how to use the built-in Apache Spark APIs for writing custom code in PySpark, Scala, and SQL for your Lakehouse ELT jobs. We discussed how to read and write functional PySpark code in your Databricks notebook to read and write Excel, JSON, XML, and URL Zip source data files that are stored in your ADLS gen2 account. Some of these data sources require the installation of Maven libraries onto your cluster. You also learned about how to use Scala and SQL user-defined functions when needed. All of these capabilities for writing custom code in notebooks with your unified data and analytics platform of choice open up the possibilities for work and customizing your ELT workloads for a variety of source data types.

PART IV

Delta Lake

CHAPTER 7

Schema Evolution

For ELT scenarios where the schema of the data is constantly evolving, you may be seeking a method for accommodating these schema changes through schema evolution features available in Azure Databricks. Frequently, customers are interested in learning more about the features of schema evolution that are available in Azure Databricks and how they can get started with building notebooks and writing code that can accommodate evolving schemas.

Since every data frame in Apache Spark contains a schema, when it is written to a Delta Lake in delta format, the schema is saved in JSON format in the transaction logs. This allows for a few neat capabilities and features such as schema validation, to ensure quality data by rejecting writes to a table that do not match the table's schema and schema evolution, which allows users to easily change a table's current schema to accommodate data that may be changing over time. It is commonly used when performing an append or overwrite operation to automatically adapt the schema to include one or more new columns. In this chapter, you will explore schema evolution capabilities and limitations with regular parquet format and explore schema evolution features and capabilities through delta format with appends and overwrites. If you are interested in following along with this example, simply create a new Python Databricks notebook and ensure that your ADLS gen2 account is mounted and that you have a running cluster.

R. L'Esteve, *The Azure Data Lakehouse Toolkit*, https://doi.org/10.1007/978-1-4842-8233-5_7

Schema Evolution Using Parquet Format

Before beginning to explore the features of schema evolution with delta format, let's understand how schema evolution applies to regular parquet files in Data Lake Storage Gen2 and what some of the limitations are. In the following Python code, a data frame containing two new columns along with sample values are created:

```
df1 = spark.createDataFrame(
    [
        (100,2019), # create your data here, be consistent in the types.
        (101,2019),
    ],
    ['newCol1', 'Year'] # add your columns label here
)
display(df1)
```

The final display() command will show the data within the data frame, as shown in Figure 7-1.

***Figure 7-1.** Display of df1 results with the new columns*

The next code would write the data frame to a parquet file within a mounted Azure Data Lake Storage Gen2 account and display the contents of the parquet file. A path would look similar to the first command of the following script. You'll need to alter your file path to your specific mount point. File paths can also be specified directly, similar to the following, "dbfs:/mnt/data/raw/evolution/file.parquet", in place of parquetpath shown in the following code:

```
# Specify parquet file path

parquetpath = "abfss://data@rl001adls2.dfs.core.windows.net/raw/delta/
schema_evolution/parquet"

# Write the data frame to the specified parquet path and show the contents
of the parquet file

(
df1
  .write
  .format("parquet")
  .save("parquetpath")
)
spark.read.parquet(parquetpath).show()
```

The objective of this test is to try to append two new columns to the existing data, which can be achieved by first creating a data frame containing the two new columns. This can be achieved by running the following Python code in a cell within your notebook:

```
df2 = spark.createDataFrame(
    [
        (200,300), # create your data here, be consistent in the types.
        (201,301),
    ],
    ['newCol2', 'newCol3'] # add your columns label here
)
display(df2)
```

Figure 7-2 shows the results of the display(df2) command. Notice that the new columns now exist.

	newCol2	newCol3
1	200	300
2	201	301

***Figure 7-2.** Display of df2 results containing new columns*

The following code is intended to append the new data frame containing the new columns to the existing parquet path:

```
df2.write.mode("append").parquet(parquetpath)
spark.read.parquet(parquetpath).show()
```

Notice from the results shown in Figure 7-3 that the new columns were created; however, schema evolution was not accounted for since the old columns were overwritten despite the fact that we specified "append" mode. Additionally, no errors were displayed using this method to either prevent or notify the error prior to the changes being incorporated.

```
df2.write.mode("append").parquet(parquetpath)
spark.read.parquet(parquetpath).show()

+-------+-------+
|newCol2|newCol3|
+-------+-------+
|    200|    300|
|    201|    301|
|   null|   null|
|   null|   null|
+-------+-------+
```

***Figure 7-3.** Python script to write the new columns to ADLS gen2*

There are fundamental limitations of regular parquet format files and schemas, and as a result, we will need to leverage delta format for true schema evolution features.

There are various other methods, as shown in the following list, for handling bad files or records in Spark when working with parquet format files after the spark.read command:

1. **Bad records path**: You'll need to specify the path to store exception files for recording the information about bad records. Network and IO exceptions will be ignored but logged in the badRecordsPath, and Spark will continue to run the tasks. Sample code: `.option("badRecordsPath", "/tmp/badRecordsPath")`

2. **Permissive mode**: Spark will load and process both the correct record and the corrupted records in a nontraditional way which may result in NULL values. Sample code: `.option("mode", "PERMISSIVE")`

3. **Drop malformed mode**: Spark completely ignores the bad or corrupted record when you use "Dropmalformed" mode. Sample code: `.option("mode", "DROPMALFORMED")`

4. **Failfast mode**: Spark throws an exception and halts the data loading process when it finds any bad or corrupted records. Sample code: `.option("mode", "FAILFAST")`

5. **Column name of corrupt record**: Spark will create the CORRUPTED column and add the corrupted records there. The corresponding correct column will contain NULLs for these values. Sample code: `df = spark.read.parquet('/mnt/file.parquet', enforceSchema=True, columnNameOfCorruptRecord='CORRUPTED')`

Schema Evolution Using Delta Format

Now that you have seen some of the limitations of schema evolution with the regular parquet file format, let's explore the capabilities of schema evolution with delta format. This section will build on the previous section where you created df1, df2, and the parquet file shown in the previous section. This section will specifically focus on Delta Schema Evolution features for appends and overwrites.

Append

Let's test the append features of Delta Lake along with the "merge schema" option using the following code within this section. The code will leverage the mergeSchema command and load data to the Delta path. Columns that are present in the DataFrame but missing from the table are automatically added as part of a write transaction when write or writeStream have ".option("mergeSchema", "true")."

```
(
df2
  .write
  .format("delta")
  .mode("append")
  .option("mergeSchema", "true")
  .save(deltapath)
)
spark.read.format("delta").load(deltapath).show()
```

From the results shown in Figure 7-4, notice the new columns that were created. Additionally, the existing columns were preserved in the schema and filled with nulls when no values were specified, which demonstrates schema evolution.

```
+-------+----+-------+-------+
|newCol1|Year|newCol2|newCol3|
+-------+----+-------+-------+
|   null|null|    200|    300|
|   null|null|    201|    301|
|    100|2019|   null|   null|
|    101|2019|   null|   null|
+-------+----+-------+-------+
```

***Figure 7-4.** Display of data frame results to add new columns in new Delta Table*

Schema auto merge can be enabled at the entire Spark session level by simply adding the following line of code at the beginning of your notebook in order to enable this feature before other code runs: `'spark.databricks.delta.schema.autoMerge.enabled = True'`. It is important to note that when both options are specified, the option from the

DataFrameWrite takes precedence. Also, schema enforcement will no longer warn you about unintended schema mismatches when enabled.

Other important considerations to note are that mergeSchema is not supported when table access control is enabled (as it elevates a request that requires MODIFY to one that requires ALL PRIVILEGES) and mergeSchema cannot be used with INSERT INTO or .write.insertInto().

Overwrite

This next example is intended to test the overwrite capabilities of delta formats when combined with mergeSchema = True by using the following code to overwrite the Delta Table with merge:

```
(
df3
  .write
  .format("delta")
  .mode("overwrite")
  .option("mergeSchema", "true")
  .save(deltapath)
)
spark.read.format("delta").load(deltapath).show()
```

The results in Figure 7-5 indicate that although the overwrite command worked and maintained the structure of the latest schema, it no longer displays any of the historical data and only shows the latest data frame that was written using overwrite mode combined with mergeSchema = True.

```
+-------+----+-------+-------+
|newCol1|Year|newCol2|newCol3|
+-------+----+-------+-------+
|    102|null|   null|    302|
|    103|null|   null|    303|
+-------+----+-------+-------+
```

Figure 7-5. *Display of data frame results to overwrite the Delta Table with merge*

Seeing some of the flaws of the previous code, let's also test this next block of code which again uses delta format; however, this time, let's use the overwriteSchema = True option combined with overwrite mode instead of mergeSchema. OverwriteSchema will address some limitations of mergeSchema such as the need to account for changing data types on the same columns (e.g., String to Integer). In this scenario, all parquet data files would need to be written. OverwriteSchema can account for dropping a column, changing the existing column's datatype, and/or renaming column names that only differ by case. In the following code, overwrite mode is used in combination with the overwriteSchema=true option:

```
(
df3
  .write
  .format("delta")
  .option("overwriteSchema", "true")
  .mode("overwrite")
  .save(deltapath)
)
spark.read.format("delta").load(deltapath).show()
```

Based on the results shown in Figure 7-6, notice that in this scenario, the entire schema was overwritten so that the old schema is no longer being displayed and only the newly written data frame is being displayed.

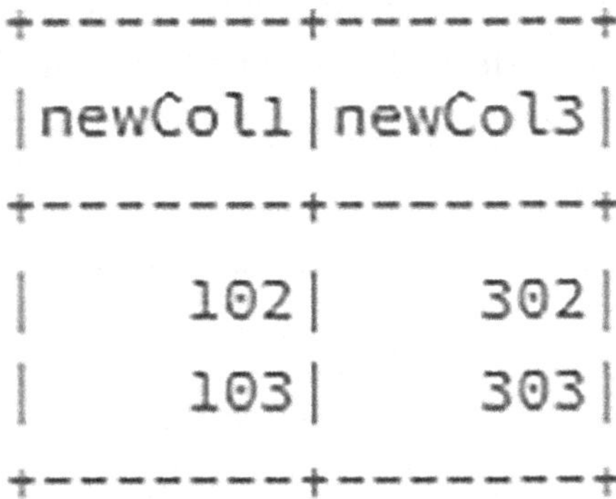

newCol1	newCol3
102	302
103	303

***Figure 7-6.** Data frame results from overwriting the Delta Table*

Summary

In this chapter, you learned more about the various Databricks-related schema evolution capabilities along with their limitations with regular parquet format. You also learned about how to explore schema evolution features and capabilities through delta format with inserts, appends, and overwrites. This opens up the possibility of building scalable and flexible Lakehouses that really take advantage of modern schema evolution features for both batch and streaming data of all volumes, varieties, and velocities.

CHAPTER 8

Change Data Feed

The introduction of the delta file format within Azure Data Lake Storage gen2 has been a modern approach to managing changing records and data since regular parquet file formats are immutable, and there is no graceful method of performing CRUD operations on these native parquet file formats. Despite the advantages of delta format files in the Data Lake, this Change Data Capture process also comes with significant overhead of having to scan and read the entire files even if only a few records within have changed. Change Data Feed within Databricks supplements this Change Data Capture (CDC) process by storing metadata about CDC records for optimized management of these changed records. Many engineers and architects are interested in learning how to get started with Delta Change Data Feed in Databricks.

Change Data Feed enables you to only read a Delta Table's change feed rather than the entire table to capture and manage changes. It requires you to manually enable a Delta Table's Change Data Feed properties and works with runtime versions of 8.2 and above. This configuration can be set at either the table for individual tables or cluster level for all tables associated with the cluster. Note that there is some additional overhead with capturing and storing additional CDC-related metadata. Change Data Feed supports batch and streaming data. In this chapter, you will learn how to implement a batch Change Data Feed process through an end-to-end exercise. Toward the end of the chapter, you will be introduced to a few streaming capabilities that could also leverage and be integrated with this Change Data Feed framework.

Create Database and Tables

The process of implementing Change Data Feed begins by creating a Databricks Cluster of 8.2 and then creating the required databases and tables with Change Data Feed enabled. For this scenario, you will learn how to create a staging table called OrdersSilver, where the Silver table is a staging table part of the Medallion

R. L'Esteve, *The Azure Data Lakehouse Toolkit*, https://doi.org/10.1007/978-1-4842-8233-5_8

Architecture coined by Databricks. The Bronze table is typically where the raw data resides, and the Gold table is the final consumption table. The OrdersSilver table has change feed enabled which will then propagate the changed records to a Gold table called OrdersGold, shown in Figure 8-1, which persists the aggregated, curated, and consumption-ready data. As a prerequisite, remember to mount your ADLS gen2 account within Databricks. You can refer back to Chapter 3 for more details on this process. Once you have created a cluster and SQL Databricks notebook, run the following script to create the database. Additionally, the script will drop tables that already exist in the database.

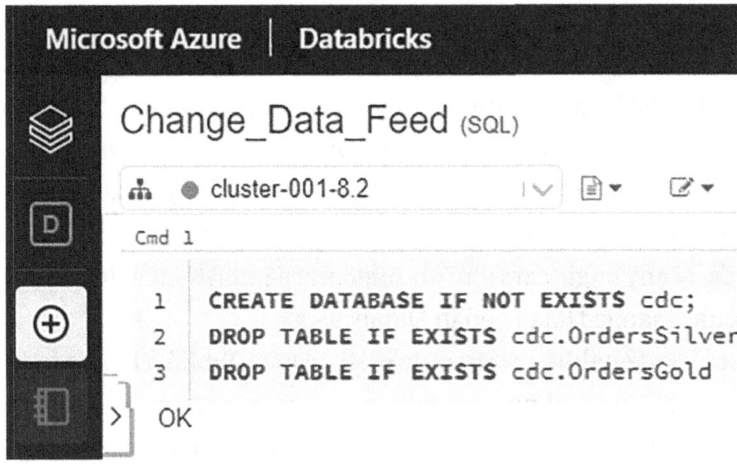

Figure 8-1. *Create the CDC database and drop any relevant tables*

Here is the script that you will need to run, as shown in Figure 8-1:

```
CREATE DATABASE IF NOT EXISTS cdc;
DROP TABLE IF EXISTS cdc.OrdersSilver
DROP TABLE IF EXISTS cdc.OrdersGold
```

Next, go ahead and create your OrdersSilver table by running the following script. Notice that the format is DELTA. Additionally, the table will be created in your Azure Data Lake Storage gen2 account which you will need to ensure it is properly mounted. Finally, notice that the table properties specify that this table must be enabled for "Change Data Feed."

```
CREATE TABLE cdc.OrdersSilver (
OrderID int,
```

```
UnitPrice int,
Quantity int,
Customer string
)
USING DELTA
LOCATION "/mnt/raw/OrdersSilver"
TBLPROPERTIES (delta.enableChangeDataFeed = true);
```

Once the Delta Table is created, notice from Figure 8-2 that it will exist within your ADLS gen2 account and will automatically have a delta_log associated with it.

Figure 8-2. *Delta OrdersSilver table in ADLS gen2*

Similarly, go ahead and create an OrdersGold table by running the following script. OrdersGold is also a Delta Table, but will not need change feed enabled since it is already enabled for the OrdersSilver table and the changes from that table will be propagated into this table. Notice also that this OrdersGold table will contain an OrderTotal column which is simply the UnitPrice * Quantity from the OrdersSilver table. The structure of this OrdersGold table is slightly different from the OrdersSilver table and is intended to be an aggregated, production-ready table.

```
CREATE TABLE cdc.OrdersGold (
OrderID int,
OrderTotal int,
Customer string
)
USING DELTA
LOCATION "/mnt/raw/OrdersGold"
```

As expected, once the OrdersGold Delta Table is created, it will appear within your ADLS gen2 account along with the associated delta_log folder, which can be seen in Figure 8-3.

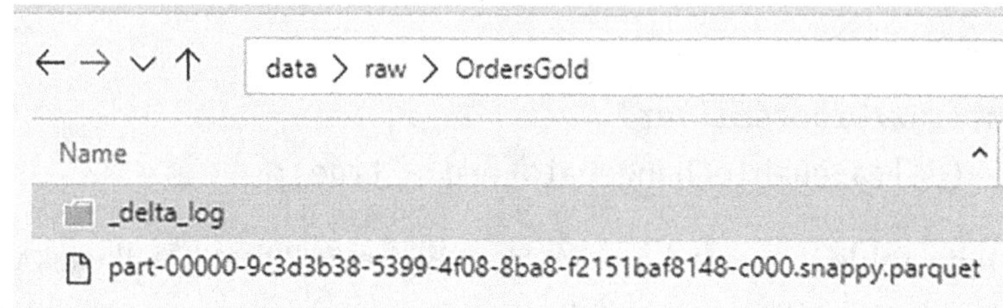

***Figure 8-3.** Delta gold table in the lake*

Insert Data into Tables

Now that you have created your Silver and Gold order tables, go ahead and run the following scriptto insert records into the OrdersSilver table:

```
INSERT INTO cdc.OrdersSilver
SELECT 1 OrderID, 96 as UnitPrice, 5 as Quantity, "A" as Customer
UNION
SELECT 2 OrderID, 450 as UnitPrice, 10 as Quantity, "B" as Customer
UNION
SELECT 3 OrderID, 134 as UnitPrice, 7 as Quantity, "C" as Customer
UNION
SELECT 4 OrderID, 847 as UnitPrice, 8 as Quantity, "D" as Customer
UNION
SELECT 5 OrderID, 189 as UnitPrice, 15 as Quantity, "E" as Customer;

SELECT * FROM cdc.OrdersSilver
```

Notice in Figure 8-4 that there are five records that will be inserted into the table.

	OrderID	UnitPrice	Quantity	Customer
1	1	96	5	A
2	3	134	7	C
3	5	189	15	E
4	2	450	10	B
5	4	847	8	D

Figure 8-4. *Insert some data to the OrdersSilver table*

Similarly, run the following scriptto insert data into the OrdersGold table:

```
INSERT INTO cdc.OrdersGold
SELECT OrderID, UnitPrice * Quantity AS OrderTotal, Customer FROM cdc.
OrdersSilver;

SELECT * FROM cdc.OrdersGold
```

Verify that the expected results match those shown in Figure 8-5.

	OrderID	OrderTotal	Customer
1	1	480	A
2	3	938	C
3	5	2835	E
4	2	4500	B
5	4	6776	D

Figure 8-5. *Insert some data to the OrdersGold table*

Change Data Capture

Since you have enabled Delta change feed in the prior steps of the OrdersSilver table, run the following script to create a temporary view which will show you the CDC-specific changes in relation to the OrdersSilver table. Notice that you also have the option to specify a range of versions. You could use this view at any point in time to retrieve a list of CDC changes for the OrdersSilver table.

```
CREATE OR REPLACE TEMPORARY VIEW latest_version as
SELECT *
    FROM
         (SELECT *, rank() over (partition by OrderID order by _commit_
         version desc) as rank
          FROM table_changes('cdc.OrdersSilver', 2, 5)
          WHERE _change_type !='update_preimage')
    WHERE rank=1
```

Now it's time to run some CRUD operations on your OrdersSilver table to demonstrate how changes are handled in relation to inserts, updates, and deletes. After running the update, insert, and delete scripts shown as follows on the OrdersSilver table, run the select statement included in the script to verify that the change type has been accurately executed:

```
UPDATE cdc.OrdersSilver SET Quantity = 20 WHERE OrderID = 1;
DELETE FROM cdc.OrdersSilver WHERE Customer = 'D';
INSERT INTO cdc.OrdersSilver SELECT 6 OrderID, 100 as UnitPrice, 10 as
Quantity, "F" as Customer;

SELECT * FROM table_changes('cdc.OrdersSilver', 2, 5) order by _commit_
timestamp;
```

Notice from the table_change metadata tracking table results shown in Figure 8-6, that update, delete, and insert operations were accurately captured along with relevant metadata.

▸ (17) Spark Jobs

	OrderID	UnitPrice	Quantity	Customer	_change_type	_commit_version	_commit_timestamp
1	1	96	5	A	update_preimage	2	2021-05-31T11:12:55.000+0000
2	1	96	20	A	update_postimage	2	2021-05-31T11:12:55.000+0000
3	4	847	8	D	delete	3	2021-05-31T11:12:57.000+0000
4	6	100	10	F	insert	4	2021-05-31T11:12:58.000+0000

Showing all 4 rows.

Figure 8-6. *Run the CRUD operations and view the table changes*

Once you have verified that the OrdersSilver has accurately captured the desired changes, run the following script to merge the changes from the OrdersSilver into the OrdersGold table using the latest_version view:

```
MERGE INTO cdc.OrdersGold og USING latest_version os ON og.OrderID =
os.OrderID
WHEN MATCHED AND os._change_type='update_postimage' THEN UPDATE SET
OrderTotal = os.UnitPrice * os.Quantity
WHEN MATCHED AND os._change_type='delete' THEN DELETE
WHEN NOT MATCHED THEN INSERT (OrderID, OrderTotal, Customer) VALUES (os.
OrderID, os.UnitPrice * os.Quantity, os.Customer)
```

After you run the script, notice in Figure 8-7 that there are three affected rows for the deleted, updated, and inserted rows.

▸ (10) Spark Jobs

	num_affected_rows	num_updated_rows	num_deleted_rows	num_inserted_rows
1	3	1	1	1

Showing all 1 rows.

Command took 3.58 seconds -- by ronlesteve at 5/31/2021, 6:14:06 AM on cluster-001-8.2

Figure 8-7. *Merge into and delete from OrdersGold table*

Once you have successfully run the script, notice in Figure 8-8 that the changes are accurately reflected in the OrdersGold table. This process has efficiently handled inserts, updates, and deletes as a result of the Delta change feed which was enabled on the OrdersSilver table.

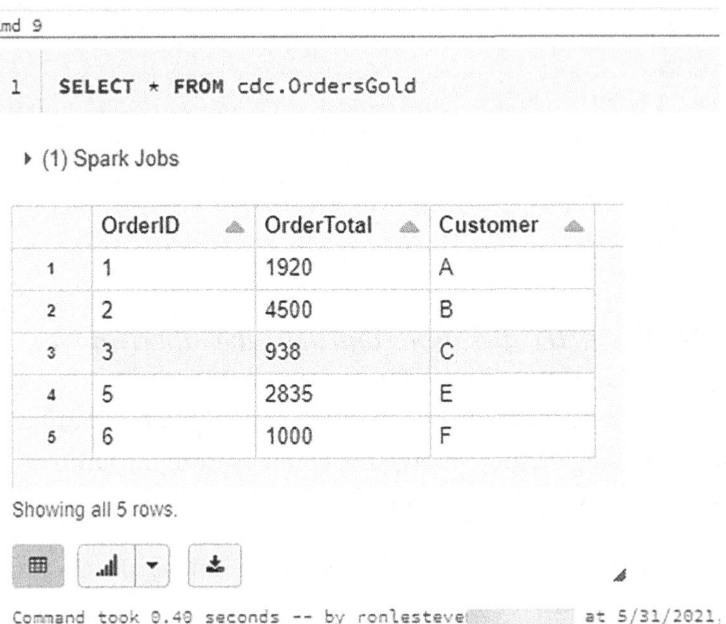

Figure 8-8. *Select and validate records in OrdersGold table*

It is important to also point out that once the Delta change feed is executed against the OrdersSilver, a new folder will appear in your ADLS gen2 Delta location, shown in Figure 8-9, which will begin capturing Delta change feed metadata.

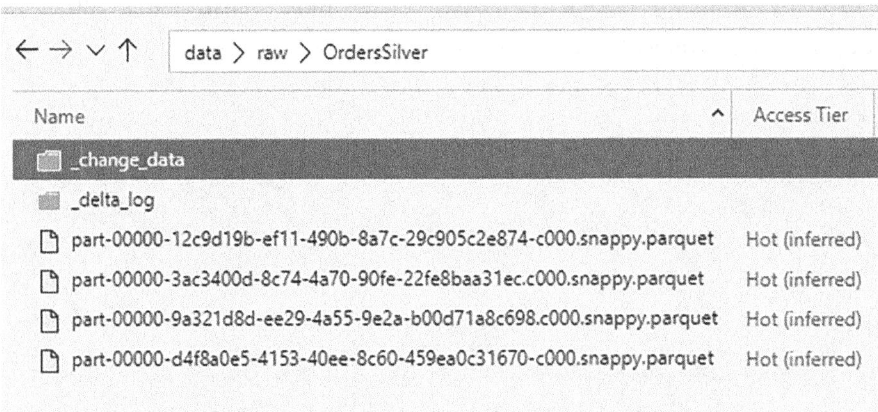

Figure 8-9. *Change data folder created in OrdersSilver table*

Notice from Figure 8-10 that the CDC-related files will begin populating in the _change_data folder. Files will be created as a result of CRUD operations that are performed against the OrdersSilver table. This additional process may create overhead and costs related to persisting CDC data in another folder. It will be important to assess whether the benefits outweigh the costs and overhead prior to progressing down this path.

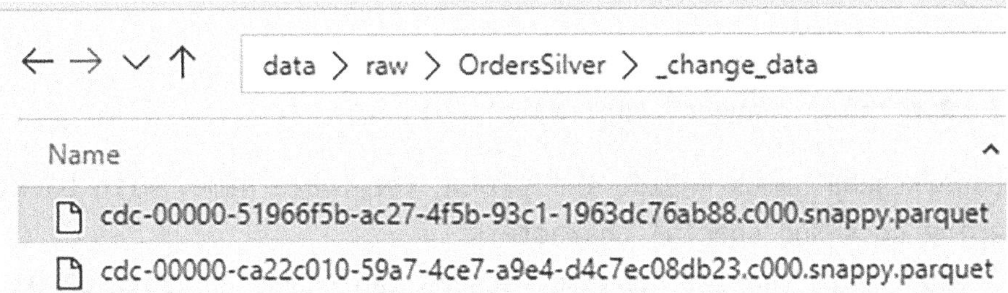

Figure 8-10. *CDC files created in OrdersSilver change_data folder*

Additionally, the _delta_log folder will also capture details related to CDC, as shown in Figure 8-11.

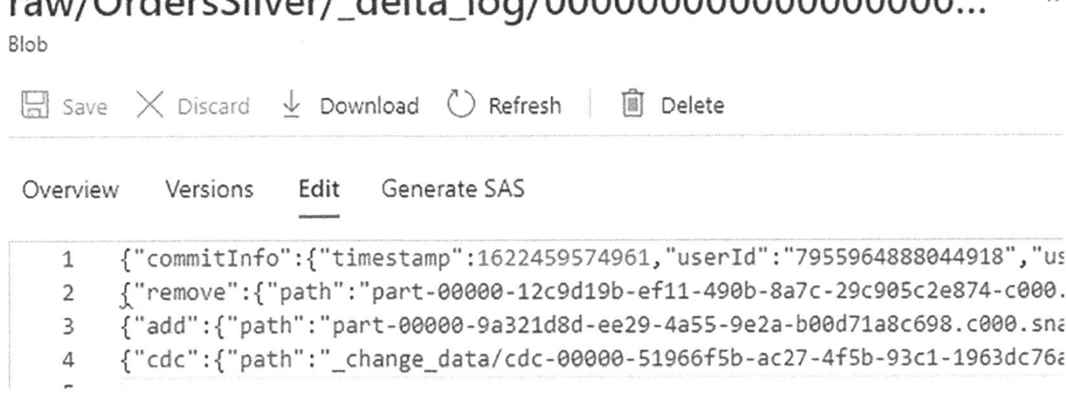

Figure 8-11. *File details for the OrdersSilver Delta logs*

You could run the following commands to read changes in batch queries:

```
-- version as ints or longs e.g. changes from version 0 to 10
SELECT * FROM table_changes('tableName', 0, 10)

-- timestamp as string formatted timestamps
SELECT * FROM table_changes('tableName', '2021-02-01 00:00:00', '2021-02-11
00:00:00')

-- providing only the startingVersion/timestamp
SELECT * FROM table_changes('tableName', 0)

-- database/schema names inside the string for table name, with backticks
for escaping dots and special characters
SELECT * FROM table_changes('dbName.`schema.tableName`', '2022-02-01
00:00:00' , '2022-02-11 00:00:00')

-- path based tables
SELECT * FROM table_changes_by_path('\path', '2022-02-11 00:00:00')
```

Once you finish this exercise, remember to drop the OrdersSilver and OrdersGold that you have created by running the script:

```
DROP TABLE cdc.OrdersSilver;
DROP TABLE cdc.OrdersGold;
```

Streaming Changes

Thus far, the Change Data Feed process described in this chapter could be applied to batch workloads. You might be asking how this can also be applied to a variety of streaming sources such as structured and unstructured data. With Spark's Structured Streaming capabilities, Azure Event Hubs can be configured through code within your Databricks notebook to stream real-time data into structured SQL tables. The velocity can be configured through triggers in the code. You can learn more about this process through a detailed step-by-step demonstration on my MSSQLTips article which can be found here: `www.mssqltips.com/sqlservertip/6781/real-time-iot-analytics-apache-sparks-structured-streaming-databricks-delta-lake/`. In Chapter 19 of this book, you will learn more about additional streaming capabilities that Databricks offers by using Auto Loader and advanced schema evolution functions.

As an example, you could read streaming data changes by running the following Python code:

```
# providing a starting version
spark.readStream.format("delta") \
  .option("readChangeFeed", "true") \
  .option("startingVersion", 0) \
  .table("myDeltaTable")

# providing a starting timestamp
spark.readStream.format("delta") \
  .option("readChangeFeed", "true") \
  .option("startingTimestamp", "2021-02-11 00:00:00") \
  .load("/pathToMyDeltaTable")

# not providing a starting version/timestamp will result in the latest
snapshot being fetched first
spark.readStream.format("delta") \
  .option("readChangeFeed", "true") \
  .table("myDeltaTable")
```

Summary

In this chapter, you learned how to get started with Databricks Delta Change Data Feed through an end-to-end exercise. You learned how to create a Delta Table with Change Data Feed enabled on a Silver table. Remember that you could also enable Change Data Feed at the cluster level as an alternative. You also learned how to create and track changes made to your Silver table and then propagate those changes into a Gold table. The table_changes from the Change Data Feed can be used to explore details related to the inserts, updates, and deletes. Additionally, you could create views and explore versions, timestamps, and granular details related to the table changes. This is an optimal process since it will not require you to read all data within your lake to identify changed records, and it is also compatible with streaming data, which supports the opportunity to design and implement highly scalable lambda architectural patterns using Delta Change Data Feed.

CHAPTER 9

Clones

With Azure Databricks 7.2 and above, there is now the capability of cloning data to create a copy of an existing Delta Table at a specified version by using the CLONE command. Many data engineers are interested in learning more about some of the features, benefits, and use cases of Deep and Shallow clones and how they can get started with using the CLONE command in Azure Databricks.

Clones have many use cases including data archiving, reproducing ML datasets, data sharing, and more. Additionally, clones can be either Deep or Shallow, and there are a few notable differences between the two. A Shallow clone does not copy the data files to clone the target, relies on the metadata as the source, and is cheaper to create. Deep clones will copy the source table data to the target location. From a streaming perspective, Deep clones have the capability of stopping any writes to the source Delta Table and continuing the writes to the cloned target location. In this chapter, you will learn practical examples of both Deep and Shallow clones, time travel, and versioning for clones. You will also learn how to read the Delta logs which capture Deep and Shallow cloning metrics.

Shallow Clones

A Shallow clone, also known as zero copy, duplicates the metadata of the table being cloned and does not copy the data files of the table. Databricks automatically runs a VACUUM operation on Spark tables as data is written. The VACUUM command recursively vacuums directories linked to the Spark table to remove uncommitted files older than a default of seven retention days. Since Shallow clones reference the original source data, if a VACUUM command is run on the original files, the Shallow clones may throw errors or become unusable. Recreating the clone will repair it. This makes Shallow clones good candidates for short experiments or testing use cases. Additionally, Shallow clones can be quickly shared with consumers without impacting cost for additional

R. L'Esteve, *The Azure Data Lakehouse Toolkit*, https://doi.org/10.1007/978-1-4842-8233-5_9

storage. Shallow clones are less costly to create since Deep clones create copies of both the data and metadata. In this section, you will learn how to create a Hive table called nyctaxi from the open source Databricks library called databricks-datasets which originally contained 400 files. By OPTIMIZE command on the table, it would optimize the layout of the Delta Lake files by condensing them into ten active files, as shown in the results of Figure 9-1. These are the ten files that will be used during the cloning process since they will be active in the table. The SQL script also includes the ZORDER command which automatically co-locates related information in the same set of files to reduce the amount of data that needs to be read. In Chapter 13, you will learn how to use the OPTIMIZE and Z-ORDER commands in greater detail.

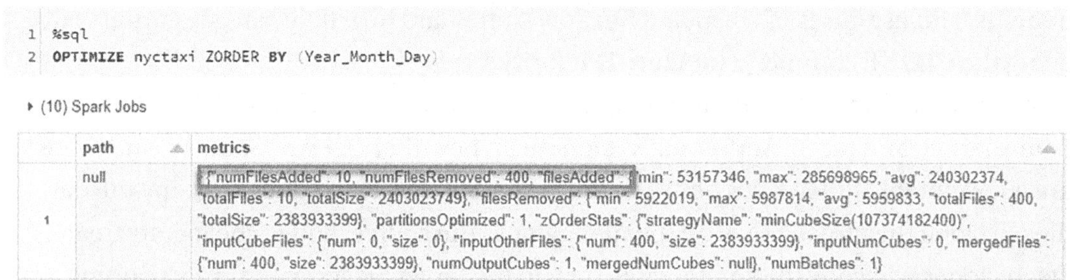

Figure 9-1. *Script to optimize the Hive table*

To confirm that you have data in the nyctaxi table, run the select statement shown in Figure 9-2 and verify the results.

```
%sql
SELECT *from nyctaxi
```

(1) Spark Jobs

	VendorID	tpep_pickup_datetime	tpep_dropoff_datetime	passenger_count	trip_distance	RatecodeID	store_and_fwd_flag	F
1	1	2019-03-16 12:39:36	2019-03-16 13:01:33	2	2.1	1	N	2
2	1	2019-03-30 12:10:06	2019-03-30 12:20:16	3	1.5	1	N	2
3	2	2019-03-12 08:13:05	2019-03-12 09:08:50	3	10.48	1	N	1
4	2	2019-03-11 18:31:13	2019-03-11 18:33:02	1	0.68	1	N	1
5	1	2019-03-27 22:25:47	2019-03-27 22:38:37	1	3.2	1	N	2
6	1	2019-03-27 08:22:36	2019-03-27 08:51:39	1	3.8	1	N	4
7	2	2019-03-05 10:21:25	2019-03-05 10:44:15	1	1.78	1	N	1
8	1	2019-03-03 11:13:05	2019-03-03 11:23:25	1	2.3	1	N	[illegible]

Figure 9-2. *Script to Select * from the nyctaxi data*

Next, you can run the following code to create the Shallow clone using the following which contains the SHALLOW CLONE command. Remember to mount your ADLS gen2 account from your Databricks notebook and include the verified file path in the following code. Remember that Chapter 3 contains detailed steps for mounting your ADLS gen2 account.

```
%sql
CREATE TABLE IF NOT EXISTS nyctaxi_shallow_clone
SHALLOW CLONE nyctaxi
LOCATION 'abfss://data@rl001adls2.dfs.core.windows.net/raw/delta/nyctaxi_
delta_Shallow_clone'
```

Within the code, there is also an option to specify the version with both Deep and Shallow clones so you can use this template for your particular use case as needed:

```
CREATE TABLE [IF NOT EXISTS] [db_name.]target_table
[SHALLOW | DEEP] CLONE [db_name.]source_table [<time_travel_version>]
[LOCATION 'path']
```

Next, run the following select SQL query to query the Shallow clone along with its source file:

```
%sql
SELECT *, input_file_name() FROM nyctaxi_shallow_clone
```

The results for the input_file_name() shown in Figure 9-3 indicate that the actual source file was not copied which goes back to our definition of Shallow clone, stating that it does not copy the data files to clone the target and only relies on the metadata as the source.

```
%sql
SELECT *, input_file_name() FROM nyctaxi_shallow_clone
```

(1) Spark Jobs

	Year_Month	Year_Month	Year_Month_Day	input_file_name()
1	201903	201903	20190316	abfss://data@rl001adls2.dfs.core.windows.net/raw/delta/nyctaxi_delta/Year=2019/part-00000-152b46ca-3fa8-4327-abe8-a98fd8695083.c000.snappy.parquet
2	201903	201903	20190330	abfss://data@rl001adls2.dfs.core.windows.net/raw/delta/nyctaxi_delta/Year=2019/part-00000-152b46ca-3fa8-4327-abe8-a98fd8695083.c000.snappy.parquet
3	201903	201903	20190312	abfss://data@rl001adls2.dfs.core.windows.net/raw/delta/nyctaxi_delta/Year=2019/part-00000-152b46ca-3fa8-4327-abe8-a98fd8695083.c000.snappy.parquet
4	201903	201903	20190311	abfss://data@rl001adls2.dfs.core.windows.net/raw/delta/nyctaxi_delta/Year=2019/part-00000-152b46ca-3fa8-4327-abe8-a98fd8695083.c000.snappy.parquet
	201903	201903	20190327	abfss://data@rl001adls2.dfs.core.windows.net/raw/delta/nyctaxi_delta/Year=2019/part-00000-152b46ca-3fa8-4327-abe8-

Showing the first 1000 rows.

***Figure 9-3.** Script to Select * from the nyctaxi Shallow clone*

Additionally, since no source data operations are confirmed, there are no physical files in the nyctaxi_delta_Shallow_clone folder, as shown in Figure 9-4.

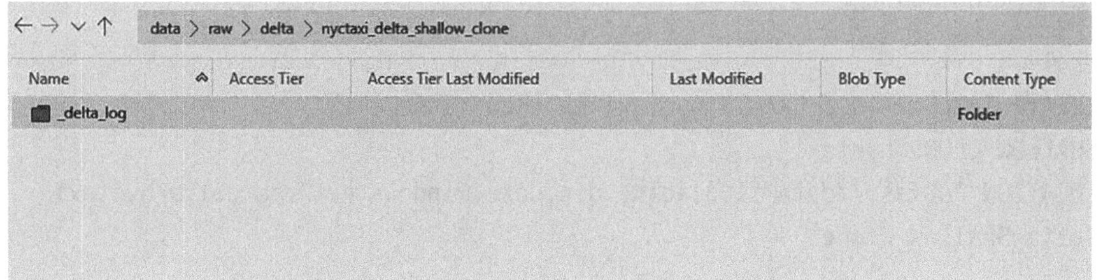

Figure 9-4. *ADLS gen2 folder showing that Shallow clone does not have any files*

On the other hand, the Delta log will contain files that capture metrics and logs around the creation of the Shallow clone, as shown in Figure 9-5.

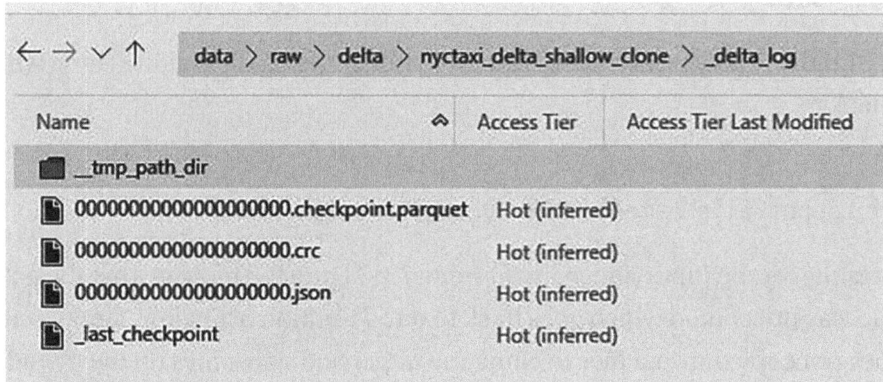

Figure 9-5. *Delta Log for Shallow clone*

Notice from Figure 9-6 that the log indicates a CLONE operation with isShallow = true.

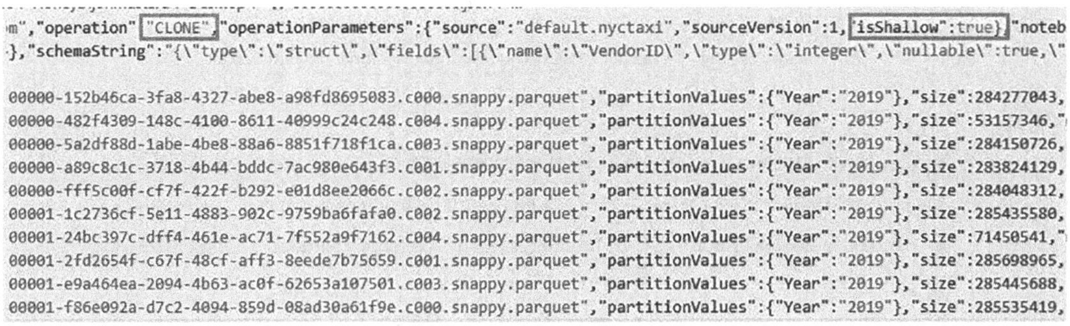

```
m","operation":"CLONE","operationParameters":{"source":"default.nyctaxi","sourceVersion":1,"isShallow":true},"noteb
},"schemaString":"{\"type\":\"struct\",\"fields\":[{\"name\":\"VendorID\",\"type\":\"integer\",\"nullable\":true,\"

00000-152b46ca-3fa8-4327-abe8-a98fd8695083.c000.snappy.parquet","partitionValues":{"Year":"2019"},"size":284277043,
00000-482f4309-148c-4100-8611-40999c24c248.c004.snappy.parquet","partitionValues":{"Year":"2019"},"size":53157346,"
00000-5a2df88d-1abe-4be8-88a6-8851f718f1ca.c003.snappy.parquet","partitionValues":{"Year":"2019"},"size":284150726,
00000-a89c8c1c-3718-4b44-bddc-7ac980e643f3.c001.snappy.parquet","partitionValues":{"Year":"2019"},"size":283824129,
00000-fff5c00f-cf7f-422f-b292-e01d8ee2066c.c002.snappy.parquet","partitionValues":{"Year":"2019"},"size":284048312,
00001-1c2736cf-5e11-4883-902c-9759ba6fafa0.c002.snappy.parquet","partitionValues":{"Year":"2019"},"size":285435580,
00001-24bc397c-dff4-461e-ac71-7f552a9f7162.c004.snappy.parquet","partitionValues":{"Year":"2019"},"size":71450541,"
00001-2fd2654f-c67f-48cf-aff3-8eede7b75659.c001.snappy.parquet","partitionValues":{"Year":"2019"},"size":285698965,
00001-e9a464ea-2094-4b63-ac0f-62653a107501.c003.snappy.parquet","partitionValues":{"Year":"2019"},"size":285445688,
00001-f86e092a-d7c2-4094-859d-08ad30a61f9e.c000.snappy.parquet","partitionValues":{"Year":"2019"},"size":285535419,
```


***Figure 9-6.** Details of Delta log for Shallow clone*

Next, let's update the Shallow clone to see how this operation impacts the logs and persisting of data by running the following script:

```
%sql
UPDATE nyctaxi_Shallow_clone
SET PULocationID = 263 WHERE PULocationID = 262
```

Notice from Figure 9-7 that there were 17 new files that were created in the Shallow clone folder since any new files created based on operations on the Shallow clone's folder will persist these files in the Shallow clone folder going forward rather than continuing with metadata pointers to the original files. This is valuable since if the Shallow clone needs to be deleted for any reason, it will have no impact on the original files. This is good for short-term experiments on a production table without affecting production workloads.

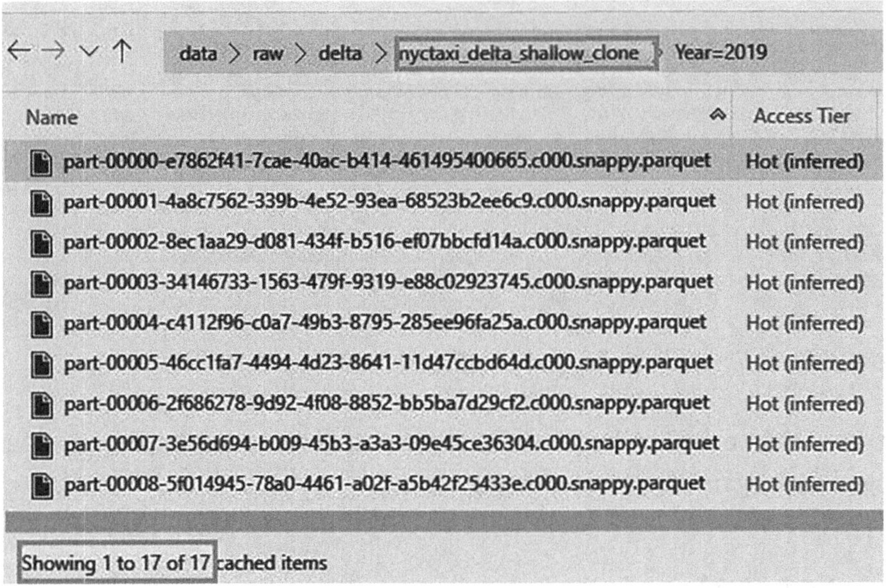

Figure 9-7. ADLS gen2 folder showing that Shallow clone now has files in folder

Based on a select with the input_file_name(), notice from Figure 9-8 that the data now points to the Shallow clone folder since there has been an update since the Shallow clone was created.

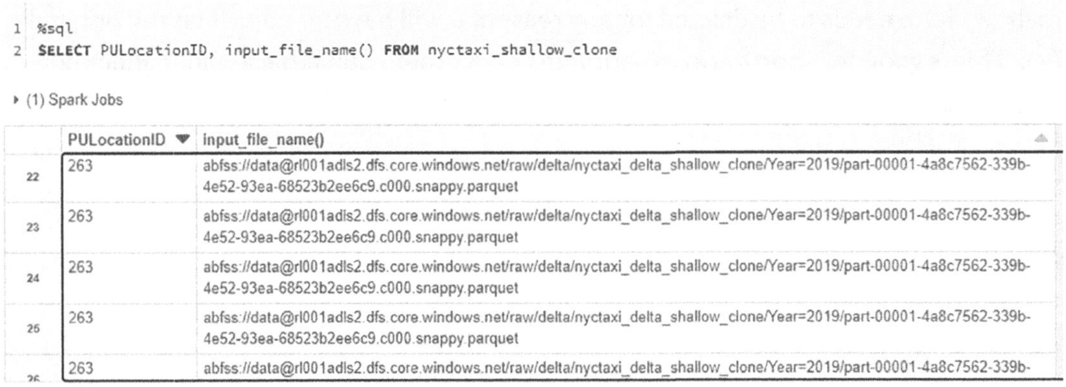

Figure 9-8. Script to list File Paths of the Shallow clones

Deep Clones

Now that you have a basic understanding of Shallow clones, let's explore Deep clones next. Deep clones create full copies of data files and metadata and are very similar to copying data using the CREATE TABLE AS SELECT (CTAS) command. It is simpler than the CTAS command since it doesn't require specifying partitioning, constraints, and more. It also supports incremental changes to the Deep clone table. In certain use cases, data may need to be archived and retained as part of either a disaster recovery strategy or due to limitations in time travel retention periods. Deep clones can support this archival of incremental updates, inserts, and deletes of data. Deep clones can be used as a long-term data sharing strategy for organizations or teams that need to tightly control data access by sharing versions of the data with a variety of stakeholders. Machine learning model testing, training, and archivals are also use cases for Deep clones. The following script demonstrates how to use the Deep clone command:

```
%sql
CREATE TABLE IF NOT EXISTS nyctaxi_deep_clone
DEEP CLONE nyctaxi
LOCATION 'abfss://data@rl001adls2.dfs.core.windows.net/raw/delta/nyctaxi_
delta_Deep_clone'
```

After running the Deep clone creation script, Figure 9-9 shows the ten active files from the original folder being copied to the Deep clone folder.

data > raw > delta > nyctaxi_delta_deep_clone > Year=2019

Name	Access Tier
part-00000-152b46ca-3fa8-4327-abe8-a98fd8695083.c000.snappy.parquet	Hot (inferred)
part-00000-482f4309-148c-4100-8611-40999c24c248.c004.snappy.parquet	Hot (inferred)
part-00000-5a2df88d-1abe-4be8-88a6-8851f718f1ca.c003.snappy.parquet	Hot (inferred)
part-00000-a89c8c1c-3718-4b44-bddc-7ac980e643f3.c001.snappy.parquet	Hot (inferred)
part-00000-fff5c00f-cf7f-422f-b292-e01d8ee2066c.c002.snappy.parquet	Hot (inferred)
part-00001-1c2736cf-5e11-4883-902c-9759ba6fafa0.c002.snappy.parquet	Hot (inferred)
part-00001-24bc397c-dff4-461e-ac71-7f552a9f7162.c004.snappy.parquet	Hot (inferred)
part-00001-2fd2654f-c67f-48cf-aff3-8eede7b75659.c001.snappy.parquet	Hot (inferred)
part-00001-e9a464ea-2094-4b63-ac0f-62653a107501.c003.snappy.parquet	Hot (inferred)

Showing 1 to 10 of 10 cached items

Figure 9-9. *Script to create Deep clones*

Similar to the Shallow clone's Delta log, there are files created within the delta_log, as shown in Figure 9-10.

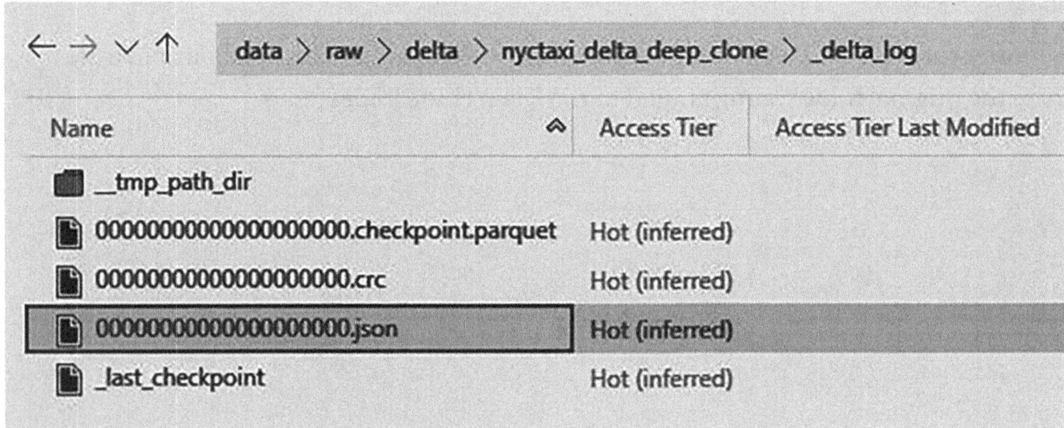

Figure 9-10. *Deep clone Delta logs in ADLS gen2*

Within the JSON log file shown in Figure 9-11, notice that this operation is a CLONE, and this time isShallow is set to False.

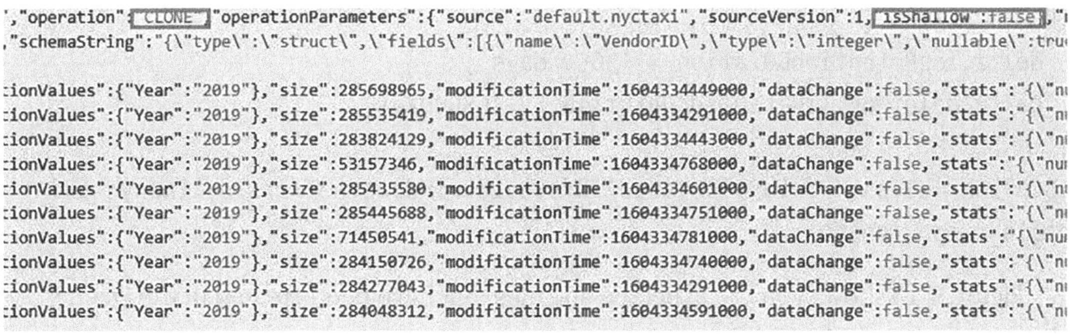

',"operation":"CLONE","operationParameters":{"source":"default.nyctaxi","sourceVersion":1,"isShallow":false},"
,"schemaString":"{\"type\":\"struct\",\"fields\":[{\"name\":\"VendorID\",\"type\":\"integer\",\"nullable\":tru

:ionValues":{"Year":"2019"},"size":285698965,"modificationTime":1604334449000,"dataChange":false,"stats":"{\"n
:ionValues":{"Year":"2019"},"size":285535419,"modificationTime":1604334291000,"dataChange":false,"stats":"{\"n
:ionValues":{"Year":"2019"},"size":283824129,"modificationTime":1604334443000,"dataChange":false,"stats":"{\"n
:ionValues":{"Year":"2019"},"size":53157346,"modificationTime":1604334768000,"dataChange":false,"stats":"{\"nu
:ionValues":{"Year":"2019"},"size":285435580,"modificationTime":1604334601000,"dataChange":false,"stats":"{\"n
:ionValues":{"Year":"2019"},"size":285445688,"modificationTime":1604334751000,"dataChange":false,"stats":"{\"n
:ionValues":{"Year":"2019"},"size":71450541,"modificationTime":1604334781000,"dataChange":false,"stats":"{\"nu
:ionValues":{"Year":"2019"},"size":284150726,"modificationTime":1604334740000,"dataChange":false,"stats":"{\"n
:ionValues":{"Year":"2019"},"size":284277043,"modificationTime":1604334291000,"dataChange":false,"stats":"{\"n
:ionValues":{"Year":"2019"},"size":284048312,"modificationTime":1604334591000,"dataChange":false,"stats":"{\"n

Figure 9-11. *ADLS gen2 Delta log for Deep clone*

After running a select on the Deep clone's Hive table using input_file_name(), shown in Figure 9-12, notice that the data is persisted in the Deep clone folder.

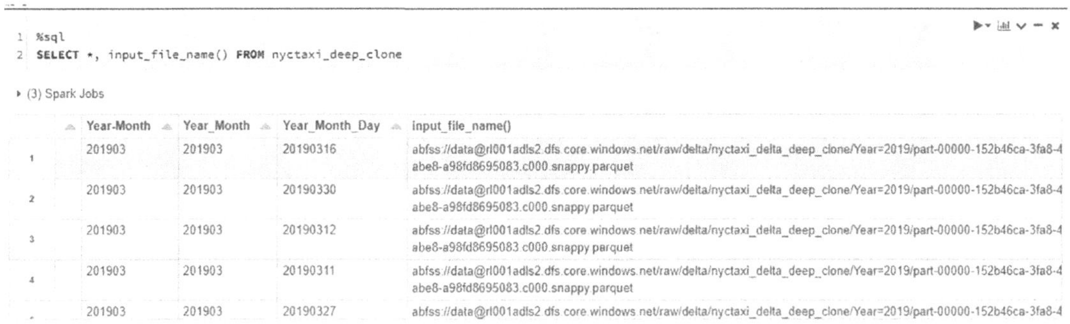

```
%sql
SELECT *, input_file_name() FROM nyctaxi_deep_clone
```

▸ (3) Spark Jobs

	Year-Month	Year_Month	Year_Month_Day	input_file_name()
1	201903	201903	20190316	abfss://data@rl001adls2.dfs.core.windows.net/raw/delta/nyctaxi_delta_deep_clone/Year=2019/part-00000-152b46ca-3fa8-4abe8-a98fd8695083.c000.snappy.parquet
2	201903	201903	20190330	abfss://data@rl001adls2.dfs.core.windows.net/raw/delta/nyctaxi_delta_deep_clone/Year=2019/part-00000-152b46ca-3fa8-4abe8-a98fd8695083.c000.snappy.parquet
3	201903	201903	20190312	abfss://data@rl001adls2.dfs.core.windows.net/raw/delta/nyctaxi_delta_deep_clone/Year=2019/part-00000-152b46ca-3fa8-4abe8-a98fd8695083.c000.snappy.parquet
4	201903	201903	20190311	abfss://data@rl001adls2.dfs.core.windows.net/raw/delta/nyctaxi_delta_deep_clone/Year=2019/part-00000-152b46ca-3fa8-4abe8-a98fd8695083.c000.snappy.parquet
5	201903	201903	20190327	abfss://data@rl001adls2.dfs.core.windows.net/raw/delta/nyctaxi_delta_deep_clone/Year=2019/part-00000-152b46ca-3fa8-4

Figure 9-12. *Script to Select folder path and data for Deep clones*

There is one more scenario that is worth testing to demonstrate the capability of time travel which allows us to revert back to a specific version of the original dataset. For my scenario, Version 1 contains 10 optimized files, and Version 0 contains 400 original files; therefore, let's specify Version 0 in the following script to create a previous version of the Deep clone. To find the version of your most recent commit, run the following Python command: `spark.conf.get("spark.databricks.delta.lastCommitVersionInSession")`. Also, notice the optional TABLEPROPERTIES overrides that can be included in the script. In this code, we can specify the log and deleted file retention period.

```
%sql
CREATE TABLE IF NOT EXISTS nyctaxi_deep_cloneV0
DEEP CLONE nyctaxi VERSION AS OF 0
```

```
TBLPROPERTIES (
  delta.logRetentionDuration = '3650 days',
  delta.deletedFileRetentionDuration = '3650 days'
)
LOCATION 'abfss://data@rl001adls2.dfs.core.windows.net/raw/delta/nyctaxi_
delta_deep_cloneV0'
```

Figure 9-13 shows you the expected 400 files that have been created in the Deep clone V0 folder within ADLS gen2.

Figure 9-13. *ADLS gen2 folder showing Deep clone created with time travel Version 0 for all files*

Additionally, Figure 9-14 shows the addition of the 400 files within the new Delta log file.

```
{"add":{"path":"Year=2019/part-00368-db69f101-7835-45cf-9c90-401a7a685b4f.c000.snappy.parquet",
{"add":{"path":"Year=2019/part-00103-58feaac0-7885-4cc5-bdb4-fb690c357021.c000.snappy.parquet",
{"add":{"path":"Year=2019/part-00115-f721e383-8537-4ebd-97d6-f8feb24f6b1c.c000.snappy.parquet",
{"add":{"path":"Year=2019/part-00150-f7622626-b8de-4fb7-badf-e440eb1bbd17.c000.snappy.parquet",
{"add":{"path":"Year=2019/part-00238-2ad4439c-10a4-4e5f-8911-161f4afbac2c.c000.snappy.parquet",
{"add":{"path":"Year=2019/part-00041-37e306a6-5ba0-4f95-af26-f56553e485b7.c000.snappy.parquet",
{"add":{"path":"Year=2019/part-00044-a3412a68-2b6f-4ba6-a827-50c79655a163.c000.snappy.parquet",
{"add":{"path":"Year=2019/part-00258-15203030-025d-4846-83f6-14a1caa031be.c000.snappy.parquet",
{"add":{"path":"Year=2019/part-00232-ea5a6dd5-eca0-42fe-875b-2416a394b50b.c000.snappy.parquet",
{"add":{"path":"Year=2019/part-00328-39cae83e-2b34-48ef-8de6-6557c7ea4856.c000.snappy.parquet",
{"add":{"path":"Year=2019/part-00235-609fae97-c993-42a7-84f6-3a7cbcf8364b.c000.snappy.parquet",
{"add":{"path":"Year=2019/part-00273-7c07dc44-0f48-44d4-82e6-1b52d11395fd.c000.snappy.parquet",
{"add":{"path":"Year=2019/part-00202-8ef7bd77-28c2-4b79-8b71-de9f0a195799.c000.snappy.parquet",
{"add":{"path":"Year=2019/part-00162-3e255f28-9269-43a6-85d5-6b871d8f639c.c000.snappy.parquet",
{"add":{"path":"Year=2019/part-00209-f7f11b97-5123-44c0-aeb8-14499c8ef39e.c000.snappy.parquet",
{"add":{"path":"Year=2019/part-00052-1d40fbae-15c5-4a60-9da8-95389526203c.c000.snappy.parquet",
{"add":{"path":"Year=2019/part-00244-e72c4057-3506-47f5-9822-92ed8cc5c845.c000.snappy.parquet",
```


Figure 9-14. *Version 0 of Delta log for Deep clone*

Summary

The possibilities and use cases for these Deep and Shallow clones are endless. Based on the use cases and value of these cloning operations, various other competitor cloud platforms are also now including similar options in their service offerings. For example, Snowflake supports a similar CLONE command on their platform which they refer to as "zero-copy cloning," which can be applied to a database, schema, or table. This operation takes a snapshot of the data and makes it available to consumers. For Synapse Analytics, the CTAS operation supports the creation of new tables based on the output of a SELECT statement.

Clones support a variety of use cases including data sharing, data and ML model archiving, testing, staging, training, and more. With Deep clones, Streaming Application transactions and COPY INTO operations are copied which enable large-scale data migrations and the continuation of workloads from where it last left off. With Shallow (zero-copy) clones, the ability to quickly clone, test, and share production data tables enables experimentation and innovation to continuously improve development efforts with minimal risk to live production data. The Shallow clones can be used as staging tables containing production data that can then be sanitized and merged back into the production tables. In this chapter, you learned about the differences between Deep and Shallow clones along with optimal use cases describing when to ideally apply each option.

CHAPTER 10

Live Tables

Building performant, scalable, maintainable, reliable, and testable live Data Lakehouse ELT pipelines in Azure is a critical need for many customers. These pipelines should support custom-defined ELT scripts, task orchestration, monitoring, and more. Within Azure, Data Factory and Databricks support many of these ELT capabilities and possess robust feature sets. Databricks Delta Live Tables enable data engineers to define live data pipelines using a series of Apache Spark tasks. Additionally, with Delta Live Tables, developers can schedule and monitor jobs, manage clusters, handle errors, and enforce data quality standards on live data with ease.

Data Factory is capable of executing both Databricks jobs and Delta Live Table pipelines through either in-built activities or the custom web activity. For executing Delta Live Tables from Data Factory, use a custom web activity configured with the Databricks API's URL. Integrating Databricks Delta Live Table pipeline with Data Factory can have a number of advantages including centralized orchestration, scheduling, and monitoring. Additionally, all parts of an ELT solution using disparate technologies can be combined into a single pipeline solution. The details for achieving this process can be found in the following Microsoft article: `https://techcommunity.microsoft.com/t5/analytics-on-azure-blog/leverage-azure-databricks-jobs-orchestration-from-azure-data/ba-p/3123862`

Delta Live Tables support the building and delivering of high-quality and well-defined live ELT pipelines on Delta Lake. With automatic testing, validation, and integrity checks along the way, Delta Live Tables to ensure live data pipelines are accurate and of the highest quality. Delta Live Tables provide visibility into operational pipelines with built-in governance, versioning, and documentation features to visually track statistics and data lineage. Additionally, Delta Live Tables support the ingestion of streaming data via Auto Loader.

In this chapter, you will learn how to get started with Delta Live Tables for building pipeline definitions within your Databricks notebooks to ingest data into the Lakehouse and to declaratively build live pipelines to transform raw data and aggregate business

R. L'Esteve, *The Azure Data Lakehouse Toolkit*, https://doi.org/10.1007/978-1-4842-8233-5_10

level data for insights and analytics. You will also learn how to get started with implementing declarative data quality expectations and checks in your pipeline, add comments for documentation within the pipelines, curate the raw data, and prepare it for further analysis all using either SQL or PySpark syntax. You will also learn how to create, configure, and run Delta Live Table pipelines and jobs.

Advantages of Delta Live Tables

There are advantages to using Delta Live Tables (DLT) for ELT as opposed to various other methods such as directly writing the ELT in a data engineering Databricks workspace and scheduling the jobs. Firstly, DLT supports data lineage graphs which make it easier to track the status of large pipelines containing multiple sources and sinks. More information can be obtained by clicking the various tables. Table schema and metadata can also be obtained by clicking the tables, which supports the need for documentation. With expectations, data quality violations can be tracked and managed easily. DLT also supports incremental loads by simply making a small syntax change. Either full or incremental refreshes can be done. While Databricks Delta keeps track of logs, DLT supports event logs within the DLT UI, and more information can be found by drilling into the specific events which also include real-time updates, automatic monitoring, recovery, and management. DLT supports multiple environments including development and production. The same code can be reused across environments easily with each environment providing features and capabilities based on the need. In addition to these advantages over regular notebook ELT, DLT is also capable of making use of the features offered by Databricks such as the Hive metastore, time travel, and more.

Create a Notebook

The first step of creating a Delta Live Table (DLT) pipeline is to create a new Databricks notebook which is attached to a cluster. Delta Live Tables support both Python and SQL notebook languages. As for environments, Delta Live Tables bring both a development and production environment to support different requirements. In the development environment, you can reuse a cluster to save on restart costs. Pipeline retries are disabled in development mode to enable quicker manual issue identification and resolution. On the other hand, production mode will instill more robust frameworks around restarts of the cluster for recoverable errors and execution retries for errors. Pipelines will run in development mode by default, but you can easily toggle between environments by using the tabs. Mode switching only impacts cluster and pipeline execution. Other configuration storage and dev vs. prod sources will need to be manually accounted for.

The following code presents a sample DLT notebook containing three sections of scripts for the three stages in the ELT process for this pipeline. The first section will create a Live Table on your raw data. The format of the source data can be delta, parquet, csv, json, and more. The source data can be linked to streaming data flowing into your Delta Lake from Auto Loader, which provides a Structured Streaming source called cloudFiles. When an input path on the ADLS gen2 account is provided, cloudFiles will automatically process new files as they arrive.

Once the first level of the DLT script runs, it will run the next dependent level of the pipeline which creates a Live Table for your staged data. In this scenario, the script defines expectations that the VendorID is not null and that the passenger_count is greater than 0 using the CONSTRAINT-EXPECT command. If a violation occurs that does not meet these criteria, those rows will fail to be inserted into this table as a result of the ON VIOLATION command. FAIL UPDATE will immediately stop pipeline execution, whereas DROP ROW will drop the record and continue processing. The EXPECT function can be used at any stage of the pipeline. The following section of the code includes the constraint to EXPECT that the vendorID must always contain a value:

```
CONSTRAINT valid_VendorID EXPECT (VendorID IS NOT NULL)
```

The SELECT statements in this staging section can be further customized to include joins, aggregations, data cleansing, and more.

The final level of the DLT script will curate and prepare the final fact table and will be dependent on the previous staging table script. This holistic script defines the end-to-end ELT multistaged flow from taking raw data to updating a final consumption layer fact table.

```
CREATE LIVE TABLE nyctaxi_raw
COMMENT "This is the raw nyctaxi dataset in Delta Format."
SELECT * FROM delta. `/mnt/raw/delta/Factnyctaxi`

CREATE LIVE TABLE Factnyctaxi_staging(
  CONSTRAINT valid_VendorID EXPECT (VendorID IS NOT NULL),
  CONSTRAINT valid_passenger_count EXPECT (passenger_count > 0) ON
VIOLATION DROP ROW
)
```

```
COMMENT "nyctaxi data cleaned and prepared for analysis."
AS SELECT
  VendorID AS ID,
  CAST(passenger_count AS INT) AS Count,
  total_amount AS Amount,
  trip_distance AS Distance,
  tpep_pickup_datetime AS PickUp_Datetime,
  tpep_dropoff_datetime AS DropOff_Datetime
FROM live.nyctaxi_raw

CREATE LIVE TABLE Factnyctaxi
COMMENT "The curated Factnyc table containing aggregated counts, amounts,
and distance data."
AS SELECT
  VendorID AS ID,
  tpep_pickup_datetime AS PickUp_Datetime,
  tpep_dropoff_datetime AS DropOff_Datetime,
  CAST(passenger_count AS INT) AS Count,
  total_amount AS Amount,
  trip_distance AS Distance
FROM live.Factnyctaxi_staging
WHERE tpep_pickup_datetime BETWEEN '2019-03-01 00:00:00' AND  '2020-03-01
00:00:00'
AND passenger_count IS NOT NULL
GROUP BY VendorID, tpep_pickup_datetime, tpep_dropoff_datetime,
CAST(passenger_count AS INT), total_amount, trip_distance
ORDER BY VendorID ASC
```

This SQL code could just as easily be written in Python if needed. You'll first need to run commands similar to the following script to import Delta Live Tables along with PySpark SQL functions and types:

```
import dlt
from pyspark.sql.functions import *
from pyspark.sql.types import *
```

Similar to the SQL EXPECT function in the preceding SQL DLT pipeline notebook script, the following commands can be used within PySpark to handle row violations based on the expectations:

- **expect_or_drop**: If a row violates the expectation, drop the row from the target dataset. For example, the following code can be used to expand upon the original expectation that we created to now drop rows with VendorIDs that are null by adding the ON VIOLATION DROP ROW command: `CONSTRAINT valid_VendorID EXPECT (VendorID IS NOT NULL)ON VIOLATION DROP ROW`
- **expect_or_fail**: If a row violates the expectation, immediately stop execution. For example, the following code can be used to expand upon the original expectation that we created to now fail the update if there are null VendorIDs by adding the ON VIOLATION FAIL UPDATE command: `CONSTRAINT valid_VendorID EXPECT (VendorID IS NOT NULL)ON VIOLATION FAIL UPDATE`
- **expect_all**: If a row violates any of the expectations, include the row in the target dataset. For example, the following line of Python code contains the various expect_all conditions: `@dlt.expect_all({"valid_VendorID": "VendorID IS NOT NULL”, "valid_VendorName": "VendorName IS NOT NULL"})`. The code shown later includes this in a sample by defining valid_Vendor as a data frame and calling it with the expect_all violation commands.
- **expect_all_or_drop**: If a row violates any of the expectations, drop the row from the target dataset. This can be seen in the code shown in the following within the section showing the following code line: `@dlt.expect_all_or_drop(valid_Vendor)`
- **expect_all_or_fail**: If a row violates any of the expectations, immediately stop execution. Similar to the expect_all_or_drop code line as shown in the following code, this expect_all_or_fail command can be interchanged or added when needed.

```
valid_Vendor = {"valid_VendorID": "VendorID IS NOT NULL", "valid_
VendorName": "VendorName IS NOT NULL"}

@dlt.table
@dlt.expect_all(valid_Vendor)
def raw_data():
  # Create raw dataset

@dlt.table
@dlt.expect_all_or_drop(valid_Vendor)
def curated_data():
  # Create cleaned and prepared dataset
```

Create and Run a Pipeline

A pipeline within Delta Live Tables is a directed acyclic graph (DAG) linking data sources to target datasets. In the previous section, you learned how to create the contents of DLT datasets using SQL queries. Once the scripts have been created, you can create a pipeline, as shown in Figure 10-1. When creating a pipeline, you'll need to fill in the required configuration properties using either the UI or JSON code. At a basic level, you'll need to specify the pipeline name, the location where the DLT notebook code is stored, the storage location, pipeline mode, and cluster specs. If your scripts are spread across multiple notebooks, these various notebooks can also be added as notebook libraries, and the pipeline will work out the lineage as long as the notebooks reference the right stages and processes. Additionally, configurations can be added to specify parameters and/or other key value-type pairs that can be referenced in the pipeline.

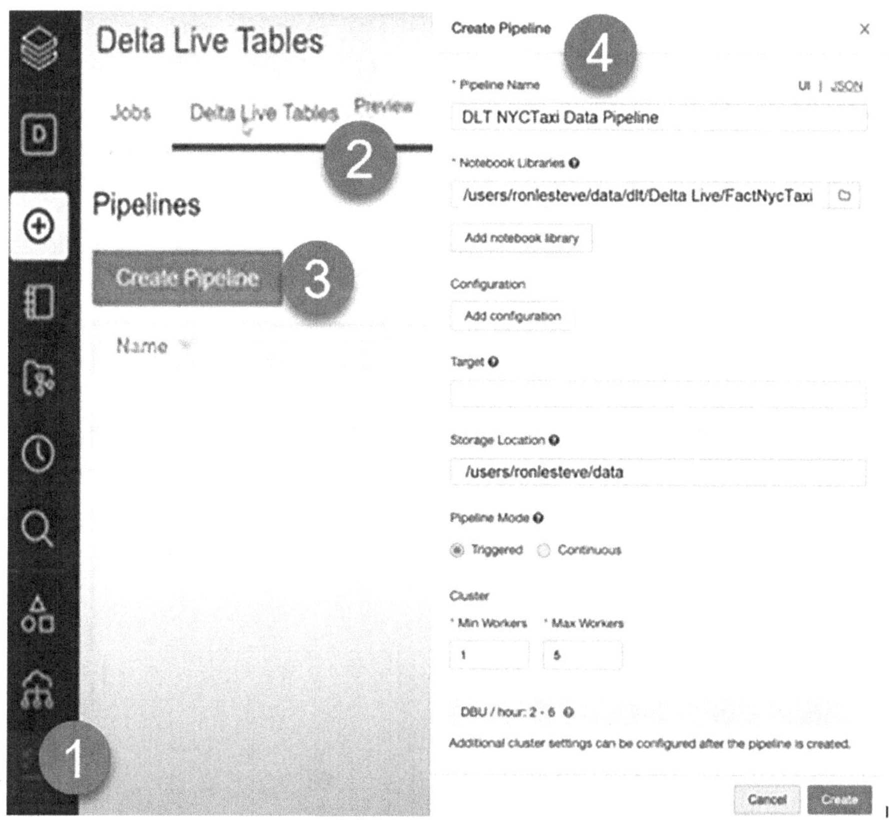

Figure 10-1. *Configuration properties for creating a Delta Live Table pipeline*

As an example, here is what the pipeline's JSON script would look like. This JSON can be further customized as needed.

```
{
  "name": "DLT NYCTaxi Data Pipeline",
  "storage": "/mnt/data/raw/Factnyctaxi",
  "clusters": [
    {
      "num_workers": 1,
      "spark_conf": {}
    }
  ],
```

```
  "libraries": [
    {
      "notebook": {
         "path": "/Users/ronlesteve/dlt/Factnyctaxi
      }
    }
  ],
  "continuous": false
}
```

After creating the pipeline, it can be further configured, started, and monitored in either your development or production environments. Notice from the Pipeline Details UI shown in Figure 10-2 that the info displays the start, run, and completing status of the pipeline steps.

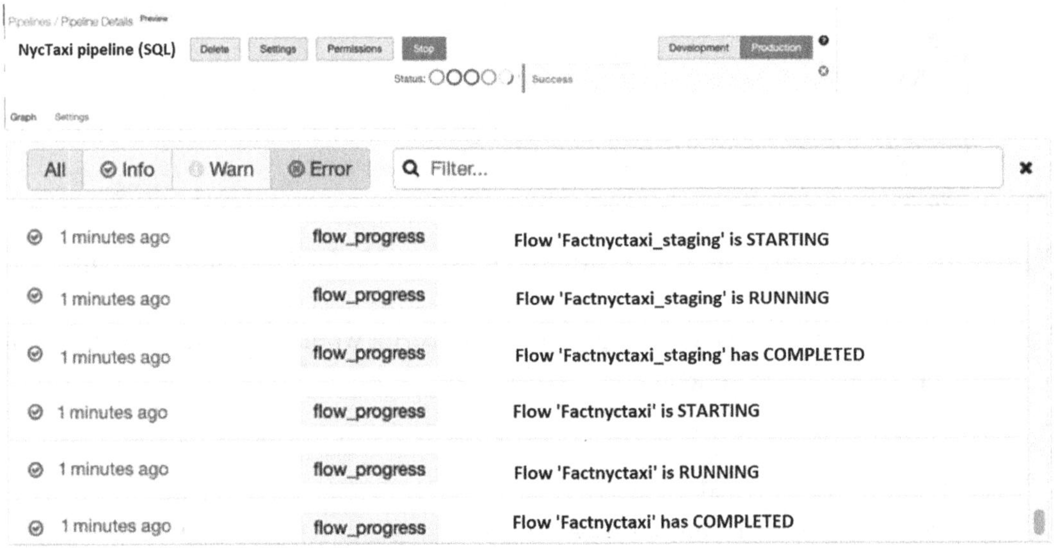

Figure 10-2. *Pipeline status for the DLT pipeline*

Notice from Figure 10-3 that the graph tracks the dependencies between jobs to clearly display the lineage. By clicking the table, you'll be able to view the defined schema of the table. While this lineage is quite simple, complex lineage showing multiple table joins and interdependencies can also be clearly displayed and tracked on this graph. This could potentially be integrated with Azure Purview by way of Purview's Apache Atlas API to capture metadata and lineage, although this is not a readily available out-of-the-box industry solution and could theoretically be custom developed.

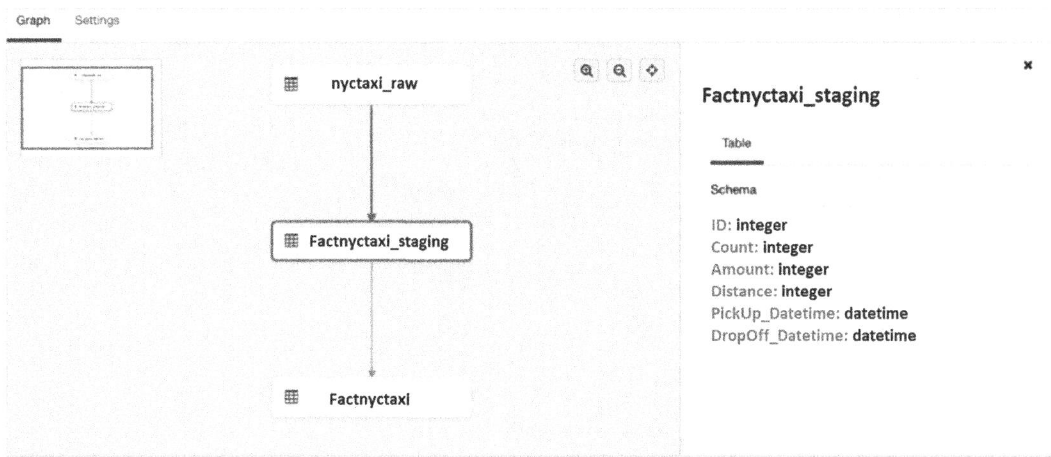

***Figure 10-3.** DLT pipeline graph showing dependencies and lineage*

Once the pipeline completes running, it will display metadata-related metrics that have been tracked for the job, as shown in Figure 10-4. Notice that it shows the number of rows that were inserted into the table along with the metrics related to any expectations for the table. For example, if records were failed or dropped, they would be tracked here.

```
    "timestamp": "2021-06-17T23:25:49.544Z",
    "message":"Flow 'Factnyctaxi_staging' has COMPLETED.",
    "level": "INFO",
    "details": {
        "flow_progress": {
            "status": "COMPLETED",
            "metrics": {
                "num_output_rows": 22509897
            },
            "data_quality": {
                "dropped_records": 0,
                "expectations": [
                    {
                        "name":"valid_VendorID",
                        "dataset":"Factnyctaxi_staging",
                        "passed_records": 22509892,
                        "failed_records": 5
                    }
                ]
            }
        }
    },
    "event_type": "flow_progress"
}
```

***Figure 10-4.** Event log metrics captured for completed DLT pipeline*

Schedule a Pipeline

After your pipeline has been created and successfully tested, you can create a job which specifies the pipeline as a task within the job. You can then customize the schedule, as shown in Figure 10-5, and the configurations even provide the capability of adding custom Cron Syntax to the job's schedule. Retries and concurrent runs can be configured as needed. Finally, you'll have the option to customize and send alerts related to job status to a specified email address. Once a scheduled job is set up, a cluster will spin up at the scheduled job time and will run through the steps of the pipeline. Remember, we mentioned previously that a cluster is entirely configurable.

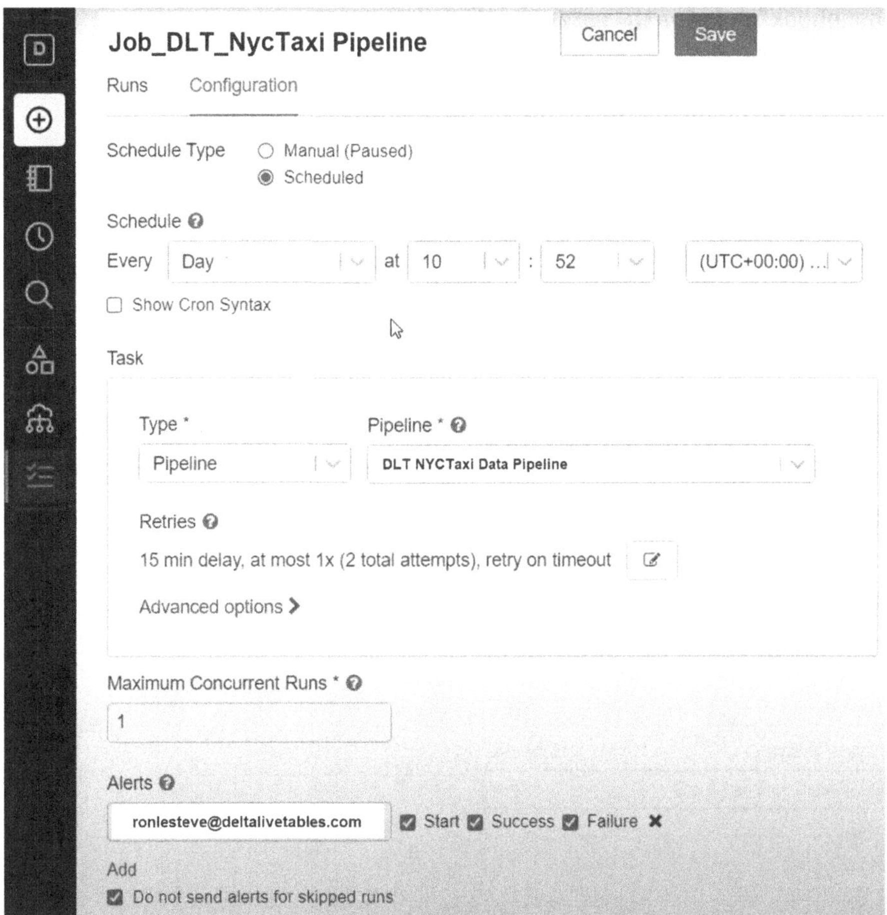

***Figure 10-5.** DLT pipeline scheduling configuration properties*

From a use case perspective, for example, if a developer has two different ETL processes that require different parameters but need to be tied to the same pipeline, they could run multiple notebooks within a pipeline, each containing their own parameters. The following code shows the JSON code to connect multiple notebooks within a pipeline:

```
{
  "name": "DLT_Pipeline",
  "storage": "dbfs:/data/raw/vendors",
  "libraries": [
```

```
    { "notebook": { "path": "/etl_1" } },
    { "notebook": { "path": "/etl_2" } }
  ]
}
```

This next block of SQL code shows how to parameterize pipelines within the notebooks:

```
CREATE LIVE TABLE vendors
AS SELECT * FROM srcVendors WHERE date > ${DLT_pipeline.startDate};
```

It is entirely possible to configure or swap the cluster once it is created and linked to a job, as shown in Figure 10-6. You could also toggle between the UI or write custom JSON code to configure the cluster.

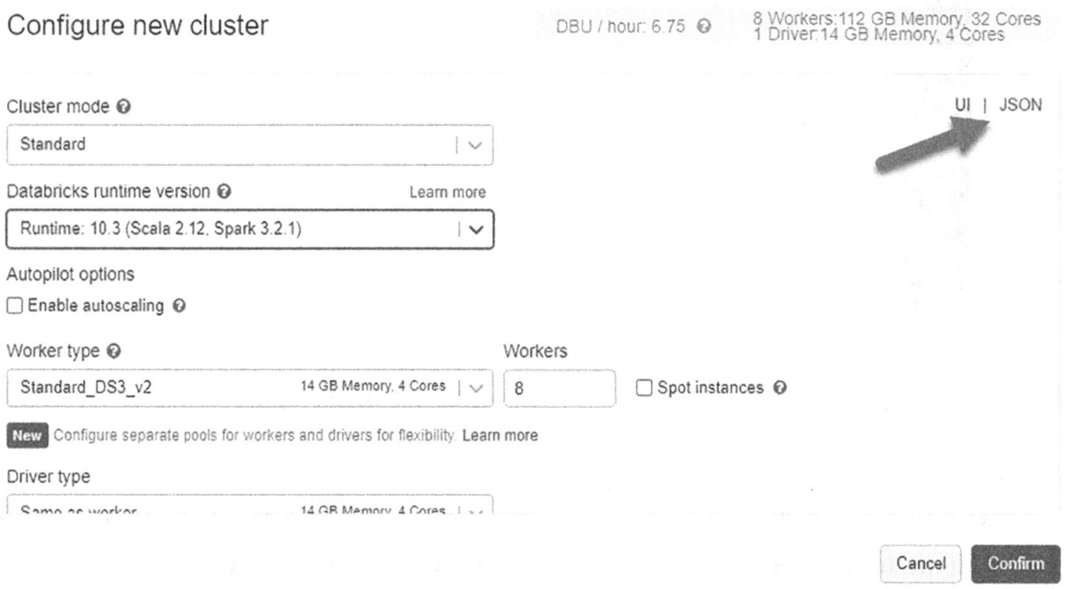

Figure 10-6. Configure DLT job cluster

Explore Event Logs

Event logs are created and maintained for all Delta Live Table pipelines and contain data related to the audit logs, data quality checks, pipeline progress, and data lineage for tracking and monitoring your pipelines. As an example, the following code creates a view for the system event metrics for the data that has been processed using the DLT pipeline.

```
ADLSg2Path = "/mnt/raw/data/NycTaxidata"
df = spark.read.format("delta").load(f"{ADLSg2Path}/system/events")
df.createOrReplaceTempView("dlteventmetrics")
```

Figure 10-7 displays the schema for some of the many fields and nested JSON objects that the pipeline captures which can be used for audit logs, quality checks, pipeline progress, and data lineage.

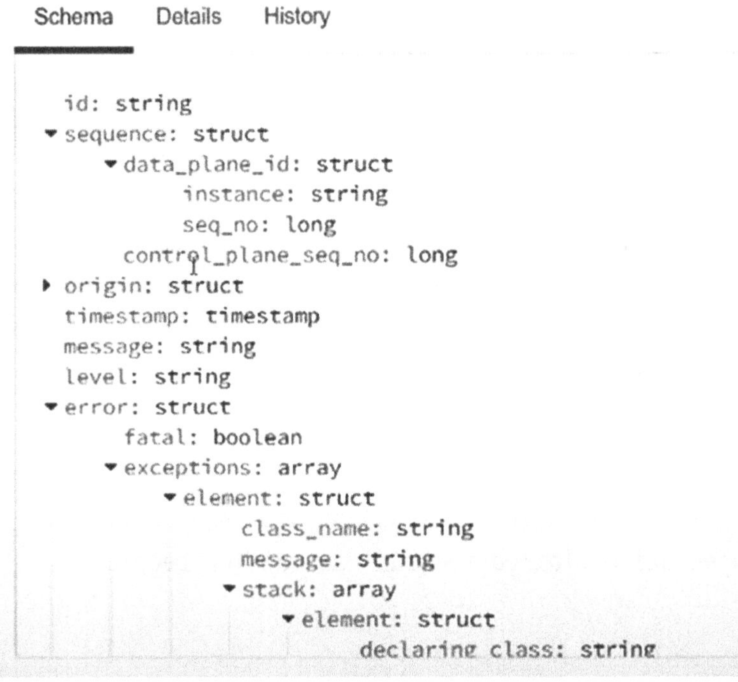

***Figure 10-7.** Schema of the completed DLT pipeline's system event logs and metrics captured*

Once the view is created, you can simply write PySpark or SQL scripts similar to the following code to display the metrics related to audit logs:

```
SELECT
        timestamp,
        details:user_action:action,
        details:user_action:user_name
FROM event_log_raw
WHERE event_type = 'user_action'
```

Figure 10-8 illustrates the results of the preceding query. This gives you an idea of some of the metrics and customized queries that you can create based on these DLT system events.

	timestamp	action	user_name
1	2021-05-20T19:36:03.517	START	ronlesteve
2	2021-05-20T19:35:59.913	CREATE	ronlesteve
3	2021-05-27T00:35:51.971	START	ronlesteve

Figure 10-8. *DLT pipeline event metrics for audit logs*

This next query is more complex and can be created on the same view to explode the nested JSON array contents to extract a more customized report on the quality of the data based on the expectations for passing and failing of the rows.

```
SELECT
  row_expectations.dataset as dataset,
  row_expectations.name as expectation,
  SUM(row_expectations.passed_records) as passing_records,
  SUM(row_expectations.failed_records) as failing_records
FROM
  (
    SELECT
      explode(
        from_json(
          details :flow_progress :data_quality :expectations,
          "array<struct<name: string, dataset: string, passed_records: int,
          failed_records: int>>"
        )
      ) row_expectations
    FROM
      dlteventmetrics
```

```
    WHERE
      event_type = 'flow_progress'
      AND origin.update_id = '${latest_update.id}'
  )
GROUP BY
  row_expectations.dataset,
  row_expectations.name
```

Figure 10-9 shows the results of the preceding query. These sorts of queries can be used in the Databricks SQL workspace to perform further customized analysis of the data quality, lineage, and audit logs. From a visualization perspective, you can create visually appealing dashboards in either Databricks or Power BI for the reporting of this data.

	dataset	expectation	passing_records	failing_records
1	Factnyctaxi	valid_VendorID	22509892	5

***Figure 10-9.** DLT pipeline event metrics for data quality tracking*

Summary

As you gain a deeper understanding of Delta Live Tables, it is important to point out a few of its additional features. Delta Live Tables support updates to Delta Tables only. Also, views in a pipeline from another cluster or SQL endpoint are not supported. Delta Live Tables perform maintenance tasks on tables every 24 hours by running the OPTIMIZE and VACCUM commands to improve query performance and reduce cost by removing old versions of tables. Each table must be defined once, and a UNION can be used to combine multiple inputs to create a table. Delta Live Tables will retain history for seven days to query snapshots of tables, with the capability of custom defining this retention period.

As you continue to advance your development of DLT pipelines, you could also parameterize the pipelines to get a robust dynamic framework that is capable of looping through a list of tables to create the pipelines in real time without having to hardcode certain fields. In this chapter, you learned more about how to get started with Delta Live Tables using Databricks notebooks, pipelines, and jobs.

Delta Live Tables support declarative ELT pipelines that can ingest and transform data sources of all varieties, volumes, and velocities. With Delta Expectations, high data quality and consistency within the Lakehouse can be guaranteed. With scheduled jobs for processing DLT pipelines, recovery, and error handling logic can be applied consistently along with robust alerting of job status. For example, advanced configuration options for pipeline retries allow you to specify the customized timeout and retry schedule. Error handling was also discussed in this chapter through violation logic checks that could be applied through either the EXPECT or EXPECT_ALL commands in either SQL, Python, or Scala. If your DLT pipelines are integrated with Data Factory, then you will also be able to use the out-of-the-box monitoring and retry features of Data Factory. Additionally, Data Factory activities support success and failure flow path to enable support for further customizations of error handling steps.

Visual monitoring of DLT pipeline steps helps with easily tracking status of data flows in the out-of-the-box UI. Additional dashboards and metrics can be created to further customize visualizations and reporting of event metrics to further track performance, status, quality, latency, etc. Delta Live Tables also support incremental loads from Auto Loader's cloud_files sources by simply specifying the Incremental in the create table statement like so: `CREATE INCREMENTAL LIVE TABLE`. Delta Live Tables support a number of unique use cases and solutions which can be found here within Microsoft's Delta Live Tables Cookbook: `https://docs.microsoft.com/en-us/azure/databricks/data-engineering/delta-live-tables/delta-live-tables-cookbook`. For a deeper understanding of Change Data Capture (CDC) techniques with Delta Live Tables, take a look at this Microsoft article: `https://docs.microsoft.com/en-us/azure/databricks/data-engineering/delta-live-tables/delta-live-tables-cdc`. It is also a good idea to check out the Delta Live Tables frequently asked questions here: `https://docs.microsoft.com/en-us/azure/databricks/data-engineering/delta-live-tables/delta-live-tables-faqs-issues`. The many capabilities which Delta Live Tables bring to the Lakehouse ELT process allow us to gain quicker insights into valuable data by simplifying and adding robust scheduling and tracking for ELT jobs and pipelines.

CHAPTER 11

Sharing

The capability of cross-organization real-time data sharing with customers, partners, suppliers, and more has been an ever-growing need. The historical challenges with securely sharing data across traditional systems have prevented seamless data sharing features. Previously, there were only a few methods of sharing data which included JDBC, ODBC, or SQL connections.

Customers are seeking secure, flexible, and open ways of connecting to a variety of data stores, types, and languages. Cloud providers are beginning to take note of this need for Data Sharing and have begun introducing new features and capabilities to the market. Snowflake has provided a capability of sharing data through its Data Sharing and marketplace offering which enables sharing selected objects in a database in your account with other Snowflake accounts. Databricks Delta Sharing provides similar features with the added advantage of a fully open protocol with Delta Lake support for Data Sharing. Customers are interested in understanding how to get started with Delta Sharing.

Delta Sharing is a fully secure and compliant open source protocol for sharing live data in your Lakehouse with support for data science cases. It is not restricted to SQL, supports a variety of open data formats, and can efficiently scale and support big datasets. Delta Sharing supports Delta Lake which contains a wide variety of features. Numerous data providers are excited about Delta Sharing and have committed to making thousands of datasets accessible through Delta Sharing. The ease of accessing this shared data promotes self-service data providers and consumers. In this chapter, you will learn about how Databricks Delta Sharing works, along with the various benefits of Delta Sharing. You will also learn how to get started with creating, altering, describing, and sharing Delta Lakehouse data using Databricks. You will also learn about a few options for consuming Delta Lakehouse data that has been shared through Databricks Delta Share. Toward the end of the chapter, I will show an example of how Snowflake's Data Sharing capability is compared to Databricks Delta Sharing.

R. L'Esteve, *The Azure Data Lakehouse Toolkit*, https://doi.org/10.1007/978-1-4842-8233-5_11

Architecture

With Delta Sharing, live big datasets in delta or parquet format within your ADLS gen2 account can be shared without needing to copy it. Since Delta Sharing is an open source capability, it supports open data format for a variety of clients, and it brings robust security, auditing, and governance features. The Delta Sharing architecture follows a simple paradigm which includes two key stakeholders, which are providers and consumers. A data provider will share their data within their ADLS gen2 account by setting up their Delta Sharing Server to grant access permissions to data recipients via the Delta Sharing Protocol. A variety of clients can then access the Delta Sharing Protocol, Delta Sharing Server, and Delta Data Table. This Delta Sharing is open source, and more information about it can be found on the following GitHub repository: `https://github.com/delta-io/delta-sharing` and at `https://delta.io/sharing/`

Once access is verified and granted, a short-lived read-only URL will be provided to the data consumer. While the initial request will be provided through the Delta Sharing Server, all subsequent requests will go directly from the client to the ADLS gen2 account where the shared data is stored. With this segregated approach to data sharing, providers can selectively share partitions or tables which can be updated with ACID transactions in real time. There are a variety of clients including major cloud providers such as Azure and open source clients including Spark, Pandas, Hive, Tableau, and Power BI that support the various capabilities of Delta Sharing within their platforms. Also, a growing number of large organizations are beginning to adopt Delta Sharing capabilities as data providers which support the monetization of their data as assets while bringing quicker time to insights for their clients. The architecture discussed in this section is shown in Figure 11-1.

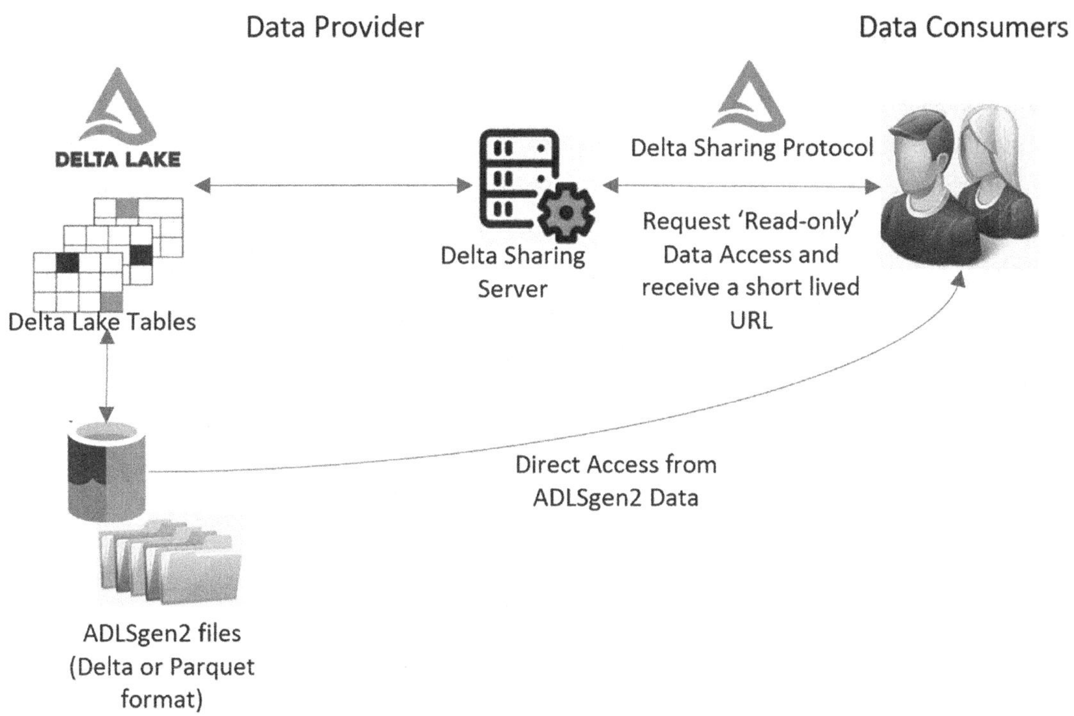

Figure 11-1. *Delta Sharing architecture diagram*

Share Data

To share data within your ADLS gen2 account from a Databricks notebook, you'll need to first mount your ADLS gen2 account within Databricks, then create a share using the `create share <MyShare>;` SQL Syntax, and then add a table to the share using the following syntax: `alter share <MyShare> add table <MyTable>;`. Note that you can run the command multiple times to add many tables to the share. Once the tables have been added to the share, you could use the `describe share <MyShare>;` syntax to view a list of tables, type, and date added to the share. A recipient can be created using the `create recipient <MyRecipient>;` syntax which will generate an activation link that can be shared with the respective data recipient. Note that `<MyRecipient>` is simply an alias to track and map the newly generated activation link to. You do not need to specify the email address of the recipient within this syntax. The following final command will grant read-only permissions on the share to the recipients specified: `grant select on share <MyShareName> to recipient <MyRecipient>;`. From the documentation, it appears that Delta Share currently only supports read-only "select" views of the data, which makes sense from a security standpoint.

Access Data

When access is granted by a data sharer, the data recipient will receive an activation link similar to the illustration shown in Figure 11-2. By clicking "Download Credential File," the data recipient will download a json file locally. Note that for security purposes, the credential file can only be downloaded once after which the download link will be deactivated. For certain technologies such as Tableau, in addition to the URL link, you may need to upload this credential file. For other technologies, you may need credentials such as a "Bearer Token" from inside this json file.

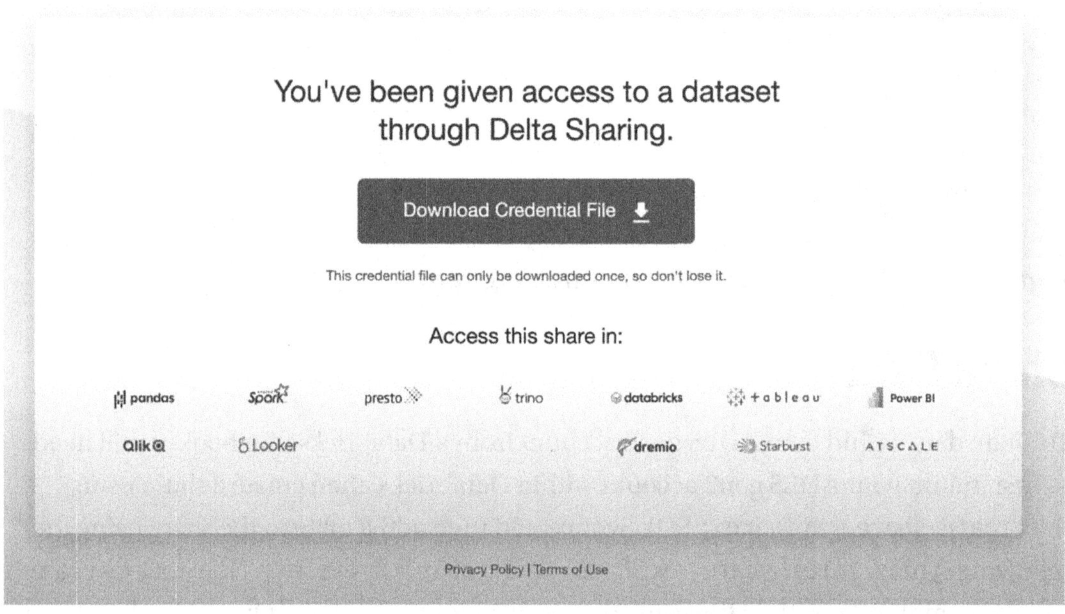

***Figure 11-2.** Download Credential File for Databricks Delta Sharing dataset*

After the credential file is downloaded, it can be referenced in a variety of different notebook types including Jupyter and Databricks to retrieve the shared data within data frames. The following commands can be run to install and import the delta sharing client within your notebook. You can also install this from PyPi by searching for "delta-sharing-server" and installing the "delta-sharing" package. After that, you can use this previously downloaded credential profile file to list and access all the shared tables within your notebook.

```
# Install Delta Sharing
!pip install delta-sharing

# Import Delta Sharing
import delta_sharing

# Point to the profile file which was previously downloaded and can be a
file on the local file system or a file on a remote storage.

profile_file = "<profile-file-path>"

# Create the SharingClient and list all shared tables.

client = delta_sharing.SharingClient(profile_file).list_all_tables()

# Create a url to access a shared table.
# A table path is the profile file path following with `#` and the fully
qualified name of a table (`<share-name>.<schema-name>.<table-name>`).

table_url = profile_file + "#<share-name>.<schema-name>.<table-name>"

# For PySpark code, use `load_as_spark` to load the table as a Spark
DataFrame.

delta_sharing.load_as_spark(table_url)
```

Within Power BI, it is easy to connect to a Delta Sharing source by simply selecting "Delta Sharing" from the out-of-the-box PBI data source options and clicking "Connect," as shown in Figure 11-3.

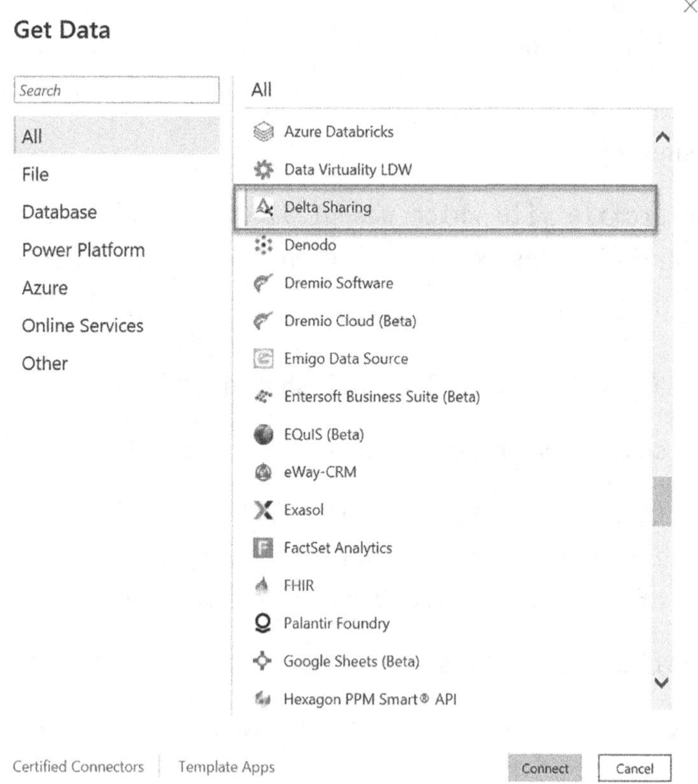

Figure 11-3. *Out-of-the-box Power BI Delta Sharing data source connector*

In the configuration section, you'll then need to enter the Delta Sharing Server URL and Bearer Token for authentication, as shown in Figure 11-4. Also notice the optional Advanced Options for specifying a row limit which enforces a limit on the number of rows that can be retrieved from the source dataset.

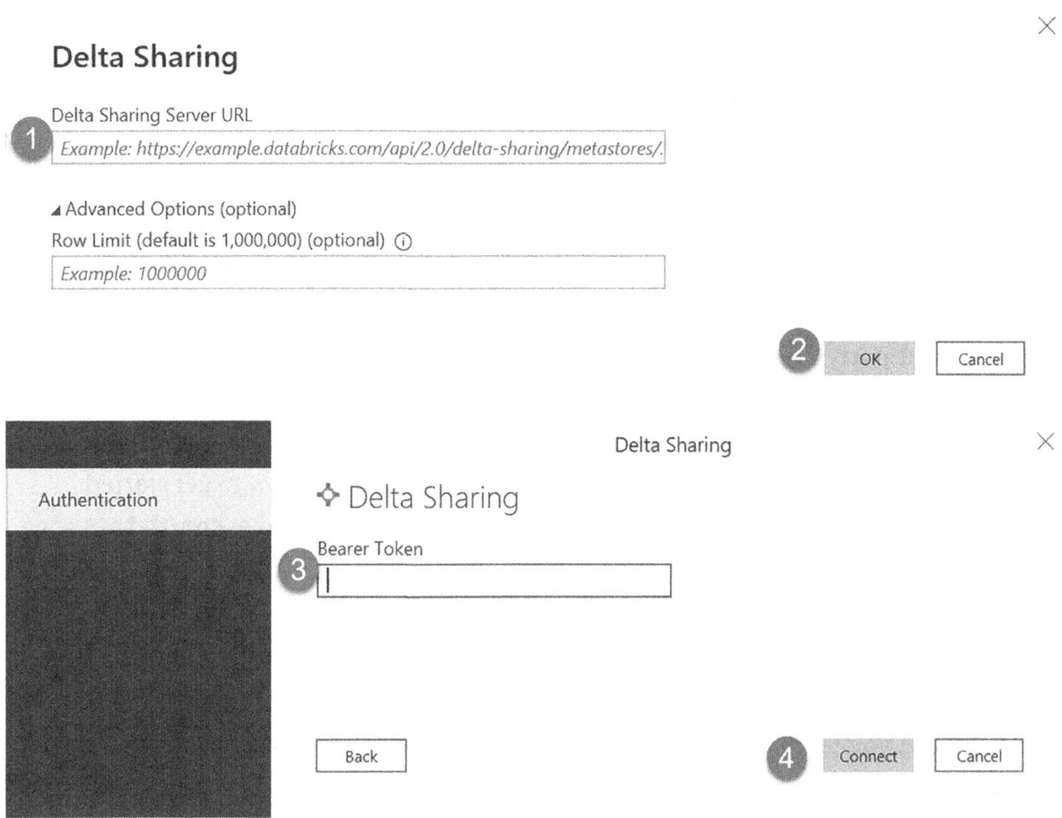

Figure 11-4. *Power BI configuration steps for Delta Sharing source*

Sharing Data with Snowflake

Most of this chapter focused on the capabilities of Databricks Delta Sharing. As we wrap up the chapter, I wanted to point out that Snowflake also has very similar data sharing capabilities as Databricks Delta Share. Snowflake may even be more mature with its data share offerings including its Marketplace which we discussed in Chapter 2. Similar to Databricks Delta Share, you would create a Snowflake data share by running the syntax `create share MyShare;`. You could then grant access to either a database, schema, or table by running SQL syntax similar to the following: `grant select on table MyDb.MySchema.MyTable to share MyShare;`. Similar to the "describe" command used in Databricks Delta, in Snowflake, you would run the following syntax: `show grants to share MyShare;`, to view details related to when the share was created, the privilege it has, what database/schema/table it has access to, and much more. Finally, permissions can be granted to allow various accounts to access the data via the following syntax: `alter share MyAccount add accounts=Account1, Account2`. This process generally assumes that the Snowflake data recipient has access to some form of a Snowflake account which was either configured by their data sharing account administrator or organization. You can find more information about working with Snowflake's data shares in their official documentation which can be found here: https://docs.snowflake.com/en/user-guide/data-sharing-provider.html

Snowflake's Data Marketplace also offers capabilities for consuming and sharing data with third-party vendors via a web UI interface. Data providers can publish free or personalized listings and share live datasets in real time without copying the data. Data consumers can consume raw or curated data from a variety of vendors. You can always find the most up-to-date information along with instructions on how to get started with Data Marketplace on Snowflake's web page here: www.snowflake.com/data-marketplace/

Summary

In this chapter, you learned more about the capabilities of Delta Sharing and how it enables data sharers and data recipients to be closely aligned through access to live data residing in a variety of sources on multiple multi-cloud platforms including Azure Data Lake Storage Gen2 and AWS S3 buckets. With its open source standards, contributors from the global developer communities can recommend or add additional connectors and contributions to the project as it continues to grow and scale. Delta Sharing reduces the complexity of ELT and manual sharing and prevents any lock-ins to a single platform. Delta Sharing has a robust roadmap for increasing sharing capabilities to support other use cases including ML Models, streaming for incremental data consumption since it already supports delta format, sharing of views, and much more. All of these secure and live data sharing capabilities of Delta Sharing promote a scalable and tightly coupled interaction between data providers and consumers within the Lakehouse paradigm.

There are other cloud providers including Snowflake and others that also have advanced sharing capabilities such as the Snowflake Marketplace and Direct Share. That being said, at the time of writing this chapter, Databricks Delta Sharing is still in its infancy and would need to address a number of existing challenges. These challenges include having the ability to revoke access to a share, support complex SQL syntaxes such as hierarchical queries which are beyond standard DML operations, and improve performance on long-running queries for small datasets.

The competitive multi-cloud Data Sharing landscape challenges the various leaders including Snowflake, Databricks, and others to constantly innovate, improve, and mature their Data Sharing offerings to support Lakehouse architectures. Until each platform is fully mature, sometimes the need to combine a variety of these technologies in a single architecture may be required to meet the objective, and that is totally ok as we all continue to mature on this multi-cloud journey. Just ensure that your solutions are scalable, maintainable, cost efficient, and performant with the eventual and iterative goal of having a simplified Data Sharing capability within your Lakehouse.

PART V

Optimizing Performance

CHAPTER 12

Dynamic Partition Pruning

Database pruning is an optimization process used to avoid reading files that do not contain the data that you are searching for. You can skip sets of partition files if your query has a filter on a particular partition column. In Apache Spark, dynamic partition pruning is a capability that combines both logical and physical optimizations to find the dimensional filter, ensures that the filter executes only once on the dimension side, and then applies the filter directly to the scan of the table which speeds up queries and prevents reading unnecessary data.

Within Databricks, dynamic partition pruning (DPP) runs on Apache Spark compute and requires no additional configuration to be set to enable it. Fact tables that need to be pruned must be partitioned with join key columns and only work with equijoins. Dynamic partition pruning is best suited for optimizing queries that follow the Star Schema models. In this chapter, you will learn how to efficiently utilize dynamic partition pruning in Databricks to run filtered queries on your delta fact and dimension tables.

Partitions

Partitioning is a database process that divides very large tables into multiple smaller parts to enable queries to run faster because they would only need to access a portion of the data. These partitioning strategies support the maintenance of large tables and improve their performance. Database table partitioning has been a mature feature of traditional SQL Server infrastructure appliances. Data in a partitioned table is physically stored in groups of rows called partitions which can be accessed and maintained separately. These partitioned tables act much like a logical table when queried. A partition key column, such as a date column, can be used as the basis of the partitions within the partitioned table. When selecting a partition key, it is important to choose a key that is frequently used as a filter within the SQL query. Traditional SQL Server

R. L'Esteve, *The Azure Data Lakehouse Toolkit*, https://doi.org/10.1007/978-1-4842-8233-5_12

appliances will then only access the relevant partitions, a process called partition elimination, for improved performance when querying large tables.

A partition function, which can be either range left or range right, can define how to partition data based on values in the partition column. With range left, the boundary values are part of the last value in the left partition. With range right, boundary values are part of the first value in the right partition.

A partition schema will map the logical partitions to physical filegroups, which contains data files that can be spread on disks. These filegroups can be backed up and restored. A partition can have its own filegroup, and an optimal partition scheme can include mapping less frequently accessed data to slower disks and frequently accessed data on faster disks.

There can be various strategies for designing partitions. The three typical strategies are horizontal, vertical, and functional partition designs. Horizontal partitioning, also known as "sharding," splits partitions into separate data stores which hold subsets of the data with the same schema. With vertical partitioning, each partition contains a subset of the fields for items in the data store split by usage patterns, such as splitting frequently accessed data in one partition and less frequently accessed data in another. Functional partitioning aggregates data by how it is used in each bounded context by splitting, for example, finance and marketing data. For more details on Data Partitioning Guidance, please read Microsoft's detailed article on the topic which can be found here: `https://docs.microsoft.com/en-us/azure/architecture/best-practices/data-partitioning`

In the scenarios shown in Figure 12-1, without dynamic partition pruning (DPP) applied, when you specify a filter on your date dimension that is joined to your fact table, all files will be scanned. Alternatively, with DPP applied, the optimizer will efficiently only prune the files that contain the relevant filter, assuming that your fact table is properly partitioned on the join key. Note that you can filter the query on a column within your date dimension that is not used in the join and it would still effectively partition prune the optimized query results.

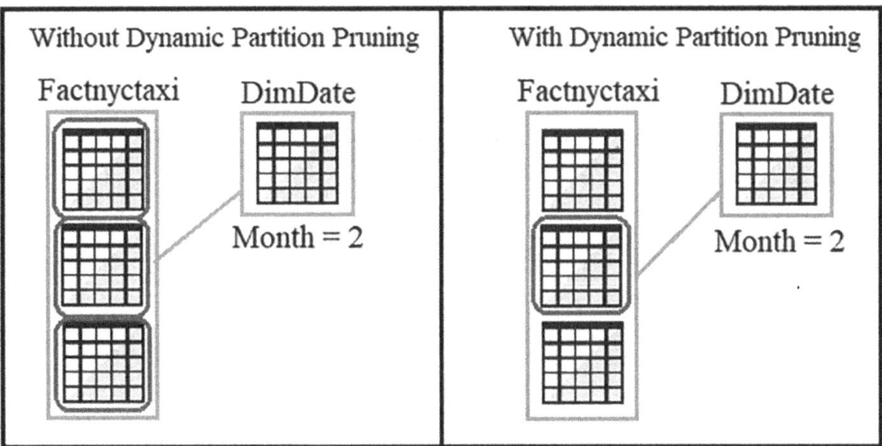

Figure 12-1. *Filter effect with and without dynamic partition pruning*

Prerequisites

For reference, here are a few dynamic partition pruning commands and their descriptions. Most of these features are automatically enabled at the default settings; however, it is still good to have an understanding of their capability through their description.

DPP Commands

- spark.databricks.optimizer.dynamicFilePruning (default is true): Is the main flag that enables the optimizer to push down DFP filters.
- spark.databricks.optimizer.deltaTableSizeThreshold (default is 10GB): This parameter represents the minimum size in bytes of the Delta Table on the probe side of the join required to trigger dynamic file pruning.
- spark.databricks.optimizer.deltaTableFilesThreshold (default is 1000): This parameter represents the number of files of the Delta Table on the probe side of the join required to trigger dynamic file pruning.

Create Cluster

To begin the process, ensure that you have created a cluster in your Databricks environment. For the purposes of this exercise, you can use a relatively small cluster, as shown in Figure 12-2.

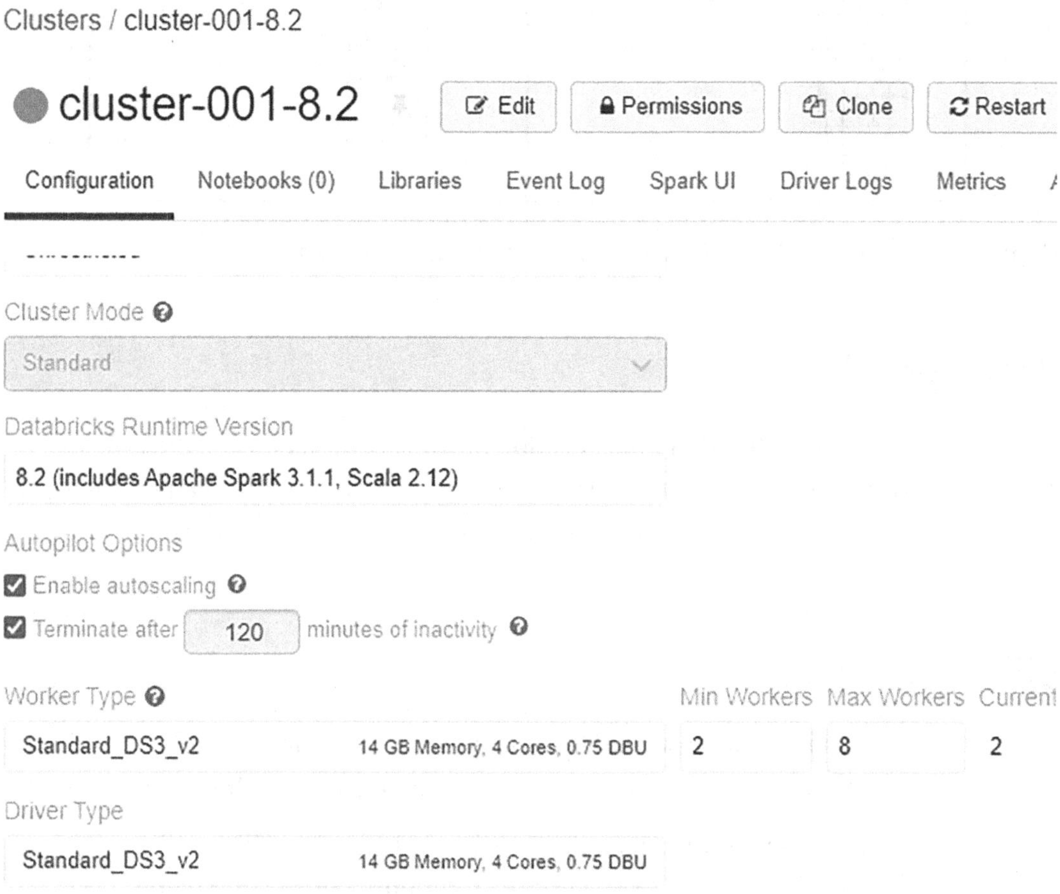

Figure 12-2. Configuration options for the cluster

Create Notebook and Mount Data Lake

Once you have created the cluster, create a new Scala Databricks notebook and attach your cluster to this notebook. Also, ensure that your ADLS gen2 account is properly mounted. Run the following Python code shown in Figure 12-3 to check what mount points you have available: `display(dbutils.fs.mounts())`

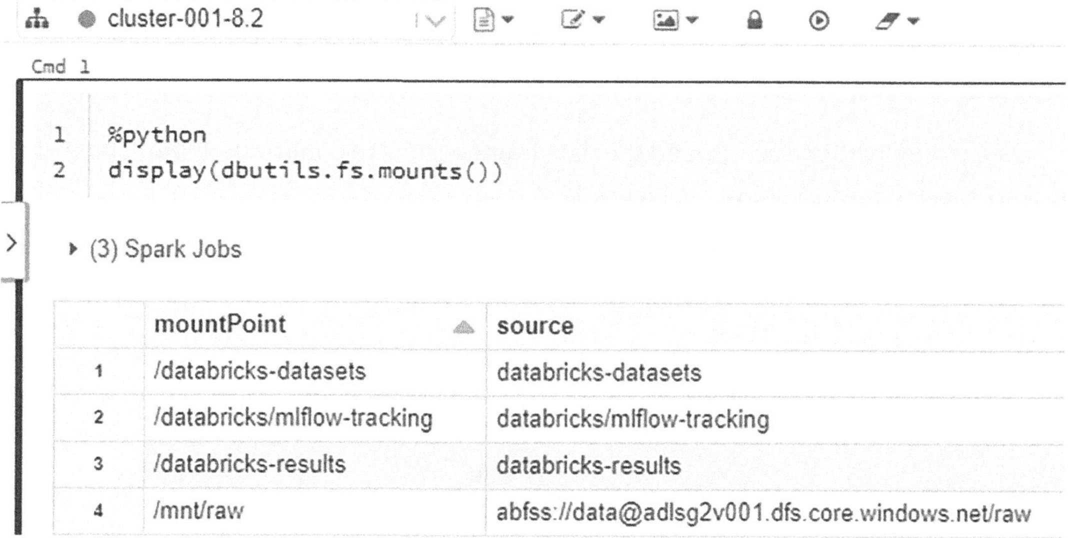

	mountPoint	source
1	/databricks-datasets	databricks-datasets
2	/databricks/mlflow-tracking	databricks/mlflow-tracking
3	/databricks-results	databricks-results
4	/mnt/raw	abfss://data@adlsg2v001.dfs.core.windows.net/raw

Figure 12-3. *Script to show all the mounts in ADLS gen2*

Create Fact Table

Next, run the following Scala code to import the 2019 NYC Taxi dataset into a data frame, apply schemas, and finally add Year, Month, and Day derived columns to the data frame. These additional columns will be used to partition your Delta Table in further steps of the process. Also, this dataset is available through "databricks-datasets" in CSV form, which comes mounted to your cluster.

```
import org.apache.spark.sql.functions._

val Data = "/databricks-datasets/nyctaxi/tripdata/yellow/yellow_
tripdata_2019-*"
val SchemaDF = spark.read.format("csv").option("header", "true").
option("inferSchema", "true").load("/databricks-datasets/nyctaxi/tripdata/
yellow/yellow_tripdata_2019-02.csv.gz")
val df = spark.read.format("csv").option("header", "true").schema
(SchemaDF.schema).load(Data)
val nyctaxiDF = df
```

```
.withColumn("Year", year(col("tpep_pickup_datetime")))
.withColumn("Year_Month", date_format(col("tpep_pickup_
datetime"),"yyyyMM"))
.withColumn("Year_Month_Day", date_format(col("tpep_pickup_
datetime"),"yyyyMMdd"))
```

After running the code, expand the data frame results to confirm that the schema is in the expected format, shown in Figure 12-4.

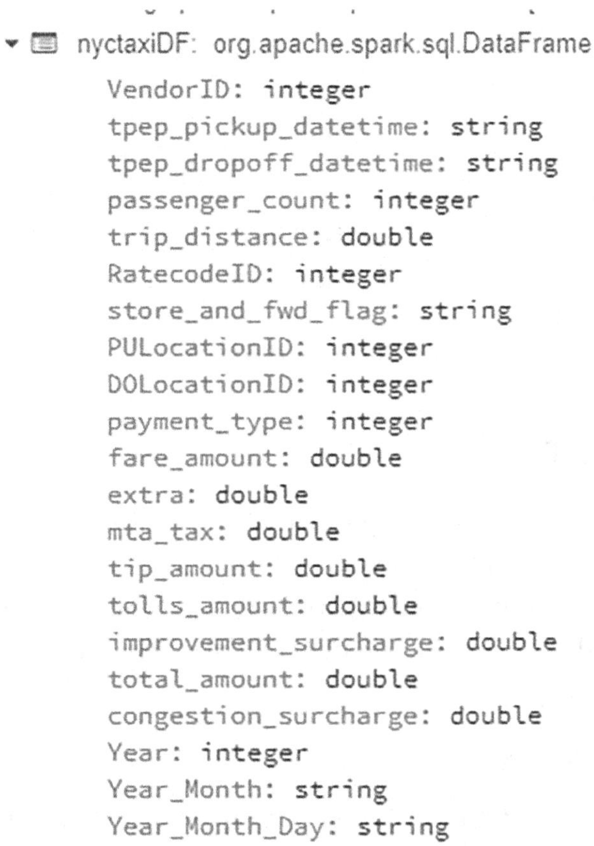

```
nyctaxiDF: org.apache.spark.sql.DataFrame
    VendorID: integer
    tpep_pickup_datetime: string
    tpep_dropoff_datetime: string
    passenger_count: integer
    trip_distance: double
    RatecodeID: integer
    store_and_fwd_flag: string
    PULocationID: integer
    DOLocationID: integer
    payment_type: integer
    fare_amount: double
    extra: double
    mta_tax: double
    tip_amount: double
    tolls_amount: double
    improvement_surcharge: double
    total_amount: double
    congestion_surcharge: double
    Year: integer
    Year_Month: string
    Year_Month_Day: string
```

Figure 12-4. *Schema of nyctaxiDF*

Run the following count of the data frame shown in Figure 12-5 to ensure that there are ~84 million rows in the data frame.

```
1   nyctaxiDF.count()

 ▸ (2) Spark Jobs

res10: Long = 84399019
```

Figure 12-5. *Count of nyctaxiDF*

Once the content of the data frame is finalized, run the following code to write the data to your desired ADLS gen2 mount point location; also, add a partition by Year, Year_Month, and Year_Month_Day. It is these columns that you will use to join this fact table to your dimension table.

```
val Factnyctaxi = nyctaxiDF.write
  .format("delta")
  .mode("overwrite")
  .partitionBy(("Year"), ("Year_Month"), ("Year_Month_Day"))
  .save("/mnt/raw/delta/Factnyctaxi")
```

In addition to persisting the data frame to your ADLS gen2 account, also create a Delta SparkSQL table using the following SQL syntax. With this table, you'll be able to write standard SQL queries to join your fact and dimension tables in further sections.

```
%sql
CREATE TABLE Factnyctaxi
USING DELTA
LOCATION '/mnt/raw/delta/Factnyctaxi'
```

As a good practice, Figure 12-6 shows how to run a count of the newly created table to ensure that it contains the expected number of rows in the Factnyctaxi table.

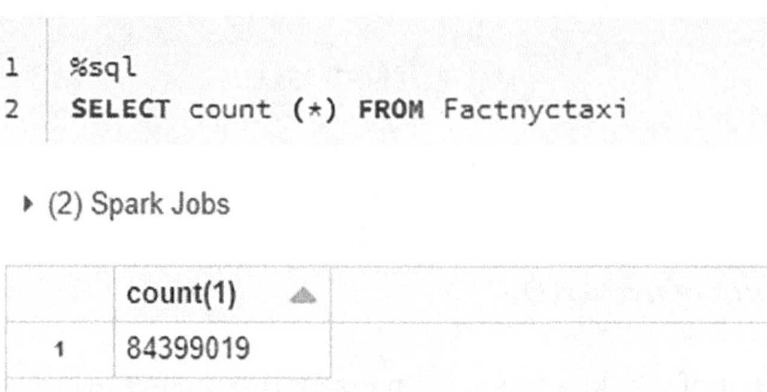

```
%sql
SELECT count (*) FROM Factnyctaxi
```

▸ (2) Spark Jobs

	count(1)
1	84399019

Figure 12-6. Script to count the Factnyctaxi SQL table

Verify Fact Table Partitions

As an added verification step, run the following SHOW PARTITIONS SQL command, as seen in Figure 12-7, to confirm that the expected partitions have been applied to the Factnyctaxi table.

```
%sql
SHOW PARTITIONS Factnyctaxi
```

▸ (2) Spark Jobs

	Year	Year_Month	Year_Month_Day
1	2019	201908	20190814
2	2020	202002	20200228
3	2019	201909	20190919
4	2019	201904	20190407
5	2019	201910	20191006
6	2003	200301	20030101
7	2018	201812	20181231

Showing all 491 rows.

Figure 12-7. Script to show partitions of the Factnyctaxi SQL table

Upon navigating to the ADLS gen2 account through Storage Explorer, notice in Figure 12-8 that the data is appropriately partitioned in the expected folder structure.

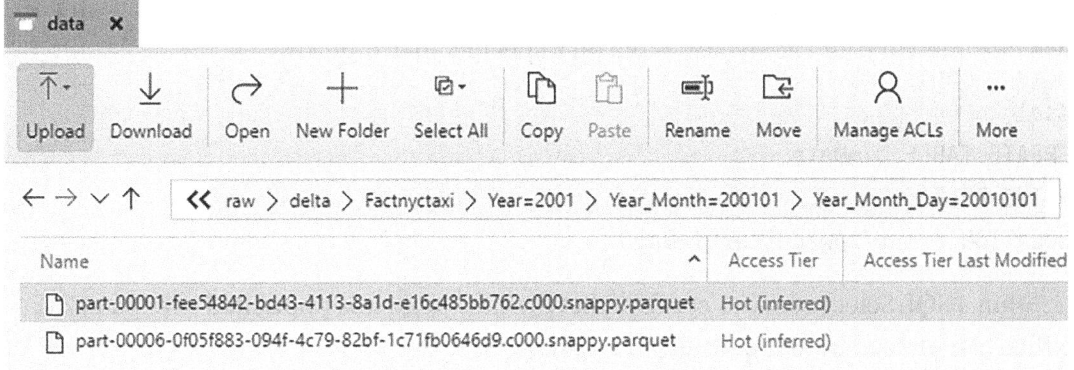

Figure 12-8. *Folder structure of the ADLS gen2 account for Factnyctaxi*

Create Dimension Table

Similar to the process of creating the Factnyctaxi table, you will also need to create a dimension table. For this exercise, create a date dimension table using the CSV file which can be downloaded from `https://support.sisense.com/kb/en/article/date-dimension-file`. Upload this file to your ADLS gen2 account and then run the following script to infer the file's schema and load the file to a data frame:

```
val dimedateDF = spark.read.format("csv")
.option("header", "true")
.option("inferSchema", "true")
.load("/mnt/raw/dimdates.csv")
```

Once the file is loaded to a data frame, run the following code to persist the data as delta format to your ADLS gen2 account:

```
val DimDate = dimedateDF.write
  .format("delta")
  .mode("overwrite")
  .save("/mnt/raw/delta/DimDate")
```

Also, execute the following SQL code to create a Delta Table called DimDate which will be joined to your Factnyctaxi table on a specified partition key:

```
%sql
CREATE TABLE DimDate
USING DELTA
LOCATION '/mnt/raw/delta/DimDate'
```

Run a SQL Select query to confirm that the date table was populated with data, which can be seen from the results in Figure 12-9.

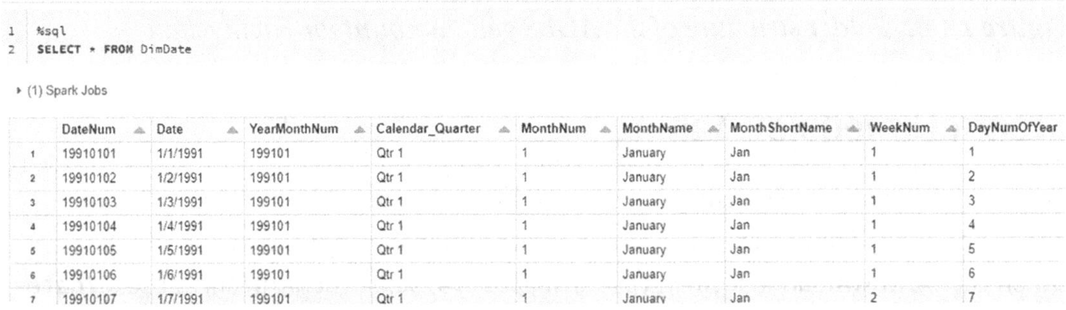

```
%sql
SELECT * FROM DimDate
```

▸ (1) Spark Jobs

	DateNum	Date	YearMonthNum	Calendar_Quarter	MonthNum	MonthName	MonthShortName	WeekNum	DayNumOfYear
1	19910101	1/1/1991	199101	Qtr 1	1	January	Jan	1	1
2	19910102	1/2/1991	199101	Qtr 1	1	January	Jan	1	2
3	19910103	1/3/1991	199101	Qtr 1	1	January	Jan	1	3
4	19910104	1/4/1991	199101	Qtr 1	1	January	Jan	1	4
5	19910105	1/5/1991	199101	Qtr 1	1	January	Jan	1	5
6	19910106	1/6/1991	199101	Qtr 1	1	January	Jan	1	6
7	19910107	1/7/1991	199101	Qtr 1	1	January	Jan	2	7

Figure 12-9. *Code to Select * from the DimDate table*

Join Results Without DPP Filter

Run the following query to join the Factnyctaxi to DimDate on the fact partitioned Year_Month_Day column for which the DateNum is the equivalent key in the DimDate table. Notice that a filter was not applied in this scenario to demonstrate from the execution plan that the dynamic partition pruning will not be activated since there isn't a filter that is being applied.

```
%sql
SELECT * FROM Factnyctaxi F
INNER JOIN DimDate D
ON F.Year_Month_Day = D.DateNum
```

Figure 12-10 illustrates the results of the query to give you an idea of the schema of the data that we are working with.

	VendorID	tpep_pickup_datetime	tpep_dropoff_datetime	passenger_count	trip_distance
1	2	2019-04-05 00:03:27	2019-04-05 00:32:08	1	3.8
2	2	2019-04-05 00:00:36	2019-04-05 00:20:50	1	4.26
3	2	2019-04-05 00:00:40	2019-04-05 00:12:44	4	2.12
4	2	2019-04-05 00:00:07	2019-04-05 00:15:46	1	2.65
5	2	2019-04-05 00:03:39	2019-04-05 00:36:18	2	7.95
6	2	2019-04-05 00:00:38	2019-04-05 00:14:32	1	5.09
7	2	2019-04-05 00:03:11	2019-04-05 00:09:35	1	0.62

***Figure 12-10.** Resulting dataset from joining Factnyctaxi with DimDate*

From the query execution plan in Figure 12-11, notice the details of the scan of Factnyctaxi. The full 936 set of files were scanned across all of the 491 partitions that were read. This indicates that since there was no filter applied, the dynamic partition pruning feature was not enabled for this scenario.

Scan parquet default.factnyctaxi +details	
number of files read	936
filesystem read data size	5.3 MB (5.3 MB, 5.3 MB, 5.3 MB)
scan time	192 ms (192 ms, 192 ms, 192 ms)
estimated repeated reads high size	294.9 KB (294.9 KB, 294.9 KB, 294.9 KB)
filesystem read data size (sampled)	10.6 MB (10.6 MB, 10.6 MB, 10.6 MB)
filesystem read time (sampled)	302 ms (302 ms, 302 ms, 302 ms)
metadata time	27 ms (27 ms, 27 ms, 27 ms)
size of files read	1536.9 MB (1536.9 MB, 1536.9 MB, 1536.9 MB)
estimated repeated reads low size	294.9 KB (294.9 KB, 294.9 KB, 294.9 KB)
number of partitions read	491

***Figure 12-11.** Details of the scan of the fact table without the filter*

Join Results with DPP Filter

Next, run the following SQL query. This query is similar to the previous one, with the addition of a where filter. Notice that this filter is not applied on any of the partition columns from Factnyctaxi, nor were they from the equivalent partition columns in DimDate. The filters that were applied were non-join key columns in the dimension table.

```
%sql
SELECT * FROM Factnyctaxi F
INNER JOIN DimDate D
ON F.Year_Month_Day = D.DateNum
WHERE D.Calendar_Quarter = 'Qtr 1' AND D.DayName = 'Friday'
```

Figure 12-12 illustrates the resulting dataset from the filtered query shown in the preceding code.

	VendorID	tpep_pickup_datetime	tpep_dropoff_datetime	passenger_count	trip_distance
1	1	2019-02-01 00:59:04	2019-02-01 01:07:27	1	2.1
2	1	2019-02-01 00:33:09	2019-02-01 01:03:58	1	9.8
3	1	2019-02-01 00:09:03	2019-02-01 00:09:16	1	0
4	1	2019-02-01 00:45:38	2019-02-01 00:51:10	1	0.8
5	1	2019-02-01 00:25:30	2019-02-01 00:28:14	1	0.8
6	1	2019-02-01 00:38:02	2019-02-01 00:40:57	1	0.8
7	1	2019-02-01 00:06:49	2019-02-01 00:10:34	1	0.9

***Figure 12-12.** Resulting dataset from joining Factnyctaxi with DimDate with filter*

From the query execution plan in Figure 12-13, notice the details of the scan of Factnyctaxi. Only 43 out of the full 936 set of files were scanned across only 24 of the 491 partitions. Also notice that dynamic partition pruning has an execution time of 95ms, which indicates that dynamic partition pruning was applied to this query.

Scan parquet default.factnyctaxi +details	
number of files read	43
filesystem read data size	5.3 MB (5.3 MB, 5.3 MB, 5.3 MB)
scan time	278 ms (278 ms, 278 ms, 278 ms)
estimated repeated reads high size	5.3 MB (5.3 MB, 5.3 MB, 5.3 MB)
filesystem read data size (sampled)	10.5 MB (10.5 MB, 10.5 MB, 10.5 MB)
filesystem read time (sampled)	544 ms (544 ms, 544 ms, 544 ms)
dynamic partition pruning time	95 ms (95 ms, 95 ms, 95 ms)
metadata time	64 ms (64 ms, 64 ms, 64 ms)
size of files read	64.6 MB (64.6 MB, 64.6 MB, 64.6 MB)
static number of files read	936
estimated repeated reads low size	5.3 MB (5.3 MB, 5.3 MB, 5.3 MB)
static size of files read	1536.9 MB (1536.9 MB, 1536.9 MB, 1536.9 MB)
number of partitions read	24
rows output	4,096

***Figure 12-13.** Details of the scan of the fact table with the filter*

Summary

In this chapter, you learned about the various benefits of dynamic partition pruning along with how it is optimized for Querying Star Schema models. This can be a valuable feature as you continue building out your Data Lakehouse in Azure. You also learned a hands-on technique for recreating a scenario best suited for dynamic partition pruning by joining a fact and dimension table on a partition key column and filtering the dimension table on a non-join key. Upon monitoring the query execution plan for this scenario, you learned that dynamic partition pruning had been applied and a significantly smaller subset of the data and partitions were read and scanned.

CHAPTER 13

Z-Ordering and Data Skipping

When querying terabytes and petabytes of big data for analytics using Apache Spark, having optimized querying speeds is critical. There are a few available optimization commands within Databricks that can be used to speed up queries and make them more efficient. Seeing that Z-Ordering and Data Skipping are optimization features that are available within Databricks, we are interested in getting started with testing and using them in Databricks notebooks.

Z-Ordering is a method used by Apache Spark to combine related information in the same files. This is automatically used by Delta Lake on Databricks data-skipping algorithms to dramatically reduce the amount of data that needs to be read. The OPTIMIZE command can achieve this compaction on its own without Z-Ordering which compacts small files into larger ones to improve the speed of reading queries from the table. This bin-packing process will produce evenly balanced data files when compared to size on disk but may not necessarily optimize on a specific column, which could be useful for scenarios where the column is used to filter queries.

Adding Z-Ordering to the OPTIMIZE command allows us to specify the column to compact and optimize on, which will impact querying speeds if the specified column is in a Where clause and has high cardinality. Additionally, Data Skipping is an automatic feature of the optimize command and works well when combined with Z-Ordering. In this chapter, I will guide you through a few practical examples of optimizations with Z-Ordering and Data Skipping which will help you with understanding the performance improvements along with how to explore these changes in the delta_logs and Spark UI.

R. L'Esteve, *The Azure Data Lakehouse Toolkit*, https://doi.org/10.1007/978-1-4842-8233-5_13

Prepare Data in Delta Lake

Let's begin the process by loading the airlines databricks-dataset into a data frame using the following script. Remember to create a Python notebook along with a running cluster that is attached to the notebook. Note that databricks-datasets are available for use within Databricks and can be found at `https://docs.databricks.com/data/databricks-datasets.html`.

```
flights = spark.read.format("csv") \
  .option("header", "true") \
  .option("inferSchema", "true") \
  .load("/databricks-datasets/asa/airlines/2008.csv")
```

Once the data is loaded into the "flights" data frame, run a display command to quickly visualize the structure of the data, as shown in Figure 13-1.

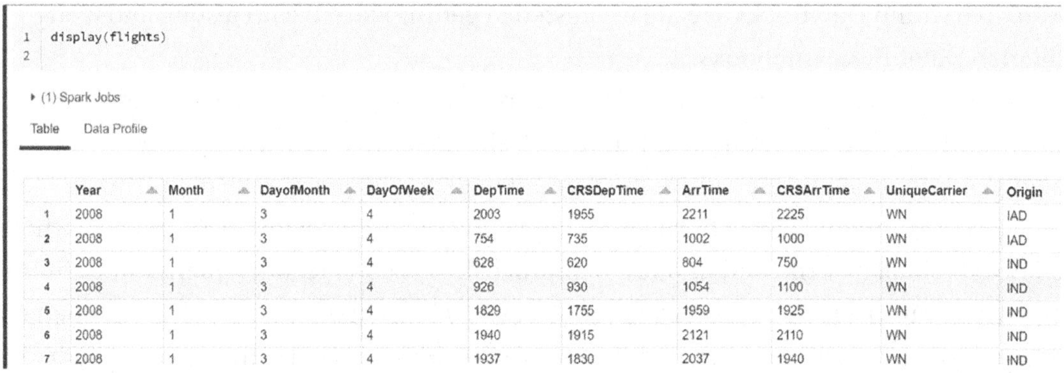

```
display(flights)
```

▸ (1) Spark Jobs

Table   Data Profile

	Year	Month	DayofMonth	DayOfWeek	DepTime	CRSDepTime	ArrTime	CRSArrTime	UniqueCarrier	Origin
1	2008	1	3	4	2003	1955	2211	2225	WN	IAD
2	2008	1	3	4	754	735	1002	1000	WN	IAD
3	2008	1	3	4	628	620	804	750	WN	IND
4	2008	1	3	4	926	930	1054	1100	WN	IND
5	2008	1	3	4	1829	1755	1959	1925	WN	IND
6	2008	1	3	4	1940	1915	2121	2110	WN	IND
7	2008	1	3	4	1937	1830	2037	1940	WN	IND

***Figure 13-1.** Code to display the flights df to see the data*

Next, run the following script which will create a mount point to an ADLS gen2 account where the data will be persisted. Ensure that the access key is replaced in the following script:

```
spark.conf.set(
  "fs.azure.account.key.rl001adls2.dfs.core.windows.net",
  "ENTER-ACCESS_KEY_HERE"
)
```

Next, run the following code to write the flights data frame to the Data Lake folder in delta format and partitioned by the Origin column:

```
(
  flights
  .write
  .partitionBy("Origin")
  .format("delta")
  .mode("overwrite")
  .save("abfss://data@rl001adls2.dfs.core.windows.net/raw/delta/
flights_delta")
)
```

As a quick aside since this section is on preparing data, as you prepare your data, you may run into scenarios where there is no clear partition key since your data contains a combined datetime value such as `'2019-03-01 00:24:41'`; you may need to break this out into various partition keys such as Year, Year_Month, and Year_Month_Day through Databricks notebook code. Let's look at a quick example of how to do this before we move onto the next section. Firstly, the following code will infer the schema and load a data frame with the 2019 yellow trip data:

```
Data = "/databricks-datasets/nyctaxi/tripdata/yellow/yellow_
tripdata_2019-*"

SchemaDF = spark.read.format("csv") \
  .option("header", "true") \
  .option("inferSchema", "true") \
  .load("/databricks-datasets/nyctaxi/tripdata/yellow/yellow_tripdata_
  2019-02.csv.gz")

nyctaxiDF = spark.read.format("csv") \
  .option("header", "true") \
  .schema(SchemaDF.schema) \
  .load(Data)
```

This next code block will add a few partition fields to the existing data frame for Year, Year_Month, and Year_Month_Day. These additional columns will be based on the datetime stamp and will help with partitioning, Data Skipping, Z-Ordering, and ultimately more performant querying speeds.

```
from pyspark.sql.functions import *
```

```
nyctaxiDF = nyctaxiDF.withColumn('Year', year(col("tpep_pickup_datetime")))
nyctaxiDF = nyctaxiDF.withColumn('Year_Month', date_format(col("tpep_
pickup_datetime"),"yyyyMM"))
nyctaxiDF = nyctaxiDF.withColumn('Year_Month_Day', date_format(col
("tpep_pickup_datetime"),"yyyyMMdd"))
```

After running a command to display the data frame, notice from Figure 13-2 that the three new columns (Year, Year_Month, and Year_Month_Day) have been added to the data frame. Notice the corresponding original datetime values to the left of the data frame. Now these new values can be used as partition values.

Table Data Profile

	VendorID	tpep_pickup_datetime	tpep_dropoff_datetime	Year	Year_Month	Year_Month_Day
1	1	2019-03-01 00:24:41	2019-03-01 00:25:31	2019	201903	20190301
2	1	2019-03-01 00:25:27	2019-03-01 00:36:37	2019	201903	20190301
3	1	2019-03-01 00:05:21	2019-03-01 00:38:23	2019	201903	20190301
4	1	2019-03-01 00:48:55	2019-03-01 01:06:03	2019	201903	20190301
5	1	2019-03-01 00:11:42	2019-03-01 00:16:40	2019	201903	20190301
6	1	2019-03-01 00:45:03	2019-03-01 00:49:38	2019	201903	20190301

Figure 13-2. *View of the newly created partition columns in nyctaxidf*

Verify Data in Delta Lake

As we head back to our original dataset, recall that you'll need to ensure that the following code completes running, which will write the flights data frame to the Data Lake folder in delta format and partitioned by the Origin column:

```
(
  flights
  .write
  .partitionBy("Origin")
  .format("delta")
  .mode("overwrite")
  .save("abfss://data@rl001adls2.dfs.core.windows.net/raw/delta/
flights_delta")
)
```

Notice from Figure 13-3 that the flight data has been partitioned and persisted in ADLS gen2. There are over 300 folders partitioned by "Origin."

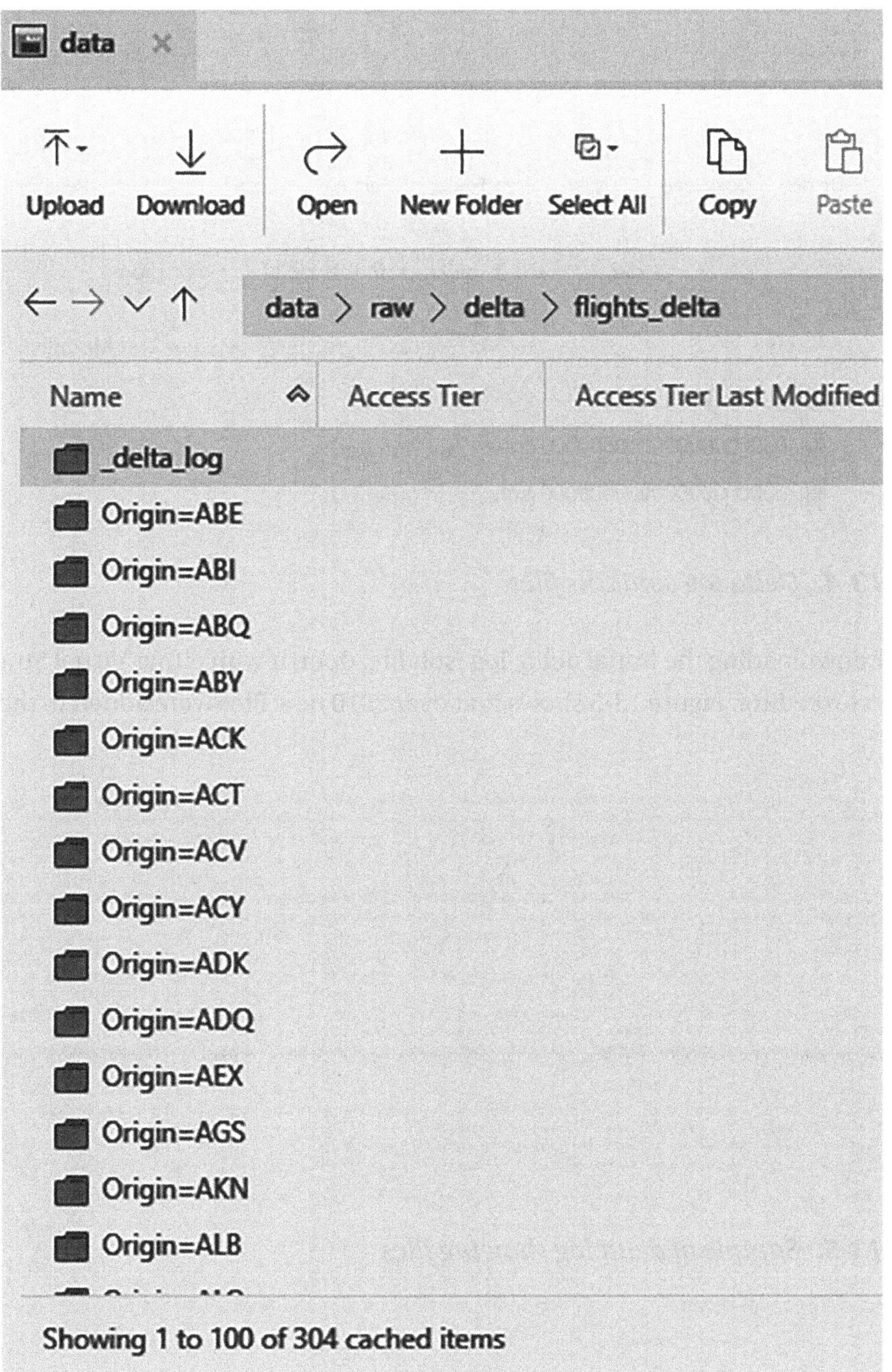

***Figure 13-3.** ADLS gen2 partitioned folders where flights were created*

Upon navigating to the delta_log, Figure 13-4 shows the initial log files, primarily represented by the *.json files.

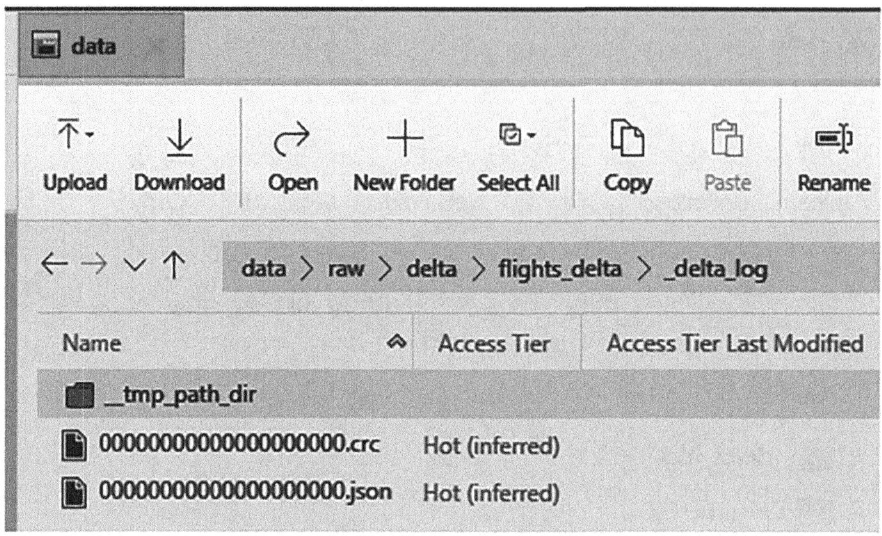

Figure 13-4. *Delta log contains files*

After downloading the initial delta_log json file, open it with either Visual Studio Code or a text editor. Figure 13-5 shows that over 2310 new files were added to the 300+ folders.


```
{"add":{"path":"Origin=SWF/part-00007-543862ac-6f39-4476-b60e-d9a39065f6ee.c000.snappy.parquet","partitionValues":{"Origin":"SWF"},"s
{"add":{"path":"Origin=SYR/part-00007-3e2e651b-2c61-4433-a671-a0e0da311983.c000.snappy.parquet","partitionValues":{"Origin":"SYR"},"s
{"add":{"path":"Origin=TEX/part-00007-f6bf58f3-5a9f-476b-bdad-5561bcbc706e.c000.snappy.parquet","partitionValues":{"Origin":"TEX"},"s
{"add":{"path":"Origin=TLH/part-00007-586a5049-3a2f-416e-bc68-357b4719c401.c000.snappy.parquet","partitionValues":{"Origin":"TLH"},"s
{"add":{"path":"Origin=TOL/part-00007-9caba796-f063-49f0-b92b-0e86c74ff22e.c000.snappy.parquet","partitionValues":{"Origin":"TOL"},"s
{"add":{"path":"Origin=TPA/part-00007-59424a2b-0c11-43bf-b04f-8039bb4501f9.c000.snappy.parquet","partitionValues":{"Origin":"TPA"},"s
{"add":{"path":"Origin=TRI/part-00007-79168c38-8c58-41bd-ab1b-1500c607fb79.c000.snappy.parquet","partitionValues":{"Origin":"TRI"},"s
{"add":{"path":"Origin=TUL/part-00007-f9f1758d-7b57-4763-be2e-92bb2af9f6f2.c000.snappy.parquet","partitionValues":{"Origin":"TUL"},"s
{"add":{"path":"Origin=TUS/part-00007-5ecf57fe-06a4-493c-915a-ab9ff4c8128a.c000.snappy.parquet","partitionValues":{"Origin":"TUS"},"s
{"add":{"path":"Origin=TVC/part-00007-72149275-1cae-4985-8dfd-b82631a250be.c000.snappy.parquet","partitionValues":{"Origin":"TVC"},"s
{"add":{"path":"Origin=TWF/part-00007-0b8ff4e9-2b07-45ec-a253-9a463706073a.c000.snappy.parquet","partitionValues":{"Origin":"TWF"},"s
{"add":{"path":"Origin=TXK/part-00007-5f1043c0-5421-4010-8d58-0190b08407cd.c000.snappy.parquet","partitionValues":{"Origin":"TXK"},"s
{"add":{"path":"Origin=TYR/part-00007-df1ad927-7672-4369-9dff-13b85b43a4ae.c000.snappy.parquet","partitionValues":{"Origin":"TYR"},"s
{"add":{"path":"Origin=TYS/part-00007-62d842bd-b41c-4253-b1cc-93483a2cdbc2.c000.snappy.parquet","partitionValues":{"Origin":"TYS"},"s
{"add":{"path":"Origin=VLD/part-00007-c1d79470-dfb8-49cd-8f51-2558a7ac76b3.c000.snappy.parquet","partitionValues":{"Origin":"VLD"},"s
{"add":{"path":"Origin=VPS/part-00007-16c3f832-840f-48e9-9117-2243d1fe24c8.c000.snappy.parquet","partitionValues":{"Origin":"VPS"},"s
{"add":{"path":"Origin=WRG/part-00007-534d0f88-edd9-4480-8d7a-1210e31e22fc.c000.snappy.parquet","partitionValues":{"Origin":"WRG"},"s
{"add":{"path":"Origin=XNA/part-00007-5716657c-08a5-4b31-9ef4-d2cb2acb2355.c000.snappy.parquet","partitionValues":{"Origin":"XNA"},"s
{"add":{"path":"Origin=YAK/part-00007-e14999bc-c92a-45b7-bd96-a62e85e80326.c000.snappy.parquet","partitionValues":{"Origin":"YAK"},"s
{"add":{"path":"Origin=YUM/part-00007-40c30ad4-0363-4042-a4f0-076be07ae551.c000.snappy.parquet","partitionValues":{"Origin":"YUM"},"s
```


Figure 13-5. *Sample of delta log showing files*

Create Hive Table

Now that you have some data persisted in ADLS gen2, create a Hive table using the Delta location with the following script:

```
spark.sql("CREATE TABLE flights USING DELTA LOCATION 'abfss://data@
rl001adls2.dfs.core.windows.net/raw/delta/flights_delta/'")
```

After creating the Hive table, run the following SQL count script to ensure that the Hive table has been created as desired `SELECT Count(*) from flights` and verify the total count of the dataset. The results shown in Figure 13-6 indicate that this is a fairly big dataset with over seven million records.

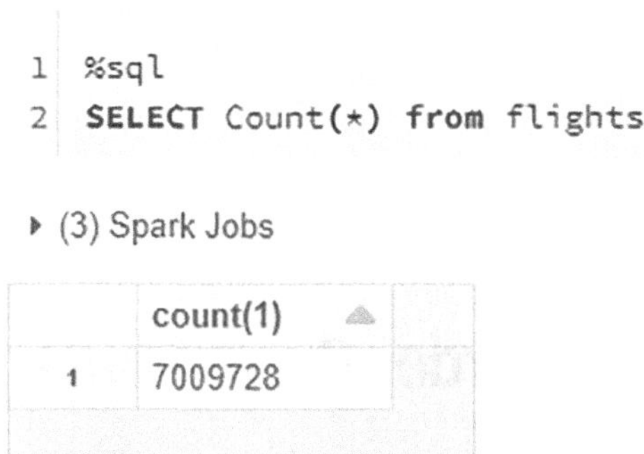

Figure 13-6. *Code to count the Hive table flights*

Next, run the more complex query shown as follows which will apply a filter to the Flights table on a non-partitioned column, DayofMonth:

```
%sql
SELECT count(*) as Flights, Dest, Month from flights WHERE DayofMonth = 5
GROUP BY Month, Dest
```

From the results displayed in Figure 13-7, notice that the query took over two minutes to complete. This time allows us to set the initial benchmark for the time to compare after we run the Z-Order command.

	Flights	Dest	Month
1	5	AVP	9
2	7	AVP	2
3	113	ONT	5
4	124	PIT	6
5	65	OMA	7
6	151	CLE	10
7	6	MLU	10
8	76	JAX	10

Showing the first 1000 rows.

Command took 2.86 minutes -- by ronlesteve at 11/1/2020, 9:13:33 PM on Standardl

Figure 13-7. *Tabular view of the previously queried Flights table*

Run Optimize and Z-Order Commands

Next, run the following SQL OPTIMZE combined with Z-ORDER command `OPTIMIZE flights ZORDER BY (DayofMonth)`, as shown in Figure 13-8. Use the column that you want to filter, which is DayofMonth. Note that Z-Order optimizations work best on columns that have high cardinality. Based on the results, 2308 files were removed, and 300 files were added as part of the OPTIMIZE Z-ORDER commands. Also, keep in mind that this is a logical removal and addition. For physical removal of files, the VACCUM command will need to be run.

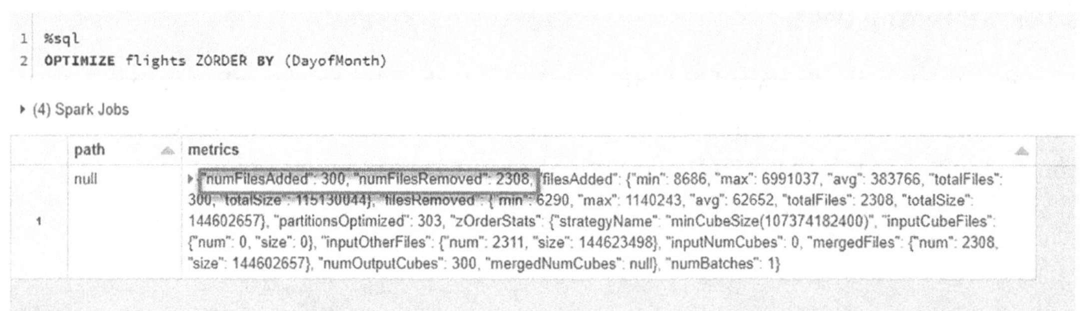

```
%sql
OPTIMIZE flights ZORDER BY (DayofMonth)
```

(4) Spark Jobs

	path	metrics
1	null	{"numFilesAdded": 300, "numFilesRemoved": 2308, "filesAdded": {"min": 8686, "max": 6991037, "avg": 383766, "totalFiles": 300, "totalSize": 115130044}, "filesRemoved": {"min": 6290, "max": 1140243, "avg": 62652, "totalFiles": 2308, "totalSize": 144602657}, "partitionsOptimized": 303, "zOrderStats": {"strategyName": "minCubeSize(107374182400)", "inputCubeFiles": {"num": 0, "size": 0}, "inputOtherFiles": {"num": 2311, "size": 144623498}, "inputNumCubes": 0, "mergedFiles": {"num": 2308, "size": 144602657}, "numOutputCubes": 300, "mergedNumCubes": null}, "numBatches": 1}

Figure 13-8. *Code and results to OPTIMIZE flights and ZORDER by DayofMonth*

Within the delta_log, there is now a new JSON format file, as shown in Figure 13-9, that you can download and open to review the results.

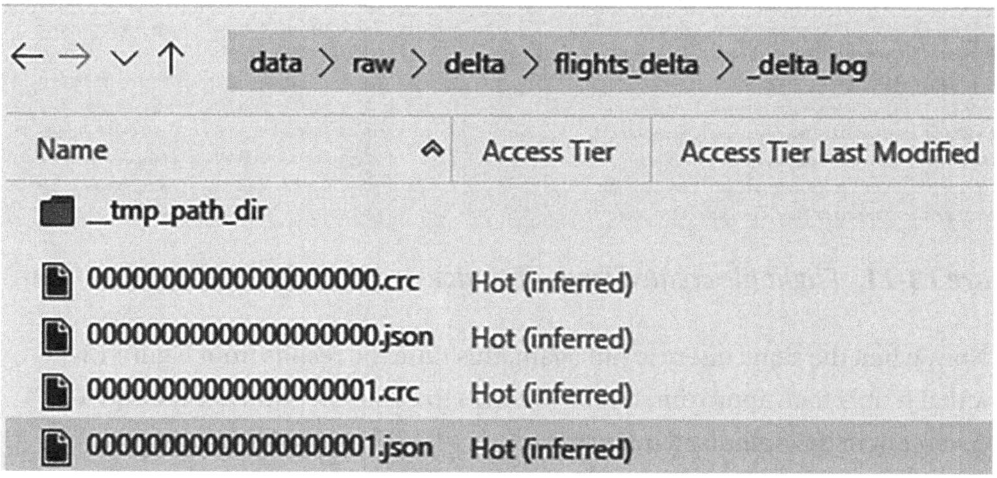

data > raw > delta > flights_delta > _delta_log

Name	Access Tier	Access Tier Last Modified
_tmp_path_dir		
00000000000000000000.crc	Hot (inferred)	
00000000000000000000.json	Hot (inferred)	
00000000000000000001.crc	Hot (inferred)	
00000000000000000001.json	Hot (inferred)	

Figure 13-9. *Delta log shows zorder changes*

As expected, Figure 13-10 shows the actions performed in these logs based on the removal and addition lines in the json file.

```
{"remove":{"path":"Origin=YKM/part-00005-37dfb5ad-1bcd-4c3f-a40a-4020061a929d.c000.snappy.parquet","deletionTimestamp":1604287124347,
{"remove":{"path":"Origin=YUM/part-00000-a7579b54-6114-4b0d-ba57-81389b274f61.c000.snappy.parquet","deletionTimestamp":1604287124347,
{"remove":{"path":"Origin=YUM/part-00001-129f5271-ca18-4423-98bf-fc343f3cb17b.c000.snappy.parquet","deletionTimestamp":1604287124347,
{"remove":{"path":"Origin=YUM/part-00002-5827ad0f-6fba-4848-80ab-35558fb390a1.c000.snappy.parquet","deletionTimestamp":1604287124347,
{"remove":{"path":"Origin=YUM/part-00003-06ac7d14-05ca-42f0-a2b8-f14bfde4907b.c000.snappy.parquet","deletionTimestamp":1604287124347,
{"remove":{"path":"Origin=YUM/part-00004-ccdddae5-559d-4357-b98a-f3e1c0d0b6ee.c000.snappy.parquet","deletionTimestamp":1604287124347,
{"remove":{"path":"Origin=YUM/part-00005-8f6e0744-c911-4b63-8b2b-bcefc80bca87.c000.snappy.parquet","deletionTimestamp":1604287124347,
{"remove":{"path":"Origin=YUM/part-00006-a95577ee-2d30-4942-b618-3edebf813cfd.c000.snappy.parquet","deletionTimestamp":1604287124347,
{"remove":{"path":"Origin=YUM/part-00007-40c30ad4-0363-4042-a4f0-076be07ae551.c000.snappy.parquet","deletionTimestamp":1604287124347,
{"add":{"path":"Origin=ABE/part-00000-d078ca82-e758-4229-b52f-a468c9c26270.c000.snappy.parquet","partitionValues":{"Origin":"ABE"},"s
{"add":{"path":"Origin=ABI/part-00001-a22c6d0f-4b06-47ee-9080-9736697cf4db.c000.snappy.parquet","partitionValues":{"Origin":"ABI"},"s
{"add":{"path":"Origin=ABQ/part-00002-fa4a1b3c-e3b1-422a-ba3c-0126ddf0626e.c000.snappy.parquet","partitionValues":{"Origin":"ABQ"},"s
{"add":{"path":"Origin=ABY/part-00003-59acd9dc-c72c-4fd2-bde3-ffdba9bd6cef.c000.snappy.parquet","partitionValues":{"Origin":"ABY"},"s
{"add":{"path":"Origin=ACK/part-00004-148f968b-5d10-4810-8d24-18cde31e9715.c000.snappy.parquet","partitionValues":{"Origin":"ACK"},"s
{"add":{"path":"Origin=ACT/part-00005-3f763002-72c9-4616-9666-457484dc00ea.c000.snappy.parquet","partitionValues":{"Origin":"ACT"},"s
{"add":{"path":"Origin=ACV/part-00006-22e21671-387e-4694-9848-2c127cac5b74.c000.snappy.parquet","partitionValues":{"Origin":"ACV"},"s
{"add":{"path":"Origin=ACY/part-00007-ef0a285a-c26f-45f4-8c47-626cdb8d20ff.c000.snappy.parquet","partitionValues":{"Origin":"ACY"},"s
{"add":{"path":"Origin=ADK/part-00008-04ea2d55-0fd7-46b2-8375-73dc41b3722a.c000.snappy.parquet","partitionValues":{"Origin":"ADK"},"s
{"add":{"path":"Origin=ADQ/part-00009-b724c5dc-499b-4eea-ba7c-b4d19c4b8031.c000.snappy.parquet","partitionValues":{"Origin":"ADQ"},"s
{"add":{"path":"Origin=AEX/part-00010-56e6267d-c353-4f81-a177-229a59d3fbfe.c000.snappy.parquet","partitionValues":{"Origin":"AEX"},"s
{"add":{"path":"Origin=AGS/part-00011-e089bca9-91e4-4665-ae52-4204bebb2519.c000.snappy.parquet","partitionValues":{"Origin":"AGS"},"s
```


Figure 13-10. *JSON files show removal and addition of files*

As further confirmation, upon navigating to within one of the partition folders, Figure 13-11 shows a new file has been created. While the Z-Order command can customize the compaction size, it typically targets around 1 GB per file when possible.

data > raw > delta > flights_delta > Origin=ABE

	Access Tier	Access Tier Last Modified	Last Modified	Blob Type	Content Type	Size
33-d9a5-4275-81de-ed92e5b0082c.c000.snappy.parquet	Hot (inferred)		11/1/2020, 8:26:47 PM	Block Blob	application/octet-stream	23.2 KB
32-e758-4229-b52f-a468c9c26270.c000.snappy.parquet	Hot (inferred)		11/1/2020, 9:29:06 PM	Block Blob	application/octet-stream	89.7 KB
f4-55fd-44b3-86a4-3123be6a0dab.c000.snappy.parquet	Hot (inferred)		11/1/2020, 8:26:49 PM	Block Blob	application/octet-stream	21.4 KB
04-c766-4e9f-8df2-d1406ed4fbb0.c000.snappy.parquet	Hot (inferred)		11/1/2020, 8:26:48 PM	Block Blob	application/octet-stream	22.4 KB
i32-7ba8-4226-ab37-52c562e7b4bc.c000.snappy.parquet	Hot (inferred)		11/1/2020, 8:26:48 PM	Block Blob	application/octet-stream	21.4 KB
:7-6ae2-43d8-ba42-1483717b2572.c000.snappy.parquet	Hot (inferred)		11/1/2020, 8:26:48 PM	Block Blob	application/octet-stream	19.6 KB
a4-8557-45c4-a532-1cb16a67e907.c000.snappy.parquet	Hot (inferred)		11/1/2020, 8:26:48 PM	Block Blob	application/octet-stream	21.1 KB
lf-555d-4dca-9ce3-761e89b1eab8.c000.snappy.parquet	Hot (inferred)		11/1/2020, 8:26:48 PM	Block Blob	application/octet-stream	23.2 KB
ed-f0a2-4a81-8790-dc9938e00814.c000.snappy.parquet	Hot (inferred)		11/1/2020, 8:26:48 PM	Block Blob	application/octet-stream	22.3 KB

***Figure 13-11.** Flight file created from optimize command*

Now, when the same query is run again, this time the results from Figure 13-12 show that it only took approximately 39 seconds to complete, which is around a 70% improvement in the optimized query speed.

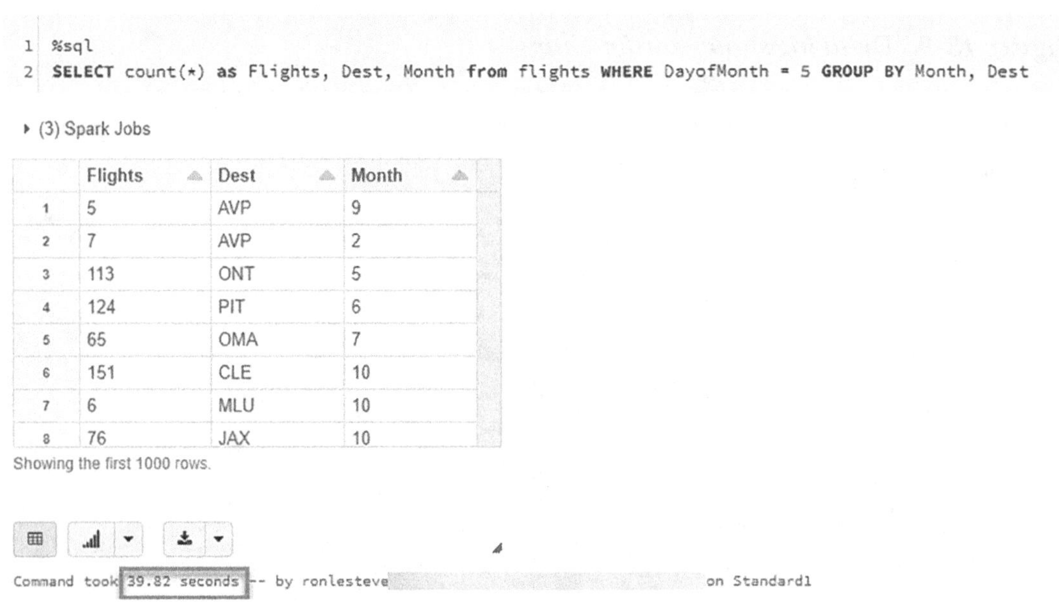

%sql
SELECT count(*) as Flights, Dest, Month from flights WHERE DayofMonth = 5 GROUP BY Month, Dest
(3) Spark Jobs
Flights Dest Month
1 5 AVP 9
2 7 AVP 2
3 113 ONT 5
4 124 PIT 6
5 65 OMA 7
6 151 CLE 10
7 6 MLU 10
8 76 JAX 10
Showing the first 1000 rows.
Command took 39.82 seconds -- by ronlesteve on Standard1

***Figure 13-12.** Optimized query only takes 39 seconds*

Verify Data Skipping

One result from optimizing your data is that Databricks puts in practice a concept called Data Skipping. Data Skipping does not need to be configured and is applied automatically when data is written into a Delta Table and is most effective when combined with Z-Ordering.

To confirm that all files are being read, run the following query `SELECT count(*) as Flights, Dest, Month from flights WHERE DayofMonth = 5 GROUP BY Month, Dest`, as shown in Figure 13-13. Follow the steps shown in Figure 13-13 to view the query plan.

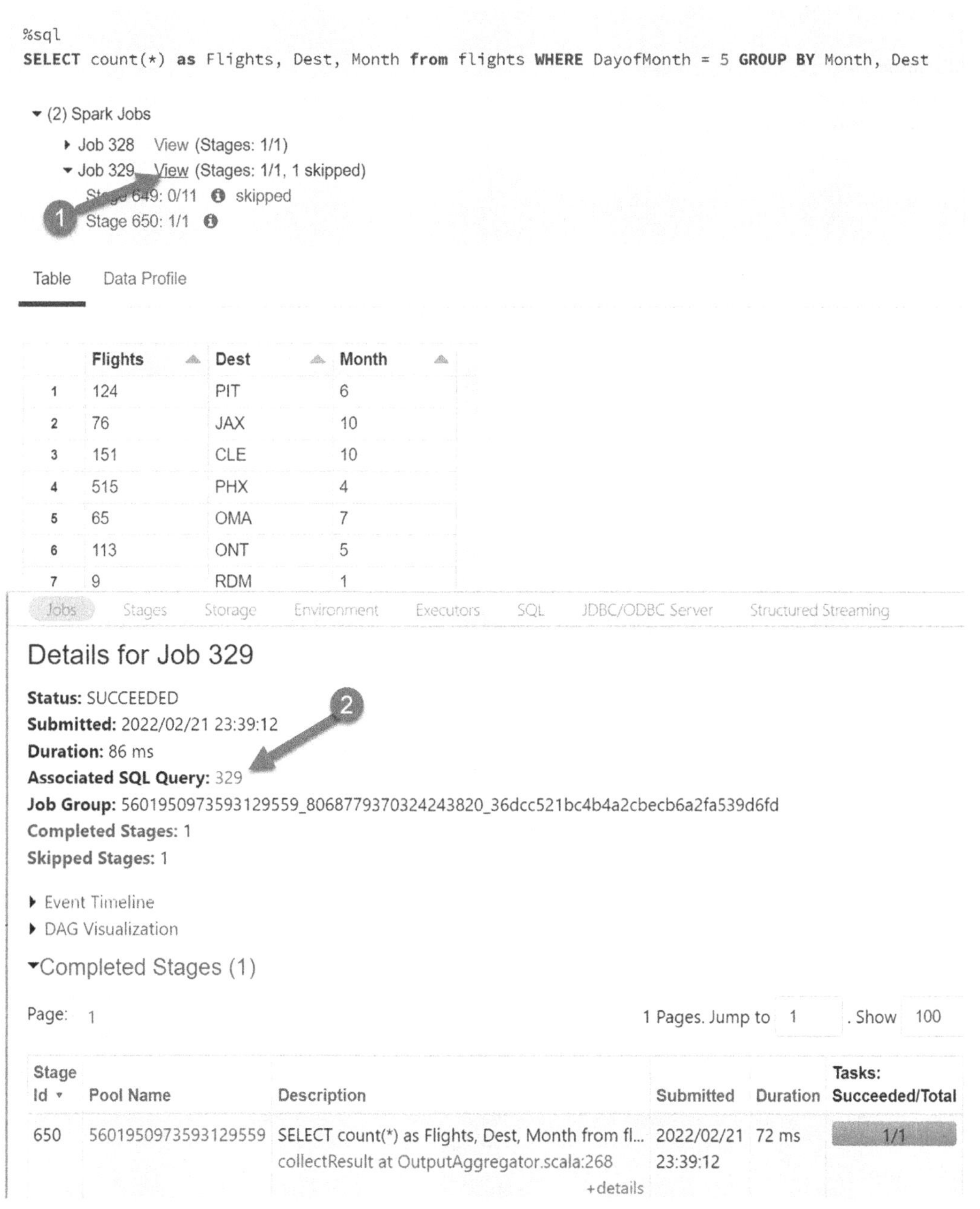

***Figure 13-13.** Steps to view the SQL Query Plan*

Notice the SQL Query Plan in Figure 13-14. Since the filter conditions applied to this query do not match the "partition by" column, all files were read.

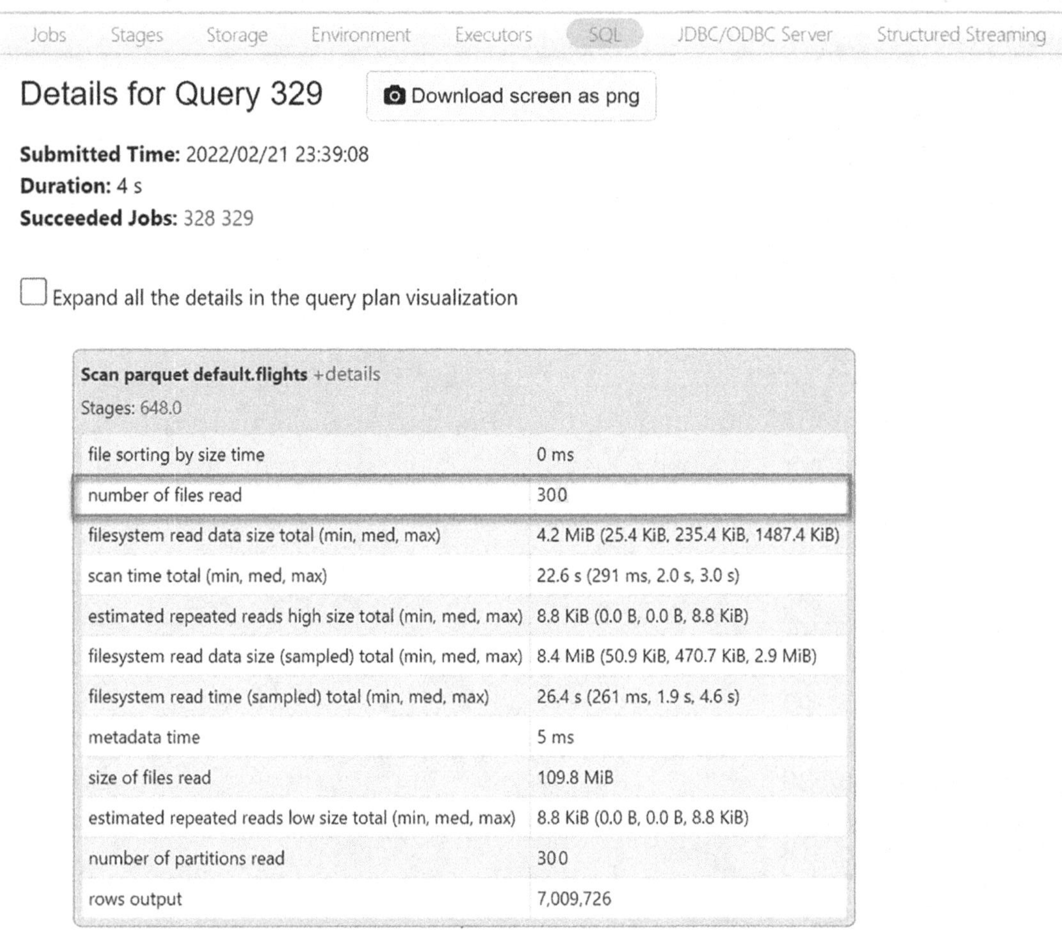

***Figure 13-14.** SQL Query Plan showing all 300 files being read*

Next, add a new filter on the "partition by" column "Origin" by running the following script: `SELECT count(*) as Flights, Origin, Dest, Month from flights WHERE Origin = 'IAD' GROUP BY Origin, Month, Dest`, as shown in Figure 13-15.

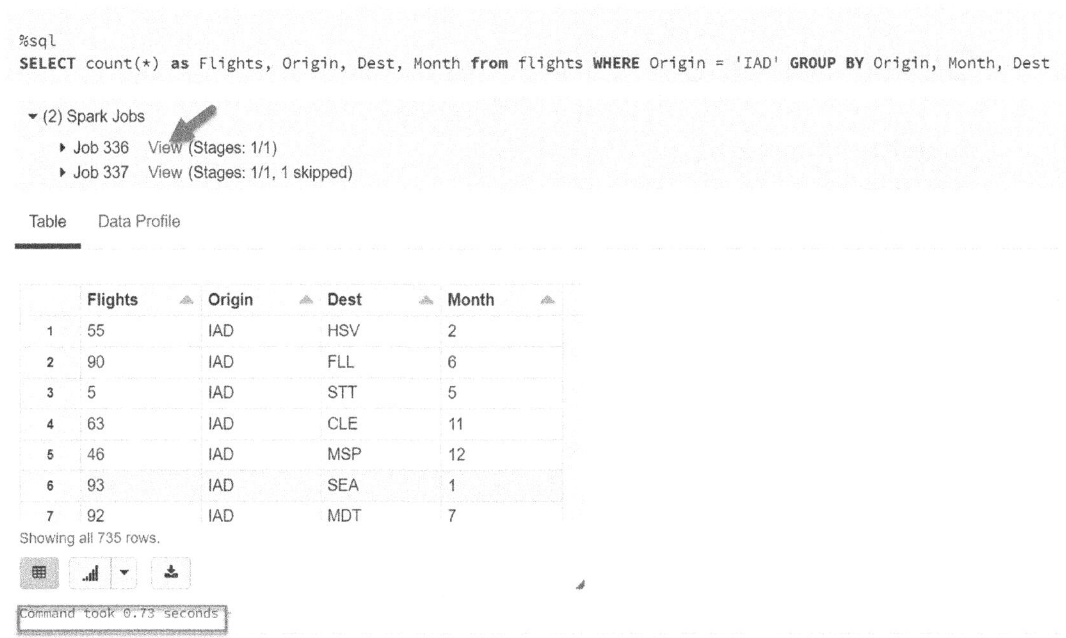

	Flights	Origin	Dest	Month
1	55	IAD	HSV	2
2	90	IAD	FLL	6
3	5	IAD	STT	5
4	63	IAD	CLE	11
5	46	IAD	MSP	12
6	93	IAD	SEA	1
7	92	IAD	MDT	7

***Figure 13-15.** Code to select from the NYC Hive table*

Based on the SQL Query Plan shown in Figure 13-16, notice that only one file was read, which confirms that Data Skipping was applied at runtime.

Submitted Time: 2022/02/21 23:49:33
Duration: 0.5 s
Succeeded Jobs: 336 337

☐ Expand all the details in the query plan visualization

Scan parquet default.flights +details

Stages: 663.0

file sorting by size time	0 ms
number of files read	1
filesystem read data size	21.4 KiB
scan time	178 ms
estimated repeated reads high size	21.4 KiB
filesystem read data size (sampled)	42.9 KiB
filesystem read time (sampled)	123 ms
metadata time	0 ms
size of files read	1235.0 KiB
estimated repeated reads low size	21.4 KiB
number of partitions read	1
rows output	76,031

Figure 13-16. *SQL Query Plan showing only one file being read*

Summary

In this chapter, you learned about ways to optimize queries in your Databricks notebooks by applying the capabilities of the Z-ORDER command which includes Data Skipping, file partitions by defined partition values, and more. It is important to note that Z-Ordering can be applied to multiple columns; however, it is recommended to take caution with this approach since there will be a cost to adding too many Z-Order columns.

There is also an Auto Optimize feature that can be applied, which automatically compacts small files during writes to a Delta Table by paying a small cost during writes to reap significant benefits for tables that are queried. Great candidates for Auto Optimize are streaming use cases, merge into statements, and create table as select or insert operations. This is enabled by default but can be enabled at the Spark session by running the `Set spark.databricks.delta.properties.defaults.autoOptimize.optimizeWrite = true;` and `set spark.databricks.delta.properties.defaults.autoOptimize.autoCompact = true;`. It can also be enabled at the table level during table creation or by running the alter command and specifying the `SET TBLPROPERTIES` with this previously listed command. For more details on Auto Optimize, please read Microsoft's documentation which can be found here: `https://docs.microsoft.com/en-us/azure/databricks/delta/optimizations/auto-optimize`

The Auto Optimize feature will not apply Z-Ordering since this will need to be done manually. Given the significant amount of time it takes to run the Z-Order OPTIMIZE command the first time, it would be recommended to consider running it sparingly and as part of a maintenance strategy (i.e., weekly) if you want better query performance for consumers. A wise strategy would be to run these commands at night when spot prices are low. Z-Ordering can be applied incrementally to partitions and queries after the initial run by running the Z Order command on the particular partitions rather than the full dataset, which would take much less time and would be a good practice as an on-going maintenance effort.

Summary

CHAPTER 14

Adaptive Query Execution

While building out a Data Lakehouse, optimizing performance of big data workloads and queries is critical to the success and scalability of your production-ready environment, in addition to maintaining high SLAs for business stakeholders that are frequently accessing data in the Lakehouse. With all the robust performance enhancement capabilities of the more mature traditional SQL data warehouses, it would be extremely valuable to have the capability of speeding up Spark SQL at runtime within a Data Lakehouse. Databricks has solved this with its Adaptive Query Execution (AQE) feature that is available with Spark 3.0 and higher.

The performance, maintainability, and scalability of a production-ready Data Lakehouse environment are what truly determine its overall success. Traditional mature SQL data warehouse systems come with the benefits of indexing, statistics, automatic query plan optimizations, and much more. The concept of the Data Lakehouse is slowly but surely maturing its capabilities and features when compared to many of these traditional systems. Adaptive Query Execution (AQE) is one such feature offered by Databricks for speeding up a Spark SQL query at runtime. In this chapter, you will learn how to get started with comparing performance of AQE that is disabled vs. enabled while querying big data workloads in your Data Lakehouse.

How It Works

Adaptive Query Execution (AQE) is a query re-optimization process that occurs when a query is executed. Since Databricks collects the most updated statistics at the end of a query stage which includes shuffle and broadcast exchange operations, it can optimize and improve the physical strategy. In the newer versions of Databricks which includes runtime 7.3 and above, AQE is automatically enabled by default and applies to non-streaming queries which contain at least one join, aggregate, or window operation.

R. L'Esteve, *The Azure Data Lakehouse Toolkit*, https://doi.org/10.1007/978-1-4842-8233-5_14

AQE is capable of dynamically changing sorting merge joins into broadcast hash joins, combining partitions into reasonably sized partitions after shuffle exchanges, and splitting skewed tasks into evenly sized tasks. AQE queries contain what is called an AdaptiveSparkPlan node which contains the initial and final plans. The query plans will change once AQE optimizations take effect. You can always find more details about AQE from Microsoft's documentation found here: `https://docs.microsoft.com/en-us/azure/databricks/spark/latest/spark-sql/aqe`

This next section will demonstrate how AQE performs on a dataset with approximately over one billion rows with joins on the query. The exercise will compare the performance of AQE enabled vs. disabled.

Prerequisites

To begin, create a Databricks cluster similar to the one shown in Figure 14-1. Notice that I have chosen relatively moderate worker and driver types, along with a runtime of 8.2 for this exercise. Obviously, the selected memory and cores will impact the query runtime, so it is important to point out the configurations used for this exercise.

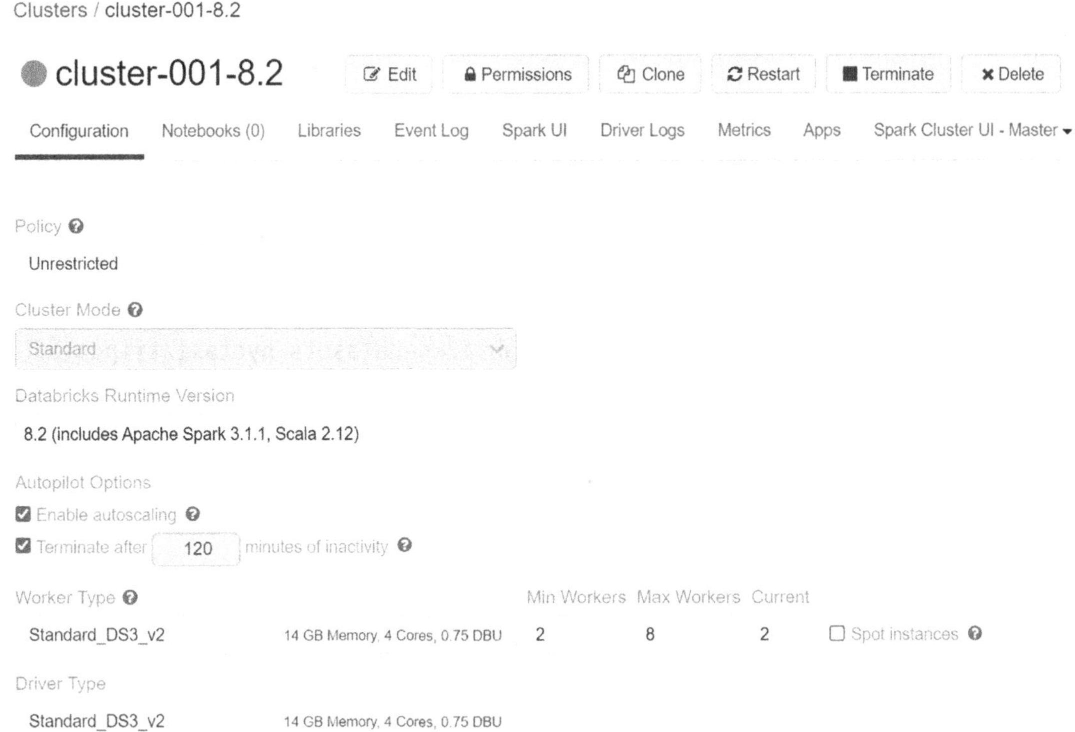

Figure 14-1. *Databricks cluster configurations*

Comparing AQE Performance on Query with Joins

In this next section, you will create a new notebook and add code to create datasets and run queries, and we will also add a new column to capture unique IDs for each row. This unique ID will be used to join two tables in the subsequent sections. This section is intended to compare the impact on AQE on a query with joins.

Create Datasets

Once the cluster has been created and started, go ahead and create a new SQL notebook; add and run the following Scala code. Notice the explode function which performs the replication of data and can be customized to your desired data volume by simply changing the number 14 in the section which contains the following: explode (array((1 until 14).map(lit): _*)). The first part of this code imports the 2019 NYC Taxi yellow trip dataset from databricks-datasets. The next part of the code will replicate the dataset

13 more times to create a much larger dataset containing over 1 billion rows. The final dataset will be saved to a data frame called nyctaxiDF.

```
%scala
import org.apache.spark.sql.functions._

val Data = "/databricks-datasets/nyctaxi/tripdata/yellow/yellow_
tripdata_2019-*"
val SchemaDF = spark.read.format("csv").option("header", "true").
option("inferSchema", "true").load("/databricks-datasets/nyctaxi/tripdata/
yellow/yellow_tripdata_2019-02.csv.gz")
val df = spark.read.format("csv").option("header", "true").schema(SchemaDF.
schema).load(Data)
val nyctaxiDF_stage = df
  .withColumn("VendorID", explode(array((1 until 14).map(lit): _*)))
  .selectExpr(df.columns: _*)
val nyctaxiDF = nyctaxiDF_stage.withColumn("ID", monotonically_
increasing_id)
```

Run the following code `nyctaxiDF.count()` shown in Figure 14-2 to count the data frame, and ensure that it contains the expected row count of over one billion rows.

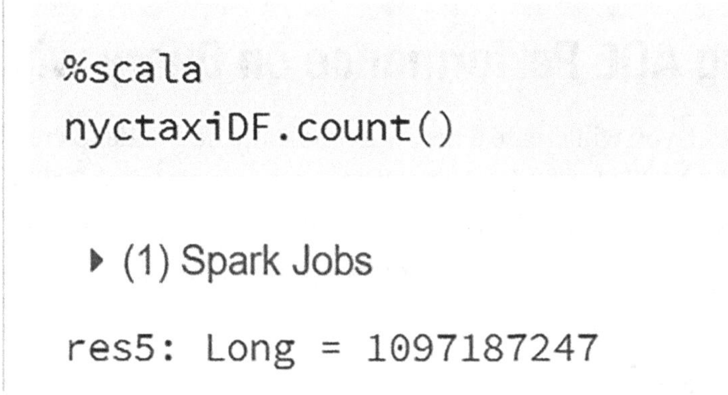

```
%scala
nyctaxiDF.count()

▸ (1) Spark Jobs

res5: Long = 1097187247
```

Figure 14-2. *Code to count the nyctaxi large dataset*

Next, you could simply run the following code `nyctaxiDF.write.format("delta").saveAsTable("dlhcore.nyctaxi_A")` to save your data frame as a delta-formatted table. Alternatively, you could run the following Scala code which will write the nyctaxiDF to your ADLS gen2 account as delta format. If you will be working through these exercises, please ensure that you have completed steps to mount your ADLS gen2 account within Databricks.

Run the following Scala code twice. For the first iteration, run the code with "nyctaxi_A" specified in the file path. And for the second iteration, run the code with "nyctaxi_B" specified in the file path. This will persist two large datasets, over one billion rows, in your specified ADLS gen2 folder path. These two datasets will be used to join each other within a query.

```
%scala

  val nyctaxiDF_delta = nyctaxiDF.write
  .format("delta")
  .mode("overwrite")
  .save("dbfs:/mnt/rcpdlhcore/datalakehouse/dlhcore/raw/delta/nyctaxi_A")
```

Similarly, run the following SQL code twice, once for nyctaxi_A and the second for nyctaxi_B, to create two Delta Tables that you will use in query joins:

```
CREATE TABLE nyctaxi_A
USING DELTA
LOCATION 'dbfs:/mnt/rcpdlhcore/datalakehouse/dlhcore/raw/delta/nyctaxi_A'
```

After creating the Delta Tables, run a count, `SELECT count(*) FROM nyctaxi_A`, on both nyctaxi_A and nyctaxi_B to verify that they both contain over one billion rows. These results can be seen in Figure 14-3.

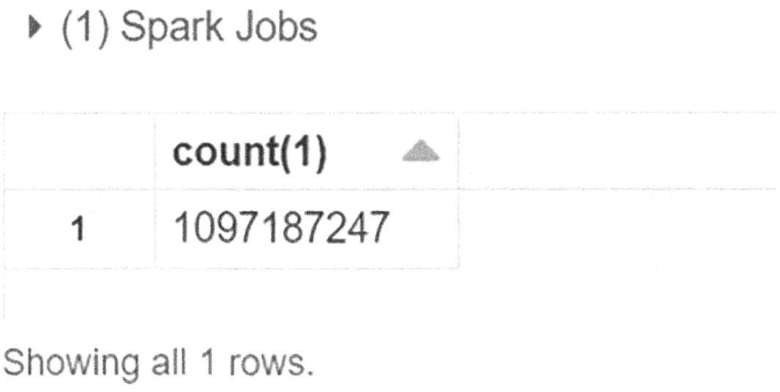

▸ (1) Spark Jobs

	count(1)
1	1097187247

Showing all 1 rows.

***Figure 14-3.** Code to count the nyctaxi dataset*

You could also run the following Select Statement `SELECT * FROM nyctaxi_A` to get a granular view of the data. Notice from the results shown in Figure 14-4 that the newly created ID column auto increments unique IDs for each row.

```
SELECT * FROM nyctaxi_A
```

▸ (1) Spark Jobs

	tpep_pickup_datetime	tpep_dropoff_datetime	passenger_count	trip_distance	RatecodeID	store_and_fwd_flag	PULocationID	ID
1	2019-03-01 00:24:41	2019-03-01 00:25:31	1	0	1	N	145	0
2	2019-03-01 00:24:41	2019-03-01 00:25:31	1	0	1	N	145	1
3	2019-03-01 00:24:41	2019-03-01 00:25:31	1	0	1	N	145	2
4	2019-03-01 00:24:41	2019-03-01 00:25:31	1	0	1	N	145	3
5	2019-03-01 00:24:41	2019-03-01 00:25:31	1	0	1	N	145	4
6	2019-03-01 00:24:41	2019-03-01 00:25:31	1	0	1	N	145	5
7								

Truncated results, showing first 1000 rows

***Figure 14-4.** SQL query to select all values from the nyctaxi_A Delta Table*

Disable AQE

To test performance of AQE turned off, go ahead and run the following command to `set spark.sql.adaptive.enabled = false;`. This will ensure that AQE is switched off for this particular performance test, as shown in Figure 14-5.

```
set spark.sql.adaptive.enabled = false;
```

	key	value
1	spark.sql.adaptive.enabled	false

Showing all 1 rows.

***Figure 14-5.** Code to disable AQE*

The following SQL query joins the two Delta Tables, applies a WHERE filter, GROUPs BY VendorID, and ORDERs BY sum_total. The EXPLAIN FORMATTED command will describe the expected plan for this query before it is run.

```
EXPLAIN FORMATTED
```

```
SELECT a.VendorID, SUM(a.total_amount) as sum_total
FROM nyctaxi_A a
JOIN nyctaxi_B b ON a.ID = b.ID
WHERE a.tpep_pickup_datetime BETWEEN '2019-05-01 00:00:00' AND '2019-05-03
00:00:00'
GROUP BY a.VendorID
ORDER BY sum_total DESC;
```

Figure 14-6 displays the results of the preceding query. These results explain the physical plan along with the corresponding exchanges, aggregates, filters, merges, and more.

	plan
1	== Physical Plan == Sort (18) +- Exchange (17) +- * HashAggregate (16) +- Exchange (15) +- * HashAggregate (14) +- * Project (13) +- * SortMergeJoin Inner (12) :- Sort (6) : +- Exchange (5) : +- * Project (4) : +- * Filter (3) : +- * ColumnarToRow (2) : +- Scan parquet default.nyctaxi_a (1) +-...

Figure 14-6. *Explain plan results when AQE is disabled*

Next, run the following SQL query. This query is simply the same query provided earlier with the exclusion of the EXPALIN FORMATTED command.

```
SELECT a.VendorID, SUM(a.total_amount) as sum_total
FROM nyctaxi_A a
JOIN nyctaxi_B b ON a.ID = b.ID
WHERE a.tpep_pickup_datetime BETWEEN '2019-05-01 00:00:00' AND '2019-05-03
00:00:00'
GROUP BY a.VendorID
ORDER BY sum_total DESC;
```

Notice from the results shown in Figure 14-7 that there are 4 stages listed and the execution time took 1.06 minutes to complete. Since AQE is disabled, once again notice the additional stages containing the 200/200.

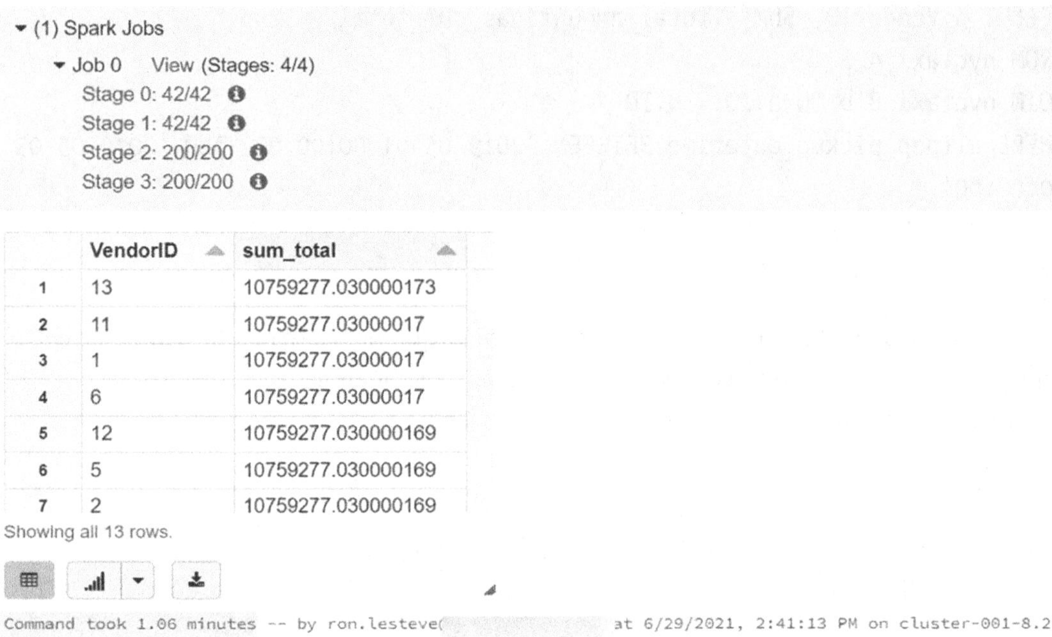

(1) Spark Jobs
Job 0 View (Stages: 4/4)
Stage 0: 42/42
Stage 1: 42/42
Stage 2: 200/200
Stage 3: 200/200
VendorID
sum_total
1 13 10759277.030000173
2 11 10759277.03000017
3 1 10759277.03000017
4 6 10759277.03000017
5 12 10759277.030000169
6 5 10759277.030000169
7 2 10759277.030000169
Showing all 13 rows.
Command took 1.06 minutes -- by ron.lesteve(at 6/29/2021, 2:41:13 PM on cluster-001-8.2

Figure 14-7. *Results from joining query with AQE disabled*

Enable AQE

Next, go ahead and enable AQE, as shown in Figure 14-8, by setting it to true with the following command: `set spark.sql.adaptive.enabled = true;`. In this section, you'll run the same query provided in the previous section to measure performance of query execution time with AQE enabled.

```
set spark.sql.adaptive.enabled = true;
```

	key	value
1	spark.sql.adaptive.enabled	true

Showing all 1 rows.

Figure 14-8. *Code to enable AQE*

Run the same code again, shown as follows, to explain the plan:

```
SELECT a.VendorID, SUM(a.total_amount) as sum_total
FROM nyctaxi_A a
JOIN nyctaxi_B b ON a.ID = b.ID
WHERE a.tpep_pickup_datetime BETWEEN '2019-05-01 00:00:00' AND '2019-05-03
00:00:00'
GROUP BY a.VendorID
ORDER BY sum_total DESC;
```

Notice in Figure 14-9 that it generates the same plan and it did with AQE disabled. This is expected because AQE will adaptively change its query plan to a more optimized plan at runtime.

	plan
1	== Physical Plan == AdaptiveSparkPlan (17) +- Sort (16) +- Exchange (15) +- HashAggregate (14) +- Exchange (13) +- HashAggregate (12) +- Project (11) +- SortMergeJoin Inner (10) :- Sort (5) : +- Exchange (4) : +- Project (3) : +- Filter (2) : +- Scan parquet default.nyctaxi_a (1) +- Sort ...

Figure 14-9. *Results containing explain plan when AQE is enabled*

Run the same SQL query that was previously provided, and notice in Figure 14-10 that the execution time took only 45.81 seconds this time, which is a pretty significant improvement in performance due to the optimized AQE plan. Notice also that there were fewer stages as a result of AQE being enabled.

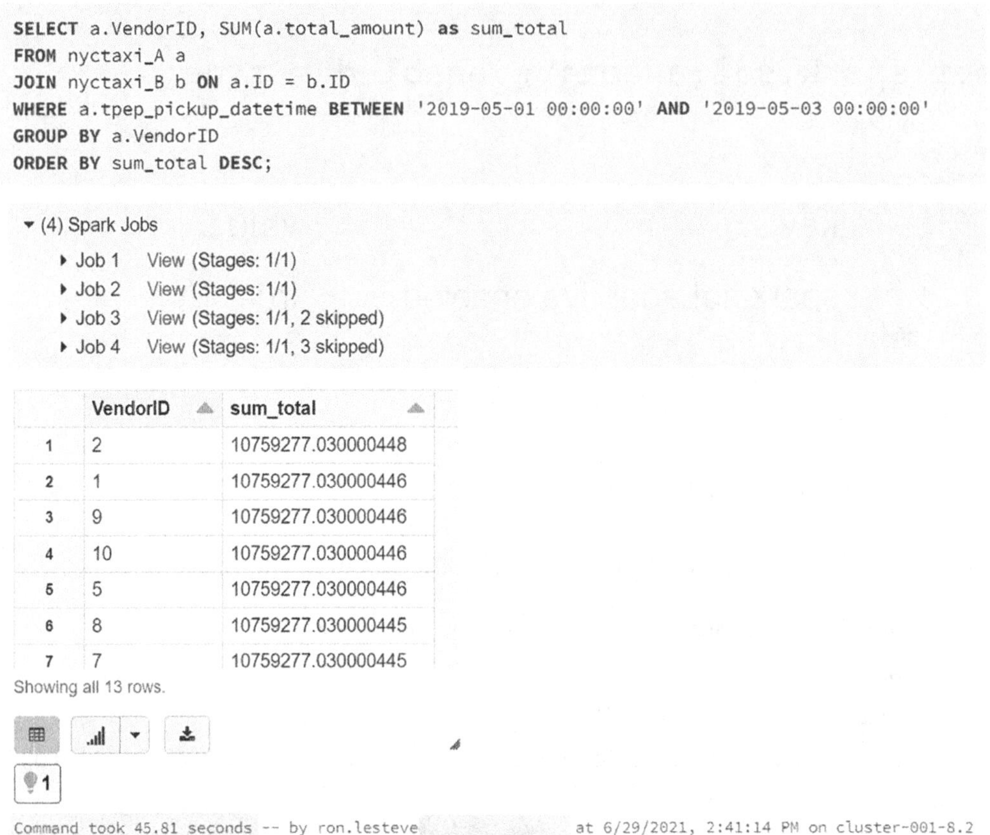

***Figure 14-10.** Query steps and time when AQE is enabled*

You can also dig into both of the query execution plans to compare and understand the differences between the plans with AQE being disabled and when it was enabled, as shown in Figure 14-11. This will also give you the opportunity to visually see where and how the AQE engine changed the plan during the execution of the query.

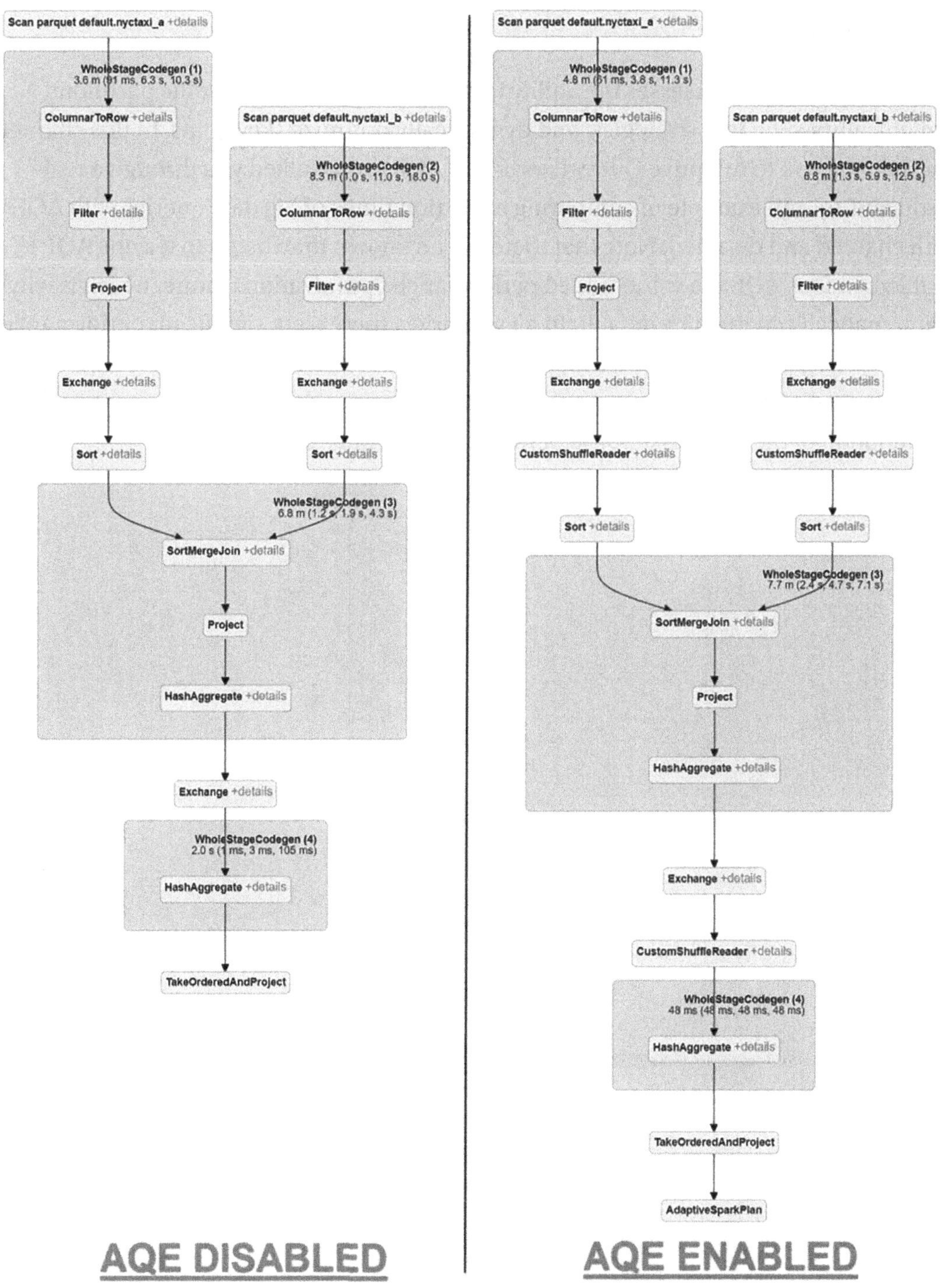

***Figure 14-11.** Comparison of query plans with AQE enabled and disabled*

Summary

The AQE framework possesses the ability to dynamically coalesce shuffle partitions, dynamically switch join strategies, and dynamically optimize skew joins. In this chapter, I introduced you to Adaptive Query Execution (AQE) and walked you through a real-world end-to-end example of comparing execution times of big data queries with AQE both enabled and disabled. Note that there are no known drawbacks to leaving AQE enabled. In fact, AQE is a value-added performance optimization feature, which is why it is automatically enabled by default. In all scenarios, there were significant performance optimization gains and benefits with AQE being enabled. The capabilities of AQE demonstrate the performance optimization opportunities that contribute to advancing the adoption of the Data Lakehouse paradigm for production workloads.

CHAPTER 15

Bloom Filter Index

Within the big data ecosystem, highly performant workloads and queries are critical for keeping customers happy and businesses running successfully. Within the SQL database realm, indexes support query performance optimization opportunities quite gracefully. Within the Data Lakehouse, there have been limited methods of applying indexes to Delta Tables. Bloom Filter Indexes are space-efficient data structures that enable Data Skipping on chosen columns. It operates by stating that data is definitively not in the file, or that it is probably in the file, with a defined false positive probability (FPP). Bloom Filter Indexes are critical to building highly performant Delta Lakehouses. In this chapter, we will address the question of how to get started with Bloom Filter Indexes.

A Bloom Filter Index is a Databricks-specific index which can be applied to a particular column in Delta Tables. It is capable of improving query execution performance by over 50% when applied correctly. In this chapter, you will learn how to create and apply Bloom Filter Index on over a one billion-row table from the NYC Taxi Dataset and then compare the query execution performance to a replica table which does not have a Bloom Filter Index applied to the same replica column. Additionally, you will learn how to tune the Bloom Filter Index options and apply Z-Order optimizations on the table.

How a Bloom Filter Index Works

A Bloom Filter Index is intended to optimize query performance and will enable Data Skipping on a column. A data file can have a single index file associated with it. An index file is an uncompressed single row parquet file stored in the `_delta_index` subdirectory. Without a Bloom Filter Index, Databricks will always read the entire data file; therefore, the advantage of the Bloom Filter Index that has been created is that Databricks first checks the index file and then the corresponding data file is only read if there is a potential filter match.

R. L'Esteve, *The Azure Data Lakehouse Toolkit*, https://doi.org/10.1007/978-1-4842-8233-5_15

The false positive probability (fpp) and numItems tuning options, which will be included in the code to create the Bloom Filter Index in subsequent sections, can be defined at the table or column level. The default fpp is 0.1 and must be larger than 0 or smaller than 1. This configuration option defines the acceptable tolerance level of having to read more data than you should, which is 10% as the default value. This could have the implication of taking longer time to write new incoming data because a fairly complex tree of indices will need to be rebuilt every time. A lower fpp will use more bits per element, resulting in greater accuracy with a potential negative impact on performance and cost.

The fpp can be tuned based on your acceptance criteria to balance the cost to maintain with the possibility of reading more data that you might need to. The numItems option defines the number of distinct items a file can contain, and the default is one million items. This option depends on a number of factors including volume of data. In the following examples, we have used 5% of the total records within a table as the numItems option. The balance between the fpp and numItems must be carefully adjusted and tuned to prevent performance issues. Sometimes, this tuning process can include a number of different factors, thus resulting in an iterative trial-and-error process to find the optimal balance.

Typically, a Bloom Filter Index is applied to an empty table, but can also be used in conjunction with the Z-Order command to rebuild the Bloom Filter Index on tables that frequently have new data being inserted. While this index is enabled by default, through the following example, you will also learn how to enable or disable this filter manually, as needed. A Bloom Filter can be dropped once it is created by using the DROP command written in SQL Syntax.

Create a Cluster

The very first step to getting started with Bloom Filter Indexes is to create a cluster in your Databricks environment, as shown in Figure 15-1. Note that Bloom Filters are automatically enabled. Nevertheless, you will see the code to enable Bloom Filter on Delta Tables in the subsequent sections. Also take note of the worker- and driver-type details for this cluster, which can be considered standard. This can be scaled as needed to further improve and optimize performance.

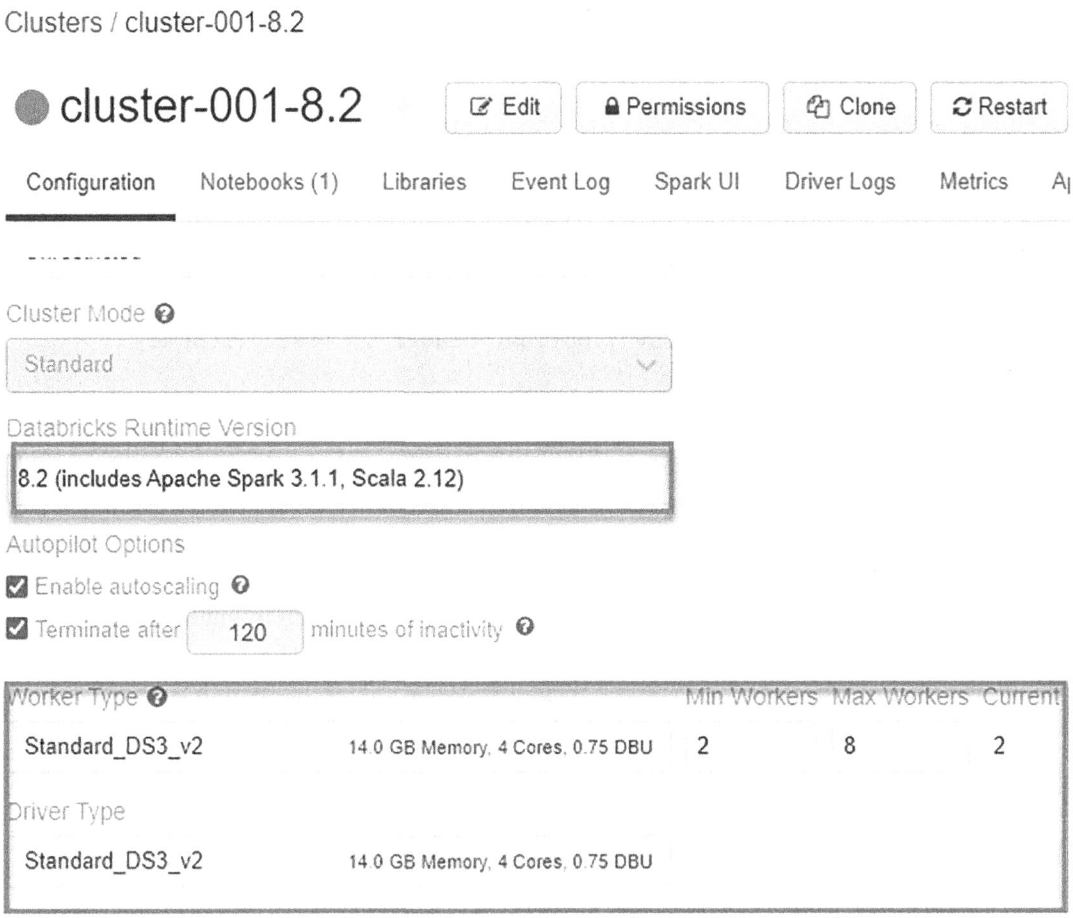

Clusters / cluster-001-8.2

cluster-001-8.2 Edit Permissions Clone Restart

Configuration Notebooks (1) Libraries Event Log Spark UI Driver Logs Metrics A|

Cluster Mode

Standard

Databricks Runtime Version

8.2 (includes Apache Spark 3.1.1, Scala 2.12)

Autopilot Options

Enable autoscaling

Terminate after 120 minutes of inactivity

Worker Type		Min Workers	Max Workers	Current
Standard_DS3_v2	14.0 GB Memory, 4 Cores, 0.75 DBU	2	8	2

Driver Type	
Standard_DS3_v2	14.0 GB Memory, 4 Cores, 0.75 DBU

Figure 15-1. *Databricks runtime version 8.2 cluster settings*

Create a Notebook and Insert Data

For this example, most of the code and commands will be run using a combination of Scala and SQL within the notebook code blocks. The preliminary code that will need to be run will extract the 2019 NYC Taxi Data csv files and schema from Databricks datasets and will store it in a data frame. The original dataset contains approximately 84 million rows of data. The additional code that includes `explode(array((1 until 14).map(lit): _*))` will duplicate the records 13 times to produce a dataset which is slightly over one billion rows. This larger dataset will prove useful when running queries, optimizing performance, and testing query times. Here is the Scala code that you will need to run to create the required dataset. You can either increase or decrease the number from 14 to size your dataset as desired.

```
%scala
import org.apache.spark.sql.functions._

val Data = "/databricks-datasets/nyctaxi/tripdata/yellow/yellow_
tripdata_2019-*"
val SchemaDF = spark.read.format("csv").option("header", "true").
option("inferSchema", "true").load("/databricks-datasets/nyctaxi/tripdata/
yellow/yellow_tripdata_2019-02.csv.gz")
val df = spark.read.format("csv").option("header", "true").schema
(SchemaDF.schema).load(Data)
val nyctaxiDF = df
  .withColumn("VendorID", explode(array((1 until 14).map(lit): _*)))
  .selectExpr(df.columns: _*)
```

Run a count using the following command on the dataset to confirm that you have over one billion rows in the dataset nyctaxiDF.count(), as shown in Figure 15-2.

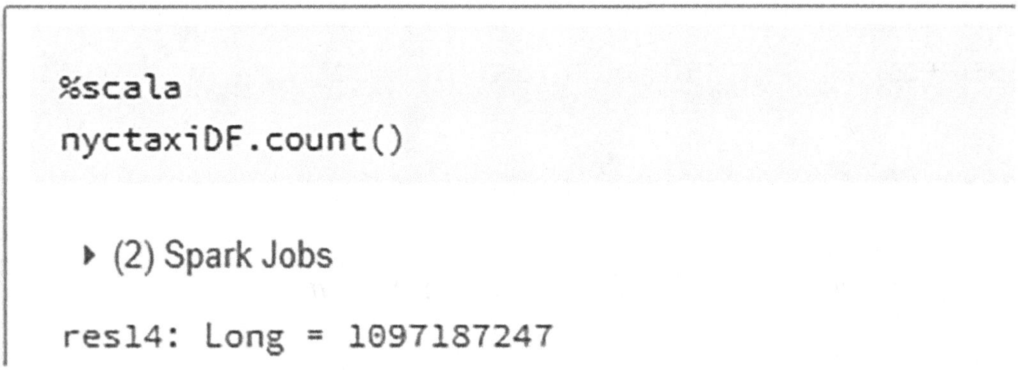

```
%scala
nyctaxiDF.count()

▸ (2) Spark Jobs

res14: Long = 1097187247
```

Figure 15-2. *Code to count data in data frame*

At this point, you are ready to persist the staging dataset as delta format to your Data Lake using the following code. In this exercise, you will be required to create two versions of this for the bloom and non-bloom tables. Let's start with the bloom data using this code. Run the following Scala code to save the dataset to your ADLS gen2 storage account. Notice that the format is set to delta and the mode is overwrite.

```
%scala

  val nyctaxiDF_bloom = nyctaxiDF.write
  .format("delta")
```

```
  .mode("overwrite")
  .save("dbfs:/mnt/rcpdlhcore/datalakehouse/dlhcore/raw/delta/
  nyctaxi_bloom")
```

Similarly, run the following code to create an isolated and duplicated version of the non-bloom data in your ADLS gen2 account. Here is the Scala code that you will need to run to create a non-bloom delta dataset in your ADLS gen2 account.

```
%scala

  val nyctaxiDF_nonbloom = nyctaxiDF.write
  .format("delta")
  .mode("overwrite")
  .save("dbfs:/mnt/rcpdlhcore/datalakehouse/dlhcore/raw/delta/nyctaxi_
  nonbloom")
```

After you run the preceding code, navigate to your ADLS gen2 account and folder structure, as shown in Figure 15-3, to confirm that the data for bloom and non-bloom has been persisted to the Data Lake.

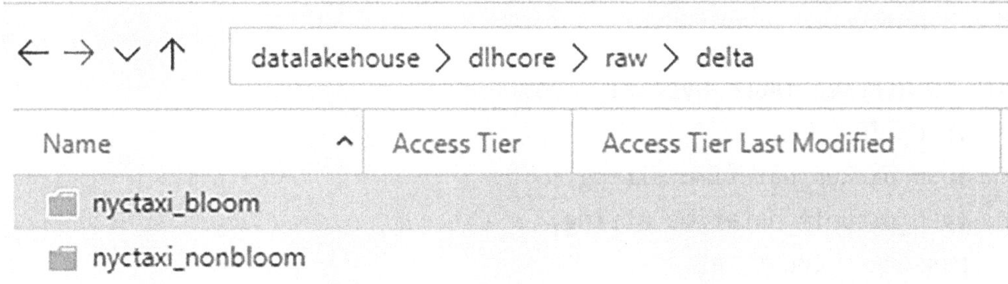

Figure 15-3. *Data written to Delta Tables in ADLS gen2*

Enable Bloom Filter Index

Now that you have some big data to work with, it is time to enable bloom filter in the notebook by running the following code to enable bloomFilter for both Spark and Delta:

```
SET spark.databricks.io.skipping.bloomFilter.enabled = true;
SET delta.bloomFilter.enabled = true;
```

By default, this Bloom Filter Index will already be enabled; however, in the event that it is disabled, it is always a good idea to manually enable this bloomFilter to ensure there are no errors caused further downstream. Figure 15-4 illustrates the resulting key-value pair which indicates that the bloomFilter Index is enabled.

	key	value
1	delta.bloomFilter.enabled	true

Figure 15-4. *Code to enable Bloom Filter Index*

Create Tables

In this section, you will need to create the required table which you will apply the Bloom Filter Index on. The following SQL code will create the Delta Table using the defined schema. Note that when you need to create an empty table, you would run the CREATE OR REPLATE TABLE command, and when you run this command, you will need to define the schema. Here is the SQL code that you will need to run to CREATE OR REPLACE the nyctaxi_bloom table:

```
CREATE OR REPLACE TABLE nyctaxi_bloom (
      VendorID int,
      tpep_pickup_datetime string,
      tpep_dropoff_datetime string,
      passenger_count int,
      trip_distance double,
      RatecodeID int,
      store_and_fwd_flag string,
      PULocationID int,
      DOLocationID int,
      payment_type int,
      fare_amount double,
      extra double,
      mta_tax double,
      tip_amount double,
      tolls_amount double,
```

```
    improvement_surcharge double,
    total_amount double,
    congestion_surcharge double)
USING DELTA
```

In the following sections, you will learn how to create a Delta Table without the need to specify the schema. The schema can be inferred by specifying your Data Lake LOCATION parameter. This assumes that your data has already been persisted to the Data Lake. You can also use the following syntax within your Python notebook to create a Delta Table directly from a data frame: `nyctaxiDF.write.format("delta").saveAsTable("nyctaxi_bloom")`. If you choose to use this method instead, remember that the newly created Delta Table will also contain data within it; therefore, for this scenario, you will also need to run the following SQL code to truncate the table to ensure there is no data in the newly created table:

```
%sql
TRUNCATE TABLE nyctaxi_bloom;
SELECT * FROM nyctaxi_bloom;
```

For our scenario, we needed an empty table to apply our Bloom Filter Index, which is why we had defined the schema within the SQL Syntax. As expected, Figure 15-5 shows that there are no records in the table upon running the following SQL count on the newly created table, `SELECT count(*) FROM nyctaxi_bloom`.

```
SELECT count(*) FROM nyctaxi_bloom
```

▸ (2) Spark Jobs

	count(1)
1	0

Figure 15-5. *Code to verify no data exists in bloom filter table*

Also, run the following SQL code to create the nyctaxi_nonbloom Delta Table. Notice that the schema is not defined here and will be inferred. Also, since you are specifying the location of the source data, the new table will be persisted with data on creation. Here is the SQL code that you will need to run to create the nyctaxi_nonbloom table:

```
CREATE TABLE nyctaxi_nonbloom
USING DELTA
LOCATION 'dbfs:/mnt/rcpdlhcore/datalakehouse/dlhcore/raw/delta/nyctaxi_
nonbloom'
```

As expected, upon running the following count of the newly created nyctaxi_nonbloom Delta Table `SELECT count(*) FROM nyctaxi_nonbloom`, notice from the count in Figure 15-6 that there are over one billion rows in the table. This table will be used to compare performance against the nyctaxi_bloom table which will have the Bloom Filter Index applied.

```
SELECT count(*) FROM nyctaxi_nonbloom
```

▸ (2) Spark Jobs

	count(1)
1	1097187247

Figure 15-6. *Code to verify data exists in non-bloom filter table*

Create a Bloom Filter Index

It is now time to create the Bloom Filter Index on the nyctaxi_bloom table by running the following SQL code. For this exercise, use the tpep_dropoff_datetime column as the one to apply the Bloom Filter Index on.

A Bloom Filter's size depends on the false positive probability (FPP) and number of elements in the set for which the Bloom Filter has been created. A lower FPP yields a higher number of used bits per element and the more accurate it will be, at the cost of more disk space and slower downloads. The default FPP of 10% requires 5 bits per element. The default numItems, distinct items in the column, is 1,000,000.

Here is the SQL code which you will need to run on the nyctaxi_bloom table to apply the Bloom Filter Index on the tpep_dropoff_datetime column. Leave the fpp to a default of 10% and apply 5% of the number of rows in the nyctaxi_bloom table as the numItems. In this case, 5% of 1 billion is 50 million.

```
CREATE BLOOMFILTER INDEX
ON TABLE nyctaxi_bloom
FOR COLUMNS(tpep_dropoff_datetime OPTIONS (fpp=0.1, numItems=50000000))
```

Run the following code to get the metadata of the table, which would include details of a Bloom Filter Index if it has been applied to any of the columns:

```
%scala
spark.table("nyctaxi_bloom").schema.foreach(field => println(s"${field.
name}: metadata=${field.metadata}"))
```

Notice from the details of column tpep_dropoff_datetime, as shown in Figure 15-7, that the Bloom Filter Index has been applied.

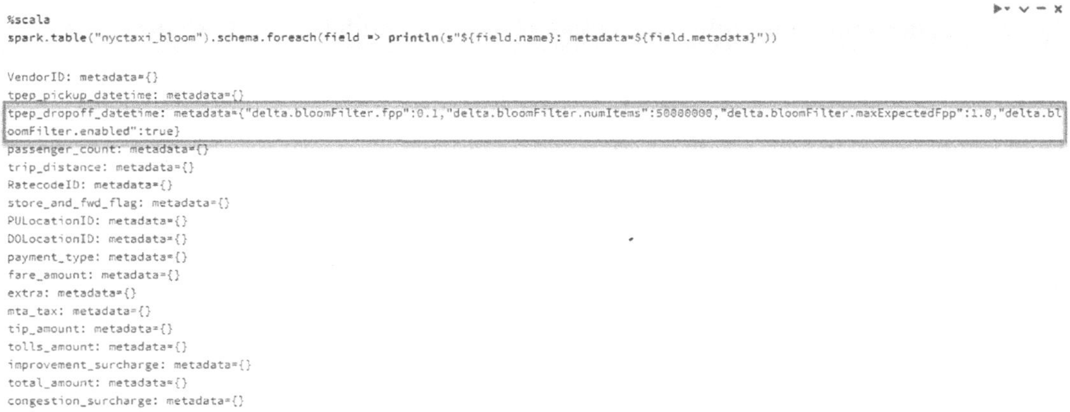

```
%scala
spark.table("nyctaxi_bloom").schema.foreach(field => println(s"${field.name}: metadata=${field.metadata}"))

VendorID: metadata={}
tpep_pickup_datetime: metadata={}
tpep_dropoff_datetime: metadata={"delta.bloomFilter.fpp":0.1,"delta.bloomFilter.numItems":50000000,"delta.bloomFilter.maxExpectedFpp":1.0,"delta.bl
oomFilter.enabled":true}
passenger_count: metadata={}
trip_distance: metadata={}
RatecodeID: metadata={}
store_and_fwd_flag: metadata={}
PULocationID: metadata={}
DOLocationID: metadata={}
payment_type: metadata={}
fare_amount: metadata={}
extra: metadata={}
mta_tax: metadata={}
tip_amount: metadata={}
tolls_amount: metadata={}
improvement_surcharge: metadata={}
total_amount: metadata={}
congestion_surcharge: metadata={}
```

Figure 15-7. *Code to view table metadata*

Next, run the following code to insert data into the nyctaxi_bloom table from the nyctaxi_nonbloom table:

```
INSERT INTO nyctaxi_bloom TABLE nyctaxi_nonbloom;
```

Figure 15-8 illustrates the results which show that the counts between the source and target match.

```
INSERT INTO nyctaxi_bloom TABLE nyctaxi_nonbloom;
```

▸ (4) Spark Jobs

	num_affected_rows	num_inserted_rows
1	1097187247	1097187247

Figure 15-8. *Insert data into bloom table*

Optimize Table with Z-Order

The last step in the process to prepare and optimize your data would be to run a Z-Order optimize command on a selected column using the following code. This is not a necessary step here but describes a specific use case to demonstrate how to re-create the Bloom Filter Index on a table that already has data within it as part of a process to keep your Bloom Filter Index fresh and regularly up to date. This can be a significant performance optimization step after inserting data into a table because it will re-optimize the nyctaxi_bloom table by Z-Ordering the data by VendorID. Note that the Z-Ordering is not done on a key that you are creating the Bloom Filter Index on. The optimized files will contain collocated data around the VendorID column, while the Bloom Filter Index will point us to the desired filtered data within these files collocated by VendorID.

```
SET spark.databricks.delta.optimize.maxFileSize = 1600000000;
OPTIMIZE nyctaxi_bloom
ZORDER BY VendorID
```

Figure 15-9 shows the results from running the Z-Order command. After the optimization completed, there are 36 files removed and 23 optimized files added. The max file size has been set to a little over 1.5 GB. Note that adding a Bloom Filter Index to a table that already has data within it will not apply the index, which is why it is recommended that the table must have the index before data is inserted. Alternatively, for data that already exists within the table, the Z-Order command will build out the

Bloom Filter Index for the new files that were added. If the files have already been optimized and you rerun the optimize command, the files will not be rewritten unless the max file size is specified. This will force a change and will update your Bloom Filter Index. This section demonstrated that the Bloom Filter Index can be used in conjunction with the Z-Order command. When the use case fits, then it should definitely be used with this Z-Order command.

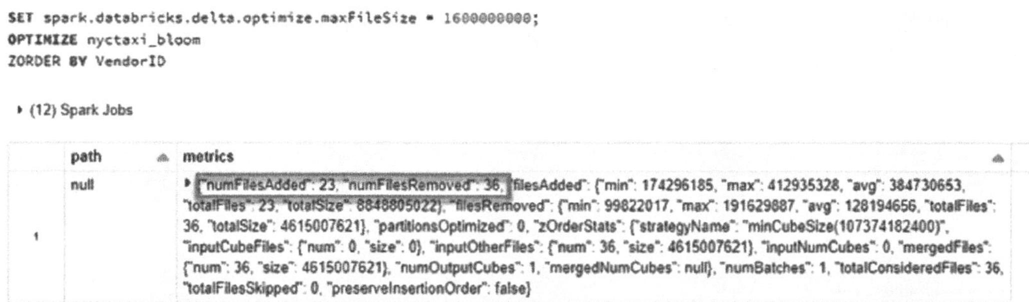

Figure 15-9. *Code to run Z-Order on Bloom Filter Index table*

Verify Performance Improvements

Run the following count query, shown in Figure 15-10, on the nyctaxi_nonbloom table with a where clause applied to the Bloom Filter Index column, and take note of the duration of the query execution.

```
SELECT count(*) FROM nyctaxi_nonbloom WHERE tpep_dropoff_datetime = '2019-01-18 20:43:08'
```

(2) Spark Jobs

	count(1)
1	39

Showing all 1 rows.

1

Command took 26.82 seconds -- by ron.lesteve(at 6/17/2021, 10:22:08 PM on cluster-001-8.2

Figure 15-10. *Code to query non-bloom table with where clause filter*

Next, run the same query on the nyctaxi_bloom table, and notice in Figure 15-11 that time has been reduced by over 10 seconds, approximately a 50% improvement in performance.

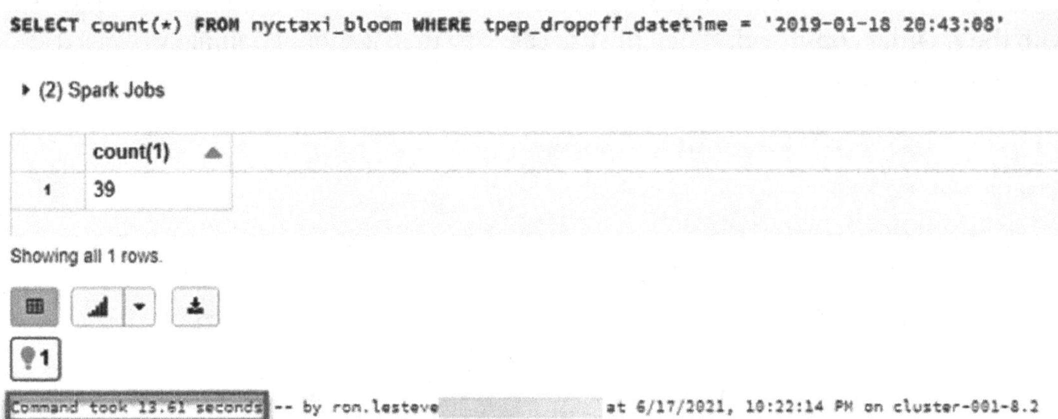

Figure 15-11. *Code to query bloom table with where clause filter*

Here is the SQL count query which you will run as part of the performance test:

```
SELECT count(*) FROM nyctaxi_nonbloom WHERE tpep_dropoff_datetime =
'2019-01-18 20:43:08'
```

Finally, for the nyctaxi_nonbloom table, try to filter on a value which you know does not exist, which in this case would be to simply append the _ symbol after the date value, and take note of the execution time, as shown in Figure 15-12.

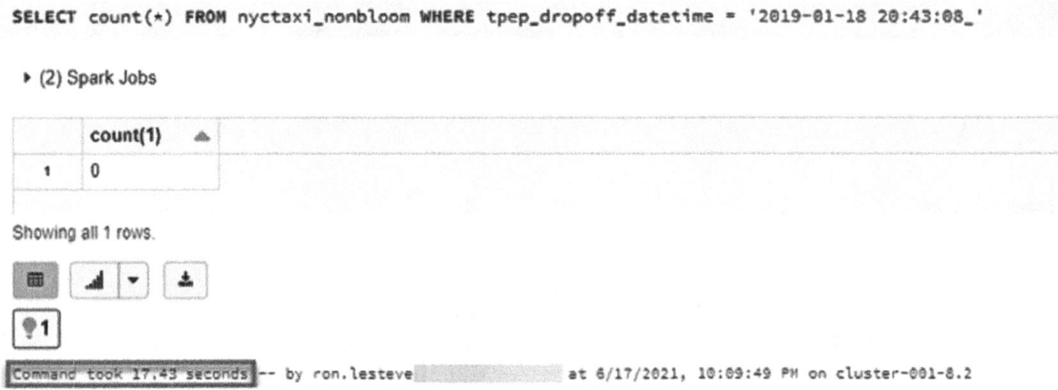

Figure 15-12. *Code to query non-bloom table with where clause filter with no data*

Once again, run the same query on the nyctaxi_bloom table, and notice in Figure 15-13 that the execution time is over 10 seconds less, an approximate 70% improvement in performance.

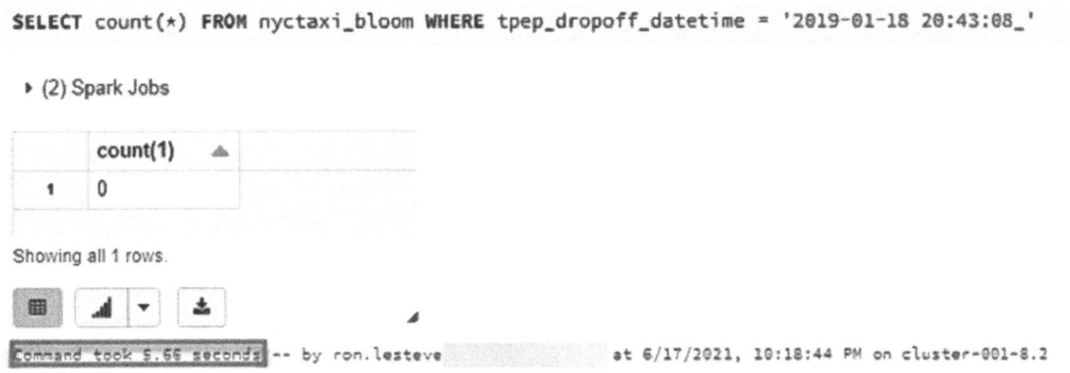

```
SELECT count(*) FROM nyctaxi_bloom WHERE tpep_dropoff_datetime = '2019-01-18 20:43:08_'
```

▸ (2) Spark Jobs

	count(1)
1	0

Showing all 1 rows.

Command took 5.66 seconds -- by ron.lesteve at 6/17/2021, 10:18:44 PM on cluster-001-8.2

Figure 15-13. *Code to query bloom table with where clause filter and no data*

Figure 15-14 shows how to view the nyctaxi table's metadata to view which columns have the Bloom Filter Index applied to it. Notice that I have added multiple Bloom Filter Indexes to columns within a single table in this example to demonstrate that it is possible for a table to have multiple Bloom Filter Indexed columns. The following Scala code, which was also run in a previous section and is also shown in Figure 15-14, will yield these results: `spark.table("nyctaxi").schema.foreach(field => println(s"${field.name}: metadata=${field.metadata}"))`. This Scala code along with more details about the Bloom Filter Index and notebook samples can be found here within this Microsoft article: `https://docs.microsoft.com/en-us/azure/databricks/delta/optimizations/bloom-filters`

```
%scala
spark.table("nyctaxi").schema.foreach(field => println(s"${field.name}: metadata=${field.metadata}"))
```

```
trip_distance: metadata={}
tpep_pickup_datetime: metadata={}
tpep_dropoff_datetime: metadata={}
total_amount: metadata={}
tolls_amount: metadata={}
tip_amount: metadata={}
store_and_fwd_flag: metadata={}
payment_type: metadata={}
passenger_count: metadata={}
mta_tax: metadata={}
improvement_surcharge: metadata={}
fare_amount: metadata={}
extra: metadata={}
congestion_surcharge: metadata={}
VendorID: metadata={}
RatecodeID: metadata={}
PULocationID_bloom: metadata={"delta.bloomFilter.fpp":0.1,"delta.bloomFilter.numItems":84000000,"delta.bloomFilter.maxExpectedFpp":1.0,"delta.bloo
mFilter.enabled":true}
PULocationID_nonbloom: metadata={}
DOLocationID: metadata={"delta.bloomFilter.fpp":0.1,"delta.bloomFilter.numItems":84000000,"delta.bloomFilter.maxExpectedFpp":1.0,"delta.bloomFilte
```

Figure 15-14. *Nyctaxi table's metadata displaying Bloom Filter Indexes*

Summary

In this chapter, I introduced you to the Bloom Filter Index and walked you through an end-to-end exercise on how to create a Bloom Filter Index to optimize performance on a filtered column. A data file can have a single Bloom Filter Index associated with it; however, there can be multiple Bloom Filter Indexes on a single table. Remember to balance the fpp and numItems options while creating the Bloom Filter Index while accounting for a number of factors mentioned in the chapter to balance performance and cost. Based on the stellar performance results demonstrated within this chapter, it is evident that the Bloom Filter Index is a promising performance booster to run "needle in a haystack" type queries which can filter extremely big datasets on a particular column. Overall, it promotes and supports highly performant Data Lakehouses and advances the Lakehouse paradigm one step closer to mature traditional data warehousing appliances.

CHAPTER 16

Hyperspace

While Spark offers tremendous value in the advanced analytics and big data spaces, there are currently a few known limitations around indexing with Spark when compared to the best-in-class SQL Server indexing systems and processes. While Spark isn't great at b-tree indexing and single record lookups, Spark partitioning attempts to address some of these indexing limitations. However, when users query the data with a different search predicate than what was partitioned, this will result in a full scan of the data along with in-memory filtering on the Spark cluster, which is quite inefficient.

Microsoft's modern Data Lakehouse now contains an open source indexing subsystem for Apache Spark called Hyperspace. There is huge potential for this Spark indexing subsystem, specifically within the Lakehouse platforms including Databricks and Synapse Analytics workspaces. Hyperspace comes out of the box with Apache Spark and is an open source service that can be called using a simple API. It also supports multiple languages including Scala, Python, and .NET. You can find more details related to quick start guides, code, and release notes on the Hyperspace page here: `https://microsoft.github.io/hyperspace/`

Similar to a SQL Server non-clustered index, Hyperspace will create an index across a specified data frame, create a separate optimized and reorganized data store for the columns that are being indexed, and can include additional columns in the optimized and reorganized data store, much like a non-clustered SQL Server index. Since Hyperspace is open source and readily available out of the box in the form API with multi-language support, it can also be used within Databricks notebooks. In this chapter, we will focus on creating a dataset in a Synapse Analytics workspace with a Hyperspace Index added on it to compare a query using Hyperspace indexed vs. non-indexed tables to observe performance optimizations within the Lakehouse.

R. L'Esteve, *The Azure Data Lakehouse Toolkit*, https://doi.org/10.1007/978-1-4842-8233-5_16

Prerequisites

This section will explain the prerequisites that are required to enable the ability to work with Hyperspace which includes the creation of a Synapse Analytics workspace, Spark Pool, and sample dataset. Please refer to the following list for detailed steps to complete these prerequisites:

1. **Create a Synapse Analytics workspace**: Prior to working with Hyperspace, a Synapse Analytics workspace will need to be created. This quick start describes the steps to create an Azure Synapse workspace by using the Azure portal: `https://docs.microsoft.com/en-us/azure/synapse-analytics/quickstart-create-workspace`. Figure 16-1 displays the overview blade of the Synapse Analytics workspace once it is created.

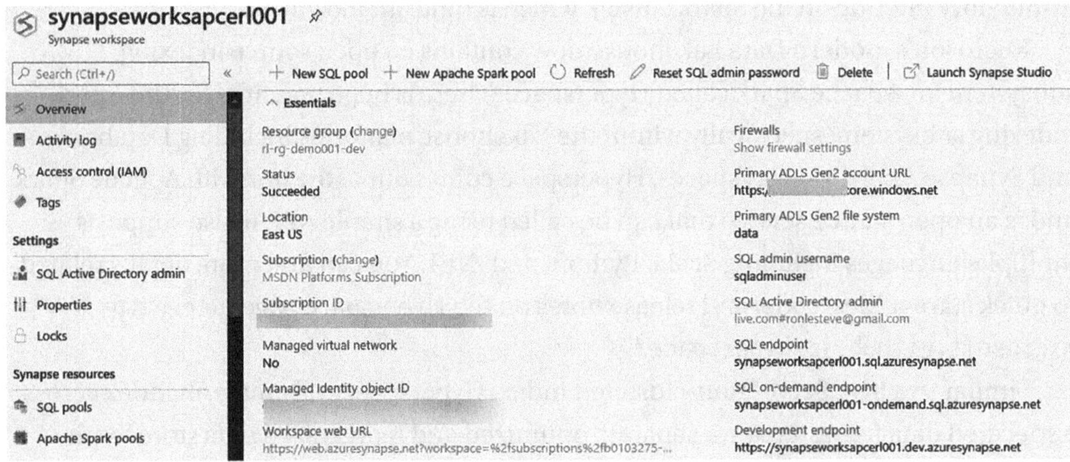

Figure 16-1. *New Synapse Analytics workspace overview blade*

2. **Create a Spark Pool**: In addition to a Synapse workspace, a Spark Pool will be needed. For more information related to creating a Spark Pool, see `https://docs.microsoft.com/en-us/azure/synapse-analytics/quickstart-create-apache-spark-pool-portal`. For this demo, I have created a Medium Node size with 8 vCPU/64 GB, as shown in Figure 16-2.

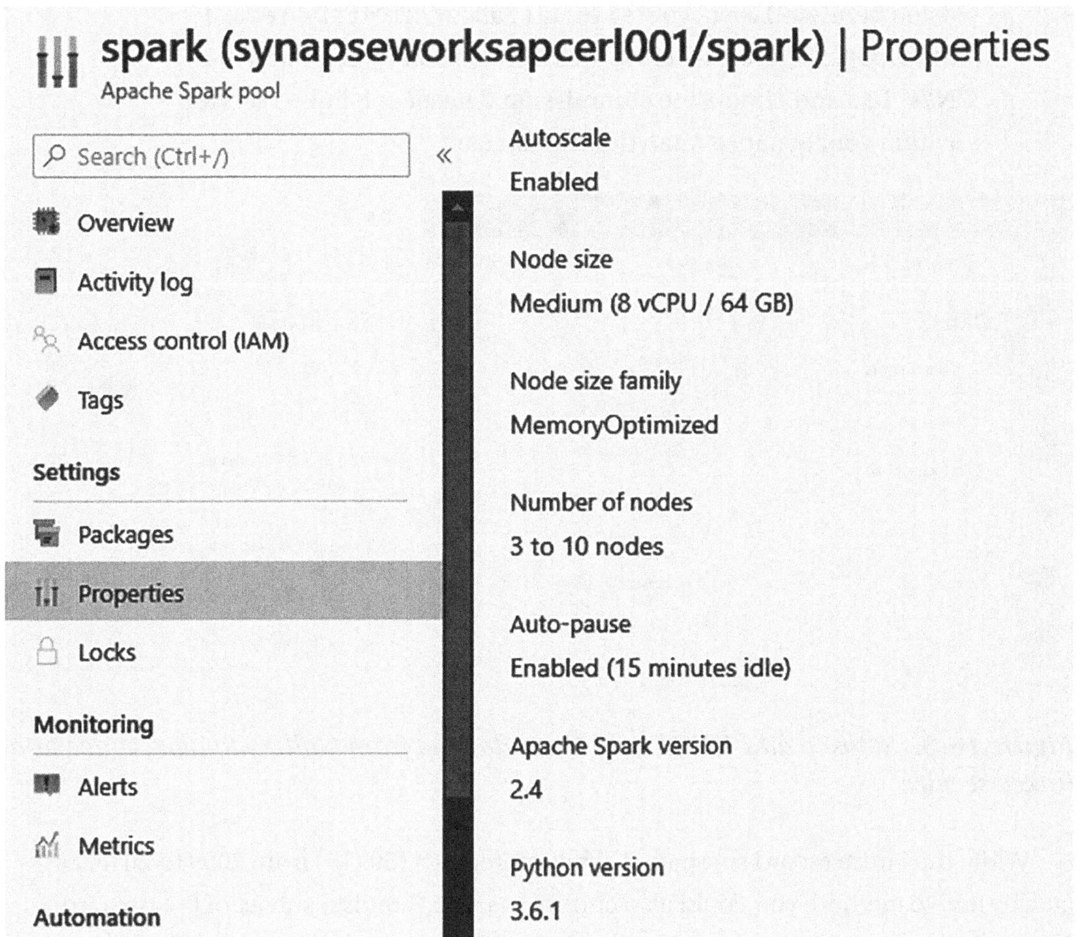

Figure 16-2. *Create a new Synapse Spark Pool*

3. **Choose a dataset**: Finally, you'll need a dataset to work with. While big datasets are always preferable, this would come with significant overhead and compute costs; therefore, for this demo, I have used a subset of the NYC Taxi and Limousine commission – yellow taxi trip records which can be found by simply searching for "nyc_tlc_yellow" from the Datasets Gallery within the Data tab of Synapse Analytics workspace. Once added, the dataset will be available as a linked service within your workspace. For reference, the entire dataset can also be found within the following website

listed here: `www1.nyc.gov/site/tlc/about/tlc-trip-record-data.page`. Figure 16-3 illustrates the steps required to add the NYC Taxi and Limousine commission dataset as a linked service within your Synapse Analytics workspace.

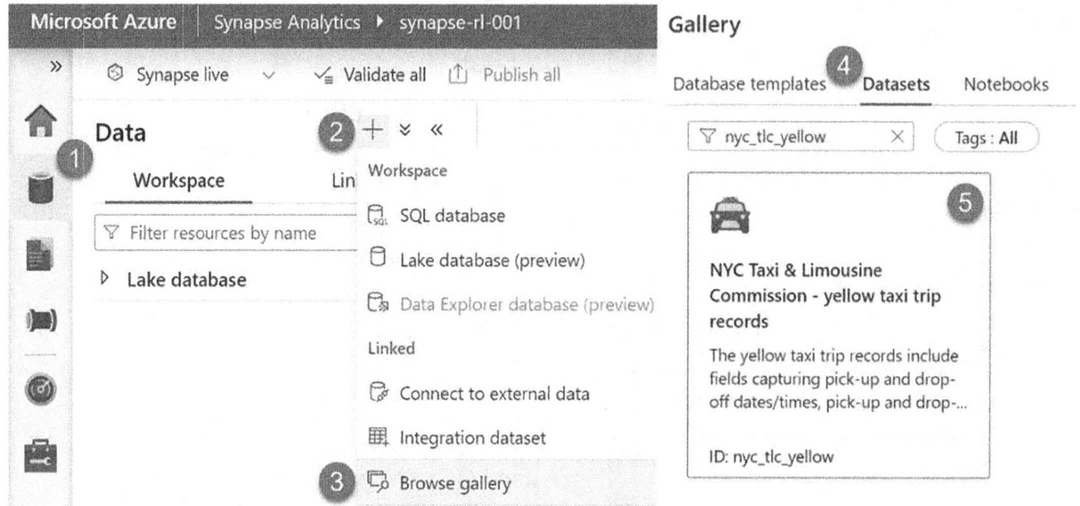

***Figure 16-3.** Steps to add NYC Taxi Yellow dataset from Gallery to workspace as a linked service*

While the entire record set spans 1.5 billion records (50 GB) from 2009 to 2018, as an alternative method, you could also choose to use a 7-month subset of the data from 2018-05-01 to 2018-05-08, which is around 2.1 million records by running the following code, which will import the NycTlcYellow data from Azure ML open datasets. There is also a parser filter for the desired dates. Finally, the code will load the data to a Spark data frame.

```
from azureml.opendatasets import NycTlcYellow

from datetime import datetime
from dateutil import parser
```

```
end_date = parser.parse('2018-05-08 00:00:00')
start_date = parser.parse('2018-05-01 00:00:00')

nyc_tlc = NycTlcYellow(start_date=start_date, end_date=end_date)
nyc_tlc_df = nyc_tlc.to_spark_dataframe()
```

Figure 16-4 illustrates the process of running the code within your Synapse Analytics workspace. Notice that the notebook is attached to a Spark Pool with two executors and eight cores and the language is PySpark(Python).

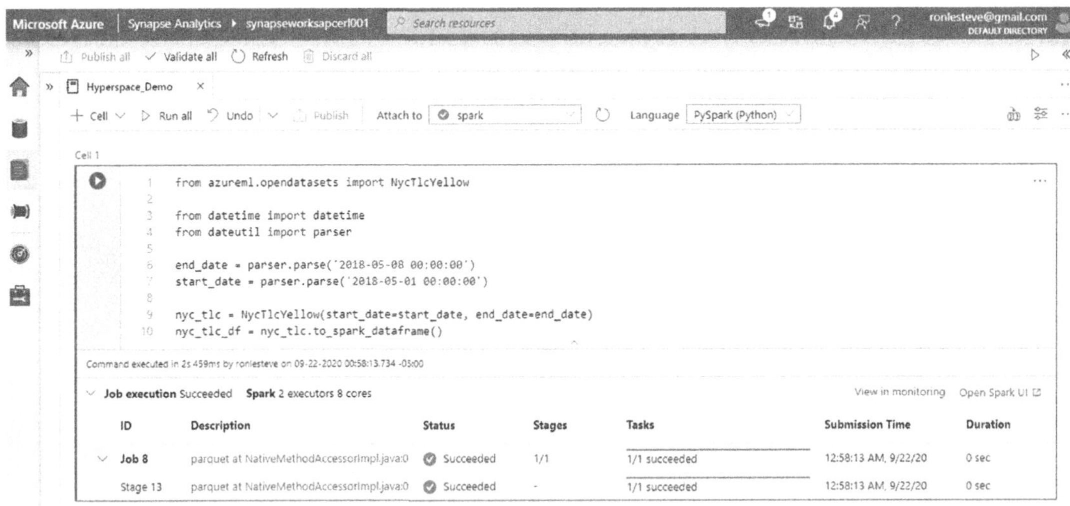

***Figure 16-4.** Import the NYC Taxi dataset*

After the job succeeds, run a select on the VendorID column to confirm that you have approximately 2.1M records using the following code: `SELECT COUNT(vendorID) FROM nyc_tlc_df`, as shown in Figure 16-5.

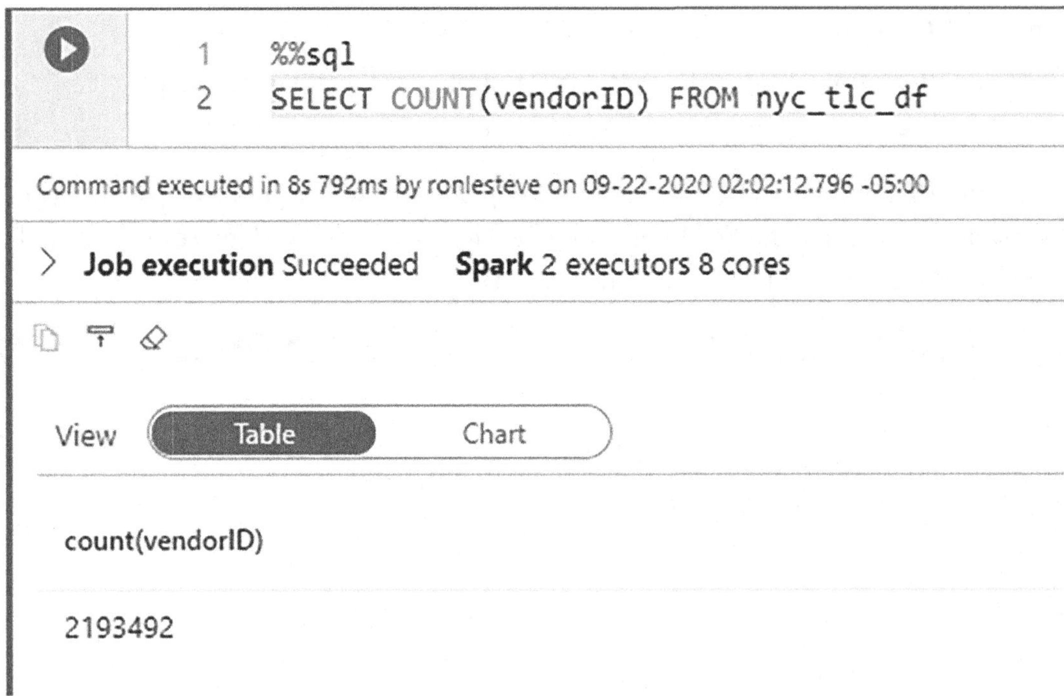

Figure 16-5. Count of records in the dataset

Create Parquet Files

Now that you have a Spark data frame containing data, the following code will create parquet files in the linked ADLS2 account:

```
nyc_tlc_df.createOrReplaceTempView('nyc_tlc_df')
nyc_tlc_df.write.parquet('nyc_tlc_df_parquet', mode='overwrite')
```

Notice from the results shown in Figure 16-6 that the Job execution succeeded.

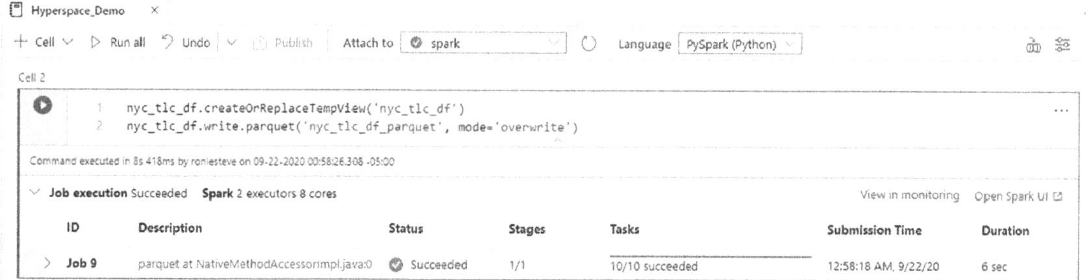

***Figure 16-6.** Create parquet files in ADLS gen2*

Finally, verify that the snappy compressed parquet files have indeed been created in the nyc_tlc_df_parquet folder within ADLS2, as shown in Figure 16-7. We will need these files later to create the Hyperspace Index.

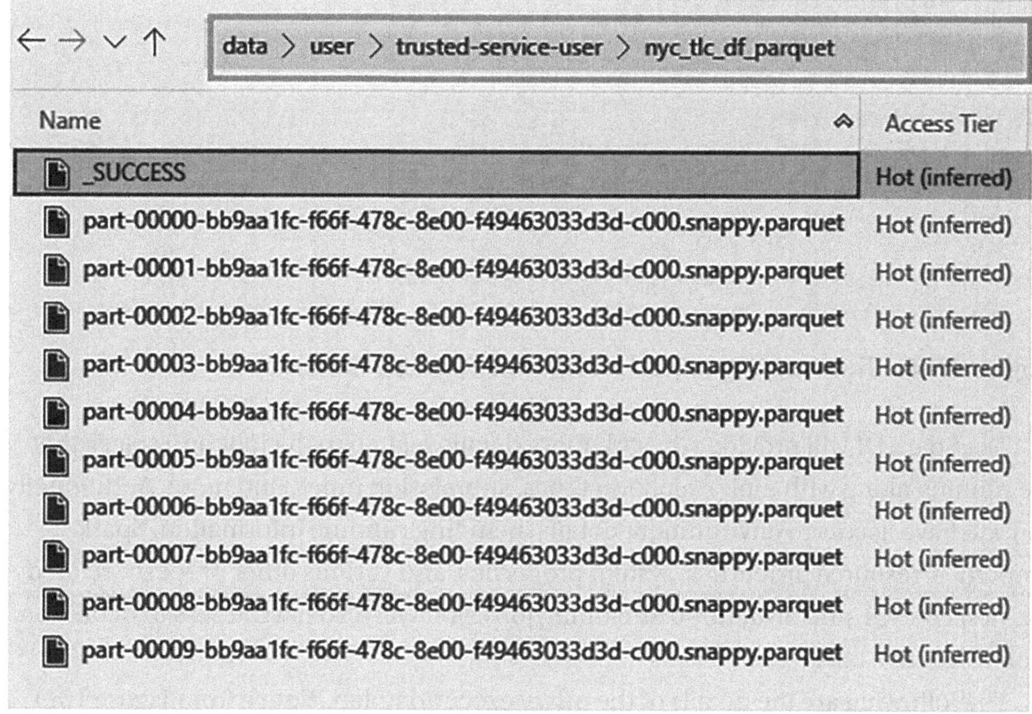

***Figure 16-7.** Image of parquet NYC data*

Run a Query Without an Index

Run the following query within your notebook to obtain a benchmark on how long the aggregate query takes to complete:

```
from pyspark.sql import functions as F
df = nyc_tlc_df.groupBy("passengerCount").agg(F.avg('tripDistance').
alias('AvgTripDistance'), F.sum('tripDistance').alias('SumTripDistance'))
display(df)
```

Based on the results displayed in Figure 16-8, this query took approximately 12 seconds to execute with 2 Spark executors and 8 cores on 2.1M data frames. To view more details related to the query, you can open the Spark UI shown in Figure 16-8.

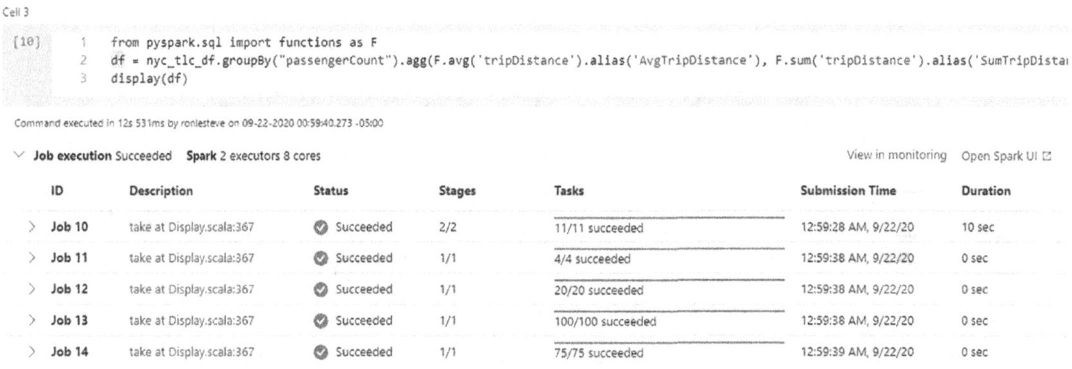

Cell 3

```
[10]
from pyspark.sql import functions as F
df = nyc_tlc_df.groupBy("passengerCount").agg(F.avg('tripDistance').alias('AvgTripDistance'), F.sum('tripDistance').alias('SumTripDista
display(df)
```

Command executed in 12s 531ms by ronlesteve on 09-22-2020 00:59:40.273 -05:00

Job execution Succeeded **Spark** 2 executors 8 cores View in monitoring Open Spark UI

ID	Description	Status	Stages	Tasks	Submission Time	Duration
Job 10	take at Display.scala:367	Succeeded	2/2	11/11 succeeded	12:59:28 AM, 9/22/20	10 sec
Job 11	take at Display.scala:367	Succeeded	1/1	4/4 succeeded	12:59:38 AM, 9/22/20	0 sec
Job 12	take at Display.scala:367	Succeeded	1/1	20/20 succeeded	12:59:38 AM, 9/22/20	0 sec
Job 13	take at Display.scala:367	Succeeded	1/1	100/100 succeeded	12:59:38 AM, 9/22/20	0 sec
Job 14	take at Display.scala:367	Succeeded	1/1	75/75 succeeded	12:59:39 AM, 9/22/20	0 sec

***Figure 16-8.** Test running a query with non-indexed tables*

The Spark UI will provide you with more details related to the jobs and stages that are running along with their execution times, submission times, and more. Additionally, you will have access to environment details including runtime information, Spark properties, resource properties, system properties, and various other property-related metrics. For SQL and Structured Streaming jobs, you will also have access to details on their respective tabs.

The following are the details of the query execution plan. Notice from Figure 16-9 that the job took approximately 11 seconds and there were no indexed tables. Alternatively, to use the Spark UI for query execution details, you could run df.explain() in a code cell to get the details within the notebook itself.

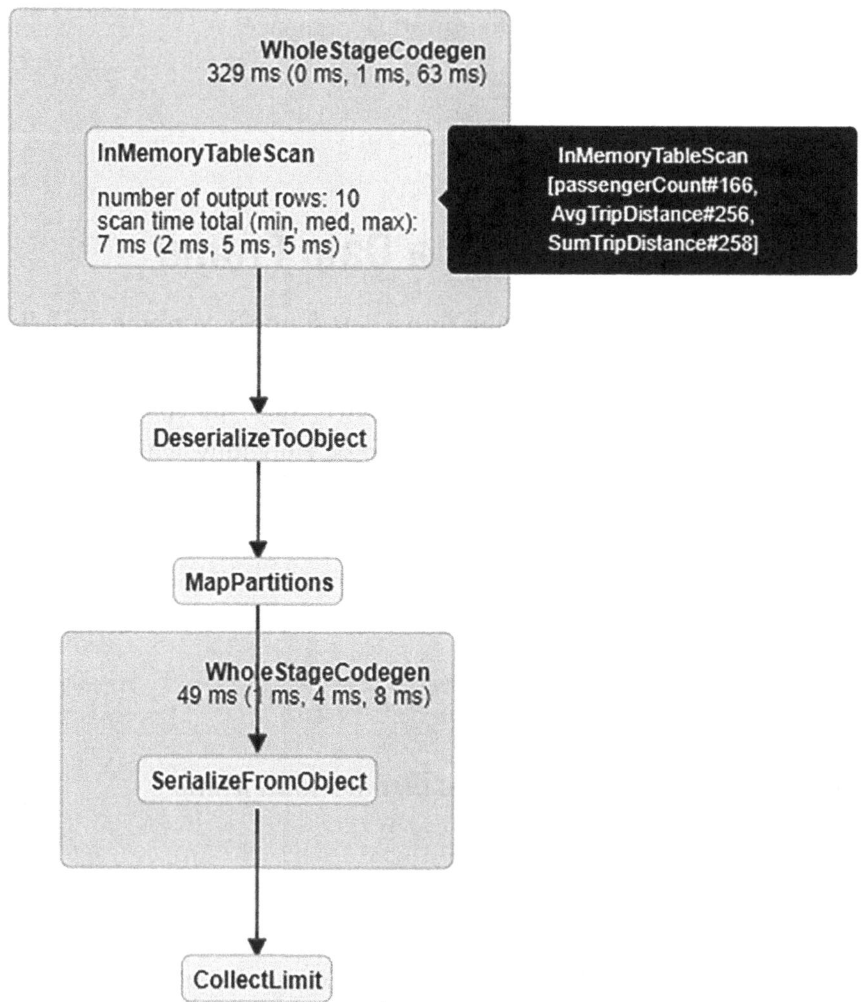

Figure 16-9. *Details of the query execution plan*

Import Hyperspace

Now that you have established a benchmark query without any indexed tables, I will demonstrate how to get started with Hyperspace in the Synapse workspace. Run the following code within your notebook to import Hyperspace:

```
from hyperspace import Hyperspace
hs = Hyperspace(spark)
```

Read the Parquet Files to a Data Frame

Next, you'll need to read the parquet files into a data frame by running the following code: `df=spark.read.parquet("/user/trusted-service-user/nyc_tlc_df_parquet/")` as shown in Figure 16-10. This is because the Hyperspace Index creation process requires the source files to be stored on disk. Hopefully, with a future release, it will have the capability of also creating indexes on in-memory data frames.

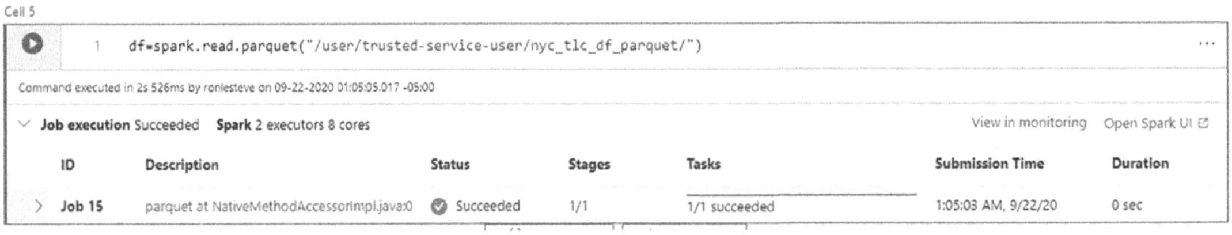

Figure 16-10. *Code to read the parquet files to a data frame*

Create a Hyperspace Index

The next step would be to create a Hyperspace Index with the following code: `from hyperspace import IndexConfighs.createIndex(df, IndexConfig("vendorID", ["passengerCount"], ["tripDistance"]))`, as shown in Figure 16-11. Note that VendorID is my indexed column. Additionally, I have included two columns that have also been used in my aggregate query.

Cell 6

```
from hyperspace import IndexConfig
hs.createIndex(df, IndexConfig("vendorID", ["passengerCount"], ["tripDistance"]))
```

Command executed in 6s 581ms by ronlesteve on 09-22-2020 01:06:49.367 -05:00

Job execution Succeeded Spark 2 executors 8 cores View in monitoring Open Spark UI

ID	Description	Status	Stages	Tasks	Submission Time	Duration
Job 17	toRdd at DataFrameWriterExtensions.scala:77	Succeeded	2/2	210/210 succeeded	1:06:43 AM, 9/22/20	4 sec

Figure 16-11. *Code to create a Hyperspace Index*

The Hyperspace Indexing subsystem will automatically create a collection of snappy compressed files in an index folder in ADLS gen2, as shown in Figure 16-12. While this adds more storage overhead costs, the benefits of a performant and optimized query may outweigh the costs. In future releases of Hyperspace, this process may be more in-memory driven.

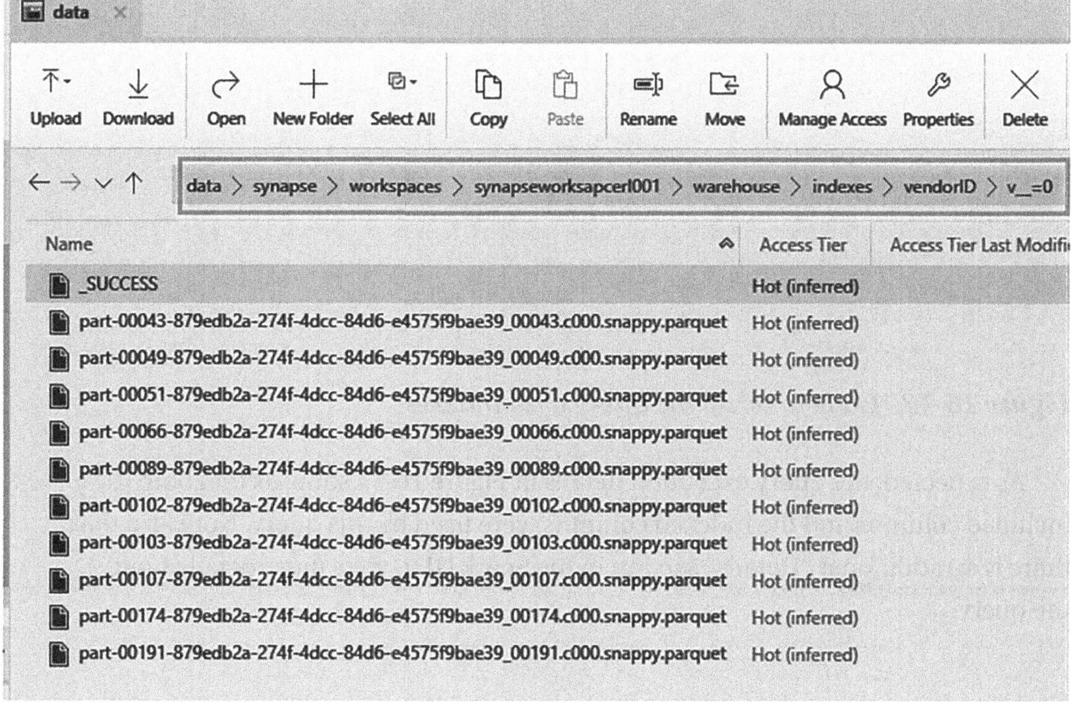

Figure 16-12. *Index files are auto created in ADLS gen2*

Rerun the Query with Hyperspace Index

Now that you have created a Hyperspace Index, rerun your original query from earlier to explore the execution time and query details:

```
from pyspark.sql import functions as F
df = nyc_tlc_df.groupBy("passengerCount").agg(F.avg('tripDistance').
alias('AvgTripDistance'), F.sum('tripDistance').alias('SumTripDistance'))
display(df)
```

This time, the query only took ~2 seconds vs. the original ~12 seconds, as shown in Figure 16-13. While the performance gains are harder to notice with relatively small 1.2M record sets, the benefits will be more notable when optimizing extremely big datasets. Once again, let's open the Spark UI to view the query details.

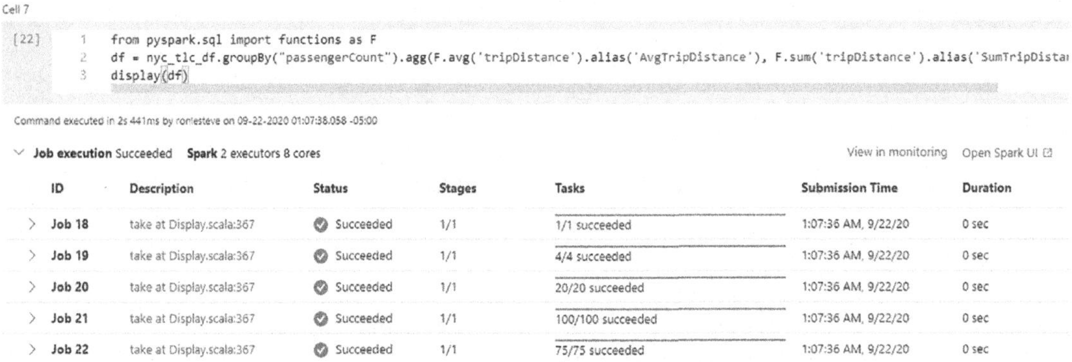

Cell 7

```
[22]
from pyspark.sql import functions as F
df = nyc_tlc_df.groupBy("passengerCount").agg(F.avg('tripDistance').alias('AvgTripDistance'), F.sum('tripDistance').alias('SumTripDistai
display(df)
```

Command executed in 2s 441ms by ronlesteve on 09-22-2020 01:07:38.058 -05:00

Job execution Succeeded **Spark** 2 executors 8 cores View in monitoring Open Spark UI

ID	Description	Status	Stages	Tasks	Submission Time	Duration
Job 18	take at Display.scala:367	Succeeded	1/1	1/1 succeeded	1:07:36 AM, 9/22/20	0 sec
Job 19	take at Display.scala:367	Succeeded	1/1	4/4 succeeded	1:07:36 AM, 9/22/20	0 sec
Job 20	take at Display.scala:367	Succeeded	1/1	20/20 succeeded	1:07:36 AM, 9/22/20	0 sec
Job 21	take at Display.scala:367	Succeeded	1/1	100/100 succeeded	1:07:36 AM, 9/22/20	0 sec
Job 22	take at Display.scala:367	Succeeded	1/1	75/75 succeeded	1:07:36 AM, 9/22/20	0 sec

Figure 16-13. *Code to rerun the query with indexes*

As expected, the query execution details in Figure 16-14 show us that both the included columns and the indexed columns were used by this query. Note also that there is an additional "Details" section in the Spark UI to view more detail about the query.

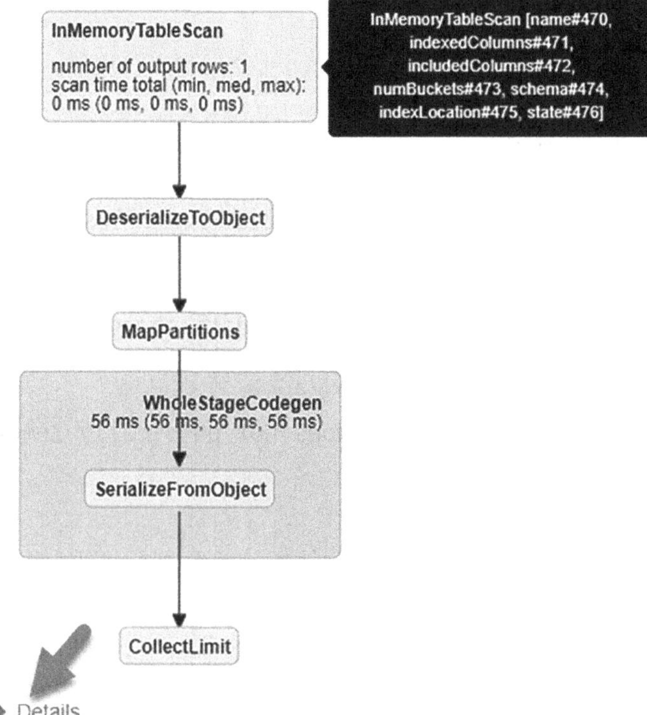

***Figure 16-14.** Execution details of the rerun query*

Other Hyperspace Management APIs

There are a few other Hyperspace Management APIs that can be used directly from the Synapse workspace. The following code `display(hs.indexes())` will display the indexes, as shown in Figure 16-15.

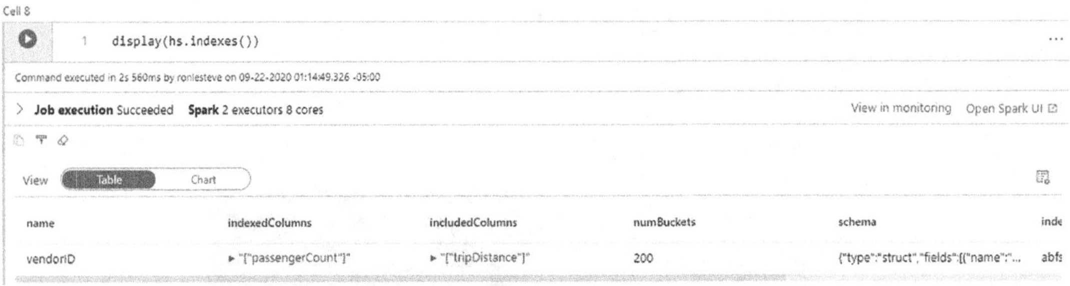

```
Cell 8
1 display(hs.indexes())
```

Command executed in 2s 560ms by ronlesteve on 09-22-2020 01:14:49.326 -05:00

> Job execution Succeeded Spark 2 executors 8 cores

name	indexedColumns	includedColumns	numBuckets	schema	inde
vendorID	▸ "["passengerCount"]"	▸ "["tripDistance"]"	200	{"type":"struct","fields":[{"name":"...	abfs

Figure 16-15. Code to display the indexes that were created

Additionally, the following scripts list out other APIs to refresh, delete (soft delete), restore and vacuum (hard delete) the Hyperspace Indexes:

```
// Refreshes the given index if the source data changes.
hs.refreshIndex("index")

// Soft-deletes the given index and does not physically remove it from
filesystem.
hs.deleteIndex("index")

// Restores the soft-deleted index.
hs.restoreIndex("index")

// Hard-delete the given index and physically remove it from filesystem.
hs.vacuumIndex("index")
```

Summary

In this chapter, you learned how to get started with creating Spark Indexes in Azure Synapse Analytics workspace by using the Hyperspace Index Management subsystem. As with any index, there comes the added trade-off with added costs to maintain additional index files and possibly even performance impacts from having to continuously rebuild indexes. On the other hand, there are numerous performance optimization capabilities of the Hyperspace Indexing subsystem that support highly performant modern Data Lakehouses. These indexes and various performance improvement technologies bring to the Lakehouse the same features that have been prevalent in many mature traditional SQL Server databases and data warehouses for decades, and they demonstrate the futuristic capabilities of the Lakehouse. Hyperspace is supported in the following languages: C#, Scala, and Python. For more details related to this Synapse Hyperspace Index subsystem, you can also refer to Microsoft's detailed documentation, which can be found here: `https://docs.microsoft.com/en-us/azure/synapse-analytics/spark/apache-spark-performance-hyperspace`. For more Lakehouse performance optimization options, please read Chapters 12 through 15 of this book.

PART VI

Advanced Capabilities

CHAPTER 17

Auto Loader

The concept of event-driven ELT paradigms has been a long-standing desire in the data engineering ecosystem and even more so as modern data architectures explore and approach the Lakehouse paradigm. While there are numerous event-driven data ingestion patterns in Azure, managing the changing schemas for streaming data has traditionally been a challenge. Additionally, the setup and management of Event Grid subscriptions, topics, and more have also been a challenge to seamlessly integrate with Spark.

Auto Loader provides a structured streaming source called cloudFiles that offers the capability of incrementally processing new files in JSON, CSV, PARQUET, AVRO, ORC, TEXT, and BINARYFILE file formats as they arrive in Azure Data Lake Storage Gen2, while also managing advanced schema evolution of this streaming data, and finally storing this data in a data frame. In addition to ADLS gen2 and Databricks File System (DBFS, dbfs:/), Auto Loader can also be configured across multi-cloud storage providers including AWS S3 (s3://), Google Cloud Storage (GCS, gs://), Azure Blob Storage (wasbs://), and ADLS Gen1 (adl://). More details about Auto Loader can also be found here on Microsoft's article: `https://docs.microsoft.com/en-us/azure/databricks/spark/latest/structured-streaming/auto-loader`

Auto Loader supports two modes for detecting new files which are directory listing and file notifications. With directory listing, Auto Loader identifies new files based on the directory within which they are inserted into. With file notifications, Auto Loader automatically sets up a notification and queue service that subscribes to file events from the input directory. While this mode requires more cloud setup permissions, it is also more performant and scalable for large input directories or a high volume of files.

R. L'Esteve, *The Azure Data Lakehouse Toolkit*, https://doi.org/10.1007/978-1-4842-8233-5_17

Advanced Schema Evolution

Auto Loader within Databricks runtime versions 7.2 and above is designed for event-driven structure streaming ELT patterns and is constantly evolving and improving with each new runtime release. With the release of Databricks runtime version 8.2, Auto Loader cloudFile source now supports advanced schema evolution. With schema inference capabilities, there is no longer the need to identify and define a schema. In this section, I will demonstrate how to get started with using Auto Loader cloudFiles through an end-to-end practical example of ingesting a data stream which has an evolving schema. Within this exercise, you will learn how to set up Auto Loader cloudFiles in Azure, work with evolving streaming data schemas, track changing schemas through captured versions in schema locations, infer schemas, and/or define schemas through schema hints.

Prerequisites

There are a few setup steps that are required for Auto Loader cloudFiles to work effectively. In this section, you will learn how to create these prerequisites which include generating the JSON files which will be used for this exercise, completing the necessary setup with Azure portal, and configuring Databricks secret scopes.

Prior to continuing this section, ensure that you have created the following Azure resources:

1. Azure Databricks
2. Azure Key Vault
3. Azure Data Lake Storage Gen2

Generate Data from SQL Database

In this section, we will use the AdventureWorks sample database to generate JSON format files for the source files that will be ingested by Auto Loader cloudFiles, since this format demonstrates a semi-structured, complex, and evolving format. You can prepare these source files by using the Adventure Works LT2019 database which is available here: `github.com/microsoft/sql-server-samples/tree/master/samples/databases`. Use the Customer table shown in Figure 17-1 to generate three source files that you will feed into the streaming Auto Loader cloudFile source.

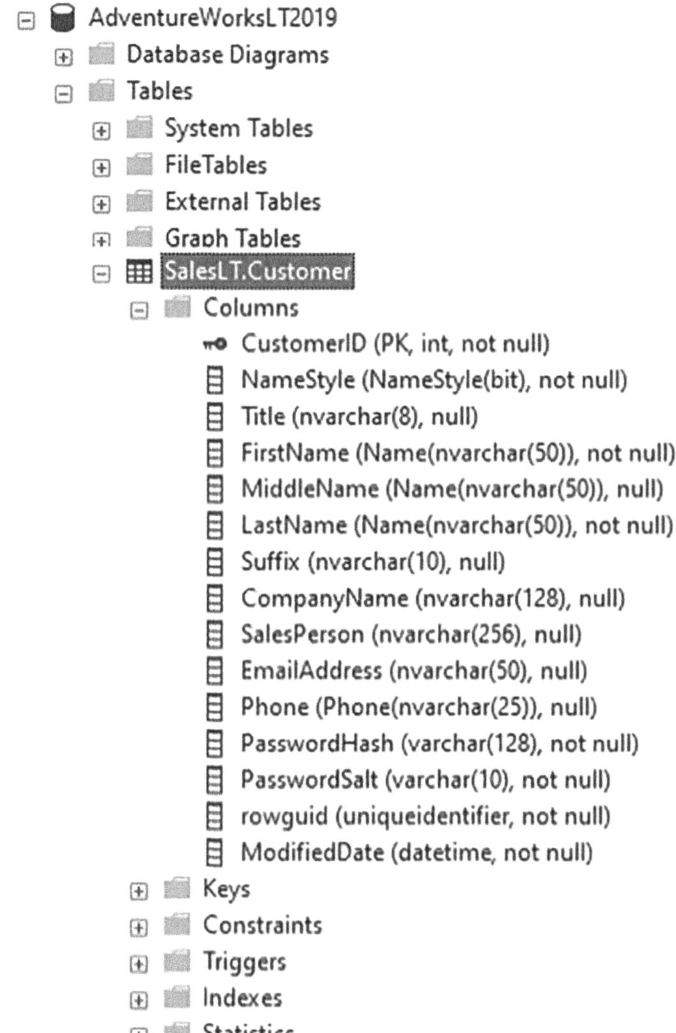

Figure 17-1. *Customer table schema*

Begin by writing the following SQL query shown in Figure 17-2, which takes a handful of columns from the Customer table and returns them as JSON format for each record per line. Save the results of this query as a JSON file which you could call Customer1.json. You will also need to repeat this exercise two more times to create two additional customer JSON files. With each iteration of the code, you will need to add additional columns to the query to truly mimic an evolving schema.

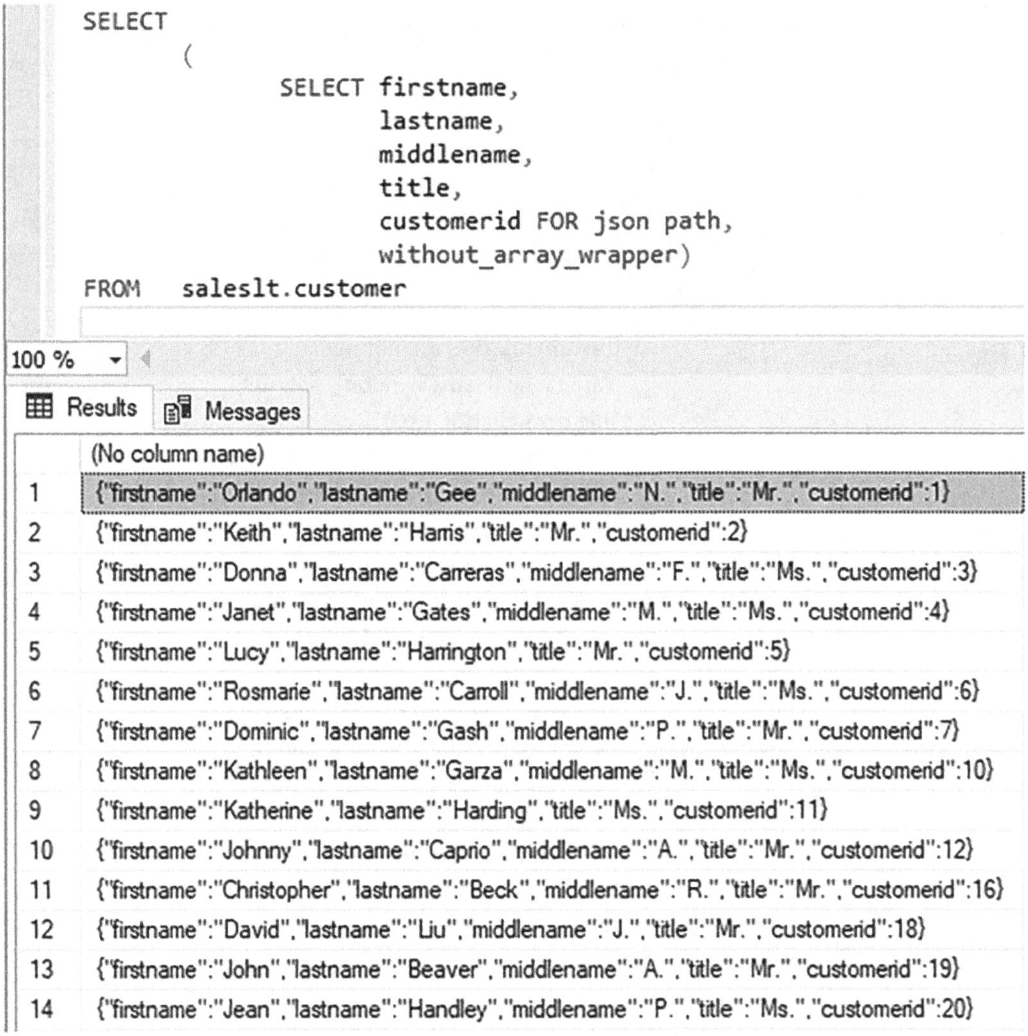

```
SELECT
        (
                SELECT firstname,
                       lastname,
                       middlename,
                       title,
                       customerid FOR json path,
                       without_array_wrapper)
FROM   saleslt.customer
```

100 %

Results | Messages

	(No column name)
1	{"firstname":"Orlando","lastname":"Gee","middlename":"N.","title":"Mr.","customerid":1}
2	{"firstname":"Keith","lastname":"Harris","title":"Mr.","customerid":2}
3	{"firstname":"Donna","lastname":"Carreras","middlename":"F.","title":"Ms.","customerid":3}
4	{"firstname":"Janet","lastname":"Gates","middlename":"M.","title":"Ms.","customerid":4}
5	{"firstname":"Lucy","lastname":"Harrington","title":"Mr.","customerid":5}
6	{"firstname":"Rosmarie","lastname":"Carroll","middlename":"J.","title":"Ms.","customerid":6}
7	{"firstname":"Dominic","lastname":"Gash","middlename":"P.","title":"Mr.","customerid":7}
8	{"firstname":"Kathleen","lastname":"Garza","middlename":"M.","title":"Ms.","customerid":10}
9	{"firstname":"Katherine","lastname":"Harding","title":"Ms.","customerid":11}
10	{"firstname":"Johnny","lastname":"Caprio","middlename":"A.","title":"Mr.","customerid":12}
11	{"firstname":"Christopher","lastname":"Beck","middlename":"R.","title":"Mr.","customerid":16}
12	{"firstname":"David","lastname":"Liu","middlename":"J.","title":"Mr.","customerid":18}
13	{"firstname":"John","lastname":"Beaver","middlename":"A.","title":"Mr.","customerid":19}
14	{"firstname":"Jean","lastname":"Handley","middlename":"P.","title":"Ms.","customerid":20}

Figure 17-2. *SQL query to create Customer1.json file*

Here is the SQL query that is used for Customer1.json in Figure 17-2:

```
SELECT
        (
                SELECT firstname,
                       lastname,
                       middlename,
```

```
                    title,
                    customerid FOR json path,
                    without_array_wrapper)
FROM   saleslt.customer
```

Similar to the previous query, here is the SQL query that is used for Customer2.json:

```
SELECT
      (
             SELECT firstname,
                    lastname,
                    middlename,
                    title,
                    customerid,
                    companyname,
                    emailaddress,
                    salesperson,
                    namestyle FOR json path,
                    without_array_wrapper)
FROM   saleslt.customer
```

Here is the SQL query used for Customer3.json:

```
SELECT
      (
             SELECT firstname,
                    lastname,
                    middlename,
                    title,
                    customerid,
                    companyname,
                    emailaddress,
                    salesperson,
                    namestyle,
                    modifieddate,
```

```
                        phone,
                        rowguid FOR json path,
                        without_array_wrapper)
FROM    saleslt.customer
```

Now that you have created Customer1.json, Customer2.json, and Customer3.json files by using the source SQL queries within this section, you are ready to upload these JSON files into ADLS gen2.

Load Data to Azure Data Lake Storage Gen2

Within ADLS gen2, you will need to create a few new folders. Create a Customer folder and load all of the Customer JSON files that you had created in the previous section into this folder. These files will be used by Auto Loader. Figure 17-3 shows the folder structure and files in ADLS gen2.

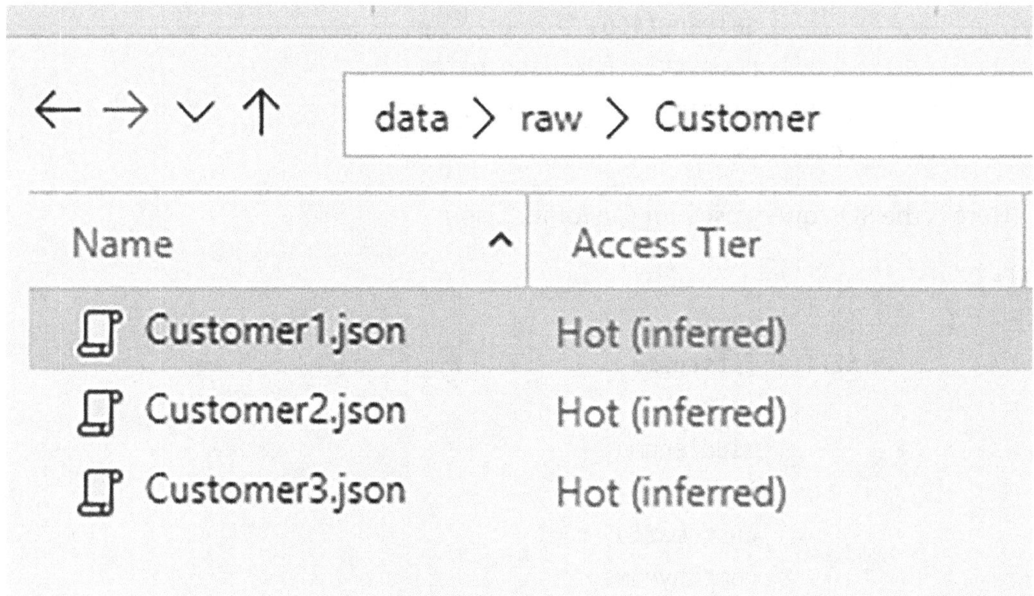

Figure 17-3. *Customer JSON files loaded to ADLS2 raw zone*

Also create a Customer_stream folder and load the Cutomer1.json file, shown in Figure 17-4. All files that will be added to this folder will be processed by the streaming Auto Loader cloudFile source.

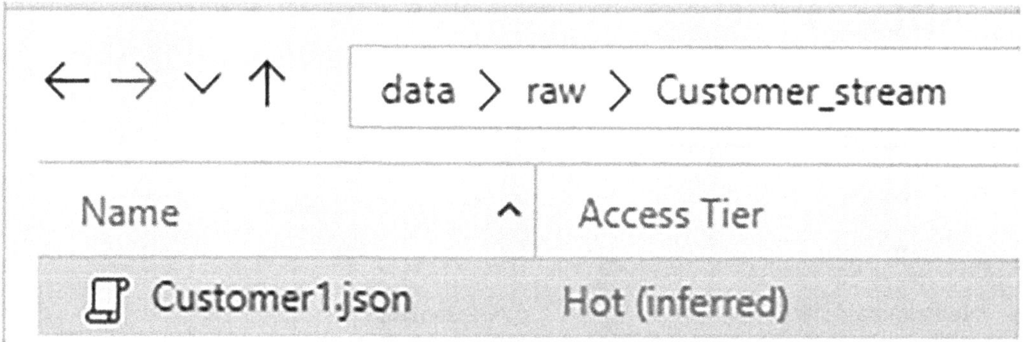

***Figure 17-4.** Customer1.json file loaded to customer_stream ADLS2 folder*

Configure Resources in Azure Portal

There are a few configurations that need to be completed in the Azure portal. Begin by navigating to Resource providers, illustrated in Figure 17-5, in your Azure subscription, and register Microsoft.EventGrid as a resource provider.

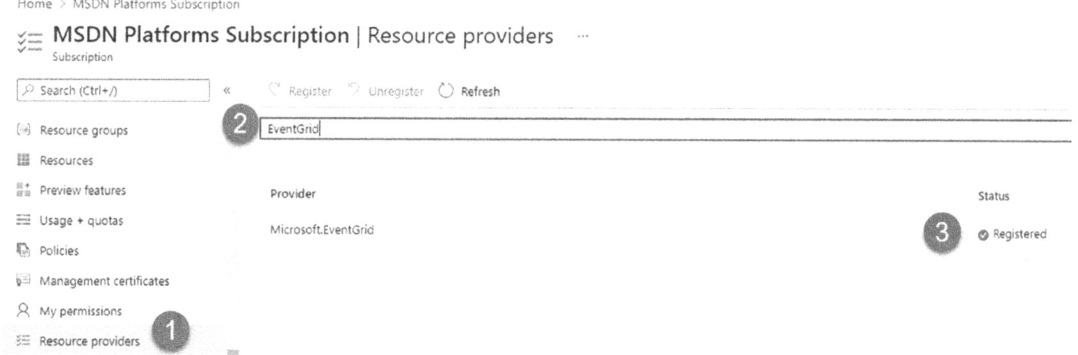

***Figure 17-5.** Register Event Grid as resource provider*

Next, navigate to Azure Active Directory and register a new application, as seen in Figure 17-6. You will need the client ID, tenant ID, and client secret of this new app and will need to also give this app access to ADLS gen2. If you need more details about this process, please see the following Microsoft article: `https://docs.microsoft.com/en-us/azure/databricks/data/data-sources/azure/adls-gen2/azure-datalake-gen2-sp-access`

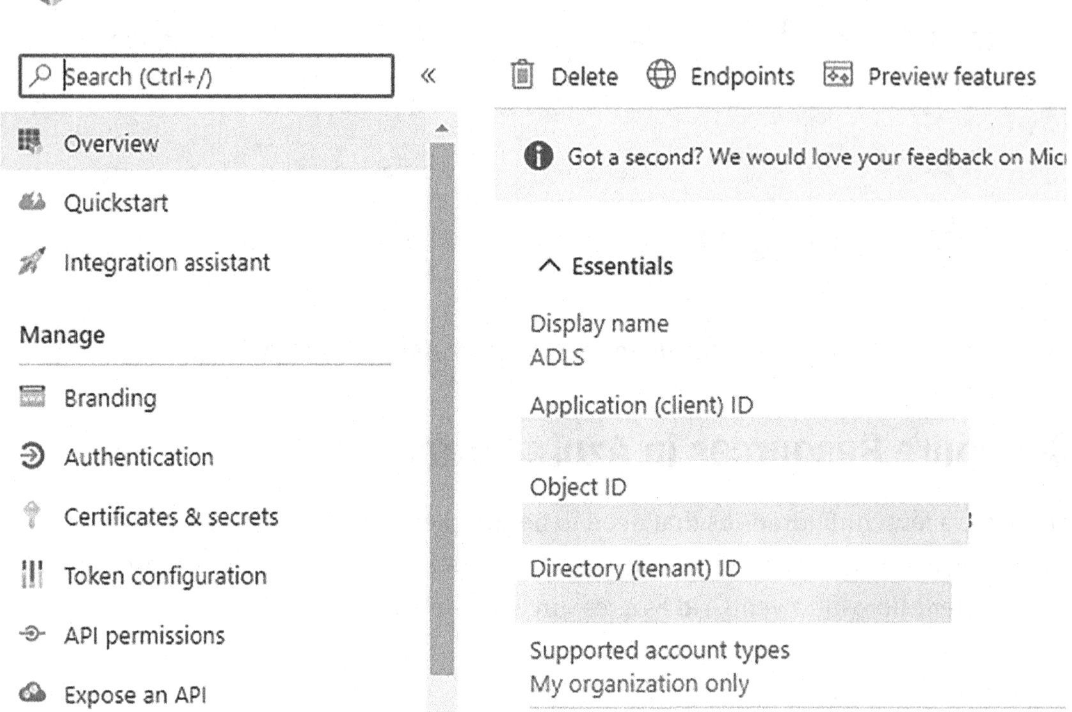

Figure 17-6. Register app that will have access to ADLS2

Once you finish registering this new app, navigate to Certificates & secrets and create a new client secret. To achieve this, follow the steps shown in Figure 17-7.

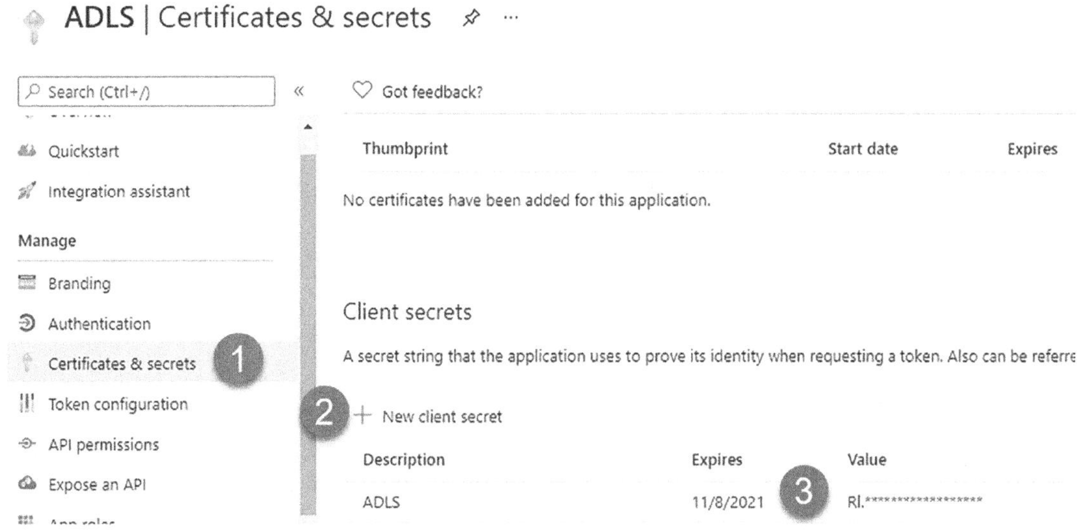

Figure 17-7. Generate a new secret for the newly registered app

Within ADLS gen2, navigate to Access Control (IAM) and add a new role assignment. Give the app that you previously registered contributor access to ADLS gen2. The steps to achieve this are shown in Figure 17-8.

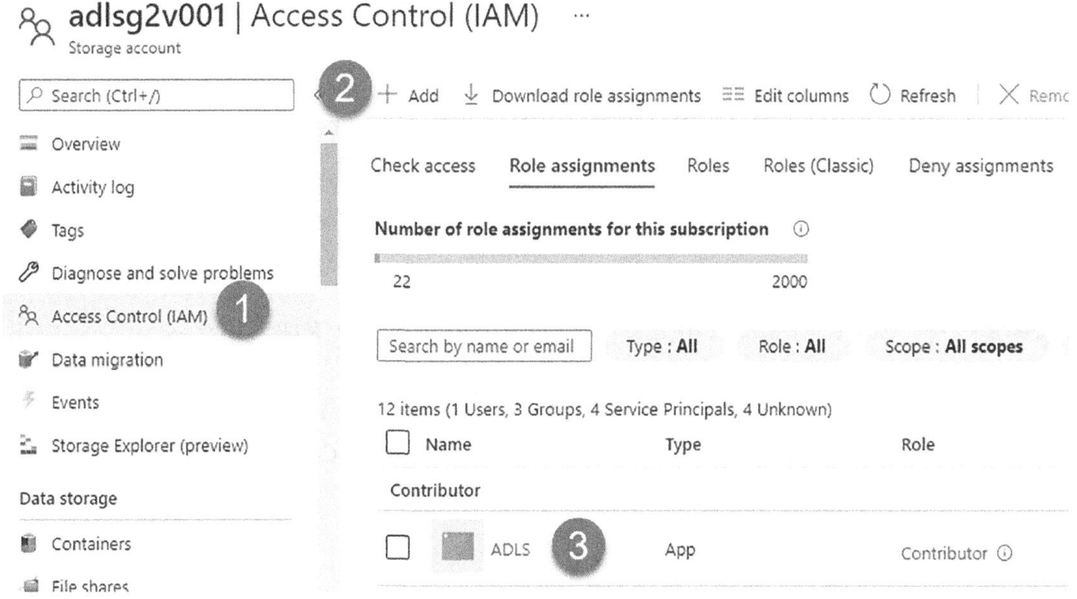

Figure 17-8. Allow the app to access ADLS2 as a contributor

At this point, begin copying the credentials and keys from the various applications so that you can store them in a Key Vault. Databricks will have access to this Key Vault, and Auto Loader will use these credentials to create Event Grid subscriptions and topics to process the incoming streaming data. Begin by navigating to the app that you registered in the previous section and copy ClientID and TenantID, shown in Figure 17-9, and save them in a notepad.

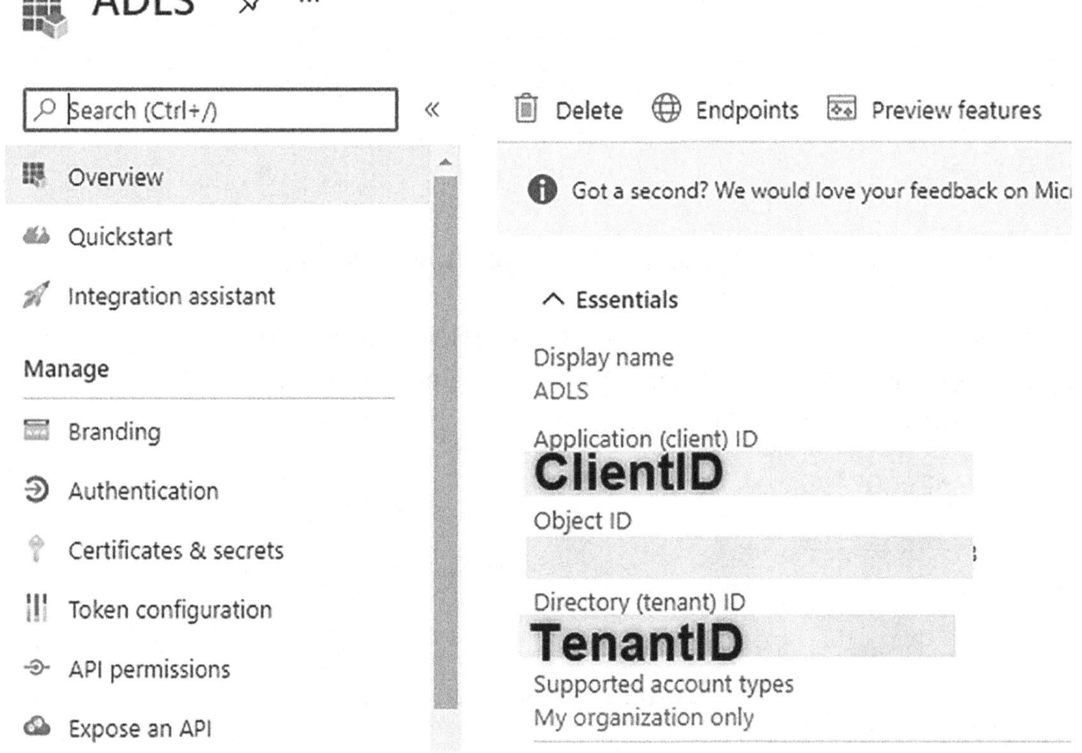

***Figure 17-9.** Copy the client and tenant IDs from the registered app*

Next, navigate to the registered app's Certificates & secrets tab, as seen in Figure 17-10, and create a new secret. Once created, copy the ClientSecret and paste this into the notepad as well.

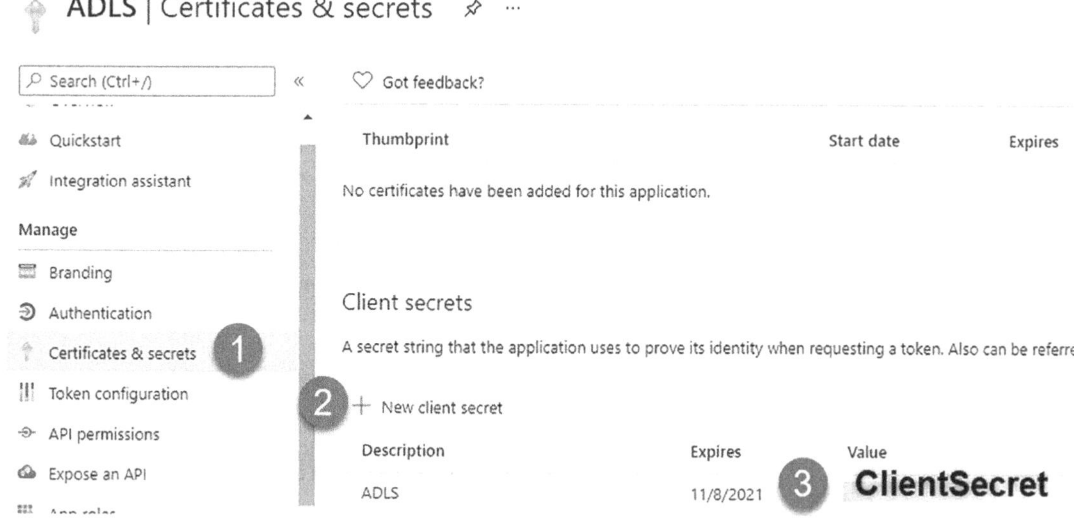

Figure 17-10. *Copy the client secret from the registered app*

You will also need to navigate to the ADLS gen2 Access keys tab, copy the SASKey, and paste it into the notepad. This can be seen in Figure 17-11.

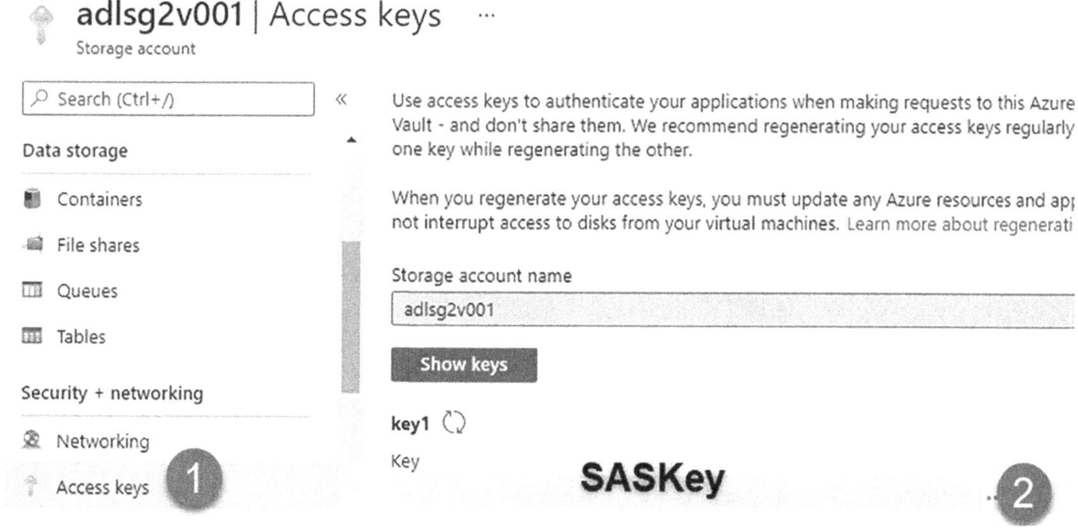

Figure 17-11. *Copy the SASKey from the ADLS2 Access keys tab*

Within ADLS gen2, navigate to Shared access signature, and ensure that the Allowed services, resource types, and permissions are configured accurately. Generate the connection string, copy it, and paste in the notepad. The steps to complete this are shown in Figure 17-12.

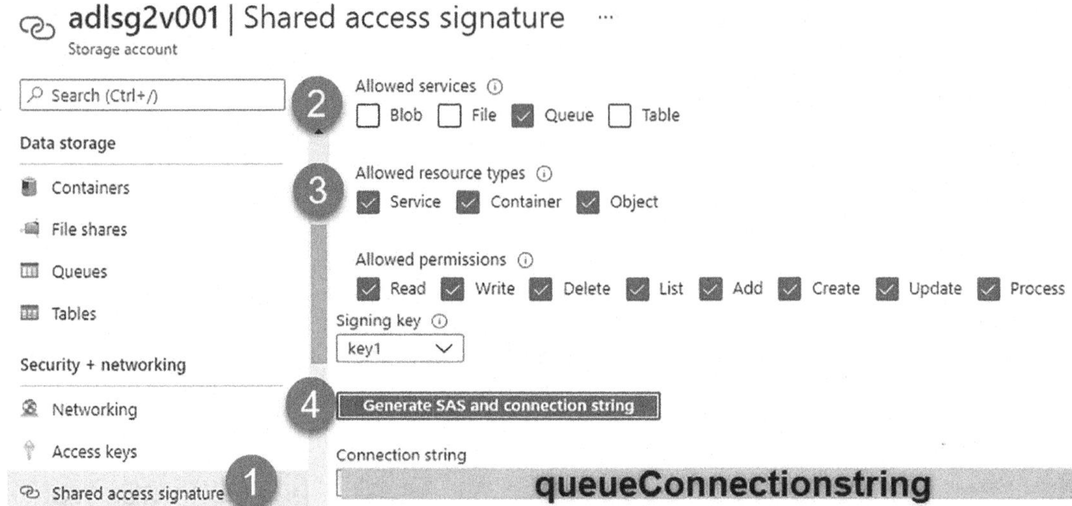

Figure 17-12. *Copy the connection string from the SAS tab of ADLS 2*

There is one final step in the Azure portal prerequisites section. Use all of the values that you have previously pasted into the notepad as Key Vault secrets. Do this by navigating to Key Vault's Secrets tab, generate a new secret, and create the following secrets. You will also need to add your resource group and subscription ID as secrets. Ensure that the following seven secrets shown in Figure 17-13 are created and enabled.

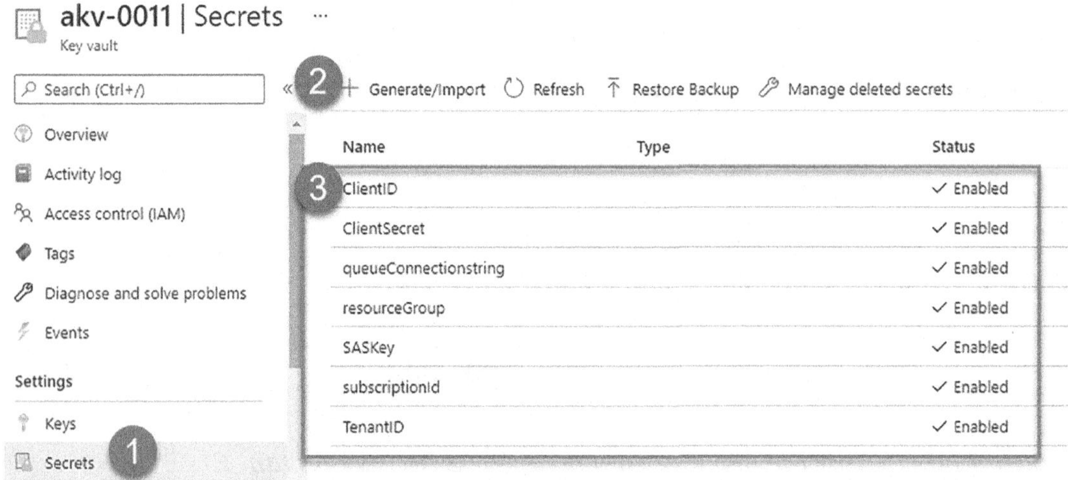

Figure 17-13. *Add the copied secrets to AKV*

Configure Databricks

In Databricks, create a new secret scope by navigating to `https://<DATABRICKS-INSTANCE>#secrets/createScope` and replace <DATABRICKS-INSTANCE> with your own Databricks URL instance. This URL will take you to the UI where you can create your secret scope. Figure 17-14 shows where you'll need to paste the Key Vault URI and Resource ID from your Key Vault into the respective DNS Name and Resource ID section.

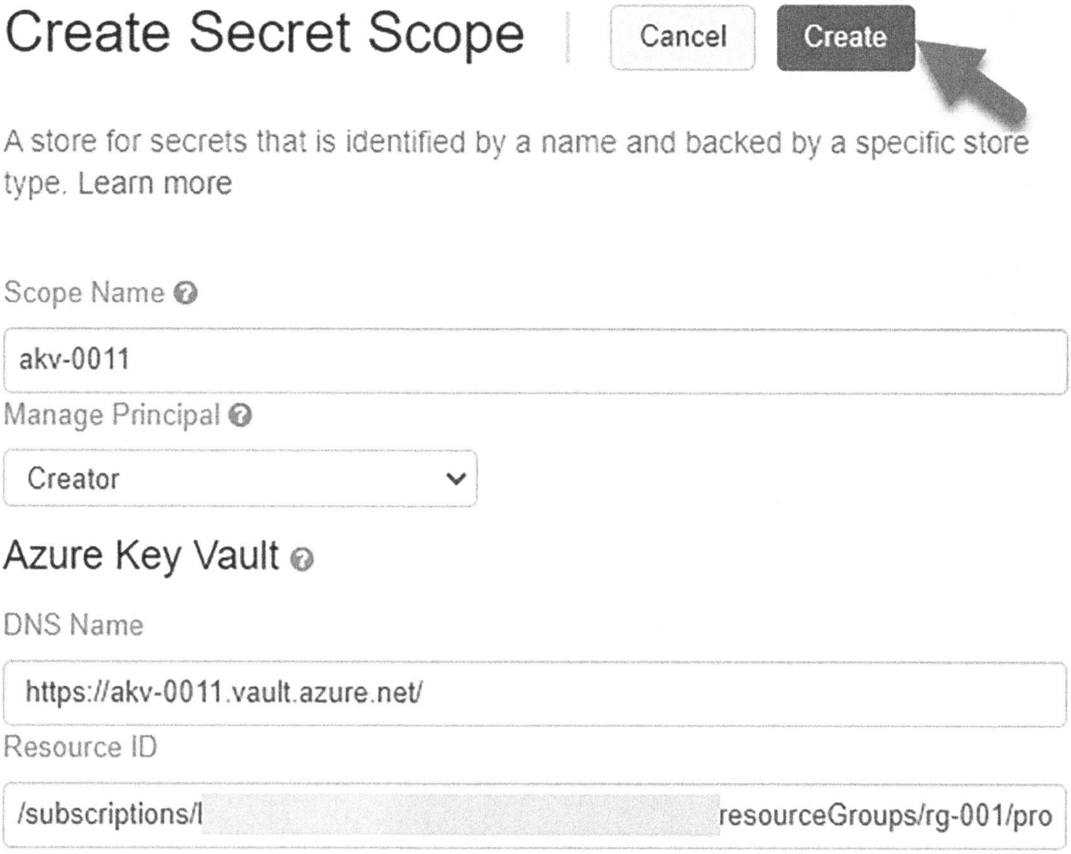

Figure 17-14. *Create a secret scope in Databricks*

Create a new cluster with Databricks runtime version of 8.2, shown in Figure 17-15. This supports the advanced schema evolution capabilities of Auto Loader cloudFiles.

Figure 17-15. *Create 8.2 runtime cluster*

To prevent any errors at runtime, also install the Event Hubs library to the cluster. This Maven library contains the following coordinates shown in Figure 17-16. Once completed, this concludes all of the required prerequisites in Databricks.

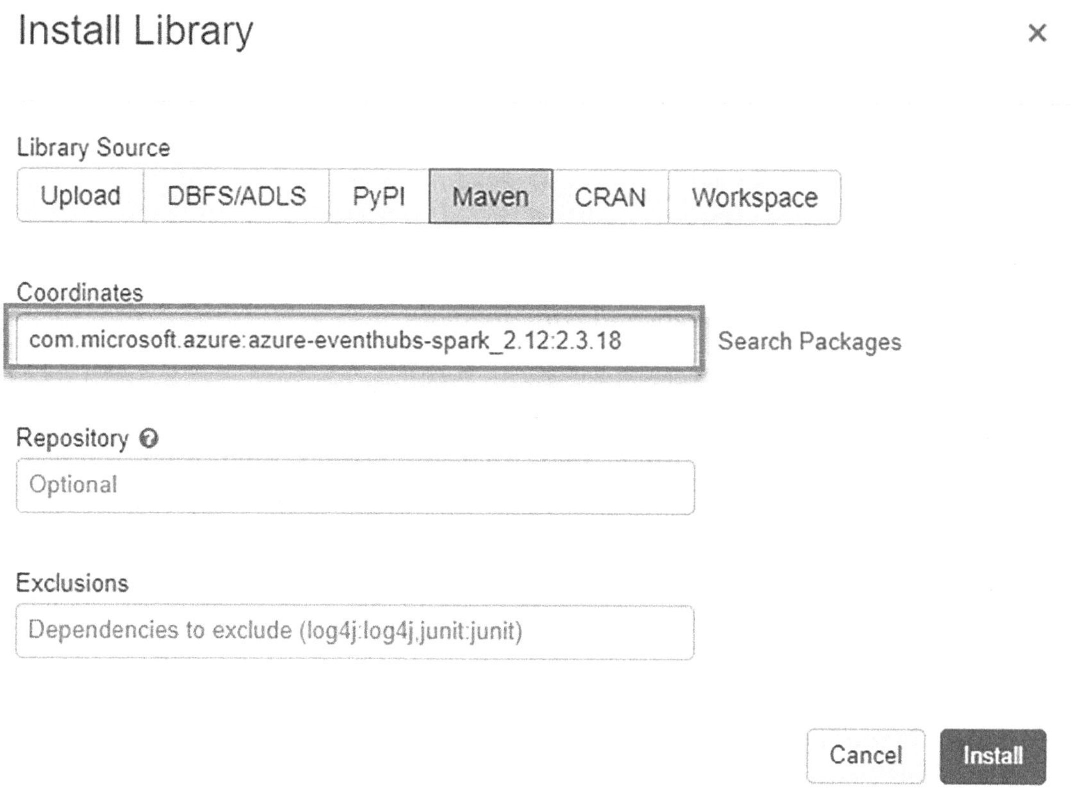

Figure 17-16. *Install Event Hubs library to cluster*

Run Auto Loader in Databricks

In this section, you will learn how to begin working with Auto Loader in a Databricks notebook.

Configuration Properties

To begin the process of configuring and running Auto Loader, set the following configuration shown in Figure 17-17, which specifies either the number of bytes or files to read as part of the config size required to infer the schema.

Figure 17-17. *Set the cloudFiles config in notebook*

Here is the code shown in Figure 17-17. Note that you could use either the numBytes or numFiles properties.

```
#spark.conf.set("spark.databricks.cloudfiles.schemaInference.sampleSize.
numBytes",10000000000)
spark.conf.set("spark.databricks.cloudfiles.schemaInference.sampleSize.
numFiles",10)
```

This next block of code shown in Figure 17-18 will obtain the list of secrets that you have created in your Key Vault.

Cmd 2

```
subscriptionId = dbutils.secrets.get("akv-0011","subscriptionId")
tenantId = dbutils.secrets.get("akv-0011","tenantId")
clientId = dbutils.secrets.get("akv-0011","clientId")
clientSecret = dbutils.secrets.get("akv-0011","clientSecret")
resourceGroup = dbutils.secrets.get("akv-0011","resourceGroup")
queueconnectionString = dbutils.secrets.get("akv-0011","queueconnectionString")
SASKey = dbutils.secrets.get("akv-0011","SASKey")
```

Command took 3.74 seconds -- by ronlesteve at 5/13/2021, 9:50:51 PM on cluster-001-8.2

Figure 17-18. *Add the dbutils secrets to the notebook*

Here is the code that is used in Figure 17-18. Since you have given Databricks access to the Key Vault secret scope, there should be no errors when you run this code.

```
subscriptionId = dbutils.secrets.get("akv-0011","subscriptionId")
tenantId = dbutils.secrets.get("akv-0011","tenantId")
clientId = dbutils.secrets.get("akv-0011","clientId")
clientSecret = dbutils.secrets.get("akv-0011","clientSecret")
```

```
resourceGroup = dbutils.secrets.get("akv-0011","resourceGroup")
queueconnectionString = dbutils.secrets.get("akv-0011","queueconnection
String")
SASKey = dbutils.secrets.get("akv-0011","SASKey")
```

Rescue Data

This next block of code seen in Figure 17-19 will build your cloudFile config. Notice that the format is listed as JSON, but could just as easily be any other format. Define the schema location within your Customer_stream folder, and set the schema evolution mode as "rescue." Rescued data is typically data that is not expected, such as different data types within the JSON blob columns. This data can be accessed later using semi-structured data access APIs. There are additional options which have been commented out in this section; however, we will cover some of these details in later sections.

```
Cmd 3

cloudfile = {
"cloudFiles.subscriptionID": subscriptionId,
"cloudFiles.connectionString": queueconnectionString,
"cloudFiles.format": "json",
"cloudFiles.tenantId": tenantId,
"cloudFiles.clientId": clientId,
"cloudFiles.clientSecret": clientSecret,
"cloudFiles.resourceGroup": resourceGroup,
"cloudFiles.useNotifications": "true",
"cloudFiles.schemaLocation": "/mnt/raw/Customer_stream/_checkpoint/",
"cloudFiles.schemaEvolutionMode": "rescue"
#"cloudFiles.inferColumnTypes": "true"
#"cloudFiles.schemaEvolutionMode": "failOnNewColumns"
#"cloudFiles.schemaEvolutionMode": "addNewColumns"
#"cloudFiles.partitionColumns": ""
}

Command took 0.03 seconds -- by ronlesteve at 5/13/2021, 10:54:38 PM on cluster-001-8.2
```

***Figure 17-19.** Add the cloud files config settings to the notebook*

Here is the code shown in Figure 17-19. Since cloudFiles will automatically create EventGrid topics and subscriptions, it will need the credentials in this code to get access to the relevant Azure resources. The _checkpoint folder will store the schema metadata and will also keep track of multiple versions of the evolved schemas.

The partitionColumns config provides the option to read Hive style partition folder structures. The schema evolution mode of "failOnNewColumns" will simply fail the job when new columns are detected and will require manual intervention to define and update a new schema. We will not be exploring this option.

```
cloudfile = {
"cloudFiles.subscriptionID": subscriptionId,
"cloudFiles.connectionString": queueconnectionString,
"cloudFiles.format": "json",
"cloudFiles.tenantId": tenantId,
"cloudFiles.clientId": clientId,
"cloudFiles.clientSecret": clientSecret,
"cloudFiles.resourceGroup": resourceGroup,
"cloudFiles.useNotifications": "true",
"cloudFiles.schemaLocation": "/mnt/raw/Customer_stream/_checkpoint/",
"cloudFiles.schemaEvolutionMode": "rescue"
#"cloudFiles.inferColumnTypes": "true"
#"cloudFiles.schemaEvolutionMode": "failOnNewColumns"
#"cloudFiles.schemaEvolutionMode": "addNewColumns"
#"cloudFiles.partitionColumns": ""
}
```

With the AdditionalOptions properties, you can define schema hints, rescued data columns, and more. In this code block, you are specifying which column to add the rescued data into.

```
AdditionalOptions = {"rescueDataColumn":"_rescued_data"}
```

In this next code block, set the ADLS gen2 config by adding the ADLS gen2 account and SAS Key:

```
spark.conf.set("fs.azure.account.key.adlsg2v001.dfs.core.windows.
net","SASKey")
```

Run the following code shown in Figure 17-20 to configure your data frame using the defined configuration properties. Notice that by default, the columns are defaulted to "string" in this mode. Nevertheless, cloudFiles is able to automatically infer the schema.

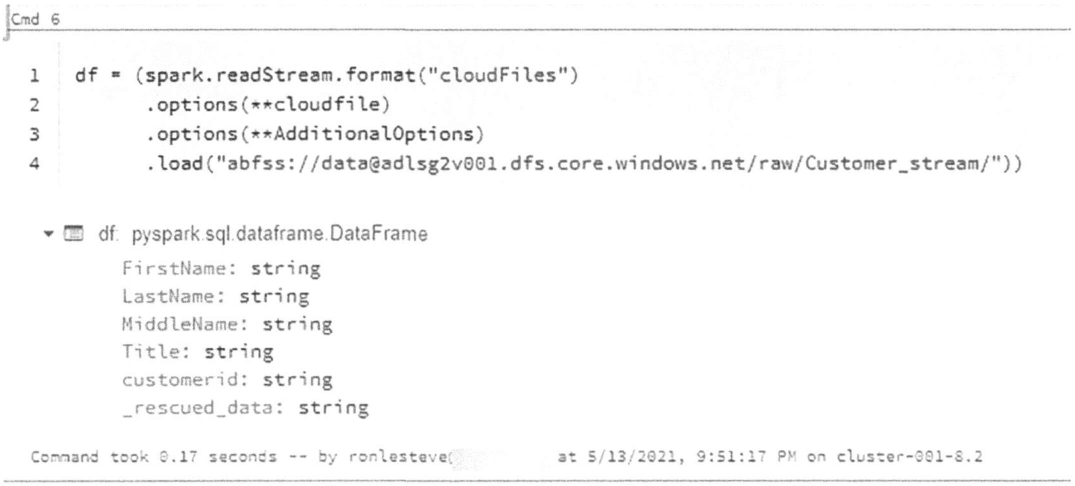

```
Cmd 6

df = (spark.readStream.format("cloudFiles")
      .options(**cloudfile)
      .options(**AdditionalOptions)
      .load("abfss://data@adlsg2v001.dfs.core.windows.net/raw/Customer_stream/"))

df: pyspark.sql.dataframe.DataFrame
    FirstName: string
    LastName: string
    MiddleName: string
    Title: string
    customerid: string
    _rescued_data: string

Command took 0.17 seconds -- by ronlesteve(          at 5/13/2021, 9:51:17 PM on cluster-001-8.2
```

Figure 17-20. *Read the stream and view the schema*

Here is the code that is used in Figure 17-20:

```
df = (spark.readStream.format("cloudFiles")
     .options(**cloudfile)
     .options(**AdditionalOptions)
     .load("abfss://data@adlsg2v001.dfs.core.windows.net/raw/Customer_
     stream/"))
```

Upon navigating to the Customer_stream folder in ADLS gen2, notice from Figure 17-21 that there is now a new _checkpoint folder that is created as a result of running the preceding code.

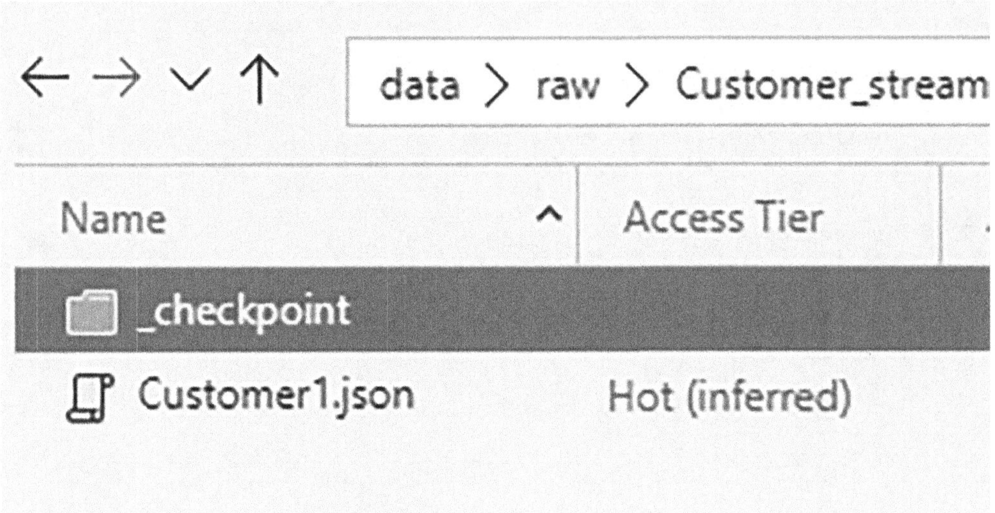

Figure 17-21. *Checkpoint folder has been created in customer_stream folder*

Within the _schemas folder, there is a file named 0, shown in Figure 17-22. This file contains the initial metadata version of the schema that has been defined.

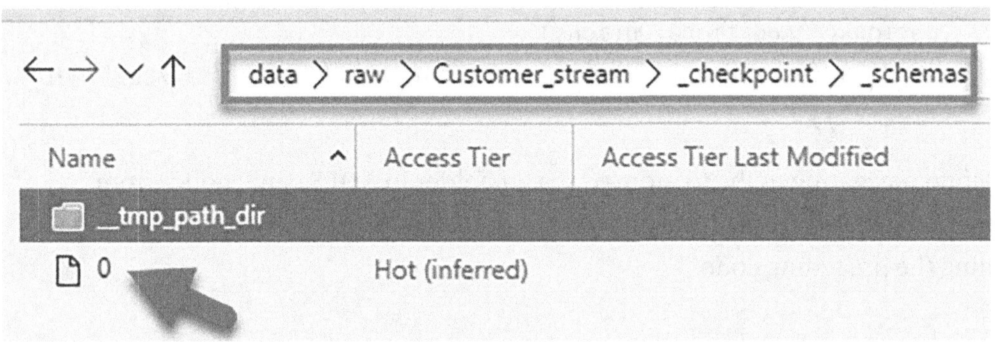

Figure 17-22. *Schema file 0 has been created which contains initial schema*

Upon opening the file, notice how it captures the JSON data frame schema structure as expected:


```
{"dataSchemaJson":"{\"type\":\"struct\",\"fields\":[{\"name\":\"FirstName\",
\"type\":\"string\",\"nullable\":true,\"metadata\":{}},{\"name\":\"LastName\",
\"type\":\"string\",\"nullable\":true,\"metadata\":{}},{\"name\":\"Middle
Name\",\"type\":\"string\",\"nullable\":true,\"metadata\":{}},{\"name\":
\"Title\",\"type\":\"string\",\"nullable\":true,\"metadata\":{}},{\"name\":
```

\"customerid\",\"type\":\"long\",\"nullable\":true,\"metadata\":{}}]}",
"partitionSchemaJson":"{\"type\":\"struct\",\"fields\":[]}"}

Schema Hints

Navigate back to the Databricks notebook and to the code block which contains AdditionalOptions. This time, add the following schemaHints. This is particularly useful if you wish to explicitly define the schema of a particular column. Here is the code. Remember to delete your _schemas folder so that the process can infer the schema from scratch once again.

```
AdditionalOptions = {
"cloudFiles.schemaHints":"customerid int",
"rescueDataColumn":"_rescued_data"}
```

Rerun the following code seen in Figure 17-23, and notice that customerid has this time been inferred as an integer rather than a string.

```
df = (spark.readStream.format("cloudFiles")
      .options(**cloudfile)
      .options(**AdditionalOptions)
      .load("abfss://data@adlsg2v001.dfs.core.windows.net/raw/Customer_stream/"))
```

```
df: pyspark.sql.dataframe.DataFrame
    FirstName: string
    LastName: string
    MiddleName: string
    Title: string
    customerid: integer
    _rescued_data: string
```

Command took 0.20 seconds -- by ronlesteve at 5/13/2021, 11:19:50 PM on cluster-001-8.2

Figure 17-23. *View schema from schema hints*

Here is the code that is used in Figure 17-23:

```
df = (spark.readStream.format("cloudFiles")
      .options(**cloudfile)
      .options(**AdditionalOptions)
      .load("abfss://data@adlsg2v001.dfs.core.windows.net/raw/Customer_
      stream/"))
```

Infer Column Types

Navigate to the cloudFile config code block, and uncomment “cloudFiles.inferColumnTypes”: “true” in Figure 17-24. This provides the capability of automatically inferring the schema of your incoming data.

```
cloudfile = {
"cloudFiles.subscriptionID": subscriptionId,
"cloudFiles.connectionString": queueconnectionString,
"cloudFiles.format": "json",
"cloudFiles.tenantId": tenantId,
"cloudFiles.clientId": clientId,
"cloudFiles.clientSecret": clientSecret,
"cloudFiles.resourceGroup": resourceGroup,
"cloudFiles.useNotifications": "true",
"cloudFiles.schemaLocation": "/mnt/raw/Customer_stream/_checkpoint/",
"cloudFiles.schemaEvolutionMode": "rescue",
"cloudFiles.inferColumnTypes": "true"
#"cloudFiles.schemaEvolutionMode": "failOnNewColumns"
#"cloudFiles.schemaEvolutionMode": "addNewColumns"
#"cloudFiles.partitionColumns": ""
}
```

Command took 0.02 seconds -- by ronlesteve(at 5/13/2021, 11:25:24 PM on cluster-001-8.2

Figure 17-24. *Enable inferColumnTypes to auto infer the schema*

Additionally, this time, remove the schemaHints from the AdditionalOptions code block shown in Figure 17-25.

Cmd 4

```
AdditionalOptions = {"rescueDataColumn":"_rescued_data"}
```

Command took 0.03 seconds -- by ronlestev at 5/13/2021, 9:51:06 PM on cluster-001-8.2

Figure 17-25. *Remove the schema hints from the AdditionalOptions code block*

Also, once again, remember to delete the contents of the _checkpoint folder in Figure 17-26 so that you are re-inferring the schema from scratch.

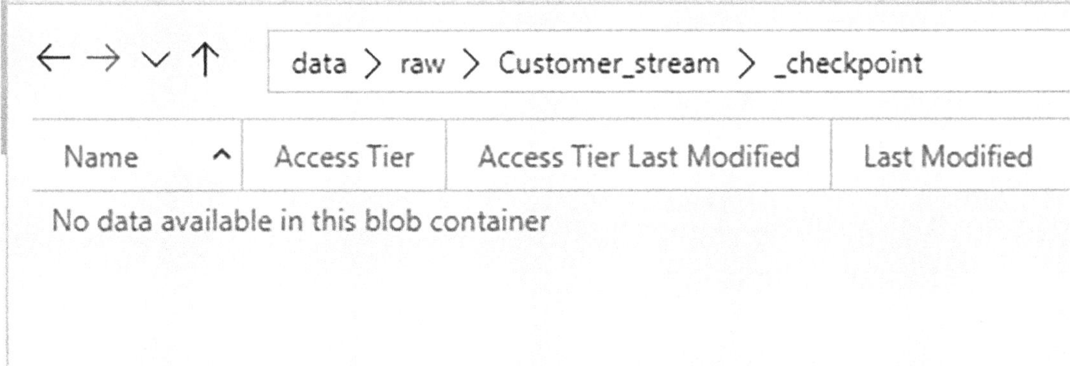

***Figure 17-26.** Delete the checkpoint file to recreate the schema file*

Rerun the following code shown in Figure 17-27, and notice that this time, without schemaHints, customerid has been inferred as "long."

```
df = (spark.readStream.format("cloudFiles")
      .options(**cloudfile)
      .options(**AdditionalOptions)
      .load("abfss://data@adlsg2v001.dfs.core.windows.net/raw/Customer_stream/"))
```

```
▸ (1) Spark Jobs
▾ df: pyspark.sql.dataframe.DataFrame
    FirstName: string
    LastName: string
    MiddleName: string
    Title: string
    customerid: long
    _rescued_data: string

Command took 0.62 seconds -- by ronlesteve@gmail.com at 5/13/2021, 11:27:54 PM on cluster-001-8.2
```

***Figure 17-27.** Read stream and notice schema is auto inferred*

Also run the following command seen in Figure 17-28 to initialize the stream and display the data.

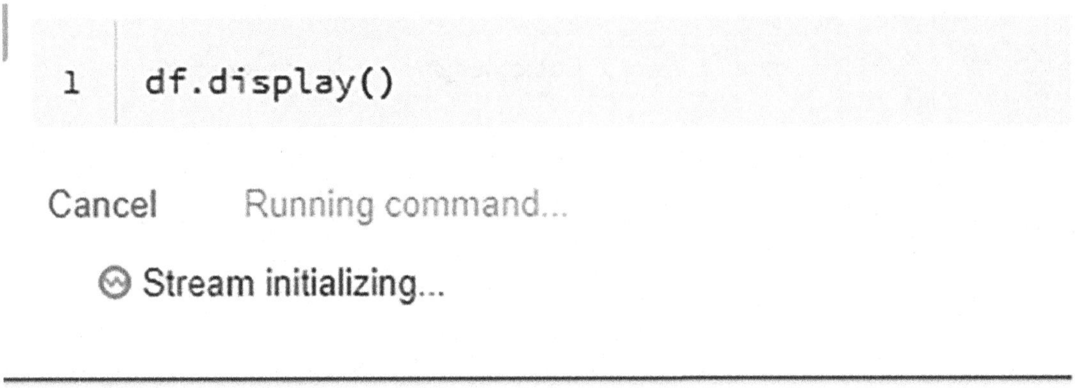

```
df.display()
```

Cancel Running command...

Stream initializing...

Figure 17-28. *Display the stream*

As expected, notice that the data from Customer1.json is being displayed in Figure 17-29. Notice that the _rescued_data column is null since there is no data that needs to be rescued yet. When you begin adding new columns from Customer2 and Customer3 JSON files, these additional columns will be captured in this column since the rescue data config properties are enabled.

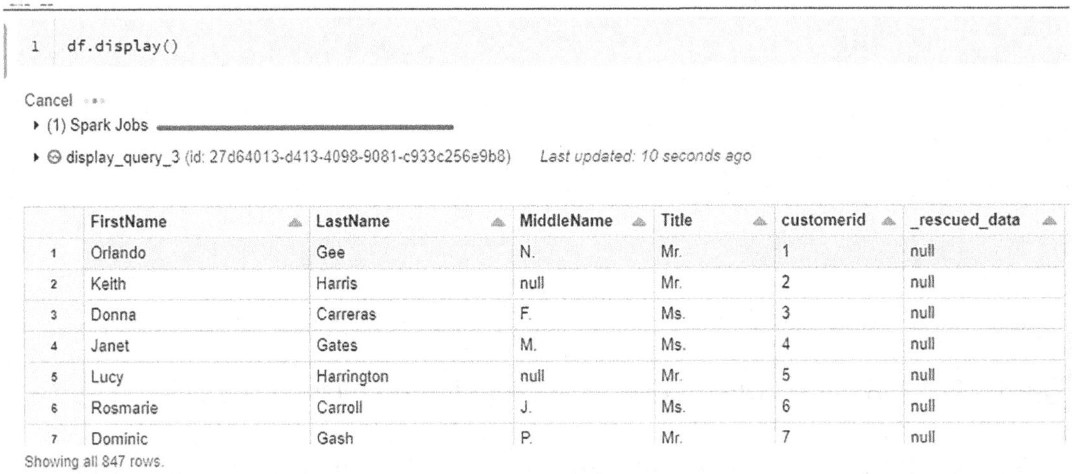

```
df.display()
```

Cancel

▸ (1) Spark Jobs

▸ display_query_3 (id: 27d64013-d413-4098-9081-c933c256e9b8) *Last updated: 10 seconds ago*

	FirstName	LastName	MiddleName	Title	customerid	_rescued_data
1	Orlando	Gee	N.	Mr.	1	null
2	Keith	Harris	null	Mr.	2	null
3	Donna	Carreras	F.	Ms.	3	null
4	Janet	Gates	M.	Ms.	4	null
5	Lucy	Harrington	null	Mr.	5	null
6	Rosmarie	Carroll	J.	Ms.	6	null
7	Dominic	Gash	P.	Mr.	7	null

Showing all 847 rows.

Figure 17-29. *The data from the stream is displayed*

Now it is time to add Customer2.json, shown in Figure 17-30, to our Customer_stream folder. Since Customer2 has more columns, it should demonstrate how schema evolution is handled by Auto Loader cloudFiles.

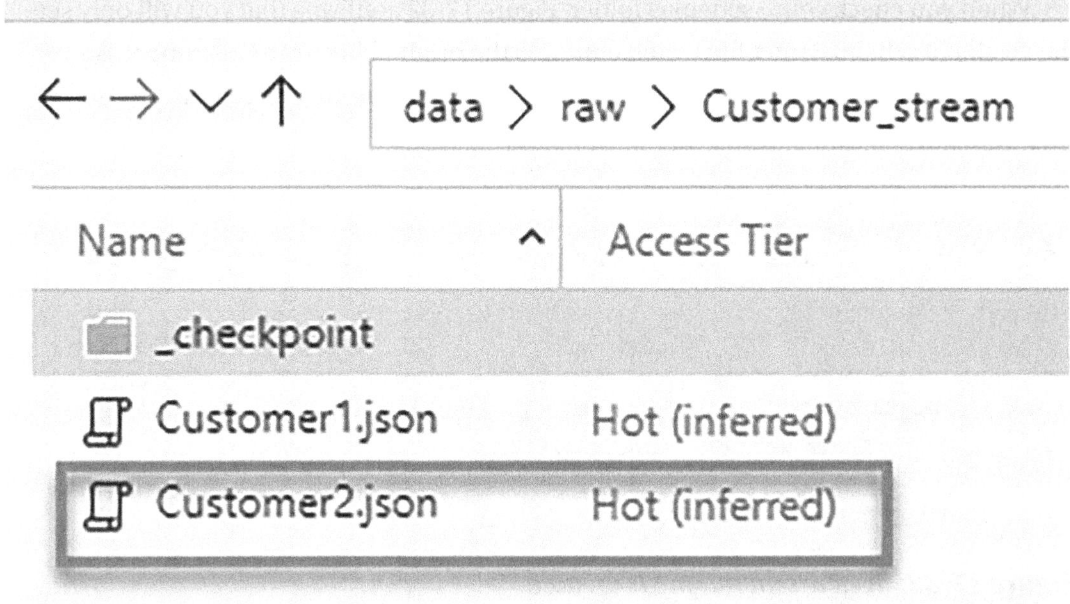

Figure 17-30. *Add the next Customer2.json file with additional columns*

After navigating back to the streaming query, notice from Figure 17-31 that the newly added columns from Customer2.json are all added to the _rescued_data column in the data frame, as expected. Since Auto Loader is constantly watching for new files, there is no need to rerun this query since the update occurs every five to ten seconds.

Cmd 15

```
1  df.display()
```

Cancel

(1) Spark Jobs

display_query_4 (id: 4d42351a-fd96-4668-a3f1-f3bab3df0223) *Last updated: 10 seconds ago*

	FirstName	LastName	MiddleName	Title	customerid	_rescued_data
861	Jean	Handley	P.	Ms.	20	{"CompanyName":"Central Discount Store","namestyle":false,"E works.com","SalesPerson":"adventure-works\\david8"}
862	Jinghao	Liu	null	null	21	{"CompanyName":"Chic Department Stores","namestyle":false," works.com","SalesPerson":"adventure-works\\jillian0"}
863	Linda	Burnett	E.	Ms.	22	{"CompanyName":"Travel Systems","namestyle":false,"EmailAdd works.com","SalesPerson":"adventure-works\\jillian0"}
864						

Showing the first 1000 rows

Figure 17-31. *Stream will pick up the new columns in the rescued data column*

When you check your _schemas folder, Figure 17-32 confirms that you will only see the version 0 schema struct file which contains the original file from Customer1.json. This is because the schema is still fixed and all new columns are added to the _rescued_data column.

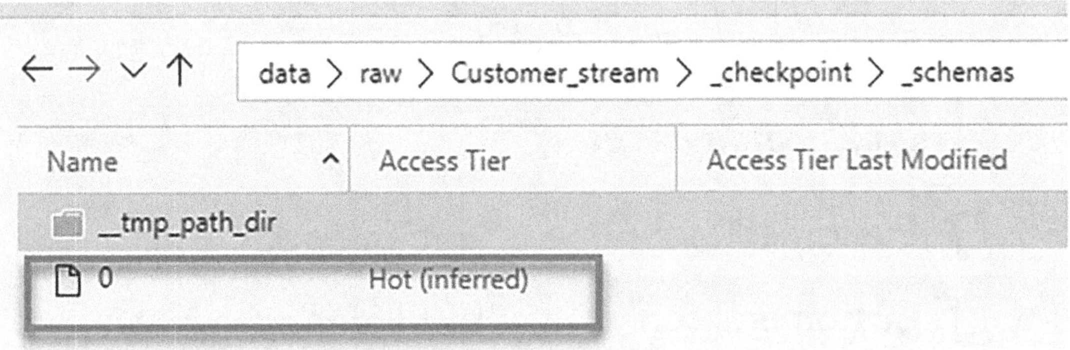

Figure 17-32. *A new schema file is created*

Add New Columns

Now that you have seen how rescue data works, Figure 17-33 shows how to enable schema evolution mode of "addNewColumns" so that you could include the new columns and now simply bucket them into the _rescued_data column. This process should now also create a new version of the schema struct file in the _schemas folder.

```
cloudfile = {
"cloudFiles.subscriptionID": subscriptionId,
"cloudFiles.connectionString": queueconnectionString,
"cloudFiles.format": "json",
"cloudFiles.tenantId": tenantId,
"cloudFiles.clientId": clientId,
"cloudFiles.clientSecret": clientSecret,
"cloudFiles.resourceGroup": resourceGroup,
"cloudFiles.useNotifications": "true",
"cloudFiles.schemaLocation": "/mnt/raw/Customer_stream/_checkpoint/",
"cloudFiles.schemaEvolutionMode": "rescue",
"cloudFiles.schemaEvolutionMode": "addNewColumns"
#"cloudFiles.inferColumnTypes": "true"
#"cloudFiles.schemaEvolutionMode": "failOnNewColumns"
#"cloudFiles.partitionColumns": ""
}
```

***Figure 17-33.** Enable option to addNewColumns in code block*

Notice from Figure 17-34 that the stream failed this time, which is deliberate since it follows the patterns of failing the job, updating the new schema, and then including the schema when the job is restarted. This is intended to follow the best practices of streaming architecture which contains automatic failures and retries.

```
df.display()
```

▸ (1) Spark Jobs

Stream stopped...

```
org.apache.spark.sql.catalyst.util.UnknownFieldException: Encountered unknown field(s) during parsing: {"CompanyName":"A Bike Store","namestyle":false,"EmailAddress":"orlando0@adventure-works.com","SalesPerson":"adventure-works\\pamela0"}
```

***Figure 17-34.** Stream job will stop since it does not match schema*

Restart the streaming job, and notice in Figure 17-35 that this time, the new additional columns from Customer2.json are included in the schema.

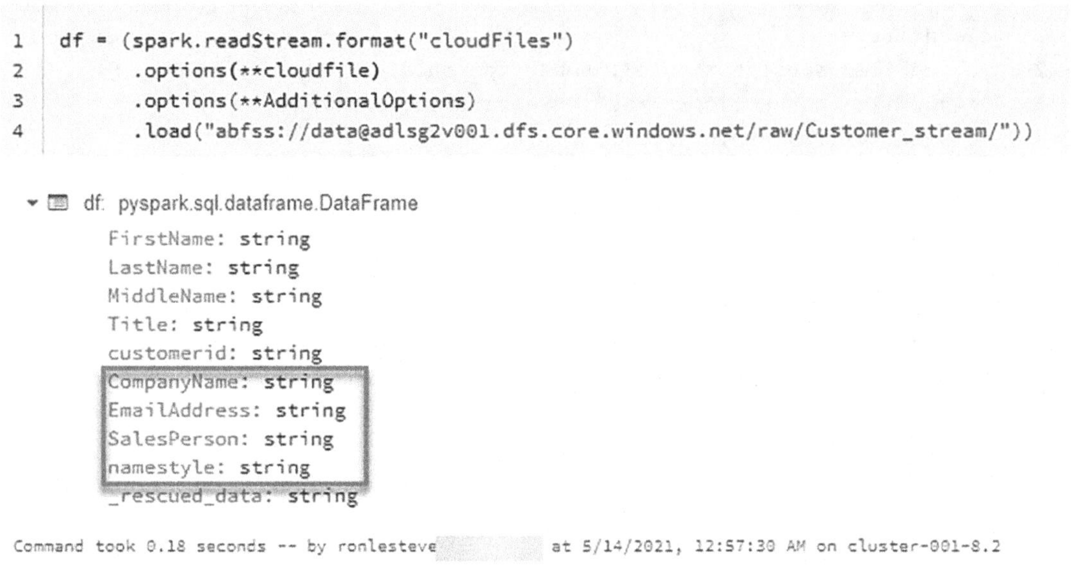

```
df = (spark.readStream.format("cloudFiles")
        .options(**cloudfile)
        .options(**AdditionalOptions)
        .load("abfss://data@adlsg2v001.dfs.core.windows.net/raw/Customer_stream/"))
```

```
df: pyspark.sql.dataframe.DataFrame
    FirstName: string
    LastName: string
    MiddleName: string
    Title: string
    customerid: string
    CompanyName: string
    EmailAddress: string
    SalesPerson: string
    namestyle: string
    _rescued_data: string

Command took 0.18 seconds -- by ronlesteve at 5/14/2021, 12:57:30 AM on cluster-001-8.2
```

***Figure 17-35.** Restart the job and rerun readstream and notice new cols*

Rerun the df.display() command, and notice in Figure 17-36 that the additional columns are displayed in the data frame.

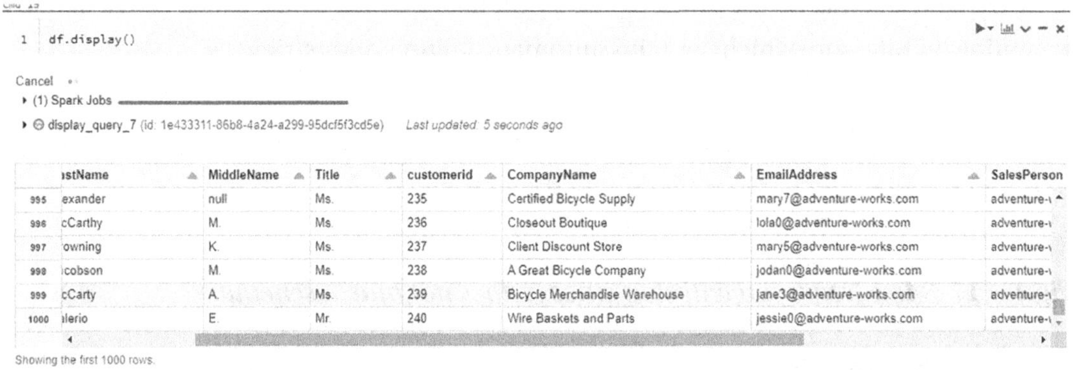

```
df.display()
```

Cancel

▸ (1) Spark Jobs

▸ display_query_7 (id: 1e433311-86b8-4a24-a299-95dcf5f3cd5e) *Last updated: 5 seconds ago*

	ıstName	MiddleName	Title	customerid	CompanyName	EmailAddress	SalesPerson
995	exander	null	Ms.	235	Certified Bicycle Supply	mary7@adventure-works.com	adventure-\
996	cCarthy	M.	Ms.	236	Closeout Boutique	lola0@adventure-works.com	adventure-\
997	owning	K.	Ms.	237	Client Discount Store	mary5@adventure-works.com	adventure-\
998	icobson	M.	Ms.	238	A Great Bicycle Company	jodan0@adventure-works.com	adventure-\
999	cCarty	A.	Ms.	239	Bicycle Merchandise Warehouse	jane3@adventure-works.com	adventure-\
1000	ılerio	E.	Mr.	240	Wire Baskets and Parts	jessie0@adventure-works.com	adventure-\

Showing the first 1000 rows.

***Figure 17-36.** New columns are added to display stream*

Upon navigating back to the _schemas folder in ADLS gen2, notice from Figure 17-37 that there is a new version (version 1) of the schema struct file.

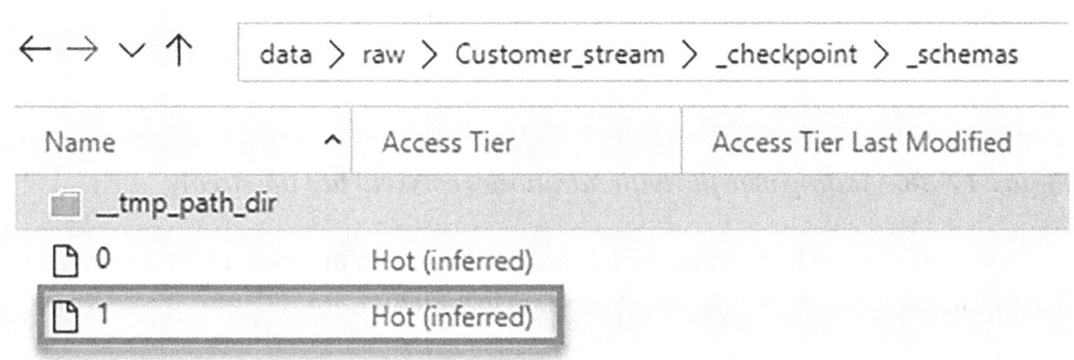

***Figure 17-37.** A new schema file is created with new cols*

Upon opening this file, notice that it contains the additional columns that were added from Customer2.json:

```
v1
{"dataSchemaJson":"{\"type\":\"struct\",\"fields\":[{\"name\":\"FirstName\
",\"type\":\"string\",\"nullable\":true,\"metadata\":{}},{\"name\":\"Last
Name\",\"type\":\"string\",\"nullable\":true,\"metadata\":{}},{\"name\":\"
MiddleName\",\"type\":\"string\",\"nullable\":true,\"metadata\":{}},{\"na
me\":\"Title\",\"type\":\"string\",\"nullable\":true,\"metadata\":{}},{\"na
me\":\"customerid\",\"type\":\"long\",\"nullable\":true,\"metadata\":{}},{\
"name\":\"CompanyName\",\"type\":\"string\",\"nullable\":true,\"metadata\":
{}},{\"name\":\"EmailAddress\",\"type\":\"string\",\"nullable\":true,\"meta
data\":{}},{\"name\":\"SalesPerson\",\"type\":\"string\",\"nullable\":true,
\"metadata\":{}},{\"name\":\"namestyle\",\"type\":\"boolean\",\"nullable\":
true,\"metadata\":{}}]}","partitionSchemaJson":"{\"type\":\"struct\",\"fiel
ds\":[]}"}
```

Similar to the previous demonstration, add the Customer3.json file to the Customer_stream folder in ADLS gen2, and notice from Figure 17-38 that the stream will fail, as expected.

```
df.display()
```

▸ (1) Spark Jobs

▸ display_query_7 (id: 1e433311-86b8-4a24-a299-95dcf5f3cd5e) *Last updated: 25 seconds ago*

```
org.apache.spark.sql.catalyst.util.UnknownFieldException: Encountered unknown field(s) during parsing: {"rowguid":"3F5AE95E-B87D-4AED-95B4-C3797AFCB74F","ModifiedDate":"2005-08-01T00:00:00","Phone":"245-555-0173"}
```

***Figure 17-38.** Adding new file with additional cols will fail the stream*

Restart the stream by running the following code shown in Figure 17-39, and notice that the new columns from Customer3.json are included.

```
df = (spark.readStream.format("cloudFiles")
      .options(**cloudfile)
      .options(**AdditionalOptions)
      .load("abfss://data@adlsg2v001.dfs.core.windows.net/raw/Customer_stream/"))
```

▾ df: pyspark.sql.dataframe.DataFrame

```
FirstName: string
LastName: string
MiddleName: string
Title: string
customerid: string
CompanyName: string
EmailAddress: string
SalesPerson: string
namestyle: string
ModifiedDate: string
Phone: string
rowguid: string
_rescued_data: string
```

Command took 0.17 seconds -- by ronlesteve at 5/14/2021, 1:04:20 AM on cluster-001-8.2

***Figure 17-39.** Restart the stream to see new cols come in*

Also, notice that the new columns from Customer3.json, shown in Figure 17-40, are included in the streaming data frame

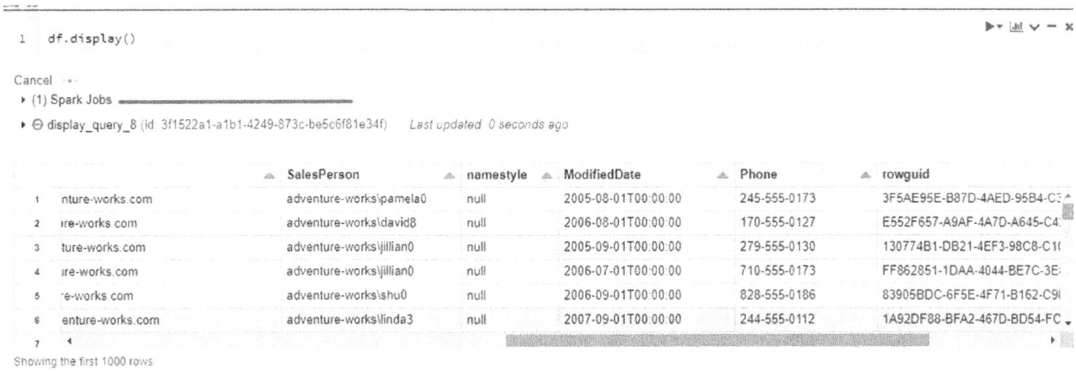

```
1  df.display()
```

Cancel
- (1) Spark Jobs
- display_query_8 (id: 3f1522a1-a1b1-4249-873c-be5c6f81e34f) Last updated: 0 seconds ago

		SalesPerson	namestyle	ModifiedDate	Phone	rowguid
1	nture-works.com	adventure-works\pamela0	null	2005-08-01T00:00:00	245-555-0173	3F5AE95E-B87D-4AED-95B4-C3
2	ıre-works.com	adventure-works\david8	null	2006-08-01T00:00:00	170-555-0127	E552F657-A9AF-4A7D-A645-C4
3	ture-works.com	adventure-works\jillian0	null	2005-09-01T00:00:00	279-555-0130	130774B1-DB21-4EF3-98C8-C1
4	ıre-works.com	adventure-works\jillian0	null	2006-07-01T00:00:00	710-555-0173	FF862851-1DAA-4044-BE7C-3E
5	'e-works.com	adventure-works\shu0	null	2006-09-01T00:00:00	828-555-0186	83905BDC-6F5E-4F71-B162-C9
6	enture-works.com	adventure-works\linda3	null	2007-09-01T00:00:00	244-555-0112	1A92DF88-BFA2-467D-BD54-FC

Showing the first 1000 rows

***Figure 17-40.** New columns from the Customer3.json file are captured in stream*

Similar to the previous example, there is yet another schema struct file included in the _schemas folder in ADLS gen2 which contains a new version that includes the additional columns from Customer3.json, shown in Figure 17-41.

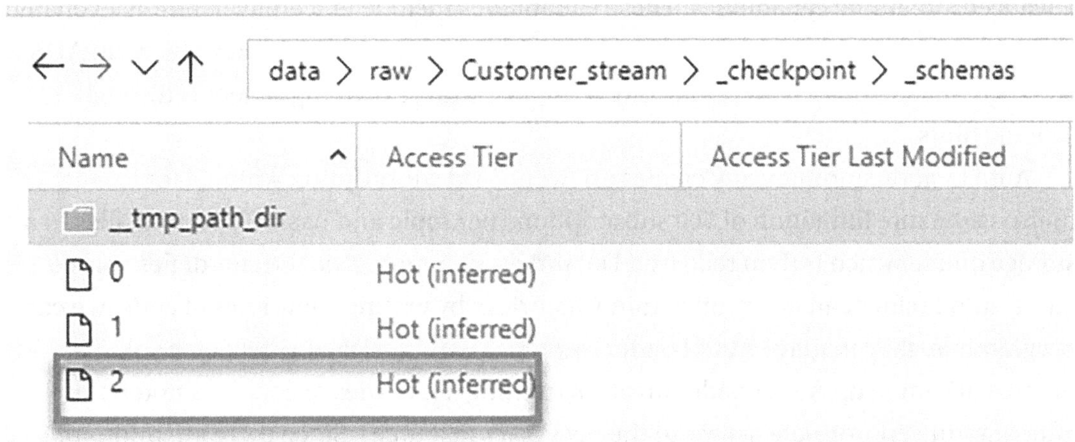

data > raw > Customer_stream > _checkpoint > _schemas

Name	Access Tier	Access Tier Last Modified
_tmp_path_dir		
0	Hot (inferred)	
1	Hot (inferred)	
2	Hot (inferred)	

***Figure 17-41.** New schema file 3 has been created with evolved schema*

Upon opening the new version of the schema struct file outlined in Figure 17-41, notice that it includes the new columns from Customer3.json:

```
{"dataSchemaJson":"{\"type\":\"struct\",\"fields\":[{\"name\":\"FirstName\"
,\"type\":\"string\",\"nullable\":true,\"metadata\":{}},{\"name\":\"LastNam
e\",\"type\":\"string\",\"nullable\":true,\"metadata\":{}},{\"name\":\"Midd
leName\",\"type\":\"string\",\"nullable\":true,\"metadata\":{}},{\"name\":\
"Title\",\"type\":\"string\",\"nullable\":true,\"metadata\":{}},{\"name\":\
```

```
"customerid\",\"type\":\"long\",\"nullable\":true,\"metadata\":{}},{\"name\
":\"CompanyName\",\"type\":\"string\",\"nullable\":true,\"metadata\":{}},
{\"name\":\"EmailAddress\",\"type\":\"string\",\"nullable\":true,\"meta
data\":{}},{\"name\":\"SalesPerson\",\"type\":\"string\",\"nullable\":true,
\"metadata\":{}},{\"name\":\"namestyle\",\"type\":\"boolean\",\"nullable
\":true,\"metadata\":{}},{\"name\":\"ModifiedDate\",\"type\":\"string\",
\"nullable\":true,\"metadata\":{}},{\"name\":\"Phone\",\"type\":\"string\",
\"nullable\":true,\"metadata\":{}},{\"name\":\"rowguid\",\"type\":
\"string\",\"nullable\":true,\"metadata\":{}}]}","partitionSchemaJson":
"{\"type\":\"struct\",\"fields\":[]}"}
```


Managing Auto Loader Resources

In the previous section, you learned about Auto Loader and cloudFiles, which have advanced streaming capabilities. These capabilities include gracefully handling evolving streaming data schemas, tracking changing schemas through captured versions in ADLS gen2 schema folder locations, inferring schemas, and/or defining schemas through schema hints.

Auto Loader automatically creates an Event Grid subscription within a topic, and there is an Azure limitation of 500 subscriptions per topic and passes incoming files to a storage queue which is then read by a Databricks data frame via the cloudFiles source. Since Auto Loader can be set up within Databricks by writing a few lines of code, we can programmatically manage Auto Loader resources within a Databricks notebook. The process of setting up Auto Loader involves running a few lines of code in a notebook after granting appropriate access to the necessary resources. Since there are numerous Azure Event Grid quotas and limits including 500 event subscriptions per topic, there are efficient methods of managing these subscriptions programmatically within a Databricks notebook to prevent some of these quotas and limits from being reached.

In this section, you will learn about methods for managing Auto Loader resources. As a prerequisite, ensure that you have created an Azure Data Lake storage account and container; loaded data into the container; created a Databricks account, cluster, and notebook; and ran the necessary Auto Loader cloudFiles scripts in the previous sections. Note that the cluster will not always need to be running and can be configured to shut down when not in use through cluster policies. Figure 17-42 shows the architectural diagram of Auto Loader for a JSON file being ingested into ADLS gen2 and processed by Event Grid, cloudFiles, and Delta Data-frame.

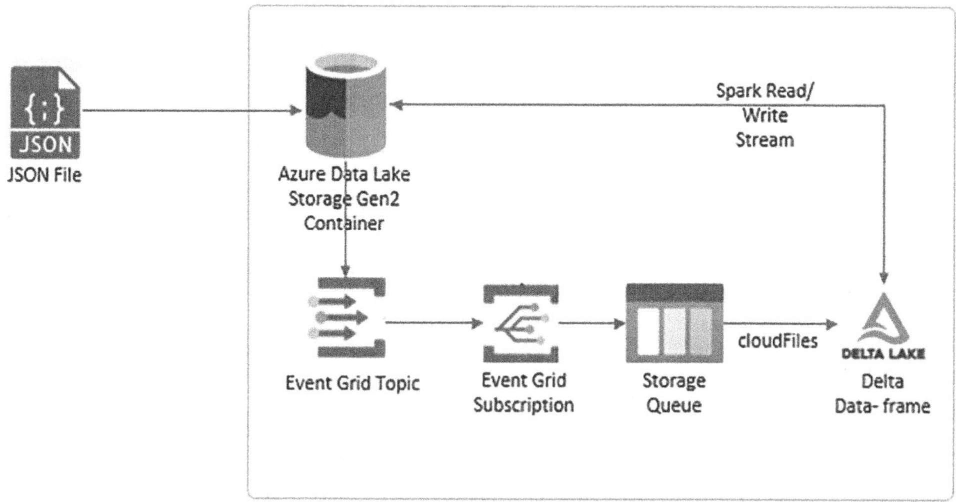

Figure 17-42. Auto Loader architectural flow diagram

Read a Stream

Once you register Auto Loader, as demonstrated in the previous section, run the spark.readStream command with the cloudFile source, while accounting for the cloudFile and additional options. You can find additional information about these cloudFile options from the following Databricks article: `https://docs.databricks.com/spark/latest/structured-streaming/auto-loader.html#common-auto-loader-options-1`

The following code will set up a data frame which will begin listening for streaming data within the defined ADLS gen2 folder path. Here is the readStream code that you will need to run by predefining the cloudFile options and storage location mount point.

```
read_df = (spark.readStream.format("cloudFiles")
      .options(**cloudfile)
      .options(**AdditionalOptions)
      .load("/mnt/raw/Customer_stream/"))
```

For the purpose of visualizing the data, run the following read_df.display() command to get an understanding of the structure of the data that is being streamed into the data frame, as shown in Figure 17-43.

▸ (1) Spark Jobs

▸ ⊘ display_query_21 (id: c1a5c26f-a430-4601-be38-a1027226dcee) *Last updated: 3 hours ago*

	FirstName	LastName	MiddleName	Title	customerid	_rescued_data
1	Orlando	Gee	N.	Mr.	1	null
2	Keith	Harris	null	Mr.	2	null
3	Donna	Carreras	F.	Ms.	3	null
4	Janet	Gates	M.	Ms.	4	null
5	Lucy	Harrington	null	Mr.	5	null
6	Rosmarie	Carroll	J.	Ms.	6	null
7	Dominic	Gash	P.	Mr.	7	null

***Figure 17-43.** Display the read stream in Databricks*

Write a Stream

One of the advantages of Auto Loader is that you have the capability of writing the stream as delta format. Note that Auto Loader is currently an append-only output mode. Here is the code that you will need to run to append the data stream in delta format to the defined location. Once you read and write the streaming data into delta format in ADLS gen2, you can begin to view and manage the Auto Loader resources programmatically.

```
write_df = (read_df.writeStream
.format("delta")
.trigger(once=True)
.outputMode("append")
.option("checkpointLocation", "/mnt/raw/Customer_stream/_checkpoint/")
.start("/mnt/raw/Customer_stream/data/")
            )
```

Once the code is run, notice from Figure 17-44 that the results will generate an ID. This ID is the unique identifier of the writeStream query. Keep track of this ID which you will use to keep track of the Auto Loader resource management process along the way within the following sections.

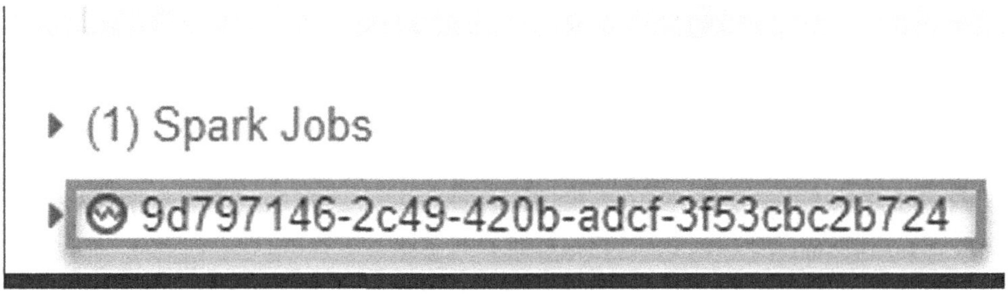

Figure 17-44. *Script to write stream in Databricks*

The following code will provide metrics about the streaming data frame which include the number of rows inserted and rows per second:

```
write_df.awaitTermination()
write_df.recentProgress
```

The results in Figure 17-45 show the unique ID of this particular query, which we have seen as follows and which we will continue to track through this process of managing Auto Loader resources.

```
Out[130]: [{'id': '9d797146-2c49-420b-adcf-3f53cbc2b724',
  'runId': '917e9609-1eca-411f-8955-5063ee719859',
  'name': None,
  'timestamp': '2021-05-20T22:55:12.566Z',
  'batchId': 0,
  'numInputRows': 847,
  'inputRowsPerSecond': 0.0,
  'processedRowsPerSecond': 52.1905231375932,
  'durationMs': {'addBatch': 9628,
   'getBatch': 39,
   'latestOffset': 5992,
   'queryPlanning': 7,
   'triggerExecution': 16229,
   'walCommit': 188},
  'stateOperators': [],
  'sources': [{'description': 'CloudFilesSource[/mnt/raw/Customer_stream/]',
    'startOffset': None,
    'endOffset': {'seqNum': 2,
     'sourceVersion': 1,
     'lastBackfillStartTimeMs': 1621551312964,
     'lastBackfillFinishTimeMs': 1621551313720}
```

***Figure 17-45.** Script to get the stream progress and metrics*

As part of the Delta writeStream process, a metadata file will be created in the ADLS gen2 _checkpoint folder, as shown in Figure 17-46. This file will contain the ID of the writeStream query that you ran in the notebook.

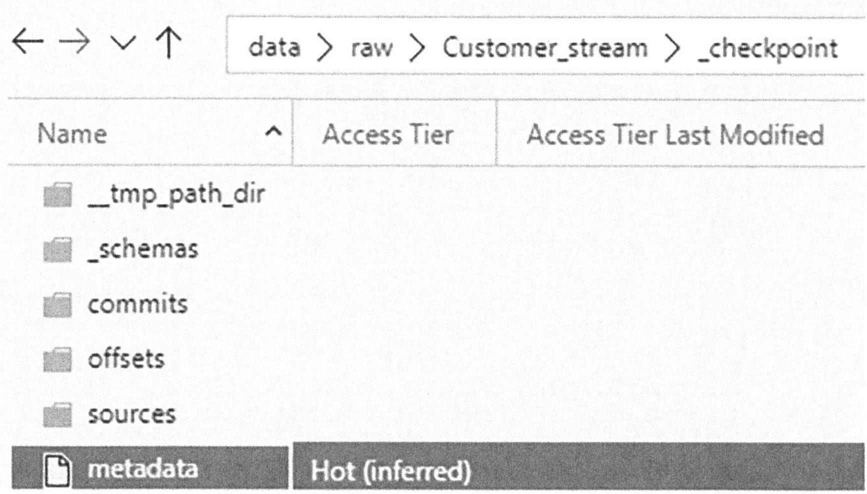

Figure 17-46. *Metadata file that is produced from write stream code*

Upon opening the metadata file, notice in Figure 17-47 that it contains the same query ID that you have been tracking thus far from you define stream query.

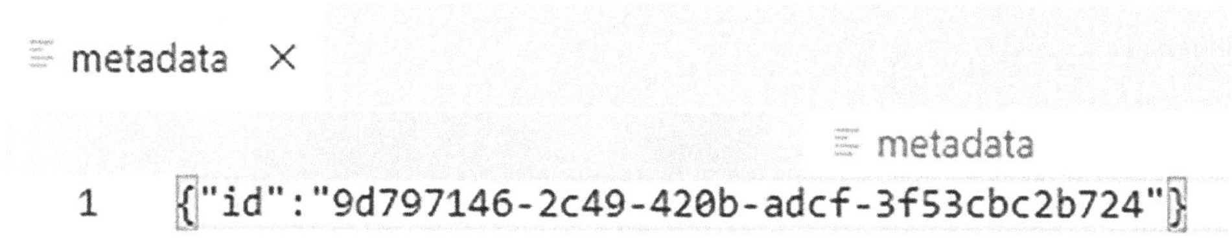

metadata ×

metadata

```
1    {"id":"9d797146-2c49-420b-adcf-3f53cbc2b724"}
```

Figure 17-47. *Metadata file contains the stream query ID*

Additionally, notice in Figure 17-48 that a new Event Grid subscription has automatically been created by the Auto Loader resources within the ADLS gen2 storage account's Event Grid topic. Notice also how it includes the same stream ID and references the Customer_stream as the prefix filter.

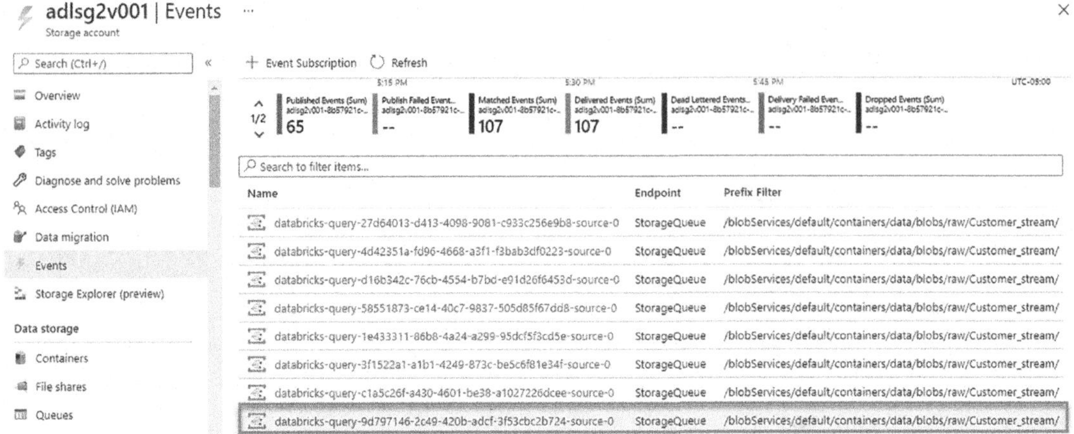

Figure 17-48. View of Event Grid subscription created by the Auto Loader

Explore Results

By drilling into the storage queues, notice that the same query has been added to the queue, as shown in Figure 17-49.

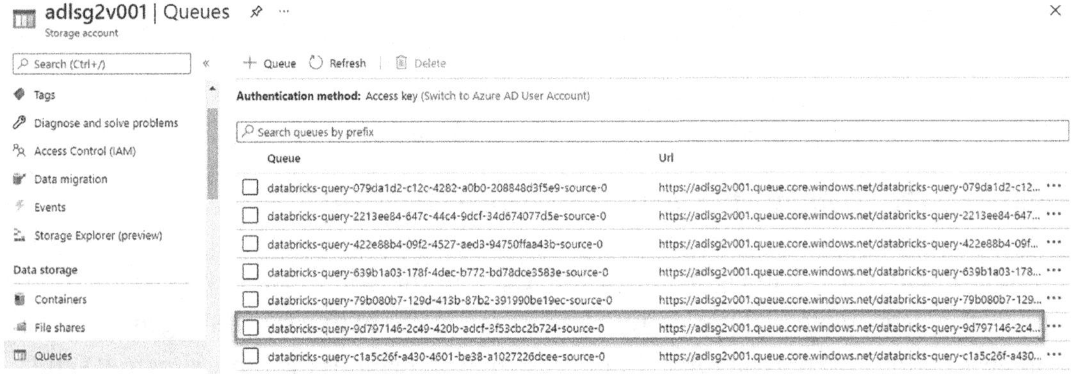

Figure 17-49. Event Grid storage queue created by the Auto Loader resource

Next, go ahead and create a new Scala Databricks notebook, shown in Figure 17-50, so that you can begin working with the Auto Loader Resource Manager programmatically. Begin by running the following command which will import the Cloud Files Azure Resource Manager.

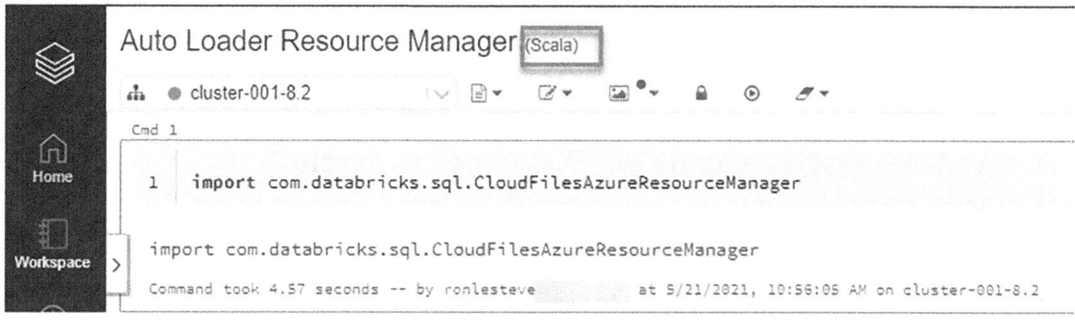

Figure 17-50. *Create a Scala notebook and import Auto Loader Resource Manager*

Here is the code that will import the CloudFilesAzureResourceManager:

```
import com.databricks.sql.CloudFilesAzureResourceManager
```

This next block of code shown in Figure 17-51 will get the secrets that are required by the Auto Loader resources. Ensure that you have created the necessary secret scope in Databricks for your Azure Key Vault. These secrets will give Auto Loader the appropriate access to be able to create Event Grid subscriptions and queues within your Azure subscription.

```
val subscriptionId = dbutils.secrets.get("akv-0011","subscriptionId")
val tenantId = dbutils.secrets.get("akv-0011","tenantId")
val clientId = dbutils.secrets.get("akv-0011","clientId")
val clientSecret = dbutils.secrets.get("akv-0011","clientSecret")
val resourceGroup = dbutils.secrets.get("akv-0011","resourceGroup")
val queueconnectionString = dbutils.secrets.get("akv-0011","queueconnectionString")
val SASKey = dbutils.secrets.get("akv-0011","SASKey")

subscriptionId: String = [REDACTED]
tenantId: String = [REDACTED]
clientId: String = [REDACTED]
clientSecret: String = [REDACTED]
resourceGroup: String = [REDACTED]
queueconnectionString: String = [REDACTED]
SASKey: String = [REDACTED]

Command took 3.92 seconds -- by ronlesteve at 5/21/2021, 10:56:14 AM on cluster-001-8.2
```

Figure 17-51. *Script to call secrets for Auto Loader to access storage account*

Here is the Scala code that will get the necessary secrets from your Azure Key Vault:

```
val subscriptionId = dbutils.secrets.get("akv-0011","subscriptionId")
val tenantId = dbutils.secrets.get("akv-0011","tenantId")
val clientId = dbutils.secrets.get("akv-0011","clientId")
val clientSecret = dbutils.secrets.get("akv-0011","clientSecret")
val resourceGroup = dbutils.secrets.get("akv-0011","resourceGroup")
val queueconnectionString = dbutils.secrets.get("akv-0011","queueconnecti
onString")
val SASKey = dbutils.secrets.get("akv-0011","SASKey")
```

You will also need to run the following CloudFilesAzureResourceManager-specific code displayed in Figure 17-52, which will take your defined secrets and then create the necessary Auto Loader Resource Manager.

```
val manager = CloudFilesAzureResourceManager
  .newManager
  .option("cloudFiles.connectionString", queueconnectionString)
  .option("cloudFiles.resourceGroup", resourceGroup)
  .option("cloudFiles.subscriptionId", subscriptionId)
  .option("cloudFiles.tenantId", tenantId)
  .option("cloudFiles.clientId", clientId)
  .option("cloudFiles.clientSecret", clientSecret)
  .create()
```

```
manager: com.databricks.sql.CloudFilesResourceManager = com.databricks.sql.aqs.autoIngest.CloudFilesAzureResourceManager@60721992
Command took 0.24 seconds -- by ronlesteve at 5/21/2021, 10:56:25 AM on cluster-001-8.2
```

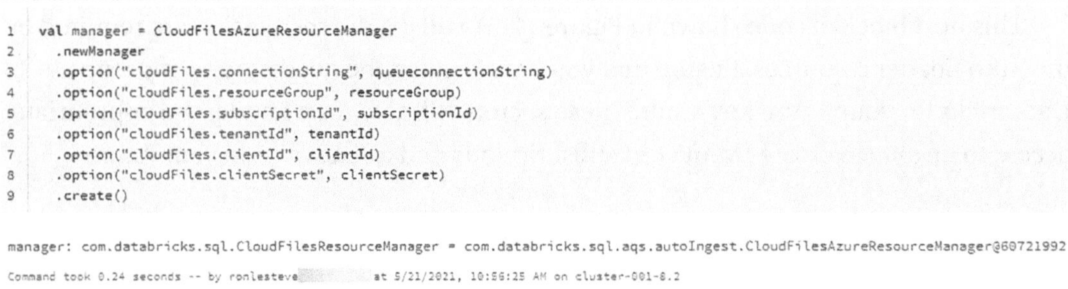

Figure 17-52. *Create a resource manager data frame*

Here is the code that you will need to run to create the necessary Auto Loader Resource Manager:

```
val manager = CloudFilesAzureResourceManager
  .newManager
  .option("cloudFiles.connectionString", queueconnectionString)
  .option("cloudFiles.resourceGroup", resourceGroup)
  .option("cloudFiles.subscriptionId", subscriptionId)
  .option("cloudFiles.tenantId", tenantId)
  .option("cloudFiles.clientId", clientId)
  .option("cloudFiles.clientSecret", clientSecret)
  .create()
```

Alternatively, you have the option of manually setting up an Event Grid subscription and storage queue by specifying the associated path in the following code. This option demonstrates the flexibility of either setting up the Auto Loader Resource Manager manually or automatically, as needed.

```
// Set up an AQS queue and an event grid subscription associated with the
path used in the manager. Available in Databricks Runtime 7.4 and above.
manager.setUpNotificationServices()
```

Run the following code shown in Figure 17-53 to list the notification services that are created by Auto Loader.

```
// List notification services created by Auto Loader
val NotificationSvc = manager.listNotificationServices()
```

```
NotificationSvc: org.apache.spark.sql.DataFrame
    streamId: string
    path: string
    checkpointLocation: string
    creationTime: timestamp
    lastUpdateTime: timestamp
    streamStatus: string
    eventSubscriptionName: string
  ▾ eventFilter: struct
        subjectBeginsWith: string
        subjectEndsWith: string
      ▾ includeEventTypes: array
            element: string
      ▾ advancedFilters: array
          ▾ element: struct
                operatorType: string
                key: string
              ▾ values: array
                    element: string
    queueName: string
    storageAccount: string
    resourceGroup: string
    subscription: string
```

Figure 17-53. *Code to list the notification services created by Auto Loader*

Here is the code that you will need to run to list notification services created by Auto Loader:

```
// List notification services created by Auto Loader
val NotificationSvc = manager.listNotificationServices()
```

Run the following display(NotificationSvc) command seen in Figure 17-54 to view this list of notification services created by Auto Loader. Notice that the Stream ID that you have been tracking previously is also displayed in this list.

```
display(NotificationSvc)
```

	streamId	path	checkpointLocation
3	d16b342c-76cb-4554-b7bd-e91d26f6453d	abfss://data@adlsg2v001.dfs.core.windows.net/raw/Customer_stream/	dbfs:/local_disk0/tmp/temporary-7b93ab03-3558-4d41
4	58551873-ce14-40c7-9837-505d85f67dd8	abfss://data@adlsg2v001.dfs.core.windows.net/raw/Customer_stream/	dbfs:/local_disk0/tmp/temporary-e7ed9ca2-3e98-431d
5	1e433311-86b8-4a24-a299-95dcf5f3cd5e	abfss://data@adlsg2v001.dfs.core.windows.net/raw/Customer_stream/	dbfs:/local_disk0/tmp/temporary-4f165a68-b02d-4e1d-
6	3f1522a1-a1b1-4249-873c-be5c6f81e34f	abfss://data@adlsg2v001.dfs.core.windows.net/raw/Customer_stream/	dbfs:/local_disk0/tmp/temporary-62a35e28-0c58-45ce-
7	c1a5c26f-a430-4601-be38-a1027226dcee	/mnt/raw/Customer_stream/	dbfs:/local_disk0/tmp/temporary-a30d1004-23a4-4fa9-
8	9d797146-2c49-420b-adcf-3f53cbc2b724	/mnt/raw/Customer_stream/	dbfs:/mnt/raw/Customer_stream/_checkpoint

***Figure 17-54.** Code to display the notification services created by Auto Loader*

Through this Auto Loader Resource Manager, you also have the option to delete Event Grid subscriptions by defining the stream IDs to delete and then running the following tearDownNotificationServices(streamId) command. Notice from the results in Figure 17-55 that the queue and Event Grid subscription have been deleted.

```
// Tear down the notification services created for a specific stream ID.
// Stream ID is a GUID string that you can find in the list result above.

val streamId = "4d42351a-fd96-4668-a3f1-f3bab3df0223"
manager.tearDownNotificationServices(streamId)
```

```
▸ (1) Spark Jobs
▸ res18: org.apache.spark.sql.DataFrame = [streamId: string, path: string ... 10 more fields]
Deleted Queue databricks-query-4d42351a-fd96-4668-a3f1-f3bab3df0223-source-0
Deleted Event Grid Subscription: databricks-query-4d42351a-fd96-4668-a3f1-f3bab3df0223-source-0.
streamId: String = 4d42351a-fd96-4668-a3f1-f3bab3df0223
res18: org.apache.spark.sql.DataFrame = [streamId: string, path: string ... 10 more fields]

Command took 29.37 seconds -- by ronlesteve at 5/21/2021, 1:27:17 PM on cluster-001-8.2
```

***Figure 17-55.** Code that will delete Auto Loader resources in Azure*

Here is the code that will delete the specified "streamID" storage queue and Event Grid subscription of the registered Auto Loader resource:

```
// Tear down the notification services created for a specific stream ID.
// Stream ID is a GUID string that you can find in the list result above.
```

```
val streamId = "4d42351a-fd96-4668-a3f1-f3bab3df0223"
manager.tearDownNotificationServices(streamId)
```

At this point, you can get more creative with your resource filtering process by running the following code which will filter your list based on a pattern. In this particular case, there are multiple queries that contain paths that reference "abfss" rather than my mount point "mnt." So, we want to list and delete the resources that were created with the "abfss" and only keep resources that were created by "mnt" location. Initially, run the following code to first identify this filtered list of queries within the Auto Loader resources:

```
val FilterNotificationSvc = NotificationSvc.filter("path like '%abfss%'")
```

Run the following display(FilterNotificationSvc) command shown in Figure 17-56 to display the list Auto Loader resources containing "abfss" paths. Notice that there are six resources listed that need to be deleted.

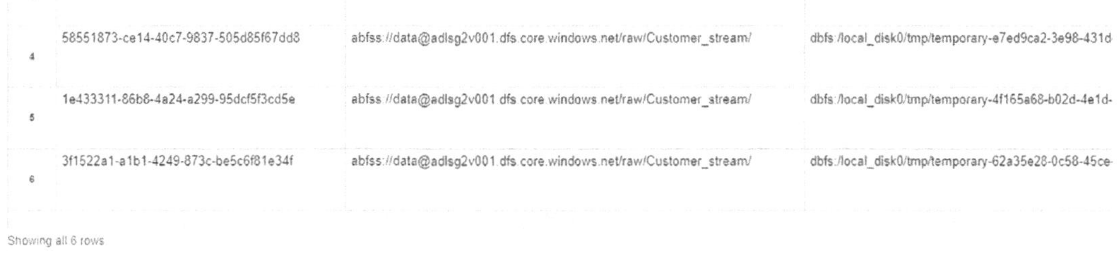

```
1 display(FilterNotificationSvc)
```

	streamId	path	checkpointLocation
1	27d64013-d413-4098-9081-c933c256e9b8	abfss://data@adlsg2v001.dfs.core.windows.net/raw/Customer_stream/	dbfs:/local_disk0/tmp/temporary-646116b4-720a-4fca-l
2	4d42351a-fd96-4668-a3f1-f3bab3df0223	abfss://data@adlsg2v001.dfs.core.windows.net/raw/Customer_stream/	dbfs:/local_disk0/tmp/temporary-5ae8fd49-759b-4554-
3	d16b342c-76cb-4554-b7bd-e91d26f6453d	abfss://data@adlsg2v001.dfs.core.windows.net/raw/Customer_stream/	dbfs:/local_disk0/tmp/temporary-7b93ab03-3558-4d41
4	58551873-ce14-40c7-9837-505d85f67dd8	abfss://data@adlsg2v001.dfs.core.windows.net/raw/Customer_stream/	dbfs:/local_disk0/tmp/temporary-e7ed9ca2-3e98-431d-
5	1e433311-86b8-4a24-a299-95dcf5f3cd5e	abfss://data@adlsg2v001.dfs.core.windows.net/raw/Customer_stream/	dbfs:/local_disk0/tmp/temporary-4f165a68-b02d-4e1d-
6	3f1522a1-a1b1-4249-873c-be5c6f81e34f	abfss://data@adlsg2v001.dfs.core.windows.net/raw/Customer_stream/	dbfs:/local_disk0/tmp/temporary-62a35e28-0c58-45ce-

Showing all 6 rows

***Figure 17-56.** Display filtered list of notifications to ensure accurate filtering*

Next, run the following code seen in Figure 17-57, which will take the filtered list of the six Auto Loader resources from the previous step and will then loop through the list and delete every Auto Loader resource that has been defined in this filtered list.

```
for (row <- FilterNotificationSvc.collect())
{
  val streamId = row.get(0).toString()
  manager.tearDownNotificationServices(streamId)
}
```

```
Deleted Queue databricks-query-27d64013-d413-4098-9081-c933c256e9b8-source-0
Deleted Event Grid Subscription: databricks-query-27d64013-d413-4098-9081-c933c256e9b8-source-0.
Deleted Queue databricks-query-4d42351a-fd96-4668-a3f1-f3bab3df0223-source-0
Deleted Event Grid Subscription: databricks-query-4d42351a-fd96-4668-a3f1-f3bab3df0223-source-0.
Deleted Queue databricks-query-d16b342c-76cb-4554-b7bd-e91d26f6453d-source-0
Deleted Event Grid Subscription: databricks-query-d16b342c-76cb-4554-b7bd-e91d26f6453d-source-0.
Deleted Queue databricks-query-58551873-ce14-40c7-9837-505d85f67dd8-source-0
Deleted Event Grid Subscription: databricks-query-58551873-ce14-40c7-9837-505d85f67dd8-source-0.
Deleted Queue databricks-query-1e433311-86b8-4a24-a299-95dcf5f3cd5e-source-0
Deleted Event Grid Subscription: databricks-query-1e433311-86b8-4a24-a299-95dcf5f3cd5e-source-0.
Deleted Queue databricks-query-3f1522a1-a1b1-4249-873c-be5c6f81e34f-source-0
Deleted Event Grid Subscription: databricks-query-3f1522a1-a1b1-4249-873c-be5c6f81e34f-source-0.

Command took 2.86 seconds -- by ronlesteve at 5/21/2021, 1:31:08 PM on cluster-001-8.2
```

Figure 17-57. *Code to delete the filtered list of defined Auto Loader resources*

Here is the code that you would run to collect and delete the list of filtered Auto Loader resources:

```
for (row <- FilterNotificationSvc.collect())
{
  val streamId = row.get(0).toString()
  manager.tearDownNotificationServices(streamId)
}
```

At this point, run the following command displayed in Figure 17-58 to re-list the registered Auto Loader resources, and notice that all paths associated with “abfss” have been deleted, as expected.

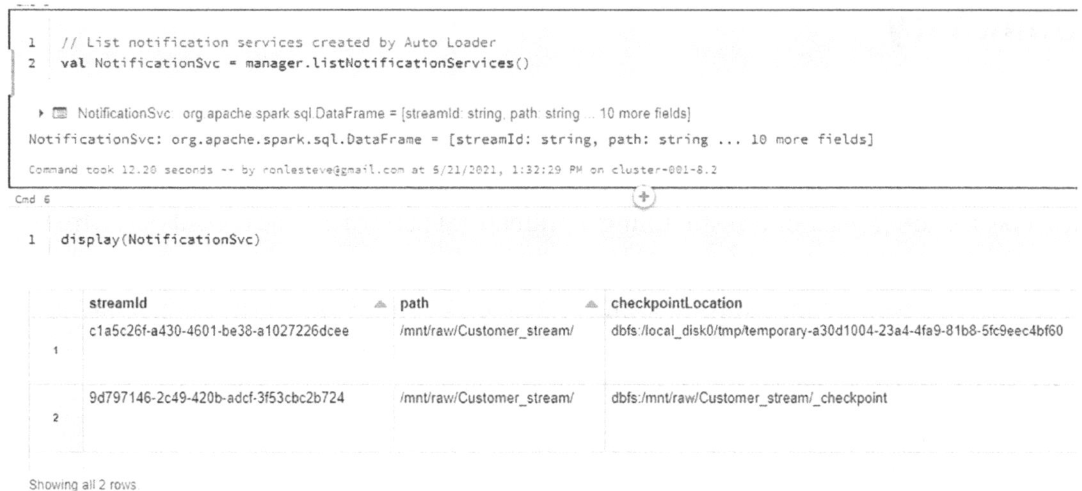

```
// List notification services created by Auto Loader
val NotificationSvc = manager.listNotificationServices()
```

NotificationSvc: org.apache.spark.sql.DataFrame = [streamId: string, path: string ... 10 more fields]

Command took 12.20 seconds -- by ronlesteve@gmail.com at 5/21/2021, 1:32:29 PM on cluster-001-8.2

```
display(NotificationSvc)
```

	streamId	path	checkpointLocation
1	c1a5c26f-a430-4601-be38-a1027226dcee	/mnt/raw/Customer_stream/	dbfs:/local_disk0/tmp/temporary-a30d1004-23a4-4fa9-81b8-5fc9eec4bf60
2	9d797146-2c49-420b-adcf-3f53cbc2b724	/mnt/raw/Customer_stream/	dbfs:/mnt/raw/Customer_stream/_checkpoint

Showing all 2 rows

Figure 17-58. *List the resources to confirm code has deleted the list of services*

As a final check, navigate to your storage account's Event Grid topic and notice from Figure 17-59 that there are now only two Event Grid subscriptions that are available and linked to the correct mount point "mnt."

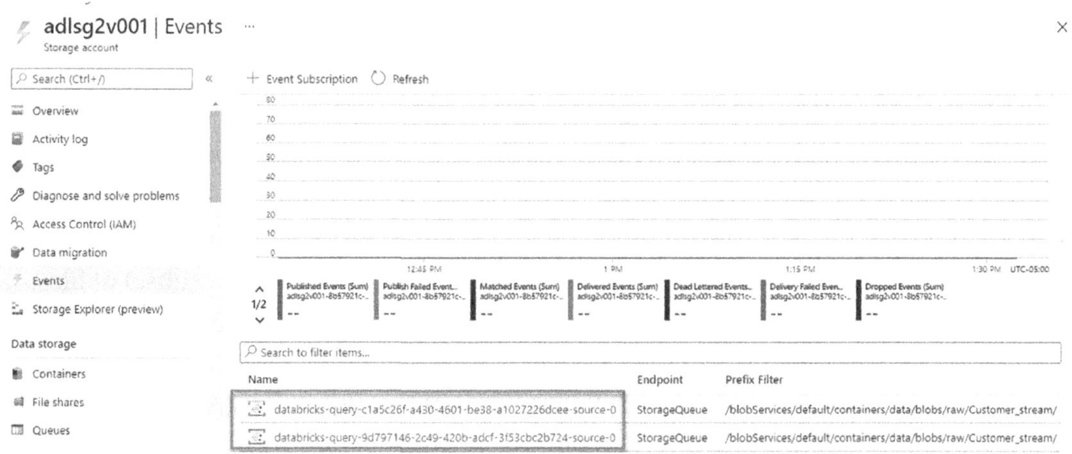

Figure 17-59. *Verify that the code has deleted the Auto Loader resources*

Summary

In this chapter, I demonstrated how to configure and run Auto Loader in Azure Databricks by using the cloudFile source. Specifically, you learned how to manage advanced schema evolution capabilities for streaming semi-structured JSON data in the first section. This modern streaming architectural pattern can be considered while building the Lakehouse architecture since it also supports writing the stream to a delta format. It can be used for both streaming and batch ELT workload processing paradigms since the cluster will shut down when there are no files in the queue to process and will restart when new files arrive in the queue. Additionally, the ease of management and maintenance of Event Grid subscriptions and topics demonstrates Auto Loader's capabilities in the modern data and analytics platform, specifically as it relates to the Lakehouse paradigm.

In the second section of the chapter, I demonstrated how to get started with programmatically working with Auto Loader Resource Manager in a Scala Databricks notebook to list, filter, and delete Auto Loader resources from your Azure subscription. This process is particularly useful to prevent any Azure Event Grid–specific quotas and limits from being reached and to properly and efficiently manage your Auto Loader resources programmatically from your Databricks notebook.

The COPY INTO command is yet another way to insert data incrementally into a Delta Table. Low-volume files that are in the thousands would be a good candidate for COPY INTO, while high-volume files in the millions or more would benefit greatly from Auto Loader from a cost and performance perspective since it can split the processing into multiple batches. For consistently evolving schemas, we've seen that Auto Loader can handle this much more gracefully. For reloading and reprocessing a subset of files, COPY INTO can be easier and more performant to manage and can run concurrently with an Auto Loader stream. Auto Loader can handle billions of files effectively which enables seamless performance and scalability. With file notification services in place, Auto Loader can discover files in a cost-effective manner.

Equipped with the knowledge of how to use this Auto Loader Resource Manager, you will be able to better control and monitor your Auto Loader resources that will be created within your Azure subscription. By having an understanding of how to implement Auto Loader Resource Manager, you will be able to bring greater value to your organization with real-time streaming analytics for big data workloads using Apache Spark within your Lakehouse, reducing the orchestration that would otherwise be necessary.

CHAPTER 18

Python Wheels

The process of packaging, sharing, and distributing Python code across teams and developers within an organization can become a complex task. There are a few methods of packaging and distributing Python code including eggs, jars, wheels, and more. In this chapter, you will learn more about ideal methods for creating a Python wheel file to package and distribute custom code. A Python .whl file is a type of built distribution that tells installers what Python versions and platforms the wheel will support. The wheel comes in a ready-to-install format which allows users to bypass the build stage required with source distributions.

There are many benefits to packaging Python code in wheel files including their smaller size than source distributions; therefore, they can move across networks faster. Additionally, installing wheel files directly avoids the step of having to build packages from the source distribution and does not require the need for a compiler. Wheels provide consistency by eliminating many of the variables involved in installing a package. In this chapter, you will learn how to create a Python wheel file using Visual Studio Code, load it to a Databricks Cluster Library, and finally call a function within the package in a Databricks notebook.

Install Application Software

The following sections list out the required prerequisites for creating a Python Package using Visual Studio Code. You will learn how to install and configure Visual Studio Code, Python, and the necessary extensions.

R. L'Esteve, *The Azure Data Lakehouse Toolkit*, https://doi.org/10.1007/978-1-4842-8233-5_18

Install Visual Studio Code and Python Extension

Firstly, you will need to install Visual Studio (VS) Code, which can be found here: `https://code.visualstudio.com/`. Once Visual Studio Code is installed, you will need the Python Extension for Visual Studio Code, which can be found here: `https://marketplace.visualstudio.com/items?itemName=ms-python.python`, and also by searching for it in the Extensions Marketplace in VS Code, as shown in Figure 18-1. While these are the Interactive Development Environments (IDEs) that are used in this chapter, you can certainly use other compatible IDEs as well, so I wanted to point out the fact that you are not entirely constrained to VS Code.

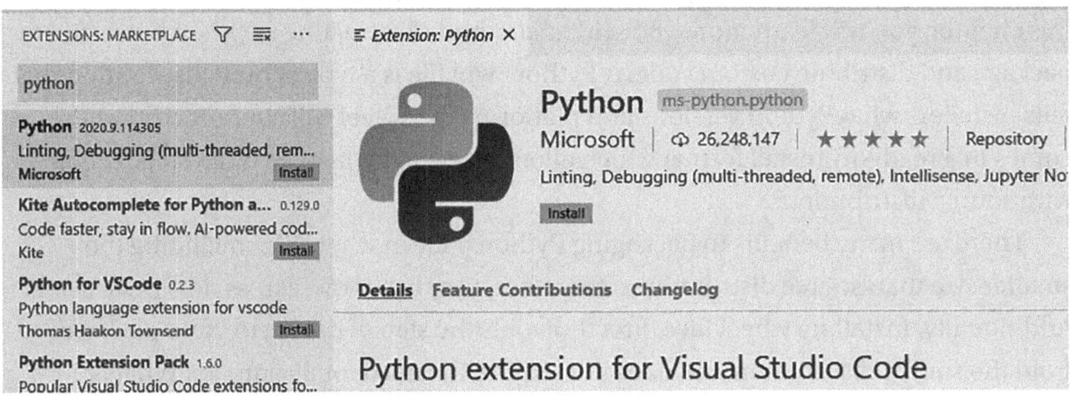

Figure 18-1. Image of Python Extension in VS Code

Install Python

You will also need a stable release of Python. For this demo, I have used Python 3.9 which is the most recently available version and can be found here: `www.python.org/downloads/`. The initial 64-bit installation UI can be seen in Figure 18-2. This process will most likely work for versions 3.9.0 or higher.

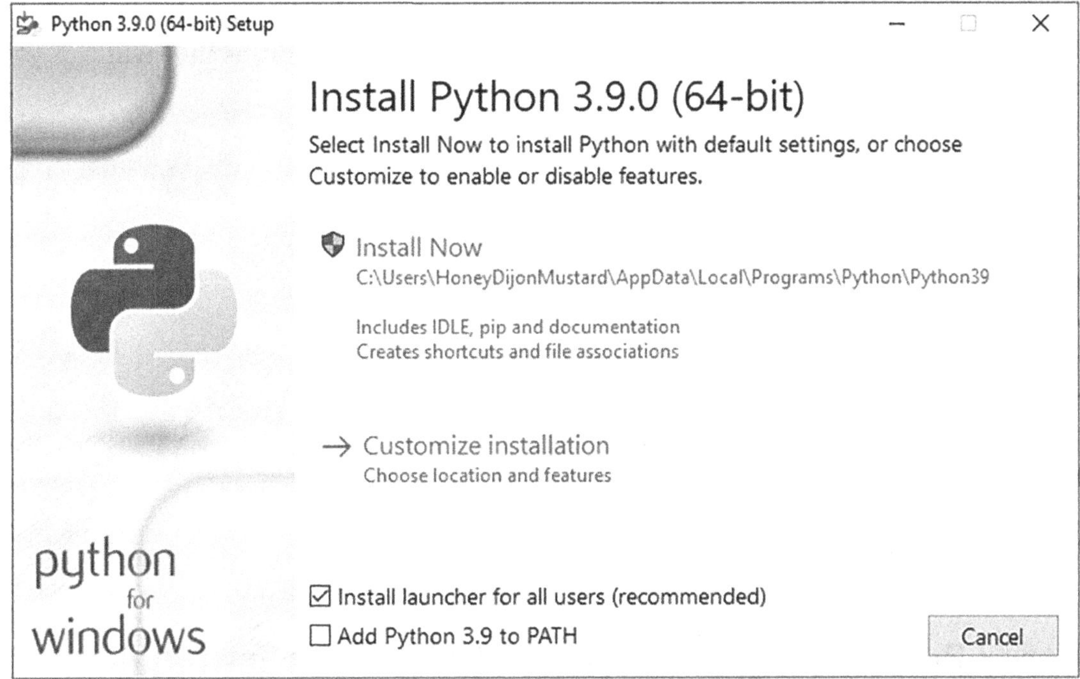

Figure 18-2. *UI to install Python 3.9*

Configure Python Interpreter Path for Visual Studio Code

Once Python is installed along with the VS Code extension for Python, you will need to set the Interpreter path to the Python version that you just installed, as shown in Figure 18-3.

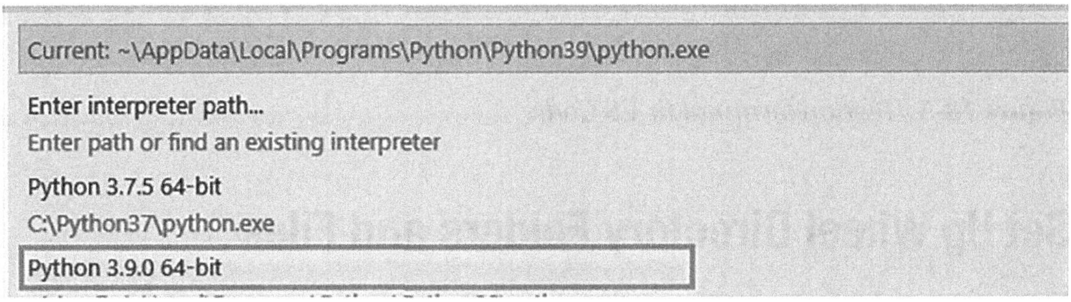

Figure 18-3. *Step to verify Python interpreter*

To verify that this interpreter path has been accurately changed, you can find it located in the bottom left-hand section of the VS Code application, as shown in Figure 18-4.

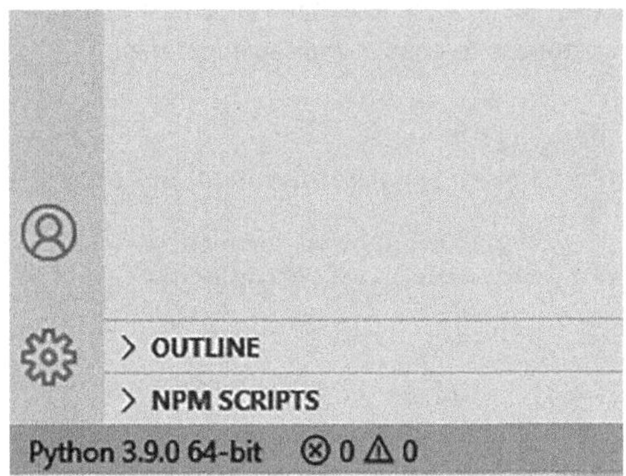

Figure 18-4. *Step to verify and change Python interpreter path*

Verify Python Version in Visual Studio Code Terminal

Next, open a new Python terminal in VS Code, as seen in Figure 18-5, and run the following command: `py -3 -version`, to verify the version of Python and confirm that it matches the version that you just installed and set.

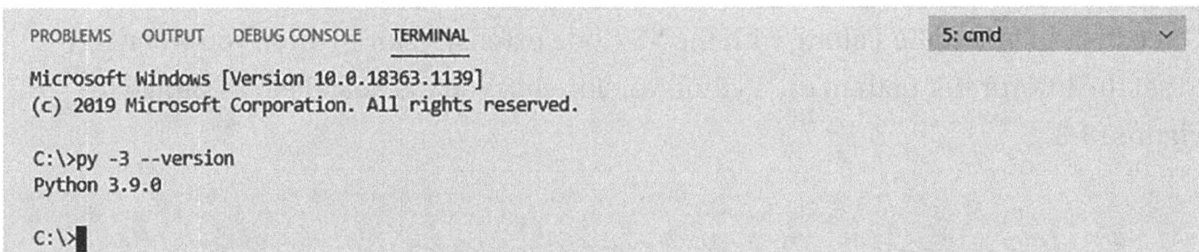

Figure 18-5. *Python terminal in VS Code*

Set Up Wheel Directory Folders and Files

Now it's time to begin creating the Python wheel file. Begin by running the following commands shown in Figure 18-6 to create a directory for the PythonWheelDemo.

```
C:\>mkdir PythonWheelDemo

C:\>cd PythonWheelDemo

C:\PythonWheelDemo>code .

C:\PythonWheelDemo>
```

Figure 18-6. *Commands to create the directory folders*

Here are the commands shown in Figure 18-6 that you will need to run:

```
mkdir PythonWheelDemo
cd PythonWheelDemo
code .
```

After the directory is created, open it in VS Code. In addition, you will need to add the following folders and files by clicking the icons outlined in Figure 18-7, as explained in the following sections.

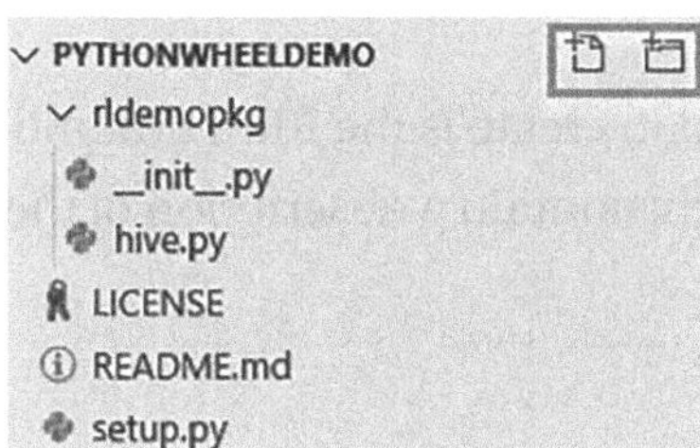

Figure 18-7. *Steps to create the Python Package files*

Create Setup File

The first file that you will need to create is the setup.py file. This file will contain all your package metadata information, which is typically similar to the script as follows:

```
import setuptools

with open("README.md", "r") as fh:
    long_description = fh.read()

setuptools.setup(
    name="hive",
```

```
    version="0.0.1",
    author="Ron LEsteve",
    author_email="ronlesteve@ronlesteve.com",
    description="Package to create Hive",
    long_description=long_description,
    long_description_content_type="text/markdown",
    packages=setuptools.find_packages(),
    classifiers=[
        "Programming Language :: Python :: 3",
        "License :: OSI Approved :: MIT License",
        "Operating System :: OS Independent",
    ],
    python_requires='>=3.7',
)
```

Create Readme File

The next file that you will need to create is the README.md file. Here are the typical contents of this file which might contain a description of the package, along with any supporting materials:

```
# Example Package

This is a simple example package. You can use
[Github-flavored Markdown](https://guides.github.com/features/mastering-
markdown/)
to write your content.
```

Create License File

You will also need to create a license file. This file will contain verbiage as follows and can be customized through the following website: `https://choosealicense.com/`. It will be important for every package that is uploaded to the Python Package Index to include a license. This tells users who will install your package the terms under which they can use your package.

```
Copyright (c) 2018 The Python Packaging Authority

Permission is hereby granted, free of charge, to any person
obtaining a copy
of this software and associated documentation files (the
"Software"), to deal
in the Software without restriction, including without limitation
the rights
to use, copy, modify, merge, publish, distribute, sublicense, and/or sell
copies of the Software, and to permit persons to whom the Software is
furnished to do so, subject to the following conditions:

The above copyright notice and this permission notice shall be
included in all
copies or substantial portions of the Software.

THE SOFTWARE IS PROVIDED "AS IS", WITHOUT WARRANTY OF ANY KIND, EXPRESS OR
IMPLIED, INCLUDING BUT NOT LIMITED TO THE WARRANTIES OF MERCHANTABILITY,
FITNESS FOR A PARTICULAR PURPOSE AND NONINFRINGEMENT. IN NO EVENT SHALL THE
AUTHORS OR COPYRIGHT HOLDERS BE LIABLE FOR ANY CLAIM, DAMAGES OR OTHER
LIABILITY, WHETHER IN AN ACTION OF CONTRACT, TORT OR OTHERWISE,
ARISING FROM,
OUT OF OR IN CONNECTION WITH THE SOFTWARE OR THE USE OR OTHER
DEALINGS IN THE
SOFTWARE.
```

Create Init File

You will also need an __init__.py file. This file provides a mechanism for you to group separate Python scripts into a single importable module. For more details on how to properly create an __init__.py file that best suits your needs, read https://timothybramlett.com/How_to_create_a_Python_Package_with___init__py.html and https://towardsdatascience.com/whats-init-for-me-d70a312da583. The following script is a sample of what is typically included in this file:

```
from .hive import registerHive
```

Create Package Function File

Finally, you will need a Python Package function file which will contain the Python code that will need to be converted to a function. In this demo, we are simply creating a function for a create table statement that can be run in Synapse or Databricks which we will call hive.py, as shown in Figure 18-7. It will accept as arguments the database, table, and location. Spark will be used to simply define the spark.sql code section. Here are the contents of this file. You can create a variety of highly customized functions depending on your use case.

```
def registerHive(spark, database, table, location):
        cmd = f"CREATE TABLE IF NOT EXISTS {database}.{table} USING PARQUET
        LOCATION '{location}'"
        spark.sql(cmd)
        print(f"Executed: {cmd}")
```

Install Python Wheel Packages

Now that you have all the necessary files in your directory, you'll need to install a few wheel packages that will be discussed in this section.

Install Wheel Package

Begin by running the following command: `pip install wheel`, within the terminal to install the wheel package. Figure 18-8 illustrates the messages that are displayed once the command runs successfully.

```
C:\PythonWheelDemo>pip install wheel
Collecting wheel
  Downloading https://files.pythonhosted.org/packages/a7/00/3df031b3ecd5444d572141321537080b40c1c25e1caa3d86cdd12e5e919c/wheel-0.35
.1-py2.py3-none-any.whl
Installing collected packages: wheel
Successfully installed wheel-0.35.1
WARNING: You are using pip version 19.2.3, however version 20.2.4 is available.
You should consider upgrading via the 'python -m pip install --upgrade pip' command.
```

Figure 18-8. *Steps to install the Python wheel package*

Possibly, you will also need to run this command: `python -m pip install --upgrade pip`, to update the pip. Figure 18-9 shows the messages that are displayed once the command runs successfully.

```
C:\PythonWheelDemo>python -m pip install --upgrade pip
Collecting pip
  Downloading https://files.pythonhosted.org/packages/cb/28/91f26bd088ce8e22169032100d4260614fc3da435025ff389ef1d396a433/pip-20.2.4-py2.py3-none-a
ny.whl (1.5MB)
     |████████████████████████████████| 1.5MB 3.3MB/s
Installing collected packages: pip
  Found existing installation: pip 19.2.3
    Uninstalling pip-19.2.3:
      Successfully uninstalled pip-19.2.3
Successfully installed pip-20.2.4
```

Figure 18-9. *Step to upgrade the pip*

Install Check Wheel Package

You will also need to install a package to check the wheel contents by running the following command: `pip install check-wheel-contents`. Check wheel contents will fail and notify you if any of several common errors or mistakes are detected. More details on check wheel contents can be found here: `https://pypi.org/project/check-wheel-contents/`. Figure 18-10 shows the messages that are displayed once the install command runs successfully.

```
Collecting pyreadline; sys_platform == "win32"
  Downloading pyreadline-2.1.zip (109 kB)
     |████████████████████████████████| 109 kB 6.4 MB/s
Building wheels for collected packages: pyreadline
  Building wheel for pyreadline (setup.py) ... done
  Created wheel for pyreadline: filename=pyreadline-2.1-py3-none-any.whl size=93844 sha256=537625cd12a309541d73460229e5b4c
262861f98b5ac5dc0e5a7b4e8093fa500
  Stored in directory: c:\users\honeydijonmustard\appdata\local\pip\cache\wheels\00\6e\d4\7c4b7bc22c090baf4f470e7f35c4f222
06277229bdb6607df6
Successfully built pyreadline
Installing collected packages: wheel-filename, verboselogs, pyreadline, humanfriendly, property-manager, toml, click, chec
k-wheel-contents
Successfully installed check-wheel-contents-0.1.0 click-7.1.2 humanfriendly-8.2 property-manager-3.0 pyreadline-2.1 toml-0
.10.1 verboselogs-1.7 wheel-filename-1.2.0
```

Figure 18-10. *Step to install the check wheel contents package*

Create and Verify Wheel File

In this next section, you will create and verify the wheel file by running a few additional commands.

Create Wheel File

To create the wheel file, run the following command in a Python terminal from the root of the project: `python setup.py bdist_wheel`. Once the command completes running, notice from Figure 18-11 that it has created the wheel file and also added hive.py to it.

```
creating build\bdist.win-amd64
creating build\bdist.win-amd64\wheel
creating build\bdist.win-amd64\wheel\rldemopkg
copying build\lib\rldemopkg\hive.py -> build\bdist.win-amd64\wheel\.\rldemopkg
copying build\lib\rldemopkg\__init__.py -> build\bdist.win-amd64\wheel\.\rldemopkg
running install_egg_info
running egg_info
creating hive.egg-info
writing hive.egg-info\PKG-INFO
writing dependency_links to hive.egg-info\dependency_links.txt
writing top-level names to hive.egg-info\top_level.txt
writing manifest file 'hive.egg-info\SOURCES.txt'
reading manifest file 'hive.egg-info\SOURCES.txt'
writing manifest file 'hive.egg-info\SOURCES.txt'
Copying hive.egg-info to build\bdist.win-amd64\wheel\.\hive-0.0.1-py3.7.egg-info
running install_scripts
adding license file "LICENSE" (matched pattern "LICEN[CS]E*")
creating build\bdist.win-amd64\wheel\hive-0.0.1.dist-info\WHEEL
creating 'dist\hive-0.0.1-py3-none-any.whl' and adding 'build\bdist.win-amd64\wheel' to it
adding 'rldemopkg/__init__.py'
adding 'rldemopkg/hive.py'
adding 'hive-0.0.1.dist-info/LICENSE'
adding 'hive-0.0.1.dist-info/METADATA'
adding 'hive-0.0.1.dist-info/WHEEL'
adding 'hive-0.0.1.dist-info/top_level.txt'
adding 'hive-0.0.1.dist-info/RECORD'
```

***Figure 18-11.** Step to verify that the Hive.py file is added in the wheel*

Check Wheel Contents

At this point, you can run the following check wheel contents command: `check-wheel-contents C:\PythonWheelDemo\dist\`, to verify that a status of OK is received, which can be seen in Figure 18-12.

```
C:\PythonWheelDemo>check-wheel-contents C:\PythonWheelDemo\dist\
C:\PythonWheelDemo\dist\hive-0.0.1-py3-none-any.whl: OK
```

***Figure 18-12.** Step to check the wheel file*

Verify Wheel File

As an additional verification step, navigate to the directory folders in VS Code and files to verify that the wheel file exists, as shown in Figure 18-13.

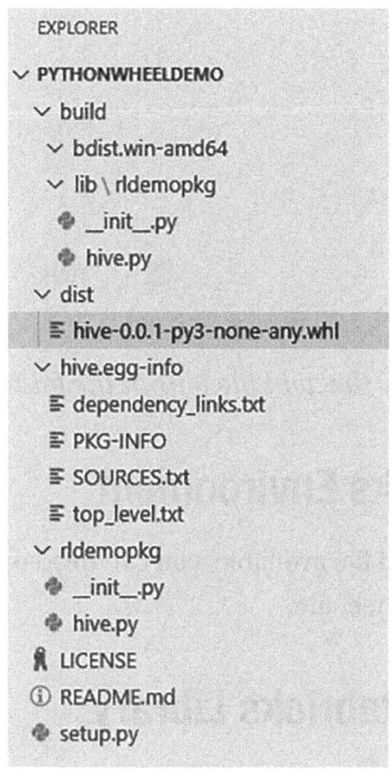

Figure 18-13. *Step to verify that the wheel exists in the dist folder*

Also, navigate to the local folder to confirm the path of the wheel file, as shown in Figure 18-14. You will need this path to upload the wheel file in Databricks.

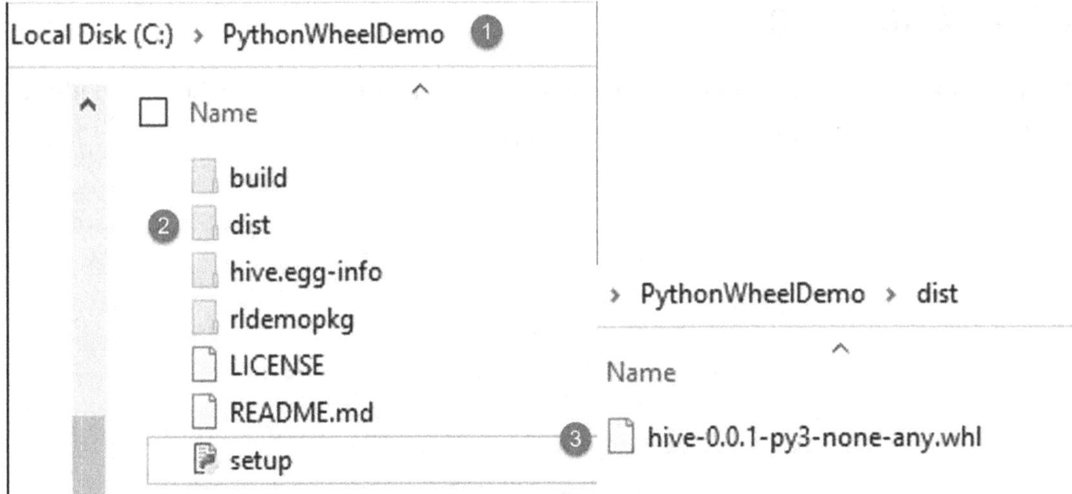

Figure 18-14. *Step to verify the .whl file within the folder*

Configure Databricks Environment

Now that you have your wheel file available, you can head over to Databricks, create a new cluster, and install the wheel file.

Install Wheel to Databricks Library

After the cluster is created, install the wheel file that you just created to the cluster by uploading it, as shown in Figure 18-15. More information on uploading wheel files and managing libraries for Apache Spark in Azure Synapse Analytics can be found here: `https://docs.microsoft.com/en-us/azure/synapse-analytics/spark/apache-spark-azure-portal-add-libraries`. However, this demo will be exclusively using Databricks. This Databricks Library installation process will install the Python '.whl' file that was created in VS Code within the cluster's library. The .whl file will automatically be installed at the cluster level when the cluster starts and will be available to all attached notebooks that utilize this cluster for running workloads.

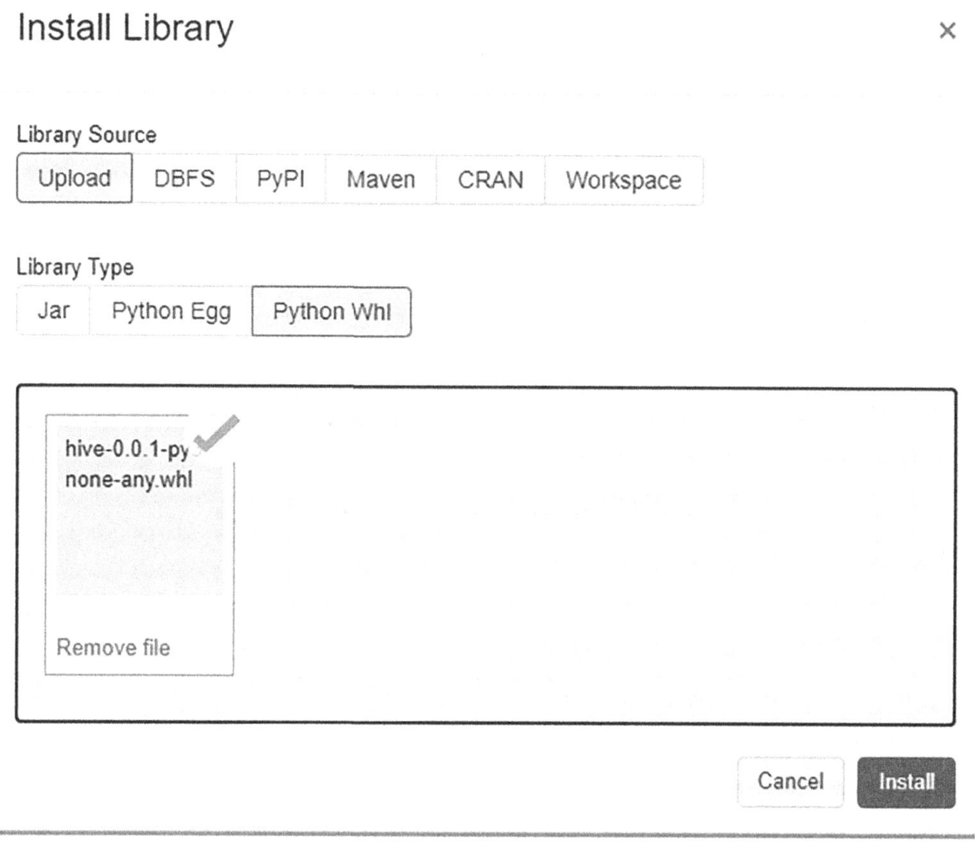

Figure 18-15. *Step to install the wheel in Databricks library*

Create Databricks Notebook

Now that you have installed the wheel file to the cluster, this section will show you how to create a new Databricks notebook and attach the cluster containing the wheel library to it.

Mount Data Lake Folder

You will need to first mount your Azure Data Lake Storage Gen2 container and folder which contains the AdventureWorksLT2019 database and files in parquet format. You can mount the location using a few methods, as seen in Chapter 3, but for the purpose of this demo, we will use a simple approach by running the following code shown in Figure 18-16.

PythonWheelDemo (Python)

Standard

Cmd 1

```
spark.conf.set(
  "fs.azure.account.key.adls2001rl.dfs.core.windows.net",
  "/                                                   mkJBB1XKe4Hve+ubds3QNscw=="
)
```

Figure 18-16. *Code to mount ADLS gen2*

Here is the code that you will need to run to begin the process of mounting your ADLS gen2 account:

```
spark.conf.set(
  "fs.azure.account.key.adls2001rl.dfs.core.windows.net",
  "ENTER-ACCESS-KEY"
)
```

Next, run the following code to list the content of the folder to locate the path containing your AdventureWorksLT2019 database within ADLS gen2. You will need to pre-upload this database to your account. The database can be found here and would need to be converted to parquet format: `github.com/microsoft/sql-server-samples/tree/master/samples/databases`

```
dbutils.fs.ls("abfss://data@adls2001rl.dfs.core.windows.net/raw/
AdventureWorksLT2019/SalesLT")
```

Create Spark Database

Now that you have mounted your Data Lake folder, create a new AdventureWorksLT2019 Spark database by running the following code, which will generate an OK message once the database is created:

```
%sql
CREATE DATABASE adventureworkslt2019
```

Verify Wheel Package

Also, run the following script shown in Figure 18-17 to verify that the wheel package was installed.

Cmd 8

```
%sh
/databricks/python/bin/pip freeze
```

```
Cython==0.29.15
decorator==4.4.1
docutils==0.15.2
entrypoints==0.3
hive==0.0.1
idna==2.8
ipykernel==5.1.4
ipython==7.12.0
ipython-genutils==0.2.0
jedi==0.14.1
jmespath==0.10.0
joblib==0.14.1
jupyter-client==5.3.4
jupyter-core==4.6.1
kiwisolver==1.1.0
koalas==1.2.0
```

Figure 18-17. *Step to verify the installed wheel file in the notebook*

Here is the code that you will need to run to re-create the results shown in Figure 18-17.

```
%sh
/databricks/python/bin/pip freeze
```

Import Wheel Package

Next, you can import the wheel package by running the following command: `import rldemopkg`. Recall from the VS Code project, rldemopkg was the root directory that contained the scripts and files.

Create Function Parameters

Next, let's define registerHive() function's parameters so that we can pass it to the function:

```
database = "AdventureWorksLT2019"
table = "Customer"
location = f"abfss://data@adls2001rl.dfs.core.windows.net/raw/
AdventureWorksLT2019/SalesLT/Customer"
```

Run Wheel Package Function

You can now run the following function from the wheel package `rldemopkg.registerHive(spark,database,table,location)`. From the printed execution results, shown in Figure 18-18, verify that the function accurately ran and created the create table statement script.

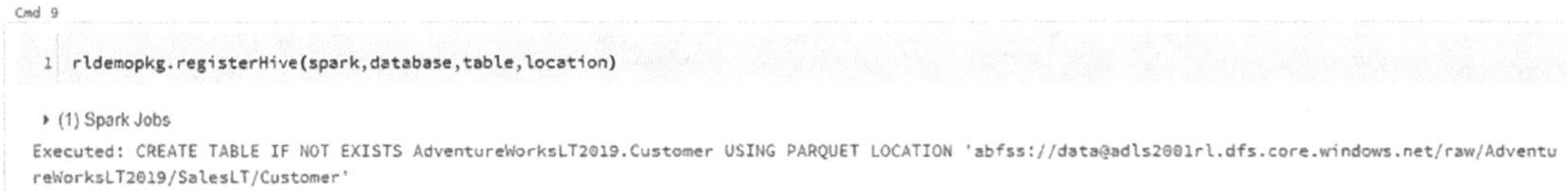

```
Cmd 9

rldemopkg.registerHive(spark,database,table,location)

▸ (1) Spark Jobs
Executed: CREATE TABLE IF NOT EXISTS AdventureWorksLT2019.Customer USING PARQUET LOCATION 'abfss://data@adls2001rl.dfs.core.windows.net/raw/AdventureWorksLT2019/SalesLT/Customer'
```

Figure 18-18. *Step to run the wheel function*

Show Spark Tables

Finally, run the show tables code again to verify that the registerHive() function did indeed create the new Customer table, as shown in Figure 18-19.

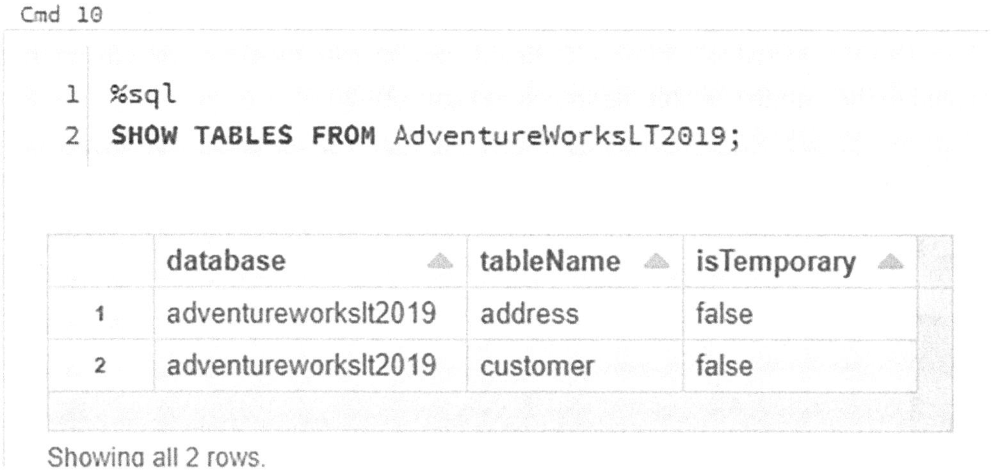

Cmd 10

```
%sql
SHOW TABLES FROM AdventureWorksLT2019;
```

	database	tableName	isTemporary
1	adventureworkslt2019	address	false
2	adventureworkslt2019	customer	false

Showing all 2 rows.

Figure 18-19. *Step to show the Spark table created by the function*

Here is the code that you will need to run to re-create the results shown in Figure 18-19:

```
%sql
SHOW TABLES FROM AdventureWorksLT2019;
```

Files in Databricks Repos

Up to this point, we have explored how to build a custom .whl file locally and then import it to your Databricks cluster. This is a great way of building your own Python libraries. As an alternative method, files for Databricks repos shift this process of developing custom Python libraries by linking the custom-developed functions to your repos which empowers developers to iterate through new code changes quickly through the development cycle by eliminating the additional process of having to uninstall the .whl file, locally update and rebuild the .whl file, and then reinstall it and restart the Databricks cluster. This process will prove challenging when there is the need to constantly update the .whl file.

Files within repos allow developers to write functions and custom libraries as .py files within Databricks and check it into the repo. These .py files can be imported, can be called directly from the notebook, and can also be synced with other branches and environments to support CI and CD processes for the code as it moves to the upper environments. This is a paradigm shift in how custom Python libraries were previously developed and imported as .whl files. To begin working with files in repos, ensure that it is enabled in the Admin Console, as shown in Figure 18-20.

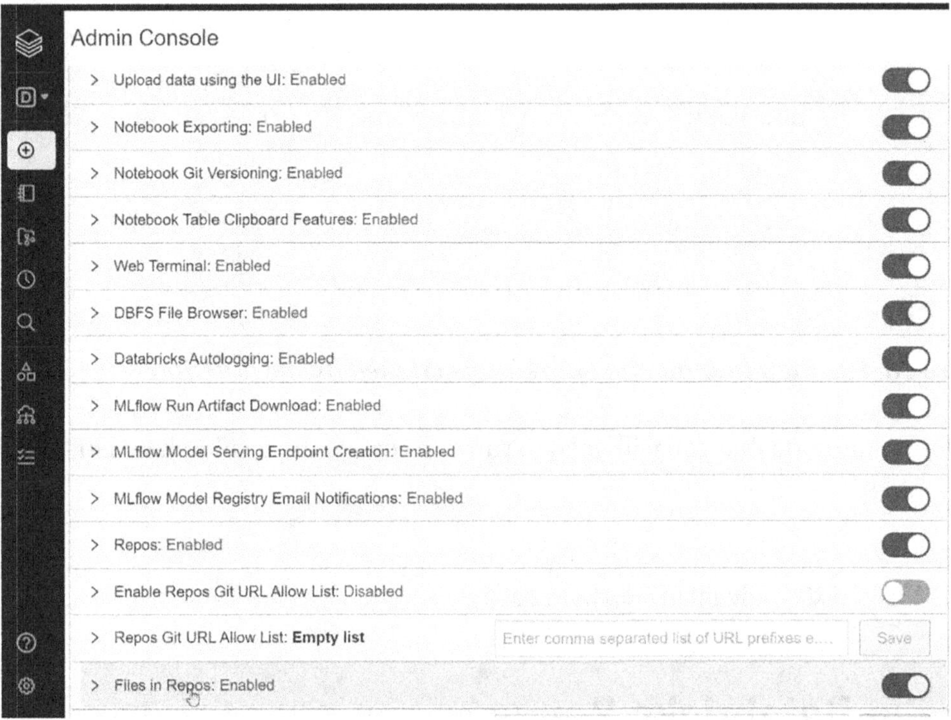

***Figure 18-20.** Step to enable files in repos in Databricks Admin Console*

While the concept seems promising, having multiple versions of code being pushed to various branches may translate into less control over having a single version of truth for your Python library. Additionally, with this approach, there are limitations around build routines related to unit testing for CI and CD that you get from building your wheel locally using VS Code and promoting it using DevOps pipelines. Creating a .py file is as simple as creating a notebook in Databricks, as shown in Figure 18-21. The contents of this file would have your Python function and can easily be called from a notebook. When deciding between .whl files built locally and .py files written in Databricks repos, consider the pros and cons of each approach when choosing the ideal pattern for your Python libraries.

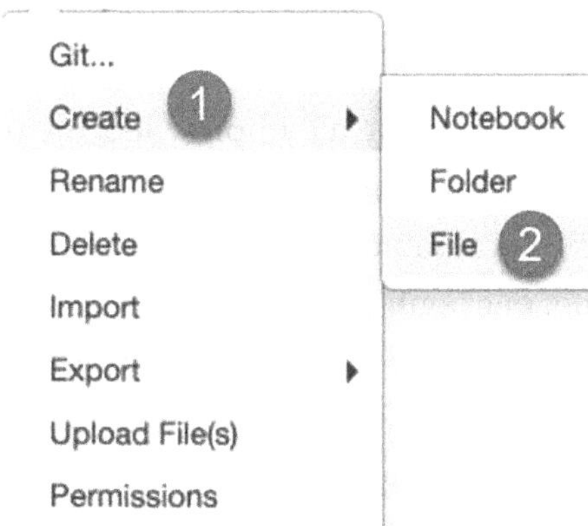

Figure 18-21. *Steps to create a file in Databricks*

Continuous Integration and Deployment

Since the topic of Databricks repos has been presented, it is worth mentioning the process of promoting notebook code to higher environments as part of DevOps continuous integration and deployment (CI/CD). Once a developer completes the development of their code and checks it into their repo, then a build pipeline can be created in Azure DevOps (ADO) through either the classic interface or with direct YAML script. Once the ADO Build Agent and build pipeline are set up, it will gather new code, run automated tests, and build libraries and Spark code. From there, as part of the release pipeline, a release artifact will be generated which will then deploy the notebooks and libraries to the higher environments. Furthermore, any automated tests and reports will be run. For more details on how to set up this CI and CD process on Azure Databricks using Azure DevOps, please see the following Microsoft article: `https://docs.microsoft.com/en-us/azure/databricks/dev-tools/ci-cd/ci-cd-azure-devops#overview-of-a-typical-azure-databricks-cicd-pipeline`

Summary

In this chapter, you learned how to create a Python wheel file using Visual Studio Code, load it to a Databricks Cluster Library, and finally call a function within the package in a Databricks notebook. This is a valuable learning exercise because it solves numerous complexities around creating, packaging, and sharing reusable code, functions, and more across developers and workspaces. While this demonstration was focused on Databricks, the concept of wheel files can also be applied to Synapse Analytics. Wheels simplify the data engineering process by promoting reusability and streamlining collaboration across developers by setting quality engineering standards for success within the Lakehouse. Finally, toward the end of this chapter, you learned about an alternate method of creating Python libraries through files in Databricks repos as an alternative to creating .whl files locally. There are pros and cons to each approach that need to be considered when selecting the solution that fits your particular use case.

CHAPTER 19

Security and Controls

Since numerous users and groups would need varying levels of access within their Lakehouse platform, Security and Controls is an important topic when administering your Lakehouse. While there are numerous Lakehouse platforms that require security and control administration, this chapter will focus on the Azure Databricks platform. This chapter will help you with understanding the various options for implementing both row-level security and other access control options within Azure Databricks. You will learn about how Databricks Administrators can begin implementing these various controls and security measures within Azure Databricks.

Azure Databricks workspace provides an interactive workspace that enables collaboration between data engineers, data scientists, machine learning engineers, data analysts, and more. Since these various groups require varying levels of security, permissions, and privileges, Databricks has a number of access controls and row-level security options that we will explore in this chapter. Note that access controls are typically available with the Databricks Premium Plan.

Implement Cluster, Pool, and Jobs Access Control

Within the Databricks workspace Admin Console, there are a variety of access control options. This section explores how to implement cluster, pool, and job access control. Once enabled, cluster access control will allow users to control who can create and manage clusters. Figure 19-1 shows how to enable this feature from the Admin Console. Simply navigate to Settings ➤ Admin Console ➤ Workspace Settings tab ➤ Enable Cluster, Pool, and Jobs Access Control.

R. L'Esteve, *The Azure Data Lakehouse Toolkit*, https://doi.org/10.1007/978-1-4842-8233-5_19

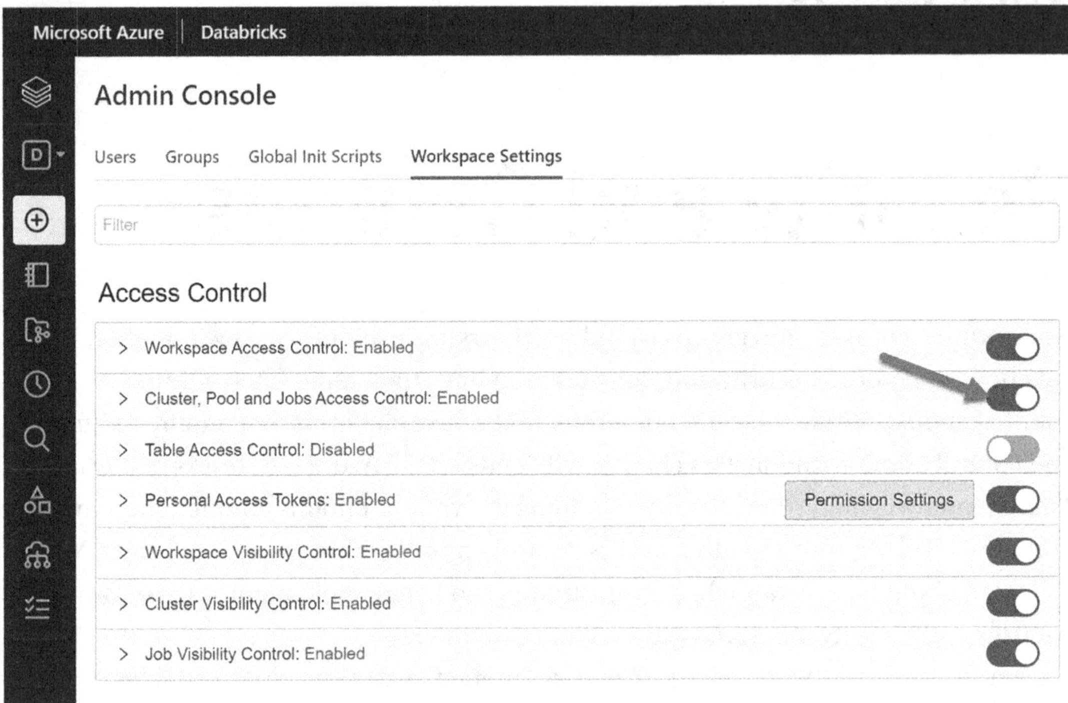

Figure 19-1. *Cluster pool in Admin Console is disabled*

Prior to enabling Cluster, Pool and Jobs Access Control, the option to allow and disable cluster creation for users is disabled, as shown in Figure 19-2.

Admin Console

Users Groups Workspace Storage Access Control Advanced Global Init Scripts

+ Add User

Username	Name	Admin	Allow cluster creation
ron.analyst@		☐	☑

Figure 19-2. *Allow cluster creation is disabled*

After enabling the "Cluster, Pool and Jobs Access Control" setting within the Admin Console, the ability to disable 'cluster creation' capability for users becomes an option, as shown in Figure 19-3. Once cluster permissions for the user are turned off, they will not be able to create new clusters.

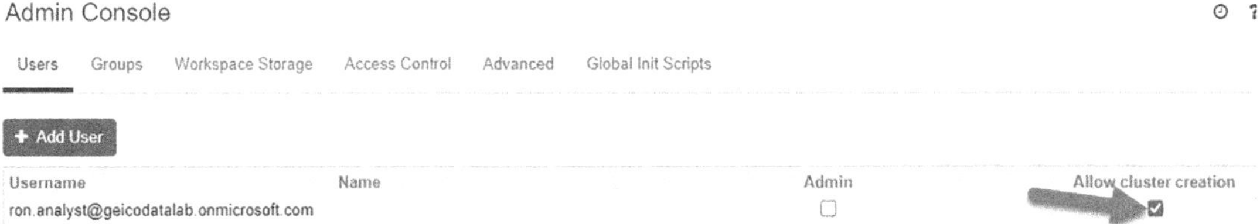

Figure 19-3. *Cluster access control is enabled*

Figure 19-4 shows that the analyst account no longer has permissions to create clusters. For more information on cluster access control, read `https://docs.microsoft.com/en-us/azure/databricks/administration-guide/access-control/cluster-acl`

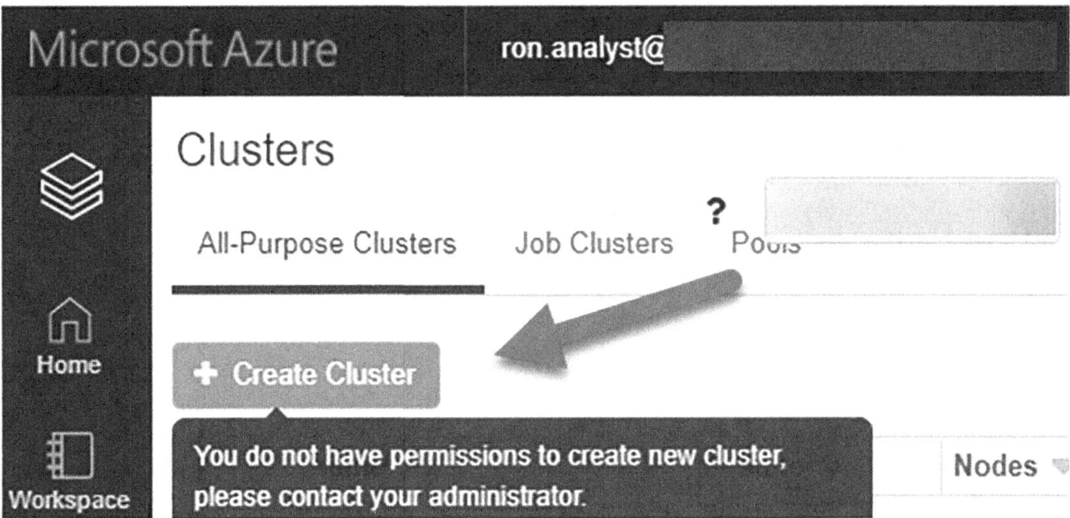

Figure 19-4. *Create cluster is disabled in analyst account*

Implement Workspace Access Control

Another available access control option within Databricks is at the workspace level, which controls who can view, edit, and run notebooks in workspaces, shown in Figure 19-5.

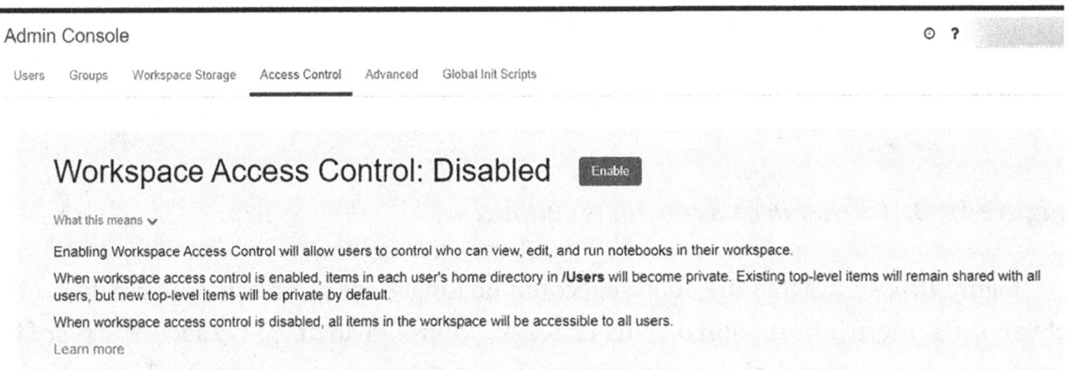

Figure 19-5. *Workspace Access Control is disabled*

Prior to enabling workspace access control, the analyst can see all of the other user's accounts and respective notebooks, shown in Figure 19-6.

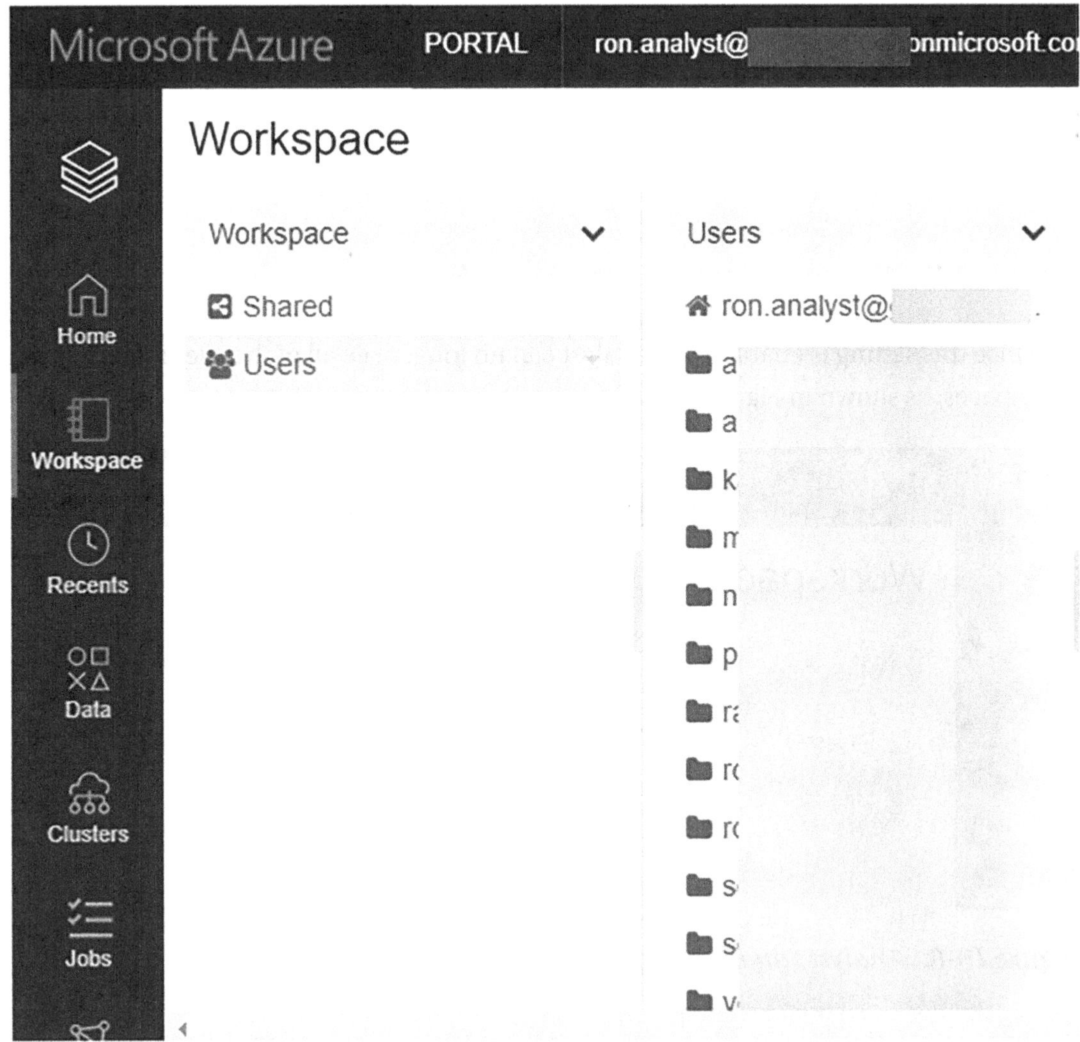

***Figure 19-6.** Analyst can see all user folders and workspaces*

After enabling the Workspace Access Control shown in Figure 19-7, the analyst can only see their workspace, and the other user workspaces are no longer visible. For more detail, read more about enabling workspace object access control here: `https://docs.microsoft.com/en-us/azure/databricks/administration-guide/access-control/workspace-acl`

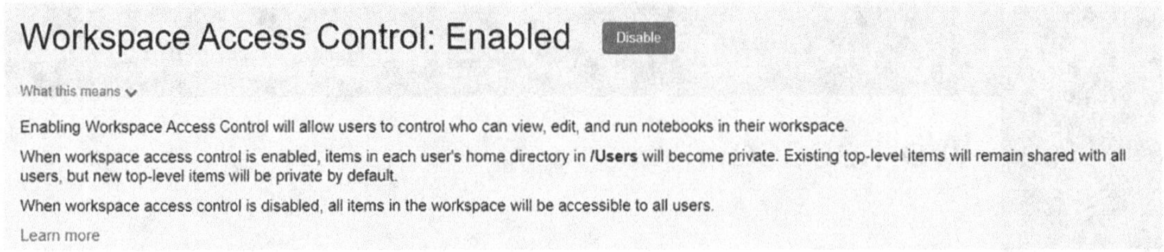

Figure 19-7. *Workspace Access Control is enabled*

Once this setting is enabled, the analyst can no longer see all of the user folders and workspaces, as shown in Figure 19-8.

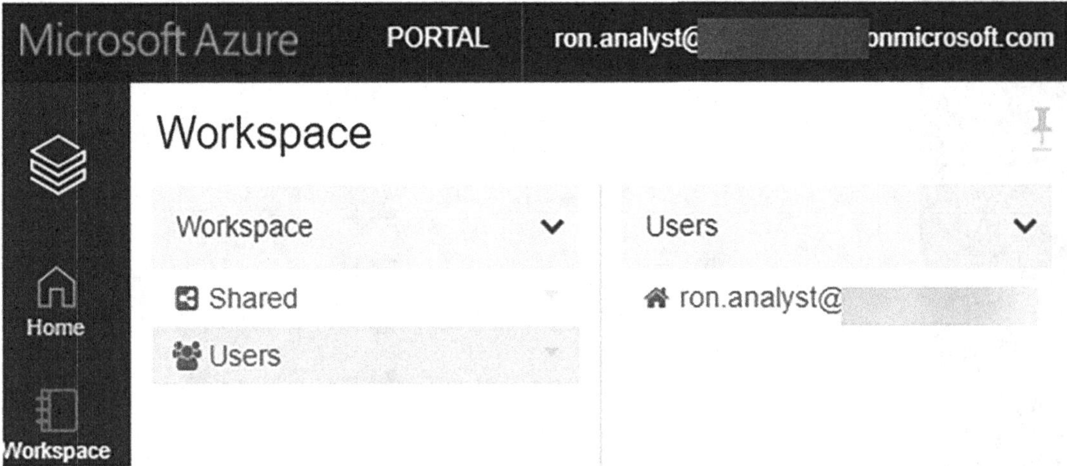

Figure 19-8. *Analyst can no longer see all user folders and workspaces*

Implement Other Access and Visibility Controls

There are a few other access and visibility controls within Databricks which add additional levels of access control which will be covered in the following section.

Table Access Control

Table Access Control allows users to control who can create, select, and modify databases, tables, views, and functions. Additionally, clusters will have additional security options for users to only be able to run Python and SQL commands on the tables and view which they have access to. From a security perspective, this option prevents users from accessing non-approved APIs or cloud storage at a cluster level. For more information on Table Access Control, read more about enabling Table Access Control for your workspace here: `https://docs.microsoft.com/en-us/azure/databricks/administration-guide/access-control/table-acl`. Figure 19-9 shows how to enable and disable Table Access Control within the Admin Console.

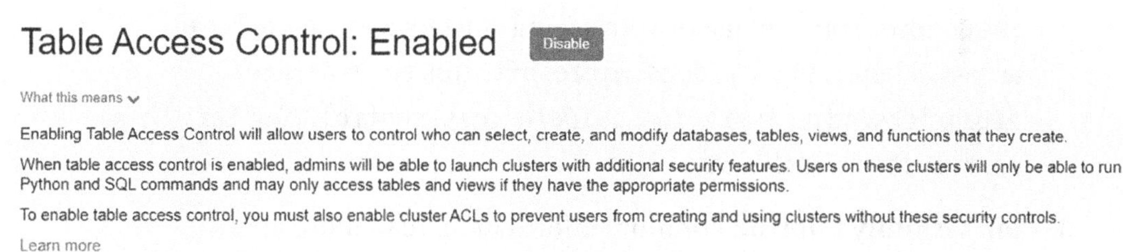

Figure 19-9. *Table Access Control within access control in Admin Console*

Personal Access Tokens

Tokens allow users to use personal access tokens to access the Databricks REST API. For more information, read more about managing Personal Access Tokens here: `https://docs.microsoft.com/en-us/azure/databricks/administration-guide/access-control/tokens`. Figure 19-10 shows how to enable and disable Personal Access Tokens within the Admin Console.

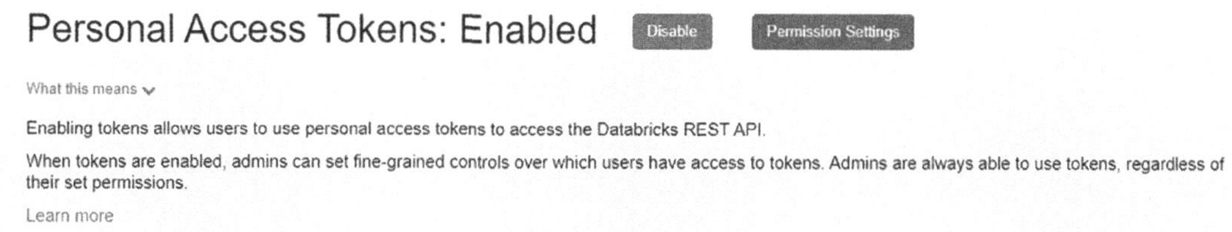

Figure 19-10. *Personal Access Tokens within Admin Console*

Visibility Controls

Access control by itself does not prevent users from seeing jobs, clusters, and filenames of workspaces, which is why there are the following available access controls related to visibility, as shown in Figure 19-11:

1. **Work Space Visibility Control**: For more information, read more about how to prevent users from seeing workspace objects they do not have access to here: `https://docs.microsoft.com/en-us/azure/databricks/administration-guide/access-control/workspace-acl#workspace-object-visibility`
2. **Cluster Visibility Control**: For more information, read more about how to prevent users from seeing clusters they do not have access to here: `https://docs.microsoft.com/en-us/azure/databricks/administration-guide/access-control/cluster-acl#cluster-visibility`
3. **Job Visibility Control**: For more information, read more about how to prevent users from seeing jobs they do not have access to here: `https://docs.microsoft.com/en-us/azure/databricks/administration-guide/access-control/jobs-acl#jobs-visibility`

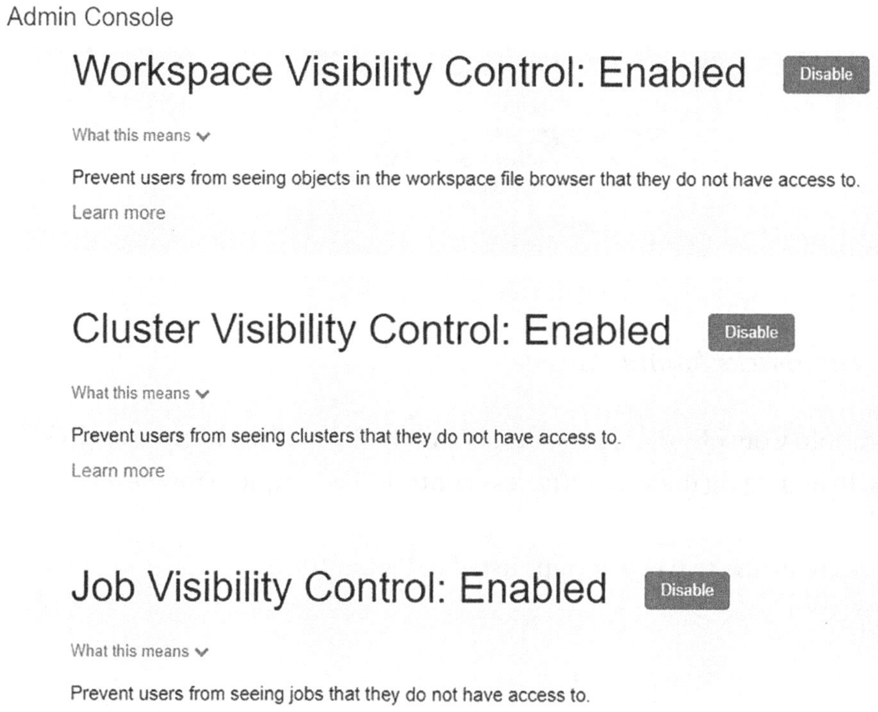

Admin Console

Workspace Visibility Control: Enabled Disable

What this means

Prevent users from seeing objects in the workspace file browser that they do not have access to.

Learn more

Cluster Visibility Control: Enabled Disable

What this means

Prevent users from seeing clusters that they do not have access to.

Learn more

Job Visibility Control: Enabled Disable

What this means

Prevent users from seeing jobs that they do not have access to.

Figure 19-11. *Visibility access control options within Admin Console*

Example Row-Level Security Implementation

In the previous sections, you learned about the various security and controls that are offered by Databricks. In the following sections, you will learn how to implement row-level security through an end-to-end example of granting row-level access to the respective vendors of the NYC Taxi dataset. You will learn how to create new user groups, load sample datasets, run queries using row-level security, and create row-level secured views and finally grant selective user access to those views.

Create New User Groups

Azure Databricks contains a robust Admin Console, shown in Figure 19-12, that is quite useful to administrators that are seeing a centralized location to manage the various access controls and security within the Databricks console.

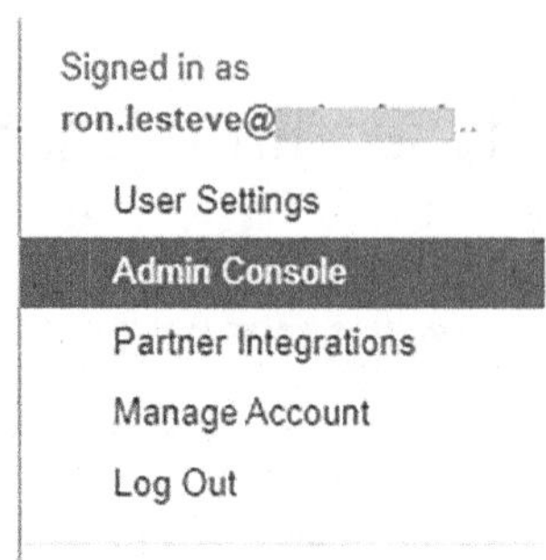

Figure 19-12. *Databricks Admin Console*

Within the Admin Console, there are a number of options from adding users to creating groups, to managing the various access controls. Let's explore row-level security within Azure Databricks by creating a few groups in the Admin Console. For the purpose of this demo, let's create the two new groups listed in Figure 19-13.

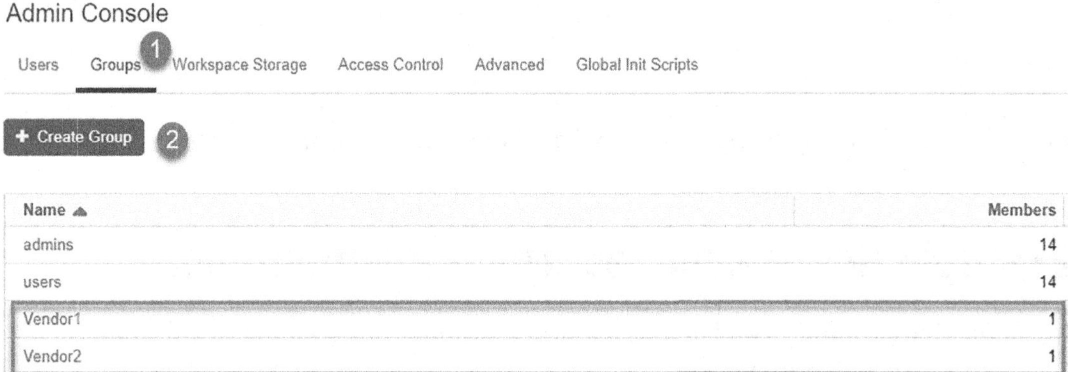

Figure 19-13. *Steps to create new groups to show row-level security*

The Vendor1 group will contain member "Ron L'Esteve" as group member with user permissions, as shown in Figure 19-14.

Figure 19-14. *Create Vendor1 group*

The Vendor2 group will contain member "Ron Tester" as group member with user permissions, as shown in Figure 19-15.

Figure 19-15. *Create Vendor2 group*

Load Sample Data

Now that we have created the groups needed to test row-level security in Databricks, you will need some sample data to test. The following code will be executed in a Python Databricks notebook and will extract the NYC Taxi Yellow Trip Data for 2019 into a data frame:

```
Data = "/databricks-datasets/nyctaxi/tripdata/yellow/yellow_
tripdata_2019-*"

SchemaDF = spark.read.format("csv") \
  .option("header", "true") \
```

```
  .option("inferSchema", "true") \
  .load("/databricks-datasets/nyctaxi/tripdata/yellow/yellow_
  tripdata_2019-02.csv.gz")

nyctaxiDF = spark.read.format("csv") \
  .option("header", "true") \
  .schema(SchemaDF.schema) \
  .load(Data)
```

Notice in Figure 19-16 that this notebook is using the "ron.lesteve" account which is a member of the Vendor1 group.

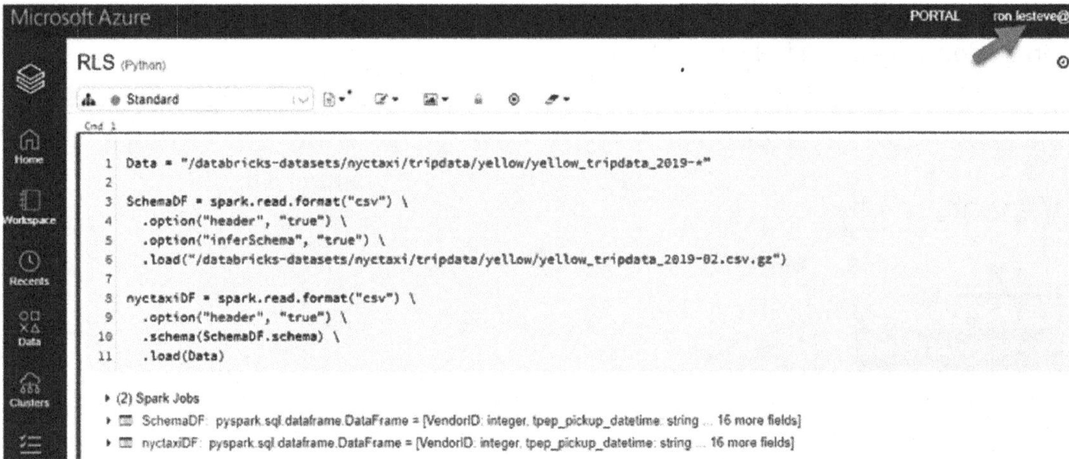

***Figure 19-16.** Load NYC Taxi dataset to df*

After loading the NYC Taxi dataset to a data frame, the following code will add a few new columns to the data frame to include a new column for the year and a new column for the vendor name which is based on a case statement referencing the vendor ID.

```
from pyspark.sql.functions import *

nyctaxiDF = nyctaxiDF.withColumn('Year', year(col("tpep_pickup_datetime")))
nyctaxiDF = nyctaxiDF.withColumn("VendorName",
      expr("case when VendorID = '1' then 'Vendor1' " +
                       "when VendorID = '2' then 'Vendor2' " +
                      "when VendorID = '4' then 'Vendor4' "
                       "else 'Unknown' end"))
```

Once the data frame is ready to be written to ADLS2 in parquet format, you can quickly display the data frame shown in Figure 19-17 to ensure that the new VendorName and Year columns are displayed as expected.

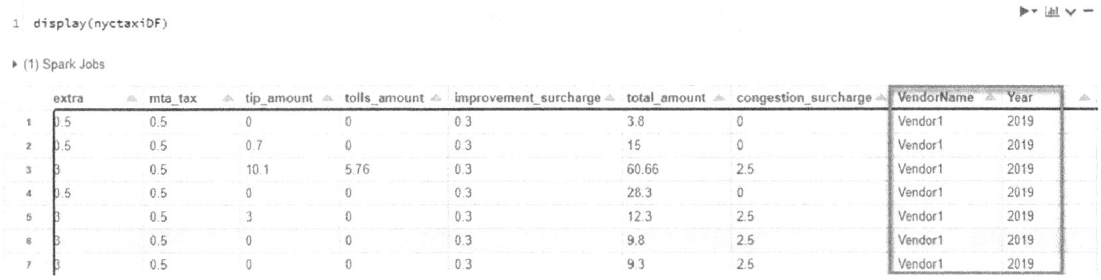

```
1 display(nyctaxiDF)
```

▸ (1) Spark Jobs

	extra	mta_tax	tip_amount	tolls_amount	improvement_surcharge	total_amount	congestion_surcharge	VendorName	Year
1	0.5	0.5	0	0	0.3	3.8	0	Vendor1	2019
2	0.5	0.5	0.7	0	0.3	15	0	Vendor1	2019
3	3	0.5	10.1	5.76	0.3	60.66	2.5	Vendor1	2019
4	0.5	0.5	0	0	0.3	28.3	0	Vendor1	2019
5	3	0.5	3	0	0.3	12.3	2.5	Vendor1	2019
6	3	0.5	0	0	0.3	9.8	2.5	Vendor1	2019
7	3	0.5	0	0	0.3	9.3	2.5	Vendor1	2019

Figure 19-17. *Display the nyctaxiDF*

Next, the data frame can be written to ADLS2 in delta format and partitioned by year with the following code:

```
(
  nyctaxiDF
  .write
  .partitionBy("Year")
  .format("delta")
  .mode("overwrite")
  .save("abfss://data@adl001.dfs.core.windows.net/raw/delta/nyctaxi_delta")
)
```

Create Delta Tables

From the delta format parquet files that were created in the previous steps, you can next create external/Hive tables using the nyctaxi Delta location with the following code:

```
spark.sql("CREATE TABLE nyctaxi USING DELTA LOCATION 'abfss://data@adl001.
dfs.core.windows.net/raw/delta/nyctaxi_delta/'")
```

The following SQL query shown in Figure 19-18 will confirm the distinct vendor names that are available in the nyctaxi external Hive table.

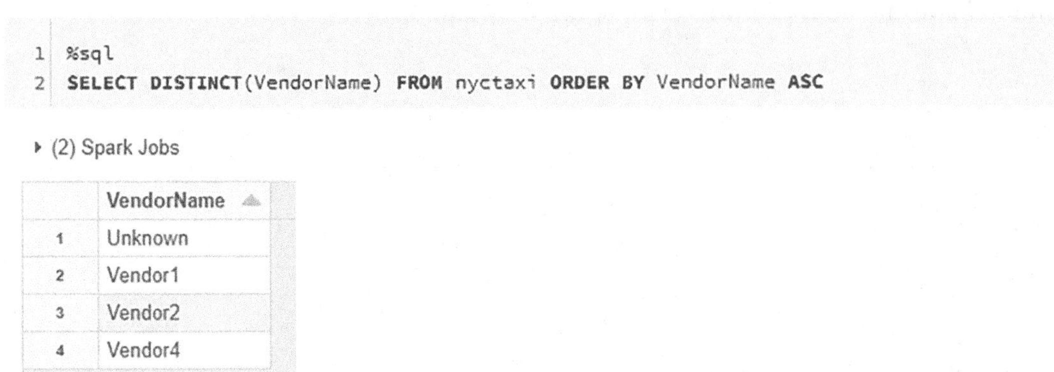

***Figure 19-18.** Select the distinct vendors from nyctaxi*

Here is the SQL query that you will need to run to re-create the results shown in Figure 19-18:

```
%sql
SELECT DISTINCT(VendorName) FROM nyctaxi ORDER BY VendorName ASC
```

Run Queries Using Row-Level Security

Databricks includes two user functions that allow users to express column- and row-level permissions dynamically in the body of a dynamic view function definition. It is necessary to create a dynamic view to see the benefits of this filter.

1. current_user(): Returns the current username.
2. is_member(): Determines if the current user is a member of a specific Databricks group

The following SQL query, shown in the following code, embeds the IS_MEMBER function in the query to verify whether the current user is in the specified group.

```
%sql
SELECT
*, IS_MEMBER('Vendor1')
FROM nyctaxi
```

From the results shown in Figure 19-19, notice that the user account is a member of the Vendor1 group since it displays "true" in the column results.

▸ (1) Spark Jobs

	x	tip_amount	tolls_amount	improvement_surcharge	total_amount	congestion_surcharge	VendorName	Year	is_member(Vendor1)
1		0	0	0.3	3.8	0	Vendor1	2019	true
2		0	0	0.3	14.3	0	Vendor2	2019	true
3		0.7	0	0.3	15	0	Vendor1	2019	true
4		1	0	0.3	10.3	2.5	Vendor1	2019	true
5		10.1	5.76	0.3	60.66	2.5	Vendor1	2019	true
6		2.56	0	0.3	15.36	2.5	Vendor1	2019	true
7		0	0	0.3	28.3	0	Vendor1	2019	true

Figure 19-19. *Select IS_MEMBER for Vendor1*

Similarly, you can also run a variation of the preceding query by changing the group member to Vendor2, as shown in the following code:

```
%sql
SELECT
*, IS_MEMBER('Vendor2')
FROM nyctaxi
```

As expected from the results shown in Figure 19-20, the "false" column values indicate that my user account is not a member of the Vendor2 group.

	x	tip_amount	tolls_amount	improvement_surcharge	total_amount	congestion_surcharge	VendorName	Year	is_member(Vendor2)
1		0	0	0.3	3.8	0	Vendor1	2019	false
2		0	0	0.3	14.3	0	Vendor2	2019	false
3		0.7	0	0.3	15	0	Vendor1	2019	false
4		1	0	0.3	10.3	2.5	Vendor1	2019	false
5		10.1	5.76	0.3	60.66	2.5	Vendor1	2019	false
6		2.56	0	0.3	15.36	2.5	Vendor1	2019	false
7		0	0	0.3	28.3	0	Vendor1	2019	false
8		0	0	0.3	7.3	0	Vendor1	2019	false

Figure 19-20. *Select IS_MEMBER for Vendor2*

This next query, shown in the following code, adds VendorName to the IS_MEMBER function, and the results indicate either a true or false:

```
%sql
SELECT
*, IS_MEMBER(VendorName)
FROM nyctaxi
```

As we can see from the results in Figure 19-21, the Vendor1 group, which I am a member of, displays "true" and Vendor2, which I am not a member of, displays "false."

	tip_amount	tolls_amount	improvement_surcharge	total_amount	congestion_surcharge	VendorName	Year	is_member(VendorName)
1	0	0	0.3	3.8	0	Vendor1	2019	true
2	0	0	0.3	14.3	0	Vendor2	2019	false
3	0.7	0	0.3	15	0	Vendor1	2019	true
4	1	0	0.3	10.3	2.5	Vendor1	2019	true
5	10.1	5.76	0.3	60.66	2.5	Vendor1	2019	true
6	2.56	0	0.3	15.36	2.5	Vendor1	2019	true
7	0	0	0.3	28.3	0	Vendor1	2019	true
8	0	0	0.3	7.3	0	Vendor1	2019	true

Figure 19-21. *Select IS_MEMBER for VendorName*

Next, add the same IS_MEMBER (VendorName) function to the where clause of the following SQL query, shown in the following code:

```
%sql
SELECT
*
FROM nyctaxi
WHERE IS_MEMBER(VendorName)
```

Notice in Figure 19-22 that it is possible to view the row-level security filtered results. Since the account is a member of the Vendor1 group, as expected, we can only see the filtered results for Vendor1. Additional views incorporating both row-level and column-level security can be implemented using this process which uses the IS_MEMBER function.

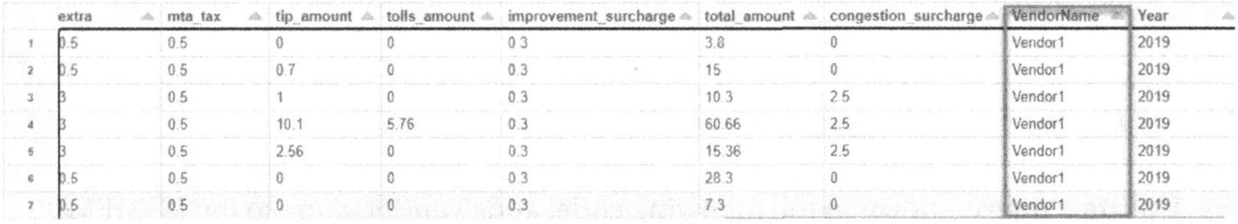

	extra	mta_tax	tip_amount	tolls_amount	improvement_surcharge	total_amount	congestion_surcharge	VendorName	Year
1	0.5	0.5	0	0	0.3	3.8	0	Vendor1	2019
2	0.5	0.5	0.7	0	0.3	15	0	Vendor1	2019
3	3	0.5	1	0	0.3	10.3	2.5	Vendor1	2019
4	3	0.5	10.1	5.76	0.3	60.66	2.5	Vendor1	2019
5	3	0.5	2.56	0	0.3	15.36	2.5	Vendor1	2019
6	0.5	0.5	0	0	0.3	28.3	0	Vendor1	2019
7	0.5	0.5	0	0	0.3	7.3	0	Vendor1	2019

Figure 19-22. *Select IS_MEMBER where Vendor1*

Also, from the physical query plan seen in Figure 19-23, notice that the partition filters utilize only the filtered groups that my account is a member of, which helps with optimizing the queries and limiting the file scans to only those which I am a member of.

```
== Physical Plan ==
CollectLimit 1001
+- *(1) Filter VendorName#6357 INSET (Vendor1,admins,users)
   +- *(1) ColumnarToRow
      +- FileScan parquet
default.nyctaxi[VendorID#6339,tpep_pickup_datetime#6340,tpep_dropoff_datetime#6341,passenger_count#6342,t
rip_distance#6343,RatecodeID#6344,store_and_fwd_flag#6345,PULocationID#6346,DOLocationID#6347,payment_typ
e#6348,fare_amount#6349,extra#6350,mta_tax#6351,tip_amount#6352,tolls_amount#6353,improvement_surcharge#6
354,total_amount#6355,congestion_surcharge#6356,VendorName#6357,Year#6358] Batched: true, DataFilters:
[VendorName#6357 INSET (Vendor1,admins,users)], Format: Parquet, Location:
PreparedDeltaFileIndex[abfss://data@gze2np1ad1001.dfs.core.windows.net/raw/delta/nyctaxi_delta],
PartitionFilters: [], PushedFilters: [In(VendorName, [Vendor1,admins,users])], ReadSchema:
struct<VendorID:int,tpep_pickup_datetime:string,tpep_dropoff_datetime:string,passenger_count:int,...
```

Figure 19-23. *Partition filters for Vendor1 name*

Similarly, after logging into the "Ron Tester" account, which is a member of the Vendor2 group, and running the same SQL query, notice from Figure 19-24 that the results are filtered to the Vendor2 records only, which confirms that row-level security is working as expected.

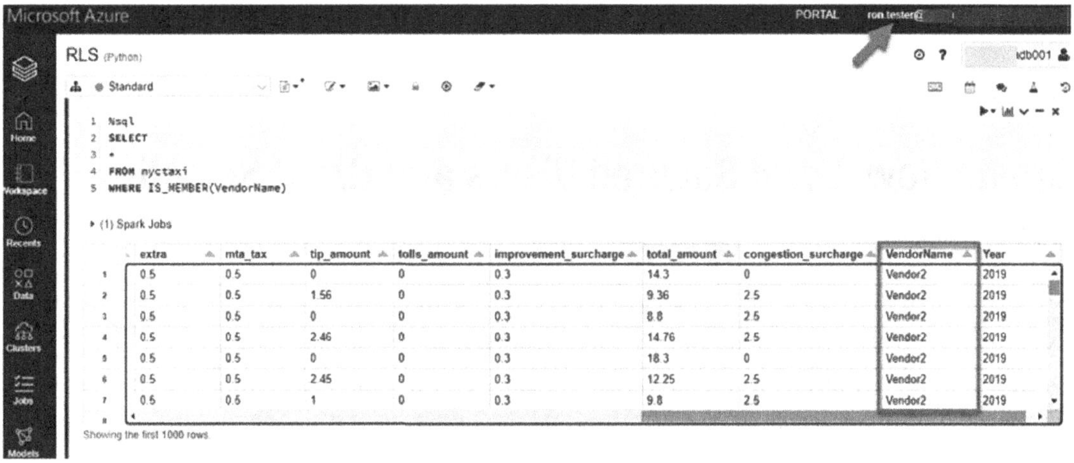

Figure 19-24. *Run a query in Vendor2 account*

Here is the query that you will need to run to re-create the results shown in Figure 19-24:

```
%sql
SELECT
*
FROM nyctaxi
WHERE IS_MEMBER(VendorName)
```

Also, this physical SQL query execution plan in Figure 19-25 shows that the partition filers are only filtering based on the groups that this member is a part of, which further optimizes the performance of the data retrieval from the query.

```
== Physical Plan ==
CollectLimit 1001
+- *(1) Filter VendorName#6735 INSET (Vendor2,admins,users)
   +- *(1) ColumnarToRow
      +- FileScan parquet
default.nyctaxi[VendorID#6717,tpep_pickup_datetime#6718,tpep_dropoff_datetime#6719,passenger_count#6720,t
rip_distance#6721,RatecodeID#6722,store_and_fwd_flag#6723,PULocationID#6724,DOLocationID#6725,payment_typ
e#6726,fare_amount#6727,extra#6728,mta_tax#6729,tip_amount#6730,tolls_amount#6731,improvement_surcharge#6
732,total_amount#6733,congestion_surcharge#6734,VendorName#6735,Year#6736] Batched: true, DataFilters:
[VendorName#6735 INSET (Vendor2,admins,users)], Format: Parquet, Location:
PreparedDeltaFileIndex[abfss://data@gze2np1ad1001.dfs.core.windows.net/raw/delta/nyctaxi_delta],
PartitionFilters: [], PushedFilters: [In(VendorName, [Vendor2,admins,users])], ReadSchema:
struct<VendorID:int,tpep_pickup_datetime:string,tpep_dropoff_datetime:string,passenger_count:int,...
```

Figure 19-25. *Partition filters for Vendor2 name*

Create Row-Level Secured Views and Grant Selective User Access

After you have defined and tested your SQL query which uses the IS_MEMBER function dynamically to apply the desired row-level security filters for users logged into the workspace, you will need to create a view, much like the following code, to ensure that the row-level security is fine-grained on a per user basis and then set up and manage appropriate administrative privileges such as "GRANT SELECT" on the view while limiting direct access to the underlying source tables. With this approach, users will be able to access the appropriate row-level secured view by running a query as simple as `Select * from vendor_nyctaxi` to retrieve the row-level data that they have access to. It will also prevent them from being able to change filters to access data that they should not be accessing.

```
%sql
CREATE VIEW vendor_nyctaxi AS
SELECT
*
FROM nyctaxi
WHERE IS_MEMBER(VendorName)
```

After the view is created, ensure that the Table Access Control is enabled from the Admin Console within the Workspace Settings tab, as shown previously in the "Table Access Control" section of this chapter. Simply enabling Table Access Control will not be sufficient, and you will also need to add the following spark config properties: `spark.databricks.acl.sqlOnly true`, to the Advanced Spark config options within the cluster, as shown in Figure 19-26, and then restart the cluster.

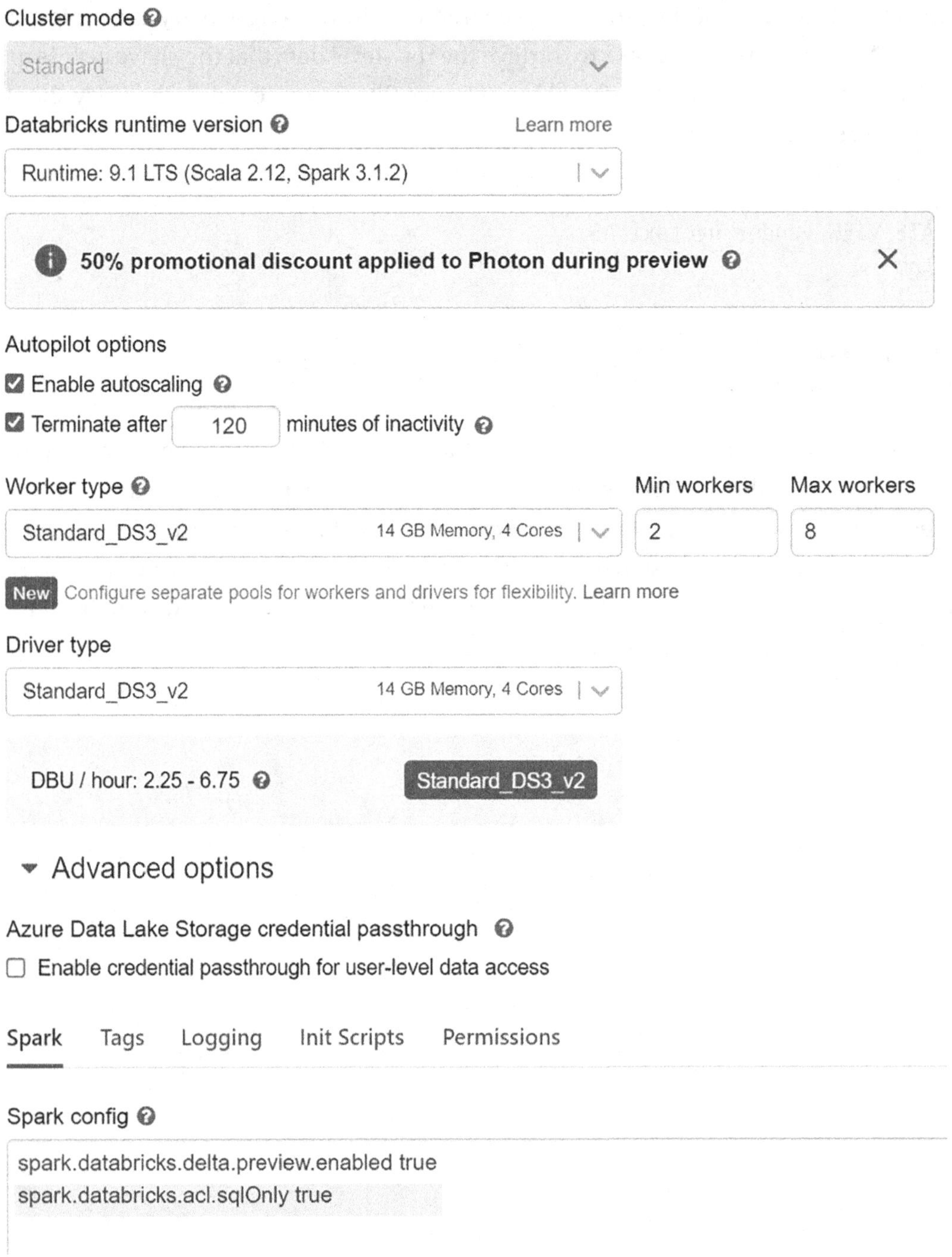

Cluster mode

Standard

Databricks runtime version Learn more

Runtime: 9.1 LTS (Scala 2.12, Spark 3.1.2)

50% promotional discount applied to Photon during preview

Autopilot options

Enable autoscaling

Terminate after 120 minutes of inactivity

Worker type Min workers Max workers

Standard_DS3_v2 14 GB Memory, 4 Cores 2 8

New Configure separate pools for workers and drivers for flexibility. Learn more

Driver type

Standard_DS3_v2 14 GB Memory, 4 Cores

DBU / hour: 2.25 - 6.75 Standard_DS3_v2

Advanced options

Azure Data Lake Storage credential passthrough

Enable credential passthrough for user-level data access

Spark Tags Logging Init Scripts Permissions

Spark config

```
spark.databricks.delta.preview.enabled true
spark.databricks.acl.sqlOnly true
```

Figure 19-26. *Step to add Cluster Access Control to the Advanced Spark options*

After completing the abovementioned steps, proceed with granting select on the views to the respective vendors, and this will ensure that only those users that have access to their respective groups will be able to see the corresponding secured row-level vendor data:

```
%sql
GRANT SELECT ON VIEW vendor_nyctaxi TO `Vendor1`;
GRANT SELECT ON VIEW vendor_nyctaxi TO `Vendor2`;
GRANT SELECT ON VIEW vendor_nyctaxi TO `Vendor3`;
GRANT SELECT ON VIEW vendor_nyctaxi TO `Vendor4`;
```

Interaction with Azure Active Directory

While access can be granularly managed through the Admin Console in the Databricks workspace, as shown within the demonstrations of this chapter, it should also be coupled with and managed appropriately through Azure Active Directory (AAD). For example, users that have valid AAD accounts should be added to an AAD group which is then granted appropriate access to the resource group within which the Databricks workspace resides. This group- and user-level administration method supports the management and maintenance of membership to the Databricks workspace much more efficiently.

Organizational users that are part of an AAD group which has access to the Databricks service will automatically have valid access to the workspace through AAD Single Sign On (SSO). Single Sign On is an authentication method which allows users to sign in using one set of credentials without having to sign in to every application separately. With this approach, these organizational users will not need to specify their username and password when they need to log into the Databricks workspace. AAD also supports methods of enabling business-to-business (B2B) accounts to integrate with AAD to access similar resources as internal organizational users. You can also add users from within the Admin Console of the Databricks workspace. With this approach, ensure that the user belongs to the AAD tenant of your Databricks workspace. For more information on sharing data with external vendors and users, read Chapter 11.

Summary

Security and controls are critical components of any modern Data Lakehouse platform. In this chapter, you learned more about cluster, pool, workspace, and job access controls. You also learned about a variety of other access and visibility controls including workspace, cluster, and job visibility controls. Finally, you explored an example on how to set up row-level security for a group of sample vendors in your Databricks workspace. All these various features offer robust security and control capabilities to promote highly secured and controlled environments and platforms within your Lakehouse.

Index

A

B

R. L'Esteve, *The Azure Data Lakehouse Toolkit*, https://doi.org/10.1007/978-1-4842-8233-5

E, F

G

Q

R

T

U

V

W, X, Y

Z

Printed in the United States
by Baker & Taylor Publisher Services